WORKING
FROM HOME

Other Books by Paul and Sarah Edwards

Best Home Businesses for the 21st Century
3rd Edition, Revised and Expanded

Finding Your Perfect Work

Getting Business to Come to You
2nd Revised Edition
(WITH LAURA CLAMPITT DOUGLAS)

Home Businesses You Can Buy
(WITH WALTER ZOOI)

Secrets of Self-Employment

Teaming Up
(WITH RICK BENZEL)

Making Money with Your Computer at Home
Expanded Second Edition

Making Money in Cyberspace
(WITH LINDA ROHRBAUGH)

WORKING FROM HOME

Everything You Need to Know About
Living and Working Under the Same Roof

Paul and Sarah Edwards

JEREMY P. TARCHER / PUTNAM
a member of Penguin Putnam Inc. *New York*

Most Tarcher/Putnam books are available at special quantity
discounts for bulk purchase for sales promotions, premiums,
fund-raising, and educational needs. Special books or book
excerpts also can be created to fit specific needs.
For details, write Putnam Special Markets,
375 Hudson Street, New York, NY 10014.

Jeremy P. Tarcher/Putnam
a member of
Penguin Putnam Inc.
375 Hudson Street
New York, NY 10014
www.penguinputnam.com

First Trade Paperback Edition 1994

Library of Congress Cataloging-in-Publication Data

Edwards, Paul, date.
Working from home : everything you need to know about living
and working under the same roof / by Paul and Sarah Edwards. —5th rev. ed.
p.   cm.
ISBN 0-87477-976-6 (alk. paper)
1. Home-based businesses.   2. Self-employed.
I. Edwards, Sarah (Sarah A.)   II. Title
HD62.5.E39   1999   98-51431 CIP
658'.041—dc21

Book design by Lee Fukui

Printed in the United States of America
7 9 10 8

This book is printed on acid-free paper. ∞

Acknowledgments

Every one of our books is the result of a team effort, although the team members usually never meet face-to-face or at the same time, and reside from coast to coast. But each has a role that deserves our hearty acknowledgment. We value and appreciate our teammates at Tarcher/Putnam, in New York. They include our beloved publisher, Joel Fotinos; our helpful and enthusiastic editor, Mitch Horowitz; his assistant, Lily Chin; the people in copyediting, production, and design, including Coral Tysliava and Claire Vaccaro; and in publicity, Ken Siman and Kristen Giorgio.

On a daily basis, our own invaluable virtual team includes our assistant, Joyce Acosta, who works with us in our home office, and our publicist, Donna Gould, who from her own home office in New Jersey is a constant source of wisdom and encouragement in her efforts to make sure the whole world gets word of our books.

Finally, we acknowledge the thousands of people we've met over the past eighteen years who have so willingly shared their personal joys and woes on the journeys to finding their own solutions for making working from home the experience they dreamed it could be.

To Shari Lewis,
whose life was a light to us and millions of others

Contents

Introduction   xi

**Part 1   New Freedom, New Choices:
Living and Working Under One Roof**

CHAPTER 1   Putting an End to Nine-to-Five   3

CHAPTER 2   Is Working from Home for You?   17

CHAPTER 3   Working for Yourself: Full-Time and Part-Time   39

CHAPTER 4   Working for Someone Else: Paychecks and
Other Possibilities   93

**Part 2   Making Your Home Office Convenient,
Functional, and Professional**

CHAPTER 5   Keeping Your Work and Personal Life Separate   115

CHAPTER 6   Finding the Right Office Space   134

CHAPTER 7   Outfitting Your Home Office with
Furnishings and Supplies   163

CHAPTER 8   Equipping and Computerizing the
Up-to-Date Home Office   199

**Part 3   Protecting Your Assets:
Legal, Tax, and Insurance Matters**

CHAPTER 9   Zoning, Permits, Regulations, and
Your Legal Decisions   247

CHAPTER 10 Claiming Your Tax Benefits 273

CHAPTER 11 Insurance: What You Need and How to Find It 314

Part 4 Managing Your Home Office

CHAPTER 12 Getting Organized and Staying That Way 351

CHAPTER 13 Managing Time: Working on Purpose 365

CHAPTER 14 Managing Money: Financing and
Cash-Flow Management 411

CHAPTER 15 Managing Information and Other Stuff:
Getting Rid of Clutter 442

CHAPTER 16 Cleaning Up: Sixty-Second Housecleaning 471

Part 5 Managing Yourself and Others

CHAPTER 17 Avoiding Loneliness 487

CHAPTER 18 Staying Out of the Refrigerator and
Away from Other Temptations 499

CHAPTER 19 Staying in Love and Saving Your Relationship 509

CHAPTER 20 What to Do About Children 530

CHAPTER 21 Getting Help When You Need It 560

Part 6 Getting Business and Growing

CHAPTER 22 Pricing: Determining What to Charge 579

CHAPTER 23 Successfully Marketing Your Home Business 605

CHAPTER 24 Moving On: What to Do When Your
Business Outgrows Your Home 640

Index 653

Introduction

This book is about living life to its fullest. It's about having your cake and eating it, too—about having the best of all possible worlds.

It's a book for everyone who's tired of the daily commute and the pressures of the nine-to-five routine. It's for everyone who dreams of economic security, more free time, a healthier or more productive lifestyle, and a chance to be closer to family and friends. It's for people who want to take charge of their day-to-day lives and their futures.

This book took root at a time in our lives when our days were full and exciting. Paul was a chief executive officer for a corporation; Sarah was an administrator for a government agency. But we both spent too many hours flying across the country, keeping tight schedules, and waving good-bye to each other in airports. We were smoking too much, sleeping too little, and leading the ulcer-prone lives that have come to characterize what our society calls success.

SARAH

I didn't feel I had many choices as a working mother. Juggling a successful career and motherhood meant being dead tired most of the time and not being able to do either job with the dedication I wanted. I was determined, however, to have both a career and a family, so I did my best in a difficult situation. I ended up in the hospital with what the doctor pronounced a stress-related illness. "You almost died here and if you don't change your lifestyle you will be back here again," he told me before discharging me.

That was my wake-up call. I knew I was stressed, but I didn't see any options without giving up my dream for both a career and a family. One day, I visited the office of one of our outside consultants. He was doing what, at the time, seemed like a most unusual thing: operating his business from his home. I took one look at his arrangement and knew with certainty: "This is for me!"

My parents grew up during the Great Depression, so I'd been raised to think that nothing in the world was better than the security of a government job. Still, two years, one master's degree, and a first-time-ever home mortgage later, I left my secure government position and opened a private psychotherapy practice in our new house.

Most people I knew predicted I would miss the benefits of a government career and regret my decision. They were wrong. I haven't regretted my decision for one day in the twenty-five years since I left the hallowed gray halls of the Federal Building.

Working from home was like having flowers delivered to me every day. I felt healthier immediately. For the first time in my son's young life, I could be a real mother and still pursue my career. I was more relaxed, and I relished working in an environment with windows and trees and the out-of-doors just a few steps away.

PAUL

Initially I was hesitant about working from home. I had concerns about the image it might create and worried that I wouldn't get my work done. So when I started my own consulting firm, I opened a downtown office and hired a secretary.

I found I'd start working at home in the morning and go into the office later and later in the day. Many days I'd see no reason to drive in at all. Eventually I closed that downtown office and set up a work space in our basement recreation room for my secretary. At first she was a bit uncomfortable with the idea of working in someone's home, but after thinking about it, she decided it was a wonderful opportunity. She could work within two miles of her own house and be closer to her children.

To me, working at home meant having all my files and books in one place. It meant saving a lot of time that used to be wasted commuting and a great deal of money that used to be spent on overhead. It meant being free to put those resources into making my home as pleasant as I wanted it to be. After all, I was working there! Most important, the saving on overhead has meant I can afford to pursue the kind of work I want to do instead of taking business just to pay the overhead.

A JOINT EFFORT

When we were first married, we were both in college and spent most of every day together. On graduating, we discovered that "growing up" and going out into the work world meant seeing very little of the ones we loved. How nice to find there's another way! We've been working from home for twenty-five years, and we see more of each other than ever before.

When we first began working from home it seemed somewhat unusual to our friends and neighbors. In fact, the neighbors thought Paul was un-employed! But soon the novelty turned to curiosity. People began asking us many questions about how we did it and how they might do it, too. As the tempo of the questions intensified, curiosity about working from home be-came the makings of a major social trend. Through our books (of which this was the first), our columns in newspapers distributed by the *Los Angeles Times* and *Entrepreneur's Home Office* magazine, our radio show of over ten years on the Business News Network, our television show that ran for four years on Home and Garden TV, seminars and speeches, our Web site (*http://www.paulandsarah.com*), and the other forums we serve, we've been able to reach millions of people from all over the world with our message: Working from home is a good life, and you can do it too.

A REFERENCE BOOK FOR PEOPLE WORKING FROM HOME

Working from Home is a reference book that will help you at every stage of having a home office, from the time you first begin considering it to the day you wonder if maybe you're outgrowing your home office. This book is a basic reference you can turn to any time a question arises or a problem de-velops.

If you're trying to decide whether working at home is for you, part 1 should be helpful. In it we address the questions of who's doing it and why, what work is being done at home, the benefits and problems you can antic-ipate, and how you can tell whether it will be difficult or easy for you. If you think you'd like to work at home but need to figure out how you can earn a living doing it, you'll find concrete ideas in part 1 for setting up your own home business or finding a job that enables you to work at home.

If you already know what you're going to do and are ready to set up your work at home, or if you're already working from home, turn to part 2. Here you'll find detailed suggestions about where to put your office, how to keep your work and personal life separate, what equipment you'll need, and how to arrange the most efficient work space.

Another aspect of getting under way, but one on which we find many new or established home-business people also need guidance, is protecting yourself from legal regulations, tax authorities, and calamities. So in part 3, you'll find the information you need on legal issues, tax matters, and insurance.

With the ever-increasing amount of information in our lives and demands on our time, working efficiently and keeping our home and office clear of all kinds of clutter can be a considerable challenge. In part 4 we provide specific guidelines for such practical matters as managing your time, your money, your information, and your paperwork.

Dealing with people and personnel is the subject of part 5. Because you may be working solo, you'll find solutions for problems like loneliness and staying out of the refrigerator. You'll discover strategies for dealing with children and family, and making sure your marriage not only survives but also thrives now that you're at home more. You'll also learn how to find employees and support services.

For home-business people, setting prices and finding customers or clients are key concerns. You'll find solutions to these challenges in part 6 along what to do if you start to outgrow your home office but want to retain the benefits of working from home while you expand or move up the professional ladder.

You'll find that many of the topics we cover—such as interior design, time management, home-office technology, and marketing—have been the subject of entire books, so we provide you with the basics for handling the core issues and refer you to additional resources if you should need them. There's a Resources list at the end of each chapter that includes recommendations for books, software, Web sites, and much more.

WORKING FROM HOME

You'll notice that our book is called *Working* from *Home*—not *Working* at *Home*. We chose to use the preposition *from* for two important reasons: first, because *from* embraces not only those whose work is done in their home but also many others for whom home is their base of operations while much of their actual work is performed on others' premises. For example, home-based salespeople, contractors, consultants, and trainers do most of their work away from home. In fact, however, four out of five home workers work *from* home.

The second reason we chose this broader definition is to communicate the importance of getting out of your home office, and reaching out to get business and participate in the broader professional and business community. Having your office in your home doesn't mean withdrawing from life. On the contrary, it's a way to become more involved in living because you're in charge of your life, released from the fatigue of being trapped for hours in a car or bus. Freed of the limits placed on your entrepreneurial spirit by traditional office structures, you become the creator of each and every day of your work life, shaping it instead of reacting to it. You can have a fuller sense of being your own person.

Sometimes we look at the days in our lives and marvel that we are living them. They are rich and varied and always full. For many years they were brightened by the sound of our son's feet as he ran in the door after school around four o'clock. Some afternoons were punctuated by a family trip to watch him play soccer. Now that he's graduated from college and off on his own, we're thankful that working from home provided us with the flexibility to enjoy his childhood. Otherwise we'd be looking back now and marveling at how quickly the time has flown by and how much we missed.

For us, having the flexibility and variety to savor each phase of our lives as it unfolds is what makes life interesting and keeps us feeling young and vital. Over the past twenty-five years, we've enjoyed three different homes in three different cities, each with its own unique home-office arrangements. There we've lived and loved and worked and played through three separate careers apiece. We've lived in the heart of a midwestern city, the suburbs of a large megalopolis, and in a seaside community just blocks from the ocean. Now, as of this writing, we're preparing to move our home office once again—this time to the mountains and a new home that overlooks a pond in small community in the midst of a national forest.

This move will herald yet another phase of our lives, but one thing remains constant and that's our sense that by living and working from home we can mold and shape the quality of our lives from the rich variety of experiences life presents to us. Our goal in writing *Working from Home* is that you, too, can feel like this when each day is done. Whatever the nature of your ideal workday, this book is dedicated to helping you create it.

PART 1

New Freedom, New Choices: Living and Working Under One Roof

CHAPTER 1

Putting an End to
Nine-to-Five

Goals

1. *Find out why there are more opportunities now to work from home.*

2. *Discover what those opportunities are.*

3. *Explore the choices others are making.*

Imagine your workday beginning with a brisk walk from the breakfast table to the den. The extra time you save every day by not commuting to work is available to do whatever you want: sleep late; work out; spend extra time with your children; garden; or get a head start on the job that needs to be done. Think of it. Even if you have only a twenty-minute commute each way, ending your daily commute is like getting an additional four-week vacation every year.

Interested? You're not alone. According to repeated surveys, one in three American workers would prefer to earn their livelihoods at home. Today we have that choice, and more and more people are choosing the work-from-home lifestyle. Of course, for most of us, going to work from nine to five, or a version thereof, has been the story of our lives. But for many, it's no longer a very satisfying way to live. For others, like the handicapped, the elderly, or parents with small children, working away from home isn't always feasible. Until recently, they had few other choices.

Since the early 1980s, however, people have begun finding new options for living and working. Today we can say good-bye to the daily commute, the dead-end job, the office politics, and the feeling that everyone else is in charge of our lives. Today we can work from home and shorten our commutes to a minute or less.

The 1980 Census found 2.2 million people working at home. By 1997, the Bureau of Labor Statistics' Current Population Survey found 7.7 million working at home, 4.1 million of whom were working in a home-based business. Private research firms find even larger numbers of people working from home. No matter which numbers one considers more believable, working from home is "in" and growing.

THE NEW DREAMS

Although our society has made strides in terms of material well-being in the past fifty years, the fast pace of the modern industrial world has not been kind to our personal lives. Work life and personal life have generally become two isolated worlds, separated in time and space by the daily commute.

Often people have to struggle to squeeze in a little "quality time" by themselves or with their loved ones—catching a few free moments between the late shuttle and the eleven-o'clock news, between the extra load of laundry and the early-morning meeting. Divorce rates remain high. Stress-related illnesses like high blood pressure, chronic headaches, back pain, alcoholism, drug abuse, heart disease, and even cancer are taking a heavy toll. Even our ability to think is affected. At a recent convention held by the American Psychological Association, a study presented by researchers at Florida Atlantic University found that people whose jobs required a thirty-mile average commute performed poorly on complex tasks and were easily frustrated. In short, many workers need a change.

From this perspective, working from home holds the promise of a new American dream—opening the door to a better way of life while maintaining or even expanding our standard of living. Of course there are problems and adjustments to contend with, but in most cases if you're looking for an alternative to the nine-to-five rat race, the advantages of creating a new lifestyle outweigh the challenges.

We call today's home-based workers "open-collar workers" because the comfort of being able to dress casually symbolizes the freedom, the convenience, and the flexibility of earning your living in your own home. Although many jobs away from home don't require that male employees show up wearing neckties or women wear high heels, open-collar workers usually wear what we've been tempted to designate as the official work-from-home uniform—sweat shirts, athletic shoes, and jeans.

"A bad commute for me is tripping over the cat."
LYNN HOOPINGARNER, SYSTEMS CONSULTANT

OPTIONS FOR EARNING
A LIVING AT HOME

Working from home is not a modern invention. During the Middle Ages and the Renaissance, European merchants set up shops and artisans their work areas on the main floors of their homes. Family living was done in a single shared room upstairs.

The mixture of work and home migrated to America. Paul Revere, like many during his time, did his silversmithing in the front of his house in Boston. You can still see his shop/house on the Freedom Trail today. Some of you may have had grandparents who operated small stores or shops and lived either upstairs or in the back of the concern. And, of course, farm families have always worked from home.

In the late 1800s, the Industrial Revolution's demand for workers drew people from their homes and farms to staff factories and offices. The advent of the automobile helped make working at home unfashionable except for writers, artists, and some salespeople. However, history has a way of repeating itself. In 1980, when we began writing the first edition of *Working from Home,* futurist Alvin Toffler, in his book *The Third Wave,* was predicting an upsurge in what he called "electronic cottagers," people who would be working from home in a computerized information age. And indeed, today's information-centered society has opened many opportunities for people to work at home, with or without computers.

Things have come so far, in fact, that we see a trend toward individualization in American business, and much of this is originating from the home. Simply put, business "firms" (companies with one or more employees) are actually shrinking, while one-person businesses are growing. According to the Small Business Administration, business start-ups are at an all-time high, but business-firm terminations are even higher. According to the *New York Times,* 43 million jobs have been permanently erased from the U.S. economy since 1979. IRS data also states that sole proprietorship tax returns continue to grow in number. In Canada, between 1989 and 1996, where the self-employed accounted for three-quarters of total job growth, nine-tenths of the growth of self-employment came from people who work alone. The individual-run business begins to emerge as the clear-cut model for small-business success at the close of the twentieth century.

AFTER-HOURS WORK

The largest number of people with home offices are corporate employees who bring their work home after normal working hours. They are generally referred to as after-hours workers, and their numbers continue to grow. A recent *Fortune* magazine poll of five hundred chief executive officers revealed that the majority expect their subordinates to put in more hours than they did ten years ago. Fifty- and sixty-hour weeks are common. The result is that legions of overstressed survivors of downsized corporations are thinking about another way of living and working.

Once someone starts taking work home and has set up a working office, it becomes tempting to spend more and more time there. So we find that after-hours work often leads to taking office work home during the daylight hours as well, and, even more frequently, to a growing number of sideline home businesses.

Ken Camp, a systems consultant for AT&T, is an example of this process. He began taking after-hours work home when AT&T offered substantial discounts on personal computers to its employees. He bought a computer and found he could leave the office around 5:00 P.M., have dinner with his family, and put in a couple of hours of work before his favorite prime-time television shows. He found he had fewer interruptions at home than at the office, so eventually he talked his supervisor into letting him work from home two days a week.

Before long, he began moonlighting. For the past two years he has made a modest profit from a part-time consulting business helping small businesses with office automation. He envisions that one day he'll leave his job and run his consulting business full-time.

WORKING A SALARIED
JOB AT HOME

As of mid-year 1998, 15.7 million employees worked at home during normal business hours, according to research conducted by Cyber Dialogue, a New York–based research and consulting firm. The research identified three categories of "telecommuters" or "teleworkers": full-time employees, contract workers, and part-time employees who telecommute informally. Full-time employees who telecommute now total 7.4 million workers. These employees work from home an average of 18.0 hours/week at home, or about 2.5 days/week. Telecommuting is the fastest growing segment of the working-from-home population with advantages for both employees and employers.

> A survey conducted by The Affiliates, a leading staffing service, said
> 14 percent of all attorneys with law firms now work from home on a
> regular basis. A full 80 percent of attorneys polled believe telecommuting will increase in the next three years.

Jane Minogue, a technical writer for CompuCorp, is such a person. She began telecommuting when she was expecting her first child. "I didn't want the stress of driving to and from work every day while I was pregnant, and I wanted to be with my baby after he was born. My boss didn't want to lose me, so when I suggested working at home, he said okay." Like many telecommuters, Jane works at home most of each week and at the office for the remainder of the time.

You don't have to use a computer or be in a high-tech field, however, to work at a job at home. "Low-tech" organizations are using the new work options as well. Pet Organics, which manufactures and distributes natural health products for pets, is entirely home based. Founder Bob Baxter runs the company from his home, and his six sales representatives work from their homes too. "It's the most practical solution economically," Bob says. "Some of my people work full-time, others work part-time. Why pay for an office when you can just as easily get the job done from home?"

The future is bright for more such opportunities. The number of telecommuters or teleworkers is growing at the rate of 15 percent a year. In chapter 4, "Working for Someone Else," we describe the best routes for taking your job home or, alternatively, finding a new job that lets you work from home.

FULL- AND PART-TIME
HOME BUSINESSES

Home-based business owners refer to themselves in a variety of ways: as small businesses, home businesses, self-employed, independent contractors, entrepreneurs, freelancers, or consultants. Bill Spees of South Bend, Indiana, is an example of this growing trend of striking out on one's own.

A licensed professional engineer, Spees with four colleagues created Legendary Systems, Inc., a successful engineering consulting firm. "We started this business after we were forced into early retirement. Except when we're traveling to consult on-site with clients, we all work at home," he reports.

Some folks have even come full circle. Ethan Winning was one of the working-from-home pioneers. Back in 1977 he already had five clients he was serving on his own apart from his corporate job as personnel director. When the sixth client appeared that October, he quit his job and set up an office at home. At the time, he had few fellow home-based contemporaries. As his business grew over the following years, so did his space requirements. "By 1982 it became obvious that we needed more space," Ethan explains. "Our kids were still young and had this 'thing' about the business taking over their bedroom." At a time when the first wave of home-based entrepreneurs was taking the plunge, Ethan moved his company out of his house into rented office space.

Ethan's business continued to flourish. In the mid-nineties, he came to yet another series of conclusions. The copy machine that once resembled a medium-sized refrigerator was now the size a of new, compact laser printer. Equipment had gotten smaller and newer. More powerful software had replaced his last secretary. "My wife, and true financial officer, asked why we were keeping the offices. We weighed the pros and cons. It came down to the fact that I was doing all my work in a ten-by-ten-foot room, made possible by 2.2 gigabytes of memory, my trusty laser printer, the phones, and a fax machine." Thirteen years after moving out of the house, he moved back in. "It's definitely helped preserve my thirty-one-year marriage, and the money we saved could be nicely put toward retirement or, even worse, fixing up the house!"

WHY IT'S POSSIBLE NOW

If you're already working from home or seriously thinking about it, you're definitely in the right place at the right time. That much is clear. But, you may be wondering, What happened? Why, all of a sudden, are there so many opportunities to work at home? Several factors account for the new options and suggest that working from home is not only here to stay but also the wave of the future.

Restructuring of the Economy

The United States has changed from a society based on an industrial economy to one based on an information and service economy. The Internet is moving further into the Information Age. With equipment running at a fraction of the cost of a car, work is done as easily in a spare bedroom as in an office.

This transformation has brought about significant changes in the way we work. Increasingly, well-educated managers and professionals seeking to climb the corporate pyramid have found midlevel positions disappearing as the corporate hierarchy begins looking less like a pyramid and more like a pancake.

Many find not only no upward mobility but also no opportunity to stay put. Even in a good economy, white-collar workers are losing jobs to downsizing, mergers, and takeovers at about the same rate as blue-collar workers. Most people know formerly high-paid managers and technical and professional workers who have been let go by companies with whom they thought they had secure futures. Many of this number are unable to replace their old jobs with work at equivalent pay or stature. Some settle for significantly lower wages; others have no luck at all and report sending out hundreds of resumes. One frustrated job searcher reported he was told everything—that he was too old, too young, too technical, too general, too specialized, in the wrong industry, obsolete, too focused, from too-diverse a background, from too small a company, from too big a company, and on and on.

The wave of consolidations of large corporations crosses most industries—from aerospace to book publishing, from home appliances to hospitals, from toilet tissue makers to telephone service. Cost savings—meaning fewer employees—are virtually always cited as a reason for a merger or acquisition.

"Category-killer" stores in office supplies, toys, home improvement, furniture result in locally owned and smaller businesses sliding down Memory Lane, leaving behind long-time employees, owners, and the sons and daughters of owners who thought the family business would become their future needing to discover new options for making their way.

As we mentioned earlier, large U.S. companies have laid off over 43 million workers since 1979. In the early eighties *Fortune* 500 companies accounted for more than 20 percent of the work force; today just 10.9 percent work for the *Fortune* 500s. In the past, layoffs included a realistic hope of being rehired when times got better. Times are very good right now, yet secure high-quality jobs with ample benefits are not coming back. And although there have been new jobs created in the new economy, few feel assured of keeping theirs, and rightly so. This is why, despite the fact that the best economic indicators are higher than in recent memory, people are more worried about money than ever before. In fact, a recent poll conducted for *USA Today* indicated that 30 percent of Americans always worry about having enough money to pay their bills—up from 20 percent in 1995.

"The job security many workers experienced in the three decades after World War II is probably gone forever."

ROBERT REICH, FORMER SECRETARY OF LABOR

Jobs Cut at 10 Large Companies in the Last 4 Years	
IBM	122,000
AT&T	123,000
Boeing	61,000
General Motors	99,000
Sears	50,000
Digital Equipment	29,800
Lockheed Martin	29,000
BellSouth	21,200
Delta Airlines	19,000
Eastman Kodak	16,800

Industrial and clerical workers have felt the job squeeze the hardest. Between 1980 and 1995, according to the *New York Times,* a full 43 percent of the manufacturing workforce was let go. That's over 24.8 million jobs. Given frequent plant closings, cutbacks in government spending, layoffs, and automation, the specter of unemployment looms over many heads even in good times. Workers who are repeatedly downsized, reorganized, purged, and merged are eager to find ways to take control of their careers.

As a result, starting a part- or full-time home business, or having a spouse start one, begins to look very attractive. And while economic restructuring is causing problems of dislocation and dissatisfaction, it's also creating the solutions. As industries consolidate into a few large corporations on the one hand and splinter into a multitude of smaller companies on the other, the mass market is narrowing into definable niche markets that can be easily served by small companies and self-employed individuals. This trend contributes to why one out of three new businesses today is started at home.

Home-Based Empowerment

Layoffs and downsizing have been part of the American economic landscape for almost twenty years now. When these trends first began, people had to scramble fast to regain their footing, and starting a home-based business turned out to be an excellent solution for many. Today, the economy is stronger than ever and employers are complaining of a scarcity in the labor pool, yet companies continue to run lean and mean. In these interesting, somewhat conflicted times, the decision to start a business or work from home isn't always a reaction to losing a job; just as often it is made from a position of empowerment. After looking at all the facts, more people are deciding to quit their corporate or industrial jobs and strike out in home-based businesses.

Tired of office politics and the constant threat of downsizing, John Harnagel decided to quit his job summarizing depositions for a midsized law firm in Los Angeles and head out on is own. He outfitted an office in his home and went prospecting. When three of his former company's best clients heard that John was out on his own, they transferred their business to him. They knew the quality of his work and were pleasantly surprised that they could get the same level of service at half the rate they had been paying to the larger firm. Needless to say, John is quite pleased with his decision. "I was a little scared to cut my ties to the salary I'd been drawing, but with my own business I now have the very real possibility of doubling my actual income yearly, which I've already done. This could never have happened if I stuck to the nine-to-five."

Jonathan Farrow was a full partner in a successful retail store that sold original art prints and other objects d'art. In order to increase sales further, he wanted to take a part of his business on line and join the thousands of entrepreneurs making sales in cyberspace. Jonathan taught himself HTML (the computer language used to create sites on the World Wide Web) and created a Web site that allowed customers to purchase his wares directly over the Internet. The Web site was so successful, it demanded his full-time attention. This allowed him to operate from home while his partner minded the store. After a year of brisk sales, Jonathan took stock of his own inventory and decided that he actually enjoyed creating Web sites and on-line sales strategies more than he liked selling artwork. It didn't take him long to reoutfit his home office to accommodate his new business interest. His new company, The Media Group, has started off on the right foot and he is already servicing accounts.

Changing Demographics

The bulk of today's population is entering their forties and fifties, and these baby boomers have reached the age when they are seeking autonomy over their lives and a higher quality of life. With American corporations cutting back and flattening out, advancement opportunities are shrinking for sea-sonal workers. So achievement-minded baby boomers are striking out into their own business ventures.

Like many women, market researcher Elizabeth Donovan bumped into the corporate "glass ceiling" in her early thirties. When she asked for a raise, she was told she was earning enough for a woman of her age. With the encouragement of her accountant, she left her job to start her own market research firm. Over the past twelve years she's realized a $600,000-a-year income working all by herself at her home-based business.

The generations following the boomers, the so-called "lost" generation now in their thirties and the "gen-Xers" now in their twenties, are making significant contributions to the home-business landscape. Historically, other generations with characteristics similar to this one have had a strong entrepreneurial talent as well, producing people like Andrew Carnegie, John D. Rockefeller, J. P. Morgan, Levi Strauss, and Dale Carnegie and in-novations like cafeterias, chain letters, comic books, frozen foods, plastics factories, shopping centers, and supermarkets. Today's entrepreneurs pro-duce developments in computers, communications, new media, and new personal service businesses like pet-sitting, wedding planning, and image consulting that can be operated at home.

Sophisticated Information Technology

The ever-decreasing cost of powerful computers, high-resolution printers, and high-speed communications has made it possible to conduct business as easily from home as anywhere. When we began working from home, the most advanced equipment suitable for a home office was an IBM Selectric typewriter and an answering machine that half of our callers hung up on. Since that time, personal computers—especially laptops—modems, fax machines, laser printers, briefcase-sized copy machines, and the Internet make working from home as productive, efficient, and competitive as it is in any office. Almost every technology leader—companies like Hewlett-Packard, Microsoft, IBM, Canon, and Sharp—are designing products specifically for home offices. It's hard to find an electronics store or mass merchandiser that *doesn't* have a home-office section.

People can live literally anywhere and transact their business in style. The owner of a skip-tracing agency does business from his home in the Virgin Islands, communicating daily by computer with his main office in Washington, D.C.

Steven Roberts, inventor, author, and computer specialist, has made his home on an "electronic bicycle." He bicycles across the country with two computers he uses to write and transmit his work to book and magazine publishers.

Tom McAnally runs his international recruiting company from his home in a tiny town in rural Montana. He operates a high-tech little house on the prairie.

Thanks to a computer, Rohn Engh also left the hassles of life in a large metropolitan area. Behind his barn in rural Osceola, Wisconsin, he now publishes *Photoletter,* an electronic newsletter that pairs photographers with photo editors of magazines and other publications. The personal computer creates hundreds of business opportunities like McAnally's and Engh's that can easily be started and operated at home. With small computers, home businesses like these have many of the capabilities once reserved only for organizations with many employees or large mainframe computers.

The computer and ever-expanding communications technology also offer job and business opportunities to those who cannot work outside the home because of physical or family limitations. Georgia Griffith, who is blind and deaf, uses her computer and a machine that prints computer Braille to work from her home in Lancaster, Ohio, as a music proofreader for the Library of Congress.

Doing word processing for American Express, through the company's Project Homebound in New York, Joseph Wynn is able to make more than three times the money he received from Social Security disability.

In tiny Reardan, Washington, Bruce Johnson produces computer graphics at home on his Apple computer. Confined to a wheelchair by a high-school football injury, he finds this a feasible and satisfying way for him to work.

The Contingent Workforce

Another result of corporate mergers and downsizing is an increasing demand for part-time or freelance consultants, researchers, and designers. This demand has created a new category of employees collectively referred to as the "contingent workforce."

Loosely defined, the contingent workforce includes part-timers, independent contractors, freelancers, leased employees, temporary workers, business services employees, and the self-employed. Contingent workers have grown from 20 percent of the workforce in the early eighties to 25 percent today. Charles Handy, author of *The Age of Unreason,* states that contingent workers comprise 50 percent of the British workforce. The U.S. is following behind with Manpower, Inc., now the nation's largest employer.

For some like Wendy Perkins, author of *Temporarily Yours,* "temping" has become a way of life, and a route to self-sufficiency. Wendy, who left her job as a stockbroker to seek greater self-expression, considers herself to be an independent contractor and has worked for more than 250 companies.

Beleaguered by the high cost of doing business, some corporations have actively helped the entrepreneurial exodus along. Rank Xerox, a London-based subsidiary of the Xerox Corporation, and Connecticut Mutual Life Insurance Company have developed programs to encourage middle managers in areas such as purchasing, personnel, and planning to quit their jobs and sign on as part-time outside contractors. A number of occupations such as medical transcription, instructional design, and graphic design work are primarily cottage industries.

New Pressures/New Values

With growing numbers of two-career couples, singles, and single-parent families, both men and women are feeling the pressure of having to juggle many conflicting demands on their personal and professional lives. Almost a third of Americans say they feel rushed, and two-thirds suffer from frequent stress. Many burn out on their jobs and on their lifestyles. And it's no wonder. Even weekends seem to be shrinking as job responsibilities, errands, and housekeeping all get squeezed into the two days that were once reserved for recreation and relaxation.

As a result of these pressures, people are looking for greater control over their time and more flexible work arrangements. Nearly eight out of ten American men and women would sacrifice rapid career advancement in order to spend more time with their families. A recent survey reported in *USA Today* showed that the love of one's family has become the value

Composition of Home Businesses

Today, home businesses cover the spectrum of providing products and services:*

TYPE OF BUSINESS	PERCENTAGE OF HOME BUSINESSES
Construction	29
Other	19
Retail sales	9
Professional services	8
Manufacturing/crafts	7
Farming	5
Wholesale trade	5
Day care	4
Finance	4
Insurance/real estate/legal	4
Engineering/computer	4
Other consulting	4
Health services	2
Education	2

* Figures provided by BIS Strategic Decisions.

Americans cherish most. So they're opting for home and hearth—family, health, and personal satisfaction.

Today's workers are also looking for new rewards from their work. They want more meaningful, satisfying work and they want to work with people they respect. These priorities have come to matter more than money or opportunities to advance.

In search of a more rewarding lifestyle, increasing numbers of people are determined to become their own boss or to work more independently. Repeatedly as we travel across the country, we hear people saying things like: "I've been told 'It's none of your business' so often that I've decided to start my own business"; or "I want to set my own hours and keep what I earn for myself. I'm tired of the rat race. I'm fed up with nine-to-five"; or "I want to succeed and excel at whatever I do. I want to work for myself even if it kills me. I am determined to work to live, not live to work!"

Gil Gordon's experience is not uncommon. After nine years, he left his position as a personnel manager to start his own telecommuting consulting firm; he had become disillusioned with corporate life. "The jobs I could be promoted to didn't look that attractive. They all involved managing rather than doing. Now I'm not working any less, but my attitude is differ-ent. I'm happy. The biggest satisfaction is knowing I'm doing something important."

New Locations

Middle-class Americans like the Enghs and McAnalys are choosing to leave the crowded urban centers and suburbs, particularly those on the coasts, and make new lives for themselves in small towns and rural areas. This trend has given rise to books and consultancies to help people relocate. We find in traveling to places like Salt Lake City and Boise a new vitality brought about by newcomers who take their skills and their expectations for culture and conveniences with them. We've been told in fast-growing areas like these and others like Springfield, Missouri; Sioux Falls, South Dakota; and Fort Collins, Colorado, that someone could start almost any one of the businesses in *Best Home Businesses for the 90s* and quickly get their business under way.

In smaller towns in which there are few industries and fewer jobs, new-comers must also bring their means for earning a livelihood. In chapter 3, we describe some ways in which they are creating livelihoods in small towns and rural areas.

Working from home holds the promise of having it all—meaningful work and more time to be with family and loved ones. The potential re-wards are great, but what is it really like and would it be right for you? In the next chapter, we'll explore these issues and suggest ways in which you can prepare yourself to work successfully from home.

RESOURCES

BOOKS

The Age of Unreason. Charles Handy. Boston: Harvard Business School Press, 1991, ISBN: 0875843018.

The Art of the Long View: Planning for the Future in an Uncertain World. Peter Schwartz. New York: Doubleday, 1996, ISBN: 0385267320.

Bold New World: The Essential Guide to Surviving and Prospering in the Twenty-First Century. William Knoke and Bill Knoke. New York: Ko-dansha, 1996, ISBN: 1568360959.

Clicking: 16 Trends That Drive America. Faith Popcorn and Lys Mari-gold. New York: HarperBusiness, 1997, ISBN: 0887308570.

The 500-Year Delta: What Happens after What Comes Next. Jim Taylor, Watts Wacker, and Howard Means. New York: HarperBusiness, 1997, ISBN: 0887308384.

The Fourth Turning: An American Prophecy. William Strauss and Neil Howe. New York: Broadway Books, 1997, ISBN: 055306682X.

Generations: The Future of America's Future, 1584 to 2069. William Strauss and Neil Howe. New York: Morrow, 1992, ISBN: 0688119123.

Release 2.0. Esther Dyson. Broadway Books, 1997, ISBN: 0767900111.

Trends 2000. Gerald Celente. Warner Books, 1997, ISBN: 0446519014.

CHAPTER 2

Is Working from Home for You?

Goals

1. Explore the pros and cons of working from home.

2. Discover who's suited to work from home and who isn't.

3. Identify what problems you personally might encounter.

4. Decide if it's right for you.

It's the only way to go! I'd never go back!" That's the spontaneous reaction many have to working from home. But others can't wait to get back; they miss the office. Are such different reactions surprising? Hardly. From the first day we started school, we've all been groomed to work in an office setting. You got up, got dressed, ate breakfast, and went to class. You sat at a desk all day long and worked at various tasks and projects with others around you. When the bell rang, you packed up your things and went home. Without the bell, this description could fit any day at the office.

When you venture into working from home, these familiar routines go the way of pep rallies and the senior prom. You get up in the morning and with just a few steps, you can be at work. Unless you have somewhere special to go that day, you don't even need to get dressed. When do you actually start working? Where is it that you'll work? Your desk? The couch? Chances are you'll be the only one there, unless your kids pop in or a neighbor drops by, and then what do you do? In every case, it's up to you. No wonder people have such diverse reactions! The whole experience is different from everything we're used to.

Some people flourish with the freedom, and others flounder. Some handle the change matter-of-factly, while others find it profoundly upsetting. Tina Lenert took to working from home like a fish returned to water. "I loved it from the moment I started. I never missed my old job for a minute. And honestly, I can't think of any real problems I've had working here."

Reporter Duane Tompkins's experience was quite different. "When the editor told us we could work from home and send in our copy by computer, I was excited. It sounded great. But it wasn't what I expected. I became disillusioned right away. I missed the hustle and bustle of the pressroom and everyone being up against the deadline together. Without anyone else around I found myself goofing off, and I was always at the refrigerator. I think I gained twenty pounds before I finally decided to move back downtown."

WHAT YOU CAN EXPECT

For those with creative business minds, working from home can be the ticket to realizing their potential. For single parents, and many women, working at home facilitates juggling family and career. For fathers, it can lead to more time and involvement with their children. For others, it's a step toward goals like financial independence, relocating to an idyllic locale, or simply escaping from the exhaust fumes, crowded trains, and congested freeways that bedevil most commuters.

Working from home can provide the means for stretching a tight budget or maintaining an accustomed lifestyle in difficult economic times. Couples who have invested time and energy in building meaningful relationships find that their investment pays greater dividends when they work from home. For the retired, or the increasing number of people considering early retirement, working from home becomes a way of contributing, of staying alive and vibrant. And for many with disabilities, it's the door to self-sufficiency and a productive future.

Working from home can be the answer to many dreams. But what can you really expect? What are the actual benefits you may enjoy and what problems might you encounter?

Most People Love It

Although working from home is not for everyone, most people doing it are quick to recommend their lifestyles. Tom Miller of Link Resources, who has been conducting the National Work-at-Home survey for years, finds that about one out of five people has a "complaint"; the rest are happy.

Home Office Computing readers are even happier. Of 4,200 readers 96 percent said they would recommend working from home to others, and 98 percent of the home-based business owners said they were happier at home than in a corporate office. An *Income Opportunities* survey found that 93.5 percent of those who work from home enjoy it most or all the time.

Telecommuters are happier at home, too, according to an AT&T and Telecommute America survey that found that 36 percent of teleworkers say they will never go back to the office again and 39 percent wouldn't go back for less than double the pay!

After giving a speech in Washington, D.C., we met a woman in the audience who does data entry at home. She told us enthusiastically, "It's the best thing that ever happened in my life." A man in the same audience gleefully joined in: "After being self-employed for several years, I'm unfit for employment now. I could never work for someone else again." These comments form a familiar refrain.

You Have Greater Freedom, Flexibility, and Control

When we ask people what they like about working from home, they tell us over and over again it's the freedom. They cherish the flexibility, convenience, and control it gives them over their lives. As Dave Green, owner of a thriving interpreting business, says: "It still amazes me that I'm able to live the way I do. I pretty much do what I want, when I want to, as long as I keep pleasing my clients."

Freedom means different things to different people, however. To Javier Ferrier, who transcribes court reporters' notes in Garden Grove, California, it means "the freedom to set my own hours. I work the hours I want."

For designer Sandra Stratton of Kahului, Hawaii, and Robert F. Dobnick of Chicago, who does space planning for wholesale showrooms, it's the creative freedom they love about working from home. Washington, D.C., housing consultant David Freed prizes the "freedom, to be able to do socially meaningful work." And Edward L. Svadlenka, who operates a carpet-cleaning and window-washing service in Hometown, Illinois, says that it "gives me the freedom to take time off." For Kim Goad, a home-based publisher in Baltimore, freedom means "I can wear my pajamas until late in the afternoon. It gives me a feeling of power when I talk to corporate clients on the telephone."

Your control extends to when you work and what you believe is the most important or pressing task. No longer do you need to react to a boss's urgency like a fire department responding to an alarm. You're not a captive of modular office systems that provide minimal privacy and require you to converse in hushed tones. You have the freedom to create an office with the lighting, color scheme, furnishings, music, and noise level of your choice.

And even though you might have family and household distractions, there are many fewer interruptions than at an office. You're away from office politics, backbiting, and the disagreeable people you would never invite into your home.

Doing It Your Way

Various surveys report that people who work from home take advantage of their newfound freedom in their own ways.

- 60% play music while working.
- Fewer than 10% work traditional 9–5 business hours.
- 53% fit time for exercising into their workday.
- Over 60% allow family members to have access to their offices.

- 81% dress casually; 6.5% don't dress at all.
- Half don't wear shoes while working.
- Nearly one in four works with the TV or radio playing.
- 11% dress in formal business attire.

"Millions have already found their productivity actually increases when they work nearer the people they're really working for—their families at home."

FORMER PRESIDENT GEORGE BUSH

You Get More Done

Research consistently indicates that productivity rises 15 to 25 percent when work is done at home in telecommuting programs, according to telecommuting consultant Gil Gordon.

It's also well established that the self-employed are the most productive people in the economy. With fewer interruptions and meetings and less office politics, it's not surprising that both the employed and the self-employed get more done at home. A study of 90,000 managers by Booz, Allen & Hamilton found that managers waste 25 percent of their time. Another study by Accountemps found that 34 percent of the average employee's day was frittered away. Still another study indicated that employers lose no less than four and a half hours a week per employee as a result of lateness, long lunch hours, or working at another job or business during office hours.

Psychological factors contribute to the productivity gains of working from home. People experience a sense of ownership of their work, gaining a new feeling of pride in accomplishment. They work at their own pace. If you're a morning person, you can begin your work bright and early to take advantage of your peak hours. Or, if your mind functions best after the sun goes down, it's your choice to burn the midnight oil. When you feel better, you do better.

Lucy and Frank Knights, who both work from home for an eastern utility company, agree with those findings: "We're surprised more companies aren't letting their people work at home. This is like owning your own business. You get more done. We're working harder than we did at the office, but we're enjoying it more."

Costs Go Down

At the same time that productivity goes up, costs go down. Here's just one example: Think what you would save if you don't drive to the office every day. Wear and tear on your car is reduced, and your auto insurance premium will probably go down. If you're putting 20,000 miles a year on your car, your mileage might drop to 12,000. Assuming the cost of driving the additional 8,000 miles a year to be 31.5 cents a mile, which is what the IRS allowed as a deduction in 1998, you'd save $2,520.00 a year, which is well over $200 a month.

Pete Silver, a marketing consultant in Miami, Florida, told us he got a note from his dry cleaner asking, "Where are you?" As people go from white collars to open collars, the washing machine takes over for the dry cleaner.

If you operate your business from home, you can usually keep your overhead down so that your break-even point is achieved far more quickly. Some businesspeople use their office rent savings to buy houses or other real estate investments.

As you'll discover in chapter 10, working from home is also a legitimate way to keep more of the money you earn from the tax collector. And you can save money on the obligatory office collections, luncheons, and the purchase of candies and cookies from other people's children. Some people miss these social functions. For them, this is a trade-off. It's a matter of whether you think of these office goings-on with fondness or as a pain in the neck.

When both husband and wife work, a Bureau of Labor Statistics Survey shows that 68 percent of the second income goes to work-related expenses. This doesn't leave much from a job paying $25,000 a year. Thus it comes as no surprise that the research firm Catalyst found that 67 percent of partners in a two-career marriage feel that having a working spouse gives them the freedom to leave their jobs. Of course, without producing some replacement income, family income falls—by 32 percent.

Even when they cover equipment costs, companies, too, usually save money by allowing employees to work at home. And for the self-employed it means only one monthly rent or mortgage payment. In cities, a cost of

$18,000 a year for office space is not uncommon. Particularly when you're starting out, the cost of office rent can mean the difference between making a profit or closing the business.

Office Rents*	
Three of the Most Expensive Cities in Which to Rent Office Space:	
Washington, D.C.	$2.70
Boston	$2.19
New York (midtown)	$2.13
Three of the Least Expensive Cities:	
Houston	$1.09
Memphis	$1.10
Louisville	$1.13

* Cost per square foot, per month

Income Can Go Up

People who work from home on their own feel a sense of financial independence. They can say good-bye to what we call the "40-40-40 plan"—forty minutes in traffic for forty hours a week for forty years. Joyce Brooks-Wiley, a computer graphics consultant and systems analyst, says, "My business has been good enough to allow me to improve my standard of living about threefold and meet lots of interesting people at the same time. I can run my office the way I like, hire and fire, wine and dine, as well as be wined and dined." Kristen Schaffner Irvin started a petroleum management business from her home and doubled her income twice in the first two years. "Everyone at my old job just waited every year for our annual performance raise. The best we could hope for was 10 percent. With my own business I basically quadrupled my income in two years!"

The sky's the limit when you run a business from your home. How much you make depends on your own ingenuity, determination, and willingness to work at it. When *Home Office Computing* magazine did a cover story on home-based millionaires, they found more home-based million-dollar businesses than there was space to list them in the article.

"One quarter of home businesses earn over $75,000 a year."

MONEY MAGAZINE

Although most home-based businesses don't reach six-figure incomes, the financial gains can nevertheless be substantial. When the White House asked us to talk about the issues concerning people who work from home, we solicited comments on line asking people to tell us what they wanted to communicate to the president. The following message from freelance writer David Palmer provides perspective on the importance to many people of what could be considered even modest income gains.

"I hope you can enlighten the folks on the Hill that self-employment is no longer synonymous with doctor, lawyer, or accountant. It also includes a growing number of displaced homemakers, single parents, factory workers, miners, and others whose skills are either no longer marketable in industry or who live in an area where self-employment is the only alternative to a service job stocking shelves in a chain drug store or flipping hamburgers. To a single parent with two or three kids, being self-employed and making $20,000 to $30,000 a year looks a whole lot better than being 'employed' at $4.50 an hour."

"Home-based businesswomen in their thirties and forties have family assets of $137,796 compared with $112,617 for those women who do not work at home."

SMALL BUSINESS ADMINISTRATION SURVEY

You Save Time

How much time do you spend commuting to work every day? Look at the chart below to see how much of your irreplaceable time is spent driving in

How Much of Your Life Do You Spend Commuting?			
DAILY ONE-WAY TRIP IN MINUTES	ROUND TRIP	HOURS EACH YEAR	EQUIVALENT NUMBER OF 40-HOUR WEEKS
5	10	40	1
10	20	80	2
15	30	120	3
20	40	160	4
25	50	200	5
30	60	240	6
35	70	280	7
40	80	320	8
45	90	360	9
50	100	400	10
55	110	440	11
60	120	480	12

rush-hour traffic. The average commute in the United States is still about twenty minutes each way. That amounts to four forty-hour weeks a year! Many people in large cities, and especially those in the suburbs, commute far greater distances. It's no longer unusual for people to tell us about one- to two-hour commutes each way. (In speaking recently to an audience of Los Angeles County employees, Paul cited a *Los Angeles Times* study that found the average commute in Los Angeles was twenty-two minutes. He never imagined that would be one of his bigger laugh lines.)

Then there's the time you spend getting dressed to go to work. Putting on your work clothes to go sit in traffic may add another five or ten hours a week. What would you do with the extra ten or fifteen hours a week you spend dressing and driving that no one is paying you for now?

What do people who work from home do with all this time they save? *Home Office Computing* found that two out of three of them use it to get more work done. Three out of five spend it exercising more. And, of course, many spend more time with their families.

What is it that people do on their breaks at the office? Have a cup of coffee, eat a snack, go to the rest room. Taking a break at home means you can pet your dog, change the kitty litter box, water your plants, wash your hair, toss a load of laundry into the washing machine, exercise, have your lunch by the pool, start your dinner, watch part of a talk show or a soap, or read a paper or business magazine.

Stress Goes Down, Health and Lifestyle Get Better

Would you like to feel more relaxed, eat a healthier diet, have more time off, exercise more, and have a better sex life? That's what the top five positive effects of working from home were, according to 4,100 *Making Money with Your Computer at Home* readers.

In contrast, nearly half of American workers worry about their jobs and feel pressure. Two in every five workers find their jobs to be "very" or "extremely" stressful, and 35 percent are thinking about quitting. *Prevention* magazine finds that the percentage of Americans who say they are under a "great deal" of stress once a week or more had risen from 55 percent in 1983 to 64 percent in the mid-nineties. Despite the generally strong economy, workers today worry more about money and feel more insecure than ever before—and with good reason: a recent poll conducted by *The New York Times* revealed that 56 percent of respondents had been laid off once in the last fifteen years, 25 percent had been laid off twice, and a startling 14 percent had been laid off three *or more* times.

Outside of job insecurity, what is the cause of this stress? One recent study found that people cite heavy traffic as the number-one cause of stress in their daily lives. Number two is frustration from interruptions at the office. Another survey indicated that the most frequent work-related stress for women is having to balance work and family demands. Working from home reduces or eliminates all these major causes of stress.

Research also indicates that the more control we feel we have over our lives, the less stress we experience. Perhaps that's the reason the one thing that people most want from a manager is autonomy. Being your own boss is the ultimate in terms of autonomy. Despite working harder and longer hours, most people report their stress level goes down once they are in charge.

Recent medical studies confirm these reports. Despite the hard work and increased productivity involved, working at home produces less stress than working at similar tasks in the office. For example, Nancy Nickel finds that having the flexibility to adjust her hours and her work pace is relaxing. "It's almost like magic. I can tailor my work to what I want to do. I can stop and take a TV break and still get more done. I feel great at the end of the day."

Common office-related stress factors, like fluorescent lights, ringing telephones, clattering equipment, buzzing conversation, and cafeteria junk food are also avoided. Financial consultant Michael Fey explains how the difference has affected him: "When I was commuting to and from work, I had to have a glass of wine when I got home to unwind." Now that he works from home he rarely has a drink outside social occasions.

Often small things make big differences in reducing stress. Open-collar workers can work in postures that are most comfortable to them. Negative attitudes of co-workers, the gossip, and the office politics that interfere with getting work done, not to mention the frequent meetings that consume a reported 45 percent of managerial and professional time, no longer need to be contended with.

> A recent survey of home-business owners and telecommuters found, among other things, that telecommuters do not smoke, drink, or use drugs as much as people who do not work at home. Telecommuters also receive promotions at a greater rate than nontelecommuters.

It's well established that lower stress means better health. Stress lowers the white blood cell count and the immune system's resistance to disease. Heart disease and high blood pressure, which affect one in four Americans, are acknowledged to be stress-related diseases. Not only do people working from home experience fewer of the major causes of stress; they also have more time to exercise and more control over what they eat. Better health is one of the greatest benefits of working from home.

Family Members See More of One Another

According to recent studies the average father spends only eight minutes a day in meaningful conversation with his children, whereas the average couple has only four minutes of closeness. Although you can expect to work more at home, you can also expect to see more of the people you love. Many mothers want to raise their children themselves. By scheduling their work when the children are at school or when they're sleeping, about 50 percent are able to be full-time parents.

The alternative in the workaday world is day care. Good day-care centers are in short supply and are expensive. Working from home may not completely eliminate child-care costs, but it can cut down on day-care expenditures which often run as much as $500 a month for each child. Because medical research finds toddlers are more at risk of getting serious infections in day-care centers, many parents feel safer having their young children at home.

According to a study we participated in developing conducted by Canon USA and the American Association of Home-Based Business Owners, 53 percent of people who work from home say it enables them to find more time for family activities.

Graphics designer Kelly Spiotto finds having her studio at home makes playing two roles in life more manageable. "When I became pregnant with my son Connor, I was working full-time at a downtown design shop. I definitely wanted to be as close to a full-time mom as possible, but I also wanted to keep working, so I split the difference and set up a home office. I made a deal with my employer that allowed me to work at home three days a week. Everything is now working out fine, I can be with Connor, share his discoveries and be an intimate part of this incredible time of his life. I can also earn a living doing what I've always loved."

For fathers, working at home means more time with family and loved ones. One parent jokingly told us he'd discovered children he'd forgotten he had. Gil Gordon says, "I feel closer to my children. Yes, it's a hassle sometimes, but I'm able to get involved with things other fathers can't."

 True Confessions

With growing concerns about street gangs, teen suicide, drugs, and alcohol, parents of teenagers are also finding working at home helps put their minds at ease. Tax specialist Alsey Graham, of Kansas City, had worked for the IRS while her daughter was in grade school, but she felt that the teen years were an important time to be there for her daughter. So she left her job to open a tax and book-keeping service from her home. "If it weren't for my daughter, I wouldn't be in business. But I'm glad I did it. You only get one chance with a child. I wanted to do it right." Sales trainer Ray Dunlop of Indianapolis would agree. He found running his business from home "made being a single parent of teenagers a lot easier."

Community Assumes New Importance

The rise of home offices makes a reemergence of community life possible. Three out of five *Home Office Computing* readers report that they participate more in community activities as a result of working at home. A survey by the American Association of Home-based Businesses (AAHBB) and Canon found that 46 percent of those who work at home spend more time volunteering in the community.

As Bob and Stephanie Wilson have found, the neighborhood takes on a new significance when you work at home. "The focus of our friendships and activities used to be in town. Now the focus has shifted. We find our friends and involvements right here in the neighborhood."

Working at home, you experience the events of life in the community. With someone on the block at home every day, the neighborhood becomes a safer place in which to live. It becomes a friendlier place, too. Not having colleagues down the hall to meet at the coffee machine, you may find yourself talking over the back fence to somebody with whom you once had only a nodding acquaintance.

Suddenly, the neighborhood is no longer just a place from which to come and go. It's now the center of your daily activities. Clients and customers, perhaps employers and co-workers, pass through it when they visit your office. You patronize nearby businesses like the copy shop, the print shop, and the office-supply store. Perhaps you have business lunches or meetings in the area. As the condition of your community becomes more important to you, you may even find yourself becoming involved in civic activities.

Working from home is helping communities in a number of other ways. It becomes easier for them to tackle air pollution and, in the process, forgo the impending gridlock on freeways and streets.

It's 100 Percent What You Make It

Whether you're salaried or self-employed, working from home means more control over your schedule and your environment than ever before. You are in charge. There is no boss standing over your shoulder. There is no time clock to punch, no bell to tell you when to start and when to stop. There is no procedures manual for working at home—it's up to you. It can be either a dream come true or a nightmare, depending on what you do. It's 100 percent up to you!

COMMON PROBLEMS

Even with these many advantages, working from home is not without its challenges, at least initially. Below is a list of the most common problems

The Pros and Cons of Working from Home

The advantages of working from home can be summarized as the 4 C's

C
osts you less to live and work
ontrol over what you do and when and how you do it
onvenience in better balancing personal, career, and family needs
loseness to those you love

The disadvantages of working from home can be summarized by the 3 D's:

D
istractions and disruptions from home, family, and friends
iscipline to get to work, stick to business, and
　　close the door on work
istinguishing your work from your personal life.

of working from home, drawn from a number of studies and surveys, including those conducted by the Roper Organization, *Home Office Computing* magazine, and us. Superseding these, however, are two problems, or challenges, that all businesses face: getting enough customers and managing money and finances. We will discuss these subjects at length in later chapters.

Expectations and Reality May Vary

Often the problems people anticipate they will have when working from home are not the same as those they actually encounter. The good news is that problems occur much less frequently than people fear. For example, whereas the largest concern expressed in one study was not having the necessary office supplies and equipment, this was not reported to be a problem for any of those who actually work from home. Other anticipated problems that were reported were far less significant than expected.

Overall, the most common problems were these: separating work and personal life, lack of space, not being taken seriously, distractions from family and friends, lack of privacy, and its inverse: feeling lonely or isolated. Other problems included working too much, lack of time, missing support personnel, child care, and staying away from the refrigerator. You'll notice that many of these common problems arise from the freedom, flexibility, and autonomy working from home provides.

Separating Work from Personal Life

Since the whole day is spent under one roof, some people report they have a difficult time juggling the demands of both home and business. They're bothered by family interruptions, housework that needs doing, deliveries and service calls, friends who drop by, barking dogs, and not having a transition period between work and play. They find it hard to switch gears from the computer to the Cuisinart and back again. The inverse is true as well. Clients may call during family time, sometimes even insist on stopping by. Deadlines are often tight and the temptation to work long hours may be difficult to resist.

Although this may sound potentially chaotic, surveys of people working at home report that 82 percent say they manage any interruptions without affecting their productivity. You'll find many creative solutions presented throughout this book for how people keep their personal and professional lives in perspective. Setting up a schedule, finding the right place for your office, achieving voice mail and telephone solutions, and arranging for proper child care are just a few you will learn about.

Being Taken Seriously

In our survey, slightly fewer than one in five home-business people reported a problem with being taken seriously by customers, clients, supervisors, co-workers, colleagues, family, or friends. To some, working from home raises the fear of missing out on promotions, losing touch with the grapevine, and being forgotten when it comes to special projects that could advance a career. Entrepreneurs worry about their professional image and whether their clients will consider a home-based business a substantial one.

Top-Ten Problems of Working from Home
1. Separating work and family life, spatially and with regard to time
2. Not enough space
3. Being taken seriously
4. Distractions
5. Lack of privacy
6. Strain on family relationships
7. Working too much
8. Feeling isolated
9. Self-discipline or self-management
10. Zoning, home and condominium association regulations

Although a few horror stories of lost clients and missed promotions are enough to cause anyone to panic, concerns about credibility are usually much more of a problem initially than in the long run. If you take yourself seriously and project a professional business image, others will take you seriously, too. Many home-based businesspeople work successfully with *Fortune* 500 clients. Employees at home, like technical writer Jane Minogue, are usually pleasantly surprised to find that they continue to advance in their careers. Jane, who initially began working from home to care for her newborn baby, was promoted to a supervisory position while there.

Surveys indicate that telecommuters are far more likely to be promoted than their office-bound brethren.

In chapter 3, "Working for Yourself," you'll find a list of specific steps you can take to create a substantial business image. In chapter 4, "Working for Someone Else," we talk about how to keep a high profile in your organization.

Self-Management

Although research consistently indicates that productivity goes up when people work from home, without the structure of a formal office routine about one in ten people in our survey has a hard time with self-discipline. They report problems with getting out of bed, getting to work, and sticking to business. Some find themselves sneaking in too much TV and taking too many trips to the refrigerator. At the other extreme, a *Home Office Computing* magazine survey shows that 15 percent have difficulty closing the door on work and leaving it behind at the end of the day. Work becomes all-consuming because it's always there.

You'll be delighted to find many creative solutions throughout this book that people have developed to help them learn how to manage themselves successfully. We call it developing the "self-management muscle." It means learning to work on a schedule of your own making, putting personal time on your calendar, and having a separate office space that is out of sight and therefore out of mind.

Feeling Isolated

While nearly a third were concerned about isolation in the Roper study, only 10 to 12 percent of those in the other surveys reported actually feeling isolated and lonely. They said they missed the social contacts of an office setting. We've found problems with feeling lonely are more likely to occur under three circumstances:

1. *A shaky start.* Problems with isolation are more common in the beginning, when new open-collar workers aren't fully clear about the direc-

tion their work is taking. They don't know whether their business or job at home will work out, and there's an initial lack of structure. Once business routines get going and they begin working with clients and colleagues, this problem disappears.

2. *Solitary work*. Sometimes problems of isolation are related to the fact that the nature of the work involves virtually no personal contact. Walter Zooi, a home-based writer and editor we frequently work with, says, "When I'm writing, whole days can go by without having any contact with the outside world whatsoever. This can be a little unnerving. I have to make sure to plan "people time," whether that's phone calls, a trip to the store, or even a little on-line discussion with colleagues or friends."

When your work demands long hours alone, however, feelings of isolation can arise whether you are working from home or in an outside office. So, it's important to take the kind of "people breaks" that Walter described. You need to have contact with others, be it meeting clients, going shopping, running errands, or chatting on line. People working from home also need to create a support network of friends and colleagues they can readily call on. You'll find more information about how to arrange for more contact and create such a network in chapter 17.

3. *A social personality*. About one-sixth of the American population is primarily motivated by the social interaction of their work. For these individuals, talking and dealing with others is the central focus and highlight of their day and working from home can become a problem indeed. Knowing this, few such people are attracted to working from home. They're only tempted to do so when illness, child-care needs, or some other necessity requires them to consider becoming home based. If you fall into this category, we recommend that you do whatever you can to stay in an office setting or, when that is not possible, arrange to have partners or employees who work with you at home.

DECIDING WHETHER WORKING FROM HOME IS FOR YOU

Despite facing these problems, experience clearly shows that the difficulties you may encounter need not be roadblocks if you are sufficiently motivated to find a way over, under, or around them.

How will you know if working from home is for you? Who is suited to work from home? We've talked in depth with hundreds of individuals to determine the answer to this question, and what we discovered surprised us.

Indeed there are certain personal qualities that seem to make working from home easier, particularly at first. As a general rule, those who are most successful are self-starters who like the line of work they're in, know what

Ten Tips for Avoiding Common Problems of Working from Home

1. Create a physically separate space for your office—a separate room, if possible. If your office must be within a room used for personal purposes, use screens or dividers to separate personal from work space (see chapter 6).

2. Get a separate number for your business, preferably a business line. This will appear more professional. Keep your personal line for your family and children to use (see chapter 8).

3. Answer the telephone with a pleasant greeting that communicates you're delighted to hear every caller and at the same time creates a professional business image. Use a mirror to make sure you smile as you answer the phone to develop your smiling voice.

4. Set goals for every day and work on those first because there is never enough time to do everything. Become an effective time manager. Don't get bogged down reacting to interruptions and demands. Think about what it means to separate *the important* from *the urgent* (see chapter 13).

5. Value your time as you value your money. Don't watch your fax machine send multiple-page documents. Instead of driving back and forth to a store to make photocopies or to hand-deliver documents, equip your home office with technology like a multipurpose office machine (priced at $500 or less) that serves as your fax, copy machine, printer, answering machine, scanner, and more. Also consider using your computer for sending and receiving faxes. You'll cut down on paper costs.

6. Save time by employing easy-to-use check-writing and accounting software, but keep paper copies of receipts, invoices, and checks. Tax records must be kept for at least six years after you've filed a return (see chapter 10).

7. Organize your filing system so that everything is easy to find. To make files stand out, use color coding for file folders and computer diskettes, etc. (see chapter 15).

8. Get furniture sized for home offices in preference to standard office furniture. A number of furniture companies are manufacturing special home-office lines. Smaller furniture is better adapted to the entryways and space available in most homes (see chapter 7).

9. Dress in a way that helps you work productively. Some people need to dress as though they were meeting clients at an office; others prefer the loose and comfortable fit of sweats and denim.

10. Have the attitude that you work from home, not at home. Hibernating is fine for bears, but not for people. Go out to make new contacts and keep old ones alive as well. Particularly if you're a naturally reserved person, remember that your home's a base, not a permanent place (see chapter 17).

they want, and are determined to achieve it. They enjoy working independently and are comfortable with minimal structure and ambiguity. They are capable of establishing and following their own schedules and deadlines.

Surprisingly, however, we find that although these attributes make it easier and less stressful to begin working from home, they are not prerequisites for success. Many people now successfully working from home did not have these attributes when they started out. Apparently, the ability to work from home and to find it rewarding is not the result of having a certain disposition or unique talents; it's more a matter of wanting to do it enough to find ways to make it work.

Like many others, home-based producer Ellie Kahn is not particularly well suited for working from home. She says, "Actually I would rather be employed and work in an office. I'm more suited to an office structure and a boss directing me and setting priorities, but my work as an oral historian is very important to me and I have yet to find anyone who will hire me to do it. So I'm learning how to be my own boss and it's worth it, because I love what I do." Had Ellie listened to conventional wisdom, she might have decided she would be unable to work from home before giving herself a chance to see what she could do.

Most of us do not initially have the mind-set, skill set, or knowledge set to work successfully on our own because we've had so little opportunity to acquire them. But research indicates that achievement is one human quality that's not determined by innate capacities; it's something we can learn from the experience of doing.

It's obvious that you have some desire to work from your home, or you wouldn't be reading this book. We suggest that instead of asking yourself whether you are already suited to work from home, ask how much you want to work from home and to what extent you are willing to learn how to do what it takes.

WHAT DOES IT TAKE?

In addition to being a producer of a good product or a provider of a good service, working from home requires that you wear many other hats, some of which may be unfamiliar to you. Whether you are self-employed or working from home on a salary, you will undoubtedly need to carry out all the following roles at one time or another.

The roles you should expect to undertake and their duties include:

• *The Executive.* Plan for the future, define and schedule what you will be doing, determine how and when you will do it, and monitor to see that you are doing it adequately.

When You Probably Shouldn't Work from Home

Although there are usually options and solutions for most work-at-home challenges, here's a list of circumstances that make it quite difficult and therefore probably not the best choice.

1. If working face-to-face on a daily basis with team members is required or preferred

2. When you really don't like your work or would rather avoid it

3. If you're someone who starts lots of things but never seems to be able to complete them

4. When you live in a discordant or otherwise unpleasant household

5. If you're a severe, chronic workaholic

6. If you are an obsessive, perfectionistic housekeeper who can't stand seeing a little dust build up, a crooked picture frame, an unwashed dish in the sink, or a pile of papers scattered on the coffee table

7. When you're struggling with a severe addiction or serious domestic difficulty

---

• *The Supervisor.* Make sure you get to work, stick to business, and don't burn yourself out overworking.

• *The Administrator and Purchasing Agent.* Equip and supply your office, handle correspondence, answer the phone, schedule repairs, run errands, file and manage financial record-keeping, obtain insurance, and so on.

• *The Security Guard.* Establish clear boundaries between work and home so that family and friends don't interfere with your work and work doesn't interfere with your personal life.

• *Public Relations, Marketing, and Sales Manager.* Get the word out about what you do and why people need you, and promote yourself so your business thrives or your career advances.

And you may have to be the janitor, too!

HOW MOTIVATED ARE YOU?

Because motivation and a willingness to learn are the most important variables for success, first ask yourself on a scale of 1 to 10 (with 1 being "not at all" and 10 being "more than anything in the world") "How much do I want to work from home?" The greater your desire above a 7, the more likely you will be motivated to do whatever it takes to master the many required roles mentioned above to succeed at working from home. The lower your score is below 7, the more important it will be that you already have the attitudes, skills, aptitudes, and knowledge you need before you start.

If you seriously want to work from home, you will probably be able to find a way to do it successfully. In fact, many people tell us that one of the greatest joys of having decided to go off on their own and work from home has been the satisfaction that comes from meeting new challenges and accomplishing things they never imagined they could do.

Here's a brief survey to help you identify what you may encounter, and some clues for minimizing problems before you go to the trouble and expense of actually moving your office to your home. If you're already working at home, the survey will provide some insight into problems or ambivalent feelings you may be having and what you might need to do to improve the situation. It takes only a few minutes to complete. Read the directions, make your choices, and then read on to interpret the results.

A Working-From-Home Suitability Survey

Below are descriptions of five offices. Choose the office in which you would most like to work. Mark that office with the number 1. Then rank the other offices from 2 to 5 in order of their interest to you. Be sure to include all the offices as you rank your preferences.

_1_ **Office A:** Walking into this warm, comfortable environment, you feel right at home. The office has a friendly, lived-in feeling. Cushioned chairs and couches are gathered around a casual seating area. The hum of conversation fills the air.

_2_ **Office B:** Everything about this office is unexpected. It's not like any workplace you've seen before. There's a sense of surprise and drama that makes just being here an adventure. The hustle and bustle of excitement fills the air.

_3_ **Office C:** The first thing you notice about this office is that there's a place for everything, and everything is in its place. There is a sense of history

and tradition about it. Everything down to the last detail is as it should be and exactly as you would expect it to be.

_3_ **Office D:** This office is first-class. There has been no compromise in quality. Excellence is clearly the standard, and from the awards tastefully displayed around the room, you know it has been achieved. Whatever is done here is done extraordinarily well.

_4_ **Office E:** This commanding office communicates a forcefulness that gets your attention. When you walk in the door you straighten up and take notice. It conveys a no-nonsense approach that demands results. The feeling of power in the office leaves a lasting impression.

Adapted from the PSE Preference Survey and Motivation Profile, _Copyright 1982, Paul and Sarah Edwards_

Interpreting Your Score

Each of the offices described in the survey represents one of the basic needs people seek to fulfill through work. By listing them in order of preference, you are indicating which needs are more important to you at this time in your life. Your choices provide some hints about how you're likely to respond to the most common concerns people have about working from home.

IF YOUR RATING WAS:

	1 OR 2	4 OR 5
Office A: *Will You Be Lonely?*	You may miss working with other people at an office. You'll probably like working from home better if your work brings people into your home or takes you out to work with others. You can create your own opportunities to get together with people. Team up with others. Schedule frequent meetings with customers and colleagues or get active in various organizations and associations. See chapter 17.	You are probably well suited for working at home. Relating to others is not the most important part of your work. You will most likely not be unduly stressed by leaving the social interaction of an office setting. But to maintain your social skills and to prevent becoming isolated from people in your field, you will need to schedule face-to-face contacts with other people.
Office B: *Will You Be Bored?*	Your work itself had better be exciting and stimulating. Otherwise, you'll find working at home might be too dull. Running your own business, however, with the challenges and risks of being an entrepreneur could keep you stimulated. See chapter 3.	You may enjoy escaping office pressures and hubbub by retreating to work in the quiet of a home office. The demands and uncertainties of running your own business could be more stimulating that you want, however, so perhaps you'd be more comfortable working from home on a salary, as a franchisee or on a long-term contract. See chapters 3 and 4.
Office C: *Will You Be Disorganized?*	You probably like a well-organized environment and value the order that comes from attention to detail. If you're able to create and stick to your own schedules	You may enjoy the freedom from imposed schedules and rules that working from home offers. At home you can work anytime, day or night; the work's always

(Continued on page 37)

(Continued from page 36)

IF YOUR RATING WAS:

1 OR 2

and organization, you may well enjoy working from home, where how you organize things is completely your responsibility. All the filing, scheduling, mailing, and cleaning will be up to . . . guess who?

4 OR 5

there. You can leave things messy or organize them as you wish. Left entirely on your own, however, you may find your desire for order will increase somewhat, and you will need to motivate yourself to be sufficiently organized to get your work done. See chapters 12 through 16.

Office D: *Will You Goof Off?*

You may be well suited to working from home because you're motivated to work hard and set high standards for yourself. You probably won't need a supervisor to keep you working all day. You may actually accomplish more with the independence of doing it all your own way. You could have a tendency to overwork, however, and if your other top choice was Office A, you may need to find a way to get recognition from others for doing a good job. See chapters 12 and 17.

You may find it difficult to work at home. You may start working later in the morning and stop earlier in the afternoon. Your attention may drift away from your work to nearby attractions like the refrigerator, the garden, or the TV. You may not be as productive as you would be with the structure and supervision of an office setting. See chapter 12.

Office E: *Will You Feel Less Important?*

You could enjoy being in command of your work and your destiny without the encumbrances of an outside organization. But you might miss motivating and directing others to action and feel limited by the confines of a spare bedroom. If so, you may want to consider building a full-fledged organization that you can run from your own home. See chapter 24.

You may feel relief from the power games and maneuvers of office politics and enjoy the freedom to work on your own.

As you can see, whether you'll find working at home a pain or a pleasure will depend primarily on you. While the survey may not determine whether working at home is right or wrong for you, it highlights some of the issues you may encounter and gives some direction on what to do about them.

Work Sheet: Special Considerations

Here are some other questions to answer when deciding to make the move home. Mark them yes or no:

____ Do you enjoy spending time in your home?

____ Is there adequate space for your work?

____ Do you like your neighborhood?

____ Do you get along with your neighbors?

____ Are the business resources you need available within a reasonable distance?

____ How will others you live with react to your working from home?

____ Will you enjoy being around them more often?

____ How will your customers or clients, your boss or co-workers feel about your working from home?

____ Can you replace the benefits you receive from your job, such as health and life insurance, disability insurance, retirement plan, paid vacation time, etc?

A strong negative response to any of these questions could mean that you may have serious adjustments to make. Fortunately, however, working from home affords great flexibility. If you want to make the move, the chances are you will be able to find some way to accommodate your particular needs and circumstances.

A trial week or even a weekend of working at home can help you discover what you need to do to make it practical for you. Once you start experimenting, you may find you'd rather fight than switch back to an outside office. The rest of this book will help you deal with the problems that can arise and with how to make the necessary adjustments for success in working from home.

CHAPTER 3

Working for Yourself: Full-Time and Part-Time

Goals
1. *Discover what it takes to make it on your own.*
2. *Know your choices.*
3. *Check out their pros and cons.*
4. *Avoid getting suckered.*
5. *Anticipate the roadblocks.*
6. *Know the start-up steps and have an entry plan.*
7. *Find start-up financing.*

I t is estimated that for every person who actually starts a business, three to ten more are thinking about it. Perhaps we all have a little bit of the entrepreneur in us, a secret wish tucked away somewhere to become a consultant, write a book, open a little shop, run a profitable Internet business, or invent a better mousetrap.

In the comfort of your living space you can now take your ideas and desires out of the back rooms of your mind and start your own business. Actually, this is the easiest route to working from home, and the business advantages are encouraging:

• **The sky's the limit on your potential income when you're your own boss.** Your business can be anything from a part-time sideline effort that brings in several hundred dollars a month to make ends meet to a multimillion-dollar enterprise like Hewlett-Packard, a company that began at home in a garage.

- *Starting a business at home keeps the initial costs down* so you can get established more easily, turn a profit sooner, and increase your chances of success.

- *You can save $8,000 to $22,000 a year* on office rental at current rental rates.

- *You can turn personal expenses like rent, furniture, and telephone costs into tax-deductible items* if you meet IRS requirements (see chapter 10).

- *You can test a new business idea without much risk,* or see whether you even like running your own business. In fact, by trying out the idea from home, you can tailor the amount of risk to meet your financial circumstances.

- *You keep more of what you earn.* We hear from people who are moving from an office to home and from their home to an office that it takes 2.5 to 3 times the gross income to produce the same net income when you work from an outside office.

Over 93 percent of people who use a home office for their business say they enjoy the arrangement.

INCOME OPPORTUNITIES MAGAZINE

WHAT IT TAKES TO GO OUT ON YOUR OWN

You've probably heard it said that entrepreneurs are a special breed. Some observers, like psychologist Alan Jacobwitz, have even gone so far as to say that entrepreneurs are born and not made, or at least that their early environment predisposes them to business success.

We agree that to succeed in your own business, you have to have the "right stuff." But today we live in an age of information, and almost anyone can acquire the knowledge and skills needed for successful self-employment. In fact, four out of five people starting home businesses aren't entrepreneurs in the classic sense of Bill Gates wanting to build a vast corporate empire. Most people working from home in their own business are slowly creating more financially and personally rewarding careers for themselves. The most important requirement is to be totally committed to starting and running a profitable home business. Men and women of all ages and backgrounds have done it.

Some were successful corporate professionals before taking the plunge. They began with the confidence, selling skills, marketing know-how, and business management experience so essential to business success. Yet many other success stories are about people who were total novices when they set out, unfamiliar with even the business basics like selling and negotiating.

What is the "right stuff"? What does it take to achieve a successful home-based business? The answers were almost as varied as the people themselves. However, our interviews do indicate that those who achieve success have several things in common:

- They enjoy what they're doing enough to keep going when times are rough.

- They are good at what they do.

- They specialize, providing a product or service that a particular group of people wants or needs.

- They have learned how to market themselves and their businesses. They know how they measure up to their competition. This helps them explain why their prospective customers should come to them and informs them how to get the word out about their businesses to just the right people.

- They stay in charge of their money.

- They are flexible enough to adapt to unforeseen circumstances and adjust their workday to the demands of the business.

- They believe in themselves and are sufficiently committed to their work, persisting until they get the job done right.

Success depends on finding the right combination of your personal preferences, talents, and skills that meet real-life needs people will pay to have met. The next step is to clearly define your business goals and develop an effective plan for reaching them. It's like putting together the pieces of a puzzle, starting with selecting the right business for you.

Will you succeed? That, of course, depends on you, but the odds are surprisingly in your favor. Contrary to the myth that nine out of ten new businesses fail within five years, home businesses do much better. Analysis of data from Link Resources, which does an annual survey of the work-at-home population, indicates that, on average, only 5 percent of home-based businesses go out of business each year. This means that over a five-year period, three out of four home-based businesses remain in business.

Why do home businesses do better than office- and store-based businesses? Probably because the risks of loss are fewer. There's no lease, and there probably are no employees, so the cost of staying in business is less. Add to this the fact that if you choose a business that you like doing, you're more apt to persist even if success is slow in coming. Although there may be many who say "I tried a home business but it didn't work out," it's been our experience that most of these folks probably didn't even take the first steps in starting their businesses, such as getting a business license or a Yellow Page listing, or joining a trade or professional association.

> *Fifty-nine percent of home businesses are operated part-time (under forty hours a week); 40 percent are full-time (forty hours+ a week)*
> INDEPENDENT INSURANCE AGENTS ASSOCIATION OF AMERICA

FOUR ROADS TO A HOME BUSINESS

Hundreds of different businesses can be started from home. Your only limitations are the space you have available and any legal restrictions that may apply. So the question becomes not so much "What's possible?" as "How do I select a business that has success potential and is right for me?" Here are four different roads you can take to answer this challenging question:

1. Starting a business on your own

2. Buying a franchise you can start at home

3. Joining a direct-sales organization

4. Buying a business opportunity

Let's consider each in greater detail.

CREATING A BUSINESS OF YOUR OWN

By far, the majority of people who have a home business started from scratch. They selected a business idea based on their unique interests, talents, contacts, and expertise and set out to serve customers and clients with their services or products.

Selecting a successful business requires that you tune in to the two most informative radio stations in the world: WPWPF ("What People Will Pay For") and WIIFM ("What's in It for Me?"). In selecting a business, you need to determine what you will enjoy and profit from, as well as what people need and will pay you money for.

Market research will help you tune in to WPWPF, and it doesn't need to be complicated or expensive. Your market research can be as simple as asking prospective customers what they need and investigating your competition. Find out what people are paying now and what advantages you can offer over the competition. Can you compete on price, service, quality, variety, or ease of use? You may even find that your competition needs you to help cover their overload.

Honor Roll of Home-Originated Companies

Amway
Apple Computer
Avon
Banana Republic
Baskin-Robbins ice cream
Ben & Jerry's ice cream
Bonne Bell cosmetics
Borland International
Brookstone Company
Cape Cod potato chips
Celestial Seasonings
Day Runner
Domino's Pizza
Electronic Data Systems
Estée Lauder cosmetics
Ford Motor Company
Gateway 2000
Gillette razor
Goldmine software
Häagen-Dazs ice cream
Hallmark cards
Hershey Foods
Hewlett-Packard
Intuit
Johnson Wax
King World Productions

Lane Bryant
Lillian Vernon catalog
Liquid Paper
Mac cosmetics
Mary Kay
Microsoft
Mrs Fields Cookies
Netscape
Nike
Northwest Bank
Pepperidge Farms
PhoneMate
Playboy
Purex
Reader's Digest
Redken
Russell Stover chocolates
Smith Brothers cough drops
SOS scouring pads
StairMaster
Steinway pianos
T.J. Cinnamon
Walt Disney
Welch's grape juice
Yahoo!

 Work Sheet: Key Questions to Ask Yourself

To tune in to WIIFM, answer these questions for yourself:

How much do you want to be directly involved with people? ___ All the time
___ Some of the time ✓ From a distance ___ Not at all

Do you want it to be a full-time or part-time business? Or are you looking for a
sideline business or a full-time calling? ✓ Full-time ___ Part-time

(Continued on page 44)

(Continued from page 43)

How many hours a week are you willing to invest in your business? 40 Be realistic. Consider your other time commitments. How much time can you commit to your business?

How important are prestige and image to you? What's your goal: ✓ Make a good income ___ Additional income ___ Have a glamorous or prestigious career and lifestyle

How much money do you need to make? You will be happier with a business that has the potential for matching your income. How much money do you want to make? 2 Each week? 8 Each month? 80 Each year?

What resources do you have available in terms of money, equipment, and know-how? These are the raw materials for turning your ideas into realities.

_____

_____

_____

_____

How much risk do you want to take? How much money can you afford to lose—or write off as an investment or "educational experience"—if the business is not successful? _____

Do you prefer a proven type of business or are you willing to take the chances of being a pioneer? ___ Proven business, please ✓ Pioneer something new

Do you want to do it your way or would you prefer a blueprint?
✓ Start my own business from scratch
___ Buy an existing business or franchise

Will you and can you get help from other people, including your family? Even when you're on your own, success is always a joint venture. The more support you can line up from family, friends, and colleagues, the easier it will be to get under way. ✓ Yes ___ Not really

Whom do you know or where can you find people who will help you? There is a wealth of resources available now, many of which are outlined at the end of this section. _____

How big is your market? Are there enough buyers that you can reach to support the level of income you desire or need? You'll need to do some homework to find this out. _____

Do you need any special licensing or training? For example, tax preparers, private investigators, and medical transcriptionists often do. ___ Yes ___ No

FINDING OPPORTUNITIES
RIGHT UNDER YOUR NOSE

With these considerations in mind, here are six possibilities for finding the ideal business for you, and they are right under your nose:

1. Turn What You Most Enjoy into a Business. If possible, turn your favorite hobby or interest into a business. There's nothing better than getting paid to do what you most enjoy. When teacher John Lewis neared retirement, he became interested in how people could remain vibrant and active after they retired. He found that knowing what to do was a problem for many retired people, so instead of retiring, he began doing retirement counseling.

Ideas for Turning a Hobby or Interest into a Business

Creating arts and crafts

Becoming a travel guide

Selling antiques or collectibles

Selling cosmetics

Interior decorating

Teaching dance and exercise classes

Maintaining a lifestyle meta site on the World Wide Web

Offering tennis lessons

Breeding, training, and grooming dogs

Giving singing or instrumental music lessons

Appraising collections (stamps, coins, art)

Running a recording studio

Corporate communications specialist Chris Richter had always loved art and popular music. After years of producing and documenting orthopedic operations and procedures for a large teaching hospital, he cured what ailed him; namely, his stifling full-time job. Now he runs a successful Web site design and multimedia production business geared to alternative music acts.

2. Turn Your Existing Job Skills into a Business. Accountants, communications specialists, engineers, graphic artists, health-care personnel, lawyers, programmers, sales and marketing professionals, scientists, secretaries, teachers—people from all walks of life—are turning their salaried jobs into profitable independent businesses. What job are you doing now? Consider how you could turn it into an entrepreneurial venture.

Gil Gordon was a personnel director; he became a telecommuting consultant. Doug Savarese is a financial software programmer and analyst; he started a sideline business writing custom software applications for fund

Work Sheet: What Would You Enjoy?

Here are some questions to help identify what you enjoy most:

- What do you get so involved in and intrigued with that you lose track of time?

- What do you do first when you get to a new city you've never been to before?

- What are you doing when you feel most like yourself?

- What are you doing when you like yourself the most?

- What are you doing when you feel most alive and energized?

- What do you like to talk about? What are other people talking about that draws you into the conversation?

- What do you take immediate action on? What do you delay doing?

- What do you do during your time off? When you're on vacation?

- What do you read? What newspaper or magazine headlines catch your eye?

- What do you collect? What mementos and photographs do you keep around your home and office?

managers. Karen Youngblood was a full-time mother; she runs a day nursery. Peggy Glenn was a secretary; she started a secretarial service, wrote a book about how others could do it, and is now a nationally known speaker, writer, and publisher.

Sometimes losing your job, or the threat of losing it, creates the momentum to start a home business. Sue Rugge started the highly successful research service, Information on Demand, after losing her job as a librarian owing to heavy cutbacks in the aerospace industry. In seven years, she and her partner turned the $250 they used to start the business into over half a million dollars' worth of sales. Reflecting back on the day she was laid off, Sue remembers, "I felt strongly that the only way I would ever have the job security and salary level I wanted was to work for myself. In other words, if you can't get a job, create one!"

"Fundamentally, all business is concerned with problem solving."

JACK NADEL, BUSINESS AUTHOR

3. Solve a Problem. Problems and complaints hold the seeds for many new businesses. People will pay to have someone do tasks they find unpleasant or need help with. Career counselor Lynne Frances had been teaching this philosophy to her students at the center where she worked.

When she decided to take her own advice, she opened a home-based cleaning service.

While Marsha Zlotnick was fighting to survive a life-threatening disease, she discovered that recovering involved many changes in what she could eat and other daily habits, but there were few places for people like herself to turn to for information, support, and assistance in making those changes. When she recovered, she turned her kitchen, dining room, and living room into a center for helping others conquer illnesses. She teaches cooking classes, offers courses in relaxation, acupressure, and massage, provides counseling, and has an extensive bookstore where people can get current information about getting and staying healthy.

Start a Business Doing Things Other People Hate to Do

- Income tax service
- Investment counseling
- Estate planning
- Real estate management
- Inventory or mailing-list management
- Selling (as an independent rep)
- Cleaning service
- Window washing
- Van and RV washing
- Shopping and gift-buying service
- Equipment repair and fix-it services
- Pickup and delivery service

---

4. Use a Hidden or Latent Talent. Sometimes the most obvious business is too obvious to notice. Karen Nestler had always given outstanding parties. She never thought of being a party planner until a friend asked her to plan a party for a family occasion. She gladly agreed and loved doing it but still didn't think of it as a business opportunity until her friend said, "That was so great, I would have paid for it." Then the light went on, and her business was born.

To unwind after a long shift of waitressing at an upscale Manhattan eatery, Amy Koza made art that involved paper and other textures. Many of her works took the form of small, intriguing books which she sometimes gave away to friends. The recipients of these gifts were so delighted that they showed them to *their* friends. The word on Amy's talents had gotten out. She now has a thriving part-time business making wedding albums and other custom-crafted gift books.

5. Use Technology and Other Resources You Have Around the House. Many people have created successful businesses with equipment and technologies they already had around the house. Conrad van de Bud turned his computer and video camera into a business taping events for broadcast on the Internet. Katherine Herman used her sewing machine to start an exclusive dress design business. Ray Jones's pickup truck became

Use Your Van or Pickup Truck to Start a Business

- Gardening or yard service
- Carpentry or house painting
- Swimming-pool maintenance
- Home maintenance and repair
- Mobile lunch wagon

- Party-plan sales (clothing, cosmetics, computers, housewares)
- Plant-care service
- Hauling or moving service
- Mobile computer-repair service
- Mobile auto-repair service

We'll Haul, a pickup and delivery service. A van or pickup truck, in fact, can be used to start a number of home businesses.

Beverly Matthews is one of hundreds of people who have turned their spare bedrooms into bed-and-breakfast inns. Two women in Texas even use their washing machines to supplement the family budget; they created a business called Washer Women, a laundry service for the crews of ships that dock in the local harbor. Your kitchen is another room that can be transformed into a wide variety of businesses.

Use Your Kitchen to Start a Business

- Catering services
- Homemade cakes and cookies
- Pet-food products
- Specialized candy
- Healthy snack food
- Hot sauces

- Cooking service for specialized diets (macrobiotic, vegan)
- Cooking school
- Herb and spice packages
- Canning gourmet fruits, jellies, and preserves

Because of their versatility, personal computers can literally become any one of hundreds of new businesses, from writing software or keeping mailing lists to helping people design personalized nutrition or exercise programs. Dorothy Baranski used her computer to start an executive service providing word processing, accounting, and bookkeeping for small businesses. Others have used their computers to start electronic shopping or referral services. We feature over one hundred computer-based businesses in our book, *Making Money with Your Computer at Home*.

Many people are using their mailboxes to start profitable businesses. Opening the mail each day to find a stack of cash orders feels great, and selling products through mail order is a growing business opportunity. Bud Weckesser actually turned a home beer-making guide he wrote into a

$700,000 mail-order enterprise. People spend over $350 billion a year on mail-order items—everything from books, clothing, and candy to housewares, plants, and sporting equipment. With the phenomenal growth of the Internet, forward-thinking entrepreneurs are creating World Wide Web/ mail order hybrids where goods are sold through Web sites but delivered through the mail. This greatly reduces the cost involved in printing and mailing traditional catalogs. People are selling unique products on their own Web sites or from an electronic mall like imall or ebay. They'll sell everything from collectibles to lingerie, peacocks to travel gear, gas masks to ghost hunting equipment.

Other Ideas for Putting Things Around the House to Work

- Use your piano for lessons, or rent practice time on it.

- Give swimming lessons in your pool.

- Turn a family room into a day-care center.

- Convert a side porch into a hothouse and sell exotic plants.

- Turn your yard into an organic vegetable garden and sell the produce.

- Dry the flowers growing in your yard and create gift sachets.

---

6. *Put What You Know To Work.* Because this is an information age, you can turn virtually anything you know into a business if enough people want to know it, too. Jeff Davis sold enough copies of a book he compiled called *1000 Adorable Names for Your Cat* to start a full-fledged pet-oriented mail-order company. Having taken singing lessons all her life, Marie Moran knew how to use her voice effectively. Noticing that a major problem people have is not projecting their voices adequately, she started a speaker's training program teaching executives how to give dynamic presentations. Wendy Perkins turned what she learned from taking temp jobs into a successful book and corporate training program on managing a contingent workforce.

If after reviewing so many business possibilities, you're still wondering just what would be the best business to pursue, here's a simple procedure developed by Mark Kleinschmidt, a Maine computer consultant, for narrowing down your choices:

Sit down and honestly make a list of what you can and can't do. Include everything you can think of. Then write a letter to yourself really bragging about your strong points.

Turn What You Know into a Business

- Plan parties and weddings.

- Become a consultant (management consulting, wardrobe or color consulting, interior decorating, home and office organization consulting).

- Write and sell "how-to" books (how to find a job, how to grow prize-winning azaleas, how to coach Little League soccer).

- Produce "how-to" tapes or video cassettes (how to buy investment property, how to sell your own home).

- Publish a specialty newsletter (backpacking news, organic gardening tips, guide to summer camps).

- Teach classes, give seminars, or tutor in your areas of expertise.

- Put your knowledge on the World Wide Web and solicit advertisers and sponsors, or charge for the content you provide.

There is no room for modesty in this procedure. When you've compiled your strengths and skills, start looking around your area and see what goods and services people are buying. Match those with what you are able to provide. This will greatly cut down the list of options. If you are lucky, you will have only two or three choices. Then ask yourself if you can run one of these businesses professionally. If you think you can, sit down and draft a plan for how you'll proceed. Show your plan to colleagues and professionals, and get ready to make some changes in it. Once you have gotten this far, you will definitely know whether or not you want to follow through.

Or pursue the 1,600 self-employment careers listed in the Appendix of our book *Finding Your Perfect Work.*

When you get to the stage of writing up your business plan, there are computer programs to help you do it, such as *Business Plan Pro* (Palo Alto Software), and for Macintosh owners, Tim Berry's *Business Plan Toolkit* (Palo Alto Software). See the Resources list at the end of this chapter.

Here is a list of start-up steps you need to take once you make a decision to proceed with a home business. In the upcoming chapters of this book you will find the details of how to carry out each step.

Start-up Steps for a Home Business

In going out on your own, it's important to do your homework and attend to the details of getting started. Here is a list of start-up steps:

- Select a business that meets the WIIFM and WPWPF tests. Expect to spend six to nine months researching and testing.

- Develop a business and marketing plan.

- Deal with the legalities—zoning, form of business, licensing, name registration, trademarks, permits, tax requirements.

- Create a financial structure—business bank account, bookkeeping system, credit, insurance, pricing.

- Set up your office—select an adequate location in your home; get needed equipment, furniture, and supplies; establish telephone service; arrange for a separate mailing address if necessary.

- Develop marketing materials—business cards, stationery, samples—and join associations.

- Establish a schedule and go to work getting business.

RESOURCES: CREATING A BUSINESS OF YOUR OWN

BOOKS

The Best Home Businesses for the Millennium: The Inside Information You Need to Know to Select a Home-Based Business That's Right for You, 3d ed. Paul and Sarah Edwards. New York: Tarcher/Putnam, 1999.

Crafting for Dollars: Turn Your Hobby into Serious Cash. Sylvia Landman. Rocklin, Calif.: Prima Publishing, 1996. ISBN: 0761504427.

Entrepreneur Magazine: Starting a Home-Based Business (Entrepreneur Magazine Series). New York: Wiley, 1996. ISBN: 0471109797.

Finding Your Perfect Work: The New Career Guide to Making a Living, Creating a Life. Paul and Sarah Edwards. New York: Tarcher/Putnam, 1996. ISBN: 087477795X.

Getting Business to Come to You, A Complete Do-It-Yourself Guide to Attracting All the Business You Can Enjoy, 2d ed. Paul and Sarah Edwards, with Laura Clampitt Douglas. New York: Tarcher/Putnam, 1998. ISBN: 087477845X.

Handmade for Profit: Hundreds of Secrets to Success in Selling Arts & Crafts. Barbara Brabec. New York: Evans, 1996. ISBN: 0871318121.

Homemade Money, 5th ed. Barbara Brabec. Cincinnati: Betterway Publications, 1997. ISBN: 1558704663.

Making Money in Cyberspace. Paul and Sarah Edwards, with Linda Rohrough. New York: Tarcher/Putnam, 1998. ISBN: 0874778840.

Making Money with Your Computer at Home. Paul and Sarah Edwards. New York: Tarcher/Putnam, 1997. ISBN: 0874778980.

The One-Page Business Plan. Jim Horan, 1997. Rent.a.CFO, 5917 Kipling Dr., El Sobrante, CA 94803; (510) 222-0805. E-mail: *rentacfo @aol.com*

The Plan: A Step-by-Step, Business Plan Guidebook. John W. Nelson III, with Karen Couto. New Ground; (800) 207-3550. Brief but useful.

Running a One-Person Business. Claude Whitmyer and Salli Rasberry. Berkeley, Calif.: Ten Speed Press, 1994. ISBN: 0898155983.

Secrets of Self-Employment: Surviving and Thriving the Ups and Downs of Being Your Own Boss. Paul and Sarah Edwards. New York: Tarcher/Putnam, 1996. ISBN: 08774778379.

Strategies for Small Business Success. Jane Applegate. New York: Plume, 1995. ISBN: 0452273528.

ON LINE

www.workingfromhome.com for hundreds of business ideas, start-up tips, special reports, updates of this book, and links to other resources.

SOFTWARE

Business Plan Pro, Palo Alto Software, Inc., 144 E. 14th Avenue, Eugene, OR 97401; (800)229-7526, (541)683-6162. Web: *www.palo-alto.com*

IdeaFisher. Idea Fisher System, Inc., 2222 Martin Avenue, Ste. 260, Irvine, CA 92612; (800)289-4332, (714)474-8111.

Tim Berry's Business Plan Toolkit, Palo Alto Software, 144 East 14th Avenue, Eugene, OR 97401; (800) 229-7526. Mac version.

BUYING A FRANCHISE

If the idea of starting a business of your own from scratch feels too scary, one way to reduce your fear is to purchase a franchise from a company that has already established a track record of success and will teach you how to use their proven methods. Of the literally thousands of franchises available today, the fastest-growing are service oriented. Over 10 percent of these can be run from home. In fact, the lower overhead of working from home makes starting a franchise even easier.

Examples of the types of service-business franchises that can be run from home include ABS Systems, which provides financial support services to small businesses, including bookkeeping, tax preparation, and financial planning; Pet Tenders, who provide boarding and walking services for pets; Computertots, which teaches computer classes at day-care centers, nursery schools, and community facilities; House Doctors Handyman Service, whose franchisees provide complete handyman services to homes; cleaning services like Duraclean International; home-inspection services like Housemasters; direct-mail advertising like Money Mailer; and directory publishing like Finderbinder/Sourcebook Directories. For a continuously updated list of home-based franchises, visit *workingfromhome.com*

When purchasing a franchise, you pay the franchiser for the right to use his or her trademark, trade name, products, and business system in exchange for an initial fee and ongoing royalties on your earnings.

In order to avoid the high costs of complying with franchising registration laws, small businesses will sometimes offer a license instead of a franchise. A license gives the start-up business person permission to use trademarks, proprietary methods, materials, or know-how and may also include training in using them in exchange for a fee and other ongoing costs of goods or materials.

The major advantage of buying a franchise is that you are purchasing a tested and proven business for which you receive training and support from the franchiser and other franchisees. In many cases you are also buying the name recognition of the franchise, which goes a long way, especially when you're starting out. This should reduce your learning curve and, theoretically, shorten the time before you start making a profit.

In franchising you are on your own, but you're not alone. With a good franchise, you get the benefit of valuable business training and support. You will have access to manuals with step-by-step instructions on procedures that have worked again and again. You should receive detailed business and marketing plans that are specific to your territory. Speaking of which, you should also get an exclusive territory. Some franchisers even offer financing for start-up fees and costs, specialized equipment and customized software, promotional materials, and continuing client referrals. With franchising, you often will enjoy the benefit of participating in national cooperative advertising. This means that all franchisees pay a certain amount (sometimes in the form of a specific advertising fee of about 1 to 3 percent of your earnings) that is pooled from all franchises for the purpose of advertising on a national level.

Franchising as an industry employs more than 8 million people in over sixty industries. Over one trillion dollars in sales were generated by franchised businesses in 1995.

Another benefit of buying a franchise is that if you do well in your business, you can often sell it because the new owner will have not only your ongoing experience but also the franchise name to help him or her get started.

In fact, buying a successful established business from an existing franchisee has several added advantages: You will have an existing cash flow, your starting income won't be a surprise because you can look directly at the books and see it, and you will also know just how supportive the franchiser has been. In other words, a lot of the guesswork is removed from starting a business.

Whether you buy a new or existing franchise, the expertise and support you receive can dramatically reduce the learning time involved in getting a business up and running. Walter Heidig of Binex Automated Business Systems, Inc., estimates that his franchisees are a full year ahead of consultants who try to run a computerized accounting and financial-planning service on their own.

Starting a home-based franchise, however, is not always peaches and cream. It usually means acquiring debt, and sometimes the franchise royalty is too high to justify the amount of money you can earn from running a one- or two-person business. You may find you're paying too much for a name that few people know. Low start-up fees that make entry easy may mean the parent company doesn't have the resources to provide you with as much support and training as you need. Lawsuits by franchisees against their franchisers for not delivering promised advertising and support are not uncommon. And if you're an independent-minded "my way" type of person, you may find the policies and procedures prescribed by the franchiser too restrictive and limiting to your creativity.

Longevity is a key predictor of a franchise's potential. Companies that were in business at least five years before franchising and four years since franchising are your best bet.

HOW TO DETERMINE WHETHER
FRANCHISING IS FOR YOU

When you buy a franchise, you are buying a successful format and the assistance to use it effectively. To help decide whether you are interested in owning a franchise, ask yourself:

• *How much structure do I need?* Are you already proficient at most aspects of running the type of business you are considering? Do you prefer to operate with a lot of flexibility and few rules? Do you work best when you make your own rules, or are you new to this business and uncertain about how you should proceed? Do you like to rely on the guidelines, policies, and procedures of someone with greater experience than yours?

• *How much am I willing to pay for the support?* Could you almost as easily learn what you need to run the business from books, seminars, college programs, or consultants, or does the franchise offer a superior or proprietary method of doing business that will give you a clear-cut advantage in attracting and satisfying your future customers and clients?

• *Do I have enough working capital to make the business work?* Generally you need at least three to six months to generate a profit. Could you start such a business for less than what the franchiser wants as a down payment? Many franchisers offer financing for a portion of the fee and the start-up costs. Others will provide you with assistance in developing a loan package. Would you be able to arrange for such financial backing if you were on your own? Franchise attorney Ira Nottonson of Sherman Oaks, California, advises that a good business opportunity should buy itself. In other words, after an initial down payment, the operating profit of the franchise should be enough to cover the payments on the balance of your loan.

For Herb and Linda Schulze, purchasing a home-based Chem-Dry franchise has worked well. Linda had been a nurse for twenty-five years; Herb, a clergyman for twenty-three years. They were both feeling "burned out" when they met at a personal-growth seminar. They fell in love, married, and began dreaming about expanding their lives in a business together. Since neither had any business background, a franchise made sense to them and they borrowed the $4,000 they needed for fees and start-up costs from Linda's parents.

Many years later, they're happy with their business. Looking back, Herb says, "A franchise means people who have never been in business can just follow the book and set up their business. We like the independence. The money is good. We made a profit immediately and paid back the loan within the first year. Best of all, we like to be of service to people."

He believes those interested in a franchise should talk with other franchisees about their experiences. For him, the most important factor has been the integrity on the part of the franchiser in following through on promises to provide strong initial training and to supply immediate technical assistance when problems arise.

---

66 Types of Franchises You Can Run from Home
(From No Fee to $50,000)

Alarm and security service	Elder care	Prenatal education
Answering service	Environmental safety	Publishing local resource directories
Balloon delivery	Executive search	Real estate advertising
Bingo publications	Financial planning	Refinishing and restoring
Bookkeeping service	First-aid training	Sales training
Business consulting	Handyman service	Screen repair
Business networking organizations	Holiday lighting and decoration	Securities and commodities brokering
Carpet cleaning and dyeing	Home inspection service	Sewer cleaning
Carpet restoration	House-sitting	Skin-care products
Catering service	Interior decorating	Sports team photography
Ceiling cleaning	Kitchen remodeling	Tax preparation
Chimney sweeping	Laminated child ID tags	Upholstery cleaning
Cleaning service	Lawncare service	Used-car evaluations
Companion service	Leak detection	Wedding planning
Computer classes for children	Loan brokering	Window-cleaning service
Computer consulting	Management training	Windshield repair
Computerized accounting	Medical claims processing	Venetian blind installation
Dance classes for preschoolers	Mobile disk jockey	Video repair
Direct-mail advertising	Newborn announcements	Video service
Drapery cleaning service	Parent education	Waterproofing
Education for children	Party planning	
	Payroll services	
	Pet-sitting	
	Photo IDs for children	

Because there are so many franchise opportunities today, you will undoubtedly be able to find one you can run from home in a field that's suitable for you. In the following Resources list you'll find additional places to look for more information on franchising.

Work Sheet: Picking a Franchise

The criteria you apply when picking a franchise should be similar to those you'd use to select any business. Ask yourself the following:

___ *Will this franchise let me do something I enjoy?* Just because someone else has made a franchise into a successful business doesn't mean you would enjoy doing it. Take the time to find out what you will spend most of your time doing in the day-to-day running of the franchise. We call this the "Core Function" of a franchise. If the actual Core Function doesn't match the Core Function you imagined, dissatisfaction and perhaps even the failure of the business could result.

___ *Am I knowledgeable about or interested in learning more about this field?* The franchisor will train you to run the business according to the methods that he or she has determined will have the greatest chance for success. Yet, successful franchisees realize that they have to take the initiative and learn as much as they can about their business and market. As more than one franchiser has said, "We provide support, but we don't run the business."

___ *Is this a business that people in my community need and will pay for?* Although the franchise may have worked elsewhere, it may not in your area. There are strong differences in the goods and services people buy from region to region. Also, a community may already have enough of a particular service like windshield repair or payroll services, for example. So make sure there's room in your area for whatever you will offer.

___ *Is the franchisor reliable, reputable, and financially solid?* We advise that you thoroughly investigate any franchise you are considering. Federal law requires all franchisers to provide prospective franchisees with a Uniform Franchise Offering Circular, or UFOC. This disclosure document will provide the basis for your investigation.

To find out if the franchisor is indeed reputable, the best place to start is by contacting those who have already purchased franchises and have been running them for some time. Don't just talk with the franchisees whom the franchisor recommends; for a full picture that includes the good, the bad, and the ugly, talk with a number of other franchisees. Also, talk with other franchisees and franchisors in the same field.

Checklist: Evaluating a Franchise

When investigating a potential franchise, here are the kinds of questions you need to be able to answer:

___ How long has the company been in business?

___ Is the franchisor new to his or her particular business but not new to franchising? (If the answer is yes, be wary; he or she may not be committed to supporting your business for the long haul.)

___ How many franchisees (franchised units) are there in the organization?

___ What is its cash position or credit rating? You can do a computer search yourself or hire an information broker to gather this information.

___ Are there any lawsuits pending from customers or franchisees?

___ Is the product or service guaranteed? Can it be sold all year long? Does the U.S. Bureau of Labor Statistics indicate that this is a growing industry?

___ Will you have an exclusive territory? Is the demand in that territory adequate to support another business?

___ Can your contract be renewed, sold, transferred, or terminated?

___ Does the company offer financing or assistance with developing a loan package?

___ What training does the franchiser provide? Is it ongoing? Can you call for help and expect to get it?

___ Does the franchise company have standards for screening applicants? Being too eager to take anyone, making big promises, and exerting pressure for a quick decision, are bad signs.

___ Is the franchisor registered to sell in your state?

___ Does the franchisor make unsubstantiated income claims?

RESOURCES: BUYING A FRANCHISE

BOOKS

The Franchise Kit/A Nuts-And-Bolts Guide to Owning and Running a Franchise Business. Kirk Shivell and Kent Banning. New York: McGraw-Hill, 1995. ISBN: 0070571252.

Home Businesses You Can Buy: The Definitive Guide to Exploring Franchises, Multi-Level Marketing, and Business Opportunities. Paul and Sarah Edwards, with Walter Zooi. New York: Tarcher/Putnam, 1997. ISBN: 0874778581.

PERIODICALS

Franchise/Business Opportunity Handbooks. Enterprise Magazines, Inc., 1020 North Broadway, Ste. 111, Milwaukee, WI 53202; (414) 272-9977.

WORLD WIDE WEB

International Franchise Association
www.ifa.org: the official site of the IFA.
www.workingfromhome.com: lists of home-based franchises with contact information.

JOINING A DIRECT-SELLING ORGANIZATION

For over 7.2 million people in the United States, working from home means being associated with companies like Avon, Discovery Toys, Fuller Brush, Mary Kay, Nu Skin, Herbalife, Rexall, Shaklee, Tupperware, Watkins, and, of course, the largest and most controversial company, Amway. These companies sell products such as cleaning supplies, cosmetics, foods, vitamins, security devices, and long-distance telephone service directly to consumers. Direct selling, at total sales of $18 billion in 1996, makes up approximately 3 percent of retail sales in the United States. Direct selling includes door-to-door sales, home-party sales, and multilevel marketing (MLM), or what is now popularly being called "network marketing."

Direct selling has advantages. It's a way of getting into your own business with little capital or sales experience. A number of companies provide extensive sales training and motivational support. And there have been enough cases of people with little education becoming wealthy through building multilevel marketing organizations to make many others see their opportunity in direct selling.

From the perspective of product manufacturers, direct selling, and MLM in particular, is a relatively low-cost way of bringing products to market. It avoids the high cost of establishing store distribution systems and national advertising. Because it costs a company less to establish an MLM organization, many companies that are longer on hope than capital come into existence. An estimated 90 to 95 percent of them, however, are out of business within two years.

Before investing your time and money in a direct-selling organization, it's important to make sure the company you're joining is worth the invest-

Locus of Direct Sales	
In the home	59%
Over the phone	15.9%
In a workplace	14.8%
At a public place*	4.3%
Other locations	6%

Fairs, shopping malls, trade show, etc.

Provided by Direct Selling Association

ment of your time and priceless energy. This means being able to distinguish a sound business from an outright scam, such as an illegal pyramid scheme, or from an undercapitalized or inexperienced company whose chances for survival are only slightly better than that of the carrier pigeon.

Pyramid Schemes

An illegal pyramid scheme exists if the majority of your profits are to come from signing people up, also known as "recruiting," rather than from product sales. A clear indicator that this is the case is when there is a cost, usually over $500, for obtaining the right to sell a company's products. If you have doubts about whether a plan is a pyramid scheme or questions about the soundness of the company, check it out with the Better Business Bureau in your community or in the headquarters city of the company. You can also check with local and state consumer protection agencies, the attorney general responsible for consumer protection both in your state and in the headquarters state of the company, the regional office of the Federal Trade Commission, the U.S. Postal Inspection Service, and the Direct Selling Association in Washington, D.C. Be aware, however, that not finding a complaint does not mean the offer is legitimate; the company may be new, or people who have paid money for the business may feel too embarrassed to complain.

Be extremely skeptical of companies that make unrealistic income claims. Ads with promises of lifelong riches for a few hours of work or that feature well-dressed people standing in front of a Rolls-Royce parked in front of a mansion with an Olympic-sized swimming pool should be considered fiction. Neil Offen, president of the Direct Selling Association, says, "The opportunity in direct sales is real but it's hard, hard work to be successful. It takes forty to seventy hours a week." Recruiting other people into an organization takes endless meetings, phone calls, cajoling, counseling, and training; and actually selling the products or services requires an equal effort.

Work Sheet: Finding the Right Opportunity

If direct selling interests you, here are some questions to ask to help you find the right opportunity.

___ **1. Would you buy the products or services the company offers yourself?** In order to succeed in direct selling you will need to be passionate about the product or service you offer. This will make you a more convincing salesperson. If you wouldn't buy the product or service, how can you expect to convince someone else to buy it or sell it for you?

___ **2. Is the company selling consumable products that appeal to most people?** Because it takes many contacts to make sales, you want a product that large numbers of people desire and use often. Products should offer some advantage—such as good price or high quality—over products available in stores or by mail, or people will turn to established brands or discounted prices in stores. High-quality products encourage repeat sales. That's important because it's easier to resell to people to whom you've already sold than continuously to find new customers.

___ **3. How long has the company been in business?** Companies that have been in business for several years are better risks. Eldon Beard, who has been involved with MLM companies for a number of years, cautions, "While 'ground-floor' and 'start-up' opportunities can be good, there is a much greater risk involved."

___ **4. Do you stand to lose much money?** Beard says, "Most legitimate MLM companies only require you to pay a small fee for a distributor kit; initial purchase of a volume of product is not a requirement for getting started in the business." If you actually stock and deliver products, does the company have a buy-back policy for the products you stock? Beard says, "A good company should offer to buy back unsold inventory for at least 80 percent of what you paid. If the company has no such policy, you could be stuck with a lot of unsold inventory should you decide to quit selling the product." In fact, you may want to select a company that requires little stocking of products. Products consume your capital, take up space, and force you to keep records and inventory.

___ **5. Are the sales, marketing, and compensation plans easy to understand?** A complex plan with a hard-to-explain commission structure will make it difficult for many people to achieve success. If you can't understand the compensation plan, how will you be able to recruit others to join the company?

___ **6. If success in the company you're considering depends on recruiting other people, do you have the ability to inspire other people's efforts and the stamina to deal with people's problems and long hours?** The skills of a sales professional are less important than those of a sales manager, and it's been found that traditional sales skills do not translate into success in multilevel marketing. This is because most people who are sold on a business opportunity drop out as distributors within sixty days.

Common Complaints

Direct sales is not for everyone. Common complaints are:

- Depending on your personality, it can be discouraging to encounter negativity from people who don't like direct sales or have themselves been involved with a failed MLM effort of one kind or another. Many people also alienate friends, family, and co-workers through the persistent sales and recruitment tactics many companies encourage.

- With the exception of major firms that have lasted for decades, most companies and their products have short life spans. Fewer than two hundred companies account for 90 percent of the sales volume in direct sales.

- With mature companies, finding potential customers and recruits can be difficult.

- The constant emphasis on recruiting new people can be disconcerting.

- Contact with sales "evangelists" who prod, spur, and classify those who do not perform as "losers" is offensive.

- Some companies restrict advertising and place limits on the way products can be sold; for example, by not permitting their sale in retail stores even if the distributor is the store owner.

- Having to attend many evening and weekend meetings and rallies can mean sacrificing home life and relations with friends and family members who, as a result, may not look favorably on your enterprise.

- Most people don't make much money. According to data compiled by the Direct Selling Association, the average gross monthly income for all salespeople in multilevel in 1997 was $178, down from $191 in 1996.

RESOURCES: JOINING A DIRECT-SELLING ORGANIZATION

BOOKS

Home Businesses You Can Buy: The Definitive Guide to Exploring Franchises, Multi-Level Marketing, and Business Opportunities. Paul and Sarah Edwards, with Walter Zooi. New York: Tarcher/Putnam, 1997. ISBN: 0874778581.

Power Multi-Level Marketing. Mark and Rene Yarnell. New Orleans: Paper Chase Press, 1997. ISBN: 1883599067.

Schemes, Scams, and Frauds: How to Protect Yourself. Wilbur Cross. New York: Harper Mass Market Paperbacks, 1999. ISBN: 0061010278.

Wave 3: The New Era in Network Marketing. Richard Poe. Rocklin, Calif.: Prima Publishing, 1994. ISBN: 1559585013.

WORLD WIDE WEB

Direct Selling Association
www.dsa.org

BUYING A BUSINESS OPPORTUNITY

Working from home is so popular today that thousands of companies are selling businesses-in-a-box, or what we sometimes call just-add-water or mix-and-stir businesses. Usually offered through television infomercials, magazine ads, trade shows, or seminars, these businesses generally are easy to understand and explain, and place a premium on your ability to sell a product or service. Popular business opportunities (biz ops) include cleaning, telephone and travel services, personalized children's books, gift baskets, and home improvement. However, others are actually in established fields or actual careers such as business arbitration, home inspection, and medical billing, and some may involve months of training.

Although many business opportunities are legitimate, others are of rather dubious value. Lee Graham, who has analyzed hundreds of such operations, says, "Eighty-five to ninety percent of the biz ops advertised have no business value. Typically, the entire 'business' consists of a cheaply produced booklet, eight to ten pages long, that contains little information of real substance." Business opportunities sold through seminars may pump you up and create group feeding frenzies with as much as $50,000 changing hands in minutes at the back of the room as the audience rushes to get one of a "limited supply" of business packages.

Business opportunities are not franchises. Although they may promise that the buyer will make money from the business activity, biz ops usually cost less, don't require payment of ongoing fees, and offer far less training, legal protection, and use of exclusive trademarks and procedures for operating the business.

We do meet people on line or at our public presentations who have made money with business opportunities. Because the price is generally under $500, buying a business opportunity can be an economical way to start a home business. One way of thinking about it is to compare the cost to the purchase of an extensive training manual or a short-term course.

We do, however, offer several cautions. Just as with a business you would start from scratch, make sure a business that sounds simple and easy is also one you will enjoy running. Chances are good that much more hard work is involved than you might imagine or are led to believe. Few businesses prosper just by placing ads in newspapers and magazines. And because business opportunities are being sold in substantial numbers, you can expect plenty of competition from other people offering the same product or service in your area. Remember: You're not buying a business; you're buying an opportunity.

Increasingly, states are passing laws that provide consumer protection for buyers of business opportunities, generally those costing more than $500 and, in some states, as little as $250. These laws are generally called Seller Assisted Marketing Plan (SAMP) laws. SAMP laws generally require that a biz op seller must give you some form of disclosure documentation as well as wait a specific amount of time, usually called a "consideration period" (typically seventy-two hours, but the period varies from state to state), before any sort of payment can be collected from you. The following states have SAMP laws in place and require vendors to register with the state and disclose information to prospective buyers: Alabama, California, Connecticut, Florida, Georgia, Illinois, Indiana, Iowa, Kentucky, Louisiana, Maine, Maryland, Michigan, Minnesota, Nebraska, New Hampshire, North Carolina, Ohio, Oklahoma, Rhode Island, South Carolina, South Dakota, Texas, Utah, Virginia, and Washington. Other states will be joining them in having laws regulating business opportunity vendors, as more and more people seek ways to maintain their middle-class standard of living into the next century.

It only makes sense that the more money and time you will be asked to invest in a business opportunity, the more you owe it to yourself to check out its validity. Some ways to check out the value of a business opportunity are:

• *Determine if the company has had complaints filed with the agencies listed on page 68 or the state attorney general's office of your own state and the state in which the company is based.* If so, has the company satisfactorily resolved all or most complaints?

• *Ask for the names and phone numbers of people who have bought this opportunity.* Call them. Check to see how long they have been in business. You want to talk with people who have been at the business for at least a year. Often the most enthusiastic people are those who are new to the business and still filled with high expectations. If there has been a training class, ask for the names and numbers of other people who were also in the class and talk with them. Check out the people you talk with to see if they have become "official" businesses, that is, have they obtained business licenses or business telephone lines. Statistically at least one in ten will have.

• *Ask the people you are talking to if they are being paid to talk with you.* Some unscrupulous companies use "singers"—people who are not actually involved in the business but are paid to say they recommend it.

• *Know what you are buying.* Are you buying a booklet, a training program, a business plan, a software package, ongoing support, special equipment, the right to sell the company's products retail or wholesale, or a license that allows you to use the company's business name? Different business opportunities may offer any one of these or any combination thereof. Assure yourself that what you receive is what you were told you would get and is commensurate with what you're paying.

Common Work-at-Home Schemes, Scams, and Rip-offs

- Stuffing envelopes. This scheme involves nothing more than selling instructions and sample ads directing you to use them to get people to pay you to find out how they can stuff envelopes.

- Chain letters. Always illegal, always a bad idea.

- Internet consulting: watch out if the business consists mainly of selling completed Web sites and space on virtual servers.

- Simple tasks like clipping newspaper coupons, keeping a diary based on watching TV or listening to the radio, reading books, taking photos, and making videos and renting time on your computer that require you to send money to register or enroll.

- At-home assembly of any kind. Often you will have to buy supplies exclusively from the seller at prices too high for you to make a profit on your sales. Many of these schemes also include draconian, arthritis-producing production quotas or minimums you must meet before you will receive worthwhile payment.

- Lists or directories of work-at-home jobs.

- Any business plan that represents that you can easily make thousands of dollars by placing similar ads yourself.

- Plans that promise that many people will send you money and instruct you to send money to the top few names on a list, removing the first name and adding your name to the bottom of the list. Beware that the scheme may be called a mailing list or mail-order business and claim to be legal.

MAKING SURE YOU DON'T
GET SUCKERED

When we decide to pursue our dreams, to go for what we truly want instead of settling for whatever comes along, we automatically become vulnerable to being suckered. Dreams are often so fragile and yet so formidable that they're easily trampled on or abandoned. So whenever someone comes along who tells us what we so much want and need to hear, we can be like putty in their hands.

Following a dream can blind us to what would otherwise be the most obvious of hucksters. We've met countless people who purchased business opportunities or signed up for multilevel programs that, to an outsider, were obviously bogus, because "it sounded so good." Even worse are the many painful stories we've heard from people who were taken in by unscrupulous partners, investors, agents, or reps who seemed to be the "answer to all their prayers." If you're a stay-at-home mother, a senior citizen, someone with a disability, unemployed, seeking a second income, or a college student, you are even more likely to be victimized, according to the Council of Better Business Bureaus.

Make sure you don't get taken. Whenever you hear someone saying the things you've been yearning to hear or things that sound so good you never dreamed you'd actually hear about anything like that, let it be a warning signal that sets off an alarm in your head with bells, whistles, and bright shiny lights saying "Proceed with caution." The minute you hear that alarm, use the following visualization:

Imagine that you're actually two people traveling in a foreign country:

- a small child who's so thirsty and hungry that he would eat and drink anything he could get his hands on. That's the part of you that's pursuing your dream and believes it will happen despite the lack of support and negative messages you've encountered.

- the parent who wants to make sure whatever the child eats and drinks won't poison or make him or her ill. That's the part of you that is objective enough to protect yourself from getting suckered.

With this image in mind, here are some guidelines that the parent part of you can use to protect your eager and hungry child from the tempting sights and smells of opportunity knocking.

Checklist: Protect Yourself

___ *Don't make decisions about opportunities from your heart alone.* Run all such "offers" through careful, objective scrutiny.

___ *Always arrange to take the time you need to make an objective, informed decision.* Do not let yourself be pressured into acting immediately.

___ *The more someone pressures you to act instantly, the more suspicious you should be.* We once had a salesman tell us, for example, that we had to sign a contract that very day after a thirty-minute phone conversation or he could not proceed. We ran like a couple of rabbits. What kind of company would want to do business with someone who would make a decision like that on the spot?

___ *Don't be tempted by special offers that prevent you from making an objective, informed decision; e.g., "My prices go up tomorrow" or "This discount applies only today."* Fine. Find out what the price will be once you've had the time you need to make an informed decision and consider that paying the difference will be well worth the investment. If the cost at that time will be prohibitive, look elsewhere.

___ *Do not do business with any company or individual who refuses to give you the names, addresses, and telephone numbers of other people with whom they have worked.*

___ *Never, never ignore that little voice in your head or that little twinge in your stomach that's telling you to proceed with caution.* That's your intuition and if you don't listen to it, you'll be saying later, "Something told me this was too good to be true. Why didn't I listen!" If you have any doubts, wait. Gather more information. Give your doubts time to surface so you can either dismiss or address them with confidence.

___ *Ask yourself, What's the worst thing that could happen?* Sometimes an offer sounds so good, you just want to throw caution to the wind and go for it. Before you do, however, make sure you're willing to live with the worst thing that could happen.

For example, if you impulsively send off $100 for a guidebook, the worst thing that could happen might be that it would sit on your bookshelf unused. But if you buy a $10,000 business opportunity at an expo, your family finances could be set back more than you can afford.

If someone requires you to sign a two-year exclusive distribution contract, you're giving up all other opportunities during that period.

These guidelines and the ones in chapter 4 should help you protect the tender, but challenging, dreams you're raising into a healthy, strapping business that will provide ample sustenance for you and your family.

RESOURCES: IDENTIFYING, REPORTING, AND GETTING HELP WITH WORK-AT-HOME SCHEMES

Better Business Bureaus are located in about two hundred communities. The Council of Better Business Bureaus, Inc., 4200 Wilson Boulevard, Ste. 800, Arlington, VA 22203, publishes pamphlets entitled *Tips on Multi-Level Marketing (How to Tell a Legitimate Opportunity from a Pyramid Scheme)* and *Tips on Work-at-Home Schemes*. (703) 276-0100. Send a self-addressed stamped envelope and include $2 for postage and handling. Web site: www.bbb.org

Consumer Fraud Alert Network is an on-line resource that offers tips on how to avoid being a victim of fraud and contains extensive links to other helpful sites. The site also contains a section that deals specifically with home-based business scams. *www.world-wide.com/HomeBiz/Fraud.htm*

Consumers' Resource Handbook from the United States Office of Consumer Affairs is the most comprehensive listing of state and local trade associations and other sources of information on work-at-home scams and other consumer issues. It is available free by writing Handbook, Consumer Information Center, Dept. 597 F, Pueblo, CO 81009; (719) 948-4000. Web site: www.pueblo.gsa.gov

Federal Trade Commission, Consumer Response Center, Sixth Street and Pennsylvania Avenue, N.W., Room 200, Washington, DC 20580; (202) 326-3128.

National Business Opportunities Bureau, 2064 Peachtree Industrial Court, Ste. 404, Atlanta, GA 30341; (800) 829-3547. Those offering business opportunities can register with this organization, although not all do. Registrants also submit their materials and agreements for use in reporting by the bureau.

Royal Canadian Mounted Police, 225 Jarvis Street, Toronto, Ontario, M5C 2M3 Canada.

U.S. Postal Inspection Service, Fraud Branch, Room 3147, 475 L'Enfant Plaza, Washington, DC 20260 or contact your local postmaster for the number of the nearest Postal Inspection office. We recommend making a habit of sending the postal inspector chain letters, underpayment of first-class postage schemes, and other questionable offers you receive in the mail or that instruct you to use the mail.

RESOURCES: BUYING A BUSINESS OPPORTUNITY

BOOKS

Home Businesses You Can Buy: The Definitive Guide to Exploring Franchises, Multi-Level Marketing, and Business Opportunities. Paul and Sarah Edwards, with Walter Zooi. New York: Tarcher/Putnam, 1997. ISBN: 0874778581.

PERIODICALS

Small Business Opportunities. Harris Publications, 1115 Broadway, 8th floor, New York, NY 10010, (212) 462-9585.

WORLD WIDE WEB

Business Opportunity News
www.business-Opps-news.com
Business Opportunities News on-line magazine. Listings of biz ops, editorials, and other resources.
www.workingfromhome.com. Lists of home-based business opportunities with contact information.

SIX ROADBLOCKS TO AVOID WHEN GOING OUT ON YOUR OWN

Our favorite questions to ask successful home-business people are: "What surprises did you have? Did you encounter any detours? Were there any land mines hiding along your path?" And, indeed, whether they start a business from scratch, buy a franchise, or join a direct-sales organization, their answers indicate similar surprises, detours, and roadblocks. Here are six of the most common problems and some ideas on how to avoid them:

1. Never Getting Started

Many who hope to start a business never get beyond the wishful-thinking stage. Under the pressure of our day-to-day responsibilities, some brilliant ideas and good intentions get put on the back burner and remain a matter of "Someday I'm going to . . ." A few of these ideas, of course, are best forgotten. Yet, unless you give them a chance, you'll never know which ones would have worked—until one day you read in the paper or see on TV that someone else beat you to it and is turning the same idea into a success story.

To avoid the death of a good idea, plan to research and test yours as soon as you get it. Begin by reading up on the subject and talking with others who know about what you want to do. Find out who's already working in the field. Tell other people about your idea and get their reactions. If the idea still seems good, set out a step-by-step plan to test it, and establish target dates to complete each step. Then put your plan into action.

By breaking your research, testing, and action steps into small chunks, you can perform some small task looking toward your future on even the busiest of days.

2. Running into Money Problems

Lack of capital and proper financial management are the most common reasons small businesses fail. Here are some of the typical financial problems home businesses encounter:

- Not having enough money to cover start-up and operating expenses
- Not having sufficient funds with which to grow
- Insufficient funds for proper marketing
- Too much debt
- Cash-flow problem
- Inadequate financial planning
- Not charging enough to make a profit
- Poor credit and collection practices
- Inadequate bookkeeping.

Start Small. Unless you have extensive experience in running a business like the one you plan to start and have contracts in hand, we advise that you keep your start-up expenses low. For example: Cynthia Post started a part-time calligraphy business with a $75 pen set; within a few months, she attained a nice side income from producing menus for local restaurants. Laura Ruhle launched Twice-Loved Treasures with only $250; she sells collectibles and dolls through on-line auction, ebay. She now processes over 140 invoices monthly, and has surpassed her former corporate salary.

Your business may demand more of an initial investment, but chances are you will be able to keep your cash outlays to under $5,000. Why? First, that's what most people do. The Small Business Administration reports that 65 percent of all businesses are started for under $5,000. Now given the fact that almost half of U.S. households have a personal computer and printer and that the cost of office technology keeps going down while its capability to help you market yourself keeps going up as the Internet provides you with access to information, low-cost communication, and customers, most of your start-up money can go into marketing expenses like association dues, samples, and software to help operate your business.

If your resources are limited, start gradually. Use your brains instead of your checkbook. Find someone in a college art class to design your logo, cards, and stationery. Use your printer and preprinted paper to print your own business cards and stationery in small quantities. Even if you're unemployed and have little savings, you may be able to use unemployment insurance funds to start your business. Because of successful pilot programs in Massachusetts and Washington, Congress, as part of the North American Free Trade Act, authorized the states to in turn pass legislation that will allow up to 5 percent of people receiving unemployment insurance to start businesses. The Washington and Massachusetts programs found that people starting businesses were able to get off unemployment more quickly than those who were looking for jobs.

Know How Much Money You'll Need and Plan For It. To determine how much money you need to have coming in, you'll need to calculate three things:

- ***Living expenses***—How much do you need to live on? This is the "salary" you must produce to support yourself and your family. Be sure to include taxes and such fringe benefits as health insurance formerly covered by your employer.

- ***Direct costs***—How much will it actually cost you to produce your product or deliver your service? This includes all expenditures for travel, telephone, and materials and supplies used in serving a specific client or customer.

- ***Overhead***—How much will it cost you to run your business? This includes all the other costs of being in business like your marketing, utilities, office furniture, and equipment.

CALCULATING YOUR SALARY. To calculate how much your earnings need to be, first identify three income figures. What you need:

- to survive $_____
- to be comfortable $_____
- to thrive $_____

It's important to know these three figures because all products or services you might choose do not have the same income potential. Also, knowing what you need and want to earn will help you set goals, price your services, and determine how many hours you will need to bill out each week.

First, unless you're looking for a way to pay for a hobby, we don't think you should even consider undertaking a business that will not enable you to at least achieve your survival income. That's why in chapter 1 we classify some of the businesses as merely part-time or add-on businesses rather than full-time ventures.

Second, while you might be willing to live at the survival level for a while, over time you probably won't be happy putting in long hours on work for an income that barely keeps you afloat. So you should also project how what you offer can provide you with what you consider to be a comfortable income within a reasonable period of time. And if the business you're considering can never produce what you'd need to thrive, even after several years of working at it, you may burn out on that business within a short time. So make sure that the business you chose has at least the potential of achieving all three of your income targets.

Identifying Direct Costs. Direct costs—those that are directly billable to your clients or customers or that you must incur up front to produce a product—are quite low for such businesses you can start with a computer as resume writing or computer consulting. Even businesses like these, however, have some direct costs—like the high-quality paper used to print out the finished resume or the cost of driving to consult with clients—so don't minimize them.

Businesses such as computer-designed T-shirts and novelties, on-line information research, or newsletter producion have higher direct costs. You must pay for the manufacturing of novelties, for example, or incur the costs of getting on-line to do research, which can be expensive. In such cases, you will need to pass these costs along to your clients by making sure you set your prices high enough or, in some cases, by billing separately for them.

At times, you may need to absorb these costs before you get paid by your clients, so calculating these expenses carefully will help you manage your cash flow. Calculating your direct costs enables you to know how much cash you need to have on hand and to plan for the time between when you do your work and when you actually get paid.

Including Overhead. By working from home you will either avoid or reduce overhead costs by nearly 40 percent of the typical expenses required for storefront or office-based businesses. You will, nonetheless, have some overhead costs, which people working from home often fail to build into their fees. Then they wonder why they always seem to be living on less than they had expected.

In the process of interviewing home-business owners for our previous book, *The Best Home Businesses for the 90s,* we discovered one reason for this common oversight. We learned that very few owners of home businesses know what their overhead is. By using money-management software like *Quicken, Quickbooks, Microsoft Money,* or *Managing Your Money,* you can quickly and easily track your overhead and therefore make sure your prices take these costs into account.

You can refer to the following work sheet, which includes standard home-business overhead items, when making your initial calculations.

START-UP COSTS. In addition to estimating your income needs and cash flow, you will undoubtedly also have some one-time start-up costs that you'll incur in getting under way. Fortunately, as we said, most businesses are started for under $5,000, and much of that cost involves computer

---

Work Sheet: Calculating Your Gross Salary Needs

For the three income targets you project, estimate how much you would need to spend each month on each item.

	SURVIVAL	COMFORTABLE	IDEAL
Auto expenses			
Clothing			
Food			
Health insurance			
Home maintenance			
Entertainment			
Education			
Medical and dental care			
Personal care			
Rent or mortgage			
Taxes (federal, state, self-employment) (see chapter 10)			
Utilities			
Other living expenses			
Total living expenses	$	$	$

Work Sheet: Calculating Direct Costs of Producing Your Product or Service

Estimate what each of the following will cost you:

Materials   _____
Travel to and from client sites   _____
Long-distance phone calls   _____
Services (e.g., printing, design,   _____
   subcontracting)
Supplies   _____
Other   _____

Total direct costs   _____

 Work Sheet: Calculating Overhead Costs for Monthly Operating Expenses

Estimate what each item will cost per month:

	SURVIVAL	COMFORTABLE	IDEAL
Insurance (see chapter 11)	_____	_____	_____
Interest or loan payments	_____	_____	_____
Marketing costs (i.e., advertising, publicity, marketing)	_____	_____	_____
Maintenance	_____	_____	_____
Office supplies (see chapter 7)	_____	_____	_____
Postage	_____	_____	_____
Professional fees (e.g., legal and accounting)	_____	_____	_____
Telephone and fax	_____	_____	_____
Utilities (above household usage)	_____	_____	_____
Other	_____	_____	_____
Total overhead	$_____	$_____	$_____

equipment and software you may already have. By working from home, your start-up costs can be considerably lower than they would be if you were setting up shop in an outside office or storefront.

In calculating your start-up costs, plan to include funds to acquire at least the following list of what we consider to be the minimum in home-office equipment you will need:

- Office furniture

- Computer hardware and software

- Printer, fax, scanner, copier, and answering machine or voice mail

- Business cards, stationery, brochures, other collateral materials, and supplies

- Other: separate business phone line, organizational dues, and any special requirements of a particular business

Such a basic setup can be purchased new for as low as $2,000 to $3,000, depending on the quality and power of the hardware you buy and the fanciness of the stationery and supplies you choose. For additional information on the details of purchasing home-office equipment, furniture and supplies, see chapters 7 and 8. Use the following work sheet to estimate your start-up costs.

To this amount, be sure to add the cash you will need to have on hand to cover initial operating expenses until you receive your first income. You'll need to have an entry plan for covering these initial operating expenses plus your living expenses while you're starting up. Once you've done these calculations, you'll have the basic information you need to develop such a plan, and as you'll see in the following pages, you have a variety of options for doing this with optimal safely and security in mind.

For information on how to make sure your fees and pricing structure cover your costs and other money-management issues, see chapters 14 and 22.

Go Easy on Loans and Investors. There are a variety of ways to finance your start-up costs. You can use your own funds, find investors, or borrow. Although it's very tempting to try to find investors or to get a loan, we advise planning to finance your business yourself to the greatest extent possible. Borrowing, even from friends or relatives, puts your new business under the additional financial pressure of having to pay back loans. Often it's difficult to get loans or investors for a start-up home business, anyway, unless you are beginning with lucrative contracts or purchase orders in hand, have an outstanding reputation in your field, or are buying a franchise or existing business that backs you up with a known name.

Work Sheet: Calculating Start-up Costs

For the three levels of income you project, estimate how much you will need to spend on each item.

	SURVIVAL	COMFORTABLE	IDEAL
Business cards	_____	_____	_____
Letterheads, envelopes, etc.	_____	_____	_____
Business licenses and other fees	_____	_____	_____
Consulting and training fees (legal, tax, computer tutor, etc.)	_____	_____	_____
Initial marketing costs of brochures, Web site, etc.	_____	_____	_____
Miscellaneous office equipment	_____	_____	_____
Answering machine or voice mail	_____	_____	_____
Computer and monitor	_____	_____	_____
Printer	_____	_____	_____
Fax technology	_____	_____	_____
Modem technology	_____	_____	_____
Scanner	_____	_____	_____
Other specialized equipment	_____	_____	_____
Office furnishings (desk, chair, storage, etc.)	_____	_____	_____
Remodeling of home (if needed)	_____	_____	_____
Software: general	_____	_____	_____
specialized	_____	_____	_____
Telephone installation	_____	_____	_____
Other start-up expenses specific to your business	_____	_____	_____
Total start-up costs	$_____	$_____	$_____

According to a 1997 Los Angeles Times *survey, more than one-third of small-business owners surveyed said that they used their credit cards to "finance everything from office supplies to inventory and equipment." This figure has doubled since their first survey, conducted in 1993.*

Fortunately, most home businesses do not involve extensive start-up costs. As a result, most people can "bootstrap" their businesses, that is, they can get under way using financial resources they have on hand such as existing earnings, savings, investment income, retirement funds, or insurance loans. Many people finance limited start-up costs with credit cards. Here is a list of possible sources of financing:

 Checklist: Six Sources of Start-up Financing

Fewer than 1,200 companies a year attract venture capital, and the median deal size is $13,000,000, with most investment taking place in Massachusetts and Northern California's Silicon Valley. Rarely is venture capital an option for a home-based business, but here are some more accessible sources of start-up cash.

___ *1. W-4 adjustment:* Since you will become eligible for some business and home-office tax deductions, reduce your W-4 withholding on your existing job and use the additional income you will see in your paycheck to cover your business start-up costs.

___ *2. Credit cards:* While you won't want to use credit cards as your primary source of major funding because credit card interest is expensive, you can use them for many types of specific start-up office equipment, printing marketing materials, supplies for filling initial orders and even postage expenses. Since you can write checks against credit cards, you can also use them to pay subcontractors or suppliers who don't take credit cards. Banks consider these to be cash advances, often with higher rates than other charges, however, so use them only when you will have income coming in soon to cover these costs.

We recommend having at least two credit cards: one for your personal expenses, one for your business expenses. It's a good idea to obtain new cards or increase credit limits while you still have a job if possible, because some companies won't issue cards to the newly self-employed person. Since you may not be able to pay off the balance in full each month at first, consider cards with low interest rates even if they have higher annual fees.

Although quicker and generally more convenient than traditional bank financing, credit card debt over the long term can be problematic, and according to Los Angeles business writer Marla Dickerson, "can be fatal to a fledgling enterprise if card balances spin out of control. So, to avoid building up a large debt at credit card interest rates, limit credit card charges to smaller costs or costs that will pay for themselves relatively quickly by generating immediate income.

___ *3. Personal loans:* If you or a spouse has an existing job and a good credit record but no track record as a business owner, banks will sometimes make

(Continued on page 78)

(Continued from page 77)

a personal loan more quickly than a business loan. Credit unions are another possible route to get a personal loan.

TIP: If you're borrowing from friends or family and are wondering how to establish an interest rate on their loan, you can visit the St. Louis Central Reserve Bank Web site (*www.stls.frb.org/fred/data/irates.html*), which lists the interest rates for one-month, three-month, and six-month certificates of deposit, which you can use as a basis for calculating a rate.

___ **4. Home equity loans:** Some people who own their own homes are able to refinance their home loan as a route to obtaining a reservoir of start-up capital. If you have a good credit history, you may be able to get a "line of credit" on your home loan that you can draw upon as needed.

___ **5. Line of credit:** If you have good credit and a good relationship with a bank, you may be able to negotiate and qualify for a line of credit. With a line of credit, you can borrow up to a certain amount on an as-needed basis. So while you're getting started, you can dip into loan funds during months when your income falls short of your needs, but you won't need to borrow the full amount you've qualified for and you can pay back what you've borrowed as you go. Many professionals start their businesses this way. Often the credit line is based on a home equity loan.

Once your business has been going for a while, you'll find growing numbers of financing options are now available to help you expand. So check out the availability of "low loc doc" loans (which entail less paperwork and faster application turnaround time) like those available through Bank of America (*www.bankamerica.com* or (800) 477-5800, ext. 700).

To check out the loans for which you can qualify, visit Quicken's Cash Finder at *www.cashfinder.com*. This is a new service, free to you as the user, that ties in with major financial institutions and allows you to shop for financing.

___ **6. Character-based microloans:** The Small Business Administration and a variety of private foundations are creating a growing number of microloan programs that make small loans (i.e., from under $100 to $25,000) to very small businesses, including home businesses. Under the federal program, money can be used to buy machinery and equipment, furniture and fixtures, inventory, and supplies, and for working capital. It may not be used to pay existing debts. The money must be repaid within six years.

These loans are based, not upon your credit history or collateral, but on good character, sufficient management ability, and commitment to making your plan successful. The Small Business Administration funds local nonprofit organizations to process microloan applications. Call or visit the nearest office of the Small Business Administration to find the agencies processing these loans in your area. You'll find a free list of them on our Web site, *www.paulandsarah.com*

Examples of Home Businesses Receiving Microloans

Accounting	Eldercare	Multimedia production
Air-conditioning	Exotic birds	Musical entertainer
Baked goods	Financial services	Organic gardening and
Beauty shop	Fishing lures	vinegar production
Bedspreads	Fitness training	Patio furniture
Bookkeeping	Forestry consulting	Pet-sitting
Business services	Fuel additives	Pig farm
Cash register sales	Graphic arts	Renovation
Catering	Greeting cards	Seamstress
Children's books	Gun bluing	Security services
Christmas wreaths	Image consulting	Seminar leader
Cleaning services	Income tax preparation	Signs in Braille
Clothing design and	Interior design	Signs and banners
creation	Inventing	Soap manufacturing
Computer services	Jewelry	Software sales
Computer training	Laundry/video arcade	Sporting goods
Computerized embroidery	Lawn care	Tour guide
Contract estimating	Legal firm	Transporting handicapped
Dance studio	Limo services	Making truck liners
Data processing	Maple products	Trucking company
Day care	Marketing firm	Utility auditing
Designer watchbands	Metal manufacturing	Video documentary
Desktop publishing	Model soldiers	Web site design
Dog sleds	Motor repair	Word processing

Develop an Entry Plan. Depending on the business you're in, it can take from six months to one year to get under way, one to three years to turn a profit, and three to five years to become self-sustaining. Covering your costs of living and doing business until you're turning a profit is one of your major expenses, and one of the biggest challenges a home entrepreneur faces.

If you have a job, keep it. Meanwhile, find out whether your business is viable. Do your homework; figure out the bare minimum you need for living expenses and business expenses. Then establish an entry plan, a way to cover that minimum until your business is going.

Sandra Oker used the moonlighting plan: she started doing career counseling in the evenings and on weekends. When she had enough clients to pay for her rent, food, and gasoline, she quit her job. John Eldridge used the part-time plan: he worked part-time in a health-food store for several hours a week while building a community theater into a viable business.

Diane Shaughnessey of Tampa, Florida, found an unusual entry plan:

when divorce left her with no income, she got a grant to start her business. Through the suggestion of a friend, she contacted the Florida State Department of Labor and Employment's Vocational Rehabilitation Division. They provide a variety of grants, including ones for starting a business, to assist such disabled individuals as displaced homemakers in reentering the workforce. Shaughnessey presented her idea for Diane Shaughnessey Productions: to create hand-built clay bowl and goddess figurines reflecting feminine spirituality and to present self-discovery workshops that assist people in moving into the creativity of sacred arts.

Skeptical at first, the representative attended a workshop Shaughnessey conducted and from that point on knew she was serious about her plans to pursue her dream of becoming a commercial fine artist and educator. They sent her to five Small Business Administration seminars on starting a business, which she attended over three months, and requested that she write a business plan. Using the knowledge she gained in the workshops and working eighteen hours a day, Shaughnessey developed and submitted the plan within thirty days asking for $35,000 in funds for equipment and initial materials. After a few months of red tape and a lot of patience and determination, the grant was approved and Shaughnessey was in business.

Although getting such a grant is for most people a long shot, depending on the kind of venture you want to fund and your background and circumstances, we've begun meeting a new breed of nonprofit or socially conscious for-profit business owners who are able to line up grants to undertake their work either full- or part-time.

Martha Ryan, for example, launched the San Francisco Prenatal Care Program to provide medical care for pregnant homeless women in 1989. A nurse practitioner working in a family shelter, Ryan realized that many homeless women were not getting prenatal care and no other community organization had plans on the drawing board to fill this need. So Ryan took a grant-writing class, wrote a grant proposal, and got a $52,000 grant from a community foundation. Getting the program under way was very difficult for the first two years because she was doing everything herself while working part-time. Now, with additional grants and fund-raising efforts, she has a staff of sixteen people and outside facilities, and she serves primarily as executive director and fund-raiser for the organization—limiting her outside work to only one day a week.

Manage Your Cash Flow. In a new home business you often must pay cash up-front while waiting for your own customers to pay for your products or services. Covering expenses while waiting for income is the bane of small businesses.

Here are three basic strategies you can use for managing cash flow wisely now:

1. **Minimize what others owe you.** Get deposits, retainers, and partial or progress payments. Take bank cards instead of giving credit. Ask for cash at the time of the sale.

2. **Get maximum benefit from cash on hand.** For example, deposit cash in interest-bearing accounts and use cash-management programs.

3. **Hold on to what you've got.** Ask for interest-free credit from suppliers. Charge your expenses on bank cards. Make timely, not immediate, payment of bills. Lease your car or truck instead of buying it.

Eight Entry Plans for Starting a Home Business

1. *The Moonlighting Plan.* Keep your full-time job and develop your business as a sideline.

2. *The Flextime Plan.* Free your daytime hours by working at a job that gives you the option of a flexible schedule. If you are established with an employer, you may need to make the case for the employer adopting flextime.

3. *The Part-time Plan.* Work at a part-time job to provide a base income while you're building up the business. When your business income equals the base income, drop the part-time job.

4. *The Spin-off Plan.* Turn your previous employer into your first major customer, or when ethically possible, take a major client with you from your previous job.

5. *The Cushion Plan.* Use a financial resource like savings, a severance package, inheritance, or divorce settlement to support yourself while you start your business. Such a cash cushion should be large enough to cover your base expenses for at least six to twelve months. Of course, time off a job can also provide a cushion i.e., you might start a business while on sabbatical or leave. Surveys show 36 percent of men and 26 percent of women have six months or more of income set aside for emergencies. Such reserves are often used to start a business.

6. *The Piggyback Plan.* If you have a working spouse or partner, cut back your expenses so you can live on one salary until your business gets going.

7. *The Have-Your-Clients-Finance-You Plan.* If you have sufficient stature in your field, you might obtain retainer contracts with clients for the first year that provide you with assured revenue in exchange for offering them services at 25 percent less than the billing rate you establish.

8. *The Gofer Plan.* While keeping your existing income, hire or have someone as a gofer to do the legwork and research needed to lay the groundwork for a successful start-up. Look for someone who charges less than you earn.

3. Inexperience

The third most common reason small businesses fail is their owners' lack of experience and knowledge. In the past this was often an unalterable limitation. Our knowledge was restricted to what we could learn at home, school, or work. Not today. Information is now available on virtually everything you might want to know.

If you're weak on sales skills, you can take courses, read books, or get private consultation on how to sell. If you're timid about negotiating contracts, you can use assertiveness-training courses, personal-growth seminars, or private counseling to improve your skills.

A survey of new businesses found that after three years of being in business, successful entrepreneurs had:

- taken six to ten months to research and to prepare for their business ventures.

- used professional advisers in setting up the business.

- taken business-related courses and read regularly about business management.

Another way you can learn about a field is by working as an apprentice. Apprenticing is a very old practice deserving a new look for those starting a new life. Apprenticing yourself can range from taking a job that will also qualify you for a license, like a private detective, to paying someone already in the business of your choice to follow him around, accompanying him for a week or longer. You may avoid paying for this real-world training by exchanging your assistance in return for experience and the ability to ask questions.

To increase your odds for success, become an information consumer in your field and in the general area of business. Read books, magazines, newsletters, and World Wide Web sources. Attend seminars, conventions, and classes. Buy and listen to tapes by experts who have the skills you need. Talk with those who can advise you in business matters.

For specific information about your business area, contact professional or trade associations. Ask your local reference librarian to recommend a reading list. You can start with the resources listed throughout this chapter.

4. Marketing Misconceptions

Making mistaken judgments about whether there are people who can and will buy your products and services is the fourth most common reason people fail in their own businesses. Accountant Susan Gwenn made the mistake so many people with new businesses make. After completing long and arduous training, she sent out announcements that she was opening her practice. Then she sat back, waiting in vain for the phone to ring. Similarly, potter Gloria Greene displayed her wares in one art fair after another only to carry most of her pots home again, wondering if she was as talented as she thought she was.

The problem in both of these cases was marketing, or the lack of it. Thinking a good product or service will sell itself is the most common marketing misconception of new entrepreneurs. Often artists, writers, professionals, technicians, information specialists, and consultants start their businesses with little knowledge, interest, or skill in marketing and selling. Without it, you have no business and, let's face it, you aren't a business until you've got business.

As researcher and author Sue Rugge found in starting Information on Demand, "Marketing is the key to everything. Doing your work is the easy part. It's the selling that's the hard part. You can never sit back. Every day you have to sell yourself again." Starting with this philosophy, Sue made "house calls." She sold her research services door to door and gave her card to everyone she knew. It was this effort that turned the $250 she and her partner started with into sales of half a million dollars.

Since most home businesses people can't hire a marketing agency in the beginning, selling yourself and your product or service will become your responsibility. Consequently, you'll need to develop what we call a "marketing mind-set," a way of thinking about business from a marketing viewpoint. This doesn't mean you have to take on a phony sales personality, but you do have to become good at letting the people who need your business know about it in a way that will convince them to buy. And you can. To learn the marketing mind-set and the skills you'll need, start with the books, tapes, and newsletters in the Resources list at the end of this chapter, and refer to chapter 23: "Successfully Marketing Your Home Business."

5. A Marginal Business Image

Think about the businesses you patronize. What do you expect from them? Of course, you want a good price, but you also want to feel confident that any business you buy from is substantial, that it will be here tomorrow. We all want to believe we can count on buying a top-quality product or service that delivers what it offers.

How do you know whether a company is top quality? Until you've bought from a business and tested it, all you have to go on is image. Image is where some home businesses fall down, however. Started on too tight a budget or operated too casually, a home business can look like an amateur effort.

Unfortunately, such a marginal business image creates a negative perception for all home businesses and leaves the impression that a home business is not a real business. And it is the fifth most common reason home businesses fail. So, in setting up your enterprise, make sure that the image you present is professional and positive. It doesn't take a big budget; it only requires attention to detail. Avoid such indicators of an amateur operation as letters printed by poor-quality printers, no one (or children) answering the phone during business hours, dirty clothes and dishes in business areas, irregular hours, unclear fee schedules, and a backlog of unpaid bills. Take conscious steps to make a professional impression.

Home-Business Code of Ethics

Because being taken seriously remains one of the top concerns of home-business owners, we recommend that all home business people consider subscribing to the following code of ethics as a way to build the credibility and image of their businesses and home businesses throughout their communities and nationwide.

1. Conduct your business in an above-board professional manner, operating within local, state, and federal laws.

2. Accurately and realistically represent what you do in all marketing, advertising, and promotional activities.

3. Undertake only that work for which you are qualified and capable of providing within the time frame and price agreed to.

4. Communicate all fees or the basis for fees in advance of providing your service or product.

5. Obtain clear, up-front agreements of precisely what you will be providing.

6. Notify clients or customers immediately if, for any reason, you cannot complete the work you have undertaken within the agreed-upon time frame.

7. When necessary, contact clients about any changes in what you will be providing them, prior to proceeding.

8. Stand behind your product or service.

9. Operate within the same professional standards and practices that you would expect from a business located outside the home.

10. Keep all proprietary information obtained from clients and customers confidential, and refrain from using such information for personal or financial gain.

11. Avoid all conflicts of interests in serving your clients or customers.

12. Work within your community and field to enhance the image and reputation of your home business.

6. Giving Up

Success has a schedule of its own. We can be masters of our own fate, but not always on our own timetable. Often those who reach the summits in life are those who are willing to proceed onward long after others have abandoned the journey. And so it is with starting a business of your own from home.

Like the "golden hour" in emergency medical care, the first year is the most critical year for business survival. It can get long and lonely. But you need to experiment, adjust, and test. As Thomas J. Watson, the founder of IBM, ironically advised, "The way to succeed is to double your failure rate." Persist until you find what works. In the meantime, make friends, and join relevant groups and organizations for support and encouragement through the rough spots. Listen to the advice of people who have been there and can make your way smoother. And always conduct your business in accord with the highest ethical standards.

TIPS FROM SUCCESSFUL HOME-BUSINESS OWNERS

In the long run, the successful entrepreneurs we talked with managed to avoid these problems and learn, not always the easy way, how to survive and grow. Here are a few of their conclusions:

- *"You have to be the best at what you do.* You can't fake it. Even if you are the best, the phone doesn't always ring on the first day. You're always three months away from a new client. You have to develop your marketing plan to ensure that the phone does ring. You have to set aside time each week for PR. I try never to ve lunch alone, for example. If I'm going to eat lunch, I eat with a business contact. I never know who a prospective client will be, so I treat everyone like a prospective client."—William Slavin, consultant, William Slavin and Associates.

- *"A satisfied customer is always your best source of business.* When you advertise, you don't have to buy a big ad. In fact, the small ads I run regularly draw more business than the several-hundred-dollar ads I ran only once. I find running an ad regularly that has some kind of logo and catchy copy draws best."—Barbara Elman, writer.

- *"Everything in business is a result of networking.* Whether it's getting an article published or finding a distributor, I keep in contact with old friends, past co-workers, and sales reps who used to call on me. I can't stress it enough—your friends and contacts are your best assets."—Gil Gordon, management consultant, Gil Gordon and Associates.

Checklist: Fourteen Money-Saving Ways to Give Your Home Business a Fortune 500 Image

Certainly one key to successes in any home business is maintaining a 100 percent professional business image even though you're at home. Here are fourteen simple steps you can follow to make sure the world knows you are to be taken seriously:

___ *1. Spring for a business telephone line.* An effective name doesn't help you much if people can't find it in the phone book or when calling for information.

___ *2. Answer the phone with finesse.* Answer after two rings with a positive professional greeting using your name or the name of your business. Have an answering service or answering machine take calls when you're not there. Call yourself to listen for the impression made by your answering machine recording or voice mail.

___ *3. Communicate quality with a custom-designed logo.* Use your own unique custom-designed logo on business cards, letterheads, envelopes, invoices, and Web site. Do not select a logo from among the standard designs offered by your printer. To keep your costs down, arrange to have a college class design your logo as a class project.

___ *4. Show substance with a federal ID number.* If you have an employee or are a partnership, use a Federal Identification number for business purposes in place of your Social Security number. It's a no-cost way to dress your business for success. To obtain a Federal ID number, simply apply at the nearest Internal Revenue Service office.

___ *5. Select a strategic location for your office.* If you have business guests coming to your home, consider locating your office so you can have a separate business entrance, or locate your office near the front or side door so business guests don't have to walk through or past personal areas of the household. Make sure that any areas through which business guests must pass en route to your office are neat, clean, and clear of overly personal items like toiletries, children's toys, photographs, and household items. Use tasteful screens, drapes, or dividers, if necessary, to separate personal areas from business areas of the house.

___ *6. Let your checks speak for you.* Use full-sized checks on business stock with your business name printed on them; they cost no more than the smaller decorated personal checks. Use a check protector device, which enters the amount in large raised numerals, or use a computer with software to print your checks.

___ *7. Create a professional Web site.* The World Wide Web is the great equalizer. With enough thought, care, and planning, your business can have a site that rivals those of the largest corporations. Pick a domain name that contains your business name (avoid the long Web addresses that come for free from your ISP;

(Continued on page 87)

(Continued from page 86)

nothing screams "small time" more loudly). Unless you are very visually inclined, have the site designed by a professional, or, have a class do it for you.

____ *8. Develop clear, professional-looking printed materials.* Whether it's your letterhead, envelopes, business cards, or brochure, your printed materials will act as your business's emissary to anyone who sees them. Make sure that everything you send out looks professional and is of a high caliber. Avoid flashy logos (unless you're in a flashy business), quirky paper stocks (see below), and iridescent colors. Whenever possible, have your stationery and marketing materials professionally designed. If you can't afford to do so, perhaps you can negotiate a trade of services with a fellow home-based designer.

____ *9. Use only top-quality paper.* Choose paper that looks and feels top grade for your letterhead, envelopes, and business cards. Fine paper doesn't cost that much more. We recommend 70-pound bond for letterheads and envelopes. Buy the paper at a printer's supply house or directly from a paper company. Then supply it to your printer as "customer stock."

____ *10. Equip your office professionally.* The cost and size of electronic office equipment today make it possible to equip your home office with the kind and quality of equipment you'd expect to find in any top-notch office in your field. Equipment that will enhance your image includes a high-quality photocopier, a laser printer or high-resolution ink jet printer, and a fax. Here's an added tip: Next time you reprint your business cards and letterhead, include your Web site address.

____ *11. Polish your correspondence.* A nationwide survey of executives by Communispond, Inc., showed that four out of five executives listed the ability to write as the most neglected skill in business. Even if your words don't flow magically from your fingers to your screen, your correspondence can be grammatically and stylistically correct using grammar-checking software. Good, clear writing skills are becoming even more important E-mail becomes a standard form of business communication.

____ *12. Incorporate for image.* Although there are several other reasons for incorporating, think about adding "Corporation" or "Inc." to your company name to enhance your business image. Before making such a change, however, consult with a knowledgeable tax professional and an attorney to determine whether this would be a wise business decision. If you decide it is, have these professionals help you select one of several options for the way your corporation will be taxed.

____ *13. Dress for success.* Although the sweatsuit may be the official uniform of the open-collar worker, dress like a successful person at the top of your field when meeting with customers, clients, and suppliers.

____ *14. Project a positive attitude.* Share the good news. Radiate confidence. Remember: self-assurance attracts; self-doubt repels.

- *"You have to really care about what you're doing.* Everything takes three times longer and costs five times more than you think it will. We wouldn't have kept going if we hadn't had a strong commitment to what we are doing."—Elizabeth Scott, developer and co-founder of Rhiannon, a software company.

- *"As you travel down this path, discomfort is sometimes a companion,* though seldom for extensive periods. And on the other side of discomfort you will discover a new high that comes with a deeper sense of your own worth. To me that is the bottom line."—Sue Rugge, co-founder of Information on Demand.

 Work Sheet: Writing a Business Plan

Writing a business plan need not be a complex and difficult process. Essentially, your home-business plan is simply a road map for what you intend to do and how you intend to do it. Unless you will be seeking a loan, venture capital, or a grant, it will primarily be for your own use to guide you in making day-to-day decisions and set priorities for your time and money. Of course, you may wish to get feedback on your plan from various legal, accounting, and business professionals. But most important, it should be a working document for your own use.

As a working document, your business plan is an evolving statement that you can update and revise as your business gets under way. You can use business-planning software to guide you step-by-step through writing your plan (see Resources), or you can create your own more informal plan by answering the following questions:

Your Business Concept: What Will You Offer?

1. What product or service will you be providing?

2. What is the mission, purpose, and vision you have for you business?

The Market: Who Will Your Clients or Customers Be?

3. Who specifically needs this product or service? (Avoid using the word *everyone* in answering this question) Why do these people need what you'll be offering? What evidence do you have?

4. Are these people using something similar now? What? How much do they pay?

5. Why would there be a need for what you plan to offer?

(Continued on page 89)

(Continued from page 88)

The Competition: To Whom Will You Be Compared?

6. Who else, if anyone, is providing a similar product or service?

7. How is what you'll offer different? Why should people buy from you?

The Finances: How Will You Make Money?

8. What costs will you have? In starting up? In running your business? In providing your product or service?

9. How will you finance the start-up and operating costs until you have enough business to cover these costs?

10. How will you support yourself while you build your business? How much income will you need?

11. What can you charge? What are others charging? What do people expect to pay? (See chapter 22.)

Getting Business: How Will You Get Under Way?

12. How will you let those who need what you offer know about your product or service? (See chapter 23.)

13. What tasks will you need to accomplish to get up and running? (Make a list and project a date for them.)

14. How much time will you have to devote each day, week, and month to starting a business?

GENERAL HOME BUSINESS RESOURCES

BOOKS

Encyclopedia of Associations. Detroit: Gale Research Company. Published annually. Available in bound volumes and on CD-ROM from the library reference sections.

Finding Money for Your Small Business. Max Fallek. American Institutue of Small Business, 7515 Wayzata Boulevard, Minneapolis, MN 55426; (800) 328-2906.

Government Assistance Almanac: The Guide to All Federal Financial and Other Domestic Programs. J. Robert Dumouchel. Detroit: Omnigraphics. Annual.

The Start-Up Guide. David H. Bangs, Jr. Chicago: Upstart Publishing Company, 1998, ISBN: 1574101153.

Thomas' Register of Manufacturers. Thomas Publishing Co., One Penn Plaza, New York, NY 10119; (212) 695-0500. Web: *www.thomasregister. com.* A multivolume affair listing the makers of many industrial products. Some companies have their product catalogs included. Useful in locating sources of supply, either for your own use or for resale. Available at most libraries.

PERIODICALS

Bootstrappin' Entrepreneur. The newsletter for individuals with great ideas and a little bit of cash. 8726 South Sepulveda Boulevard, Los Angeles, CA 90045; (310) 568-9861.

Entrepreneur. 2392 Morse Avenue, Irvine, CA 92714; (800) 926-6995. E-mail: entmag@entrepreneurmag.com, Web: *www.entrepreneurmag.com.*

Working at Home. P.O. Box 5484, Harlan, Iowa; 51593; (800) 352-8202. Published by *Success* magazine.

WORLD WIDE WEB

Better Business Bureau
www.bbb.org
Official site of the Better Business Bureau.

Business @ Home
www.business@home.com

paulandsarah.com
www.paulandsarah.com the place to be . . . on your own but not alone . . . practical information, inspiration, and support for making it on your own. Daily business and marketing tips, personally answered Q&A, daily motivational messages, free special reports, FAQ's, book updates, chats, and links to lots of other resources.

Small Business Administration
www.sba.gov
Official site of the SBA and an excellent resource for information and guidance.

Bootstrappin' Tip of the Week
www.kimberlystanseil.com

COURSES

Entrepreneurship 101
An on-going tutorial developed by Debra Esparza, director of the USC Business Expansion Network, and written by *Los Angeles Times* business writer Vickie Torres that helps budding businesspeople with information on financing, accounting, planning, marketing, and other crucial issues. The tutorial can be found on the *L.A. Times* Web site at: *www.latimes.com/ smallbiz*

GOVERNMENT AND COMMUNITY RESOURCES

Small Business Administration (SBA):
The Small Business Administration offers a variety of services that, although primarily focused on larger small businesses, can also benefit home-based businesses. These include:

- Advice and technical assistance through Small Business Centers operated by universities and chambers of commerce, the Service Corps of Retired Executives (SCORE), and Small Business Information Centers in major cities. To contact the Small Business Administration for the locations of these services in your area, look in your telephone directory under U.S. Government for your local SBA office or call the Small Business Answer Desk at (800) 8-ASK-SBA ([800] 827-5722).

- Publications. To find out about current publications and prices, write for order forms 115A and 115B, Small Business Administration, P.O. Box 15434, Ft. Worth, TX 76119.

- Microloans processed by local nonprofit organizations. Contact the nearest SBA office for programs in your area.

- SBA Online is on their Web site at: *www.sba.online.sba.gov*

Department of Defense:
The Department of Defense has a Small Business Innovation Grant program. To get information, call the Defense Technical Information customer help line at (800) 225-3842.

Internal Revenue Service:
New Business Tax Kit. Available in local IRS offices or phone (800) 829-8815 for further information.

STATE AND LOCAL SOURCES

Most parts of the United States and Canada provide some assistance to small businesses. These include:

- state and provincial economic development agencies
- local colleges
- public libraries
- chambers of commerce

RADIO

Working From Home. Hosted by Paul and Sarah Edwards (Sundays at 10 P.M. Eastern, 7 P.M. Pacific) on the Business Radio Network and available with a satellite dish on Digital: Satcom C-5, Transponder 15 and Analog: Satcom C-5, Transponder 3. Web site: *www.paulandsarah.com* for cities and program information.

CANADIAN RESOURCES

Home Business Report magazine, Impact Communications, Ltd., 2949 Ash Street, Abbotsford BC V2S4G5. Voice: (604) 854-5530, Web: *www.strategis.ic.gc.ca.* Impact Communications also publishes *Guide to Creating a Home-Based Association* and specializes in helping Canadian micropreneurs bring products to the marketplace.

SOHO Central provides networking. For a full sense of their services, see the Web site: *www.soho.ca.* For BC/Alberta, contact: SOHO Business Group, # 242-757 West Hastings Street, Vancouver, British Columbia V6C 3M6; (604) 929-8250. The rest of Canada: SOHO Business Group, 2255B Queen Street East, Ste. 3261, Toronto, Ontario, M4E 1G3; (416) 693-7646, E-mail: *soho@istar.ca*

CHAPTER 4

Working for Someone Else: Paychecks and Other Possibilities

Goals

1. Determine if your job is one that could be done at home.

2. Convince your boss to let you bring your job home.

3. Find a new job at home.

4. Avoid work-at-home scams.

5. Negotiate a work-at-home agreement.

Every three hours every day of the year for many years, someone has visited us on line to seek information about how to find a job he or she can do at home. Others seek advice on how to get their managers to let them take their jobs home. They are looking for ways to combine the security and benefits of a job—health insurance, a pension plan, sick leave, paid holidays, and, above all, a paycheck—with working from home. They tell us:

"I like my job, but with all the interruptions at the office it's hard to get anything done. I'd like to convince my supervisor we would all benefit if I could work at home part of every week."

"I'm the sole supporter of my kids. I need a steady income I can count on every week, but I'd sure like to be there when they get home from school."

"I've thought of starting my own business, but I think I would have a hard time getting customers. With my disability, it's hard for me to get out of the house. I know both Excel and Paradox inside out, though, and if an employer could get the work to me, I'd be ready to go."

"I'm in a bind. Next year my husband will be transferred to a city three hundred miles away. I'm going with him, but I hate to leave my job. I could do almost everything the job requires with a telephone, modem, and a computer terminal. Maybe I can arrange to stay on and work long distance."

"I hate losing one to two hours commuting in traffic and another hour getting dressed up every day. And I cannot say enough bad things about having to wear high heels to work."

Fortunately, there is a contingency within many companies and government agencies that allows employees to work from home. A Bell Atlantic study found that approximately 2 million businesses in America support formal telecommuting programs of some sort. At one point, AT&T and IBM were even making work from home mandatory for thousands of salespeople. This movement toward taking salaried work home is most often called telecommuting (substituting commuting for communications) and less often referred to as teleworking (working from a distance). Whatever you choose to call it, it's been growing at a rate of 15 percent a year over the past five to seven years. Over 11 million people now telecommute, and that number is predicted to grow to over 23 million by the year 2000. Here's an example of the many kinds of jobs that are being done from home.

The opportunity to work at home spans all levels of office hierarchy, from vice presidents to data-entry workers. Writers, Web professionals, designers, accountants, researchers, lawyers, and computer programmers can easily do it. So can many clerical, data-processing, and communications personnel. Technical jobs that require a lot of reading and report writing are well-suited, as are jobs that require a great deal of travel or fieldwork. Managerial or supervisory positions in areas such as purchasing, pensions, sales, and planning can also be done away from the corporate office.

There are an ample number of jobs that can be done at home, and it's getting easier to find one. There are two primary routes to getting a job at home. Convincing your present employer to allow you to start working from home is the best place to start. If that's not possible, you can start from scratch and search for a new job that will allow you to work at home.

BRINGING YOUR CURRENT JOB HOME

Nick Sullivan, formerly of *Home Office Computing* magazine, himself a teleworker, says, "In general, I think it's easier to get a job and then talk about doing it at home." And we agree. Although it's still not the norm, more companies are allowing employees to work at least part-time from home.

Salaried work at home grew at an estimated 20 to 30 percent a year during the 1980s. In a study of corporate plans for the nineties by the Conference Board, a business research firm, it was reported that 56 percent of corporations plan to allow home-based work in the future. Increasingly,

Salaried Jobs You Can Hold at Home

Accountant	Illustrator	Public relations
Actuary	Indexer	professional
Advertising copywriter	Instructional designer	Purchasing agent
Advertising sales	Insurance agent	Real estate agent
representative	Insurance claims	Records manager
Answering service	adjuster	Researcher
operator	Interpreter	Reservation agent
Architect	Interviewer	Sales representative
Assembly worker	Inventory control clerk	Secretary
Auditor	Lawyer	Social worker
Booking agent	Market research analyst	Software engineer
Bookkeeper	Marketing planner	Speechwriter
Budget analyst	Medical records	Stockbroker
Buyer	technician	Technical writer
Computer programmer	Medical reviewer	Telemarketer
Computer systems	Medical transcriptionist	Telephone order
analyst	Multimedia producer	taker
Cost estimator	News reporter	Transcriber
Customer service	Operations research	Translator
representative	analyst	Travel agent
Data entry clerk	Paralegal	Urban planner
Database administrator	Patent searcher	Utility rate forecaster
Desktop publisher	Personnel analyst	Video editor
Economist	Pollster	Webmaster
Editor	Print production	Web site designer
Environmental analyst	supervision	Web site fulfillment
Financial analyst	Probation or parole	Web site reviewer
Graphic designer	officer	Word processor

companies are finding it makes more sense to move the work than to move people. Some companies institute formal work-at-home programs for which you apply in order to work at home; however, the majority of companies that allow employees to work at home do so on a more informal basis. According to telecommuting consultant Gil Gordon, "The telecommuting trend for companies is becoming more fluid. Instead of rigid telecommuting policies, smart employers will allow employees to work where they work best. For many, this will be working from home."

The extent to which you can work from home without a formal program depends on what arrangement you can make with your supervisor. Whether done on a formal or an informal basis, being able to work at home means first proving that you are a capable and reliable self-starter. Even then, you can still expect to have some convincing to do.

> *"Before asking your boss if you can begin telecommuting, put yourself in his position. Ask yourself if you can be trusted to work without direct supervision. Be honest with yourself. If you don't feel you're ready, don't ask your boss. If you feel you are ready, begin by demonstrating that you can be trusted."*
>
> GIL GORDON, TELECOMMUNICATIONS CONSULTANT

CONVINCING YOUR EMPLOYER
TO LET YOU WORK AT HOME

Even if your job can be done at home, why should your company allow you to work there? Don't plead your case to be home with your kids or to take care of Grandma. Although these goals are important to you, think about what would motivate a company to step outside convention and try something new. Employers need to see that the benefits to them of letting you work from home will be worth the risks. Here are several of the primary reasons companies are allowing employees to work from home. Think about which of the following benefits will motivate your management:

- Increase in productivity. After studying over two hundred companies with work-at-home projects, Gordon reports that "company productivity rises as much as 30 percent when people work at home." These gains are possible because employees work more quickly without office interruptions and socializing. Also, they can work at their own pace and during their peak energy hours. Work hours generally increase due to time saved commuting.

- Staff shortages can be alleviated. Whenever the demand for skilled workers exceeds the supply, as is often the case with secretaries, programmers, medical transcriptionists, designers, and software engineers, the alternative of working at home is one way for companies to attract prospective employees. Employees working at home can also reduce the cost of "temps."

- Turnover can be reduced. Because of high job satisfaction, salaried at-home workers rarely quit their jobs. And by allowing valued employees to work at home, companies don't lose them if they move (or the company relocates), or if they decide to start a family, or need to care for someone who becomes ill. Not having to train new employees can result in considerable savings for a company.

- Absenteeism can be lowered. Studies show that telecommuters are healthier than their office-bound counterparts, so sick time is reduced. Employees can work at home in bad weather, with sick children, despite automobile problems, or while waiting for home deliveries and service calls that would otherwise cause them to miss work.

- Costs can be reduced. Companies can save on space and parking. Savings of $5,000 or more per employee are not unusual. Growing companies do not need to have their growth limited by the cost and lost time involved in finding additional office and parking facilities. Companies with their own buildings can even consider leasing the space made available by employees who are working at home, and the rental income can increase profits.

- Use as an incentive. Allowing people to work at home is an alternative to promotion in companies where reorganization or downsizing provides fewer management positions. It can also be used to acknowledge and reward valued employees.

- It's good for the environment. Telecommuting reduces air pollution, fuel consumption, and the ozone-depleting CFCs that all those automobile air conditioners spew into the atmosphere. In today's image-conscious (and to be fair, environmentally conscious) times, companies like to say that they're doing their part in promoting a greener world. Allowing employees to telecommute is a low-investment, high-return way for companies to be able to make these claims.

Once you are aware of the factors that may motivate your company to let you work from home, your next step is to consider carefully the feasibil-

---

From the Boss's Point of View

A Telecommute America survey of 1,000 executives reported the following advantages they saw in allowing employees to telecommute:

Higher morale	79%
Reduced cost/space needs	64%
Employee retention	63%
Reduced stress	63%
Reduced absenteeism	61%
Increased productivity	59%

ity of doing your job at home. Which tasks can be done at home? Which ones require you to be in the office? What are the difficulties that might develop, and how would you handle situations such as suddenly needing information that's only available at the office?

For most managers to consider having employees work at home, the work must be easily measured. You and your manager need to know without a doubt when the work you do has been completed. Each task or project should have a precise beginning and end and require minimal face-to-face contact with co-workers. Before proposing a permanent plan to work at home, build a track record of working from home informally. Many of you are probably already doing this in the form of take-home work you are doing evenings and weekends. Occasionally ask to take your work home for the afternoon. Then try proposing to work at home on a specific project for a day or two.

Only take work home when you feel confident you can do an outstanding job. Keep in touch by phoning in each day to find out if anything has arisen that you need to handle. Follow up on all messages immediately, so no one will feel you are inaccessible.

Consultant Gil Gordon suggests that even after doing your homework and building a track record, "don't go for broke all at once. Approach management with the idea that you'll work at home on a small scale—perhaps starting one or two days a week at most—for the first two to three months."

OPPORTUNITIES ON THE NETS:
BOTH INTER AND INTRA

One of the most exciting developments in telecommuting has been the growth of the Internet and smaller, private networks called Intranets. The Internet, the worldwide public network of computers, phone lines, and modems that we've all heard so much about these past few years, has given companies and their employees any number of powerful options. The Internet makes electronic mail, E-mail, available to anyone with the required equipment. E-mail allows telecommuters to stay in closer touch with the office than ever before. If a company has a site on the World Wide Web, the most popular area of the Internet, employees working in Cyburbia can check it frequently for company news, developments, and much more. The Internet also allows for inexpensive video conferencing so you can have face-to-face meetings with office staff while you're home and they're still at the office.

Intranets are private networks and are the exclusive domain of the company who maintains them. Through an Intranet, a company can post confidential messages, manuals, standards, plans, and many of the other resources that could formerly only be accessed at the office. Home-based employees can refer to these resources at any time directly through their computers. Another development in Intranets is the increased power and scope of *GroupWare*. *GroupWare* is specialized communications software that allows employees in different locations to all work together simultaneously on the same documents. *GroupWare* also facilitates secured E-mail and video conferencing.

How to Determine Whether Your Job Can Be Done at Home

- Does your job require little face-to-face contact?

- Can needed face-to-face contact be scheduled into a weekly time at the office?

- Can needed face-to-face contact be conducted with teleconferencing over the Internet?

- Are the expectations for what you produce and when you produce it clear?

- Is your performance easily measurable?

- Can you work without physical access to resources and materials at the office?

- Can needed access to resources and materials be scheduled into a weekly time at the office?

- Does the job require a great deal of concentration without interruptions?

- Is there adequate security at your home for your work?

Each "yes" answer you can give increases the likelihood that your job can be done at home.

FINDING A NEW JOB TO DO AT HOME

Although taking your existing job home is your best chance of working from home on a salary, there are several ways to find a job to work at at home.

Long-standing home-based jobs. Salespeople and repair and customer service personnel in some industries, such as publishing and pharmaceuticals, have long used their homes as work headquarters. But these are generally work-from-home jobs as distinct from work-at-home jobs.

Personal contacts. Your most likely way to get a new job that allows you to work at home is through people you know or meet. Nearly two out of three people hired to work at home are employed by firms with fewer than a hundred employees. Your best chance to work at home, therefore, is with a small company in your hometown. Such a job might consist of word processing, desktop publishing, something having to do with Web site content or the technical side of the Internet, billing for a doctor's office, taking telephone calls, or bookkeeping.

You find these jobs the same way you find any other kind of job. Research by the National Center for Career Strategies indicates that fully 70 percent of all jobs are obtained through personal contacts, or what is called "networking." As one employer who hires people to work at home told us, "The only way to get work is to ask for it." Networking is a way to make contact with the people you need to ask.

To locate the likely companies and get the interviews you need, tell everyone you know that you're looking for a job you can do at home and describe the type of work you can do. Attend professional and trade association meetings in your field. Look up the various forums, Web sites, chat rooms, and newsgroups on the Web and jump in. Ask for ideas and suggestions. Follow up on any leads you get until you are successful.

To land the position you want, you might offer to work at home under contract on a specific project, or to provide overload services during emergencies. Do outstanding work and the company may call on you again and again, or even put you on salary. Many specialized temporary agencies today will find situations that allow skilled freelancers or contract workers such as technical writers, designers, Web professionals, word processors, and others to work at home.

Make your work at home a bargain. One of the most creative ways of finding a work-at-home situation was accomplished by a Los Angeles writer. In negotiating a job offer, her soon-to-be employer asked her how much she expected to earn. She gave him two figures. The first was what she needed to earn to work at the company office. The second, although still a good salary, was $10,000 less—provided she could work at home. Her new employer developed a brand-new attitude about the benefits of employees working at home.

Classified ads in newspapers. Newspapers regularly list ads for telemarketers in their Help Wanted sections. Telemarketing includes selling by telephone as well as taking incoming phone calls. Many of the 800 and 888 numbers you see used for ordering products, making reservations, and contacting customer service are phoned into people's home offices. Even if the ad doesn't say so, you may be able to persuade prospective employers in some fields to let you work from home. If you have a special talent or training, you may be able to work for a specialized phone-based service or some sort of phone-based counseling or advice-oriented service. The vast majority of people working for these services receive their calls at home.

Home assembly. Despite many sham offers of this type, there are some home-assembly companies that do provide income-producing work, according to Ruth M. Howard, who has made a study of home-assembly opportunities. She publishes a booklet, video, and newsletter naming and evaluating the companies that deliver what they promise. Potential earnings from legitimate companies doing piece-rate work range between $100 and $400 to $500 a month. To earn $500 a month, someone with good manual skills can expect to work full-time. Remember this is work for which the earnings are below minimum wage and employee benefits are nonexistent—and there are sharks who do not deliver on their promises.

Lists of work-at-home jobs. Many ads labeled "Apply Now" are simply selling lists of companies that will supposedly hire people to work at home. Some urge you to mail money, others to call a 900 number. The lists virtually always prove disappointing because, first, companies that are hiring almost always want people in their local area and, second, once a company's name appears, so many people contact the company that even if there were jobs, they're quickly gone and subsequent applicants either find their calls answered angrily or their letters ignored.

Companies that market home workers' services. There are companies that seek to provide businesses with personnel who work at home. We believe this is a terrific concept. Over the years, however, we've seen well-intentioned entrepreneurs attempt to provide this service, and we know of none that have succeeded. In fact, all those we know of have gone out of business. What does this mean? It means that ultimately everyone must sell him- or herself for work-at-home jobs. On-line listings can give you leads, and we know people who have found hourly and salaried work at home through lists and contacts made on line. But ultimately you must establish your own credibility. It simply doesn't work like a temp agency, where some company can just line up work for you just because you work from home.

Virtual corporations. *Business Week* was among the first to describe a change in American business when it did a cover story called "The Hollow Corporation." This new way of working is also referred to as the "virtual corporation" in a book by that name by William Davidow and Michael Malone (New York: Harper Business, 1992). A virtual corporation, unlike the traditional hierarchical organization, has a small core of permanent employees and uses independent workers who may never see the inside of the corporate office or meet face-to-face with co-workers. Work is more project oriented than permanent. Debbie Dewey, who herself has operated from her home serving a number of companies, defines a virtual corporation as "a group of people with different areas of expertise working together as a team, remotely or locally, to provide a service/product to meet a business need with specific predefined goals."

With the advent of improved Internet-based videoconferencing and GroupWare (file- and application-sharing software), many home-based and small businesses have formed their own virtual businesses. Some arrangements are formal, many others, less formal. In your personal and on-line networking be aware of the possibility of joining an existing virtual organization or forming one yourself.

WORK-AT-HOME EMPLOYMENT SCHEMES

Some ads are outright schemes to take your money. A typical one might read: "COMPUTER—do you own or have access to a personal computer? Up to $35/hour. Full/part-time, starting immediately." It sounds like a job but asks you to send money for what turns out to be worthless information. Other types of work that have proved to be scams are clipping coupons and newspapers, data entry, envelope stuffing, listening to the radio, making neckties and sewing, typing, and watching TV. Envelope stuffing is the most common of these schemes. Stuffing envelopes sounds like easy work, but in actuality it is always a pyramid-like sales scheme in which you get a set of instructions telling you "to place ads similar to the one to which you responded."

How to Spot Work-at-Home Schemes

First, work-at-home schemes require you to send money before you even receive an explanation of how you are going to make money; an ad for a real job opening will not ask for money before you learn the details. Second, if an opportunity sounds too good to be true, it probably is. If you suspect a scheme, check it out with the Better Business Bureau, local consumer protection offices, state consumer protection and attorney generals' offices, the Federal Trade Commission, and the U.S. Postal Inspection Service. Addresses and phone numbers for a number of these can be found in chapter 3.

If you feel the urge to send in your money, follow the advice of Sidney Schwartz, who has made a study of these schemes. Here are his suggestions:

- Keep copies of all ads, claims, and guarantees. If the only guarantee is on the order form, photocopy it before sending it in.

- Pay with a charge card instead of by check or cash. This allows you to dispute the charge if you feel you've been taken.

- Save the envelope or package the merchandise is shipped in so you will have a dated postmark.

WORKING FOR SOMEONE ELSE **103**

- Send all correspondence by certified mail. Should you return the merchandise, always get a signed return receipt as proof of delivery.

- Remember, when you respond to one of these ads, you're gambling. Don't bet more than you can afford to lose.

WHAT KINDS OF COMPANIES HAVE AT-HOME EMPLOYEES?

Companies with fewer than 100 employees and *Fortune* 500 corporations are the ones employing the most home-based workers. The reasons for this are that large companies and agencies are able to accommodate specialized work arrangements; and small companies are willing to be flexible in order to compete for qualified personnel and to save money.

Assuming your skills enable you to work in a job that can be done at home, let's consider the characteristics of the companies that are most likely to allow people to work at home.

Information-Intensive Organizations

Often, but not always, jobs in these information-intensive companies are computer or communications oriented and involve data entry, word processing, telemarketing, or teleordering. Representative industries and companies with employees working from home include:

- *Banks and financial institutions:* American Express, Citibank, First Chicago Corporation, Mellon Bank.

- *High-technology companies:* Ameritech Corporation, Borland International, Inc., Digital Equipment Corporation, DuPont, Hewlett-Packard, Honeywell, Hughes, IBM, Sun Microsystems, Xerox.

- *Governments:* City of Los Angeles; County of Los Angeles; City of Portland; City and County of Denver; states of California, Arizona, Colorado, Hawaii, and Washington, and various federal agencies.

- *Insurance companies:* Aetna Life & Casualty, Allstate, Blue Cross/Blue Shield of South Carolina, Blue Cross/Blue Shield of Maryland, Equitable Life Assurance, Hartford Insurance Group, John Hancock Mutual Life, New York Life, Travelers.

- *News organizations:* Time Warner, Gannett, United Press International.

- *Retailers:* JCPenney (customer service), Bell Atlantic, Montgomery Ward, Sears.

- *Telephone companies:* AT&T, Bell Atlantic, GTE, New England Telephone, New York Telephone, Pacific Bell, US WEST.

- *Translation and transcription:* Berlitz Translation Services, Globalink Language Services, Journal Graphics.

Sales Organizations

Sales organizations have customarily allowed, or sometimes required, representatives to work from home. Businesses making extensive use of sales reps include insurance, publishing, real estate, printing, pharmaceuticals, and other product manufacturers.

Fast-Growing Small Businesses

Instead of renting office space or having employees come into the founder's home, growing businesses like Escrow Overload of Los Angeles and Letter Perfect of Baltimore, both of which began as home-based businesses, prefer to hire employees who will work from their homes. Such small businesses need employees to do secretarial jobs, sales, bookkeeping, product assembly and shipping, art, public relations, and computer programming.

SPECIAL ADVICE FOR THE DISABLED

The disabled are a minority group, now numbering 43 million Americans, that anyone can join at any time. Being or becoming disabled does not extinguish the need or the desire to work. We have heard from dispirited and sometimes angry disabled people who, despite repeated attempts, have been unable to find work. This problem persists despite the fact that thanks to personal computers and adaptation devices developed by companies like IBM and Apple, they can now work effectively from virtually anywhere. Such hurdles would be discouraging for anyone. But the road to finding a job under these circumstances demands persistence. You have to become a "squeaky wheel." As Brian Wettlaufer, who operates a consulting practice in Miami called Handicap Placement Services, Inc., advises, "Don't give up. There are opportunities."

If you have a rehabilitation counselor, consider working with him or her to develop a "rehab" plan. Such plans may be funded by federal, state, and local resources and may allow you to work at home either as an off-site worker, an employee, or as a self-employed individual. Plans may include training to enable you to develop new skills. Although funds are limited, occupational and vocational rehabilitation agencies have provided equipment.

Once someone has identified a work possibility, the Job Accommodation Network, funded by the President's Committee on Employment of People with Disabilities, provides consulting on methods and devices directed at working out problems necessary to make the situation work. The network may be contacted by phone at (800) ADA-WORK or on the Web: *http://janweb.icdi.wvu.edu.*

An important resource for the disabled is the Handicapped Users Database on the CompuServe Information Service. Created and managed by Georgia Griffith, herself blind and deaf, this immense collection contains resources for employment arranged by state and a list of local bulletin-board systems that enable local networking.

NEGOTIATING SATISFACTORY COMPENSATION

Some critics, primarily from labor unions, fear that "electronic cottages" could become the sweatshops of the future, with low-paid employees slaving over computer terminals and being paid on a monitored piece-rate basis. Electronic Services Unlimited, which conducted a study to explore the potential of telecommuting, did not find this fear to be a reality, however.

In speaking across the United States we've met a wide variety of employees working from home, but never one who complained of abuse. To avoid problems with compensation and benefits, however, get a clear agreement about your employment status.

Among salaried positions at home there are differences in benefits, support services, and equipment and supplies provided by the employer. Let's discuss a variety of possible arrangements.

Salaried Teleworkers

Teleworkers/telecommuters are salaried employees who do part of their work at home during normal working hours. Teleworking has been growing at an annual rate of 10 to 15 percent a year, reaching 11 million American workers in 1997, according to FIND/SVP. However, the vast majority of these telecommuters are operating informally. For example, someone taking work home an afternoon or two a week is considered a telecommuter, but the worker's company does not have a formal policy covering working at home. One of the pioneering telecommuting studies was conducted by the state of California back in 1988 and 1989. The state of California program involved 150 people. The conclusions reached by program analysts are still indicative of the results that most telecommuting programs bring:

- Productivity increased from 9 to 10 percent according to supervisors and from 20 to 30 percent from the standpoint of employees. State offices that did the best job of supporting and managing telecommuters showed productivity gains double those of other offices.

- The program paid for itself in thirteen months, and at the end of two years the benefit-to-cost ratio was 20 to 1.

- Only 40 percent of teleworkers needed personal computers for their work, but 64 percent used them.

- Thirty percent of the work done by California state employees can be done at home.

The research on California government employees was followed by a study by the University of San Francisco's Institute of Distributed Work of office workers employed by private companies who telecommuted one to two days a week. These workers increased their productivity by an average of 16.8 percent.

The 1994 Los Angeles earthquake jolted traditional managers in Southern California into rethinking their opposition to allowing employees to work at home. The underlying opposition many managers have to working at home is based on: (1) losing the feeling of control over employees that comes from direct observation, and (2) the often-mistaken belief that they can adequately monitor only employees in their sight. For most, it takes something as powerful as a major earthquake to change.

> The two most important ingredients for successful teleworking are self-motivation on the part of employees and positive management support on the part of employers.

Commissioned Positions

Gilda Silvani works from home, overlooking the blue Pacific at Laguna Beach, California. As an employment counselor for Escrow Overload, she specializes in providing temporary personnel to savings and loan associations, banks, and real estate companies.

Gilda interviews prospective personnel, checks out their backgrounds, and follows up on marketing done by the company's corporate office in Los Angeles County. As companies call her with needs for temporary workers, she matches the people from her files with the requirements of the job. She's among the home-based workers who are paid on a commission.

When working on commission, alternative arrangements are possible. On straight commission, you simply receive a percentage of every sale you make. Sometimes you can get hired into a position that provides salary plus commission and fringe benefits. And some companies offer an advance, or "draw," against your future commissions so you will have some income while you are getting started or when business is slow. Ken Worton, for example, works as a salesman for a wholesaler of housewares, hardware, and sporting goods. He receives a $1,800 draw each month toward his sales commission, which is 3 percent of the profits on what he sells, or 15 to 17 percent of the selling price.

The percentage of commission varies depending on the price of the product or service you are selling and your employment arrangement. Generally, when you are an independent contractor representing a company, the percentage of commission will be higher than if you work for a company that offers salary plus commission and fringe benefits. Bob Baxter of Pet Organics pays his independent sales reps a 20 to 25 percent commission plus an incentive if they reach their dollar sales goals. He says his commission is higher than most.

Owing to savings on overhead, some employers pay substantially more to commissioned employees who work at home. Escrow Overload, for example, can pay their employment counselors 4 to 8 times the commission of their competitors because of the savings in overhead they realize by having staff work at home. Customarily, temporary-help agencies pay commissions of 25 cents to 50 cents per hour of employment booked. Escrow Overload is able to pay $2 per hour booked, enabling some workers to make as much as $1,000 per week.

Benefits and support services also vary from employer to employer. Most certainly the company should provide you with a territory, sales leads, or a route to cover, as well as promotional materials, samples, and any backup information you need in order to sell the product or service adequately. Although benefits often are not included, the better-commissioned position will include group insurance coverage, a car, or travel expenses.

NEGOTIATING A WORK-FROM-HOME AGREEMENT

Whichever payment arrangement you negotiate, make sure to confirm such points as:

- The hours you will work and how often you are expected in the office

- The method of payment: salary, hourly wage, piece rate, commission

- Which benefits are included, such as health insurance and employer's share of Social Security
- Whether you are covered under workers' compensation
- What liability insurance you'll need on your home and who will pay for it
- The process used to determine when work is completed
- The amount of work expected
- Which equipment and supplies you'll need and who will pay for them
- Method and degree of supervision and performance evaluation
- The training available to you
- Opportunities for wage increases and career advancement
- Requirements and opportunities to return to work at the office

> Better than three out of five companies with official telecommuting policies surveyed by the Business Research Group of Newton, Massachusetts, provided either a portable or desktop computer to their at-home workers.

KEEPING IN CONTACT

Feelings of isolation can be more of a problem for home-based employees than for home-based entrepreneurs. Those whose work requires them to sit at home and work alone all day at a computer are the most susceptible. Anyone, however, who is away from the office long enough can start to feel like an outsider. As time passes, company shop talk can begin to sound like a foreign language, and you may discover you've missed out on special projects because no one thought of you when assignments were handed out. After all, out of sight, out of mind.

There are several solutions to this problem. Some lie with the employee; some with the organization and the supervisor.

Certainly E-mail and frequent telephone contact can help. In her book *Virtual Office Survival Handbook*, Alice Bredin, author and small-business consultant, suggests several ways to keep in touch including staying in contact with the receptionist or department secretary to remain current with goings-on in the office. We also advise encouraging people to contact you at home and finding a "buddy" who will keep you informed as well. Finally, the best solution is to spend at least one day a week in the office, if possible. Many teleworking programs require this.

ARRANGING OFFICE SUPPORT

Working from home can feel like living on an island. Office support—like supplies, secretaries, copy facilities, and special equipment—that used to be outside your door is now ten to thirty or more minutes away. You may miss having a copy machine down the hall or someone to handle all your appointments, phone calls, and filing. But some of the support you need can be provided during your day in the office or perhaps by an expense allowance to cover the cost of buying stamps or having copies made in your neighborhood. Often handling such details can be thought of as a trade-off for the freedom and flexibility of being at home.

GETTING APPROPRIATE SUPERVISION

Management consultant Marilyn Miller points out that in many offices "you can be in the upper fifty percent of your field if you just show up at work, the upper thirty percent if you show up on time, and the upper ten percent if you show up on time with your eyes open." Obviously, managing home-based workers requires something besides seeing them in the flesh.

Like other employees, work-at-homers need information, guidance, feedback, and support from their supervisors. Sometimes, however, because your supervisor can't see you in the hall or hear about difficulties you might be running into as an at-home worker, you have to take a more active role by asking for the information and direction you need.

BEING AWARE OF POSSIBLE FAMILY CONFLICT

One survey showed that family conflict is more often a problem with those employed at home than with those who work for themselves. While the self-employed are more likely to list family closeness as one of the chief benefits of working from home, those on jobs at home are more likely to list it as a problem.

We suspect this may occur because more people working at home on a job are doing so out of necessity, while most people who start a business do so because they want to. Family conflicts are also more prevalent when the kind of work you do keeps you from getting out of the house, as is more usually the case if you're employed than if you work for yourself.

The best safeguard against family conflict is to be aware of how working at home will affect those you live with. To minimize or avoid problems, set up your office and workday in the manner described in the subsequent chapters of this book.

If you plan your office space and work schedule with your family in mind and have open, honest family relationships, the period of adjustment can be brief and manageable. For example, the biggest problem telecommuter Sharon Miller faced was having to work at times when her family didn't want her to. But her husband would help out by fixing dinner or taking the family out to eat. Specific suggestions for easing family tensions when working at home are discussed in chapters 19 and 20.

Certainly, working from home is not for every employee. There are workers like Sophie Wojicik, who tried working for a bank from home but eventually went back to the main office because she missed a traditional office environment. But there are also employees like Sharon Miller, who will change jobs to spend more time working from home, and like Gilda Silvani, who describes her situation as "heaven on earth."

So although securing a job at home may be a challenge, if you think you're suited for it, persist in your efforts. Aside from the other advantages, the satisfaction of strolling from your desk out to your own mailbox where your paycheck lies waiting will make the effort worthwhile.

RESOURCES

BOOKS

The Age of Unreason. Charles Handy. Boston: Harvard Business School Press, 1991. ISBN: 0071033114.

Making Telecommuting Happen. Jack M. Nilles. New York: Van Nostrand, Reinhold, 1994. ISBN: 0442018576.

Telecommute! Go to Work Without Leaving Home. Lisa Shaw. New York: Wiley, 1996. ISBN: 0471118206.

The Telecommuter's Advisor. June Langoff. Newport, R.I.: Aegis Publishing Group, 1996. ISBN: 096327905X.

The Telecommuter's Handbook: How to Earn a Living Without Going to the Office. Debra and Brad Schepp. New York: McGraw-Hill, 1995. ISBN: 0070571023.

Teleworking Explained. Mike Gray, Noel Hodson, and Gil Gordon. New York: Wiley, 1993. ISBN: 0471939757.

The Underground Guide to Telecommuting. Woody Leonard. Reading, Mass.: Addison-Wesley, 1995. ISBN: 0201483432.

The Virtual Corporation: Structuring and Revitalizing the Corporation for the 21st Century. William H. Davidow and Michael S. Malone. New York: Harper Business, 1993. ISBN: 0887306578.

Virtual Office Survival Handbook. Alice Bredin. New York: Wiley, 1996. ISBN: 0471120596.

REPORT

California Telecommuting Pilot Project Final Report. Stock No. 7540-930-0400-6, State of California, Department of General Services, Publications Unit, P.O. Box 1015, North Highlands, CA 95660. $10.90. (Provide a street address as this comes via UPS.)

MAGAZINES AND NEWSLETTERS

Home Working: Essence Communications Inc., 1500 Broadway, Ste. 600, New York, NY 10036; Phone: (212) 642-0600. Web: *www.homeworking.com*

Telecommuting Review: Gil Gordon Associates, 10 Donner Court, Monmouth Junction, NJ 08852. Web: *www.gilgordon.com*

Tele-News: The American Telecommuting Association, 1220 L Street, NW, Ste. 100, Washington, DC 20005; Phone: (800) ATA-4-YOU. Web: *www. knowledgetree.com/ata-nl.html*

Work Times: New Ways to Work, 785 Market Street, Ste. 950, San Francisco, CA 94103. Phone: (415) 995-9860. Web: *www.nww.org*

ORGANIZATIONS

American Telecommuting Association, 1220 L Street, NW, Ste. 100, Washington, DC 20005; Phone: (800) ATA-4-YOU. Web: *www.knowledgetree. com/ata.html*

Canadian Telework Association: a nonprofit organization of Canadian private- and public-sector associations dedicated to promoting telework programs in Canada. Web based: *www.ivc.ca*

International Telework Association and Council: 204 E Street N.E., Washington, D.C. 20002, Phone: (202) 547-6157. Web: *www. telecommute.org*

INTERNET

Gil Gordon & Associates: *www.gilgordon.com* A comprehensive site dedicated to telecommuting research, news, issues, and ideas.

NET, Inc. Telework Solutions: *www.netinc-usa.com/Telework.* This site is dedicated to a focus on telework centers. Extensive national and international links to centers and resources.

Telecommute America! *www.att.com/TELECOMMUTE_AMERICA/* A nationwide public-awareness, information, and education program focusing on the benefits of telecommuting and nontraditional work environments.

Telecommuter's Digest *www.tdlgest.com* Weekly compendium of job openings, mainly programming, data entry, medical transcription, and word processing.

The International Teleworking Association. *www.telecomute.com* Advisory organization with local chapters.

Newsgroups

misc.jobs.offered
misc.jobs.contract

PART 2

Making Your Home Office Convenient, Functional, and Professional

CHAPTER 5

Keeping Your Work and Personal Life Separate

Goals

1. Set boundaries.

2. Maintain privacy.

3. Manage phone calls, visitors, deliveries, and pets.

A peaceful marriage of home and office depends on establishing effective boundaries. The office, with its phone calls, mail, paperwork, noisy equipment, and business visitors, can invade the sanctity of the home. In the same way, friends, neighbors, kids, barking dogs, soap operas, and peanut butter sandwiches of home can clutter up the halls of business. Creating effective boundaries preserves the character of each.

Fortunately, the boundaries you set up to maintain the privacy of your home will also help create a professional business atmosphere and, as you'll see in chapter 10, may help you qualify for valuable tax deductions. Recognizing the boundaries you need to create is a first step in making practical decisions that will ultimately affect the success of your home office.

SETTING BOUNDARIES BETWEEN YOUR HOME AND OFFICE

There are many tools and techniques for setting boundaries between your home and your work. Walls, doors, windows, lighting, furniture, and clothing are all material means you can use to define the boundaries you want to create. How you organize your time and arrange your space—your office location, work schedules, and household rules—are other more subtle means at your disposal.

Financial consultant George Gaines separates work and home by a single door. He lives alone and detests housework. "My kitchen may be stacked with dishes and the bedroom a shambles, but that's okay. That's 'my' space. I keep it any way I want. On the other side of the living-room door, it's a different world. It's always neat as a pin because that's where I meet with my clients. It's my office."

Programmer William Keen keeps work in bounds with a basement telephone. "I could work in the middle of a tornado. Nothing bothers me. I just tune it all out. Actually, I work best if two or three things are going on at a time. But if my boss or a business contact calls, they don't think so highly of the stereo blaring or the kids yelling in the background, so I have a little office in the basement for my business phone."

Joan Cullen creatively defines the boundaries between her work and home with a bed sheet. As an editor who works several days each week at home, she keeps her office on the dining-room table, which she has covered with a king-size sheet. The table is piled with manuscripts in various stages of editing. When she's ready to put the work away and claim her apartment for herself again, she stacks all her materials in the center of the table, carefully marking off each project with a rubber band or colored paper, folds and ties the four corners of the sheet over the pile, and puts her whole "office" in a closet.

We use these examples because they illustrate how personal and how simple establishing useful boundaries can be. Whether you prefer the peace and harmony of a monastic retreat, the intensity and excitement of a politician's campaign office, or something in between, the essential task is to define boundaries that can keep both your household and work space the way you want them.

Let's consider some of the basic decisions you need to make about the boundaries of your home office. By answering these questions, you will begin to recognize which types of boundaries you will need to set for yourself and the others in your household.

Slightly more than 31 percent of U.S. households have dedicated some of their homes to a home office, according to a 1998 survey by the public opinion polling firm Wirthlin Worldwide. That's up 7 percent from two years earlier.

If you answer "yes" to seven or eight of the questions on the following work sheet, you'll want an office that is as separate as possible from the rest of your household. If feasible, consider a separate structure or at least a separate entrance for business guests. Soundproofing your office in one of the ways suggested in chapter 7 may also be necessary. If you live with oth-

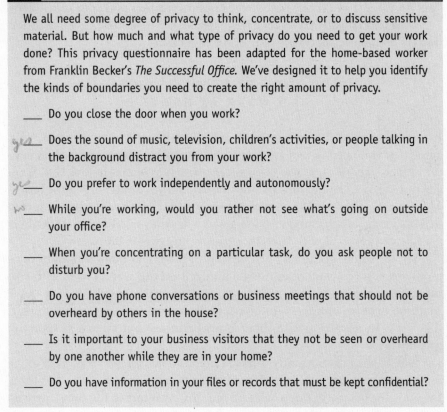

 Work Sheet: How Much Privacy Do You Need to Work Productively?

We all need some degree of privacy to think, concentrate, or to discuss sensitive material. But how much and what type of privacy do you need to get your work done? This privacy questionnaire has been adapted for the home-based worker from Franklin Becker's *The Successful Office*. We've designed it to help you identify the kinds of boundaries you need to create the right amount of privacy.

____ Do you close the door when you work?

yes Does the sound of music, television, children's activities, or people talking in the background distract you from your work?

yes Do you prefer to work independently and autonomously?

_no_ While you're working, would you rather not see what's going on outside your office?

____ When you're concentrating on a particular task, do you ask people not to disturb you?

____ Do you have phone conversations or business meetings that should not be overheard by others in the house?

____ Is it important to your business visitors that they not be seen or overheard by one another while they are in your home?

____ Do you have information in your files or records that must be kept confidential?

ers, you'll need to establish clear rules as to when they can and cannot interrupt you.

If you answered "yes" to just four to six of these questions, involvement with people and other activities is important to you, yet a separate work space might still be required. You'll likely want a door to your office, but you'll also want ready access to what's going on outside the door at different times during the day. If you work alone at home, arrange at least weekly contact with colleagues, co-workers, friends, or clients.

If you answered "yes" to only one to three of the questions, you'll probably prefer your office in the midst of plenty of activity. In fact, you may want an open office space in the heart of the household. If you work alone at home, occasionally try to take your work out to your clients' sites or to a public place like a restaurant, library, or hotel lobby. Try to have contact each day with customers, clients, co-workers, family, or neighbors. If there's nothing going on at home, you may even want to create some noise and activity there by turning on music or the TV.

If you answered "yes" to question 7, arrange to have a double entrance into your office or schedule your appointments carefully. If you answered "yes" to the last question, have locks put on your files and your office door.

Now let's consider the other basic decisions you'll need to make in setting up boundaries between your home and office.

DO YOU LET PEOPLE KNOW YOU WORK AT HOME?

Eighty percent of the people we've talked with say, "Sure, why not?" We agree that you needn't feel any stigma about working from home. As a matter of fact, according to the most recent figures released by the U.S. Census Bureau, over half of all small businesses in the country are home based. Most people whom you inform about your status won't care where your office is so long as you can do a good job at what they need you to do. Others are likely to respond with friendly curiosity and even a bit of envy.

Yet, for some, not telling people that they work at home can help solve problems. One consultant expressed his decision this way: "I work with *Fortune* 500 companies. They're used to working with consultants who have Madison Avenue addresses. I don't actually know what they would think if they knew I was talking with them in my bathrobe, but I'd just as soon not find out."

Jack Gibbs intermittently works at home so he can get away from office interruptions at the public relations firm that employs him: "The last thing I want is for people to know where I am. My secretary is the only one who knows—and my supervisor, of course."

If for these, or any other, reasons, you feel at all uncomfortable with people knowing you work from home, usually there's no need to tell them. By arranging outside business meetings and having a business phone and special mail service, you can just as easily appear to be working in a regular office setting. And when business contacts ask where you're located, chances are they're referring to the area of the city or county you're in, not whether you're in a home office.

DO YOU WANT BUSINESS VISITORS COMING TO YOUR HOME?

Sooner or later most people who work from home are confronted with this decision. Half of the people working from home prefer to meet with business visitors away from their home offices. The other half have business visitors coming to their homes at least occasionally. The decision is a personal one. Here are several points to consider in making the choice.

Security

Will you and your premises be safe if your business brings strangers into your home? Recording studio owner Randy Tobin never gives his address out to callers interested in his services. He interviews them, asks for a phone number, and calls them back before he discloses his location. Instead of having new psychotherapy clients come to her home office, Cheryl Smith arranged to do her initial interviews at a nearby clinic.

Privacy

Will you feel as though your inalienable right to privacy has been taken away or that your home is being invaded by strangers? How much space you have and how you arrange it will probably determine whether business visitors feel like intruders. For Kitty Friedman, who lives and writes in a one-room guest house, there is no way to close off her personal space from business guests, so she makes most of her business contacts by phone or meets clients at a publisher's office.

When you have a little more space than Kitty does, closed doors or separate business entrances work to retain your privacy. Graphics designer Mary Stoddard didn't like having customers come into her office when it was in the living room. She felt her home had become too public, so she converted her garage into a studio/office and had a separate entrance installed. This created the boundaries she needed to keep business from invading her home.

Image

Is your office space appropriate for business meetings, and do you want to keep it looking presentable for clients or customers? Thomas Kerr thought not. He didn't feel his small apartment would convey the image he wanted to project as a management consultant. His solution was to join a private club where he could hold business meetings. Some people join airline clubs for this purpose.

Designer Kelly Spiotto has her own prohibitive factor to contend with: a lively, rather vocal two-year-old. "It's a three-ring circus!" she says. "Sometimes I pick up and deliver, but whenever I can, I have clients E-mail me their manuscripts or send them via courier."

Toti O'Brien solved a similar problem for the dance classes she teaches in her loft apartment. "After my son was born, I found that even with a nanny or my husband watching him, I was distracted when teaching." The building she lives in has a small gym. "I asked them if I could hold my classes there, and since no one uses it much, the manager said 'why not?'"

If you decide your home office doesn't convey the right image for business meetings and appointments, another option is to rent an office suite on a part-time basis from an organization like HQ, which provides all the professional office services you need, including conference facilities and office space, at a cost lower than that of renting an office full-time. You use the facilities only when you need them. These office-rental organizations can also provide secretarial services, take phone calls, and receive mail for you.

Or like personal coach Mavis Page, you might rent space from colleagues. Page holds group sessions three nights a week in space he rents by the hour from a psychotherapist who sees clients only during the day.

Before jumping to obtain outside space because a client requests a site visit, however, marketing consultant Laura Douglas suggests exploring why clients want to come to your office. If they want to make sure you're a real business, she advises, "Don't try to mislead them. Be straightforward. Tell them that your business is home based." On the other hand, Douglas points out, "it's possible that the reason clients want to come to your office is simply to get out of theirs. They could want to feel free to discuss something with you they don't feel comfortable discussing in their own office or they might just want an excuse to get out of their cubbyhole for a while. If that's the case, figure out somewhere you can meet like a restaurant, hotel, or airline club where you can get together without setting up a separate office facility."

What to Do When You Don't Want to Meet Business Visitors in Your Home

1. Offer pickup and delivery services.

2. Meet at the customer's, client's, or employer's location.

3. Transact business by mail, telephone, or on line.

4. Meet in neutral territory, such as a restaurant, hotel lobby, or club.

5. Rent a hotel suite or conference room.

6. Consult with a friend or associate who has an office complementary to the service or product you offer and make an arrangement to exchange referrals or services for occasional use of their office space.

7. Rent an executive office suite by the hour, day, or month. Such services provide office space, conference or meetings facilities, as well as mail, phone, and secretarial services.

8. Use a fax machine.

But if the time comes when you definitely need more space, you still have a variety of choices of how to expand without losing the benefits of working from home (see chapter 24).

HOW DO YOU HANDLE BUSINESS PHONE CALLS?

According to freelance cameraman Steve Haines, the best thing about working from home is that he never misses a phone call. "Crews are notorious for calling at all times of the day and night. Many times I've gotten the job because I am the only one who answers the phone no matter what time it is."

Of course, not everyone is as willing as Steve to be available day and night for business calls. Lynne Frances, for example, felt differently about taking customer calls for her cleaning service. "When you have your business at home, there's no respect for your personal life. People knew I would be at home, so they disregarded my business hours and called me anytime they wanted. For my own peace of mind, I had to find a way to limit business calls to business hours." She got a private line and hired an answering service for her business number.

As Lynne found out, the dilemma in setting up home-office phone service is how to make sure you don't miss important business calls without becoming a slave to the telephone twenty-four hours a day. The following is what we recommend:

1. Have a separate telephone line for business. We recommend that this second line be a business rather than a residential one so that:

- People who call Directory Assistance to ask for you by your business name will get your number.
- You will have a listing, sometimes two, in the Yellow Pages.
- You can avoid having to take personal calls during business hours.
- You can choose whether to take business calls after business hours, thereby protecting your private life.
- You can leave your residential line free for other family members to use without interfering with your business.
- Business telephone costs can be claimed as a tax deduction.

Switching a residential line to a business line usually costs about half of what installing a new business line does. Some people use one line for incoming and the other for outgoing calls, and, increasingly, people are installing separate lines for their fax and modem use. This keeps voice calls separate from "machine calls."

2. *Locate your business phone away from household noise.* Unless you're providing child care, pet care, or cleaning services, household noises that can be picked up over the receiver are disruptive during business conversations. Since you can't always predict when the neighbor's dog will bark or the kids will turn on the stereo, your best bet is to locate the business phone away from such activity and use good sound-control techniques. (See chapter 7 for ideas on soundproofing your home office.)

3. *Answer your business phone in a formal manner.* Use either your own name or your company name. The way you answer your business phone will often determine whether or not the caller perceives you as a professional who is at work.

If you don't have a secretary answering your phone, you will be the one to create the proper impression. To put forth a positive professional image, many business owners we know greet callers with "Good morning" or "Good afternoon," followed by their name. It always works to their advantage to put a "smile" in their voices when they answer.

Do not have young children answer your business phone. If you want other adults in the household to take business calls, instruct them to use the same professional procedure as you do.

4. *Use an answering machine, answering service, or voice mail.* Whether your goal is to free yourself from constant business calls or to be sure you don't miss any, your home business needs these resources to preserve your peace of mind.

You can think of voice mail as an electronic substitute for a secretary. It operates just like the systems used by large corporations. It turns your phone into a sophisticated answering machine that gives callers choices. Callers can select one number on their phone pad that instructs the computer to take a message, another to obtain information you've recorded for them, or a third to have the computer forward their calls to you or someone else. Voice mail can also tell callers that all lines are currently busy and ask them to stay on the line until you're free. There are many inexpensive software programs that allow your computer to act as a voice-mail system. Most regional phone services such Pacific Bell and Atlantic Bell offer a voice-mail service to which you can inexpensively subscribe.

If you use an answering machine or voice mail, create a polite and businesslike message. Avoid the temptation to record anything "cutesy." And don't start an answering-machine message with "Hello," followed by a pause. This leaves callers feeling foolish when they realize they've responded to a greeting from a machine. An answering machine or voice-mail message should:

- Begin by giving the name of your business (e.g., "You have reached . . .").

- State that you're away from the phone right now.

- Ask that the caller leave a name, number, and the time of the call.

- Assure the caller that you will return the call as soon as possible.

- Keep voice-mail choices simple, offer no more than four, and make instructions easy enough for any seventh-grader to follow.

If you decide to use an answering service, check to be sure it is courteous, prompt in answering, and accurate when taking messages. We suggest periodically calling the service yourself, as if you were an unknown customer or client, to see how you are treated.

5. *Take advantage of phone company services such as call-forwarding, conference calling, and call-waiting.* By being more readily available during standard business hours, you will increase the likelihood that your customers and clients won't feel the need to reach you after hours. A cellular phone is also effective for this purpose.

In chapter 8, we'll examine these and other new telephone features that can facilitate your work.

DO YOU USE YOUR HOME ADDRESS FOR BUSINESS PURPOSES?

The majority of people who work from home use their home address for both personal and business mail. There are no special arrangements you need to make, nor should you encounter any difficulties with the post office, regardless of how much business mail you receive.

However, if you're concerned about giving your home address to strangers or if you have an address on Sheep Dip or Sleepy Hollow Lane and don't like the business image it conveys, you can make other arrangements for mail delivery. If you're employed, use your employer's address and have your mail forwarded. If you're self-employed, you can rent a post-office box or an address from a mail-receiving service like Mail Boxes, Etc. Mail-receiving services provide you with a street address and a suite number instead of a post-office-box number. This removes the doubt created in many people's minds when they see a post-office box as a business address. The cost is usually less than twenty dollars a month.

For Victor Herrera, changing his mailing address meant business. Having had a background as an investigator for the county coroner's office, he opened his innovative mobile autopsy service, 1-800-AUTOPSY, only to find that people were turned off by his address in a low-rent area. So he rented an address through a mail-receiving service in a high-rent commercial district. Business boomed and has been growing rapidly ever since.

 Warning!

If you decide to use a private mail-receiving service, keep in mind that if you move, the post office will not accept a mail-forwarding order on a private post-office box and often the private post office will forward for only thirty days. And they will charge you for the postage on forwarding your mail.

An advantage of a post-office box for businesses that receive a high volume of mail is that mail is sorted and placed in postal boxes several times a day; however, courier services, such as Federal Express, will not deliver to a post-office box. To get the advantage of a post-office box and still receive courier deliveries, include both your street address and post-office box as follows:

Anytown, NY 10222-0909
Your business name
Your street address
P.O. Box 415
Anytown, NY 10222-0909

If you use this format, approved by the U.S. Postal Service, your regular mail will be sent to the post office box, but your street address directs courier deliveries to your home address and shows you are not just a mail drop.

Private firms like Airborne, DHL, Federal Express, or United Parcel Service will, of course, provide door-to-door delivery to your residence. For a modest fee, they will also pick up outgoing mail from your home office.

ACCEPTING DELIVERIES WHEN YOU'RE AWAY

Imagine this. You get a rush order for four hundred custom-designed hats. The materials arrive by overnight mail. But you're out on a delivery, and when you come home the hallway of your New York co-op is stacked floor to ceiling with boxes and on your door is a note from the owners' association proclaiming that your business is a hazard.

It happens. And even worse, you could find one of those little notes that say "We tried to deliver your packages today. We'll try again tomorrow" and miss your delivery date. Only one out of three home business owners works *at* home. Most of us work *from* home. We spend a good portion of each day out meeting clients, serving customers, working with associates, or making deliveries.

So, the hassles of missing important deliveries are a common inconvenience. To avoid the problem, you can prearrange with a delivery service to leave your packages whether or not you are there. But security and weather conditions can be a concern.

Some people rent an executive suite, warehouse their materials elsewhere, or make arrangements with a mail-receiving service. Of course, these solutions won't work for everyone and in all circumstances, for example, when clients are picking up or delivering work to you after business hours.

If you have a neighbor who's a fellow work-at-homer, you can offer to accept deliveries for each other. In some cases you can provide pickup and delivery services yourself to get important materials to clients on time.

If none of these solutions fills the bill, check out Smart Box (816/472-8881; *www.smartbox.com*). It's a secure, climate-controlled home-delivery device that you can install in a garage, porch, or side door. It allows those

How to Help Business Visitors Locate Your Home and Feel Welcome

1. If your residence is at all difficult to find, send directions by fax, E-mail, or regular mail in advance describing how to get there. If possible, use a separate entrance for business visitors.

2. If you live in a multifamily dwelling, cut out the typeset name from your card or stationery, have it laminated, and post it on your own door or on the building directory. If you live in a single-family house where the address is difficult to see or confusing to find, consider a simple yard sign by your front walk displaying your name and address. Although business signs are usually prohibited in residential areas, signs like the one shown in Figure 5-1 should pose no problem and can greatly assist visitors.

3. Arrange for a convenient and easy-to-remember place to put guests' coats, hats, and packages. People are often unaccustomed to business meetings in the more relaxed atmosphere of a home office, so be sure they've retrieved their belongings before they leave or you'll soon have a closetful of assorted wraps and umbrellas to return.

4. Have coffee, tea, or water available as you would in a traditional office, and offer it to guests when they arrive.

5. Keep bathroom facilities fresh and supplies available. Although a guest bathroom is certainly preferable, if guests must have access to a facility used by other household members, make sure personal toiletries remain out of sight.

6. Clear areas where your business visitors come of personal items like children's toys, dirty dishes, and laundry baskets so that they don't feel they're intruding on your personal life.

Figure 5-1

you authorize to leave or pick up items when you're not there, and it's Internet-enabled. If you wish, your clients, colleagues, customers, or delivery people can access a unique code for each delivery, confirm access authorization, and verify that the delivery has been made—all on line.

SETTING BOUNDARIES FOR OTHER PEOPLE

When you're working in a traditional office, the assumption is that while you're there, work has priority. This assumption generally defines how, when, and in what way people interact with you. When you're working at home, however, there is no single assumption about what you're there for. After all, it's a place where you play many roles: worker, neighbor, friend, mate, parent, citizen.

Under these circumstances, it isn't always easy for others to know how to interact with you. Therefore you need to set limits and define boundaries so they will know when you're working and when you're not. It's up to you to let them know what you expect and to help them feel comfortable with an unfamiliar situation. Here are some tips to help you accomplish this with various kinds of people.

Business Visitors

Let colleagues, co-workers, customers, and clients know specifically when they can call you. For example: "Call me on weekdays between nine and five." "Please call me after twelve o'clock." "Call me anytime and leave a message with my service. I check in every hour, and I'll call you back." To reinforce this boundary, do not answer your business phone after work hours. If you wish, you can put your answering machine or service on your business phone so you can return calls after hours the next morning.

If customers come to your home, clearly define business hours. We suggest having customers call before leaving. Set a time to meet with them and give them an idea of how long the meeting should last. "We can meet from nine to ten tomorrow morning." "If you could simply drop the papers by, I would certainly appreciate it. I don't have much time right now." Again, to reinforce your limits, avoid making too many exceptions to transacting business before or after the hours you've set.

A study at the University of Southern California found that when you have regular business visitors, a separate outside entrance works best. Of course, having a separate structure will further separate your home life from your business life. For example, David Palmer erected a prefab building in his backyard for about one-fifth the cost of adding on to his home.

When having business visitors come to your home, be prepared for them. Once they arrive, make them feel welcome and comfortable. If family members are present when business visitors arrive or while you're meeting, take the initiative in introducing them briefly to your guests, and let them know you will be working and wish not to be disturbed.

Because you're not in a traditional office setting, cueing guests that it's time to leave can be an awkward moment. Sometimes they wonder whether

Introducing Business Visitors to Family Members

Follow these simple rules of etiquette when introducing business visitors to family members and staff.

Men are introduced to women. For example, when introducing a male visitor to your wife, you would say, "Marjorie, I'd like you to meet Jim Evans. Jim, this is my wife, Marjorie." Or, when introducing a female visitor to your husband, you would say, "Jill, this is my husband, George. George, this is my client, Jill Rose."

Younger persons are introduced to older persons. For example, you would introduce your son to a business visitor with "Jim, this is my son John. John, this is Mr. Evans."

People with less status are introduced to people with more status. For example, you introduce the vice president of a company to your secretary like this: "Georgia, I would like you to meet my secretary, Susan Scott. Susan, this is Georgia McGuire of Holt Advertising."

to stay and chat after the meeting. To ease the situation, stand up, or move toward the door to let visitors know it's time to leave. Thank them for coming and, when necessary, tactfully remind them you have more work to do.

Neighbors and Friends

As Mary Smith, a production manager for a telecommunications project, has found, "Sometimes it's hard to go into the study and shut the neighbors out."

Let friends and neighbors know your work hours and when you are available. Say "Come by after five," for example, or "Let's visit over lunch. I'll come over at noon." Tell them when they can call. If they call while you're working, politely say you'll call them back when you're finished. Do not start a conversation. If you wish, you can put voice mail or an answering machine or service on your personal line while you work.

Of course, you don't want to antagonize people in the process of getting them to respect your work boundaries, but as writer David Goodfellow found, you do have to be hard-nosed about it. "My family and friends know that during business hours my office is strictly private, but I had to get downright unfriendly to make that happen. It worked, though, and with no lasting hard feelings."

To keep bad feelings from building up and still be firm about boundaries, psychotherapist Ellen Barker uses the "not now, but when" approach to telling people not to bother her while she's working. Instead of just turning people away, she tells them exactly when she will be available.

Family

Plan your work schedule and go over it with your family to show them when you will and will not be available. Do not assume anything. Let them know at what times and for what reasons you can be interrupted.

Set rules for your family about your business telephone and your equipment. Let them know the kind of help or support you need and expect. Discuss which types and levels of noise you can and cannot tolerate, which areas must be left neat and tidy, and what they are to do when you have business guests.

Employees

If you have workers coming into your home, help them feel comfortable in what may be an unfamiliar setting by explaining exactly what you expect. Because working from home may feel much more informal than working in an office, it is particularly important to establish a businesslike manner.

Set clear hours. Define when employees can take breaks. Show them which areas of the house are open and which bathroom to use. Make it clear whether or not they can use your business phone, your dishes, your refrigerator, or your food. Chapters 19 through 21 go into more detail about working at home successfully with family members and employees.

SPECIAL CONSIDERATIONS
FOR PET OWNERS

Having the family dog snoozing at your feet or the cat curled up in your lap can be one of the best things about working from home. Still, managing pets while working from home can sometimes be a challenge. First, if you have customers or clients coming to your house, remember that a small but significant number of people are allergic to dogs and cats, and some people are afraid of dogs. In fact, a survey of three thousand Americans found that dogs are their tenth most common fear. So keeping your pets in a yard or another part of the house away from your business visitors may make good sense, even if your animals "wouldn't hurt a soul."

Another problem faced by dog owners who work at home is when the dog begins barking loudly right in the middle of an important phone conversation. So much for the professional business image!

Short of keeping your dog away from the work area, a mute or hold button on your telephone, preferably both, can help. The mute button allows you to hear the person you're talking with but prevents him or her from hearing you as long as you're holding the button down. The hold button keeps the caller on hold and frees you to leave the phone and take care of the disturbance. With these features, simply say, "Just a moment. There's a dog barking outside my window. Let me close it." These buttons are also ideal for unexpected disruptions from children or other household emergencies.

Veterinarian Roger Kuperways points out to home-based pet owners that pets will raise a fuss when you change the rules on them. He recommends that when you start working from home, sit down with your family and decide what the rules will be for your pet now that you're working from home. Make a definite list of what your pet can and cannot do: e.g., be in the house during working hours, get on the office couch, come in your office, sleep under your desk, jump up on guests, sit on your lap while working. Then get everyone to agree to stick to these rules.

Whenever you set new rules for your pets, if they involve major changes, be ready for a month or two of whining, barking, and other forms of protest. Pets will want to do what they've been used to doing, but if you and everyone else are consistent during this period, they will get used to the new rules and settle down. If you need help with a problem pet, having a trainer can help. Interview several and find one both you and your pet like. Remember, though, as all good trainers will tell you, they're training you, not the pet. To change a pet's disruptive behavior you will have to follow through consistently on what you learn.

True Confessions: Home Office Canine Etiquette

Until we started working from home we'd never let ourselves have a dog. They're such social animals that we felt guilty at the thought of leaving one all alone five days a week. So, as soon as we started working from home, we promptly got a dog. At times we've had three dogs in our home office.

Over the years we've gone from having Scotties to whippets, to an Italian greyhound and now a toy Manchester terrier. And if the truth be known, as much as we've enjoyed them all, sharing a home office with a dog has been a challenge for us indulgent pet owners. To maintain a professional work environment with dogs underfoot, we've had to learn the basic rules of Home Office Canine Etiquette.

Our first lesson was literally the most painful. We had a temperamental Scottish terrier. Occasionally he snapped at strangers when they reached down to pet him. We tried telling everyone who came to our home, "Our dog does bite, so don't try to pet him." Unfortunately, there were always a few overly confident people who'd assure us that dogs never bit them, and before we could intervene, they'd stick their hand in our dog's face. Thus we learned:

Home Office Canine Etiquette Rule #1: If you have clients coming to your home office, you can't have a dog that snaps.

No matter how carefully you try to keep your dog away from visitors, there's always a chance they'll encounter each other. And even if you have a dog that *never* bites, it's still wise to have liability insurance that covers business guests.

Whippets are among the friendliest and most easygoing dogs you can imagine, but even with the sweetest, most loving of dogs, you'll inevitably have business guests coming to your home who are deathly afraid of dogs or allergic to them. So we've learned:

Home Office Canine Etiquette Rule #2: Find out how your business visitors feel about dogs before allowing yours to join you in greeting guests at the door or letting them sit in on your meetings.

Of course, this means that you need to have a place in your home where you can isolate your dog(s). In previous homes we've had a pantry, a kitchen, or basement area where we could keep our dogs away from guests who'd just as soon not meet them. Our current home, however, is quite open, so we've had to find more innovative solutions.

We've installed a child-safety door, for example, between our loft office and the rest of the house. When we don't want the dogs to join us at the door or in the living room with guests, we close the safety door and keep them in the office. We've also put a Dutch door on our assistant's office, so the dogs can stay with her while guests are visiting.

(Continued on page 131)

(Continued from page 130)

Barking has proven to be a more difficult challenge, however. Of course, it's not professional for a dog to be raising a ruckus in the midst of an important business call. So, for unavoidable emergencies, we learned:

Home-Office Canine Etiquette Rule #3: Get a telephone with a mute button.

A mute button allows you to hear the people you're talking with but prevents them from hearing anything on your end of the line. More important, we learned:

Home Office Canine Etiquette Rule #4: Train your dog.

Teach it not to bark, socialize it to be friendly with strangers but not to jump up on them, and make sure it will come to you when called. Now, you may be wondering, how on earth will you ever do that? Until recently our dogs had always been so well mannered by nature that not much socializing was needed. Then, we got Billy, our toy Manchester terrier. Although he's our favorite dog of all time— friendly, loyal and loving—he didn't come with the best of manners. He barked brazenly, more like a rooster than a dog, at every household and office noise from the phone ringing to the doorbell chiming and even at the musical cue announcing that Windows has booted up on the computer. And, especially, he barked when strangers came into the house. Then, once he made friends, he would pester them incessantly for attention. That's when we learned:

Home Office Canine Etiquette Rule #5: Get professional help if you need it.

We turned to dog trainer Dana Miller and learned it wasn't our dog she'd be training; it was us. Here's the process she taught us:

The Three Steps to a Well-Behaved Dog

Professional trainer Dana Miller taught us how to teach our dog to behave using a basic three-step process:

1. Interrupt bad behavior by getting the dog's attention using a leash or long line.

2. Correct the dog's behavior by using a command like "hush" or "down."

3. Praise the good dog as soon as it produces the desired behavior.

Of course you have to go through these three steps consistently hundreds of times before the well-behaved dog emerges.

(Continued on page 132)

(Continued from page 131)

As you can imagine, this process took some time and it was disruptive of our work schedule for a while. During Billy's training, we had to keep him on a leash so we could correct him. And we've had to be persistent about never letting undesirable behavior go uncorrected. But the investment has paid off. We now have a well-behaved office mate, and, most of the time, a peaceful home office. To find a professional trainer in your area, Miller recommends asking your veterinarian for a referral and interviewing several trainers to find one you feel confident and comfortable with. She also suggests reading *Good Owners, Great Dogs,* by Brian Kilcommons (Warner Books, 1992). Meanwhile, we've discovered:

Home Office Canine Etiquette Rule #6: Keep the door closed to the laundry room if you don't want to discover your dirty unmentionables scattered around your home office.

KEEPING YOUR OFFICE SPACE IN BOUNDS

By necessity, most home offices are confined to a relatively small space, but work projects don't always fit neatly in small spaces—especially as your business activities at home grow. Defining boundaries helps you maintain the best aspects of a home and an office. Fortunately, as we'll discuss in the next chapter, you have options as to where you locate your office. Entire industries of products, supplies, and consultants are now available to help you keep your office space sufficiently organized to prevent its overtaking the rest of your home.

Tips For Keeping Your Home And Office Space Separate

1. *Clearly demarcate your work space* by using a separate room, partition, bookcase, screen, or room divider so that you and everyone else will know precisely where the home stops and the office begins. Make sure you can close your office off when you're working.

2. *Set definite work hours* and let everyone know precisely when you will be available for business and when you are free for personal activities.

3. *Have a signal that makes it clear when you do not want to be disturbed;* for example, when the office door is closed or when you put up a DO NOT DISTURB sign.

(Continued on page 133)

(Continued from page 132)

4. **Learn how to say "No, I'm working now"** firmly, but politely, and stick to it so that everyone will know you mean what you say.

5. **Use a separate business telephone line** and have an answering machine or answering service to screen calls or record messages when you are not available.

6. **Soundproof your office** by using a solid-core door and other materials and equipment that reduce noise.

7. **Dress in a particular way when you're at work.** You need not resort to coat and tie or hose and heels, but wearing work attire can help you and others know it's time for business if doing so becomes a problem.

8. **Organize your office** so you can keep work materials, paper, and equipment in clearly defined office spaces.

9. **Have a separate outside office entrance** for the ultimate in privacy, or locate your office in a converted portion of a garage, a guesthouse, or a separate building.

RESOURCES

BOOKS

Feng Shui: The Book of Cures: 150 Simple Solutions for Health and Happiness in Your Home or Office. Nancilee Wydra. Lincolnwood, Ill.: Contemporary Books, 1996. ISBN: 0809231689.

Good Dog, Bad Dog. Mordecai Siegal and Matthew Margolis. New York: Henry Holt, 1997. *www.matthewmargolis.com*

Healing Environments, Your Guide to Indoor Well-Being. Carol Venolia. Berkeley, Calif.: Celestial Arts, 1994. ISBN: 0890874972.

Home Safe Home: Protecting Yourself and Your Family from Everyday Toxics and Harmful Household Products. Debra Lynn Dadd. New York: Tarcher/Putnam, 1997.

When Good Dogs Do Bad Things. Mordecai Siegal and Matthew Margolis. New York: Little Brown, 1986. *www.matthewmargolis.com*

HOME DELIVERY DEVICE

Smartbox, 2018 Swift, N., Kansas City, MO 64116; Phone: (816) 472-8881. Web: *www.smartbox.com*

Finding the Right
Office Space

<table>
<tr><td>

Goals

1. Decide how much space you need.

2. Find a place for everything.

3. Set up an office that matches your work style and lifestyle.

4. Make the most of available space.

5. Add on or remodel if necessary.

6. Use professional help.

</td></tr>
</table>

Lynne Frances's cleaning service started out in her bedroom, but ended up in the living room. She didn't like waking up in the middle of the night and being reminded of the work she had to do.

Gary Eckart's stained-glass factory started out in the den and ended up in an RV parked beside his house. His toddlers were too interested in his tools and the brightly colored glass.

Mary Stoddard's graphics studio started out in the living room and ended up in the garage. She found she didn't like strangers entering the privacy of her home.

Tom Girard began his translation service on the kitchen table and ended up converting the basement into an office. He didn't like the breakfast table piled with his papers or his papers adorned with telltale jelly stains.

In fact, almost every problem people have in working from home—whether it's overeating, too many interruptions, or not getting enough work done—is either aggravated or alleviated by where they put their offices. The location of your office can even be the solution to problems that seem to be unrelated to office location. The McNaughtons are a case in point.

Bill McNaughton is a professor and has worked at home part-time for many years. As a high-school teacher, his wife, Bonnie, had always worked away from the house. But when she left teaching, she completed a degree in instructional design and opened a business at home writing technical manuals.

She set up her office at the top of the stairs in a bedroom left vacant when the kids moved out. But from the very beginning, this arrangement didn't work. Two, three, or maybe four times a morning her husband would come into her office to ask a question, share some news, or just say hello. She kept urging him not to interrupt her and please to wait until lunch to talk. He would apologize and agree to leave her alone but then interrupt her again. She tried being tolerant but, once distracted from her work, she would lose her momentum and find it hard to get started again.

On the verge of renting an office, Bonnie decided to have one last talk with her husband. The more they talked, the clearer the problem became. Because her office was right at the top of the stairs, he had to walk by it as he went to and from his office in the den. This happened quite often since he was used to pacing while thinking. Seeing her office, even with the door closed, was too much of a temptation for him. He couldn't resist dropping in to visit.

They solved the problem by trading offices. From the bedroom office, he could walk up and down the stairs freely, as many times as he wished. With his wife's office out of sight down the hall, it was also out of mind. She got her work done and they chatted over lunch.

Like so many of us, Bonnie hadn't really given much thought to where she'd put her office. The spare bedroom at the top of the stairs had seemed only natural. Yet this location created unnecessary problems, as unplanned office sites often do.

Finding the right space for your office is a matter of putting together several factors and coming up with the best possible location. The right space meets the demands of your particular job. It matches your personal work style and budget and qualifies you for tax benefits you're entitled to. And it fits in with your household environment. The object of this chapter is to help you identify the office location that will work best in your situation.

MINIMUM HOME-OFFICE SPACE REQUIREMENTS

An *Income Opportunities* magazine survey found that most home offices are squeezed into three hundred square feet or less and that not having enough space was the number-one complaint among their readers! We've found that to work effectively at home, most people need these basic work areas:

1. Space for a desk and chair, where you can do paperwork and make phone calls.

2. Space where you can work with a computer, typewriter, calculator, or other equipment.

3. Contemplation or conversation space with chairs or a couch, where you can collect your thoughts or hold business meetings.

4. Storage space for filing cabinets, books, and reference materials.

5. Shelf space for storing supplies and infrequently used equipment.

6. Large work space for activities like assembling or producing materials and doing mailings or shipping.

In addition to these basic work areas, consider your needs for specialized space. Do you need room for particular equipment? Work space for employees? A waiting area for customers or clients?

All these work areas needn't be in the same room. Attics, basements, garages, or enclosed back porches make good storage spaces. A closet makes an ideal out-of-the-way but handy place for a bank of filing cabinets,

---

Finding a Place for Everything

Because everything obviously can't be kept in your immediate desk area, use this formula adapted from Stephanie Winston's book *Getting Organized* to decide where to keep what. On a scale of 1 to 7, rate the item you're storing or filing in terms of how frequently you use it. Give items you use every day a 1; those you use once a year, a 7. Place the items in the following locations according to how you rate them:

1—place all items you rate as a 1 within arm's reach of your desk area.

2–3—keep items you rate as a 2 or 3 within your immediate office space in files or cabinets, on countertops or shelves.

4–5—store items you rate as a 4 or 5 in nearby cabinets or closets, or on shelves outside your office space.

6–7—store those items you use only once or twice a year in remote locations like an attic, basement, or garage.

and a linen closet makes a great place for stocking supplies. The living room is a good meeting room. The dining room can serve as a conference room.

Plan, however, to choose areas that are arranged so you can use them conveniently. Everyday supplies should be as near as possible to your work space, while less frequently used equipment and files can be kept in more remote areas.

From our experience, here's a final tip: Plan to add at least 10 percent of whatever office space you think you need for storage space.

MATCHING YOUR WORK STYLE

It's very tempting to recommend locating your home office in a separate room with a sturdy door. In fact, the most popular place for a home office is a spare bedroom. Not everyone has a spare bedroom, however, and a separate office is not always possible. We've found so many successful home offices that break this standard mold, though, that you needn't be limited to the most conventional solution.

You've heard the saying "Home is where the heart is." It applies equally to home offices. The best office space will be one where you want to work. We all have our idiosyncrasies and preferences, and the right place for one person can be a disaster for another. Elizabeth Forsythe Hailey, Noel Cavanaugh, and Magdelena Chaney, for example, are all writers who work at home, but each prefers writing under quite different circumstances.

Elizabeth likes to write in the kitchen so she "can keep an eye on things." Noel locks himself away in a basement hideaway: "Everyone knows if I'm downstairs they'd better not interrupt me unless a new baby or a million-dollar check has just arrived. When I'm writing, I can stay down there for twenty-four hours at a time." Magdelena likes to move around when she writes. She may type at her desk for a while in the sunny office she had built over her garage. Then she may get up and stroll outside to think and jot down some notes, and afterward resume writing in the comfort of the living room.

Work Sheet: What's Your Style:

So how can you know what the best place for you is? Here are several decisions you can make to help you match your office space to your personal preferences and work style. Check where you fall on each of the following continua.

Private? _____ **or** _____ **Public?**

This is probably your most important space decision. Do you like or need to work in an exclusive private space away from all other noise and activity? Or do you like to work in the midst of it all? The privacy questionnaire in chapter 5 should give you a good idea of where you are on this continuum.

At one extreme is Dr. Richard Ricardi, whose office is located in a separate building behind his garage. As a psychiatrist, he finds that "a separate location helps my clients feel this is definitely a professional office and not a social setting. I also find by walking back to the office in the morning I 'go to work' and then at night I close the door and I 'go home.'"

At the other extreme is Brenda Rosetta, who runs her cookie company entirely from her spacious state-approved kitchen. She says of her kitchen office, "I'm always at the heart of the action and never miss out on a thing that's going on."

Shared? _____ **or** _____ **Exclusive?**

Can your office space serve other household purposes when you're not using it for business? Over seven out of ten home offices are used exclusively as offices, according to *Income Opportunities* magazine. Sometimes, of course, you don't have a choice about this one. The question often becomes which room can be used both for an office and for household purposes, without totally disrupting the operations of either.

At one extreme is Mary Stoddard, who sets up and takes down her graphic-design studio every workday. Each morning she moves the cars out of the garage, pulls down tables that are hinged to the walls, and starts working. Every evening she puts her work away, folds the tables up, and drives the cars back into the garage. For her, sharing this space on a daily basis works out fine.

At the other extreme is William Lecker, who will not share office space with other household activities, even on an infrequent basis. When he started creating handmade jewelry, he thought the guest room could easily serve as his workshop, because guests used it only once or twice a year. He found instead that his metals and stones could neither be put away nor moved without considerable difficulty, even for a weekend. He decided to move his workshop into an unused breakfast room where he could work and visit with his wife when she was in the kitchen. Keep in mind if you do share your office space with other activities that you risk losing your home-office tax deduction. (See chapter 10 for the details of how to protect your tax deduction.)

(Continued on page 139)

(Continued from page 138)

Windows? _____ **or** _____ **No Windows?**

Over eight out of ten home offices have at least one window, but some people find windows distracting; they can't keep their eyes and their minds on their work. Others feel almost claustrophobic in a windowless office.

As a data-entry clerk, Helen Gilles sits at her computer most of the day. To minimize glare problems, she likes an interior room without windows.

Jack Gates works in sales so he's on the road most of the week. He doesn't look forward to the reports and other paperwork awaiting him on the weekend, but it becomes almost enjoyable as he does it near the large sliding glass door in his office, which looks out onto the backyard. "We have one of the most beautiful jacaranda trees I've ever seen. I like to look at that tree and see the sunlight flooding through it into the office. It relaxes me. I even enjoy watching the kids play out there with the dog."

Compact? _____ **or** _____ **Spacious?**

You may like a lot of elbow room, space to spread out your things while you work. Or you may prefer keeping everything close at hand.

When Sharon Kirkpatrick started working as a seamstress, she set up a sewing room on an enclosed porch off her living room. It was a big, open space and seemed ideal. She could spread out her patterns and tackle many projects at once. But she ended up feeling as if she were working in a giant wastebasket. Thread and scraps, patterns and half-cut garments, pins and tape were everywhere. She was embarrassed to bring people in there for a fitting.

So she decided to move her sewing room to a large walk-in closet, where she sews on one piece of work at a time. The porch, which she put back in order, is a space she now uses to store her materials, cut her patterns, hang finished garments, and have fittings.

MAKING THE MOST OF
YOUR AVAILABLE SPACE

We've known a few people who've moved to a new home just because it's better suited for a home office. But most of us are limited to making do with what we've got. The space you have, however, is probably not as limiting as you think. As we've said, you can consider working in almost any part of your home. You can convert or remodel your space into something more suitable. And if all else fails, you may be able to expand or add on. Let's review some of these options, beginning with the most commonly used rooms.

True Confessions: Fitting an Office into Your Household

Once you have a picture of the type of office most suitable for you, you can match your needs with what goes on in your household.

Engineer Jeff Knoghton set up his office in the den off the family room. The den was a natural place. In fact, one of the reasons he bought the house was that he saw the den as the place he would one day use to start a consulting practice. When that day finally arrived, he proudly set up his desk, files, and comfortable chair and went to work.

Everything was fine until 3:00 P.M. when the kids came home. From that hour on, the television was playing or the children were laughing and carrying on with friends in the family room nearby. At Jeff's request, they became pretty good about keeping the TV set turned down, but every once in a while, usually just as he was on an important call or in the midst of a crucial thought, he would be assaulted with make-believe high-speed chase sounds replete with mock police sirens and screeching brakes. Despite efforts at restricting viewing hours and other creative "solutions," household tensions increased until he finally moved his office to an upstairs bedroom.

A careful review of household activity patterns before deciding on his office location would have helped Jeff avoid the problem in the first place. So spend a day or even a week noticing what goes on in your home before deciding where to put your home office. Keep notes about who does what during which hours.

Is the living room the most likely place for a romantic evening with a date? Would the answering machine and computer equipment interrupt the mood there? When and where do family members or roommates use noisy equipment like power tools, the lawn mower, the dishwasher, or the vacuum cleaner? To which room do other people gravitate when they come over? Where do the kids play? What are the traffic patterns through your home and the noise patterns outside your home? Does someone in the neighborhood practice the piano, or even worse, the drums? Will the kids run down the hall past your office on the way from the living room to their bedrooms? Do you have to walk past your office on the way to your bedroom? With this kind of information, you're in a good position to decide on the best use of the space you have.

The Spare Bedroom

The spare bedroom is still the most popular candidate for a home office. Because it is a spare room, the work space can generally be used without sacrificing a great deal of living area. In fact, you may find it possible to continue using the room for other purposes when you want to. If there's a sofa bed in the room, it can still be a guest room or, if it has ample bookshelves, it can serve as a library. As we mentioned, though, using the room for nonbusiness purposes jeopardizes your home-office tax deduction, as you will see in chapter 10.

Spare bedrooms are often far enough away from the mainstream of household activities to offer some kind of privacy, yet accessible enough to make having business guests or running out for occasional household chores convenient. The most important consideration, however, is that a spare bedroom is usually large enough to feel like a real office and not like a makeshift work space.

The Living Room

For the right business, a living-room office has many advantages. As long as you keep your desk neat, the living room can serve as your home office by day and return to its role as a living room after working hours.

Because the living room is usually the most spacious area of the home, it is more easily divisible into a separate office space with partitions, bookcases, screens, or furniture. It is almost always near the front entrance, which makes it accessible to business visitors. It is usually designed as the public part of the home, so personal areas are located away from it. It is often the most formal part of the home and, as such, is suitable for creating a business image. In addition, closets and guest bathrooms are usually found nearby.

In some houses with a family room or den, the living room is actually anything but a "living" room. It's reserved for holidays or the arrival of special guests. If this is your situation and you don't need a more isolated office area, the living room can be an excellent choice.

The Family Room

If you have both a family room and a living room, you can use the family room for your office and move activities that used to take place there into the living room.

Family rooms are generally located near the kitchen and back entrances and therefore make good workshops, studios, or labs. They're somewhat removed from the sound of street traffic. But often they open onto other living areas. This can be an advantage if you like to be in the center of activity, but a disadvantage if you're seeking a more secluded work space.

The Kitchen

Since the kitchen is such a central part of any home, locating your office there will put you at the heart of household activity. Water, food, and cooking grease may gum up your office space and equipment. But if you need access to plumbing, electricity, or, of course, cooking equipment, this may be the right location for you.

Figure 6-1. Breakfast room converted into an office.

A breakfast nook can often be turned into an office (see Figure 6-1). Sometimes the kitchen itself can be divided to create a separate office area.

Beware, though, of the temptation to snack your way through the day, and of a possible negative effect on your business image. A professional atmosphere in the kitchen is possible but often difficult.

The Dining Room

Many people get along quite well without ever using their dining rooms, preferring to eat in the kitchen, family room, or breakfast nook. This infrequent use, along with the size and location of most dining rooms, makes them excellent candidates for home offices.

Sometimes the dining area is an alcove off the living room. For a business like consulting, this can be a particularly attractive setting, with the living room serving as a meeting or waiting room for the office beyond. Or the dining room can become a second office for employees you hire, with your primary office located in the living room.

Closets, Dressing Rooms, and Storage Spaces

An area twenty-four to twenty-seven inches deep and five feet wide allows enough room for work or filing space. Therefore, walk-in closets, long closets with sliding or louvered doors, storage rooms, nurseries, guest bathrooms, or spaces beneath and along stairways are areas that can be transformed into home offices.

The advantages of these tiny, hidden areas are that they create a compact, self-contained work space, and one that is out of the way when not in use. The disadvantages, of course, are that such work areas may be too small, poorly ventilated, and quickly outgrown.

The Bedroom

Sometimes bedrooms are large enough to be divided, partitioned, or screened off for separate office space (see Figure 6-2).

Generally, however, we discourage people from using their bedrooms as home offices. Your bedroom is probably your most private and personal space, a place of retreat. Working in your bedroom, you may feel that you can't ever get away from business, even when you're ill. And if you're married or living with someone else, an office in the bedroom you share may mean your work will be invading somebody else's private space too. Some couples we interviewed had declared the bedroom off limits for business, to preserve this one area of their home for intimacy and relaxation.

CONVERTING OR REMODELING

When existing space doesn't lend itself to a home office, you may be able to transform it into space that does. This transformation can be as simple as using screens, partitions, shuttered folding doors, furniture, or wall units, or as complex as putting up or tearing down doorways and turning a dusty attic into a skylit studio. The costs can range from a $50 screen to thousands of dollars for a major renovation.

Decorative screens like those available through mail-order catalogs like

Figure 6-2. Sometimes bedrooms are large enough to divide or partition off.
A storage wall can create office space without disrupting the room.

the Bombay Company ([800] 829-7789) or Topix Innovative Gallery ([800] 478-4703) are attractive, affordable, and practical. For maximum flexibility, Herman Miller has an expandable home-office screen in three heights, which diffuses glare and can extend up to six feet or fold back when you want the space open (phone: [800] 646-4400; Web: *www.hermanmiller. com*).

Another option is to use one of the open-plan modular systems popular in today's offices. In the past, most of these systems were too cumbersome and expensive to use at home, but today manufacturers like Bush Furniture, O'Sullivan Industries, and HON offer modular office systems for the home office (see Figures 6-3 and 6-4). These units include desktop, file drawers, shelves, and space for a computer and printer all built in. They can be assembled in various floor plans. Some can be assembled yourself; others must be set up by a professional upon delivery.

Or you might even explore movable walls available from companies like

New Space-Making/Space-Saving Resources

Products to help you organize your home office. Manufacturers such as GMI, Rubbermaid, and O'Sullivan Industries are creating a rich array of clever products for the home office that provide innovative ways of organizing lots of material in cramped or under-furnished spaces. For example, the SOHO Adjustable Workstation, available from OfficeMax, allows you to place your computer equipment—including printer, software, books, and other office supplies—in a space-saving integrated cart with wheels.

Shelves and wall units like the Rubbermaid Storage Cabinets feature floor-to-ceiling shelves in various sizes. Poliform USA, located in New York, offers a versatile shelving unit that can act as a room divider or a wall unit.

Plexi-Craft has created a rolling lucite computer cart that enables you to move your office from place to place. ([800] 24-PLEXI). Products like these are available at office superstores, via mail and Web order, and in hardware and home-center stores.

Integrated equipment. The trend in home-office equipment is toward combining functions performed by many pieces of equipment into one space-saving, multifunctional unit. Manufacturers like Canon, Hewlett-Packard, Panasonic, Xerox, and others offer a wide variety of multifunction units combining fax/printer/copier, and fax/printer/copier/scanner all in one.

Professional organizers. Over the past twenty years an entire consulting specialty—the professional organizer—has emerged to help us all fit more into tight spaces. These information-age specialists offer space planning and design, paper management, storage systems, and general office organization. Often they specialize in home offices, and they have access to many creative ideas and products that enable the person cramped for space to use every square inch to its maximum advantage. They charge from $50 to $125 an hour to help you set up your office in a way that maximizes your space.

For monthly updates on the latest home-office products like these, visit our Web site, *workingfromhome.com*

USG Corp. (phone: [312] 606-4000; Web: *www.usgcorp.com*). These walls go up quickly; can be taken down, moved, and reused; come in various sizes, fabrics, or finishes; and fall into the same tax category as furniture and equipment.

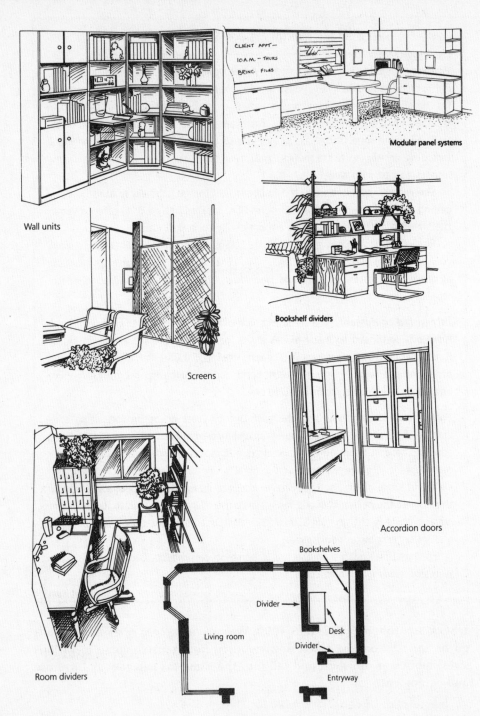

CLIENT APPT—
10 A.M. - THURS
BRING FILES

Modular panel systems

Wall units

Bookshelf dividers

Screens

Accordion doors

Bookshelves

Divider

Desk

Living room

Divider

Room dividers

Entryway

Figure 6-3

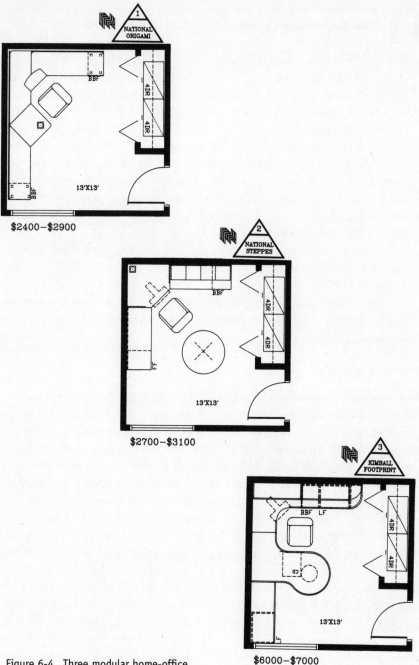

Figure 6-4. Three modular home-office
system layouts, available through Desks
Incorporated, Commercial Furnishings and
Systems, 1385 South Santa Fe Drive, Denver,
CO 80223; (303) 777-8880.

True Confessions: Personal Organizer to the Rescue

Voice and communication coach Sandra McKnight, for example, hired a professional organizer when she found that her growing business was taking over her one-bedroom apartment. She decided that the $475 she paid organizer Susan Rich was worth every penny. Six hours and sixteen trash bags after Rich arrived Sandra discovered she actually had plenty of space. She just hadn't been using it well. She describes the process as follows: "Susan rearranged my desk, phone, and filing cabinets so I have easy access to everything. Then she turned some of my kitchen cabinets into an office supply area. Most important, however, she created a system for me to get my desk cleared off and keep it that way. Now I can immediately process the endless amounts of paper that come across my desk and quickly access what I need when I need it."

To locate professional organizers in your area, write to the National Association of Professional Organizers, NAPO News, 1033 La Posada Drive, Ste. 220, Austin, TX 78752-3880; *www.napo.net*

When simpler space-making ideas like these don't meet your needs, you might consider some of the more extensive remodeling options described below.

Converting a Garage

To completely transform a garage into an office, you'll usually need to remove the garage door, build a new wall and install a standard door, upgrade the floor, and put in necessary insulation and waterproofing. Then you'll need to refinish the interior and exterior and add any necessary utilities like heating, air-conditioning, and plumbing. If the weather in your area is particularly severe and your garage is detached from the house, you may want to add a breezeway or covered walkway between your home and garage/office.

Usually, garage conversions mean giving up car space; however, converting only part of the garage or using an attached garage storage area instead may save enough space for a daytime office and a nighttime garage.

If all this sounds like a big job, it is. When you're finished, however, you'll have a spacious home office that provides ample privacy and a separate entrance for business visitors. Joetta and Jerry Moulden were able to convert their twenty-by-twenty-foot two-car garage in Houston into a fully functioning office and guest bedroom. They replaced the garage door with a wall of sliding glass doors and built two closets into a wall of bookcases that house two fold-down twin beds.

Converting an Attic

If you haven't used your attic in a while or removed the inevitable cobwebs, its initial appearance may be a little off-putting. But don't let appearances stop you from considering this space option. An attic/office is removed from the rest of the house, can provide a large work and storage area, and may even offer a view.

If you're interested in remodeling your attic, take a look at the current design of the room. Generally, building codes will allow you to convert your attic to living space if the ridgepole (the horizontal timber at the top of your roof to which the rafters are attached) is at least seven feet above the subfloor (the rough, unfinished floor of your attic).

The higher the ridgepole, the more comfortable your space will be. As a rule of thumb, at least one-half of the usable space needs to be seven feet high in order for the attic to be considered a viable home-office option. The remaining lower-headroom areas can be used to create efficient storage space.

A frequent problem with attic conversions is access to the office. To build a stairway leading there, you need to have two feet by ten feet of space on the floor below and in the attic itself. A longer space would be needed if your ceiling is higher than eight feet. If you don't have this much space, you can consider a spiral staircase, which usually requires an area of four to five square feet. Please note that it may be difficult to get equipment up to the office on a spiral staircase.

Since the attic is subject to extreme temperatures in summer and winter, working conditions in an attic/office will be intolerable without proper insulation and an efficient means of heating and cooling. For both floor and ceiling, using fiberglass insulation batts, packed between the structural supports, is reported to be one of the most effective ways of controlling the room temperature. You can also use portable heaters and fans, but take safety into consideration before you purchase any portable appliance.

Converting a Basement

If you have a basement, that, too, can be turned into an office. Again, don't be put off by appearances. Clear it out, clean it up, and then look at the possibilities. Like attics, basements are removed from the flow of household activities and can offer you a quiet, private place to work. However, in addition to the inconvenience of stairs, the image of going "down" to see you could be less than desirable for business visitors.

The biggest problems in remodeling a basement are water leakage and humidity. You can waterproof the walls with commercial water sealant painted onto the inside of each exterior wall. Wood-textured board can then be placed between the exterior walls and a final covering of wall paneling or plasterboard.

If you decide to paint the walls, make sure you use waterproof paint and add a mildew retardant to the paint. If the room continues to feel damp, you may want to install one or two air vents that lead outside or to

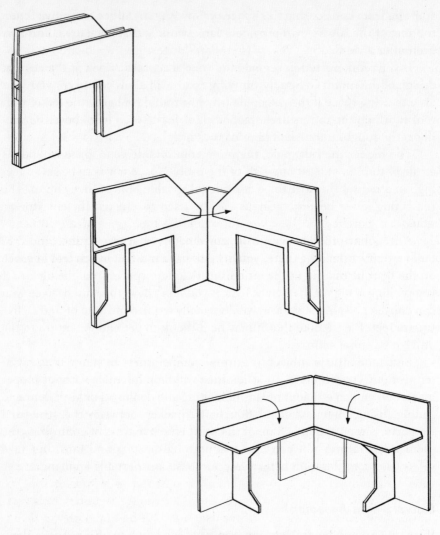

Figure 6-5

the house. Heaters, of course, will greatly help reduce the damp feeling, as the heat will cause the moisture to evaporate. Dehumidifiers are also available that work around the clock to reduce humidity.

Since most basements have concrete floors, you may want to install a warmer-looking surface like wooden boards or carpeting. With proper padding and insulation, a carpet can enhance the atmosphere and provide further protection against cold and dampness.

Basements are generally rife with exposed pipes, unconcealed wiring, and conspicuous utility meters. You can turn these eyesores into "architectural elements" using some bright paint over pipes, ducts, or other out-croppings to make them match the background or to create a colorfully pleasing design. Ceiling tiles, plasterboard, or textured wallboard can also be used. Make sure, however, that all the ducts and pipes are properly sealed and leakproof before you cover them.

You might set up a useful partition or movable screen (see Figure 6-3, p. 146) in front of the harder-to-hide heaters, meters, or wire boxes. Cabinets and freestanding closets can also be cleverly placed to conceal a number of these unsightly objects, as can room dividers.

Converting a Patio or Porch

Patios and porches can become functional, attractive, and airy offices. These areas have the advantage of providing an exterior entrance and are usually set off from household activity. As with an attic, an enclosed porch or a patio requires adding insulation, heating, and cooling.

ADDING ON

When your home simply isn't big enough, you may have the option of adding on to what you've got. When adding on, you have three choices: you can build up, out, or down. The first step is to begin mentally breaking down walls, imagining rooms where there are none, figuratively digging out new foundations, and filling the yard or sky with a bigger house or perhaps separate structures.

You can begin by drawing a map of your house and the surrounding property, experimenting with different additions. Let your imagination go. Don't limit your ideas to office space. Consider adding on other areas that will free your existing space for office use. A master bedroom off the living room, for example, can become an ideal office when you've added a new (and improved, of course) master bedroom into another part of the house.

To help plan changes in the layout of your home and office, you can use computer software like *Design Your Own Home,* by Abracadata, Ltd., or *Floorplan Plus,* by ComputerEasy, to try out various space-making alternatives.

After you've generated as many ideas as you can, check how feasible they are with more than one construction professional. Talk over your ideas with friends, relatives, or others who have added on.

When we realized we would have to add on, or move at least one of our offices out of the house, we began analyzing every possibility. We thought of building a second story over the garage, adding space off the living room, or constructing a separate building in back of the house. We weren't satisfied with any of these ideas until Sarah's mother suggested an ideal alternative we never would have thought of—leveling the redwood cathedral ceiling in our family room and building a second-story bedroom for our son over it. This freed up his smaller room off the living room to become Sarah's counseling office and gave him the equivalent of a private suite, perfect for a teenager.

A Dormer

If you have a steep roof, you can add work space to existing rooms or create new rooms by building single, double, or full dormers (windowed projections built into the roof). (See Figure 6-6.)

Raising the Roof

You can expand your available space by raising one or both sides of your roof. A small attic space can become a loft/office or a second floor over one or several rooms.

A Loft

A loft can make an ideal office space because it is usually removed from the mainstream of household activity. Since lofts typically involve raising the roof above existing space or opening ceiling space from rooms below, they do not afford privacy. Doors can be fashioned, however, to slide over a loft opening to solve this problem.

A Second Story

You can have a second story constructed over all or only a part of a single-level house. Of course, building a second story is a major project that is both costly and time-consuming. Also, the living space below the new story will be out of use while building is going on. This can create considerable disruption to both your household and your work. So we recommend moving out of the house during construction, if possible.

Despite these drawbacks, adding a second story can double your space as it did for us when we built a second story over our family room.

A Basement

If you have a partial basement or a crawl space under your house, you can convert this area into a full basement and a viable home office. If you have no basement, you can create one under all or part of your house.

Creating a basement is another complicated and expensive option, but it is possible. It requires specialized knowledge of construction, so when considering this option locate a general contractor with previous experience and a proven track record doing such excavation.

A daylight basement can become a pleasant alternative to a damp and dingy underground basement/office. A daylight basement has all or part of one wall open to ground level, with windows that allow substantial light to enter into the office area. This windowed wall, which can be made of double-insulated glass, may also create an interesting entry. With sliding glass doors, it can even provide a patio extension to your office in warmer months.

The only requirement for a daylight basement is that there be a full-height foundation wall that is large enough for a door or at least a good-sized window at ground level. The amount of excavation and reconstruction of your foundation depends on the slope of your yard. Most homes can have at least a partial daylight basement built into the foundation.

A Separate Building

If you do not have the extra space, you can build or buy a separate structure. This structure can be attached to your house by a covered walkway or breezeway if you desire.

Because you're starting from scratch, building a separate structure can be more expensive than adding on. For some people, the advantages of adding a new, separate home office may be worth the investment, however. Construction doesn't disrupt the household, and when the building is finished you can have business visitors without their intruding into the privacy of your home. Your office will be completely self-contained.

If building a separate structure is outside your budget, you might consider prefabricated or precut construction kits. These kits cost anywhere from 20 to 40 percent less than comparable custom-built units—and they serve the purpose just as well. The sizes vary according to style and manufacturer, but most lines include models that are at least 9 feet by 12 feet. To locate them, refer to the "Building" listings in your local Yellow Pages. Or you might want to consider Home4Me, a one-room modular 15-by-15 foot stand-alone house. It's designed to accommodate all the essentials into 225 square feet, including kitchen, bath, walk-in closet, and storage loft. Built from standard building materials, it uses electric heat. Price: $13,500 plus $2,500 delivery charge and your cost to connect sewage and electricity.

Mobile homes or recreational structures can also be relatively affordable office sites. Even mini storage units like those offered by Mobile Mini (phone: [800] 950-6464; Web: *www.mobilemini.com*) and others can serve as workshops, warehouses, or places to stock inventory, surplus, or records. Public relations consultant Jennifer Ash came up with one of the more creative office-space solutions we encountered. She occupies a two-room cottage with a large decked terrace off the living room. When she couldn't find

Figure 6-6.

Side porch became this sunny office.

Back porch off kitchen became this handy office.

Patio converted into studio

Loft office

Dormers

Raising the roof

Adding a wing

Installing a yurt

a workable space for her desk in either room, she literally pitched a tent on the deck.

Her canvas gazebo, manufactured by Moss Tent Works, is totally self-contained and waterproof. By day it provides adequate work space for her and one associate. At night, Jennifer merely zips up the tent and "comes home for the evening," carrying her phone along with her.

Another choice is a yurt, a freestanding structure of Mongolian heritage made available by Pacific Yurts, Inc., which also can make a self-contained external home office (see Figure 6-6).

Making Space When You're Renting or Can't Add On*

1. **Use your imagination.** If you start with the assumption that there's always more room somewhere, our experience is you'll find it. We thought we 'd used every inch of space in our office storage room, for example, until it occurred to us that we could double the number of filing cabinets in the room by folding up the legs on our 6-foot worktable and putting it on top of a row of five additional 29-inch-high filing cabinets.

2. **Convert dead space into office space.** The space under stairwells can make an excellent storage and supply closet. Unused space between wall supports can be carved out for built-in storage units. Space above filing cabinets also makes a great location for storage racks and cabinets. A forty-eight-inch round table tucked into a corner can become a conference table.

3. **Use wall units and bookshelves to quadruple your storage area.** All walls in your office can be turned into usable space by lining them with floor-to-ceiling shelving. This shelving doesn't need to be expensive. Avatar makes reasonably priced ready-to-assemble units, and there are retail stores that specialize in creative and inexpensive wall unit arrangements.

4. **Convert closet space.** A whole office can be tucked into a walk-in closet. Linen closets make ideal supply cabinets. Open up more space in the center of the office by taking the doors off the closets and using them as a recessed area for your or your employee's desk. Conceal file cabinets in closets by building a frame around the space and closing it off with sliding doors.

5. **Divide an existing room with a room divider or screen.** Custom shutter and blind companies can build a custom-designed wood divider with shutters that can be opened for light and visibility or closed to put your home office completely out of sight.

(Continued on page 159)

(Continued from page 158)

6. **Turn any existing room into an instant office with a folding desk unit,** like Origami, a desk unit designed especially for home offices by National Office Furniture (see Figure 6-5) or the folding computer table from Globe. Small when folded, opened, they become a full-blown desks with lots of storage and filing space. Use Herman Miller's Scooter, a tiny movable stand that can be tucked under any surface and pulled out to be used as a keyboard holder, writing surface, or notebook computer stand. A folding desk can also be built to fold down from a small closet with ample storage built in along the back wall of the closet.

7. **Make furniture serve multiple purposes.** Recognizing that home-office space can be tight, manufacturers are developing multiple-use furniture. Herman Miller, for example, has filing cabinets that can serve as nightstands, a table desk that can become a buffet service, and drop-leaf desktops that expand or fold down as needed.

* If you rent, remember to check your lease and talk with your landlord about any physical alterations.

GETTING A PROFESSIONAL OPINION

If your budget allows, consider getting advice from professional builders, designers, and architects. Lloyd and Suzanne Faulkner of Encino, California, are examples of designers who specialize in creating attractive and workable home-office spaces. They've helped clients with such innovative solutions as turning a pool table into a desk and finding a coffee table that can be raised, when needed, to desk level. They've even designed rolling desks for those who are confined to their beds. Aside from specialists like the Faulkners, various other professionals can be helpful:

Architects

- Prepare detailed plans and specifications for bids on the work to be done.

- Draw up all plans in accordance with local health, safety, and engineering codes.

- Provide workable plans to contractors.

- Supervise all construction work.

- Inspect the completed work.

Draftsmen or Building Designers

- Draw up plans for straightforward and fairly simple remodeling.

General Contractors

- Work with the architect, designer, or owner in meeting all specifications for materials and construction of the work to be done.

- Hire subcontractors to handle specific phases of the job and ensure that each phase is completed.

- Set up all work schedules.

- Secure all building permits and arrange for all necessary inspections.

- Purchase all materials and supplies.

- Furnish all tools and equipment required.

✔ **Checklist:** Hiring a Contractor

____ Always get at least three to five detailed estimates in writing before making a decision.

____ Prepare a drawn plan and a materials list for each contractor to base his or her bids upon.

____ Always ask contractors for references and be sure to call them, or even stop by and inspect the work yourself.

____ Check out a contractor with the local Better Business Bureau.

____ Make sure the contractor is licensed and bonded. Call your state workers' compensation insurance office to ensure the contractor is paid up. (If not, you may be financially responsible for any injuries sustained by the contractor or her employees.)

____ After choosing a contractor, have him draw up a detailed contract that outlines the scope of the work, payment schedule, and time of completion.

____ Never allow yourself to be pressured into signing a contract.

____ Never pay a contractor in cash. Use checks or credit card.

____ Never pay more than 10 percent up-front. Set up a payment schedule.

Interior Designers or Decorators

- Assist you in utilizing your existing space more creatively or efficiently.

- Assist you in furnishing and decorating the space.

- Purchase furniture and decorator items at a discount.

Depending on your eye for design and the extent of your skills, you may be able to implement many of the ideas in this chapter yourself. Whenever remodeling or adding on to your home, however, contact your local city or county government to determine the permits and specifications required, and call on a licensed contractor of good reputation to carry out any extensive work.

 True Confessions: The Ever-Evolving Home Office

Recognize that finding the right office space may become an ongoing process, as it was for author-photographer David Goodfellow.

"Ten years ago," he explains, "I divided a twelve-by-twelve-foot spare bedroom in half and turned one half into an office for technical writing and the other half into a darkroom, but both areas soon became too small. Five years ago I sealed in our carport, the top of which doubled as a patio deck. It became a twelve-by-eighteen-foot office, a twelve-by-six darkroom, and a twelve-by-twelve junk room."

"To keep water from dripping down my neck when it rains, I had to have a composition roof put on the deck. Then our central heating didn't have enough selectivity to keep the office warm. So I bought a space heater."

"The advantages of his new arrangement are many, however. "First," he points out, "a nice percentage of my house is a tax write-off. Second, the new office is far enough away from the kitchen to make munching a real effort. Third, the office is bright and comfortable, which makes working there a joy."

So whether you find the right space for your home office immediately or, like David, create it over time, finding an arrangement that suits you can make a positive difference in your productivity and how you feel about your work. And remember, the costs involved in creating your office space are deductible, so keep your receipts. The next challenge becomes setting it up in the best way possible for your business.

RESOURCES

BOOKS

Adding On: How to Design and Build a Beautiful Addition to Your Home. Roger Yepsen, (ed.). Rodale Home Improvement Books, Emmaus, Pa.: Rodale, 1996. ISBN: 0875967698.

Adding Space Without Adding On. Jane Cornell, Timothy Bakke, ed., David Jacobs, Mark Feier. Creative Homeowners Press, 1996. ISBN: 1880029855.

Corporate Interiors (Corporate Interiors Design Book Series, No 1). Stanley Abercrombie. New York: McGraw-Hill, 1997. ISBN: 0070182434.

Ergonomic Living: How to Create a User-Friendly Home and Office. Gordon Inkeles and Iris Schencke. New York: Simon & Schuster, 1994. ISBN: 002093081X.

Healing Environments, Your Guide to Indoor Well-Being. Carol Venolia (see chapter 5 Resources for full citation).

Home Storage: Projects For Every Room. David H. Jacobs. New York: McGraw-Hill, 1994. ISBN: 0070324042.

Making the Most of Work Spaces. Lorrie Mack. New York: Rizzoli International Publications, 1995. ISBN: 0847818977.

The Ultimate Home Office: Designing, Planning, and Creating the Perfect Workspace for Your Home or Apartment. New York: Time Life, 1997. ISBN: 0783549482.

SOFTWARE

Custom Home, Sierra On-Line. P.O. Box 85006, Bellevue, WA 98015; phone: (800) 757-7707. Web: *www.sierra.com*

Imagine Your Interior. Showoff! Software, 2301 Burlington, Ste. 220, North Kansas City, Missouri 64116; phone: (888) 374-6963. Web: *www.showoff.com*

Complete Home 3-D. Sierra Software, P.O. Box 53210, Bellevue, WA 98015; phone: (800) 757-7707. Web: *www.sierra.com*

ON-LINE RESOURCES

Manufactured Housing Global Network. *http://mfdhousing.com*

OTHER RESOURCES

The American Society of Interior Designers. 608 Massachusetts Ave. NE, Washington, DC 20002; (202) 546-3480.

Pacific Yurts, Inc. 77456 Highway 99 South, Cottage Grove, OR 97424; phone: (541) 942-9435. Web: *www.yurts.com*

CHAPTER 7

Outfitting Your Home Office with Furnishings and Supplies

In the not-too-distant future, we'll live in "smart houses" that will monitor and manage the lighting, temperature, humidity, telephone system, security, air, even the art hanging on the walls and the music being played. Bill Gates, Microsoft's president, has already built one. Without the resources of Mr. Gates at our disposal, however, we must still attend to and configure our home offices to meet our preferences manually.

Unfortunately, many people take a "ready, fire, aim" approach to setting up their home offices. Eager to get under way and keep costs down, these folks just make do with whatever's around the house. Others go after bargains that don't hold up to daily use and end up costing more because they need to be replaced far too soon. Still others spend a lot of time and energy trying to set up a professional office only to find when the furniture and equipment they selected arrives, it doesn't fit their home-office-sized space.

Too often, open-collar workers put up with the mistakes or oversights they make when first setting up their offices and suffer through backaches, headaches, eyestrain, and other irritations and inconveniences. Yet having the wrong office setup can be even more serious.

> *Ergonomic disorders are the fastest growing category of work-related illness, according to the Bureau of Labor Statistics. They account for 56 percent of all illnesses reported to OSHA.*

Dramatic increases in the use of personal computers with their keyboards, mice, and monitors can result in cumulative trauma disorders like carpal tunnel syndrome, bursitis, ganglion cysts, tendinitis, epcondylitis, thoracic outlet compression, tenosynovitis, myositis, and other equally unpronounceable disorders. At their worst, these illnesses can incapacitate someone to the point of paralysis.

Aesthetician Lori Tabak discovered this the hard way. Several months after obtaining new facial equipment for her home-based salon, she strained her back muscles so severely that she was unable to work for over a month. Only gradually with careful attention to ergonomics and the help of medical professionals was she able to slowly resume a regular workweek. Such ailments have become common occupational hazards for home-businessed professionals like medical transcriptionists and writers.

At the other extreme, research by Dr. Mark Peltier and Dr. Robert Baron has shown that an ideal home-office environment can have the same invigorating effect as stepping outside on a beautiful morning after a good rain. Working in an optimal environment has been proven to result in a more positive mood, greater efficiency, a better memory, higher goal setting, and a pattern of appropriate risk taking!

Fortunately office furniture and equipment manufacturers have responded to the needs of home office workers. Most manufacturers now offer furniture, supplies, and equipment just for the home office, with ergonomics among their top considerations. To fully benefit from these many resources, we must stop settling for a "make do" office and outfit our place of business as effectively as we can. In this chapter we'll provide some guidelines for cost-effectively creating a productive, safe, and healthful office.

Of course, setting up an effective home office is not just a matter of avoiding problems. To find out what matters most to people about their home offices, we interviewed both veteran homeworkers and the professional organizers who get called in to help when a home-office setup is problematic. These veterans and experts repeatedly listed four bottom-line criteria for making a home office functional:

* *Convenience*—the setup needs to save you time and simplify your work. You should be able to come in and just start working.

* *Comfort*—the office needs to satisfy you physically and emotionally, and cause you no pain or strain while you're working.

• *Functionality*—work needs to flow smoothly, with items used every day within arm's reach.

• *Privacy*—the office space needs to be free of intrusions and disturbances.

With these standards in mind, we've organized this chapter like a department store. We'll offer as much variety as possible in addressing these major considerations, while taking into account both appearance and finding bargains in the process. Let's begin with the furniture department.

CHOOSING YOUR FURNITURE

Furniture is one of the things on which home-office workers tend to over-economize, at least at first. Marge Abrams, who calls herself a Paper, Space, Possession, and Time Management Consultant, says, "Until people are 'successful' in a home business, they don't spend a lot of money on furniture. They use what's in the house. I've done the same thing."

If you're like over half the office workers surveyed in a Louis Harris poll, however, you spend over 75 percent of your day sitting at your desk. This tells us that it is crucial to put time and money into finding the best desk and chair. The wrong desk and chair, more than any other items in your office, can make you vulnerable to all ailments mentioned above. And the effects are not always physical. Fatigue, loss of concentration, and irritability are some of the more subtle problems traced to the wrong furniture. On the other hand, productivity gains of up to 40 percent are possible once the right office furniture has been found. More specifically, one-third of workers interviewed listed a comfortable chair as one of the top two contributors to their productivity. Designer William Strumpf suggests approaching chairs, desks, and other important office furniture as if the piece were a garment: "It should be proportioned to fit the person who's using it."

Not all designers are like Strumpf, however. According to a survey reported in *Interior Design* magazine, interior designers rank aesthetics over comfort in selecting office furniture (77 percent to 45 percent), so if you call on a designer to help you select your office furniture, be sure you choose one who believes in safety and comfort first. You can use the following Worksheet to identify the furniture you need. Then consider the information that follows in making the best choices in office furniture.

The Desk

Desk surfaces need to be different heights for different tasks. While writing surfaces should generally be 30 inches off the ground, typing or computing surfaces are usually 26 inches high. Of course, you can have both a writing

---

Work Sheet: What Furniture Do You Need?

___ Desk

  ___ Appropriate width and depth
  ___ Different heights for different tasks
  ___ Suitable style
    ___ Solid
    ___ Cube
    ___ Open table

___ Chairs
  ___ Desk Chair
    ___ Supportive back
    ___ Firm seat
    ___ Breathable material
    ___ Firm armrests
    ___ Adjustable height
    ___ Footrests
    ___ Tilt mechanism
    ___ Rollers
    ___ Easy chair

___ Side or conference table chairs

___ Filing Cabinets
  ___ Legal size
  ___ Standard size
  ___ Vertical cabinets
  ___ Lateral cabinets
  ___ Hanging files
  ___ Non-hanging files

___ Tables
  ___ Worktable
  ___ Conference table
  ___ End or coffee table
  ___ Other:

___ Couch
___ Bookcases
___ Storage racks
___ Lamps

---

desk and a separate computer desk, but today some desks are designed to include surfaces of more than one height. Others can be adjusted up and down or tilted to the position you desire as you change tasks.

Besides height, other desk features that should be tailored to you and your home office are width and style. Unless the office is 20 feet or more across, choose a desk no wider than 7 feet. Larger desks will overpower and crowd the room. Even the style of your desk affects how large it will seem. Available choices are solid, cube, or open-style desks. In smaller offices, a table desk will appear to take less space than a cube desk of the same size.

And if you're thinking you need to have a lot of space to have an ergonomically designed office, think again. The Laptop Desk is possibly the smallest ergonomic desk unit in existence. This ergonomically adjustable desk is designed for a laptop computer. Although it could fit in the tiniest of closets or corners, it has room for not only your computer but also your mouse, copy holder, task lamp, printer, disks, documentation manuals, pencils and pens, coffee cup, surge protector, and more (American Business Concepts; phone: [800] 877-4797. Web: *www. sail2000.com*).

According to Techline, a manufacturer of an array of home office desks, someone setting up a first-time home office will spend around $300 for a simple, basic desk unit. Within time, however, they're shopping for a more sophisticated desk system that provides additional workspace, storage space, and room for added equipment. So they might want a desk that includes an L-shaped arm extension, a corner unit, and shelving and spend around $1,000 and up.

The Desk Chair

A fully adjustable ergonomically designed chair can help avoid just about every physical problem we've discussed. Conversely, a poorly chosen chair may not only aggravate these problems, but can cause muscle strain, swelling of the lower legs, reduced blood circulation (which in turn diminishes your ability to think), and varicose veins. According to William C. Isenberg, furniture industry analyst, many desk chairs claiming to be ergonomic are merely imitations of actual ergonomic designs. These chairs keep the price down but often create problems that are far more expensive. It is essential that you educate yourself to determine which chairs are truly ergonomic. The best way to start is to sit in any chair you're considering to personally evaluate the back, seat, arms, and optional features.

The back of the chair should provide support for the base of the spine, helping it hold a slight forward curve. The backrest should be high enough to allow you to relax against it, and rise to at least the lower part of your shoulder blades. The chair should also distribute your weight evenly, thus minimizing pressure on your thighs.

Chairs with tilt mechanisms work with the seat and back fixed or with a separately adjustable seat and back. A chair with a five-pointed base, rather than the customary four legs, will help you avoid tipping over if you lean back too far.

The seat of the chair should be rounded so it won't dig into your thighs and restrict blood flow in the legs. The seat should also be adjustable up and down over a range of six to nine inches, so you can adapt it to different work tasks. Preferably, the adjustment can be made by gently pressing a button or lever under the seat from a sitting position.

When your chair is properly adjusted, your feet should be flat on the floor and the seat should be parallel to the floor. If you are short, you may need a footrest to keep your legs from dangling.

Often people assume that a soft seat is the most comfortable. Actually, the comfort only lasts a short time, because a too-soft seat limits the natural S curve of your spine. The seat material should be a rough, porous fabric that lets body heat dissipate.

The arms should have a hard surface that wears well and resists soiling,

How a Bad Chair Can Cut Your Earnings

If you're using an uncomfortable or ill-fitting chair, it can easily cost you 5 minutes an hour in lost productivity. Here's what that costs you a year, based on a range of hourly rates you might earn or pay an assistant working 2,000 hours (8 hours a day, 5 days a week, 50 weeks a year).

HOURLY RATE	ANNUAL COST
$10	$1666.66
$15	$2499.99
$20	$3333.32
$25	$4166.65
$30	$4999.98
$35	$5833.31
$40	$6666.64
$50	$8333.30
$75	$12499.95
$100	$16666.66

but preferably should not be made of metal, which feels cold and slick. The arms should be low enough not to rub the underside of the desk or hit other furniture.

A chair with rollers will enable you to move from one work area to another. Make sure that the rollers have self-locking casters that travel smoothly over carpeting but not too quickly over wood or linoleum. "Dual-wheel" casters are preferable to the "ball" type because they move more smoothly, distribute weight more evenly, and don't cut into the flooring.

Most people find that spending from $400 to $1,000 on a good chair is worth the investment. Fortunately more and more manufacturers are creating high-quality furniture scaled to the size and the budgets of the home office. For example, Haworth, a leader in top-of-the-line office chairs, has introduced the new Accolade line of ergonomic chairs with home-office budgets and needs in mind.

But keep in mind, the higher cost of the chair does not necessarily mean the chair will be better for you. One person, for example, who has been experiencing a lot of lower-back pain, traded in his expensive designer chair for a $135 chair and the back pain went away. There's perhaps nothing more individual than a chair. Case in point, a lawyer took his entire office staff in to select new desk chairs. Each person chose a different chair!

Remember, the more adjustments a chair has, the more closely it can

Features-to-Look-for Checklist: Choosing an Ergonomic Chair

The best way to know if you're getting the ergonomic chair you think you are is to discuss your needs with the vendor, and of course, give it a try. Here's a glossary of terms provided by Dr. Leonard Kruk of Westinghouse Furniture Systems to help you talk about the ergonomic features you want:

❑ *Static ergonomic chair*—a chair without controls to adjust back, seat, and arms that has been designed ergonomically to fit the dimensions of the average body type. Poor choice for anyone who doesn't fit the norm.

❑ *Active ergonomic chair*—has controls for manually changing the positions of the back, seat, and arms precisely to each individual. Good for everyone who will take the time to fiddle with the controls to get them just right. Studies show most people don't.

❑ *Passive ergonomic chair*—automatically adjusts ergonomically to the body of the person who sits in it. Especially good if anyone else uses your desk chair.

❑ *Posture-back chair*—has an adjustable back and a stationary seat.

❑ *Posture-tilt chair*—has a back that tilts back twice as far as the seat, reducing pressure at the back of the knees when tilting.

❑ *Swivel-tilt chair*—has back and seat that tilt and swivel together.

❑ *Pivot-tilt chair*—prevents the front of the seat from rising when the chair tilts back, keeping the feet on the floor and reducing pressure on the back of the knees for better circulation.

❑ *Forward-tilt locking chair*—the chair can be locked so it won't tilt, keeping the sitter in a forward position. Good for keyboard-intensive work.

❑ *Pneumatic chair*—has a gas cylinder you can control by a button or lever that will lower or raise the chair while you are sitting on it.

be customized to your body; but the more complex it is, the less likely most people will be to use it. Unfortunately most people don't take advantage of the ergonomic features of their chairs.

Finally, whatever combination of features you choose, even the best chair isn't designed for long-term sitting, so get up and move around every twenty minutes or so while working!

Filing Cabinets

Just as you can never have too many friends, you can also never have too many filing cabinets. Whether you need two file drawers or a bank of cabinets, you have several basic choices to make:

Size. Because of Paul's law background, our files are legal size, but the more convenient option is the standard letter size.

Shape. Although lateral files have gained in popularity, they can take up a substantial amount of floor space, and we find them less convenient to use than vertical cabinets. A lateral cabinet can, however, be functional as a room divider as well as a spacious storage unit.

Filing features. Hanging files fit on racks in a standard file drawer. Although they make your folders easy to see and manipulate in the file drawer, the folders are clumsy to handle when removed from the cabinet.

Locking. If you have confidential material, locks are a requirement for your cabinets. In fact, you may want to get even stronger file cabinets that are burglar- and fireproof as well.

Quality. Whatever kind of file cabinet you buy, stick with recognized brands such as HON, Steelcase, and Litton. As Stephanie Winston points out in *The Organized Executive,* cheap cabinets jam easily. Their drawers may slip off the tracks or fall out completely, and their tendency to tip over makes them dangerous.

Isenberg points out that a five-drawer vertical file is not very accessible to a short person. He recommends mobile files mounted on casters that can move from place to place.

CREATING AN ERGONOMIC HOME OFFICE: SAVE YOUR BODY—YOU CAN'T WORK WITHOUT IT

When you're working on your own, there's no one looking after office safety but you. So here's a list of tips other home office workers have passed along for setting up an office in a way that keeps you working comfortably. Because everyone is different, not every tip may be helpful to you. Products like those mentioned are available through office supply stores and catalogs unless otherwise indicated.

1. Use a visorlike hood over the top of your monitor or a glare screen to reduce glare. Some screens, like those from Glare/Guard Safe Technologies Corp., have form-fitting shields ([800] 262-3260)

that are plug-in devices for protection against electronic field radiation. Safe Technologies also offers ELF Pro Tech bands that wrap around your monitor to reduce electric field radiation emitted from the back, sides, and top of your monitor.

2. Try out an ergonomic keyboard like the TRU-Form with touchpad (eliminates the need for a mouse) by Adesso. This keyboard has a built-in wrist rest and allows the elbows to rest at shoulder width, taking pressure off wrists, elbows, and shoulders. A study by office manufacturer Haworth, Inc., found using an ergonomically designed keyboard increased keystrokes by 25 percent and reduced typing errors by 50 percent.

3. Build up the strength and dexterity of your fingers, hands, wrists, and forearms with a kneading ball like Eggercizer by ACCO.

4. Place your monitor 16 to 28 inches from your face, and position it so that the top of the monitor is at eye level or slightly lower. To get your monitor in the right place, you can place it on an adjustable monitor arm. To get your monitor at the right height you can use an adjustable stand, or simply place books underneath it. Input-Ez ([800] 227-0810) has created a compact retractable tabletop unit that sits on a standard desk or table and houses your computer, monitor document tray, and keyboard at a proper angle.

5. Use a copyholder to save crooking your neck when entering data from another document. Position it as close to the screen as possible within the same arch of vision as the monitor and keyboard. PerfectData has six models from monitor side mounted to easel based ([805] 581-4000). The Input-Ez desktop unit described above has a built-in document tray.

6. Make sure your feet are on the floor while working at your desk and that your elbows are at a 90-degree angle to your keyboard. If necessary use a footrest that keeps your feet flat and eases strain on the legs, feet, and lower back.

7. Equip your phone with a headset so you can write or keyboard while talking on the phone. GN Netcom ([800] 995-5500) has a variety of models including ones with a microphone that filter out noise. Or Bell Atlantic offers the Earphone, a hands-free Touch-Tone phone, with an ultralight one-ear earpiece that you can use alone, with your own phone, or a 15-inch cord to talk on the phone while you compute, write, file, cook, etc.

8. Use a wrist rest that sits under your keyboard and keeps your hands/wrists/arms in a straight line up to the elbows instead of bent while you keyboard. Or use a lap keyboard pillow with a built-in wrist rest, which allows you to rest your keyboard on your lap. One worker created his own rest using a $1 piece of tubular foam pipe insulation held in place with a rubber band.

9. Take frequent breaks, blink, and fidget. (Various studies show that short, regular rest breaks alone can increase productivity from 7 to 10 percent; and, according to the *New England Journal of Medicine,* computer users blink less and keep their eyes open wider when looking at the screen, which results in eyestrain.)

10. Try cushions or foam padding to support your back.

11. Protect your wrist from mouse stress with an ergonomically designed mouse like Microsoft's J-Mouse. American Packaging Corp. has wrist rests for mice, keyboards, and calculators ([503] 852-5577; E-mail: *ampak@onlinemac.com*). You might also do as Paul did and switch to using your other hand. When Paul, who is right-handed, started using his left hand to work the mouse, all the strain problems he'd been having disappeared.

12. If a mouse gives you too many aches and pains, try a track ball. Kensington Turbo Mouse is a track ball with customizing software ([800] 535-4242; Web: *www.kensington.com*).

13. Wear a wrist splint while keyboarding. Many people do this routinely to prevent problems.

14. Because working at a computer monitor can be hard on your eyes, uncorrected or improperly corrected vision can result in fatigue and other problems. So talk to your eye specialist about whether you would benefit from special glasses or lenses. Reading glasses are not always appropriate for computer work, but special glasses just for working at the computer or monofocal, full-width bifocal, flat-top, or progressive additional lenses may be of value.

15. Consult with a chiropractor or other specialist familiar with ergonomics. Our chiropractor corrected many posture and seating problems we would never have recognized. One man was able to stop wearing a splint at the keyboard within a month of implementing his chiropractor's advice.

NOISE CONTROL

Noise, among all environmental factors, has the strongest correlation to job stress and dissatisfaction in an office, according to a Columbia University study. Even moderately high noise levels cause higher blood pressure, faster heartbeat, and other symptoms of stress. Excessive noise causes fatigue, distraction, and errors in work. Actually, noise may have consciously or unconsciously played a role in your choosing to work from home.

Although too much noise certainly interferes with work, a total absence of sound is also stressful. As one person who moved his office home says, "The first thing I noticed was the silence. I never realized how much I appreciated the sounds of the office."

Just how much sound do you need to stay mentally alert? Probably not more than thirty decibels, about the sound of a normal air conditioner. Even better would be twenty decibels of sound, about equivalent to leaves rustling in the breeze.

The average office has a noise level of about fifty decibels. The sound of an average conversation is about sixty decibels, while the vacuum cleaner in your home runs at about eighty decibels. Prolonged exposure to over seventy decibels may result in hearing impairment.

Sound-Control Techniques

To keep the sound levels in your office down to a comfortable level, you can simply increase the distance between your office and outside activity. Doubling the distance between your office and outside activity will decrease the noise that travels between the two points by six decibels. If this is impossible, you can use one or more of these sound-control techniques:

1. Draperies over windows. For maximum effectiveness, these need to be floor length and lined

2. Ceiling treatments that don't reflect noise, such as acoustical tile or commercially applied sound-absorbent material

3. A thick pile carpet with an underpad to absorb noise in the room

4. Weather stripping on doors and windows to keep unwanted street noise out and prevent noises that might bother neighbors from traveling

5. Relocating noisy equipment to a separate room or closet

6. Using flashing lights or a soft ring setting on telephones

7. In-room barriers such as room dividers or acoustical screens

8. Outdoor barriers like a concrete block wall over five feet high, shrubs, and foliage

9. Solid-core doors in place of hollow-core ones

10. Double-glazed windows

11. Wall coverings such as fabric or cork. Armstrong Soundsoak is a fabric over acoustical fiberboard that will absorb 60 percent of noise.

12. Acoustical drywall and paneling on top of your existing walls, with thick insulation placed between the studs of the new wall

Of course, you can always use earplugs or a headset like NoiseBuster Extreme by Noise Cancellation Technologies ([800] 278-3526; Web: *www.nct-active.com*) if you're unduly distracted by household or outside noise.

Sound-Masking Techniques

Also before you spend a lot of money or time on any sound-control measures, find out if the undesired noise is coming through a heat or air vent. If it is, using one of the sound-"masking" techniques described below will be more effective. Because these sounds are rhythmical, they will also help mask noise you can't screen out by other measures.

These methods can also be used to produce enough sound to keep yourself alert when working from home alone:

1. A stereo playing low.

2. A gurgling fish tank with a water filter and air pump.

3. A cage of songbirds, such as canaries.

4. A "white noise" generator like those available from Sharper Image ([800] 344-5555) or Hammacher Schlemmer ([800] 233-4800). These machines, about the size of portable radios, play restful countryside and seaside sounds as well as pure white noise.

Keeping Noise Down While on the Phone

If you're having problems with bothersome or inappropriate noise while talking on the phone (e.g., barking dogs, rattling dishes, giggling children), try one of the following solutions:

1. A mute button on your telephone will block out a temporary disruption like reprimanding a barking dog or telling a child to turn

down the television. With the button down, you can hear the other party on the line, but they can't hear you.

2. For continual noise from equipment, conversations, nearby children playing, etc., you might consider a product like the Confidencer, by Roanwell Corporation ([212] 989-1090; Web: *www.roanwell.com*), which fits into the mouthpiece of your telephone handset and cancels 80 percent of the background noise normally picked up through the telephone. Not only can you be heard better; you can also hear better.

3. Some headphone models like those from Plantronics include a microphone that filters out background noise ([800] 544-4660; Web: *www.plantronics.com*).

 True Confessions

Tudor Barker of Dorset, England, made soundproofing his home office into a low-cost do-it-yourself project. He began with the floor by laying half-inch-thick polystyrene tiles along the floor, covering them with hardboard, and sealing the gap between the floor and the walls with silicone. Then, to soundproof the windows, he bought the thickest glass panes he could afford, triple-glazed each frame at a slight angle, and once again sealed the edges with silicone.

LIGHTING YOUR HOME OFFICE

According to a Harris poll for Steelcase, lighting is the number-one contributor to productivity. The amount and type of light you need depend on your age, the kind of work you do, and your preferences.

Generally, the more detailed your work, the more light you need. So if you're a cartographer making maps, you'll need more light than someone taking notes while on the telephone. Also, as you age you need more light. A person over fifty may need 50 percent more light than a younger person, and a person over sixty may need 100 percent more.

When using a computer at any age, however, you may need less light, not more, in order to avoid glare on your computer screen, because readability of a computer screen depends on the contrast between onscreen characters and the screen background.

Here are some general guidelines to follow when considering the best lighting for your office.

Use Natural Light When Possible

The best light for your office is also the cheapest—daylight. Daylight provides the truest color and is the least tiring. It is also the best kind of light for preventing eyestrain. This means you will be more productive in natural light. The quality of daylight, however, is affected by a number of factors: direction of exposure; the color and texture of your walls, ceiling, and furnishings; the arrangement of your work space; and, of course, the time of day and the weather.

Daylight entering from the north is usually a soft, indirect light, shining steadily most of the day. Artists and craftspeople prefer this type of natural light, especially when it hits pale-colored interiors. Because of its lack of glare, northern light is best for operating a computer, too. More direct light enters from an eastern or western source and, to a lesser degree, from the south, and will not only cause more glare but also unbalanced illumination.

One way of getting nonglare daylight is to add clerestories, or windows that are installed high up on a wall. Clerestories throw diffused light into the center of a room, providing balanced illumination without glare, and because of their height they also provide privacy. Installing clerestories in an existing building is likely to be expensive, however. Skylights are another attractive and more affordable way of bringing additional daylight into offices where it is blocked or nonexistent. Various skylight styles enable you to direct light to a work area or diffuse light evenly throughout your office.

Supplement with Artificial Lighting

Of course, it's impossible to work by daylight all the time, even in an ideal room. At night or on gray days you have to turn on the lights. The most common types of artificial light are incandescent and fluorescent lighting. Both have their advantages and disadvantages.

Incandescent lights are usually small and have a high degree of intensity, so they can be used for task lighting—that is, supplementary lighting focused directly on your work. A desk lamp provides task lighting, as do track lights. Used in conjunction with ceiling fixtures, a desk light can eliminate shadows on your work.

The color emitted by an incandescent bulb is warm toned. It is softer, reflects better on the skin, and is gentler on the eyes than fluorescent light, although newer types of fluorescent lighting provide color rendition that is as good as or better than that of incandescent bulbs. Incandescent light is also the most expensive form of lighting, consuming the most electricity for the light produced. It also converts much of this energy into unwanted heat.

Fluorescent lighting is diffused, produces little heat, and provides a steady, highly efficient light source. It generally requires large, relatively expensive fixtures, however, and cannot easily be used to spotlight specific areas. Fluorescent lights also blink, and if you're near enough to the light source to notice the blinking, you're apt to experience eyestrain and fatigue.

Comparison of Incandescent and Fluorescent Lighting			
Light Source	Power Required	Light Output (lumens)	Approximate Lifespan
Incandescent	150 watts	2,880 foot-candles	750 hours
Fluorescent	50 watts	3,200 foot-candles	12,000/-20,000 hours

Because incandescent and fluorescent lighting both have advantages, you may want a balance between the two. If you use fluorescent lighting, the most desirable kinds of bulbs for a home office are full-spectrum bulbs, which are most like natural daylight. One source of such bulbs is the Harmony 7th Generation Catalog, 1-800-456-1177.

Compact fluorescent bulbs are now being made that fit into standard lamps. These bulbs offer long life (approximately 7,000 hours) and use only about one-fourth the energy of a conventional incandescent bulb. Though compact by fluorescent standards, these bulbs are still more than twice the size of an incandescent bulb and may not fit within enclosed fixtures. Another innovation, halogen bulbs, provide a white light, last about 2,000 hours, and use about 10 percent less electricity.

We are making use of Chromalux bulbs made with neodymium. These bulbs produce the color rendition of natural sunlight with a 99.6 percent rating. The bulbs fit standard lamps and last about 3,000 hours. You may be able to find these new bulbs only at stores specializing in lighting fixtures.

AVOIDING EYESTRAIN AND FATIGUE

Fatigue can result from adjusting your eyes to varying levels of light in a room. Therefore, to avoid eyestrain, set the general level of light in the room equal to the level of light on your work.

One option for keeping this balance is to use dimmer switches to adjust the level of light in the room. They also save electricity and can change the mood from a bright work setting to a softer conference-room atmosphere. Installing a dimmer switch for incandescent lighting is simple and inexpensive, but for fluorescent lighting it is costly. It's more economical to install dimmer-switches on fluorescent lights when they are first installed.

Another cause of eyestrain is glare. The more illumination you have in an office, the greater the risk of glare. Therefore you need to find a balance between having too little light and too much. You can reduce glare by making sure lightbulbs are not in your line of sight and by avoiding light that reflects off shiny surfaces such as picture glass, mirrors, and the like. Another simple way of reducing glare is to have several small light sources rather than one bright light. A Cornell University study found that indirect light bounced off the ceiling is better than fluorescent lighting for working at your computer. Workers with standard overhead lighting experience greater lethargy.

A simple way to enhance lighting in your office is using color to your advantage. Dark colors absorb light; light colors reflect it back into the room. One of Paul's previous offices had redwood paneling on about half of the wall area; while the other half was white. At night, there was a noticeable difference in the level of light needed in each area: where the wall was darker, we had to increase the amount of electricity we used. So one way of cutting down your electric bill is to have light-colored walls and ceilings.

Best Ways to Deal with Static Electricity

1. Antistatic mats
2. Aerosol spray
3. Humidifier
4. Plants in your office
5. Uncarpeted floors

CREATING AN ENVIRONMENTALLY CONSCIOUS HOME OFFICE

We believe every open-collar worker is entitled to a bumper sticker that reads "I save air, water, and energy—I work from home."

By not commuting to a job, you are not contributing to air pollution. As former President George Bush pointed out to the California Chamber of Commerce, in the first speech in which a president endorsed working from home, ". . . if only five percent of the commuters in Los Angeles County telecommuted one day each week, they'd . . . keep forty-seven thousand tons of pollutants from entering the atmosphere." By working at home, you're also probably using less water than if you were at an office.

People working from home can conveniently practice additional conservation measures. Here are eighteen things you can do:

1. Use halogen and compact fluorescent bulbs that produce more light, last longer than ordinary incandescent bulbs, and use less energy.

2. Install low-flow toilets; they use only one-third to one-fourth as much water as standard toilets.

3. Use the "print preview" feature in your word-processing or publishing software to see what your printed page will look like upon printing. This will reduce the number of test copies you need to make.

4. Use personal-information-management software instead of making notes on paper.

5. E-mail or Fax information instead of mailing, hand-delivering it, or using a messenger service or an air-freight company. You'll save on fuel and energy. Choose plain-paper fax machines instead of those that rely on nonrecyclable, chemically treated thermal paper.

6. Make use of an internal fax in your computer, so you can send and receive faxed messages without having to produce printed pages.

7. Store information and documents on computer disks or external drives instead of in paper files.

8. Use outdated stationery to make notepads instead of throwing it away.

9. Buy products made from recycled paper.

10. When it will not create confusion, use the back sides of paper for lists and scratch paper.

11. Save shipping boxes, plastic foam balls, and other plastic packaging materials and reuse them to avoid generating nonbiodegradable trash. Or create your own packing material by buying a paper shredder designed for the home office. GBC's Shredmaster 405 at only $29.99 shreds three to five sheets at once into long strips, while Fellowes' Power Shredder at $159.99 is larger and shreds up to seven sheets at once into cross-cut pieces. Shredders are available at office superstores.

12. Consolidate as many errands as possible into one trip. Use your own shopping bags, rather than plastic ones.

13. Be environmentally conscious about the office products you use. Use paper, for example, made from 100 percent postconsumer waste recycled, never bleached.

14. Without decreasing your productivity, reduce air-conditioning by scheduling your work for other than the hottest hours of the day,

using attic fans and skylights that open. Heat only the rooms you need to use in winter.

15. Recycle everything from your PC to your toner cartridges. Hewlett Packard's Toner Cartridge Recycling Program allows you to send in your used cartridges for reuse and recycling. For more information, call (800) 340-2445.

16. Use mugs rather than plastic foam cups.

17. Retro-fit lights with fixtures that use much less energy. Generally, such lighting increases lighting quality and yields a 20 to 30 percent annual return. Turn off lights whenever you leave a room. The EPA says it's a myth that turning lights on and off wastes energy.

18. Many cities, municipalities—even utility companies—offer free energy and water use evaluations where a certified inspector will come to your location and assess your home and office. The inspector will show you where you can save resources and money and offer specific suggestions on how to do so.

19. Use environmentally friendly materials like cleansers, paints, glues, furniture, and carpets that can be found in environmental directories and many natural-food stores.

20. Never improperly dispose of household or office hazardous waste, such as paints and supplies, photo-developing chemicals, petroleum products, etc. This includes not placing hazardous materials into your regular garbage. Most cities and municipalities have special facilities for such waste. Take your hazardous waste to these facilities.

Through the Green Lights and Energy Star programs, the EPA offers information on energy-efficient office equipment that's easy on both your budget and the environment. Using such equipment can cut your electric bills by as much as 50%. Visit *www.epa.gov/smallbiz*

PROVIDING SECURITY
AND FIRE PROTECTION

Home offices increase and decrease your security risks. On the one hand, you have added equipment and material to protect. You may also be bringing strangers into your home. On the other hand, you are at home more often or at least away at irregular times. This reduces your chances of being burglarized, because thieves avoid houses where someone might be home.

Here are thirteen ways to further protect yourself from theft and to safeguard confidential materials.

1. Secure your doors and windows. The more difficult you make entry into your home, the less chance that someone will go to the trouble of breaking in. In addition, since thieves have often been in a house as visitors before they burglarize it, you can substantially reduce your risk by having prominent safety features like dead bolts and good locks. Even if potential burglars figure they can get into your home, getting things out will appear difficult.

2. Light your premises well, both inside and outside. Motion-activated superbright halogen lights, for example, will flood outdoor areas at night if intruders enter your property, startling them and alerting you without running up your electricity bill. These motion-detecting sensors can be purchased at most hardware and home-center stores. If you hear a suspicious noise outside at night, don't turn on your inside lights so someone can see you; turn them on so you can see them.

3. Get a dog that barks at strangers. Convicted burglars who were surveyed rate a dog as the most effective deterrent. Although some would disagree, we still believe a barking dog when strangers approach while you're away puts off intruders other than the professional burglar.

4. When you're away from home, create the appearance that someone is there. Arrange to have someone take in your newspaper and mail, use timers to turn sprinklers on and off during the day and to switch lights on and off automatically in different rooms at night. Store garbage cans out of sight, have your phone answered by voice mail, an answering machine, or answering service, and if you'll be gone for a considerable period, have the lawn mowed during that time.

5. Hire a house-sitter when you're going out of town. At least be certain the newspaper and mail are picked up every day. Students at theological seminaries, for example, are reliable house-sitters.

6. Have a security inspection. Some police departments offer free security inspections, or you can hire a security consultant.

7. Hire a private patrol service, or participate in a Neighborhood Watch program on your block. These operations have cut crime in some areas by as much as 40 percent.

8. Purchase a safe like one of the many Sentry Fire-Safe Security Safes, for important papers, money, valuable tools, photographic plates, computer disks, and so on. Just having a safe may prevent theft, because the police estimate that most burglars are in and out of the house in six minutes, and breaking into a safe takes time. Safes can be fireproof, waterproof, and even explosion-proof.

9. Install a burglar alarm system. To protect a two-thousand-square-foot home, you can get a reasonable measure of security for as little as a few hundred dollars. For example, infrared sensors that detect intruders by sensing changes in infrared radiation or heat cost from $25 to $125 each. One device can cover several rooms. Because they don't emit sound or light waves, they are less apt to trigger false alarms and are fairly easy to install. Also easy to install is a wireless system using sound and motion detectors with a remote control. Other devices are sensitive to changes in air pressure. Some people use an inexpensive computer to create a sophisticated alarm system for themselves. If you have pets, you can get motion detectors with a "pet alley" that scans only above the height of your pet. If you need to protect only one door or a specific object like a safe or filing cabinet, you can get a self-contained alarm for under $50.

Instead of doing it yourself, you can also get your house wired by companies like Protection One, Brinks, Sears (which uses local contractors), or by a local independent firm. Charges vary dramatically for basically the same work from installer to installer so it's wise to get several bids. Often companies will offer a lower price if you sign up for a monitoring contract. Keep in mind that the monitoring station is in a distant city so you cannot inspect its operation. It's also a good idea to check with the Better Business Bureau or other consumer agencies because some alarm services use outdated equipment that is easily set off by a dog's bark and that triggers false alarms that can lead to your being fined.

10. Place a pair of size-16 work boots outside your door.

11. Install smoke detectors and make sure to have your electrical service checked routinely to protect your home office against fire damage. When we moved into our first house and needed additional wiring for the porch we were enclosing, our horrified electrician discovered we had a slow fire in our fuse box.

12. Install a surveillance camera so you can see who's at the door or elsewhere on your premises.

Aside from these common precautions, you can also keep small fire extinguishers on hand and buy fireproof filing cabinets. However, they are seven or eight times as expensive as conventional office files.

CREATING THE IMAGE AND DECOR YOU WANT

The way your office looks can make the difference between feeling productive and motivated or disorganized and demoralized while working. If employees, customers, co-workers, or clients come to the office, appearances can be important for gaining their respect and trust. This is especially true of a home office, where establishing a professional atmosphere is more of a challenge than in a traditional office building. A Herman Miller study of home offices found, however, that trying to mix home and office decor was often a visually jarring experience as fine wood family antiques mingled in the same room with steel filing cabinets and metal printer stands. With a little thought and planning, however, this need not be the case, especially now that manufacturers are designing furniture and accessories especially for the home office. Here are five basic steps you can take to achieve the image you want:

1. *Take a fresh look at your office space.* Imagine you're starting a new job and seeing your new office for the first time. Ask yourself if this is a place where you would feel like working and could be productive. Decide if it looks too homey or too stark.

Rooms that look fine in a home may be too "busy" for an office, because of too many bright colors, fussy wallpaper, too much clutter, or too little space. On the other hand, if you've cleared everything out of a room, attic, or basement, and all you have is a desk and a chair in an empty room, the space may be too large, drab, or cheerless for productive work. Take a look at your office from the viewpoint of the people who will be coming there as clients, customers, employees, or business associates. Consider their expectations and the statement your office makes about you and your business. If you're an accountant, for example, does your office convey the attention to order and detail that suggests you give careful advice about money? If you're an artist, does your office look like a creative place?

2. *Decide on the look you want.* Choose the tone or overall impression you want to impart:

Practical	Elegant	Creative	Homespun
Classic	Casual	Contemporary	High tech

If you aren't sure about the look you want, think about the offices of people you respect and admire in your field. How do their offices look? Go through some decorating magazines and clip out photos you like. Remember offices you've worked in before and what you liked or disliked about them.

3. *Use color to create coordinated look and feel.* The furniture, the wall covering, the floor covering, the colors you use, the lamps, the ceiling,

the window treatments, any wall decorations, and even the equipment and supplies should all work together to send the same message. Color can help you do that.

Color will have a particularly strong influence on the overall effect of your office. The colors you choose will affect you and those who come into your office both physiologically and psychologically. Color helps determine whether people feel their surroundings are cramped or spacious, and how hot or cool the room feels. For a sense of excitement, cheer, and relief from boredom, use warm colors. Reds, oranges, yellows, and browns increase heart rate and respiration. There are indications that yellow also results in higher productivity in the workplace, while reds contribute to tension.

If you want to create a calmer, more serene and restful environment, use cool colors. Blues, greens, and grays slow down bodily responses. There is evidence that natural wood reduces stress while the color gray is experienced as depressing. Gray carpeting, however, will hide dirt, lint, and spills better than other colors, so if you want to take advantage of gray carpeting, balance it by using warm colors elsewhere in your office.

4. Decide what has to go and what can stay. You don't have to start from scratch. Decide which present furnishings are consistent with the image you want. Often you can re-cover, refinish, repair, or repaint what you now have. Or you can leave it all as is and purchase items consistent with your new look piece by piece as your budget allows.

5. Consider consulting an interior decorator, designer, or feng-shui consultant. Such professionals can not only help you select a new decor

---

How to Make a Small Room Look Larger

- Use one light color, such as an off-white or pastel, for walls as well as for drapes or curtains.

- Cover the floors with bright wall-to-wall carpeting.

- Keep the furnishings simple and uncluttered.

- Use mirrors (but remember they reflect light).

How to Make a Large Room Look Smaller

- Use bold colors and contrasting wall and floor coverings and furniture.

- Use large, heavy furniture.

- Use area rugs to define one or more sections of the room.

but also show you how to make the most of what you have. In fact, they often will save you money by suggesting a few inexpensive accessories to tie in what you have available with the look and feel you want. Of course, they can also guide you through the labyrinth of decorating and placement options by adding new floor or wall coverings, painting your office, and moving things around. Addressing these simple elements suggested by Florida-based feng-shui expert, Nancelee Wydra, for example, changed her client's home-based graphic design studio from a dreary, uninspiring place to meet with clients into an environment that projected confidence and capability. The designer could see the positive effect of these changes immediately.

MAINTAINING ADEQUATE TEMPERATURE, HUMIDITY, AND AIR QUALITY

Studies show that people work better when temperature and humidity are at comfortable levels and the air is clear and fresh. You can usually maintain these optimal working conditions without much effort.

Although climate is a matter of individual preference, people are most comfortable and productive in temperatures between 68 and 75 degrees, with the humidity between 40 and 50 percent. In other words, if you're sweating it out without an air conditioner during the summer, buying one can be good for your productivity as well as your comfort. Studies have shown that when the office temperature rises to the mid-eighties, mental performance becomes impaired.

If you have a problem room that's always too hot or too cold, there are a number of possible solutions. The human brain works in such a way that even though the temperature remains constant, we can use color to make ourselves feel cooler or warmer. You'll feel cooler in a room decorated with blues, greens, and grays but warmer in one decorated with pinks, reds, oranges, yellows, and browns. To get the effect you want, you needn't paint or paper your entire office with these colors. Use them in accessories like large wall-hangings, graphics, or pillows and even change them with the temperature of the season.

Air Cleaners

To keep the air in your office clean and fresh, you can install an electrostatic air filter, also called an electronic air cleaner. Adding these devices to most heating and air-conditioning systems costs approximately $500. Buying a portable air cleaner for the room will cost less. The most effective room air cleaners use high-efficiency particulate air filters called HEPA filters. True HEPA filters remove 99.97 percent of all particles down to 3 microns in size: Many HEPA air cleaners also include carbon filters that

To Warm Up a Home Office

1. Add solar panels to capture heat from the southern and/or western walls.

2. Install skylights and arrange your work area in their light path.

3. Carpet the home office and use ⅝-inch padding.

4. Plant deciduous trees outside windows for sunlight in the winter and shade in the summer.

5. Draw curtains, drapes, or blinds to retain heat when there is no direct sunlight.

6. Use insulated glass and make sure walls as well as ceilings are properly insulated to a standard of R-19.

7. Install a room heater.

8. Add a room humidifier to make the existing temperature seem warmer.

To Cool Off a Home Office

1. Place bookcases on all southern and western walls.

2. Use fluorescent lights.

3. Shut off appliances and lights when room is not in use.

4. Plant evergreens outside walls and windows with southern or western exposures.

5. Use indoor plants to shade direct sunlight.

6. Install a window air conditioner.

7. Use roof ventilating fans.

8. Arrange work areas in the direct path of circulating air.

9. Use blinds or curtains to block out direct sunlight.

10. Tint windows that receive the full glare of the sun.

11. Install heat-absorbing double windows.

remove odors and some organic chemicals. The *Enviracaire* portable air cleaner from Reliable Office Supply ([800] 735-4000), for example, comes in light- and heavy-duty models.

Either option removes smoke and cleans your air of microscopic particles that create a film on surfaces. The operating cost of an air cleaner is about the same as that of using a 60-watt light bulb. For a buyer's guide to room air cleaners, including ratings, filters, features, and pricing, visit *www.dulley.com*

An ionizing air filter can also improve air quality. These filters are useful in rooms without access to outside air, in areas where smog is a problem, or in rooms with electronic equipment such as office machines, television sets, and computers.

Houseplants That Clean the Air

According to research conducted by the National Aeronautics and Space Administration, common houseplants can also help purify the air. Not only do plants such as English ivy, dracaenas, and palms freshen stale air, they also remove toxins such as benzene, formaldehyde, and carbon monoxide that can build up in any home office from the use of paper products, cigarette smoke, cleaning and office supplies, natural gas, and so forth. NASA researcher B. C. Wolverton recommends that plants be included in your operating expenses, like pencils and fax machines. Although any plant will help, research has shown that Gerbera daisy, mother-in-law's tongue, pothos, and spider plant absorb the most toxins. Wolverton claims that eight to fifteen plants will "significantly improve" the air quality in the average home. That's about one plant per 100 square feet.

Aromatherapy

Finally, the odor of a work environment is normally overlooked unless fumes become consciously unpleasant or obnoxious. Research is pouring in, however, that fragrance can have a significant effect on the workplace, affecting alertness, performance, stress levels, and even heart rate, muscle tension and blood pressure. The Japanese are already using scents in the workplace, and in one experiment worker errors dropped 21 percent when the air was scented with lavender, 33 percent when jasmine was added to the air, and 54 percent when a lemon aroma was used. Here's how research is showing that you can assist your performance by adding scents to the air:

- **Improved work efficiency:** lavender, jasmine, and lemon

- **Learning aids:** basil, rose, bergamot, and cardamom

- **Reduce anxiety:** basil, bergamot, cedarwood, and hyssop

- **Reduce stress:** rose and tangerine

- **Relaxing:** lavender, chamomile, apple, and spice

- **Stimulating and invigorating:** lemon, jasmine, pine, eucalyptus, and rosemary

You can create these effects with potpourris; also, the Origins stores ([800] 723-7310) sell a line of essential-oils aromas called Sensory Therapy along with diffusers for subtly filling the air with positive fragrances, and White Rose of Provence offers a line of essential oils and diffusers in room or whole house models (800) 677-2368. Also JoAnn Bassett's Bassett Aromatherapy offers a line of fragrances and diffusers via mail (800) 738-8678 or on the Web at *www.aromaworld.com*

At the other extreme, to rid your home of unpleasant, embarrassing, or unprofessional household odors you can use a line of products called Kruegers' NonScents ([800] 942-8565) to control any odor, including those from pet accidents or lodged in carpets, furniture, floors, air vents, cars, laundry hampers, ashtrays, etc. These products have no fragrance. They absorb the undesirable odors. To freshen the air, research suggests using basil or peppermint.

Dust Busters

1. Dust your office regularly.

2. Use tacky dust cloths available at drugstores.

3. Spray your monitor with an antistatic spray like STAX made especially for electronic equipment.

4. Use an air filter. They range from $16 to $299 for ones that trap particles by charging them electronically so they stick to the filter.

5. Have a service come in to clean your air-conditioning and heating ducts and vents annually.

PURCHASING OFFICE SUPPLIES AND SMALL EQUIPMENT

When you first set up your office, we suggest you generate a list of the minimum equipment and supplies you'll need. If you're currently working at a job, a good way to start is to go through your office and list what you find on top of your desk, in your drawers, and in your cabinets. If you have a secretary, find out and list the common supplies he or she keeps on hand. Otherwise, review the equipment and supplies listed below.

For special time-saving supplies, accessories, and equipment for organizing and running your home office, see chapters 13 and 15. For special supplies and materials for marketing your business, see chapter 23.

Checklist: Basic Office Supplies and Small Equipment

Supplies

___ Accordion files	___ Jiffy padded mailing bags
___ Business cards	___ Mailing labels
___ Business envelopes	___ Paper, laser, and copier
___ Calendar or calendar software	___ Paper clips, fasteners
___ Computer diskettes	___ Pens, pencils, erasers, markers
___ Cleaning kit for disk drives and	___ Postage stamps
disks	___ Priority mail and overnight
___ Cartridges or ribbons	mailing envelopes
___ Correction fluid	___ Ring binders
___ Dust-Off air-spray canister	___ Rubber bands
___ Envelopes and shipping boxes for	___ Rubber stamps
air-express companies you use	___ Staples
___ File folders	___ Stationery: letterhead, billhead
___ File labels, tabs	___ Tape: cellophane, packaging
___ Glue, rubber cement	___ Tyvek mailing envelopes
___ Index cards	

Small Equipment

___ Calculator	___ Paperweight
___ Check protector (businesslike and	___ Pencil holder
inexpensive)	___ Postage affixer or a digital
___ Flip chart (for brainstorming and	___ Postage meter (saves time)
planning)	___ Postage scale (improves accuracy
___ In- and out-boxes	and saves money)
___ Letter opener	___ Pencil sharpener
___ Letter tray	___ Ruler
___ Mouse pad	___ Scissors
___ Organizer for CD-ROMs	___ Staple remover
___ Paper cutter	___ Stapler

WHERE TO BUY

With the growth of the small office/home office (SOHO) market, you have more choices than ever before of where and how to buy office furniture, supplies, and equipment. You can roam the aisles of office superstores like Office Depot, Office Max, and Staples; computer megastores like CompUSA; specialty stores like Crate and Barrel; and specialty departments in larger stores. And while local stationery and office-supply stores are giving way to the "power retailers," you may still be able to get a discount as well as personal service by paying a visit to your local mom-and-pop or independent store. But you don't even need to leave your home office to get nearly everything you need; you can also get good service and prices buying by mail and on line.

We recommend taking a tour through office-supply mail-order catalogs and also specialty paper house catalogs. You'll find everything from pre-printed four-color designed papers for letterheads, envelopes, presentation folders, and business cards to papers for postcards, coupons, news releases, newsletters, gift certificates, presentation folders—all of which you can color-coordinate and customize with your computer and printer. You'll find lists of these various catalogs among the resources at the end of this chapter.

At one time, mail-order catalogs were thought to offer the best prices, and sometimes they still do. But there are many times when you just can't beat office superstore prices. And if you live in a city large enough, walk-in paper dealers, such as Kelly Paper and Kirk Paper in Arizona, California, and Nevada, may offer a larger variety of papers at better prices than you'll find in office-supply stores. Of course, price isn't the only factor to consider in deciding where to shop. Convenience, variety, availability, and service count too. Let's look at some of the factors to consider in deciding where to shop.

No matter where you buy your furniture, equipment, and supplies, there are some cautions you should always exercise. For instance, don't buy anything in broken or torn packages unless you have a chance to inspect the product or the opportunity to return it. Sometimes you can save money buying seconds or damaged merchandise, but be certain that the product is still usable. Because such items are generally sold as is, you probably won't be able to get a refund or make an exchange.

Buying by Mail

If you buy from a mail-order catalog, you may find some products at bargain prices. Keep in mind, however, that you will also have to pay for shipping and, often, insurance. When these costs are added to the order, you may not save much money, particularly when compared with prices at office superstores.

Moreover, shipping can be delayed, especially during the holidays. If you have to return an item, it may take as long as two weeks before the return is processed. Finally, judging a product from a photograph is not quite the same as seeing it in person. Unless you're already familiar with the product, you may find it smaller, clumsier, or not quite the same color you had in mind. That's why it's important to read product descriptions, including measurements, and to check model numbers carefully before ordering.

Features to Look For: Buying from Office Supply and Office Superstores

- Variety and quality of products offered

- Availability. Is merchandise on hand or must it be special-ordered from a catalog?

- Delivery. Is it offered? Free or for a charge? Is it same day, twenty-four hour or less?

- Convenience of store location and of merchandise in the store

- Toll-free 800 number to place phone orders

- Offer to match or beat lowest advertised price

- Membership required for best prices? Membership free or for a charge?

- Helpfulness and expertise of store personnel

- Return policies: no return, money back, or store credit?

- Truth in advertising. Do you often go in to buy highly desirable advertised items which are sold out by the time you get there?

Most catalog companies offer liberal return policies and will refund or exchange products to the customer's satisfaction. This, however, is not always the case, so review the return policy before buying. In other words, read the fine print, which should state the return policy next to, or on, the order form. When you have to pay return or exchange expenses, an item can end up costing more than if you had bought it locally.

Because of a lack of local suppliers or the specialized nature of an item, the only way to get some supplies may be through a catalog. Even in Los Angeles, we've found it easier to order some things by mail than to find a local supplier. In ordering such items, we suggest you keep a three months' supply on hand at all times and order quarterly.

For quick service, make sure to place your orders either before or considerably after a holiday rush. Actually, mail-order firms report that their busiest times are January 1–15, April 1–15, September 1–15, and the entire month of December.

Ordering by mail is a common cause of complaints to consumer agencies. To guard against having a problem yourself, order from a known firm with a good reputation. Before ordering, check out who's responsible for damage during shipment and look for the following:

What to Look For: Buying from Mail-Order Vendors*

- Toll-free order number

- Shipping costs

- Other handling fees

- Always offer their lowest prices

- Next-day delivery

- No quibbles on money-back guarantee

- Shipping paid on returns

- One-year or lifetime guarantee on all items

* *According to* What to Buy for Business

In addition, if you're responding to an advertisement, phone or write the magazine in which the advertisement appeared to find out if the mail-order business has a record of complaints. Other excellent places to check on a company as well as on a product you're considering buying are on on-line forums and newsgroups.

Unless the company has stated a specific time for delivery, it must ship within thirty days of receiving your order. If the company fails to do so, it must notify you and give you the choice of receiving a refund or agreeing to a new shipment date. You automatically have the right to cancel and get a refund if you don't receive your order within the required time. On the other hand, by ignoring the first notice of a delay, you imply that you are willing to accept later delivery. You must be notified of any further delays, however, and you must specifically agree to them.

To protect yourself from problems when returning unsatisfactory products, pay by credit card rather than by cash or check. Then should you have a problem, you can often get the charge reversed. Sometimes when you can't get sellers to respond to your concerns, simply advising them that you will be asking their bank to credit your bill will spur them to action. While banks do not usually advertise this service, it is one that was brought about by the federal Fair Billing law, and the wise buyer takes advantage of it. The ability to protect yourself against problems of nondelivery or defective merchandise is reason enough to have at least one credit card.

One further tip: If the problem with a product is its quality, keep in mind that quality is always arguable and somewhat subjective. You will have more success by describing your problem as "not having been delivered in accordance with the agreement." Calling a problem a "billing error" rather than a "dispute" also increases the likelihood you'll get the charges reversed. And when the goods you've ordered by mail arrive, watch for any labels or stickers on the boxes that read Warranty Void. You may be wise to return the package unopened.

How to Handle a Problem with a Mail-Order Company

Here are some agencies you can turn to with a complaint:

The Postal Inspection Service. You can locate the postal inspector in the seller's area by contacting your local postmaster or postal inspector. The post office has a mediation service for settling disputes; phone: (800) 275-8777.

Better Business Bureau. To find out the address and phone number of the bureau in the seller's area, contact the Council of Better Business Bureaus, Inc., 4200 Wilson Boulevard, Ste. 800, Arlington, VA 22203. *www.bbb.org*

Direct Marketing Association. If you are unsure about a particular mail-order company, you may want to see if they are members of the DMA. 1120 Avenue of the Americas, New York, NY 10036-6700; phone: (212) 768-7277. *www. the-dma.org*

In California. The agency responsible for consumer complaints is the Department of Consumer Affairs, Complaint Assistance Unit, 1020 N Street, Sacramento, CA 95814. *www.dca.ca.gov*

In New York City. Contact the Complaints Division, Department of Consumer Affairs, 42 Broadway, New York, NY 10006. *www.ci.nyc.ny.us/html/dca/home.html*

If you charged your purchase on a credit card, contact the issuer of the card in writing to get a credit on your account. You're entitled to withhold payment. Federal law and regulations provide extensive procedures for resolving disputes, and you will receive this information once you have notified the credit card issuer.

Mail-order companies that have the best reputations for prompt delivery and customer satisfaction appear under Resources at the end of this chapter.

Buying On Line

Buying on line by computer has become big business. Almost every manufacturer of furniture and office supplies maintains a site on the World Wide Web. Smaller merchants sell through on-line shopping malls as well. So to find what you're looking for, do a search for the company name to find the

URL of the site. Often you will be able to order merchandise directly from the Web site.

In addition, the major services—America Online, CompuServe, and Prodigy—all offer extensive electronic shopping. For example, the Electronic Mall on CompuServe offers goods and services in fifteen departments such as Computer Hardware, Computer Software, and Office Supplies/Business Services. Well over a hundred different merchants sell through the on-line shopping mall. These include large companies like AT&T and Sears selling home-office products to Hammacher Schlemmer selling its selection of innovative products. AOL has several "channels" devoted to on-line business services and equipment and supplies shopping.

 Warning! Beware Office-Supply Telephone Scams

Watch out for office-supply telemarketing scams. These solicitors try to get you to buy common items of poor quality at high prices by confusing you into thinking that they are your usual supplier or that you or someone else in your office already placed an order with them. Sometimes they will send you the items and bill you for them later, so you just routinely pay the invoice. We have made it a policy never to order from a telephone solicitor. We always ask them to send a catalog or written material for us to consider. That usually takes care of it; they don't have one. But we would also immediately return anything neither of us ordered marked Return to Sender.

---

20 WAYS TO FIND HOME-OFFICE BARGAINS

1. Ask for a business discount. Usually you will need no more identification than a business card. Ask for discounts for cash or early payment.

2. Use recycled products. Companies like Computer Recyclers, (800) 635-2816, Marine Park Computers and Electronics, (800) 262-0163, and NWCD, (800) 773-6923 sell high-quality remanufactured fully warranted computer systems, printers, and accessories. Recycled toner cartridges for both printers and copiers can save 25 to 40 percent of the cost of new ones. They are available from companies like Data Products, (800) 232-2141, and Nashua, (800) 258-1724.

3. Shop at business liquidation sales advertised in the classified section of most newspapers.

4. Shop at estate sales.

   5. Go to police auctions.

   6. Buy checks directly instead of from your bank. They can cost 50 percent less from companies like Checks-in-the-Mail, (800) 733-4443, Current, (800) 533-3973, and Image Checks, (800) 562-8768.

   7. Look for moving sales when large companies change locations; shop at garage sales and bazaars or at secondhand stores, including veterans' rebuilt-merchandise shops.

   8. Use erasable products like disk and file labels you can use again and again.

   9. Shop at discount retail warehouse clubs that offer 25 to 30 percent discounts to members. Membership fees for clubs like Costco, Pace, and Sam's cost about $25 to $35.

   10. Buy unfinished furniture, unassembled furniture, or furniture kits.

   11. Build your own furniture with basic carpentry tools, using patterns or suggestions in popular "do-it-yourself" books and magazines.

   12. Find slightly damaged furniture from shipping companies.

   13. Investigate buying furniture that has been abandoned at storage companies.

   14. Shop in rural or out-of-the-way sections of the country.

   15. Buy seconds or furniture with manufacturers' errors.

   16. Look for discontinued styles, specials, clearance sales, inventory sales, and "loss leaders" used to draw people into a store.

   17. Shop in the want ads or in "bargain" newsletters for items being sold because a company is remodeling or redecorating.

   18. Look for floor samples or demonstrator models sold at reduced prices.

   19. Look for mill ends and remnants at carpet and flooring stores.

   20. Shop at federal government auctions for surplus equipment and supplies. To learn about bidding on these items, write to the Federal Supply Service, General Services Administration, Washington, DC 20406, or contact them on the Web: *www.gsa.gov.* Also try the Department of Defense Surplus Sales, P.O. Box 1370, Federal Center, Battle Creek, MI 49016.

   For more ideas on saving money, subscribe to *Pocket Change Investor* ([914] 758-1400, [800] 255-0899) or look in back issues of the *The Tightwad Gazette* ([207] 524-7962), the bible for dedicated penny-pinchers.

RESOURCES

BOOKS

Buy Wholesale By-Mail 1998 (serial). Lowell Miller and Prudence Mc-Cullough, eds. New York: Harper Collins. 1997. ISBN: 0062734385.

The Complete Book of Essential Oils and Aromatherapy. Valerie Ann Worwood. San Rafael, Calif.: New World Library, 1991. ISBN:0931432820.

The Complete Home Lighting Book: Contemporary Interior and Exterior Lighting for the Home. James Davidson. New York: Overlook Press, 1997. ISBN: 0879517662.

Design Sense: A Guide to Getting the Most from Your Interior Design Investment. Linda Blair. New York: Wiley, 1996. ISBN: 0471141046.

Directory of Home-Based Business Resources. Priscilla Y. Huff. Babylon, N.Y.: Pilot Books, 1997. ISBN: 087576200X.

Ergonomic Living: How to Create a User-Friendly Home and Office. Gordon Inkeles and Irish Schencke. New York: Simon & Schuster, 1994. ISBN: 002093081X.

Ergowise: A Personal Guide to Making Your Workspace Comfortable and Safe. William A. Schaffer and Rab Cross. New York: AMACOM Books, 1996. ISBN: 0814479073.

The Green PC, Making Choices That Make a Difference, 2 ed. Steven Anzovin. New York: Wincrest/McGraw-Hill, 1994. ISBN: 0070030073.

The Healthy House: Creating a Safe, Healthy and Environmentally Friendly Home. Sydney Baggs and Joan C. Baggs. New York: HarperCollins, 1997. ISBN: 0732256682.

Home Design from the Inside Out: Feng Shui, Color Therapy, and Self-Awareness. Robin Lennon and Karen Plunkett-Powell. New York: Penguin USA, 1997. ISBN: 0140195394.

Home Office Design: Everything You Need to Know About Planning, Organizing, and Furnishing Your Work Space. Neal Zimmerman. New York: Wiley, 1996. ISBN: 0471134333.

Home Offices: Your Guide to Planning and Furnishing. John Riha. New York: Better Homes & Gardens Books, 1997. ISBN: 0696207281.

Home Safety and Security, Home Repair and Improvement, Vol. 13. Editors of Time-Life Books, New York: Time-Life Books, 1996. ISBN: 0783538995.

150 Things You Should Know About Security. Louis A. Tyska and Lawrence J. Fennelly. Portsmouth, NH: Butterworth-Heinemann, 1997. ISBN: 0750698330.

Organized to be Your Best. Susan Silver. Los Angeles, Calif: Adams Hall Publishing, 1995. ISBN: 0944708366.

Outfitting Your Home Business For Less. Walter Zooi and Paul and Sarah Edwards. New York: AMACOM Books, 1999. ISBN: 0814479936.

Taming the Office Tiger: The Complete Guide to Getting Organized at Work. Barbara Hemphill. New York: Times Books, 1996. ISBN: 0812927125.

MAGAZINES

Consumer Reports (monthly) and *Consumer Reports Buying Guide Issue* (annual). Consumers Union, 256 Washington Street, Mount Vernon, NY 10553.

In Business, The Magazine for Ecological Entrepreneuring. 2718 Dryden Drive, Madison, WI 53704-3086; (608) 246-3599.

AUDIO

Inner Peace Music. P.O. Box 2644, San Ansalmo, CA 94979; phone: (800) 909-0707. Web: *www.innerpeacemusic.com*

MAIL-ORDER OFFICE AND COMPUTER SUPPLIES

DATAPRINT 700 S. Claremont Street, Ste. 205. San Mateo, CA 94402; (800) 227-6191; Web: *www.dataprint.com*

Hello Direct. 5893 Rue Ferrari, San Jose, CA 95138; (800) 444-3556 (telephone products). Web: *www.hello-direct.com*

Inmac PC Select. 55 United States Ave., Gibbsville, NJ 08026; (800) 547-5444.

Lewis & Lewis. 1600 Callens Road, Ventura, CA 93003; phone: (800) 342-3607. Web: *lewisnlewis.com* (Hewlett-Packard printer supplies).

MacWarehouse, (800) 255-6227, and **Micro Warehouse,** (800) 367-7080, 1720 Oak Street, Lakewood, NJ 08701; Web: *www.warehouse.com*

OfficeMax Catalog 3605 Warrensville Center Road, Shaker Heights, OH 44122; phone: (800) 788-8080. Web: *www.officemax.com*

PC Connection, (800) 800-0004, and **Mac Connection,** (800) 800-0002, 730 Milford Rd., Merrimack, NH 03054; Web: *www.pcconnection.com*

Penny Wise. P.O. Box 487, Bowie, MD 20718; (800) 942-3311; Web: *www.penny-wise.com*

Quill. 100 Schelter Road, Lincolnshire, IL 60069; (847) 634-4800; Web: *www.quillcorp.com*

Reliable Home Office. P.O. Box 1501, Ottawa, IL 61350; phone: (800) 869-6000. Web: *www.reliable.com*

Viking Office Products. 950 W. 190th St., P.O. Box 61144, Torrance, CA 90502; phone: (800) 248-6111 and (800) 421-1222. Web: *www.vikingop.com*

Wholesale Supply Company. P.O. Box 23770, Nashville, TN 37202; (800) 962-9162.

SPECIALTY PAPER AND LABEL SOURCES

Idea Art. P.O. Box 291505, Nashville, TN 37229; phone: (800) 433-2278. Web: *www.ideaart.com*

Laser Label Technologies. 1485 Corporate Woods Parkway, Uniontown, OH 44685; (800) 882-4050.

Paper Direct. P.O. Box 1514 Secaucus, NJ 07096; phone: (800) A-PAPERS. Web: *www.paperdirect.com*

Queblo. P.O. Box 8465, Mankato, MN 56002; phone: (800) 523-9080.

CHAPTER 8

Equipping and Computerizing the Up-to-Date Home Office

<table>
<tr><td>

Goals

1. Review features of the latest popular home office technology and software.

2. Decide what you need for your office.

3. Use handy feature-to-look-for checklists when you shop to be sure you get what you need.

4. Find resources for protecting and maintaining your equipment.

</td></tr>
</table>

Hundreds of thousands of people have started home offices with nothing more than a desk, a telephone extension, and a filing cabinet. Some people begin with even less. When we began working from home in 1974, very little real office equipment was available or affordable for a home office. So we began operations with two desks, an answering machine, and an IBM Selectric typewriter. Consequently, we depended on outside services for photocopies and for turning our rough manuscripts into copy we could submit to clients and publishers. Now these are all things we routinely do ourselves because of the wealth of equipment that has become the heart of our home office.

The typical home office today has at least one personal computer, a printer, fax capabilities, a modem, an answering machine, and a variety of special telephone features. Many home offices also have a copy machine and a scanner as well.

Why this high-tech transformation in home offices? First, the prices of electronic equipment have come way down. By shopping carefully, you can now get all the equipment mentioned above for under $2,500. Second, equipment is becoming increasingly compact, perfect for small office spaces. Third, to be competitive today, a home business needs to use as much of the latest equipment as possible. In fact, the growth of personal computers has gone hand in hand with the growth of working from home, as you can see in Figure 8-1.

So what equipment do you need? You need enough to do business efficiently and remain competitive. But you don't need to get everything at once. Most people start with the items that will make the biggest difference in terms of getting ample business, doing their work more effectively, and projecting the most professional image. Then, as those items pay for themselves by assisting your business to grow, you can add the next most useful item and so forth until you have everything you need to be most efficient and effective.

In this chapter, we're going to take you on a verbal tour of the well-equipped home office and prepare you to shop confidently for your own home-office equipment. You can actually take the **Features-to-Look-For**

 Work Sheet: The Well-Equipped Home Office

Check off the equipment you already have and put an asterisk* by the equipment you need and will want to be adding to your home office at some time in the future. You might also wish to prioritize the equipment you need to get as those you need immediately or as soon as possible and those you will defer for the future.

___ Two-line cordless telephone

___ Answering machine or service

___ Voice mail

___ Pager or cellular phone

___ Fax or fax/modem

___ Computer: desktop and portable

___ Laser or ink-jet printer

___ Modem

___ Copier

___ Scanner

___ Digital Camera

___ Other: _____

Technology Enables People to Work from Home

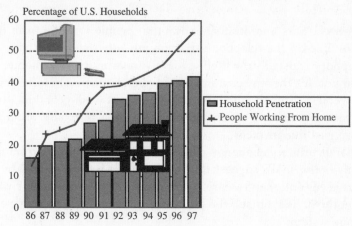

Percentage of U.S. Households

Household Penetration
People Working From Home

86 87 88 89 90 91 92 93 94 95 96 97

Sources: Consumer Electronics Manufacturers Association & IDC/Link

Figure 8-1

Checklists you'll find in this chapter with you when you shop to make the selection process easier.

We consider the items that appear on the following checklists in bold-face type to be important features of equipment that will be used at home for business purposes. Items in italics are "nice to have," but not vital. We must caution you that the features and models of products for the home office change rapidly—faster even than those for automobiles or stereos! So keep in mind that the checklists are constructed as of this writing for 1998 models. What we describe as state-of-the-art may well be surpassed by the time you read this book.

Also, costs, models, features, and even manufacturers of home-office equipment change almost daily. Generally speaking, prices and sizes are going down, and quality and the number of features available are going up. Something you think is unaffordable as you read this chapter will probably become a bargain in six month's time. When you shop, you may also find that features you want that aren't mentioned here or are said to be unavailable may be awaiting you. In fact, unless something unforeseen intervenes, all these goodies are the very least you can get!

To get up-to-the-moment information and reviews of specific equipment, you need to check recent issues of publications, both print and on line, that conscientiously evaluate new products. These publications are in the Resources list at the end of the chapter.

Let's imagine now that we're going shopping to equip your home office. We'll be taking a tour of the kind of equipment that you'll find either in successful people's home offices or on their wish lists. Let's start with the telephone: the lifeline of most home offices.

TELEPHONES: WHAT DO YOU NEED?

Research (ours and others') shows that people working from home spend more time on the telephone than on any other single activity. In fact, the telephone is usually the lifeline for anyone working from home. More often than not, it's the way customers and clients reach us in the first place. It's the vehicle through which much of our paid work gets done, from setting up appointments to reading E-mail, faxing a purchase order or tracking down past-due invoices.

Your primary challenge will most likely be choosing from among your many options. We suggest that the quickest way to start is by identifying your needs and then researching the services that will most cost-effectively meet them. Ask yourself the following questions to set up your optimal telephone system:

1. How often do your work or personal activities take you out of your home office during times when clients and customers will be calling you? How will you make sure you don't miss those calls?

2. Do you want certain callers to be able to reach you while you are at locations other than your home office? How will they reach you without disrupting your activities at these other locations?

3. How much time do you spend talking on the phone each day? How frequently will other calls be coming in while you are on the phone? What will you do to be sure that important business callers don't get repeated busy signals?

4. Will there be times during the workday when you will be working in your home office but don't want to be interrupted by phone calls? How will you screen and record these calls?

5. What personal telephone needs do you have going on in your home? Will family members or roommates be making and receiving calls? How will you separate these other household telephone needs from your business phone needs? Is there more than one location in your home where you will need to pick up your incoming business calls?

6. Do you use or will you be using a fax and/or a modem? How will you make sure you can send and receive such transmissions without interfering with your voice calls?

With your answers to these questions in mind, review the following service and equipment options and contact your local telephone company to find out how they can best meet your needs.

Why You Should Have at Least One Separate Telephone Line for Your Business

Whether you are self-employed or telecommuting, if you are working from your home on a regular basis full-time or part-time, we believe you should have at least one separate line for your business activity. Many people, at least in the beginning, rely on their one residential line for their business phone, but here's why we believe that, as soon as possible, you should have a separate line, and if you plan to use your fax machine or the Internet on a regular basis, why we recommend two separate lines.

- *Keep personal and business life separate.* A separate phone line will help you better manage your personal and business life. For example, your children can let your business line ring through to voice mail or an answering machine. Your family can use the personal line while leaving the business line free for incoming business calls. You can put an answering machine, service, or voice mail on either line when you want to be free to work or enjoy your personal life uninterrupted.

- *A more professional image.* A separate business line will provide you with a more professional business image. For all the reasons just mentioned above, a separate business line will convey that you are a "real" business. With a business line, you can answer your calls with a professional greeting and have a service, answering machine, or voice mail respond appropriately when you cannot answer personally.

- *Help you get more business.* A separate business line will help your clients and customers reach you. A separate business line will enable you to have a Yellow Page listing and to be listed in the Business White Pages. When someone looks up your business in the phone book or calls the information operator, your business will be listed. Often, home-business owners who don't get a separate business line lose out on an undeterminable amount of business when people cannot locate them through the phone company.

- *Better manage voice and data needs.* With an additional line for your data communications (fax and modem) you will be able to receive and make calls while on line or using your fax machine. This adds considerable efficiency to your operations.

VOICE-MAIL CHOICES

Voice mail answers your calls and takes messages like a sophisticated answering machine, but it offers additional advantages. First, because most large companies use voice mail, a home business with voice mail becomes

Checklist: Finding Solutions
to the Top Four Home-Office Phone Needs

Not all the service options listed on this checklist are available from all telephone companies; at this time, however, most have them on the drawing board. The names of these services vary from one phone company to another. So describe what you need to your phone company, and they will tell you about the services they have.

1. Taking messages when you're busy or out of the office

Answering machine
Answering service
Voice mail—from the phone company
— private voice mail services
— voice mail on your computer
Call-forwarding
Fax in or fax back
Caller ID

2. Receiving calls when you're out of the office

Call-forwarding—delayed call-forwarding
— remote call-forwarding
— priority call-forwarding
Cellular phone
700 number
Paging system

3. Handling incoming calls while you're on the phone

Voice mail
Callwaiting with call-cancel and three-way calling
Call-return
Busy call-forwarding
Call-forwarding of call-waiting
Call-hunting

4. Screening your calls while you're working

Answering machine
Special call acceptance
VIP alert
Distinctive ringing
Fax/phone/answering machines
Fax/modem switches
Call pickup
Integrated equipment
House-wide systems

virtually indistinguishable to callers from *Fortune* 500 companies. And in many ways voice mail is like having a receptionist because it can carry out many of the tasks a receptionist would provide. For example, in addition to simply leaving a message, callers can choose from among a variety of options. They can listen for a list of your services, receive directions for getting to your office, or obtain instructions for ordering a product. Having such information available on a prerecorded message saves you the time of taking or returning such calls and provides your callers with immediate access to frequently requested information.

Voice-mail systems generally offer the ability to set up different outgoing messages that can be programmed to run at various times of the day. In addition, voice mail enables you to set up individual "mailboxes" where you can leave private messages for different people in addition to your generic greeting. Each mailbox has its own ID-coded extension that you can assign to those people with whom you want to stay in touch. The value of mailboxes is that you can leave detailed messages for any individual with whom you may need to communicate, and thereby avoid playing phone tag with hard-to-reach people. Also, with an answering machine, you can pick up your voice-mail messages wherever you are by dialing your own number.

One of the best features of voice mail is that it will pick up incoming calls while you are on the phone, so your callers will never get a busy signal. Some services will even answer multiple calls at the same time. The only limitation, however, is that you can't "screen" your calls the way you can with an answering machine. Sometimes you won't know you had a second call coming in until you complete your call and check to see if there were any calls while you were on the phone. Here are three different ways you can add voice mail to your home office.

Add the Best Features of an Answering Machine to Your Voice Mail

Solo Point's *Voice Mail Manager* supplements the voice-mail system you sign up for through your local telephone company with the features you miss most in your answering machine: a message waiting light, "line" call-screening capabilities, and push-button controls for play, save, delete, fast forward, and rewind for under $80. Call toll-free (888) SOLOCALL (765-6225) or visit *www.comversens.com*

Voice-Mail Answering Machines

More sophisticated digital answering machines offer many voice mail–like features such as voice-mail boxes, selected outgoing messages, call-forward capability, and much greater voice recording time.

Voice Mail Through Your Phone Company

Most local telephone companies are now offering voice-mail service for a modest monthly charge through your existing phone and phone number. For example, Bell Atlantic has Answer Call, which for under $10 a month provides the ability to record thirty to forty-five minutes of voice messages. As with an answering machine, you can access your messages from a remote location, save some of the messages to replay at a later time, and erase others. A similar service is GTE's voice mail, Personal Secretary; US WEST offers Voice Messaging; Pacific Bell's service is called Message Center; Ameritech's is Call Minder; and BellSouth's is Memory Call. Note, though, that the voice-mail systems offered through specific phone companies may not have all the features described above.

Private Voice-Mail Services

If a voice mail–like answering machine or voice mail through your phone company doesn't meet your needs, another choice is to sign up with a private voice-mail service. In the short term, using one of these two methods is probably the most simple, effective, and least expensive option for most home businesses. You will pay from around $5 to $20 a month, depending on the number of mailboxes and other options you select.

Voice Mail on Your Computer

A more versatile and cost-effective solution over the long haul might be to set up a voice-mail system on your own computer using specialized software and a voice-mail card that you install in your computer. The voice-mail card digitizes your voice so that it can be stored on your hard drive just as if it were computer data. When a call comes in, it is picked up by the voice-mail card, the caller hears your greeting, and the person's message is recorded on your hard disk.

You can set up your own voice-mail system using a reasonably priced system like Symantec's *CommSuite* or *PROCOMM Plus* from Quarterdeck, which combines fax, E-mail, telephone answering, and pager communications.

To accommodate any of these systems, you will need a large-capacity hard drive, because the outgoing greeting or messages you leave combined with any incoming messages from callers require about ten megabytes per hour of high-quality speech. Although some voice-mail systems offer a low-quality recording speed that doesn't take as much disk space, if you will be using voice mail while you are working at your office, you will probably want to buy a computer that you can dedicate to your voice-mail system.

ANSWERING SERVICES

Answering services provide a person to take your calls and, according to some surveys, most people prefer a warm body on the other end of their telephone calls. Nevertheless, we find most home-based businesspeople do not use answering services. The cost is one factor. An answering machine or voice mail is a one-time cost instead of a monthly fee that adds to your overhead each month. In addition, answering service personnel are sometimes rude and abrupt.

If you decide to use an answering service, start by considering those you've enjoyed speaking to when you've called others. Here are a few ways to do some comparison shopping. Visit the answering service's office without an appointment. Notice how many times the phones ring before they're answered. Are the operators courteous? Do they personalize their conversations around their customers' businesses? Most services have many switchboards with different operators. Insist on an operator whose manner you like and be specific about how you want your phone answered. Many are now actually automated voice-mail and pager services. So find out if real people are taking messages or if it is a voice-mail/pager service.

Ask for the names of three or four of the service's customers, preferably people with businesses similar to yours. Call to find out if these customers

What to Do About Telephone Tag

Two out of three business calls aren't completed on the first try. One party calls the other, who is not available; the second party returns the call, and the first party is not there; and so on. This back-and-forth calling has been calculated to amount to two years over a lifetime. To avoid playing telephone tag:

- Use E-mail when possible and appropriate.
- Set up a telephone appointment, and agree on a specific time to call.
- Determine when the person you're calling will be in the office. State that you will call again at that time.
- Use a voice-mail box, fax-in, and fax-back to take care of communication that doesn't actually require you to talk person-to-person to confirm a meeting, provide directions, get a price list, etc.
- Have your calls forwarded to your cellular phone.
- Leave a message on your answering machine or voice mail that specifically tells callers when you will return to the office.

are satisfied. Ask if they receive their messages reliably. Find out if their customers complain about the service and how well the service handles urgent phone calls. Once you've started with the service, occasionally call your number to be certain your customers are receiving the treatment you want them to have.

Naturally, you can combine a variety of these many telephone products and services to arrive at the best solution for your business. Your telephone company can help you find creative combinations that will meet your personalized needs for a top-notch home-office phone system.

TEN WAYS TO SAVE MONEY AND TIME ON YOUR TELEPHONE BILL

1. Dial direct. This can save you 60 percent of the costs of operator-assisted calls.

2. Place long-distance calls during off-hours whenever possible. The rates are lower when you call before 8 A.M. or after 5 P.M. on weekdays. Take advantage of time differences in placing calls to people in other areas. Remember, if your call extends beyond the off-hours, you pay the full day rate.

3. If your long-distance calls amount to more than $10 a month, use a discount calling plan, such as AT&T's Reach Out America, MCI's Prime Time, or Sprint's Sprint Plus. Frequently carriers also offer special discount programs as part of new promotions.

4. To find out the current best rates for the major long-distance carriers, obtain the research of organizations like the Telecommunications Research and Action Center or Consumer Reports, which do impartial cost comparisons. Factor into your decision additional benefits like sign-up bonuses and getting frequent-flyer miles for using particular services.

5. To keep track of different types of calls, use more than one long-distance carrier. Then you can differentiate personal from business calls, one client from another, or one business from another. To gain access to the three major long-distance carriers, use these codes prior to dialing the long-distance number: AT&T, 10288; MCI, 10222; and US Sprint, 10333. Calls will be listed by company on your telephone bill.

6. Use "800" numbers whenever possible. When you're calling an out-of-town business, it's a good idea to check an 800 directory or call information: 1 (800) 555-1212.

7. Check your telephone bills for errors. If you find them, call and get credit.

8. If you spend more than six hours a week making phone calls, use an automatic phone dialer in the form of hardware or software.

9. While your business is first getting under way, use only one telephone line with distinctive ringing for both your business and personal telephone calls. Most companies will allow you to turn your distinctive-ringing number into a separate business line at any time without changing the number.

10. Use the Internet for long-distance calls with products like *NET-Phone*.

 Features-to-Look-for Checklist: Telephone Hardware

Telephone equipment is keeping pace with all the new telephone services and offering myriad phone configurations with useful styles and features for complementing the many new phone services. You can buy a telephone with a variety of combinations of the following features:

❑ Mute button turns off your microphone to screen out sounds, like a dog's barking, while your caller continues talking.
❑ Adjustable ring volume.
❑ Automatic redial calls back the last number you called.
❑ Recall calls back the last number that called you. Important if you let a call go by during call-waiting or didn't make it to the phone for some reason before the party hung up.
❑ Hold button puts your caller on hold.
❑ Call-on-hold indicator reminds you that you have a caller holding.
❑ Message-waiting indicator tells you that you have a voice-mail message, a must if you have voice mail that picks up your incoming calls while you're on the phone.
❑ Programmable memory keys provide one-touch dialing to frequently called numbers or immediate access to phone features like call-forwarding, three-way calling, or call-waiting.
❑ Speakerphone lets you talk on the phone without using the handset.
❑ Call-forward indicator reminds you that your calls will be forwarded to another number.
❑ Call I.D. display shows the phone number of your caller (not allowed in all states, however).
❑ Call log stores incoming phone numbers so you have access to the numbers of people who have called you.

Other telephonic options include two-line phones, cellular phones, cordless phones, and two-line cordless phones. And if you don't like using a speakerphone, you can get a telephone headset.

TWO-LINE TELEPHONES

We strongly recommend getting one or more two-line telephones: one line for your business number and one for your personal number. With two-line phones you will be able to easily answer each line appropriately no matter where you are in your house, without the added clutter of having two separate phone sets. Do you want to be running from room to room to answer calls on your various lines, especially if your house has several floors? We have a two-line phone in our office, which is on the third floor of our town house, another in the kitchen, which is centrally located on the second floor, and a third in the bedroom, which is on the first floor. Two-line phones are available in both corded and cordless models.

CORDLESS TELEPHONES

We also highly recommend a cordless telephone for the home office because you can take it with you anywhere, indoors or out. This comes in especially handy when a delivery arrives in the middle of an important call, an important file you want to attend to is out of reach of your desk phone, or other personal matters need attention during the business day. It's not uncommon, for example, for the phone to ring while we're outside getting the mail or taking the dogs for a walk. Keep the cordless in your pocket, and you won't miss a call.

A cordless phone is almost an essential for parents working with children at home, according to home-based writer Rosalind Resnick. Her three-year-old is at that age where she has just discovered how to climb out of her playpen. With a cordless phone, Resnick can trail her toddler from room to room, safeguarding not only her daughter but her own peace of mind as well. Using the intercom on his cordless phone, computer consultant David Moskowitz has been able to work in his office downstairs and still take care of his daughter when she's home sick from school. Whenever she needs anything from Dad, she just "beeps."

Be aware, however, that if the electricity goes out, so will your phone service on a cordless phone. So always have at least one corded phone for both your personal and business lines. Cordless phones, as Newt Gingrich will tell you, are not secure. Anyone with a special scanner can tune in to your conversation. Cordless phones also present difficulties if you live in a hilly area or near radio or television transmission towers. 900Mhz cordless phones provide better, stronger signals over much longer distances. They do cost more, but are well worth the additional expense.

CELLULAR PHONES

Cellular phones are becoming a staple for the four out of five people who work from home a majority of the time, as opposed to at home. Fortunately, prices on cellular phones continue to drop as do their size and weight. You can have calls forwarded to your cellular, or with the digital phones or those with "DTMF"—tone-dialing sound—you can pick up your answering-machine or voice-mail messages. You can even receive faxes over your cellular phone.

A cellular phone also makes working from home easier for parents who

---

 Features-to-Look-for Checklist: Cellular Phones and Service

Phones:

❏ *Size and weight.* The smaller and lighter, the better, of course. But often smaller and lighter means more costly. The heavier and bulkier, the more wattage and therefore the better the range.

❏ *Wattage.* Zero-point-six watts is adequate in major metropolitan areas but can be a problem in outlying regions. Blaupunkt has a portable that has a 1.2-watt output. Car kits can be equipped with 3-watt boosters.

❏ *Battery power.* Most are NiCad batteries, although some use a newer, more desirable battery called NiMH. It typically takes eight to ten hours to recharge, but you can buy a rapid-recharge accessory that can do it in under two hours.

❏ *Battery life.* Typically you can expect about sixty minutes of talk time and about twelve hours in standby, but this varies. Some vendors offer longer-life batteries, but they are heavier.

❏ *Fuel gauge.* If possible get a phone that will show you how much battery power is left, because if you recharge before the battery runs down, you reduce the battery's life. An indicator that shows exactly how much power remains is better than a low-battery light.

❏ *Call timers.* Most cellulars display how many minutes you've been talking, but you can also get a one-minute alarm beeper inaudible to the other party to alert you to wrap up before starting another minute of costly airtime.

(Continued on page 212)

(Continued from page 211)

❑ **Call-in-absence indicator.** This feature lets you know if someone tried to call while you were away from the phone. Some indicate how many calls. But most phones don't know who called, so a few let the caller leave a phone number, like a display pager. Muratec has a model that has a built-in voice-messaging capability, like an answering machine. You leave a message, and the caller can leave a very short message on a voice chip in the phone.

❑ **Alphanumeric memory dialing and displays.** Almost all cellulars have a memory dialing feature that allows you to store commonly called numbers (100 is typical), but who can remember what numbers go with what codes? Alphanumeric memory stores the names of the people so you can scroll down and pick the one you want to dial.

❑ **Scratchpad.** This handy feature lets you enter a phone number someone gives you during a phone conversation into a "holding pattern," without any sound to the caller. Then you can dial that number by pressing a single key once you've finished with the first call.

❑ **Auto credit card dialing.** If you make long-distance calls on your cellular, you may want to charge them to your long-distance carrier instead of to your cellular bill. This feature automates entering the long-distance carrier access numbers and account data. It can also be used for checking your voice mail.

❑ **Data link.** This allows you to link your PC with your cellular so you can send or receive data or faxes. However, according to *What to Buy for Business,* this feature isn't always reliable as yet and digital cellular will do better. If you want this option, look at Motorola, Nokia, OKI, and Fujitsu.

❑ **Car kits.** Although not necessary, car kits give you several valuable features: you can talk without holding the handset, and some have a hands-free dialing feature, automatic answer, better reception, wattage booster, and even a feature that will honk your horn if you have a call coming in while you're out of the car!

❑ *Service:*

- Separate rates for peak and off-peak hours
- Make sure at least thirty minutes are included in your monthly service fee.
- National coverage
- Long-distance coverage
- Detailed billing
- Voice-mail alert
- Display messaging
- Weekend calling packages
- Call-waiting, call-forwarding, conference calling, caller ID

want to remain in touch with clients while chauffeuring kids to and from school, watching a daughter's soccer game, or waiting at the tennis court while a son trains for an upcoming competition. And vice versa, your children can reach you in an emergency, even while you're out of your home office.

The cost of cellular phones runs from free to $300 and above. You can get the best deals on phones when you sign up for a cellular service. The phone will often be free of charge if you sign a contract committing to a service for a specified length of time, usually two years. If you want to buy a new phone after you've signed up, you can pay as much as several hundred dollars more. So when you're ready for a new phone, cancel your existing service and start a new one. You might have to change carriers to do this.

The price of cellular calls, both incoming and outgoing, is still high— around 25 to 45 cents per minute, up to 90 cents in some areas, in addition to your monthly access charge and an initial setup fee. To keep costs down, you can be selective in giving out your car phone number. Or, instead of giving out your cellular number at all, you can use a service like Priority Call Forwarding to forward to cellular only those calls you urgently want to receive.

To make using your cellular phone more convenient Ora Electronics has a recharger that restores power to your phone in minutes. Called the *Quick Charger*, it also refreshes and recycles your phone's battery, restoring it to full capacity. It comes with an AC adaptor or vehicle adaptor (phone: [818] 772-2700; Web: *www.orausa.com*).

TELEPHONE HEADSETS

A headset frees both your hands for writing, using your computer, or carrying out other activities while you talk. Of course, a speakerphone accomplishes the same task, but many people hate talking to someone on a speakerphone; the room noise gets carried along with your voice and, of course, there's a loss of privacy. A headset, on the other hand, provides both the voice privacy and quality of your handset.

Plantronics has been a leader in telephone headsets since 1961, and they have a wide variety of models ranging from $99 to $240 (phone: [800] 544-4660; Web: *www.plantronics.com*). Recently they've introduced their StarBase 2000 telephone with a built-in headset that saves desk space and reduces cord clutter in an already-crowded home office. It comes with many of the state-of-the-art telephone features we've mentioned like automatic redial and speed dialing.

If you want to use a headset with a cordless phone, you can use a cordless/headset combo, so you can clip your phone to your waistband and walk about the house talking with your hands free (for current models, phone: [800] 444-3556; Web: *www.hello-direct.com*).

ANSWERING MACHINES

At one time, an answering machine was just about the only cost-effective way for many people working from home to make sure they didn't miss important calls. Today, having an answering machine remains a popular and economical solution, although using one these days can identify you as a small operation. Larger companies have a live operator or, more frequently now, voice mail. To overcome this limitation, some lines of answering machines have added multiple message capability and voice-mail boxes that enable them to resemble voice mail. Still, if a "corporate" image is vital to your business, an answering machine may no longer be the best solution. Certainly it is no longer your only option.

The good news about answering machines is that fewer people hang up on them now than in the past. In fact, in some parts of the country it's considered rude not to have an answering machine. And some people prefer an answering machine to an endless litany of voice-mail selections.

As the prices of answering machines have come down, our experience is that they have become more prone to mechanical failure. If you decide to use an answering machine, don't buy a flimsy one just to save money! Once you have your machine, it's a good idea to call home periodically to make sure the machine is working properly and messages are being recorded.

Features-to-Avoid Checklist: Answering Machines

❑ Pause by speaker halts recording or hangs up line.

❑ Machine stops recording if speaker's voice is too soft.

❑ Outgoing message slurs or speeds up your voice.

❑ Extended delay before resetting to answer after a previous call.

❑ A complex sequence of commands to retrieve messages remotely.

❑ Messages automatically erased upon rewind.

FAX MACHINES

A fax, short for "facsimile," allows you to transmit information over the phone lines instantly to another fax machine or to a computer that's capable of receiving faxes. Using a fax saves time over conventional mail, costs a fraction of what messenger and overnight-delivery services cost, and is often more direct than E-mail. It takes less than twenty seconds to fax a page of text, so a three-page fax will require only a one-minute phone call even if sent to the other side of the world. From coast to coast, sending a short document by fax costs less than sending it by U.S. mail for 33 cents. After a computer and a telephone, a fax is probably the next most important piece of equipment to have in terms of enabling you to work effectively from home.

Fax technology is available in two basic forms: a stand-alone machine or a board or card that's placed inside a personal computer. The advantages of a fax that's mounted on a computer board are that it takes up no additional desk space, generally costs less, enables you to transmit documents created in your computer without first printing them out in hard copy and, because a document sent by your computer doesn't need to be scanned, the document received by the person to whom you send it will look better. You can, however, *only* transmit documents stored inside your computer through a fax board. If you want to fax a receipt, a copy of a magazine or newspaper article, or any other unique document, you must use a stand-alone fax or a first scan the document into your computer. A stand-alone fax can also be used as a backup photocopier.

Devotees of each method feel strongly about their choice. One person told us that he thought using a stand-alone fax was the equivalent of using a typewriter instead of a computer. He especially values his ability to compose a document in his computer and, with his internal fax, automatically send it to one thousand people simultaneously. He likes being able to convert and edit faxes he receives and return them to the senders. He likes having a fax board in his laptop so that he has fax capability on the road.

On the other hand, we know people who feel equally strongly about their stand-alone faxes. They don't want to leave their computer on in order to get faxes while they're gone. They don't like faxes clogging up their disk space, which can become full while they're away from the office and cause them to miss incoming faxes. They don't like not being able to send off a clipping or memo that's not stored in their computer. Obviously, there are pros and cons of each and the choice is highly personal, depending on your needs. An increasing number of people are solving the problem by having both. That's what we do. Paul prefers an internal fax; Sarah likes the external; but we each use both, depending on the circumstances.

If you decide to go with a freestanding fax machine, here are other features to consider:

Features-to-Look-for Checklist: Fax Machines

❑ *Paper type:* Thermal or Plain Paper

❑ *Resolution quality.* Sufficient to your needs. Graphic designers need higher resolution than most businesses. Measured in dots per square inch, popular models range from 200 to 400 dpi. Measured in gray scales, 16 is typical; 64 is high quality, permitting transmission of photos, illustrations, and graphics.

❑ *Image enhancement.* Resolution relates to the image of your outgoing faxes. Image enhancement, also called image smoothing, enables your machine to improve the quality of incoming faxes.

❑ *Document size.* Thermal faxes can receive a document of any length. Most plain-paper faxes receive only letter-sized paper. If you receive a legal-size document, the machine will either reduce it to letter size or carry the extra copy over to a second page. If you want to receive on different paper sizes, you can select a model with a dual on-line cassette. The machine will automatically select the appropriate page size for the incoming fax. Some models will also take documents eleven inches wide for ledger sheets.

❑ *Document feeder and handling.* On low-end models document feeders may be manual, which you must feed page by page, or automatic, in which case the machine feeds up to twenty pages. Higher-end models go up to fifty. If you send multiple-page documents, feeding them by hand or by cluster is time-consuming. In poorer models multiple sheets may feed through together, requiring you to refax. In fact, misfeeding is the number-one gripe that *What to Buy for Business* hears from owners of low-cost fax machines.

❑ *Paper supply.* Trays for receiving plain-paper faxes typically have a 200-to-250-sheet capacity; some go up to 500. If you travel or are out of the office, you will miss faxes once your paper supply runs out. If the fax has sufficient memory, however, your machine can store incoming faxes when the fax runs out of paper. Memory in typical budget faxes stores 7 to 20 pages.

❑ *Footprint.* Personal faxes range in size from 13 to 30 inches wide, 4.5 to 14 inches high, and 7 to 20 inches deep, so in some cases your choice will be limited by the space you have available. Canon has an upright fax, for example, that's perfect for a narrow shelf, ledge, or credenza. It stands upright and is only 8 inches deep and 9 inches tall. Lanier, on the other hand, has a model that's 4.5 inches high but 12 inches deep, perfect for fitting under a low shelf or even stacking on a rack. Some, however, are nearly the size of personal copiers.

(Continued on page 217)

(Continued from page 216)

Dialing:

❑ *Automatic redialing.* Also called auto-retry, this feature enables the fax to keep dialing a busy number at intervals of two or three minutes until it answers.

❑ *Speed dialing.* As on the telephone, speed dialing lets you program frequently used numbers so you can send them with the touch of one or two keys.

❑ *Voice request.* If you want to talk to the person after faxing, this feature will not hang up immediately.

Memory:

❑ *Size of memory.* Usually 7 to 20 pages, but you can upgrade to 100 to 200 pages. This is important for storing incoming faxes when paper runs out and for broadcasting.

❑ *Broadcasting.* This is a real time-saver if you will be faxing the same document to several people. The fax stores the document in memory, and you tell it all the numbers you want it sent to.

❑ *Fast scan.* If memory is sufficient, the fax can scan in documents in as few as two seconds; more commonly, it's five to six seconds. This is important when sending multiple pages or for broadcasting.

❑ *Dual access.* Also called transmission reservation, this feature lets you do more than one thing at a time on your fax. You can copy something while dialing an outgoing fax or, while receiving an incoming fax, you can set up to send an outgoing one, walk away, and once the line is free, the outgoing fax will go through.

MULTIFUNCTION UNITS: USING ONE PIECE OF EQUIPMENT TO DO THE WORK OF MANY

Between business and personal phone lines, fax modem lines, answering machines, fax machines, and printers, your home office could start looking more like an electronics store than a residence. But today's office equipment is getting smaller and smaller, and one piece of equipment may do what once took two, three, or more pieces to accomplish. Using such integrated equipment can save you money as well as desk space.

Although you have a growing selection of space-saving integrated equipment like two-line cordless phones, speakerphones, and single- or two-line telephone/answering machines and combinations. With a fax/phone/

answering machine, you can have one line serving three purposes. By having all three of these devices in one, when you are not available or in your office, the machine answers incoming calls and detects if a fax or voice call is being received. Voice calls trigger the answering machine and, of course, the fax machine receives faxes.

 Warning!

To date, people who try to combine voice and fax on one line report that they do miss some faxes and, of course, call-waiting will interrupt fact transmission—although some machines let you program in a dialing prefix to deactivate call-waiting before sending a fax.

A wide variety of other multifunction units combine plain-paper fax, laser printer, copier, phone, answering machine, and modem. Units like the Hewlett-Packard OfficeJet All-in-One enable you to produce color documents as a printer, fax, scanner, or copier, and it sells for under $600.

The disadvantage of buying a multifunction machine is that one component, the printer or copier, for example, may become too small or inefficient to meet your growing needs. Instead of having to a replace just this component, you will have to replace your unit to replicate your capabilities. Also, if, for example, the fax component needs to be sent in for repair, you will lose your printing, copying, answering machine, and other capabilities as well.

 Tip: To consolidate, use ISDN

To get multiple uses from your phone line, you can have an ISDN line installed. One ISDN (that is short for Integrated Service Data Network) line enables you to have two telephone lines on the same line. There is a hefty installation fee for an ISDN line, and the monthly rate is higher but not as high as paying for multiple lines separately. Talk to your phone company.

COMPUTERS

You can think of a computer as your staff-in-a-box, the equivalent of having four or five people working for you, enabling you to perform many of the tasks a secretary, bookkeeper, receptionist, marketing manager, business planner, and tax advisor would do for you. The right computer and software can keep your overhead down and your profits up in the following ways:

- If you're working alone, add a computer and you can double or even triple business without hiring staff.

- If you're working with a secretary as your only employee, add a computer and you may never need to hire additional staff.

- If you're working with a secretary and a bookkeeper, add a computer and your staff of two can do the work of three or more.

Clearly computers have become like telephones: a staple of office life. Your choices today for finding a computer or computer network that meets your needs are more abundant than ever before. In addition to a variety of standard desktop models, you also have a rich array of notebook computers as well as subnotebooks, palmtops, and personal organizers to choose among.

A notebook computer will not only fit in a briefcase, but many are sufficiently powerful to run your entire business from home on the road, or on your clients' premises. Also a considerable fraction of the power of your desktop computer can now fit in the palm of your hand, or at least in your purse, by using a mini-notebook, palmtop, pocket organizer, or personal digital assistant.

Mini-notebooks are lighter and smaller than notebooks, weighing 1.8 to 3 pounds with some only slightly more than an inch high yet can feature Pentium processing power, a full keyboard, and most everything you'd find in the much larger desktop machines.

Palmtops are smaller and less expensive than mini-notebooks, have even smaller screens, more cramped keyboards, and less than full-powered processors, but some run a scaled-down version of Windows called Windows CE. This allows you to create memos, reports, and spreadsheets that can be easily imported into full-featured Windows programs. You can also check E-mail and surf the Web with a palmtop.

PDAs (Personal Digital Assistants) fit into your pocket and purse and enable you to keep track of your calendar, appointments, address book, notes, memos, and planning. Using a PC link, you can transport data to and from your desktop and you can back up data as well as add functions with RAM cards.

If you want a small computer that can go with you when you leave your home office, compare the models you're considering with the criteria we set for desktops and notebooks and come as close as you can, compromising on those features that make the least difference to you and what you need it to do.

Features-to-Look-for Checklist: Desktop Computers

❑ *Operating system.* Current choices include the latest version of Windows, Windows NT, MAC, and UNIX. DOS with Windows is the most popular operating system at this time for home-office and home-business purposes.

❑ *Processor.* The equivalent of your computer engine, processor choices for Windows and Windows NT today include Pentium, Pentium with MMX, and Pentium II, each being progressively more powerful.

❑ *Processing speed.* Although a variety of factors affects the speed at which your software will run, not all processors operate at the same speed. Each has a processing speed that is measured in megahertz (MHz). The higher the speed, the faster it will run. Aim for at least 200MHz to 233MHz.

❑ *Disk drives.* We recommend having a floppy-disk drive (3.5 inches). You also need a hard-disk drive capable of storing a minimum of 1.2 gigabytes (GB) of data. If you underestimated the disk space you need, however, you can buy software utilities that will compress the size of files and free up additional space; however, to then access the files, you have to decompress them. Of course, you can also scrap an old hard drive and buy and install a bigger one. Disk-drive speed, measured in milliseconds (ms), is also important. Most manufacturers are using drives under 16 ms. Try to get an access speed of 12 ms or less.

❑ *CD ROM drive.* CD ROM drives are a must these days. Almost every new desktop system is sold with a CD ROM as standard equipment. Try to obtain one that will perform as quickly as possible. Today's standard is 24X (times) sampling, although 100X sampling and beyond devices are just around the corner.

❑ *Random Access Memory (RAM).* Absolute minimum memory for today's business software is 16MB; however, we recommend 32MB. You can always add additional megabytes of RAM fairly inexpensively.

❑ *Ports.* You need at least two serial (RS 232) ports for accessories like an external modem, a mouse, a label printer, or business card scanner and one parallel port for your printer. Within limits, additional ports can be added.

❑ *Expansion slots.* Vacant expansion slots make it possible for you to expand the capacity of your computer internally—for example, by adding network communications, a television card, or advanced sound card, so that you can keep pace with technological advances without having to buy an entirely new computer. Three or four open slots should be adequate.

❑ *Footprint.* The size and shape of PCs vary widely from standard desktop models that average about 6 inches high by 21 inches wide by 16.5 inches deep to small-

(Continued on page 221)

(Continued from page 220)

er footprints that are about 4 inches. Slimlines are a couple of inches shorter, and towers and minitowers save desk space by sitting on the floor.

❏ *Video performance.* The video adapter or video card that comes standard with your computer is what links your computer's processor to the monitor. Most users require a PCI video card that has at least 2 MB of RAM on board. If you plan on working with a lot of graphics or animation, we recommend a 3D card with at least 4MB of S-G-RAM. CPU speed and, of course, the monitor you select also have a major impact on video quality.

❏ *Sound-capability.* Most machines today come standard with a set of speakers and a 16-bit sound card of some sort. If you plan on using your computer for heavy-duty sound recording or multimedia purposes, you have to do some in-depth research on the many high-quality options available.

❏ *Modem.* Machines today come standard with at least a 33.6K modem/fax card. If you can, try to get a system with a 56K modem, which is slightly faster.

❏ *Software or peripherals,* such as the latest version of Windows, various office programs, and a mouse, are included in the price.

❏ *Low noise.* Noise is caused by the cooling fan inside the system's unit, and if it's too loud, it can become an ongoing subtle source of irritation.

❏ *Service.* Everything that runs breaks, so select a computer that has local or on-site service.

❏ *Warranty.* Get a computer with a reputation for reliability, and one with a twelve-month or longer warranty. To double your warranty up to another twelve months, purchase your equipment with Gold MasterCard, Visa, or American Express. We advise doing this even if you have to pay an additional small percentage of the sales price to cover the dealer's bank charge.

❏ *A toll-free hot line* to manufacturer for free technical assistance for as long as possible and ongoing Web support. Expect to pay a fee after the initial free support runs out.

❏ *Understandable and complete documentation* that tells you how to set up and use the computer.

Features-to-Look-for Checklist: Monitors

❑ *Resolution.* The better the resolution on your monitor, the sharper the image and the easier on your eyes. Most PCs sold today are equipped to support monitors with SVGA graphics, which provide at least 1024 x 768 at a 75 Hz refresh rate. Graphics and multimedia are more satisfactorily rendered at resolutions starting at 1280 x 1024 lines of resolution refreshed at 114Hz.

❑ *Size.* As the resolution of monitors increases, so does the size. But the larger the monitor, the more dramatic the increases in price. A realistic size for a home office is 15 or 17 inches measured on the diagonal; 20-inch monitors, however, will help reduce eye strain.

❑ *Flicker.* Whether your screen will have a flicker depends on how often the screen is redrawn, or refreshed; this is measured in hertz (Hz). A flicker-free monitor needs what's called a "refresh rate" of no less than 70 to 75Hz.

❑ *Flatness of the screen.* Although no screen is completely flat, the more curved the screen the more distortion there will be at the edges.

❑ *Ergonomic and safety features.* Look for monitors with adjustable tilt-and-swivel stands, front-access controls, and low electromagnetic field emissions that meet Swedish MPRII specifications.

What-to-Look-for Checklist: Where to Buy a Computer

Long ago, if you wanted to buy a computer you went to your friendly local computer store, who provided you with whatever support and service you could get, even repair. Today, you have many additional choices.

You can order directly from manufacturers like Dell, Gateway, Micron, and others by mail order and over their Web sites. (Dell and Gateway even allow you to custom-configure your own system and order it through their Web sites.) You can shop at consumer electronics outlets and national office supply warehouses like Office Depot, Staples, OfficeMax, and computer superstores like CompUSA. They generally don't provide service and support, (leaving that to the manufacturers), or you can buy from "super channel" computer mail-order catalog companies like PC Connection ([800] 800-0004), Micro Warehouse ([800] 367-1080), CompUSA Direct ([800] 669-4727), Insight Computer Systems ([800] 998-8036), and USA/Flex ([800] 477-8323). (These "super catalogs" often offer lowest price guarantees, thirty-day money-back guarantees, as well as other support services of their own.)

(Continued on page 223)

(Continued from page 222)

Here are several factors to consider in deciding where you want to buy your computer:

❑ *Price.* Some sources will meet lowest offers. Mail order is still your best for getting the lowest price. Dealer prices are lowest in big cities.

❑ *Delivery time.* Although some mail-order companies have same-day shipment, others can take one to three weeks for delivery, depending on the product. At a dealership you walk out the door with your computer.

❑ *Money-back guarantee versus hands on.* Usually money-back guarantees are available only through mail and Web order to compensate for the fact that at a dealer you can see and try out the computer firsthand.

❑ *Pre-purchase information.* Some sources are only "order takers." They know little or nothing about the technicalities of the sophisticated products they are selling. Others, especially the ones you encounter when ordering directly from the manufacturer, are highly trained specialists. Also consider whether you have access to product literature.

❑ *Availability of accessories.* Try to buy from a source that will carry the supplies and accessories that you may need later; for example, added memory, cables, or extra batteries. Or be sure you've lined up another source.

❑ *Support.* Manufacturers, in general, will be your main source of support for the equipment you purchase.. All major mail-order manufacturers have technical-support phone lines. Some mail-order dealers do, too. The availability of the support varies, however. Check out the hours: twenty-four hours a day or business hours only; seven days a week or only during the work week. Access time: How long you need to wait on hold. Cost: Is the line toll-free? Do you pay for the call, or is it a 900 number? Some manufacturers also offer on-line support through their Web sites or via E-mail.

❑ *Warranties and repair.* Most computers come with a one-year warranty supplied by the manufacturer. Some dealers offer an extended warranty option. Find out if service will occur at your site, at the local dealer, or if the equipment must be shipped back to the manufacturer. Some local dealers will provide you with a loaner machine while yours is away. What is the turnaround time: same day? next day? two days?

❑ *Credibility and reputation of vendor.* Proceed with caution when getting an incredible deal from an obscure vendor.

How to Keep Your Costs Low and Other Ideas for Getting a Computer When You Can't Afford One

1. Buy a computer with bundled software, provided the software is what you need.

2. Order proven hardware by mail from reputable mail-order companies that have the lowest price offers, but take into account shipping and other charges.

3. Buy a computer that includes peripherals, such as printer and modem, in the purchase price.

4. Buy last year's model, but be sure you will be able to get service, software, and peripheral devices locally.

5. Buy a used computer, after having it checked out. Disk drives are the most likely sources of problems.

6. Buy a factory-reconditioned machine.

7. Comparison-shop. Prices among sources vary.

8. Ask your clients, customers, or employer to buy you a computer or give you one on a lease/purchase basis. Show them how such an arrangement could save them money or otherwise benefit them.

9. Consider leasing.

10. Buy at computer-show prices. Typically, exhibitors will offer special prices if you buy at the show, and these prices are often good.

SOFTWARE: A BARE-BONES HOME OFFICE LIBRARY

Throughout this book we recommend software for just about every aspect of operating a home office, such as word processing, bookkeeping, contact management, voice and data communications, design, and database management. Which of these many kinds you need and which package you'll choose depend entirely on your needs.

Some people build their software library one by one as the need arises. Others go out and buy everything they think they'll need. Still others aren't sure what they'll need, so they get an integrated package, or suite, of programs like Microsoft *Office*, Corel *Professional Office*, or Lotus *SmartSuite*. Such packages include a bundle of software programs that are fully-integrated and perform a number of important business functions such as word processing, spreadsheet, database management, organization, and many more. Whichever approach best suits you, here's what we consider to be the basic software any home office should be using to operate most efficiently and competitively at this time.

- Word processing (All the popular programs include extensive desktop publishing, even Web publishing capabilities)

- Financial management (Your choice: check writing, accounting, or spreadsheet. See chapter 14)

- Contact database (Your choice: mailing list, contact management, information management, time management, or full-fledged database. See chapter 15)

- Communications (Linking you to the on-line world of the information highway. See pages 231-33 in this chapter)

- Tax preparation (with links to your financial management program)

To start building your library you might wish to review the activities your business requires you to spend the most time doing and what percentage of your time is devoted to these activities. Then explore software options to help carry out your most time-consuming activities more quickly and easily.

After you have obtained basic software, you can add software as particular needs or problems arise. For example, when you:

- land an especially large project: project management software could help.

- send out a lot of packages through UPS and you're tired of writing addresses on multiple sheets and labels: most contact managers, such as *ACT!* and *Goldmine,* by Goldmine Software, have built-in label-printing capabilities.

- keep losing track of which E-mail goes with each job: a personal information manager (PIM) such as *Maximer,* by Maximer Technologies, or Lotus *Organizer* allows you to sort and track electronic documents and correspondence just as you would paper files.

- need to link up with your desktop while you're away: A program like Symantec's *pcANYWHERE* lets you call in to your computer at home and work from it on your notebook.

FINDING AND BUYING SOFTWARE

There are a variety of resources designed to help you find programs that meet your needs. Many magazines publish lists of the best-selling software, review new products, and rate software packages. You may want to read reviews of the same packages in several magazines because software reviewers, like movie critics, notice and report on different characteristics and come to different conclusions. User groups, on-line bulletin boards, and searches on the World Wide Web can also be helpful for finding out if there's software that does something you need. You can join the growing numbers of people who shop on the Web both from stores that sell exclusively on line as well as from vendors who operate stores and/or send out mail-order catalogs. In at least one case (Egghead), a former store chain now sells exclusively on the Web (*www.egghead.com*).

If you like to see and touch what you are going to buy, you can go to computer stores like CompUSA or Inca or to office superstores like Office Depot, OfficeMax, and Staples. Of course, you buy from these same stores on line from their Web sites (*www.officedepot.com, www.officemax.com,* and *www.staples.com*). The superstores generally offer free delivery.

If catalog shopping is convenient, there are Micro Warehouse ([800] 367-7080), MacWarehouse ([800] 255-6227), PC Connection ([800] 800-5555 or *www.pcconnection.com*), The PC Zone ([800] 258-2088 or *www.pczone.com*), Tiger Direct ([800] 888-4437 or *www.tigerdirect. com*), and Midwest Micro ([800] 455-9068 or *www.mwmicro.com*), among others. The office superstores have mail-order catalogs, too. You can also order a variety of computer items from catalogs that specialize in computer supplies, like Global Computer Supplies ([800] 227-1246 or *www. globalcomputer.com*) and Inmac ([800] 547-5444 or *www.inmac.com*).

Catalog companies commonly take orders twenty-four hours a day, seven days a week, and some offer overnight delivery and a thirty-day no-risk guarantee, often making mail order one of the cheapest and most efficient ways to buy software.

Sometimes the best way to find the right combination of software is to hire a computer consultant, many of whom are operators of home businesses themselves. A consultant can offer personal, affordable service and advise you as to which packages to select, install them for you, and help you get up and running with them. You can locate computer consultants through the Yellow Pages or contact the Independent Computer Consultants Association (see Resources at the end of this chapter).

Free Software

Public domain software is free. It's been developed by computer enthusiasts who want to share their accomplishments. Alfred Glossbrenner describes public domain software and its availability in his book *How to Get Free Software*.

Features-to-Look-for Checklist: Software Checklist

❑ Does it do what you need?

❑ Reputation (popular proven programs are a sure bet)

❑ Does it avoid things you dislike?

❑ Is what it will do worth the money?

❑ Does it run on your machine?

❑ Does it run quickly enough on your machine?

❑ Will it conflict with anything else on your computer?

❑ Is it easy to learn and use?

❑ Is the documentation clear?

❑ Do the package and the manufacturer have a good reputation?

❑ Is user support provided? How so?

❑ Is this version compatible with older versions you might have?

❑ Toll-free support?

❑ Call-at-your-cost support?

❑ 900 number support?

PRINTERS

You may have noticed that The Well-Equipped Home Office Work Sheet on page 200 includes a laser or ink-jet printer. The reason for this is clear. Laser and laser-quality printers have come down in price so dramatically that no one should sacrifice the professional quality they need as a home-based business. You can get a high-quality ink-jet printer for as low as $200 and a laser for as low as $400. You can even get a color ink-jet printer with near laser quality for a few hundred dollars.

Working from home still results in enough problems with being taken seriously that it just doesn't make sense to look like anything less than the very best—especially when you can look so good, so affordably. So let's talk about how you can have a *Fortune* 500 look without spending a fortune. You have two choices for achieving that top-quality look: a laser or an ink-jet printer.

- Laser printers form their images out of tiny dots. The more dots, the higher the resolution and the better the print quality. The higher the resolution, the more your document looks as though it had been typeset at the print shop instead of on your own printer. Lower-cost laser printers, the ones around $300 to $450, have 300 x 300dpi (dots per square inch), while higher-cost home-office lasers offer 600 x 600dpi to 1,200 x 1,200dpi.

- Ink-jet printers squirt ink directly onto the paper. This means that if you're using paper that absorbs ink, your image may not be quite as sharp. With nonabsorbent paper, the image can smudge right after printing and later if the paper gets wet, although Hewlett Packard has ink-jet printers that don't smudge. Also, ink-jet printers run as low as $200 and have almost as good print quality as the 300dpi lasers. Where ink-jet printers really shine is when it comes to color. You can get beautiful color documents and overheads with ink-jet printers priced as low as $200! Laser color, at as low as $2,500, may still be beyond many home-office budgets at this point but expect this to come down too.

For most business purposes, a 600 x 600dpi printer is fine, so a laser printer like the Hewlett-Packard LaserJet 6Lse will present a most impressive image for your business. Certain businesses like graphics or desktop publishing, resume writing, and word-processing services where the quality of the print image is very important will most likely want a 600dpi printer with image enhancement and extra memory for large graphic images.

If space is a consideration, Alps offers a side-writer line of Micro Dry laser-quality printers that stand only 14 inches high and have a very small footprint.

There are a variety of portable printers available, too, so you can use your notebook to print while on the road. Citizen offers a reasonably priced (less than $200) model, the PN50, that prints on any paper stock.

Here is an encapsulation of features you will want to consider in choosing your printer.

Features-to-Look-for Checklist: Printers

❑ *Print method.* Laser, ink jet, bubble jet.

❑ *Print resolution.* 300dpi, 600dpi, 1,000dpi, 1,200dpi. Postscript option.

❑ *Price.* Typical ink jets run about one-third to half the price of the lower-end lasers. But when considering price, don't forget to factor in the cost of copies (see below). The printers we've been discussing are in the $200 to $800 range.

❑ *Cost of copies.* Cost per black-and-white laser copy typically ranges from 2 to 3 cents per page. For color ink jets, the cost is about 2 cents per page when printing a sheet with 5 percent monochrome coverage and about 13 cents per page when printing a sheet with 15 percent color coverage.

❑ *Speed.* Laser speeds are measured in pages per minute (ppm), with models at the prices we've been discussing ranging from 5 to 12ppm. The typical ink jet will run about half as fast as an entry-level laser. Ink-jet speeds are also measured in pages per minute. Models range from 3 to 8 ppm for black and white and 1.2 to 3 for color.

❑ *Footprint.* Ink jets take up slightly less space than lasers, ranging in size from around 6 to 13 inches high, 13 to 17 inches wide, and 10 to 23 inches deep. If you are tight for space, models do vary in width, height, and depth.

❑ *Memory.* Laser printers come with at least 1MB of random access memory (RAM). Many have 2 to 8 Megabytes or more. The amount of memory affects not only the speed of your printer, but also what type of printing you can do. For a full page of graphics, you need at least 2MB (think ads, presentations, and overheads). For Postscript, you need a minimum of 3 to 4MB; 4 to 8MB is better. You can always add memory, but memory upgrades often run more than it would have cost to purchase additional memory initially.

❑ *Paper handling.* Of course, the more paper a printer holds, the less often you will run out and need to refill it. Ink-jet trays have a standard paper supply of from 100 to 150 sheets. Some have manual feed slots. Lasers have cassettes like copiers that hold from 100 to 250 sheets. Lasers can have manual feed slots, too, which is handy for feeding envelopes, special paper, etc.

❑ *Paper size.* Most laser and ink-jet printers take both letter- and legal-sized paper. A few will accommodate ledger paper.

❑ *Toner cartridges.* Laser toner cartridges generally print from 3,000 to 6,000 pages, depending on the model. Cartridges can be recycled.

(Continued on page 230)

(Continued from page 229)

❏ *Envelope feeders.* Feeding envelopes into printers can be problematical, although just about all lasers can take standard-sized envelopes fed in one by one or in a special envelope cassette. But your software will have to be able to transpose the image vertically. If you need to print a lot of envelopes, get a model with an envelope feeder. They run about $300.

❏ *Color.* Ink jet, thermal heat transfer, laser.

❏ *Warranties and service.* As is true of computers, the best discount prices on printers are offered by mail-order dealers, computer warehouse stores, and office warehouse stores, although local computer dealers also have special discount offers—so watch for ads. Two-year warranties are common, especially for ink jets. Most warranties cover repairs only if you send the printer back to the dealer's or manufacturer's service depot, often a two-week process. Some dealers will do repairs themselves. Fortunately lasers are remarkably reliable. Most leading manufacturers have customer support service lines with specialists who will walk you through problems.

❏ *Documentation.* Look for clear and easy-to-understand instructions, especially for explaining how to install drivers and fonts, and for troubleshooting.

❏ *Manufacturers.* Epson and Hewlett-Packard have dominated the ink-jet market; Hewlett-Packard leads the laser market. There are many other reputable manufacturers, too.

SCANNERS

Although certainly not a must for every home office, scanners have uses for everyone. A scanner makes it possible to get an image from a piece of paper into your computer and incorporate it into reports, proposals, presentations, newsletters and flyers, even Web sites.

There are three basic configurations for scanners: flatbed, sheetfed, and handheld. With prices on flatbed scanners coming so far down (some as low as $100), the only reason to use a sheetfed or handheld is if your space is severely limited. If you haven't seen one, flatbed scanners are about 12 inches wide by about 18 inches deep. You can scan images and text from almost any source—books, flyers, photographs, etc.—by placing them directly on a glass platen, similar to a copy machine. The scanner will scan the image in full color and send it to a graphics program where you edit it and then import it into a word-processing, desktop publishing, or other program.

As with printers, scanner resolution, or quality, is determined in dots per inch (dpi). The greater the dpi, the better the image resolution and the more expensive the machine. If you only need to scan images for inclusion into documents that you will print using your laser or ink-jet printer, or will use in multimedia presentations or on a Web site, a 300 x 300dpi color scanner will do just fine. If you plan to use a scanner as part of a graphic-design or other business where image resolution needs to be of print quality, you will need a scanner of much higher resolution, at least 1,200 x 1,200 dpi.

One particularly useful type of scanner is a business card scanner like CardScan for the IBM pocket-sized PC. These little devices instantly update business card information into your database address book. You simply insert the business cards you collect into the scanner and it picks up and places the pertinent information in your contact management database.

Scanners can be obtained from all the sources we listed for computer systems. The same tips and cautions apply as well.

ONLINE ACCESS

With a modem communication software and an on-line service or Internet Service Provider, your computer becomes a research library, message delivery service, and a communications center to the world. A modem which now comes bundled into virtually all computers is the doorway to the Information Highway, it links you to the World Wide Web and other online services. The key feature to look for in a modem is speed, measured in kilobytes per second (Kbps). At the time of this writing 33.6Kbps is the standard modem speed. 56Kbps modems, providing a seemingly much faster speed, are available, but none seem to be performing at anywhere near that speed. Just remember, no matter what the going rate, the faster the better.

A cable modem, available through your local cable company, offers the fastest access to the Internet for the money. But at this writing cable access is available to only 10% of U.S households.

An Internet Service Provider (ISP) gives you the software and inter-connectivity you need to go on line, either for a straight monthly fee, or a per-hour charge, depending on the company or plan you select. Through an ISP, your modem makes a local call into their system. Their computer then connects you to the Internet itself. This is done so quickly and easily it will appear seamless to you. There are basically two kinds of ISPs:

Straightforward ISPs

These companies provide no-frills access to the Internet and give you at least one E-mail account. They are often very easy to use and are generally cheaper per month than the on-line services; however, they don't begin to offer the informational and networking resources of on-line service providers. Well known ISPs include Earthlink (Web: *www.earthlink.net*; phone: 800-395-8425), MindSpring (Web: *www.mindspring.com*; phone: 800-719-4660), and NTR.NET Corporation (Web: *www.ntr.net*; phone: 800-962-3750).

On-line Service Providers

On-line service providers offer a gateway into the Internet in addition to a plethora of their own information resources, discussion groups, bulletin boards, and much more. On-line service providers are part library, part newsstand, part broadcast network, and part town square and meeting place. The original content they provide is unique and separate from the Internet itself and can only be accessed by "members." Monthly fees and hourly charges tend to be higher for on-line service providers than for ISPs.

The "big four" on-line service providers include:

- America Online (Web: *www.aol.com*; phone: 800-827-6364)

- CompuServe (Web: *www.compuserve.com*; phone: 800-848-8990)

- Microsoft Network (Web: *www.msn.com*; phone: 800-386-5550)

- Prodigy (Web: *www.prodigy.com*; phone: 800-776-3449)

 Features-to-Look-for Checklist: Choosing an ISP*

The right ISP can make your on-line life much easier and give you the most conducive set of services for the money you have to spend. How do you begin? The first thing to do is to identify your own needs in terms of services. Then determine how much you can comfortably afford to spend each month on your connection. Your ISP answer lies between these two points.

Use the following criteria when assessing the merits of national and local ISPs:

❏ **Price** There are almost as many pricing plans as there are ISPs. First and foremost, make sure the ISP offers you a local access phone number, or toll free number, to dial the service. If the dial-up access number is a long-distance or toll call, look elsewhere. Secondly, consider the ISP's price plan carefully. Many ISPs offer plans like five hours for $9.95 and $2.95 for each additional hour. If you only plan to spend five hours a month online, these are good options. If you

(Continued on page 233)

(Continued from page 232)

think your time online will probably be more, you may wish to consider a plan that offers more hours, or better yet, unlimited hours for a single monthly fee. America Online, for example, offers unlimited access time for $19.95 per month.

❏ *Online Resources.* Many local and national ISPs offer unlimited access time for generally lower monthly fees. The interfaces they provide are usually not as complete or user-friendly as those of the big four. If you are fairly computer savvy, these plans might be right for you. You will enjoy looking for the additional software required to fully access all of the Internet, such as a browser, browser "plug-ins" for multimedia, etc., E-mail program, Newsgroup reader, FTP, and more. But if you are new to computers or don't have the time to configure your on-line environment, you may want to turn to one of the "big four" on-line service providers. They provide easy-to-use, all-in-one interfaces that include all the software required to handle Internet navigation and E-mail. They also provide extensive original content as described in the above section. As competition for your on-line dollar becomes fiercer, we predict the monthly and hourly fees of the big four will come down.

❏ *Dependable connection.* Look for an ISP that provides connections at a number of modem speeds. The current standard of 33.6Kbps is quickly being replaced by the faster 56Kbps, and many telephone companies are offering good rates for home-based ISDN (an even faster connection, up to 128Kbps, that requires a special phone line) lines. An ISP should offer connections at any of these rates. Ask the ISP how many subscribers they have and what their "customer to modem" ratio is. This refers to how many customers are routed through each modem in the company's system. The more customers per modem, the slower your access time will be, and the more frequently you will encounter a busy signal when trying to access the provider. Look for a customer-to-modem ratio of no higher than 12 to 1.

❏ *Service.* Find out about the ISP's customer service logistics. Do they have an 800 phone number for technical support? Do they have on-line support where you can ask technical questions of a live support person? The big four have comprehensive support logistics as do the larger, national ISPs like Earthlink.

Once you've found an ISP that's right for you, a simple phone call will allow you to open an account with them. The company will usually then ship you a software package which you will install. You will then be ready to conquer the online world.

* From our book Making Money With Your Computer at Home, 2d edition (Tarcher/Putnam)

COPY MACHINES

When we first started working from home, the smallest copy machines were bigger than most closets and way outside the budget of a fledgling home office. But all told, we undoubtedly spent the equivalent of several years in time traveling to and from copy stores, waiting in line, and groaning over copies flecked with spots from overused and smudged machines. Now, not only can you get a copy machine the size of a briefcase for under $300, but laser printers have become so affordable, fast, and of sufficient quality that some people are simply bypassing copiers altogether. Others are even opting to let their faxes do double duty as copiers.

Yet, in many situations there is truly no substitute for having your own copier. First, your fax can only meet the most minimal of copy needs, and using your laser printer has only limited usefulness. In fact, it can tie up your printer, wear out your cartridge faster, and ultimately slow you down as photocopiers generally produce more pages per minute. And, of course, you can't use your printer to make copies of anything that isn't already in your computer without taking the time and energy to scan it in.

The price and size of minicopiers are dropping while their features are expanding. It doesn't take many trips to the copy store to pay for a copier. For example, let's say your time is worth $25 an hour and it takes you thirty minutes to get to the copy store, wait in line, make your copies, and return home. If you do that only three times a week, you'll pay for the copier in just over ten weeks!

You can get a minicopier for as little as $300 or as much as several thousand, depending on the number of copies you need to make and the features you want. Quality minicopiers in all price ranges make excellent copies, as good as or better than those you get at the copy store. They are surprisingly easy to use, reliable, and require virtually no maintenance. On the average, making your own copies will run you about 4 to 5 cents each, less than most copy stores charge for one or a low volume of copies. Cartridges, however, are not cheap, running around $75, and need to be replaced after about 1,500 to 4,000 copies, depending upon the model of copier.

Popular lines of minicopiers include Canon, Minolta, Sharp, and Xerox. Which one will be best for you generally depends on how many copies you need and the type of documents you're reproducing. The very low volume copiers that cost as little as $300 have minimal features, but if you need to make only a few copies a week and usually require limited numbers of copies for each document, these copiers can serve you adequately. The Canon PC320, for example, is one of the smallest copiers (costing around $400) and weighs about sixteen pounds.

If you need to make over 500 copies a month or even a few copies of many-paged documents, this is still considered low-volume in the copier world, but you'll need one of the more sophisticated models. These copiers run around $1,500 to $3,000 and can produce from 800 to 3,500 copies per month, but they are definitely desktop copiers with a home-office-sized footprint. There are many models in between with a variety of features. Here's what to look for:

Features-to-Look-for Checklist:
Copiers for Under 1,000 Copies a Month

❏ *Quality of copy.* Produces high-quality copies on plain paper as well as on different weights of paper such as letterhead, card stock, label sheets, and transparencies. Copy quality varies, so take in samples of the types of originals you will be copying and try them out.

❏ *Recommended maximum volume.* Be sure the model you buy is designed to produce the volume of copies you expect to make each month. Otherwise, you could damage the machine. It's true. We did it. Late one night we pushed our machine beyond the call of duty for an early-morning meeting and although it finished the job, it was never the same! Models range from 500 to 3,500 copies.

❏ *Copy speed.* Quoted speeds are based on continuous copying of 8.5-by-11-inch paper from an original. Good low-volume copiers usually make around twelve to twenty copies per minute. But if you most frequently make just one copy, the speed you're most interested in is the time involved in making the first copy. This can range anywhere from five to twelve seconds.

❏ *Ease of use.* Make sure the control panel keys and the means of getting the toner into the copier are easy to use. Copiers with toner cartridges are much more convenient than those requiring you to load toner from a bottle. Not all cartridges are as easy to use as others, however. The easiest are single user-replaceable cartridges.

❏ *Type of cartridge.* Most copier cartridges simply replace the toner. Others involve periodic serving of other elements. Canon, however, has a Single Cartridge System: each cartridge includes not only the toner but also the drum and the development unit, making their copiers virtually service free. Each time you replace the cartridge, you're essentially getting a new copier.

❏ *Reliability.* Sources of information on reliability are the User Ratings of Copiers by Datapro Research Corporation, Copier Selection Guide with Durability Ratings by Buyers Laboratory, Inc., and What to Buy for Business.

(Continued on page 236)

(Continued from page 235)

❑ *Readily available service.* You should receive some sort of service guarantee with your purchase. Service is either on-site, or carry-in.

❑ *Moving or stationary platen.* The top of lower-priced copiers often moves back and forth while making a copy. The copies are just as good, but the machine requires more space than is immediately apparent.

❑ **Reduction and enlargement capability.**

❑ **Paper input tray capacity.** Models range from 50 to 250.

❑ **Cartridge life.** Generally from 1,500 to 3,000 copies.

❑ **Manual light and darkness adjustment.**

❑ **Multiple paper trays for different sizes of paper.**

❑ **Automatic document feeder.** A rare feature on a desktop copier.

Buying a Used Copier

Be aware of some common buzzwords in selling used copiers. A "refurbished" copier has received a good cleaning and some new paint. A "reconditioned" machine has been newly painted and upgraded internally to match the manufacturer's new products. A "remanufactured" copier has gone back to the factory assembly line and had all worn parts replaced, in addition to getting a new paint job and internal enhancements. You decrease your chances of buying someone else's troubles with a remanufactured copier.

DIGITAL CAMERAS

It's well known that a picture is worth a thousand words, and most self-employed individuals would love to add color photos to promotional materials. But until lately that has been too costly to do as much as you might like to. No longer. Not with a digital camera. By teaming a digital camera with your computer and a color ink-jet printer, you can pop promotional photos on postcards, business cards, and flyers You can put photos in proposals, newsletters, and brochures and even print them on glossy paper. You can show your stuff to the world by posting photos on your Web site or E-mailing them to those you want to impress.

If you're not familiar with the technology, digital cameras allow you to snap a picture that's completely within the digital realm. The image you capture is stored as a digital file (primarily .jpg) that can be instantly viewed on a computer, included within a word-processing or desktop-publishing document, or incorporated into a Web site. There is no need to scan an image taken with a digital camera; it's already scanned.

These cameras function in much the same way as traditional film cameras, except that there's no film. Images are stored directly in the camera's internal memory. You still must set the focus, lighting, and other parameters associated with traditional photography. If you're no pro at getting the perfect shot, don't despair. The newer digital cameras have a built-in liquid crystal display that will allow you to see the image just as you've captured it and discard shots until you get ones you like that show you in action, highlight your products, or feature your satisfied customers.

When you get a shot that looks promising, using image-editing software like Adobe's *Photoshop* or *PhotoDeluxe,* Microsoft's *Picture It,* or *Kai's Super Goo,* you can crop, enhance, distort, resize, rotate, and recolor your photos to greatest impact. With the new megapixel cameras like Fuji's MX700, Kodak's DC260, or Nikon's Coolpix 900, even amateurs can produce photo-quality shots.

If you're on a tight budget, you'll be pleased to know that prices of digital cameras are dropping while their quality is rising. Prices for megapixel cameras run from $500 to $1,000 yet offer the quality once limited to top-of-line professional cameras costing $2,500 to $15,000 and more. If that still sounds too high, keep in mind that we've interviewed people who are happily making money on their Web sites from shots they've taken of merchandise with $250 to $300 digital cameras.

Color ink-jet printer prices have dropped dramatically, too, going as low as $250.

The Difference Between a Digital Camera and a Scanner

You can't take a scanner on the floor with you and take pictures of your newest shipment. You can do this with a traditional camera, but you'd then have to send the film to be developed and have the images scanned. With a digital camera you can snap your newest arrivals and have them posted on your Web site within minutes.

Although digital cameras have the considerable advantage of being portable, they don't replace the traditional flatbed scanner. Unless you have a copy stand and considerable patience, digital cameras are an awkward, time-consuming way to capture existing images from books, magazines, and other printed sources. Flatbed scanners far outperform digital cameras when it comes to scanning documents for OCR, or text recognition, purposes as well.

If you're no techie, getting your images from the camera to your computer has become easier, too, although it can still be a chore for a novice. But to circumvent this challenge, Fuji and Kodak have film-processing centers where you can "pick up" your photos on paper, on disk, or via E-mail.

If you don't have your own Web site and don't want to spend the time, money, or expense to create one, you can have your photos posted on line for thirty days on an access-protected site through services like Fujifilm.Net or Kodak's PhotoNet. This means you could set up an on-line exhibit and invite prospective clients or customers to come take a look.

WHAT TO LOOK FOR: DIGITAL CAMERAS

The main reasons for a general business to purchase a digital camera are inventory cataloguing and enhancing graphic presentations. Unless you have a graphics-intensive business, you will not need a camera offering the highest resolution; the Web and most business printers still don't support it. Because image resolution is fairly low, especially as compared with traditional 35mm cameras, you also don't need to be too concerned about lens quality.

The features you do need to be concerned about are similar to those within the digital world in general: memory, storage capacity, and pixel resolution. When you take a picture with a digital camera the image is stored in a digital format, either in internal memory or in some sort of removable memory. Many camera manufacturers use the CompactFlash flash memory card. Memory capacity is expressed in Megabytes (MB). Look for cameras that offer at least 2MB of memory. This will allow you to store approximately thirty-five to fifty images in "economy" (low resolution) mode or about ten images in standard quality (passable resolution) mode.

Although resolution is much lower, in general, than that of traditional cameras, look for a camera that provides a minimum resolution of 1040 x 768 pixels, 24-bit color in high quality modes.

Also look for a camera that comes with photo-finishing or image-editing software. The software should not allow you to manipulate your images but will download them easily from your camera's memory into your computer.

Viewfinders on digital cameras are much more like video camcorders than traditional cameras. Your subjects are presented to you on a small screen. After your image has been captured, you view it instantly on the screen. Many cameras will allow you to do some rudimentary image editing on the spot using the same screen. To reduce eyestrain and improve image quality, the camera should have an LCD screen no smaller than 1.8 inches.

Minimum Specification for a General-Business-Use Digital Camera

- *Memory:* 2MB

- *Resolution:* 1040 x 768 pixels, 24-bit color

- *Storage:* 50 frames in "economy" mode, 10 frames in "standard" mode

- *Lens:* glass lens

- *Focal length:* 7.9 inches to infinity

- *Viewing screen:* 1.8 inches or larger LCD color

- *Software:* Image editing/photo finishing software that also allows images to be ported to a computer. Also make sure it has a TWAIN driver for PCs.

RESOURCES: HOME-OFFICE EQUIPMENT AND ACCESSORIES

A List of Vital and Helpful Peripherals, Accessories, and Utilities for Protecting Your Equipment and Data

• *Be safe: back up.* You don't have to hassle with backing up all your data on floppy disks or on a cumbersome tape drive. The easiest and surest way to back up your disk drive just in case it should crash is to add a removable hard drive to your computer onto which you can back up significant chunks of your entire drive. For example Iomega's popular Zip (100 MB of storage) and Jaz (1 GB of storage) drives and Syquest's SyJet (1.5 GB of storage) allow you to store quite a bit of data onto removable cartridges.

• *Don't lose files from a goof-up.* So you hit the wrong key. All that work is gone. Not necessarily. Get a file-recovery utility like *Norton Utilities, PC Tools,* or *MacTools.* It may save you from a disaster.

• *Diagnose the problem.* When something's gone wrong with your computer, you may be able to find and correct the problem yourself. Before calling for help, use programs like TouchStone's *CheckIt* to search out and correct the problem if they can.

• *Immunize your computer from getting a virus.* Get virus-protection software like Norton *AntiVirus* and run all new software through it before loading it into your computer. New viruses develop and spread quickly, especially if you spend a lot of time on line. You will have to update your virus checker often.

• **Don't lose it all when the lights go out.** Get a backup power supply, called an uninterruptible power supply (UPS). Basically it's a battery that will keep your computer running when the electricity goes out, for anywhere from five minutes to an hour. It at least gives you the chance to save what you're working on and turn off your system.

• **Surge protector.** Don't allow a power surge to fry your equipment. Protect it with a surge protector like the Filtered Strip SP-700, by Curtis Manufacturing (sold where office supplies are sold or call [800] 321-5386). The SuperMax 6 All Path Protection Platform is modular and has under- as well as overvoltage protection. This device is sold at office-supply and electronic stores or you can call Panamax (800) 472-5555. You can also get a whole-house surge suppressor mounted on your breaker panel, as a snap-in circuit breaker or as an electric meter socket adapter. Prices range from $75 to $500.

• **Don't let valuable data go up in smoke.** Keep disks or backup disks safe from fire with the Security Chest by Sentry. It will store up to sixty 3.5-inch disks in a fireproof, heat-proof, humidity-proof safe that will protect them in temperatures up to 1,550 degrees Fahrenheit for a half hour.

HANDY HELPERS

• **Share your printer.** You and your partner or assistant can share a single printer with an auto switch or a manual switch available from most computer supply catalogs and stores.

• **Network your home office computers.** Setting up a small network so your office computers can share applications and files is fairly easy and cost-effective. Products from Netgear and ArtiSoft's LANtastic are great low-cost solutions.

TRAVELING WITH YOUR OFFICE

• **Pack your office for the road.** Pack your notebook, portable printer, disks, and cellular phone in one handy briefcase like the Galizia Compac-Case, an office in a briefcase ([800] 883-2273). Or pick out one of the Kensington notebook carrying cases ([800] 535-4242) that come in various sizes, depending on how much of your office you want to take with you.

• **Retrieve faxes while you're away.** COMMUNICATE! from 0/1 Communique, Inc., allows faxes to be stored in your computer while you are away so you can retrieve through a data/fax/voice card anywhere you might be.

• *Make labels the easy way.* Seiko's line of smart label printers quickly prints labels on up to two-inch-wide labels.

KEEP YOUR EQUIPMENT CLEAN AND IN WORKING ORDER

• *Eliminate cord clutter.* Keep the space behind and beneath your desk from looking like a cord jungle with a cord manager like Rip-Tie from The Rip-Tie Co. ([800] 348-7600), which neatly bundles cords with Velcro strips.

• *Clean equipment inside and out.* Keep all your office equipment looking good and working well with Dust-Off Office Care Kit, which contains eight items for cleaning your phone, computer, keyboard, monitor, laser printer, and fax (Falcon Safety Products [908] 707-4900).

DO IT YOURSELF

• *Tinker tools.* Sometimes documentation on office equipment will tell you to turn a screw or change a knob, or you may be so bold as to replace a chip or install a card or new drive. The MiniKit by Jensen Tools should be in your desk drawer for just such times. It's a little zippered-case tool kit filled with twenty tiny home-office electronics-sized screwdrivers, pliers, and the like ([800] 426-1194).

BOOKS

Build Your Own Multimedia PC: A Complete Guide to Renovating and Constructing Personal Computers. Ian Robertson Sinclair. Portsmouth, N.H.: Butterworth-Heinemann, 1997. ISBN: 0750628553.

Computer Guide: Personal Computer Reference and Training. Charles Portland. Portland Publishing, 1997. ISBN: 0965592405.

Computer Telephony: Automating Home Offices and Small Businesses. Ed Tittel and Dawn Rader. San Diego: Ap Professional, 1996. ISBN: 0126914117.

The Hand-Me-Down PC: Upgrading and Repairing Personal Computers. Morris Rosenthal. New York: McGraw-Hill Computing, 1997. ISBN: 007053523X.

How to Use Computers. Lisa Biow. Emeryville, Calif.: Ziff Davis, 1997. ISBN: 1562765663.

The Indispensable PC Hardware Book: Your Hardware Questions Answered. Hans-Peter Messmer. Reading, Mass.: Addison-Wesley, 1997. ISBN: 0201403994.

Internet Research Companion. Geoffrey W. McKim. Indianapolis: Que Education & Training, 1997. ISBN: 1575760509.

Making Money with Your Computer at Home. Paul and Sarah Edwards. New York: Tarcher/Putnam, 1997. ISBN: 0874778980.

PC Magazine Computer Buyer's Guide (annual). Emeryville, Calif.: Ziff Davis. ISBN: 1562764349.

Outfitting Your Home Business for Less. Walter Zooi, Paul and Sarah Edwards. New York: AMACOM Books, 1998.

MAGAZINES

Computer Shopper. Ziff-Davis, 1 Park Ave., New York, NY 10016. *www.zdnet.com*

Home Office Computing. Scholastic, Inc., 555 Broadway, N.Y., NY. The periodical for home-based businesspeople, covering both business and technology. *www.smalloffice.com*

MacUser. Ziff-Davis (for full citation, see above, under Computer Shopper).

NetGuide magazine. CMP Publications, 600 Community Drive, Manhasset, NY 11030. *www.netguide.com*

PC/Computing. Ziff-Davis (see above).

PC magazine Ziff-Davis (see above).

Windows magazine. CMP Publications, 600 Community Drive, Manhasset, NY 11030. *www.winmag.com*

MAIL-ORDER EQUIPMENT CATALOGS

Computer Discount Warehouse: (800) 599-4239

Insight Computer Systems: (800) 998-8036

Micro Warehouse: (800) 367-7080

PC Connection: (800) 800-0004

USA/Flex: (800) 477-8323

MAIL-ORDER SOFTWARE CATALOGS

MacWarehouse: (800) 255-6227

Micro Warehouse: (800) 367-7080

The PC Zone: (800) 258-2088

PowerUp Direct: (800) 851-2917

COMPUTER HARDWARE AND SOFTWARE DIRECTORIES

Directories Available in the Reference Section of Libraries:

Business Software Directory. Published by Learned Information.

Datapro–McGraw-Hill Guide to Apple Software. Published by Datapro Research Corporation.

Datapro–McGraw-Hill Guide to IBM Software. Published by Datapro Research Corporation.

ON-LINE COMPUTER INFORMATION AND RESOURCES:

Buysmart. Advice ranging from how to buy a color printer to choosing the best long-distance carrier. *www.buysmart.com*

Computer.com. CNET's information for a wide variety of digital equipment: from computers to digital cameras. *www.computer.com*

CNET. A daily news service that covers computing and on-line issues and new technologies. Also includes product reviews and buyer's guides. *www.cnet.com*

MacMillan Computer Publishing Online. "The authoritative encyclopedia of computing." *www.cmp.com*

Ziff-Davis Online. Searchable product reviews, buyer's guides, and access to all Ziff Davis's computer publications. *www.zdnet.com*

ON-LINE SHAREWARE LIBRARIES

Melosa. A metasite containing links to over three hundred shareware libraries on the Web.
http://earth.vol.com/~drcello//sharelib.htm
www.jumbo.com
www.shareware.com

ON-LINE DIGITAL PHOTOGRAPHY SITES

File companies with assistance on producing digital images from traditional film: *www.fujifilm.net; www.kodak.com; www.filmworks.com*

Digital camera resources: News and links to reviews. *www.dcresource.com*

Digital photography reviews: Reviews of digital cameras, scanners and imaging software, and digital photography basics, *www.inconference.com/digicam/index.html*

Message board: A user group for digital-photography buffs. *rec.photo.digital*

PHOTO-EDITING SOFTWARE

Adobe Photoshop

Adobe Photodeluxe

Microsoft Picture It

Kai's Super Goo by Metacreations.

ON-LINE PHOTOFINISHING

Fujifilm Album, www.fujifilm.net

PhotoNet Online, www.photonet.com

PictraNet Album, www.pictranet.com

Seattle FilmWorks, www.filmworks.com

TECHNICAL HELP

Independent Computer Consultants Association, 11131 South Towne Square, Ste. F, St. Louis Mo. 63123; phone: (800) 774-4222. Web: *www. icca.org*

PART 3

Protecting Your Assets:
Legal, Tax, and
Insurance Matters

CHAPTER 9

Zoning, Permits, Regulations, and Your Legal Decisions

Goals: Know

1. Which zoning permits and other regulations apply when you're working from home

2. What you can do if you're not zoned to work from home

3. How to set yourself up as a business entity

4. Whether to incorporate or not

5. About trademarks, copyrights, and contracts

6. How to find a lawyer

T he law's made to take care o' raskills," wrote George Eliot in *The Mill on the Floss* in 1860. More recently, home-based businesspeople have come to regard laws, and sometimes their interpretation and administration, as the work of rascals. Although home-based businesses usually do not face all the laws and complicated regulations larger businesses must deal with, they nevertheless encounter regulation from all levels of government.

At the city and county level, zoning, business licenses and permits, and fictitious name registration may shape your business actions. Many cities now require home-based businesses to register and pay a special yearly fee. State law may require you to obtain a professional or occupational license to pursue your chosen work, collect sales tax for your product or service, and prohibit certain types of businesses from being conducted from your home. The federal government requires licenses of specific types of businesses; also, more recent laws, such as the Americans with Disabilities Act (ADA), may apply to your home business.

In this chapter, we'll discuss contracts and whether or not it would be beneficial for you to incorporate your business. We'll also talk about when to consult and how to select a lawyer. The terms we'll be using as we describe these legal issues may be different in your state or locality, but the general principles will be similar.

IS IT LEGAL FOR YOU TO WORK AT HOME? ZONING ORDINANCES, OTHER LAWS, AND RESTRICTIONS

Fortunately with the growing popularity of home business, many communities have updated their zoning regulations during the eighties and nineties to expand their revenue base and encourage economic development. But while zoning restrictions are becoming less problematical in some places, they remain outdated in others.

But in some cities and suburbs the answer to whether it's legal for you to work at home is no, because zoning ordinances often prohibit you from using your home for business purposes. In a few situations, state or federal laws and home association regulations may also limit the business use of your home.

Although zoning originated in Roman times, current ordinances that restrict the business use of homes arose from a desire to protect neighborhoods from the smokestacks of the Industrial Revolution. Some of today's zoning ordinances were written back in Civil War times. Now, over a century later, yesterday's good intentions often no longer apply.

No matter how outdated an ordinance or regulation may be, violating one can be risky business. If you are operating illegally, you may be forced to stop conducting your business, and you will certainly find yourself faced with the discomfort of playing legal hide-and-seek. You may find yourself unable to complain about justifiable problems neighbors are creating, such as noise, for fear they'll retaliate by reporting you. It is essential that you find out whether it is legal for you to work at home and how to register your business.

ARE YOU ZONED TO WORK AT HOME?

Zoning ordinances are created at the city or county level of government and vary widely from one locality to another. In Sierra Madre, California, for example, home businesses are permitted if you take out a business license. In adjacent Pasadena, however, you must apply for a home occupation permit before you can get a business license. In nearby Los Angeles, you must pay an annual registration fee. You can find out about your situation by answering these three questions:

1. *Does your city or county have zoning ordinances?* Some areas of the country, like the city of Houston, do not have zoning. To find out about your area, contact your city or county government. To figure out which department of government is responsible for zoning, use this rule of thumb: If you would call the police in an emergency, you're governed by the city. If you would phone the sheriff, you deal with the county.

Within city or county government, zoning is usually handled by either the Building Inspector or the Planning Department. Otherwise, your area may have a special Zoning Administration you can contact.

2. *How is your property zoned?* Zoning ordinances divide the city or county into four basic classifications: Residential, Commercial, Industrial, and Agricultural. Each of these areas includes further distinctions, such as Residential-Single-Family Units, and Residential-Multiple-Family Units. Also, the types of activities that can be carried out in each area vary by locality. However, certain general observations can be made.

Most home businesses can be operated in an area zoned for agricultural use. After all, farming was the original "home business."

Many cities prohibit any residential use of buildings in an area zoned for industry. This causes problems for work-at-homers like artists who might want to rent warehouses or other industrial buildings to work and live in. A common exception to this restriction allows a guard to work and sleep on a building's premises in order to provide security. Consequently, some artists arrange to work as watchmen by night and painters or sculptors by day.

Most zoning codes allow buildings in commercially zoned areas to be used for both residential and business purposes. In fact, a familiar part of American tradition has been the neighborhood mom-and-pop shop, with the family living upstairs or in the back.

Residential zoning restrictions present the most problems for people working at home. Some localities either allow no business uses in residential areas or limit the nature and scope of business activities that can be done at home. Sometimes communities allow more latitude in multiple-unit residential areas with apartment buildings and condominiums.

To find out which kind of zone you live in, locate your property on the official maps at the government office responsible for zoning. Chances are you live in a residential area and face a number of possible restrictions.

3. *Specifically, what is and is not allowed in your zone?* Nine out of ten localities restrict using residences for offices or businesses in some way, according to a study entitled *Home Occupation Ordinances*, done by Jo Ann

Butler and Judith Getzels for the American Planning Association. Some communities distinguish between a business and a profession.

In such cases, businesses generally cannot operate from a home, but recognized professionals like physicians, lawyers, dentists, musicians, artists, architects, and counselors can maintain home offices. What qualifies as a profession, however, may vary from one locality to another. For example, barber or beauty shops are considered professions in some places but not in others. Photography, real-estate brokerage, interior decorating, dance instruction, and roofing have been classified as businesses by some courts, while the giving of singing and music lessons has usually been found to be a profession.

What particular zoning ordinances restrict and allow reflects the tastes of the local personalities responsible for the ordinances. As a result, contradictions between communities abound. For example, some communities prohibit a separate entrance for a home office; others require it. Irksome restrictions may limit the hours you can work and prohibit using your address in advertising, including Yellow Page listings, and using outside buildings, such as garages, for your office. So before adding or remodeling an outside building for use as a home office, it's important to check your community's zoning and building codes.

Despite many variations in zoning codes, the American Planning Association study found some patterns. The following are the most common restrictions on home offices and home businesses (the percentages represent the percent of communities having the particular restriction):

- Restrictions limiting increases in vehicular traffic (46%)

- Restrictions on use or size of outside signs (42%)

- Restrictions on on-street parking (33%)

- Limitations on employees (33%)

- Limitations on the amount of floor space used (20%)

- Restrictions on retail selling times on the premises (13%)

- Prohibitions on outside storage of materials (11%)

- Restrictions on inside storage of materials (8%)

You can look up the restrictions in your community yourself by going to the office in city hall or the courthouse that administers zoning. If you're on line, you may wish to consult your city's Web site. First, locate your home on a zoning map. This will either be mounted on a wall or contained in a book of zoning maps; it may be a large book. You will find the classification for your home indicated on the map. With this in mind, then read the zoning ordinance or get a copy of the zoning regulations to take with you either free or for a small fee. Read the regulations to determine what specifications apply to the type of zone in which you live and the type of business activities you intend to carry out in your home. This is public information, and you do not have to answer any questions to obtain it.

What Happens When You're Charged with a Zoning Violation

If authorities find you are in violation of a zoning ordinance, they will send you a notice ordering you to stop. After receiving such a notice you must stop or file an appeal immediately, because each day you continue can be a separate violation.

If you do not comply with the order, authorities have two alternatives. Typically, they seek an injunction: an order from the civil court prohibiting you from continuing the violation. As in other civil lawsuits, you will be served with a notice of a hearing and have the opportunity to hire a lawyer or defend yourself. Violating an injunction, once it's issued, puts you in contempt of court and is punishable by fine or imprisonment.

The authorities can also choose to prosecute the violation of a zoning ordinance as a municipal misdemeanor. This type of proceeding is usually a last resort, however. It begins with issuing a warrant or bill of complaint from the municipal court. If found in violation at the ensuing trial, the offender can be fined and/or imprisoned.

WHAT YOU CAN DO IF YOU AREN'T ZONED FOR BUSINESS

Many people living in areas that aren't zoned for business just ignore the law. They figure no one will know and there will probably be no problems. Often this is the case, because zoning officials usually don't have the time to go looking for violators. This is simply a fact, not encouragement to ignore zoning laws. There are many ways of solving zoning problems without violating the law. In any case, officials can find out about violations in a variety of ways.

Most commonly, zoning violations are reported by unhappy neighbors who call with complaints of too much noise, traffic congestion, or cars parked in front of their homes. Feuding neighbors might call just out of spite. This happened to a man in the Pacific Northwest who was operating a contracting company from his home.

Each morning, four or five men would meet at his home office and he would send them out on their assignments for the day. They met inside, were not noisy, and did not congest parking. Yet the neighbors complained, and zoning officials forced the contractor to stop doing business from his home. He then sold his house, moved to another county, and began operating his business from his new home. Pursuing him, his old neighbors checked the zoning regulations, found he lived in another area not zoned for business, and reported him once more. Again he was stopped from doing business.

Obviously, good relations with neighbors are important in avoiding zoning problems. But there are other ways city officials find out about violations. Something as simple as an application for a business license or sales permit can call their attention to violators. A Web site designer who worked from her apartment discovered this the hard way when she tried to lease some new equipment. The lease required that she get a business license, which she did. Subsequently, a report of the license went to the zoning department and she was cited for a violation.

Similarly, the owner of a word-processing service discovered she had to pay state sales tax on some of her services. Applying for a sales tax permit meant the city would be notified of her home business, but failure to apply would put her in the position of violating state law. Too often, ignoring zoning ordinances leads to one of these legal double binds. A journalist even found the zoning inspector at his door within days of having a business telephone installed in his home.

The best strategy is to avoid zoning problems by taking preventive steps. Following are ten ways to prevent problems and to deal with them if they arise.

1. Establish and maintain good relations with neighbors. Find out how your neighbors feel about your working from home. Often neighbors feel safer knowing someone will be in the neighborhood during the day. Some are glad to have your business nearby. When your neighbors are supportive of your work, they can be valuable allies should you need special permits or a variance to work at home.

If they are opposed to your working at home, carefully note their concerns—both those they state explicitly and those you discern from their nonverbal communication. Respond to them positively and nondefensively. Offer assurances and guarantees.

A fear that is often behind neighborhood opposition even when the home business would not create noise and traffic—the two primary concerns neighbors have—is that property values will suffer. The fact is that developers of new upscale homes are now as a matter of course customizing rooms that can be used for home offices. Home offices and higher property values go hand in hand.

Judith Corbett, who successfully obtained a variance after having been cited by Los Angeles's Building and Safety Department, had served her neighbors as the chair of their Neighborhood Watch. As a result, her son was able to get nearly all her neighbors to sign petitions supporting her in getting a variance. A man in another city operates a million-dollar mail-order business from his home in an upscale neighborhood. Big semi trucks make deliveries to his home at least once a week. At his peak season, he has eight employees, but no one complains to the zoning authorities. Why? Every family has had a teenager or stay-at-home mom who has been employed by him at some time.

2. *Know specifically what business activities you can and cannot do* at home and adjust your business to meet the restrictions. If retail sales are prohibited on your premises, for example, distribute your wares through sales representatives, over the Web, or via mail order. If employees other than your immediate family are prohibited from working in your home, contract with an outside secretarial service or have your employees work from their homes instead.

3. *Rent a private mailing address or office suite* to use as your official business address. *Before* doing this, find out if a physical inspection of your business is a prerequisite of obtaining a city business license. Also, over twenty states have consumer protection laws that require any business using a post office box address or private mail-receiving service to disclose in all advertising and promotional materials, including order blanks and forms, the complete street address from which business is actually conducted.

4. *Contact your local Chamber of Commerce.* Chamber staff may know how others have solved similar zoning problems.

5. *Consult with an attorney who specializes in zoning matters* and who wins most of his or her zoning cases. You may be able to get the name of one from staff at the zoning office.

6. *Apply for a use permit,* which will allow you to use your home as a business. You may be able to get a use permit from community officials after an investigation of your business plans and facilities. Use permits usually do not require a public hearing.

7. *Apply for a variance.* You can ask the local zoning board for a waiver of zoning restrictions in your case. Variances are exceptions granted by a zoning board, a planning board, or an appeals board. Variances are escape valves built into the system. No one has an inherent right to a variance, and zoning boards do not like granting them. In fact, boards will only consider variances under certain circumstances. Filing fees are charged to initiate the process. These fees may range from hundreds to thousands of dollars, whether your application is approved or not.

You may have a case if you can show that what you are doing is comparable to a permitted occupation. For example, someone tutoring children in how to use computers might be able to show how this new occupation is similar to teaching children to play the piano, which has traditionally been allowed at home.

You also may have a case if you can show that literal enforcement of the ordinance would deprive you of your livelihood and cause a hardship for you. For example, a single parent with three small children at home might be able to show that there is no other way either to provide or to care for the children.

Finally, you may have a case if you can show that there would be no harm done to the neighborhood or larger community. Because getting a variance requires a public hearing, such an approach is often your best bet. Poll your neighborhood. Find out how people feel about your working at home. Honor their concerns, get them on your side, and bring them to the hearing. If many neighbors come out to support you, and no one opposes you, it certainly will help.

Public support from people other than your neighbors can also make a difference. For six years after he retired as first violinist of the Boston Symphony, Herman Silberman taught violin in his condominium in San Diego, California. Then the homeowners' association reported his business to zoning authorities and they ordered him to cease and desist from teaching in his home.

Silberman's students, however, effectively used the appeals process and obtained a variance so he could continue offering his lessons. They circulated a petition on his behalf and won over the six-person planning commission.

Learning the history and operations of the planning commission or zoning authority deserves your attention as well. Identify the members and review their voting records to discover what they usually allow and what they deny. Attend zoning board meetings on other cases to see how the hearings are conducted, how the board operates, and who is most influential.

In larger communities, board members may represent special political or economic interests. In smaller communities, the people on the zoning boards are generally citizens like yourself. Whatever the size of your community, understanding the board members should help you build the best case for yourself.

Regardless of how well prepared you are, it's wise to consult an attorney. Legal expertise can help you in evaluating your situation and planning your appeal.

8. *Get your community's zoning ordinance amended.* Since some zoning ordinances are still antiquated, you might consider mobilizing other home businesses in your community to get the ordinances amended. Artists in Los Angeles and New York, for example, successfully mobilized to get changes in zoning that allow them to live and work in studios located in industrial areas.

David Hughes of Colorado Springs, Colorado, rallied residents using his computer bulletin board. The result was that nearly two hundred people packed a city council meeting and a more permissive ordinance ended up being passed than the one that had been headed for enactment.

When Ron Miller's wife wanted to start providing translation services in her Melbourne, Florida, home, he checked their zoning and found that the city prohibited home-based businesses. He went to the city manager, who wrote Ron, "The prohibition has been carefully reviewed by City Council twice in recent years, and both times the Council has voted to make no changes." Ron then went to work. He wrote a draft ordinance for the city council, obtained statistical information, and found that 12 percent of the county's population worked at home. He collected copies of all ordinances regulating home occupations from nearby cities; he wrote thoughtful letters to the council members after each vote. A major story on his battle was printed in a local weekly newspaper. He enlisted the support of the local home-business association. In the end, by a 6-to-1 vote, Melbourne voted to allow home-based businesses.

Ways to locate fellow open-collar workers in your area are through civic organizations, professional and trade associations, Yellow Pages, local newspaper advertising, and on line through forums and newsgroups and utilizing search engines (using popular home-based occupations and your city as search terms). You can join together to propose an amendment either through the zoning commission or directly to your city council or county legislature.

In drawing up the proposed amendment, enlist the help of a lawyer who believes in your cause.

The box below lists the types of provisions a reasonable zoning code might include. You can use these as guidelines for proposing an ordinance, or for reviewing a proposed ordinance or amendments to an existing code.

9. Get a change in state law. This is based on the fact that states regulate their cities and counties. Vermont was the first state to require its cities to allow home-based businesses and Oregon was the second. Vermont's law is short and to the point:

> Protection of home occupations. No regulation [referring back to local zoning] may infringe upon the right of any resident to use a minor portion of a dwelling for an occupation which is customary in residential areas and which does not change the character thereof. 24 V.S.A. 4406(3).

As the number of people working from home continues to grow, the political climate will be ripe for similar laws in many states.

Reasonable Provisions for Zoning Regulations of Home Offices

1. The home office or business is clearly secondary to the use of the dwelling as a residence and does not change the residential character of the dwelling or the lot in any visible manner.

2. The work done in the home office or business creates no objectionable odor, noticeable vibration, or offensive noise that increases the level of ambient sound at the property lines.

3. The home office or business does not cause unsightly conditions or waste visible off the property.

4. The home office or business does not cause interference with radio or television reception in the vicinity.

5. The home office or business has no more than two full-time employees who are not residents of the household. Special permits may be granted to allow more employees.

6. The home office or business has no signs visible from the street that are inconsistent with signs allowed elsewhere in the zoning regulations.

7. The home office or business sells no articles at retail on the premises that are not raised or grown on the premises.

8. The home office or business occupies no more than 40 percent of the dwelling.

9. The ordinance should recognize that parking requirements for businesses that serve clients, patients, or customers are different from those for home offices where the only business visitor is apt to be an occasional overnight courier.

10. The home office or business does not create a volume of passenger or commercial traffic that is inconsistent with the normal level of traffic on the street on which the dwelling is located.

11. Parking of a truck(s) or van(s) should be allowed to the extent they do not interfere with the residential look of the neighborhood.

10. Home-business associations can lobby city planners and home developers to include provisions allowing home-based businesses both in covenants that run with the land in single-family-home developments and in the bylaws and covenants, codes, and restrictions (CC&Rs) of condominiums.

Open-collar workers are now a viable bloc of any local economy. In Pittsburgh, for example, 40 percent of all business start-ups are home based. As a result, the media are likely to be favorable to the home-business cause. Find news reporters who will cover zoning-related stories. In larger cities, coverage may be harder to get, so you may need to use your imagination to create a story suitable for TV and print that is more than talking heads. Crowds of people create interest, but what if home-based business-people operating with zoning problems themselves are not willing to be recognized or to identify themselves? Why not have them board a bus in a remote location and arrive en masse at city hall wearing disguises—like a mustache, a bandana, or a mask of some sort? If people are not willing to do this, how about using mannequins, dolls, or even signs to indicate witnesses afraid to show their faces? Emphatically make the point that these zoning violators are among a community's most productive citizens who are aching to be able to pay city license taxes in exchange for their legitimacy.

HOMEOWNERS' ASSOCIATION REGULATIONS

Sometimes homeowners' and condominium association regulations are included as covenants that run with the land and restrict homes in the area from being used for business purposes. A deed with this kind of restriction can preclude your working from home if challenged by the association. To ensure your ability to work from home, find out about any such limitations before buying a new home. If one exists, determine whether it can be waived and have your waiver acted upon as a condition of your purchase.

STATE LAWS

A number of states have Industrial Homework laws. These laws were generally passed in the late 1930s to protect women and children from abusive labor practices. The laws are concerned with people employed in manufacturing products, and sometimes certain home businesses are prohibited entirely. For example, some states, such as California, Illinois, Pennsylvania, and New Jersey, prohibit the preparation of food and drink for commercial purposes, as well as articles used in serving food and drink. Such prohibitions make catering businesses in which the food is prepared at a home kitchen against the law. Other items that often cannot be manufactured at home include drugs, poisons, bandages, toys, and dolls. Illinois forbids the manufacture of metal springs, while Massachusetts doesn't allow the manufacture of clothing, except for women's hosiery and hats. California says "no" to making clothing for children under the age of ten, as well as to making toys and dolls.

Aside from prohibiting the manufacture of particular items, states with Industrial Homework laws require a potential employer to get a permit for such work, the workers to get certificates, and homeowners to permit inspection of their homes. New York specifically excludes clerical work, such as typing, transcribing, and bookkeeping, from the requirements of its law. California has a law requiring talent agents to be licensed but forbids granting a license if the business is to be conducted "in rooms used for living purposes." No doubt this was intended to curb exploitive "casting couch" situations. In all likelihood, these state laws should not affect you. To find out about such laws in your state, however, consult with your attorney, or if your state has an agency that helps small businesses, contact that agency.

States with Laws Regulating Home-Based Work	
California	Ohio
Connecticut	Pennsylvania
Hawaii	Rhode Island
Illinois	Tennessee
Indiana	Texas
Maryland	Washington
Massachusetts	West Virginia
Michigan	Wisconsin
Missouri	
New Jersey	District of Columbia
New York	Puerto Rico

FEDERAL LAWS

Under the Fair Labor Standards Act, the federal government requires companies engaged in interstate commerce to provide all employees working at home, including clerical personnel, with "homework handbooks" in which the employee must keep detailed records of hours worked. Some states, such as California and New Jersey, also require the use of home work handbooks by businesses not covered by federal law. Also under federal law, the U.S. Department of Labor may prohibit categories of home work, and, since the 1940s, it has banned the manufacture of women's apparel in workers' homes. The rationale for this ban is to protect workers against minimum-wage violations, abuses of child labor laws, and the harrowing conditions of sweatshops. The Wage and Hour Division of the Department of Labor enforces these regulations.

In addition, some occupations that can be based at home, such as investment advisers and firearm dealers, require federal licensing. Also, if you serve the public in your home office, as a professional practice would do, employ seven or more full- or part-time people, or are engaged in interstate commerce, the Americans with Disabilities Act applies to you.

BUSINESS PERMITS, REGISTRATIONS, AND LICENSES: WHAT'S REQUIRED?

Other than observing the ordinances, laws, and regulations governing business use of the home, operating a home business on a full- or part-time basis requires taking the same legal steps as operating a business anywhere else. In some cases, however, home-based businesses may need more permits than other businesses. For example, a home business may require a general business license, a home occupancy license, and a specialty license for some kinds of businesses. The permits, registrations, and licenses vary greatly from locality to locality. They also depend on the nature of your business. Use the following checklist as a guide for identifying which legal steps you need to take. Then consult a lawyer or appropriate government agencies if you're not sure how these requirements apply to your business or locale.

 Legal Checklist

Depending on your type of business and your state and local requirements you may need to:

____ Obtain an employer's ID number with Form SS-4, if you have employees, are a partnership, or are incorporated

____ Obtain a federal license if required by federal law

____ Obtain any trademarks, copyrights, patents needed

____ Incorporate, form a limited-liability company, or file a statement of partnership if not a sole proprietor

____ Register business name (in some states)

____ If needed, obtain seller's permit—also known as Certificate of Authority or Resale Certificate

____ Obtain state trademark if needed and available

____ Obtain any required state licenses

____ Check your zoning

____ Obtain a local business license

____ Register your business name if using a name other than your own or a variation of your name

Work Sheet: Should You Incorporate Your Business?

A common question people ask when starting a business is "Do I need to incorporate?" Depending on whom you ask, you will get different answers. Even accountants and attorneys, the experts on this subject, disagree. As a single-person business, your choice is between a sole proprietorship or a corporation. If you're going into business with one or more persons, you can choose among a partnership, a corporation, and possibly a limited-liability company. There are other forms of business organization, but they would be less usual for a home-based business. These are limited partnerships, joint ventures, and professional corporations. In considering each of the main options, take into account:

___ The cost in dollars and time to start and maintain each form of business organization

___ Your business image and your ability to get work

___ The risk to your personal assets and future earnings

___ Your goals for the size of your business and whether you want the business to extend beyond your lifetime

___ If you need or want financing, the ease of obtaining loans and investors

___ How much government regulation you will experience

___ How much taxes will cost you

The following section outlines the pros and cons of each of the major choices for a home business.

SOLE PROPRIETORSHIPS

As a sole proprietor, you and the business are one and the same: your business's income is your income; your business debts are your debts. If you move to another city, the business moves with you. If you die, the business ends. Sole proprietorships are by far the most common form of small business, whether home based or not.

Advantages of Sole Proprietorships:

• *Inexpensive.* Because sole proprietorships involve little in the way of forms, licenses, and legal requirements, they're the least expensive of the business structures.

• **Less complicated.** Sole proprietorships are less complicated to set up and operate.

• **Complete control.** You have complete control in all aspects of running your business. There are no partners to consult, no boards of directors to answer to, and no shareholders to keep happy.

• **You keep all profits.** You are the sole proprietor of the business; the money you make is your own.

• **Easier to terminate.** You can terminate your business; almost as easily as you started it.

Disadvantages of the Sole Proprietorships:

• **Liability.** In a sole proprietorship, your freedom also comes with responsibility. You will be personally liable for any debts or damages your business incurs.

• **Financing will be more difficult.** Because your business begins and ends with you, banks and other financial institutions are reluctant to provide financing to sole proprietorships.

• **Perception.** If your competition will be mid- or larger-size companies, not having an "Inc." after your business name might put you at a disadvantage.

PARTNERSHIPS

Partnerships enable you to share the work and responsibility of a business with someone else. Partnerships cost less than corporations to form and, because there are few government regulations to contend with, they are also easy to start. Although informational tax returns are required of partnerships, they do not pay income taxes.

Anyone entering into a partnership should have an attorney draw up a partnership agreement first and obtain partnership insurance as soon as the agreement goes into effect. (For further details on insuring your business, see chapter 11.) These precautions are important because it's as difficult to find a truly suitable partner as it is to find a good mate. Because partners can have difficulty sharing authority or have clashing values, partnerships terminate at an even greater rate than marriages, 50 percent of which end in divorce.

Even your best friend can be a disaster as a partner. That's what one person found out. The now–former friend and partner took charge of the partnership books. He subsequently withdrew most of the profits for himself and left his former friend having to pay taxes on money he never received! The partner discharged his debts by declaring bankruptcy. A partnership agreement might have provided some protection for the wronged partner.

Advantages of Partnerships

• *More capital.* Any partner or partners should bring their own share of start-up or additional capital to the table.

• *Teamwork and support.* People working together toward a common goal generally accomplish more than those working singly.

• *Less governmental control.* As with the sole proprietorship, partnerships enjoy fewer regulations and less paperwork than corporations. Income, after it has been distributed to the partners, is treated like personal income. You can deduct losses in the partnership from other sources of income when you complete your income tax forms just as you can for a sole proprietorship.

• *Share in profits.* All partners share in the profits.

Disadvantages of Partnerships

• *Partners frequently disagree.* Partnerships, as we stated, are like marriages. And as in marriages there are frequent disagreements, even breakups. Partners often don't perform as you might expect.

• *Group decisions.* Any decision of consequence that needs to be made must be made by all partners. This can slow things down and lead to internal strife.

• *Messy breakups.* If you, or any of partners, tire of the business, rewriting your articles of partnership can be sticky. Often, partners must be bought out to keep the business going. This can be expensive and put a serious bind on cash flow.

• *Time investment.* Making joint decisions, keeping communication open, coordinating joint activities, and collectively solving problems take additional time and energy.

LIMITED-LIABILITY COMPANIES

Originated to meet the legal and tax needs of large corporations engaged in joint ventures, limited liability companies (LLCs) can also be used by home-based businesses. To use an LLC, your state must have passed legislation authorizing them; so far, over thirty states have done so. A few states do not allow limited liability companies to be used for some professions and occupations.

Because some states (Alabama, California, Connecticut, District of Columbia, Florida, Iowa, Kansas, Kentucky, Massachusetts, Nevada, New Jersey, North Carolina, Ohio, South Dakota, Tennessee, and Wisconsin) require LLCs to have at least two members, a limited liability company is not a substitute for a sole proprietorship. On the other hand, many states allow corporations to be formed by only one person. An LLC is more like a partnership and can be used where a limited partnership or an "S" corporation won't work or is impractical. (An S corporation, like a partnership, pays no corporate income taxes. Earnings are passed on to shareholders in proportion to their ownership, which is advantageous if the individual tax rate is lower than the corporate tax rate.) For example, some states, like California, don't recognize Subchapter S corporations, which means that even though a corporation may pay no federal tax as an entity, it must fully pay state corporation taxes. The limited-liability company allows income and deductions, as in a partnership or an S corporation, to flow through to its members.

Advantages of LLCs

• *Limited liability.* Like corporations, LLCs limit your personal liability from debts and damages incurred by the business.

• *Tax benefits.* Depending on the ways your business operates, you may benefit from slightly lower taxes by forming an LLC.

Disadvantages of LLCs

• *Complexity and expense.* Because LLCs are fairly new structures and complicated to set up, you will mostly likely need to hire the services of an attorney. (You can cut your costs, however, or even give it a shot yourself, by referring to books like *Form Your Own Limited Liability Company,* published by Nolo Press, *www.nolo.com*)

• *Limited tax benefits.* Although some businesses will pay slightly lower taxes, most home businesses will probably wind up paying more with an LLC.

• *The Limit on Limited Liability.* As with a corporation, insurance is one's best protection against insurable losses. The cost of a serious lawsuit can wipe out your business. Also, as with a corporation, an LLC does not shelter your personal assets from the reach of tax agencies collecting delinquent employee and payroll taxes.

• *A limited-liability company generally dissolves upon the death or withdrawal of any member.* A limited-liability company is formed by filing "articles of organization" with the state and is governed by an operating agreement that is comparable to a partnership agreement.

CORPORATIONS

The words *corporation* and *incorporated* suggest strength, stability, and reliability. For a small business, this may mean having an easier time getting the attention of prospective customers and investors. The appearance of substantiality that comes with being incorporated even attracts con artists as a cover-up for their schemes.

In the past, many small businesses incorporated in order to take advantage of tax benefits; however, since 1986 the tax advantages of being incorporated have lessened or disappeared. In fact, some corporate tax rates, particularly for personal service corporations, are higher than individual tax rates.

Forming a corporation may limit your liability if something goes wrong, but keep in mind that you are personally responsible for your own actions, whether you are incorporated or not. Also, most lenders will require the owners of corporations to execute personal guarantees for loans and mortgages. Being incorporated may protect you from personal liability for the acts of your employees; however, insurance is the only meaningful form of protection because if you are sued, whether you win or not, the high cost of defending yourself can put you out of business. Bear in mind, though, that becoming a corporation may raise your insurance costs.

A reason for incorporating that can overshadow all other considerations is preserving your self-employment status for tax purposes. If your work is such that you work for only few clients during a year or are in an industry being targeted by the IRS for classifying of independent contractors as employees, there's another better reason to incorporate. It can enable you to preserve your self-employment status and avoid being classified as a common-law employee by the Internal Revenue Service or a state revenue agency. Further, if you work for companies who fear that working with an independent contractor might make them vulnerable to costly penalties and back taxes if you are reclassified as a common-law employee, your ability to market yourself may depend on being incorporated. Maintaining your status as an independent contractor is discussed in chapter 10.

Being employed by your corporation may enable you to obtain workers' compensation for yourself as a form of disability insurance. A corporation may have advantages for you for sheltering retirement benefits if your net income is high enough. It also offers better opportunities for raising capital if you choose to expand your business. Ownership can be more easily transferred. A corporation has a separate legal identity from your own, so it can survive beyond your lifetime. If you are using your home as a launching point for a company you plan to build into a much larger enterprise, it may cost much more to change an ongoing business into a corporation than it costs to incorporate at the outset of your operations. Another reason that prompts some to incorporate is that appearing to be employed, even though the employer is your own corporation, may make it easier to obtain credit or buy a home or a car.

On the other side of the ledger, corporations are much more expensive to start. They involve extensive paperwork and record keeping, are closely regulated, and may be subject to double taxation because some states do not recognize S corporations. This means you may be paying state corporate taxes as well as state and federal individual income taxes.

We believe that when all the factors are taken into consideration, most people—other than those whose work places them in danger of being classified as common-law employees—are best advised to begin as a sole proprietorship. If you do decide to incorporate, once your annual gross receipts reach $100,000 we advise seeking legal and tax advice from professionals experienced with small businesses.

Although we recommend getting advice on incorporating from an attorney or accountant, consider this: Of the nation's 501,000 attorneys listed in Yellow Pages in the USA, 281,000 filed sole proprietorship returns and 134,000 were covered by partnership returns in 1995. This means that virtually nine out of ten attorneys are not organized as corporations. Accountants similarly choose sole proprietorships and partnerships as their form of business. It's fair to ask professionals advising you if they are incorporated and, if not, why not.

Finally, although it's relatively easy to set up a corporation with an incorporation kit (available in office-supply stores) by using a service, or even over the Web, it's easier to make costly mistakes in attempting to make the legal and tax decisions involved in incorporating yourself. Companies that provide incorporation services are quite familiar with forming Delaware corporations, but may not be so conversant with the corporation laws of other states. Keep in mind before incorporating in Delaware that you will have to register as a foreign corporation in your own state and pay taxes both where you live and work, and in Delaware. You can learn more about incorporating from *How to Form Your Own Corporation*, available in many states from Nolo Press (*www.nolo.com*).

Advantages of Corporations

• *Limited Liability.* With a corporation, your liability is limited to the amount of your investment in the business. Creditors cannot touch your personal funds, assets, or other holdings.

• *Corporate benefits.* As a corporation, you and other members in your business will be able to take advantage of fringe benefits such as pension plans, insurance, company cars, and so forth.

• *Permanence of existence.* A corporation has a life of its own and continues to exist even after the death or illness of the principal officer in the corporation.

• *Easier to get financing.* Financial institutions prefer lending to corporations because the very existence of the company does not rest on just one person or persons, as with partnerships and sole proprietorships.

Disadvantages of Corporations

• *Expensive to start.* Corporations are complicated structures that involve the guidance and advice of professionals. This generally creates considerable additional expense over other forms business.

• *Difficult to change.* When you start a business, sometimes it's hard to foresee what your needs will be in the future. Corporations, once established, are difficult to change or modify. You could get caught in a structure that no longer meets your needs or objectives.

• *Negligible tax benefits.* Under current tax structures (see next chapter) many forms of small business do not benefit from a lower corporate tax rate.

TRADEMARKS

One way to protect your business identity is with a trademark or service mark. A trademark is a distinctive word, name, symbol, or combination of these used to distinguish a product or service from those of competitors. Historically, trademarks were developed to indicate the origin and authenticity of products. A service mark is simply a trademark for services.

Anyone can, as intellectual property lawyer Gerry Elman says, "place a ™ or ℠ symbol next to any word, words, or logo that one regards as the trademark of his business. One doesn't need to get governmental permission. . . . It's just like staking your claim in the gold rush. But the next step in the gold rush is generally to go to the government office and register the claim one has staked out." Registration provides benefits that include being able to bring suit in a federal court without satisfying the usual jurisdictional requirements as well as the possibility of being awarded attorneys' fees and treble damages. You can use the ™ or ℠ symbol as soon as you adopt it, but you must wait to use the ® until your mark is approved for federal registration.

Registering a trademark is different from registering a trade name. A trade name is used to identify a business, and the laws and procedures are different. In some states, such as California, you cannot protect an unincorporated company name on a statewide basis, but you can protect a trademark. Trademarks can be registered either with the U.S. Patent and Trademark Office for nationwide protection or with your state government, if state law permits.

In the past, you could only get a federal registration of your trademark if you were actually using it in interstate commerce. Now you only need to allege that you intend to use the mark in interstate or foreign commerce. A trademark registered with the federal government can use the "small R in a circle" as a notice that your mark is protected. An additional advantage of registration is that federal law makes it "incontestable" after five years, which does not happen with state trademarks.

For trademark information and applications, you can phone (800) 786-9199, or (703) 308-HELP. You may write for information as well: U.S. Patent and Trademark Office, Washington, DC 20231 (*www.uspto.gov*). For copyright information, you can phone the Information Line at (202) 707-3000 or write Copyright Office, Library of Congress, Washington, DC 20559-6000 (*http://lcweb.loc.gov/copyright/*). Patent applications may be obtained from the Superintendent of Documents, Government Printing Office, Washington, D.C. 20402, or downloaded directly from the U.S. Patent Office Web site at *www.uspto.gov/web/forms/*

Additional resources include *The Copyright Handbook* (book with disk), *Trademark* or *Patent Copyright & Trademark,* available from Nolo Press (*www.nolo.com*).

To Obtain a Universal Product Code (UPC) Symbol

If you are going to be producing a product, you may find that retailers require that UPC labels be printed on your packaging. UPCs are the familiar vertical bars in varying widths that are on most products now and are scanned when we go through a checkout line in most stores. The codes are also used for inventory control.

To obtain Universal Product Codes for your products, contact the Uniform Code Council in Dayton, Ohio, at (937) 435-3870; Web: *www.uc-council.org*

WHY AND WHEN YOU NEED CONTRACTS

Contracts are the job descriptions and pay scales of the self-employed. When you work from home, they are your most important safeguards against problems with customers and clients, and they help ensure that you are taken seriously as a business. Take heed from stories like these.

 True Confessions

Artist Mary Kennelsworth was employed by a greeting card company when she decided to do sideline freelance work at home. Having been employed with an established organization, she didn't realize that potential customers might not take her small business seriously. "Perhaps it was because I was so new at this," she told us. "I didn't get anything in writing until one client decided not to proceed with a project after I'd already done all the work. From then on, I got everything in writing, including partial payments up-front."

Management consultant Eric Paine had a similar experience: "When I first began consulting, I was so eager to get some business I didn't even think about a contract. The company I was talking with wanted to explore what I could do for them, and I was eager to show them. At first, things went very well. I completed the work over a three-month period, during which they seemed satisfied.

"When I submitted the final report with my bill, however, they asked for a few revisions. I made the revisions and resubmitted my bill. I didn't hear anything from them for a couple of months, and when I called they told me they were still reviewing it and might want more revisions. Now it's six months later. I haven't gotten any money and they aren't returning my phone calls."

Certainly Eric is not without any recourse, but the amount of time and energy he spent trying to collect or entering into a lawsuit may be so great that it's not worth the effort. Better to offset such possibilities up-front by signing a contract before taking the work.

Eric now uses a "letter of agreement" for his management-consulting contracts. He meets with his clients to work out the specifics of the consulting he will do and afterward sends them a detailed letter indicating everything they agreed to in the meeting. He sends two copies and asks that one be signed, dated, and returned to him.

Whatever your business, be it selling knickknacks, catering, or computer programming, you should definitely create a standard contract to use with your clients or customers. In it, spell out your business agreement with specifics such as what you will provide, when you will provide it, what it will cost, and when they will pay you.

Contracts can be verbal or written, but written ones are certainly preferable. They can be as simple as a signed order form. Greg Rohan has clients fill out and sign a basic client information form (name, address, phone number, and so on) and at the bottom is a payment contract that reads:

"I understand I am to pay for services at the time they are rendered unless I have made other arrangements, and agree to pay for appointments I do not cancel at least 24 hours in advance."

He reviews this statement verbally to be sure the person understands and agrees. Whenever he makes other financial arrangements with clients, he writes these agreements on the form before they sign it. He attributes never having problems with collecting fees to this procedure.

Cathy, a designer and marketing consultant, includes contractual language along with the estimates she provides. The estimates detail the exact services she will render and the price for each service. The contractual language includes her terms of payment. When customers sign her estimate, they also sign an agreement that specifies when and how Cathy will be paid.

The best way to develop contract agreements that are customized to your needs is to consult a lawyer. You can also talk with colleagues about the contracts they use, ask your professional or trade association for information, or attend a workshop on contracting. Pro forma contracts are now available on computer software.

Sometimes your clients or suppliers will offer you a contract. When this happens, review the terms carefully. Ask questions about provisions you do not understand. The contract should cover all important points you have discussed. Contract terms must be correct as well as clear and specific; ambiguous language can lead to conflict later on. Usually these contracts are presented as a "standard form," so they appear to be unchangeable. Actually, a contract is always negotiable. Read the fine print and feel free to write in modifications. And bear in mind that any handwritten modifications need to be signed or initialed by both parties.

In most cases, we suggest having a lawyer look over the contract agreements you negotiate at first. Later, you may feel familiar enough with the way contracts are written to make informed changes on your own.

SELECTING A LAWYER

Some people only go to the dentist when they're in agony with a toothache. Then, too often they're faced with extensive, expensive, and time-consuming dental work. Its the same with going to a lawyer. In either case, the better approach is to go in for periodic checkups and avoid developing emergencies.

You can call on a lawyer to:

- Help you decide upon and set up the form of business you want to establish (a sole proprietorship, partnership, or corporation).

- Advise you on regulations affecting your business and assist you in filing for necessary licenses, permits, and registrations.

- Advise you on insurance you need and refer you to a good agent.

- Review contracts and other legal documents.

- Help you with collection problems. Sometimes a letter on a lawyer's letterhead is enough to get payment from a debtor.

- Provide you with advice and help you take action to avoid lawsuits.

- Represent you in unavoidable lawsuits.

Whether you need a lawyer right now or not, find one you can trust who understands your business situation. You may actually consult your lawyer infrequently, but when those times come, you'll be a step ahead if that person already knows you and your business.

The best way to find a lawyer is through referrals from others with businesses like yours. If you don't already know such business owners, contact them through professional and trade associations or the Chamber of Commerce. Then talk with the lawyers you've been referred to. Tell them about your business situation and select the lawyer you feel best understands and reflects your business interests.

You can obtain legal services through prepaid legal plans that cater to businesses. For an annual fee, usually around $200, you may get unlimited telephone consultation with an attorney, the writing of collection letters and letters to government agencies on your behalf, review of contracts and other documents, and provision of partnership agreements and articles of incorporation, all at no additional charge. For more involved legal matters, you can obtain legal representation at greatly reduced rates. However, our personal experience would indicate that the old adage about getting what you pay for applies. So other than for the most routine matters, we advise finding an attorney who specializes in serving small and home-based businesses.

Once you've selected a lawyer, think of that person as an essential part of your business team. Go to him or her for professional advice to avoid legal problems, just as you would call on an accountant to avoid an audit. Law, like taxes and insurance, is an area where you can use experts to help you keep your business on track.

RESOURCES

BOOKS

American Jurisprudence Pleading and Practice Forms Annotated, published by the Bancroft Whitney imprint of Lawyers Co-op Publishing Company, is a set of books containing thousands of forms. It is updated with pocket supplements and can be found in law libraries. Law libraries are usually located in courthouses. There you will find many other books of forms and documents, some localized and some for legal specialties.

Basic Law for Small Businesses. Susan S. Jarvis. Belmont, CA: West/Wadsworth, 1997. ISBN: 0314201394.

The Contract and Fee-Setting Guide for Consultants and Professionals. Howard L. Shenson. New York: Wiley, 1990. ISBN: 0471506605.

Getting Business to Come to You, 2d ed. Paul and Sarah Edwards, with Laura Clampitt Douglas. New York: Tarcher/Putnam, 1998. ISBN: 0-87477-845-X (pp. 199–277). This book contains material on selecting and protecting a business name.

Inc. Yourself, 8th ed. Judith H. McQuowan. New York: HarperCollins, 1996. ISBN: 088730821X.

Legal Guide for Starting and Running a Small Business, 3d. ed. Fred S. Steingold, Mary Randolph, and Ralph Warner, eds. Berkeley, CA: Nolo Press, 1997. ISBN: 087337374X.

Neighbor Law. Cora Jordan. Nolo Press, 950 Parker Street, Berkeley, CA 94710; (800) 728-3555, or visit their web site at *www.nolo.com.* 1998. ISBN: 0873374258.

Nolo Press publishes a line of self-help legal books that are also used by lawyers and judges. Among the titles they publish are: *How to Form a Limited Liability Company, Form Your Own Corporations, Everybody's Guide to Small Claims Court, How to Form a Nonprofit Corporation, Patent It Yourself, The Partnership Book,* and *Simple Contracts for Personal Use.* Most of these books are written for national readerships; others for specific states such as California, Florida, New York, and Texas. Many of their books have disks with software that provide forms. For a free catalog, write Nolo Press, 950 Parker Street, Berkeley, CA 94710; (800) 728-3555 or visit their web site at *www.nolo.com.*

155 Legal Do's (And Dont's) for the Small Business. Paul Adams. New York: Wiley, 1996. ISBN: 047113161X.

SOFTWARE

Custom Forms. American Software, 500 Birch St., Suite 5600, Newport Beach, CA 92660; (714) 708-0700; Web: *www.ameri-soft.com*

Patent it Yourself (Windows). David Pressman. Nolo Press & Electronic Data Systems Corporation, 950 Parker Street, Berkeley, CA 94710; (800)

728-3555. Up-to-date information (e.g., Provisional Patent Application Program and GATT changes), expert advice, forms, letters, and contracts. *www.nolo.com/category/Software.html*

ON LINE

ContractMaker. Digital Contracts, Inc. Software and on-line businesses can draft contracts directly on the Web with this service. *www.digicontracts.com*

Free Advice. Free legal advice on 100 topics available twenty-four hours a day along with a list of lawyers who will provide free initial consultations to local potential clients. *www.freeadvice.com*

On-line services, including America Online, CompuServe, and the World Wide Web itself, have legal forums and resources. Although attorneys will not give specific legal advice, the conversation and documents, such as full texts of Supreme Court cases, can be valuable.

Quickform Contracts. Automated drafting of documents for the computer industry, Internet commerce, and general business transactions. *www. quickform.com*

Web*Law Partner Legal and Business Forms Online. *www.legal-businessforms.com*

OTHER FORMS OF LEGAL HELP

Caldwell Legal, USA. P.O. Box 245778, Sacramento, CA 95824; (800) 222-3035. Provides a prepaid legal plan for businesses for $420 a year. Caldwell also has affiliates in British Columbia, Manitoba, and Ontario. *www.caldwell-legal.com*

Halt: An Organization for Legal Reform. 1612 K Street, NW, Suite 510, Washington, DC 20002. One of the few organizations that looks out for clients who run into trouble with their lawyers. (202) 887-8255; Web: *www.halt.org*

Martindale-Hubbell Law Directory. The most complete source of lawyers' names, lising attornies by state and specialty. Available in libraries or on line at *www.martindale.com*

Tele-Lawyer provides advice about small business and consumer matters by phone. You can call a 900 number or use a charge card. In some cases, they make referrals to local low-cost providers of legal help; (800) 835-3529 for information (*www.telelawyer.com*).

CHAPTER 10

Claiming Your Tax Benefits

Goals

1. Find out if you qualify for the home-office deduction and why you should take it.

2. Know what other deductions you're entitled to and make sure you qualify for them.

3. Protect yourself from being audited.

4. Learn what taxes you are required to pay.

5. Set up a retirement account.

6. Avoid common tax traps and pitfalls.

7. Keep adequate records.

8. Get the tax help you need.

When you become self-employed, your experience as a taxpayer changes dramatically. As one person reflected, "My biggest shortcoming was in not researching my tax situation. I was totally unprepared for the responsibility of shepherding part of my income to the IRS. Consequently . . . I worried all my hair out."

Whether taxes cost you your hair or turn your hair gray—or you enjoy the experience of watching formerly nondeductible parts of your cost of living become tax deductions—depends on getting the information you require and acting on it. This chapter will guide you through the basic conditions you will need to become aware of as a self-employed person—the benefits, the requirements, and the traps.

At times, we will not present the conventional views you may have heard or read. We will provide you with the IRS citations, however, for the unconventional information some tax advisors will tell you is wrong. We advise you to find a tax counsel who truly knows this area of tax law. Some do not. With the information in this chapter, you can check a tax professional's knowledge or willingness to learn.

Our intent in this chapter is not to turn you into a tax expert, but to give you a general overview of what you're entitled to under the law. You should neither overlook items you can deduct nor exaggerate your deductions recklessly. Your best position is to take a smart, realistic middle ground.

According to recent surveys, only 37 percent of U.S. taxpayers prepare their own returns.

First, let's consider the tax benefits of working from home. Fundamentally, the tax system of the United States recognizes what President Calvin Coolidge said in 1925: "The business of America is business." Yet, hungry for tax revenue, Congress is eliminating business deductions. In 1994, the meal and entertainment deduction was reduced to 50 percent. Club dues deductions are now gone (including airline, athletic, and country clubs), even though your only reason for being in a club may be business. The share of the dues you pay a professional or trade association that is used for lobbying is also not deductible (and it's up to the association to notify you of what percentage of your dues goes to lobbying).

Nevertheless, there remains a wide range of business deductions. You need to take full advantage of them in order to help offset lost fringe benefits like health insurance, pension plan, sick leave, and vacations. These "fringe benefits" are worth between 25 to 50 percent of an employee's wages. So if you were earning $30,000 a year as a salaried worker, your benefits were worth between $7,500 and $15,000. In this chapter you will learn of some of the major deductions you are entitled to and why you should take everything you can.

One positive recent tax development has been the virtual elimination of the consequences of the Soliman case. A few years back the Supreme Court of the United States dealt home-based businesses a painful blow in the *Commissioner of Internal Revenue v. Soliman* case, by interpreting the law so that it took away the home-office deduction from hundreds of thousands of people who work *from* home rather than *at* home. This was a contentious ruling, to say the least. If the same standard applied to home-based businesses in the Soliman case were to apply to all businesses, entities that principally serve their public away from their headquarters—taxi companies, home health-care providers, ambulance companies, airlines, locksmiths, installers of all kinds, mobile everything—would not be able to deduct their offices, garages, storefronts, and warehouses! Fortunately, under the 1997 Taxpayer Relief Act, as of 1999 any home office that is the business's sole office and is used regularly for the administration of essential activities will qualify for a home-office deduction.

Despite such victories, you will read things in this chapter that will make you angry (they make us angry), but they reflect the nature of the forces that have an impact upon us. What we can do is treat our tax lives as

Judge Learned Hand wrote was expected of us: "Anyone may arrange his affairs so that his taxes shall be as low as possible. He is not bound to choose that pattern which best pays the treasury. There is not even a patriotic duty to increase one's taxes. . . . Nobody owes any public duty to pay more than the law demands; taxes are enforced exactions, not voluntary contributions."

TWO CATEGORIES
OF DEDUCTIONS

In general, the deductions you can claim when working from home fall into one of two categories: *home-office expenses* and *ordinary business expenses*. You can claim ordinary business expenses whether your office is in a downtown building, a suburban storefront, or in your home. Since the primary tax advantage the home-based worker has over other taxpayers is home-office deductions, let's turn first to how you can qualify for these.

MEETING THE IRS CRITERIA
FOR A HOME-OFFICE DEDUCTION

As long as you meet the necessary criteria, whether you live and work in a house, an apartment, a condominium, a cooperative, a mobile home, or even a boat, you can deduct the cost of operating and maintaining the part of your home that you use for business. The Internal Revenue Service has two basic criteria your home office must meet in order to qualify as a tax write-off. The first is that the portion of your house you wish to claim as a business expense must be used exclusively and regularly for business.

Exclusive Use

"Exclusive use" means that the portion of your home you're claiming as a deduction is used only for business. Your home office may be an entire room you have given over to that purpose or it may simply be an alcove in your living room or a breakfast nook off your kitchen (one, however, that is not used for dining). It need not be separated from the room by a partition, but it must be a separately identifiable space. So for tax purposes, think of your home office—your business space—as an entity separate from the part of your home given over to personal use.

If people must pass through your business area on the way to another room, does your home office fail to meet the exclusive use test? No, according to the case of *Hughes, Jr. v. Commissioner* (T.C. Memo 1981-301).

Currently there are two exceptions to the exclusive-use rule. You may take a deduction for space used to store inventory or product samples and for space used as a day-care facility. For example, if you're in direct sales of cosmetics, gift baskets, health products, or household cleaning products and meet the following criteria, you can take a deduction on space used for inventory, even if that space, in a laundry room or basement, for example, is also used for nonbusiness purposes. To qualify for this exception, however:

- Your business must involve wholesale or retail sale of products.

- The inventory must be kept for use in your business.

- Your home must be the only fixed location of your business.

- You must use the storage space on a regular basis.

- The space you use must be separately identifiable as space suitable for storage.

For the day-care exception, you can be caring for children, people who are physically or mentally handicapped, or people over the age of sixty-five. Your day care must meet your state's requirements for licensing or registration. You can deduct rooms that the people you care for regularly use even though you use those rooms for personal purposes when those in your care go home. You calculate your deduction on the basis of the percentages of both space and time that the room is used for day care.

Regular Use

"Regular use" refers to using the business segment of your home on a continuing basis. Let's say you have space set up as a photo lab in a bedroom and you use it exclusively for that purpose once every several months. This would be what the IRS calls "incidental or occasional use" and would not qualify you to take a home-office deduction. However, if your business is seasonal, you can still meet the regular-use test.

Whereas the exclusive-use test is strict in not allowing you to mix personal and business uses in a single space—such as a guest bedroom for occasional visitors if you have a roll-away bed or having computer games on your computer—the few court cases on "regular use" suggest that the regular-use test is more flexible.

The second criterion your home office must meet in order to qualify as a tax write-off is that the portion of your home you use exclusively and regularly for business must be either your principal place of business or a place where you meet with customers or clients in the normal course of business.

Possible Deductible Home-Office Expenses

- Cleaning a home office

- Condominium association fees

- Household furniture converted to use in the home office

- Household supplies used in the business space

- Mortgage interest (partial)

- Real estate taxes (partial). Note that in some states, like Colorado, a home-business owner who converts rooms into business space may get a higher tax bill for the space that is then deemed "commercial."

- Repair and maintenance of office portion of home

- Security system

- Telephone line used exclusively for business if it is a second telephone line. The basic local service for a first line, including taxes, is not deductible; however, business long-distance calls on the personal line are deductible and services added for business use like call-waiting may be deductible.

- Trash collection

- Utilities attributable to business use of home (electricity, gas)

Principal Place of Business

To better understand this criterion, here's a little background on its history. After years of conflicting tax-court and appeals-court decisions, the Supreme Court ruled in January of 1993 that for a home office to qualify as a principal place of business, it must be the place where the most important functions of the business are performed. This means where the revenue is generated.

The Supreme Court also ruled that if it's not clear where the important activities that lead to delivering goods and services take place, then the time spent in the home office and elsewhere are to be compared. If it still isn't clear where the principal place of business is, the presumption is that the home office does not qualify for a deduction.

Because surveys indicate that four out of five home-based businesspeople do most of their income-producing work outside their home offices, under this ruling, millions of people who had no office other than their home could not take a deduction for the cost of having an office. This ruling was considered unfair and contrary to the best interests of small business, and the economic interests of a wide cross section of the political and business spectrum of the country.

In 1995, delegates to the White House Conference on Small Business began working on a definition for home offices that would be both clearer and fair. Soliman, upon whose situations the tax ruling was based, was an anesthesiologist with a six-figure income. (It takes that kind of salary to be able to afford to bring a case before the Supreme Court.) He was taking a $5,000 home-office deduction. Most home businesspeople can ill afford to lose that kind of deduction. So, after careful study, conference delegates recommended that the tax definition be updated to include any home-based business where the home office is used as the principal place of regular administrative duties, regardless of where actual income is generated.

Signed into law as part of the Taxpayer Relief Act of 1997 and becoming effective in 1999, this updated definition will help millions of home-based businesses enjoy a significant tax benefit. With the new law, a home office will qualify if it meets the Solimon test or is used as your administrative or management headquarters. This also means that even if you conduct some business activities away from home in places like your car or a hotel room that are not fixed, your home can still qualify as your principal place of business.

We provided this background so that if a future Congress is looking for a way to raise revenues by eliminating the exception to the Soliman definition of principal place of business, you will understand the stakes.

Exception: a Place for Meeting

Even if your home office is not your principal place of business, you are also entitled to deduct home-office expenses if in the normal course of your work, you see clients, patients, or customers face-to-face at home. Lawyers, doctors, psychotherapists, and management consultants are examples of people who might maintain outside offices yet also see clients at home. The space used for meeting clients, not for doing paperwork or other activities, is deductible.

Exception: a Separate Building

Here's another exception. If your home isn't your principal place of business but you have on your property a separate freestanding structure—a barn, a greenhouse, a workshop, a studio, a detached garage, a cabana, or anything physically detached from your home—and it is used exclusively and regularly for business, you can claim the home-office deduction for the use of that space. If a literary agent has a downtown office where she does most of her business but has converted a guest house on her property into an office where she works every Monday and Friday, she will be able to take the deduction for her home-office space. You should be able to show this by

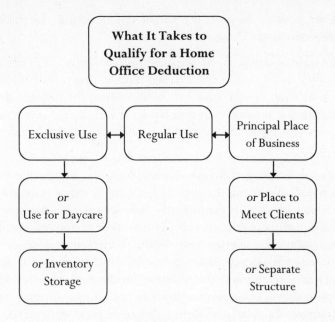

Figure 10-1

doing things like putting your home address and phone number on your business card and marketing materials, and keeping a calendar or other records showing the meetings and appointments at your home office.

WHY YOU SHOULD TAKE YOUR HOME-OFFICE DEDUCTION

If you qualify for a home-office deduction, claiming it can mean a considerable savings. A typical American home averages about 1,600 square feet, is worth $110,000 and, including utilities, insurance, repairs, and property taxes, costs a homeowner about $10,000 a year. A 200-square-foot bedroom (12.5 percent of the home) used for a home office will result in about a $1,600 home-office deduction, including depreciation. Figuring that our typical homeowner is just getting started and is only in a 15 percent income tax bracket, combined with paying less in self-employment taxes, the home office deduction is worth about $500 a year. That would pay for a month or two of health insurance, buy a multifunction fax/printer/scanner, or enable our home-based businessperson to make a modest investment in marketing to get more business.

For many people who spend more on housing or are in a higher tax bracket, the home-office deduction is worth more each year. Renters particularly benefit because, unlike homeowners who can deduct mortgage interest and property taxes on Schedule A, renters get no such deductions.

There are reasons beyond the initial dollar savings for taking your home-office deduction. These are:

• *To be able to deduct your business auto mileage.* You need to take the home-office deduction in order to begin deducting business mileage on your vehicle as soon as you leave home; otherwise, the mileage deduction doesn't start until you reach your first business location. If you make only a single business stop, you are entitled to no deduction for what in reality is a business trip.

• *To avoid keeping time-consuming logs.* If you qualify to take a home-office deduction, you do not need to keep a log of your use of your computer if you use it only for business. In fact, using it for nonbusiness purposes risks having your home-office deduction disallowed because that would violate the exclusive-use test. Without the home-office deduction, the computer is considered "listed property," and to deduct it and other equipment, you must answer the question on the back of Form 4562 that asks "Do you have evidence to support the business use/investment claimed?" Answering this "yes" means you need to have kept a log of the business and personal use of your computer.

• *To avoid a catch-22 penalty.* If you qualify to take a home-office deduction and fail to take it, thereby overstating your income for self-employment tax purposes, you are subject to penalties (Revenue Rulings 56-407, 57-538 and 79-396). The idea is that the government does not want you qualifying for higher Social Security benefits than you are entitled to. So unless you claim all allowable deductions in figuring net earnings from self-employment, you may be penalized later.

• *To avoid being taxed twice.* When you sell your home, you will be responsible for paying tax on the portion of your gain relative to the amount of your home used for business, whether you took the home-office tax deduction or not. As stated by IRS Publication 587, "If you used any part of your home for business, you must adjust the basis of your home for any depreciation you were allowed for its business, even if you did not claim it." If you think about it, if you do not take the home-office deduction, you are paying taxes on the same money twice—once when you don't take the deduction and then again when you sell your home. To avoid this quagmire,

 Caution

Be careful that the steps you take to prove you have a legitimate home office do not conflict with your zoning or homeowner association rules; for example, no commercial yard signs.

don't qualify your home office for a deduction by not meeting the three criteria outlined above. This may be wise if you plan to sell your home in the near future. Of course, you lose the benefits.

. . . AND WHAT ABOUT RISK OF AUDIT?

Many tax advisers advise against taking the home-office deduction for fear of increasing the risk of being audited. Taking a home-office deduction does increase one's chances of being audited, but considering all the benefits is it a risk worth taking? The truth is the IRS targets self-employed people anyway. This is because the self-employed are one of the largest groups of nonfilers. In short, you do yourself no favors when you don't take the home-office deduction if you are entitled to it.

There are a variety of steps you can take to help prove your home office is a legitimate one. For example, you can have a separate business telephone number, put a sign on your mailbox or door, have clients or customers regularly come to your office, keep a log or have them sign a "guest book," use your home address on your business card, and receive mail there.

The Scoop on Home-Office Audit Risk

Self-employed taxpayers who filed Schedule C's in 1994 had the following chances of being audited:

4.3%	Less than $25,000 in gross earnings
3.57%	$100,000 and more in gross earnings
3.01%	$25,000 to $100,000 in gross earnings

DEDUCTING HOME-OFFICE EXPENSES

When you qualify for a home-office deduction, you can also deduct a variety of expenses in addition to your regular business expenses.

Direct expenses for the business portion of your home—such as painting your office or fixing a leak in it—are fully deductible. But you should be aware that the IRS makes a distinction between capital improvements (like adding a room that you use for business, installing customized cabinets in your home office, or designing space for your computer) and repairs that you'd make in the normal course of maintenance (like fixing a broken window or repainting your office). Repairs are deductible. Capital improvements, however, are depreciated, which means that the deduction must be spread over a period of a number of years.

Indirect expenses related to the entire home—such as mortgage payments, insurance, utility bills, exterior painting, roof repair, depreciation—are deductible in part. To calculate the part of these expenses you can deduct, divide the square footage of your office space by the total square footage of your home. Thus, if the office measures two hundred square feet and the whole home measures sixteen hundred square feet, your office takes up 12.5 percent of the total space and you can deduct 12.5 percent of your indirect expenses.

Determining the Square Footage of Your Home

If you don't know the square footage of your home, here are some guidelines for how the real estate industry calculates square footage:

Square footage can be measured from exterior walls. Although the space between the exterior and interior walls is not inhabitable, it does contain the wires and pipes that make a house livable.

Detached houses—the finished square footage is the sum of the finished areas on each level measured at floor level.

Town houses—each level is measured from the exterior finished surface of an outside wall or from the center lines between dwellings.

Openings between floors are not included, but stairs and landings are.

To be included, finished areas must have a ceiling height of at least seven feet, except under beams, ducts or other obstructions, and stairs.

Alternatively, if the rooms in your house are about the same size, you can calculate the deductible portion by dividing the number of rooms used for business by the total number of rooms in your home. It's a good idea to draw up a floor plan of your house to indicate the portion used for your home office. This will provide documentation of your use of a portion of your home for business purposes if you need the verification.

The amount of home-office expenses you deduct cannot exceed the amount of gross income you've earned from your work at home. So to ensure that you will not be using a home-office deduction to offset the income you've earned from a business, you must calculate the deduction in a particular sequence of steps. This makes the calculation somewhat complicated, but IRS Publication 587 entitled *Business Use of Your Home*, which comes out each year, contains instructions, a work sheet, examples, explanations, and references to other IRS publications for calculating your deduction. If you complete your own tax return, we recommend that before filing you show the result to a tax specialist at least the first time you claim a home-office deduction. Figure 10-2 is an example of a completed Form

Form **8829**

Department of the Treasury
Internal Revenue Service (5)

Expenses for Business Use of Your Home

▶ File only with Schedule C (Form 1040). Use a separate Form 8829 for each home you used for business during the year.
▶ See separate instructions.

OMB No. 1545-1266

1993

Attachment
Sequence No. **66**

Name(s) of proprietor(s) *Kelly Martin*

Your social security number *123 :45:6789*

Part I Part of Your Home Used for Business

1	Area used regularly and exclusively for business, regularly for day care, or for inventory storage. See instructions	1 *200*
2	Total area of home	2 *1,600*
3	Divide line 1 by line 2. Enter the result as a percentage	3 *12.5* %

- For day-care facilities not used exclusively for business, also complete lines 4–6.
- All others, skip lines 4–6 and enter the amount from line 3 on line 7.

4	Multiply days used for day care during year by hours used per day	4	hr.
5	Total hours available for use during the year (365 days × 24 hours). See instructions	5	8,760 hr.
6	Divide line 4 by line 5. Enter the result as a decimal amount	6	.
7	Business percentage. For day-care facilities not used exclusively for business, multiply line 6 by line 3 (enter the result as a percentage). All others, enter the amount from line 3 ▶	7	*12.5* %

Part II Figure Your Allowable Deduction

8	Enter the amount from Schedule C, line 29, **plus** any net gain or (loss) derived from the business use of your home and shown on Schedule D or Form 4797. If more than one place of business, see instructions	8	*30,000*

See instructions for columns (a) and (b) before completing lines 9–20.

		(a) Direct expenses	(b) Indirect expenses		
9	Casualty losses. See instructions	9			
10	Deductible mortgage interest. See instructions	10	*6,000*		
11	Real estate taxes. See instructions	11	*1,300*		
12	Add lines 9, 10, and 11	12	*7,300*		
13	Multiply line 12, column (b) by line 7	13	*913*		
14	Add line 12, column (a) and line 13			14	*913*
15	Subtract line 14 from line 8. If zero or less, enter -0-			15	
16	Excess mortgage interest. See instructions	16			
17	Insurance	17	*500*		
18	Repairs and maintenance	18 *400*	*1400*		
19	Utilities	19	*1,800*		
20	Other expenses. See instructions	20	*1,200*		
21	Add lines 16 through 20	21	*4,900*		
22	Multiply line 21, column (b) by line 7	22	*613*		
23	Carryover of operating expenses from 1992 Form 8829, line 41	23			
24	Add line 21 in column (a), line 22, and line 23			24	*1,013*
25	Allowable operating expenses. Enter the **smaller** of line 15 or line 24			25	*1,013*
26	Limit on excess casualty losses and depreciation. Subtract line 25 from line 15			26	*28,074*
27	Excess casualty losses. See instructions	27			
28	Depreciation of your home from Part III below	28	*260*		
29	Carryover of excess casualty losses and depreciation from 1992 Form 8829, line 42	29			
30	Add lines 27 through 29			30	*260*
31	Allowable excess casualty losses and depreciation. Enter the **smaller** of line 26 or line 30			31	*260*
32	Add lines 14, 25, and 31			32	*2,186*
33	Casualty loss portion, if any, from lines 14 and 31. Carry amount to **Form 4684**, Section B			33	
34	Allowable expenses for business use of your home. Subtract line 33 from line 32. Enter here and on Schedule C, line 30. If your home was used for more than one business, see instructions ▶			34	*2,186*

Part III Depreciation of Your Home

35	Enter the **smaller** of your home's adjusted basis or its fair market value. See instructions	35	*110,000*
36	Value of land included on line 35	36	*30,000*
37	Basis of building. Subtract line 36 from line 35	37	*80,000*
38	Business basis of building. Multiply line 37 by line 7	38	*10,000*
39	Depreciation percentage. See instructions	39	*2.6* %
40	Depreciation allowable. Multiply line 38 by line 39. Enter here and on line 28 above. See instructions	40	*260*

Part IV Carryover of Unallowed Expenses to 1994

41	Operating expenses. Subtract line 25 from line 24. If less than zero, enter -0-	41	
42	Excess casualty losses and depreciation. Subtract line 31 from line 30. If less than zero, enter -0-	42	

For Paperwork Reduction Act Notice, see page 1 of separate instructions.   Cat. No. 13232M   Form **8829** (1993)

Figure 10-2

8829, using the typical data given in this chapter. Form 8829 must be used by people who report their business income using a Schedule C.

Note that the home-office deduction can be used to bring the taxes on what you earn at home to zero, but it can't be used as a loss to reduce taxes on the income you earn at a full-time job or from other sources. However, you can carry forward to future years the home-office expenses you were not able to deduct.

Underused Home-Office Deductions

- *Medical expenses for spouses working together.* For very small, family owned business, 100 percent of noninsured medical costs are deductible. Although the qualifying and record-keeping requirements are strict, exploring Section 105 of the tax code can provide you a considerable deduction for medical expenses not covered by your insurance. (Hint: if you're healthy, consider reducing your medical insurance to a high deductible catastrophic plan and pay for routine medical costs yourself, then deduct them.)

- *Medical savings accounts.* As part of health-care reform, the Federal Government has allowed individuals to establish a special tax-free savings account to be used exclusively for medical expenses. The monies that you deposit into such an account are considered tax-exempt. The account must be administered by a financial institution much like an IRA. See the box in Chapter 11.

- *Purchasing a large cargo or passenger van.* By purchasing a cargo van, passenger van, or sport utility vehicle weighing over 6,000 lbs., you will not be confined to standard limitations on the amount by which you can depreciate the vehicle.

TAX TRAPS AND PITFALLS

Here are several other issues you should consider in deciding whether to take a home-office deduction.

- If you use your home office for more than one business or business purpose, failure to meet the qualifications for all business activities will disqualify the entire deduction. For example, if you have a home business and you also bring home work from your job but you can't qualify it as an employee business expense, you could lose your otherwise-legitimate home-office deduction. But you can use an office for multiple purposes and get the home-office deduction if all the businesses would qualify for it. This applies to one person doing multiple things at home as well as two people, like a husband and wife, using the same office.

- Whereas you may qualify for a home-office deduction if you are in a partnership, a limited liability company, or a Schedule S corporation, if you incorporate your business as a Schedule C corporation, you lose the home-office deduction. Some people consider having their partnership or corporation own their residence so as to avoid the limitations on the home-office deduction, but IRS regulations are written so that this doesn't work out in the taxpayer's favor. However, as an employee of your Schedule C corporation, if you can qualify your home office expenses as an employee business expense, you can have your corporation reimburse you for them and the corporation can deduct what it reimburses you. You may also have the corporation pay you rent, which unlike wages, would not be subject to social security taxes. But check with your tax professional, as it's easy to make mistakes in this area.

- Finally, if you own your own home and are entitled to a home-office deduction, consider this pitfall: Suppose you paid $80,000 for your home and now plan to sell it for $140,000. Generally the $60,000 increase in value will not be taxed because of the exclusion from taxes allowed by the 1997 Taxpayer Relief Act of gain (up to $500,000 for a married couple) you realize in selling your principal place of residence. But let's say you have been entitled to a home-office deduction of 15 percent. When you sell your house, you will need to pay a tax on 15 percent of the increase in value (or $9,000). This is the catch in the home-office deduction that tax professionals will warn you about. This is because the Taypayer Relief Act provides that you must recognize gain to the extent of any depreciation *allowable* with respect to the business use of your home. So if you qualify your home office as deductible, be sure to include depreciation as an expense because you will be paying a capital gains tax whether you actually take depreciation or not. And be sure to work with a qualified tax professional who may help you minimize that gain.

THE HOME-OFFICE DEDUCTION
FOR SALARIED AND COMMISSIONED EMPLOYEES

If you are a salaried or commissioned employee of someone else but work from home, you may still be eligible for the home-office deduction. An employee's home-office expenses, like other unreimbursed employee business expenses, are deductible only to the extent that they exceed 2 percent of ad-

The Taxpayer Relief Act of 1997

As of May 6, 1997, the Taxpayer Relief Act stipulates the following changes in capital gains taxes that will affect the profit you make on the sale of your home:

- A maximum tax rate of 18 percent has been set for sales of property acquired after December 31, 2000, that will have been held for more than five years at the time of the sale.

- A 25 percent ceiling on real estate depreciation recapture that is treated as capital gain.

- The current 28 percent maximum capital gains rate will continue to apply to sales property held for more than one year but not more than eighteen months.

- The Taxpayer Relief Act allows taxpayers to exclude up to $250,000 of gain ($500,000 for married couples filing a joint return) realized on the sale or exchange of a principal residence occurring after May 6, 1997. Unlike the "one time" exclusion provided under prior law, the exclusion is allowed each time you sell or exchange a principal residence, although the exclusion generally may not be claimed more frequently than once every two years. Also unlike under prior law, you are not required to reinvest the sales proceeds in a new residence to claim the exclusion. To be eligible, the residence must have been owned and used as the taxpayer's principal residence for a combined period of at least two years out of the five years prior to the sale or exchange. You must recognize gain to the extent of any depreciation allowable with respect to the rental or business use of such principal residence for periods after May 6, 1997.

justed gross income. Like anyone claiming a home-office deduction, you must meet the exclusive- and regular-use tests, and your home must be your principal place of business or a client meeting place. In addition, however, your employer must expect you and require you to use your home for your work. Using your home for your work must be for your employer's convenience. To support this claim, get a statement in writing to this effect from your employer.

What does this mean in practical terms? A concert musician needs a practice room thirty hours a week but, because the orchestra does not provide a space for individual practice, he uses a room at home as a studio. The studio qualifies for a home-office deduction. If, on the other hand, you merely take your briefcase home at night and do some work in the evenings, you are not entitled to the deduction.

DEDUCTING ORDINARY
BUSINESS EXPENSES

Ordinary business deductions include expenses that are necessary for the operation of your business but are not included in the home-office deductions described above. If you are a salaried employee, these are expenses required for your employment but not reimbursed by your employer.

Let's discuss such business expenses in more detail.

Everyday Expenses

The most common types of expenditures are items or services used in the day-to-day course of your work: the telephone, office supplies, Internet charges, postage and shipping costs, printing and duplicating expenses, advertising and promotion charges, fees for professional services. Not all deductible expenses are quite this obvious, however. A fashion consultant who subscribes to *Vogue* or a painter who buys books on art history can deduct these expenses because it's allowable to deduct the cost of books, magazines, and newspapers related to your work. Furthermore:

- If you're a dance instructor, you can deduct the records and tapes you use for your classes.

- If you're a psychotherapist, the cost of any personal-growth seminars you attend in order to evaluate their suitability for your clients is deductible. (So are the facial tissues your clients use.)

- To a caterer, cookbooks are a business expense.

- If you're a restaurant critic, your meals out are deductible.

- If you hold sales meetings at your home, the coffee you serve— and the sugar, too—are write-offs.

- A color or wardrobe consultant can deduct the cost of mirrors in the office.

- If you're a journalist, you can deduct the daily newspaper.

- A swimming teacher giving lessons at home can claim a portion of the pool expenses.

- If you are a professional speaker, you can deduct your audio and video equipment.

- An entertainment-industry musician can deduct the cost of going to movies, subscribing to cable television, buying records, and attending entertainment-industry seminars. These are all research-related expenses that enable such a musician to keep abreast of the profession and get ideas for future work.

"Above-the-Line" Tax Deductions

Above-the-Line tax deductions are ones that reduce your Adjusted Gross Income (AGI). They are often more valuable because Adjusted Gross Income is used as the basis for calculating your self-employment tax, for establishing whether you will be able to deduct large medical expenses and casualty losses, and for Roth IRAs calculations.

Here are common AGI deductions that some people miss or that you may want to consider because of their added value:

- Keogh, SEP, and SIMPLE contributions

- Medical Savings Account

- Moving expenses

- Penalty on early withdrawal of savings

- Self-employment health insurance deduction

- Self-employment tax (one-half)

- Student loan interest

Travel

Whenever you leave home to meet with business contacts, do work-related research at the library, buy office supplies or postage, negotiate a contract, or attend a work-related class or meeting, you are making a business trip. If you happen to stop at the dry cleaner or grocery store en route, the entire trip still counts as business. You will, however, need to keep a log of your business and nonbusiness travel if you also use your car for trips that are exclusively personal.

If you use public transportation such as buses, subways, or taxis (a taxi driver will give you a receipt if asked), record the date, destination, cost, and purpose of each trip in a travel diary. If you travel primarily in your own vehicle, log all business-related mileage. Then deduct the cost in miles (in 1998, the IRS is allowing 31.5 cents per mile, plus parking and toll fees).

The alternative is to calculate what percentage of your overall car use is devoted to business, and take that percentage of your total automobile expenses (including gasoline, repairs, maintenance, insurance, and depreciation) as your deduction.

Check List: Ordinary Business Expenses

Check off any of the following ordinary business expenses that apply to your business. Review this list with your tax advisor to be sure you're not overlooking applicable deductions:

___ Accounting and bookkeeping fees
___ Advertising expenses used for prizes and contests
___ Attorney fees
___ Automobile expenses including:
    ___ Auto club membership
    ___ Garage rental
    ___ Loss on sale of auto
___ Bad debts
___ Bank service charges
___ Bankruptcy
___ Books and periodicals related to business
___ Business conventions including those on a cruise ship
___ Business meals (50%)
___ Capital expenditures (Section 179, Internal Revenue Code)
___ Career counseling costs
___ Commissions to agents or sales reps
___ Consultant fees paid to reduce cost of business
___ Copyright costs
___ Depreciation
___ Dues for professional and trade associations
___ Education expenses for maintaining or improving required skills
___ Electronic mail services
___ Financial counseling fees
___ Furniture and equipment (office)
___ Gifts (business), but limited to $25 per recipient per year

___ Health insurance*
___ Insurance expenses (including portion of homeowners')
___ Interest on trade or business debts
___ Internet services
___ Legal fees
___ License fees and taxes
___ Messenger services
___ Office furniture and equipment
___ Office supplies
___ On-line services used for business
___ Operating losses in a prior year
___ Organization expenses of corporation (amortizable over not less than 60 months)
___ Passport fee for a business trip
___ Pension/retirement plan contributions
___ Postage and shipping
___ Printing and duplicating
___ Professional association dues
___ Professional books and journals
___ Repair and maintenance of business property
___ Social Security taxes (50%)
___ Start-up expenses (amortized over 60 months)
___ Tax preparation of business tax return
___ Taxes, state and local taxes on business
___ Theft losses of business property
___ Travel expenses

45 percent may be deducted in 1999, 50 percent in 2000 and a full 100 percent by 2007

Entertainment

Home-based workers can deduct not only restaurant meals, drinks, and tickets to events such as concerts and plays—but also expenses incurred while entertaining business associates at home, such as wages for hired help, the cost of flowers, and the cost of food and drink. However, this deduction is limited to 50 percent of their total cost, and there are strict rules for deducting business meals, such as the requirement that the business discussion be directly preceding, during, or directly following consuming the meal or beverage. Besides these typical entertainment expenses, business gifts are also deductible, up to $25 per business associate, the limit since 1962.

The IRS will disallow any expense that you can't substantiate, however, so be sure to keep receipts as well as a record of people in attendance at each event, their business relationship to you, a summary of the business discussion of the event, and the date. In other words, saving a credit card receipt from a restaurant is not enough; you must fill out the reverse side with the names of the people you entertained and a summary of the business discussion, in order for the IRS to accept it as a deduction.

Business Property: To Deduct or Depreciate?

When it comes to the way tax law deals with business property, we're in the arena of depreciation and capital-expense deductions. These are terms of confusion to many people who are innocent of our labyrinthine tax system. Our purpose in the next few paragraphs is to help you think about these things so you can take maximum advantage of them.

If furniture in your home office and the equipment you require for your work can be used for three years or more, the property may be depreciated. To depreciate means that rather than deducting the entire cost of your new printing equipment in a single tax year, for example, you spread the deduction over the life of the equipment. You can also take furniture that was previously for personal use, put it to use in the business portion of your home, and depreciate it.

The decision to depreciate is a strategic one. Suppose you spend $1,500 on a color laser printer for your business. If you buy it in a year when your earnings are high, you may want to take the large deduction all at once in order to bring your taxable-income level down. If, on the other hand, you have a year when your earnings are low, you might be better off spreading out the deduction over a period of years. (The IRS, by the way, has guidelines for the amount of time over which you depreciate particular kinds of property.) Also consider that because depreciation expenses lower your gross income, they may lower the amount of self-employment tax you pay, too.

Because a computer may be the most expensive item of business equipment you buy, we'll use it as an example of how to deduct business property costing more than $100.

If you use your computer more than 50 percent of the time for business, you have two options for deducting its cost. You can deduct the cost in the year you purchase the computer, as a Section 179 capital expense, or you can depreciate it over five years. You are allowed up to $18,000 as a Section 179 capital-expense deduction. If you spend more than the maximum amount eligible for a capital-expense deduction, the excess amount can be depreciated. But the amount of property that can be taken as a capital expense cannot exceed the taxable income from a business. In other words, you cannot offset income from a job or other source using the capital-expense deduction.

Your other option is to depreciate your computer. You can use the Modified Accelerated Cost Recovery System (MACRS). Or you can use straight-line depreciation. This method spreads out the time you depreciate your equipment. Automobiles and light trucks must be depreciated over five years, and stringent limits are placed on automobile deductions each year.

A word of caution is in order here. If you use your equipment partly for business and partly for personal reasons, you will need to substantiate your deduction with adequate records proving business usage.

RENT, LEASE, OR BUY?

Virtually anything you can buy today can also be rented or leased. Your choice is a business decision of which the tax consequences may be less important than other considerations. For instance, does leasing enable you to obtain equipment you could not afford to buy? Because leasing is normally equivalent to 100 percent financing, does it let you have more money on hand for working capital? Does leasing allow you to pay for equipment or other items out of your earnings rather than using your savings or a home-equity loan? Of course, you must qualify for a lease, which means you must have good credit, though probably not as flawless for leasing office equipment and furniture as is needed to lease a car. As a general rule, you will need to have been in business for at least a year.

In terms of taxes, when you rent on a daily, weekly, or monthly basis, you are incurring an ordinary business expense; whereas a purchase is subject to being depreciated or, if it qualifies, being a Section 179 capital expense deduction. Because Congress and the IRS are constantly revising the tax code, we suggest you consult with your tax specialist before making a decision about leasing.

A lease can be another name for a rental, in which case it's called an operating lease. It can also be a way to finance a purchase, in which case it's called a capital or finance lease. Ownership remains in the name of a third party (usually a leasing corporation) for the term of the lease. A thousand dollars is the minimum fair market value—the equivalent of the purchase price—for most capital or finance leases. At the end, you can purchase the leased item for an agreed-upon percentage of the purchase price. From then on, it's yours.

How much that agreed-upon percentage is will determine the tax treatment you get. If you only pay 1 percent or 2 percent, it will be considered by the IRS as a purchase, and you need to either take it as a Section 179 capital expense deduction or depreciate it. If you pay 10 percent or more—21 percent to be safe—you should be able to deduct your lease payments as ordinary business expenses.

Leasing has a cash advantage over a purchase on credit because a lease usually requires little or no down payment, whereas a credit purchase may require 20 to 30 percent down. However, a disadvantage of leasing is that it's much more expensive than buying, since the leasing corporation includes charges to cover its overhead and make a profit. For example, *Consumer Reports* calculated that buying a $2,500 computer would cost $3,019 with a twenty-four-month lease, $2,969 if you paid for it on a credit card with an 18.8 percent interest rate, and $2,552 if you paid cash. The cash price includes a 3 percent cost of lost opportunity for the use of your money and factors in a small residual value of $188.

Technological obsolescence is often a reason cited for leasing. At the end of a lease period, you can give back what may be obsolete equipment that may have little market value. On the other hand, if you're in a business like desktop video, multimedia production, or presentation graphics, in which capability is rapidly improving while costs are declining, you may want to turn over your equipment before the lease is up. If it's a purchase structured like a lease, you could find yourself at the end of a lease with obsolete equipment you can't resell for a reasonable price.

If you do decide to rent or lease, make certain you understand the contract—especially the fine print. Rental and lease agreements are printed so that customers will think the terms are fixed. But remember, everything is negotiable, even the terms of contracts with major corporations like IBM or Xerox. The contracts are written to their advantage, not yours. Elaine Re, a national authority on negotiating, says that superior power in a negotiation isn't based on the size of the business, but on how attractive or unattractive it is for a party to make or not make a deal. Your contract may mean the difference between a salesperson's meeting a quota or qualifying for a bonus. So you do have some leverage in negotiating your contracts.

Taking into account all the ways leasing might have an impact on the operation of a particular business, you can see there is no stock answer as to whether renting, leasing, or buying is best for everyone. And it's a decision you may well want to make with the assistance of your tax advisor.

✔ **Check List:** Negotiating a Rental or Lease Agreement

Here are some points to negotiate:

___ The exact nature of the financing agreement—does it have liens or restrictions

___ The amount of each payment

___ Who is responsible for insurance, maintenance, and taxes? Usually the lessee.

___ What happens to the leased item at the end of the lease?

___ Renewal options

___ Cancellation penalties, if any

___ Disadvantageous terms and conditions

___ Length of the lease period

START-UP COSTS

Prior to the time you begin business, the money you spend is considered by the IRS as a capital expense and cannot be deducted in the current tax year as you would the ordinary business expenses described earlier in this chapter. Some of these expenses, however, can be amortized over sixty months, which means that you'll take expenses as spread over a period of years. You must file an "election" to amortize these costs, or else they cannot be recovered until you sell or close the business. This is done in conjunction with Form 4562 and an attached statement.

Money you spend investigating and preparing to begin business—like initial office supplies, market surveys and research, consultants, professional services, travel for securing customers, suppliers and distributors, organizing a corporation or partnership, occupational licenses, officially filing your business name with the county or state, and sometimes franchise fees—all qualify for amortization.

When does business begin so that you can deduct money you spend in the current tax year? For a store, it's generally when the doors open; for a partnership or corporation, it's when it begins the activities for which it is organized; for a home-based sole proprietorship, it's certainly when you make a sale but it can begin earlier if you can show you began business activities. For example, a specialized temporary help service that starts advertising for people to be included in its database and sends out notices to prospective customers that it has temps should be able to make the case that it has begun business. It might also be the act of obtaining a business license or registering your assumed business name.

If you claim expenses that should have been amortized as ordinary business expenses and they are disallowed, you lose the ability to amortize them with no deduction until you end the business. So it's a good idea to get professional advice so you can maximize your deductions at this stage and avoid costly mistakes.

MONEY FOR YOUR RETIREMENT

Because no corporate or government job is funding a pension plan for you when you're on your own, it's important to put money aside for the years when your earning ability will decline. As a self-employed person, even with a part-time business, you can provide for your own retirement and in the process reduce how much income tax you owe.

You can do this with either a Simplified Employee Pension (also called a SEP-IRA) account or a Keogh or HR-10 plan. A Keogh requires enough paperwork that most people need professional help to have one, but a SEP-IRA is much simpler. You can usually start a SEP simply by completing a Form 5305-SEP, which will be provided by any of the various vendors happy to have you invest your money with them, including banks, savings and loans, insurance companies, brokerage firms, and mutual funds.

Currently, the most you can deduct each year for a contribution to a SEP-IRA plan for yourself is the smaller of either 13.04 percent of your "net earnings from self-employment" up to an inflation-adjusted yearly maximum dollar amount. Your net earnings from self-employment are the amount on which you pay self-employment tax reduced by the amount of the self-employment tax. (This calculation leads to your not being able to reduce the amount of self-employment tax you pay, but it does reduce your federal income tax.) If you have a bad year, you can reduce or skip paying into your SEP. Keep in mind that if you have employees with either of these plans, you will be contributing to their retirement, too.

A variation of a Keogh plan, called a "money purchase plan," has a $30,000 limit because it allows up to a 20 percent deduction of net self-employment earnings. For more information on retirement plans for the self-employed, obtain IRS Publication 560. It's also a good idea to get counsel from a financial planner, which is itself a popular home-based business.

TAX RESPONSIBILITIES
OF THE SELF-EMPLOYED

As a self-employed individual you have a variety of tax obligations in addition to filing the customary annual federal and state income tax. You will need to estimate your federal taxes and pay them quarterly, for example. Also you will need to pay a Self-Employment Tax to cover Social Security and Medicare, which, if you were on a salary, your employer would deduct for and contribute to. And there are additional state and local taxes to consider, which may include sales taxes. Let's look at each of these responsibilities individually.

Estimated Tax Payments

If you are a sole proprietor, a partnership, or a shareholder in a Subchapter S corporation, you are considered self-employed. Since you don't have an employer deducting taxes from your pay throughout the year, you are responsible for making advance payments of your estimated federal income tax. If you estimate that you will owe $1,000 or more in income taxes (upped from $500 by the Taxpayer Relief Act), you are required to make estimated payments. Estimated tax payments are due quarterly—on April 15, June 15, September 15, and January 15—and are filed on a Form 1040-ES. At the end of the tax year, you will file a final Form 1040 with a Schedule C, which itemizes your business expenses for the whole year.

To avoid underpayment penalties—which are substantial—individuals whose adjusted gross incomes were under $150,000 need to have paid at least 100 percent of their prior year's tax bill. People whose incomes were over $150,000 need to have paid 110 percent of the amount they owed in the prior year.

It's in your interest to make your estimated tax payments during the year. This system also keeps you from owing a large sum of money all at once, which can be overwhelming. If your state of residence has income taxes, as most do, you will have to make estimated tax payments throughout the year for state taxes as well.

Self-Employment Tax

Your estimated tax payments will also include the federal self-employment tax—Social Security and Medicare. If you were employed by someone else, your employer would pay half of your Social Security and Medicare and the other half would come out of your paycheck. Self-employed people must pay the full amount themselves; however, 50 percent of the self-employment tax is deductible on the 1040 form.

What if you are a salaried employee and you operate a home-based business as a sideline? In this case, you'll be filing both the usual Form 1040 and a Schedule C for your home-business deductions; you may also have to pay additional self-employment tax. No matter how little your sideline income is, you should be aware that it is subject to tax—although by taking advantage of the home-office deduction, you may find you owe little or no taxes.

Employment Taxes

Home-based workers who employ others must comply with many additional tax requirements. IRS Circular E, Employer's Tax Guide, covers the federal regulations, and your state tax agency can inform you of state requirements for employers with regard to income, state unemployment, and workers' compensation taxes.

If you employ your children or grandchildren, their earnings are deductible. Family businesses do not need to pay Social Security or unemployment taxes on minor children, and the children pay no income taxes on the first $3,000 of earned income. To substantiate this claim, keep time records of their work (the records will be more believable to the IRS if a nonrelative keeps them), note the work done, and pay family at the rate you would pay a non-family member for the same work.

State and Local Taxes

Depending on where you live, you will face a variety of state and local tax requirements. All but seven states—Alaska, Wyoming, Nevada, Florida, South Dakota, Texas, and Washington—have state personal-income taxes (New Hampshire and Tennessee only tax income derived from stocks and bonds). But even those may have taxes on businesses. For example, Florida levies an income tax on corporations. Some cities, like Kansas City, have earnings taxes apart from the state income tax; others have unusual taxes on business. New York, for example, taxes unincorporated businesses.

Sales Taxes on Goods and Services

If you sell taxable goods and services from a home-based business, you must pay state sales tax in all states but New Hampshire, Delaware, and Oregon, which manage to stay afloat without a sales tax. Handicrafts, antiques, silk flowers, and pet products are all examples of taxable goods; if you operate a repair service, the parts you use may be taxable.

Taxable services are difficult to pinpoint and vary greatly from state to state. In California, for instance, taxable services include printing, audiotape duplication, videotape rental, and some aspects of word-processing services. This is a tricky area; you may think the services you are providing are not taxable, when in fact they are. And since state tax authorities are very serious about collecting their sales taxes, it's important to check with your local agency to find out whether your work falls into a taxable category.

One woman we met ran a graphics business without being aware that her work was subject to sales tax. After five years in business, she was audited—and the amount she owed for five years' worth of sales tax plus penalties and interest was so high that it forced her to close up shop.

Check rates, too. They vary within states because many cities, counties, and special districts collect sales tax; it's been calculated that there are over 10,000 different sales tax rates in the United States.

MAKING SURE YOU QUALIFY
FOR YOUR BUSINESS DEDUCTIONS

Just because you and your clients consider you to be self-employed does not mean the IRS will agree. As companies rely increasingly on consultants, freelancers, outside services, and independent contractors instead of hiring permanent employees, the IRS is taking a growing interest in assuring that such arrangements are not just a way for both parties to avoid paying conventional taxes.

Should the IRS decide that you are an employee masquerading as an independent contractor, you will find yourself in the worst of all possible worlds. You will receive neither the fringe benefits that accompany employment nor the tax benefits available to the self-employed.

Therefore it's increasingly essential, unless you are working from home as a salaried employee, to take every precaution to set yourself up in a way that clearly demonstrates that you are an independent, self-employed individuals in business for yourself. In fact, one magazine was sufficiently alarmed that they featured a headline proclaiming "The IRS Wages War on the Self-Employed." Every week two thousand or more people who may have considered themselves to be self-employed individuals working as independent contractors for their clients are being reclassified as employees.

Some industries are being targeted more aggressively than others, specifically the computer field, construction, entertainment, health care, and travel. In the data-processing industry, for example, a survey showed that because of this problem, three out of four companies had reduced or eliminated contracts with independent engineers, consultants, and other technical people. Some state agencies are taking a more aggressive stance in this area as well; e.g., California, Colorado, Georgia, Illinois, Michigan, Pennsylvania, New York, and Texas.

A video director told us, "I've got one client now who refuses to deal with me on any basis other than as an employee. I submit a time card and my company invoices separately for equipment rental." As the director observed, "Since I only work for them occasionally, can you imagine what would happen to our business relationship if every time I completed a project with them, I went down to file for unemployment!"

Whether or not you're in these industries or these states, if you have only one or two clients, especially if one of your clients is your former employer, you should be aware of what can happen should the IRS decide to reclassify you as an employee. Here's what happens.

When you are reclassified as an employee, the company you've been working with, your client, will be assessed for the back taxes it didn't withhold for you as an "employee" and will be slapped with a 100 percent penalty for not having withheld taxes from your wages—even though you paid them yourself. You, on the other hand, will owe back taxes, because:

- You took off business expenses before calculating how much you would pay in self-employment tax (Social Security and Medicare) and therefore you paid less federal income tax than you would have if you were an employee.

- If you were paying for health insurance, you may have taken the 45 percent deduction you were allowed as a self-employed person. As an employee, this deduction would be disallowed and you would owe the difference.

- As a self-employed person, you may have put money aside in a retirement plan, such as a SEP, and deducted this from your federal income tax. Once you're classified as an employee, you can only deduct the $2,000 allowed for an IRA, so you may be penalized for overcontributing.

- Due to the loss of these deductions, you may have underpaid your estimated taxes and could then be assessed a penalty for underpayment.

 Caution

You should also know that if you are reclassified by the federal government, they will report it to your state agencies and, if you were reclassified by a state agency, they will report it to the IRS.

Obviously, any self-employed person who for any reason may be vulnerable to being reclassified needs to take specific steps to protect his or her right to remain in business. The following checklist outlines the criteria the IRS looks for in determining whether someone is an employee or self-employed. The more of these criteria you meet, the safer you will be.

Work Sheet: Preserving Your Independent Contractor Status

The key to who is employed and who is self-employed is essentially a matter of control—who calls the shots with regard to how you work. Following is the text of the twenty issues contained in IRS Publication 937 that serve as guidelines for determining this issue of control. Below each issue are examples of specific measures you can take to demonstrate that you are in fact an "independent" businessperson and not an employee. Language from the IRS publication is in italics, followed by our recommendations. See how many you can check off:

___ 1) *Instructions. An employee must comply with instructions about when, where, and how to work. Even if no instructions are given, the control factor is present if the employer has the right to control how the work results are achieved.*

Whenever possible, take the initiative to be the one who spells out the contract between you and your clients. Have a standard contract that you can modify for each project that is printed on your letterhead and that clearly spells out the terms of your agreement. Focus the agreement on the results or service you agree to produce.

___ 2) *Training. An employee may be trained to perform services in a particular manner. Independent contractors ordinarily use their own methods and receive no training from purchasers of their services.*

Take on work that you are clearly already trained to carry out. If prospective work requires additional training, secure your own training from an outside source and pay for it yourself.

___ 3) *Integration. An employee's services are usually integrated into the business operations because the services are important to the success or continuation of the business. This shows that the employee is subject to direction and control.*

Outsourced work is increasingly becoming a mainstay in the operations of many companies. Entire business functions such as public relations or office management are now outsourced and, of course, there is nothing an independent contractor loves more than to become indispensable to a client's operations. But to protect your independence, make your "outsider" status apparent.

Avoid having office space set aside for you on your client's site. Use your own equipment as much as possible. Do not give out your client's phone number as a place where you can be reached. If you must take calls while on a client's premises, have your calls forwarded from your own business number rather than giving out your client's number. Hold as many meetings as possible on your own premises or at a third location.

___ 4) *Service rendered personally. An employee renders services personally. This shows that the employer is interested in the methods as well as the results.*

(Continued on page 300)

(Continued from page 299)

As a sole proprietor you will most likely be rendering your services personally, so everything you do to meet other criteria is that much more important. One of the most significant things you can do is incorporate. Although this can be expensive, it establishes a separate business identity for you.

Provide a copy of your certificate of incorporation to your client. Having evidence in your client files is important because IRS and state agencies audit companies, and you may not even know that this is happening. So providing your clients with tangible evidence can make your case for you when you're not there.

Whether you incorporate or not, use a business name distinct from your own.

Have a business telephone line that is listed on your business card and letterhead. Obtain a business license and provide a copy to your clients. If you have a truck or car that you can have your business name on, have it photographed and appear in a brochure or at least provide a snapshot to your clients. Have a separate business bank account in the name of your business into which you deposit payments from clients. The endorsement with your business name is more evidence of your independence.

Never use a resume. That communicates "employee."

____ 5) *Hiring assistants.* *An employee works for an employer who hires, supervises, and pays workers. An independent contractor can hire, supervise, and pay assistants under a contract that requires him or her to provide materials and labor and to be responsible only for the result.*

Again, as a sole proprietor, you may not have any plans to hire others to carry out any particular aspect of your contracts, but you can and, when feasible, it is to your advantage to do so. Nonetheless you most likely will use other outside services, such as printers, travel agents, or graphic or secretarial assistance. Keep track of receipts and checks covering such costs related to each project. And although it might help your bottom line, don't be tempted to rely routinely on your client's employees as your support staff. This will also help you avoid the impression of your being an integral part of your client's workforce.

____ 6) *Continuing relationship.* *An employee generally has a continuing relationship with an employer. A continuing relationship may exist even if work is performed at recurring although irregular intervals.*

We all hope to have a continuing relationship with our best clients and customers. To protect your independent-contractor status, however, make sure that each project is clearly time and/or task defined and that each new project with past clients is rebid, renegotiated, and occurs under a new and separate contract.

____ 7) *Set hours of work.* *An employee usually has set hours of work established by an employer. An independent contractor generally can set his or her own work hours.*

(Continued on page 301)

(Continued from page 300)

With a personal organizer or software like Lotus *Organizer,* you can keep track of time spent on projects for various clients to help you demonstrate that your time is divided among your clients and that it varies week by week or month by month according to your own priorities and demands.

____ 8) **Full-time required.** *An employee may be required to work or be available full-time. This indicates control by the employer. An independent contractor can work when and for whom he or she chooses.*

Always having more than one client simultaneously is one of the best ways to protect your independent-contractor status. Therefore whenever you are working primarily with one particular client, you should make sure to consistently invest both time and money in marketing for additional clients. Document both the time and money you spend marketing and administering your business.

____ 9) **Work done on premises.** *An employee usually works on the premises of an employer or on a route or at a location designated by an employer.*

The more work you are able to do in your own home office, the better. This is also now critical to making your home office your principal place of business in order to qualify for a home-office tax deduction as well. Hold client meetings at your home office or at conference facilities that you pay for, and track the hours spent working on each project in your home office to help demonstrate your independence.

____ 10) **Order or sequence set.** *An employee may be required to perform services in the order or sequence set by an employer. This shows that the employee is subject to direction and control.*

Make sure that the contract or letter of agreement you have with your clients spells out what you will do but does not define the order, sequence, or method by which you will do it.

____ 11) **Reports.** *An employee may be required to submit reports to an employer. This shows that the employer maintains a degree of control.*

Although informal or formal progress reports may be essential to some contracts or to keep clients happy, in negotiating a contract, when possible limit required reporting to a final report to be delivered upon completion of a project or make report preparation a discrete billed activity.

____ 12) **Payments.** *An employee is paid by the hour, week, or month. An independent contractor is usually paid by the job or a straight commission.*

Although you may use hourly fees to calculate your final bid or quote, working on a flat fee basis better safeguards your independent status. This means that carefully tracking the time it takes to complete each project you undertake is vital so

(Continued on page 302)

(Continued from page 301)

that you have a history upon which to estimate accurately flat fees that realistically reflect the amount of time you actually need to complete a new project. Cases, however, have been won when the worker was paid on an hourly basis.

___ 13) **Expenses.** *An employee's business and travel expenses are generally paid for by an employer. This shows that the employee is subject to regulation and control.*

To safeguard your independent status, build as many expenses as possible into your flat fee rather than billing for them separately. Or charge a per diem to cover travel and expenses instead of billing by the item. This means, of course, that you need to obtain firm quotes on your business expenses, so that you don't end up eating unexpected costs and losing money on a project.

___ 14) **Tools and materials.** *An employee is generally furnished significant tools, materials, and other equipment by an employer.*

Outfit your home office with the equipment and tools you need to carry out your work without having to rely on the resources of your clients. Purchase all materials used on a project yourself and build the costs of these materials into your fee structure.

___ 15) **Investment.** *An independent contractor has a significant investment in the facilities he or she uses in performing services for someone else.*

Setting up, equipping, and supplying your home office adequately is an investment that demonstrates your independent status. A separate business telephone line, a separate business bank account, and a variety of accounts with vendors and suppliers are all indications of your investment in your own business.

___ 16) **Profit or loss.** *An independent contractor can make a profit or suffer a loss.*

One consequence of getting paid a fixed fee rather than working by the hour is that, indeed, there is the potential of incurring either a profit or loss depending upon whether you have accurately estimated your costs and time.

___ 17) **Works for more than one person or firm.** *An independent contractor is generally free to provide his or her services to two or more persons or firms at the same time.*

Once again, having multiple clients for whom you work at the same time on a schedule at your own discretion is one of your best protections. Just be sure to document time spent working for your various clients, especially if you are concerned about being able to meet other criteria. Provide clients with nonconfidential information in a letter or memo about other clients you serve that is kept in a company file.

(Continued on page 303)

(Continued from page 302)

___ 18) *Offer services to the general public.* *An independent contractor makes his or her services available to the general public.*

The more visible you are as an independent business, the more clearly you meet this criterion. The more high profile your marketing efforts, the better; advertising, listings in professional and trade directories, active participation in business organizations as a business, a Yellow Pages listing, or other ongoing advertising all show you are actively offering your services in the marketplace. Be sure to provide evidence of these to your clients for their files.

___ 19) *Right to fire.* *An employee can be fired by an employer. An independent contractor cannot be fired so long as he or she produces a result that meets the specifications of the contract.*

Make sure you have contracts that clearly spell out the terms of your agreement so that, in fact, you cannot be let go until completion of a contract as long as you are meeting the specified terms. Building in a cancellation fee is also a good idea.

___ 20) *Right to quit.* *An employee can quit his or her job at any time without incurring liability. An independent contractor usually agrees to complete a specific job and is responsible for its satisfactory completion or is legally obligated to make good for failure to complete.*

Again, be sure to have a clear contract covering what you will provide and under what circumstances you can cancel a contract. Be scrupulous about meeting contractual obligations.

Be able to demonstrate how you could, or have, called upon others to work under your auspices to carry out aspects of contracts when you have been unable to do so yourself. Be able, in other words, to demonstrate that you have reliable backup to handle overload or emergencies as a business would.

 Caution: Form 2208

We have described many things you can do to protect your independence. Now let's mention something you are probably best advised to avoid. You're apt to see or hear about IRS Form SS-8. This form is used by companies to get a determination from the IRS as to whether someone is an employee or an independent contractor. SS-8 has three pages of questions and specifies a variety of documents to be submitted with it. The complexity of SS-8 will help you understand why so much effort is needed to make it clear you are a business. Reportedly 90 percent of IRS SS-8 determinations find that someone is an employee. These are not good odds, so what you need to do is to establish yourself so clearly as an independent business that your client company will not be tempted to get an SS-8 determination.

Caution: The Hobby Rule

The IRS presumes an enterprise is a hobby (and not eligible for deducting losses to offset income from other sources) if it does not show a profit for three years out of five. So to meet IRS standards, the business needs to be showing a profit by its third year; however, this presumption may be rebutted.

If you can show a calendar or other records to document that you have put in a substantial amount of time and are serious about making a profit; if your losing money is due to circumstances beyond your control or is normal for the type of business you have chosen; if your activities show a businesslike approach (see "Fourteen Money-Saving Ways to Give Your Home Business a *Fortune* 500 Image" on page 86); and, of course, if you are depending on the business for your liveli-hood (and getting by through borrowing, living on earnings, etc.), you may still be able to claim your business deductions. Be prepared to prove to the IRS that yours is a serious business and not a hobby.

When You Mail Something to the IRS

When you mail a tax return or any important document to the IRS, use certified mail, return receipt requested. This is acceptable proof that you filed the required documents even if the IRS loses them.

KEEPING ADEQUATE TAX RECORDS

Clear, complete records of your income, expenses, assets (such as a computer or fax machine), and liabilities (such as loans or notes) enable you to minimize your taxes and to defend yourself in the event you're audited. The IRS does not specify what form your records should take, but you must be able to substantiate any claim you make.

Think of your records as footprints; the written documents—invoices, bank statements, canceled checks, deposit slips, and especially receipts—are the paper trail that your business operation leaves behind. You can either maintain your records yourself, hand over the task to a professional, or use some combination of the two.

Receipts are particularly crucial because they back up your claims for business expenses. Get in the habit of obtaining receipts by paying with a check or credit card (there's automatically a paper record), asking for a receipt, or creating one immediately upon expenditure. Suppose you make a long-distance business call from a pay phone—no receipt. Then create your own, writing down the expense and its business purpose on a piece of paper, in a logbook, or on an appointment calendar.

Some people consider it sufficient to place all their receipts and tax records in one box or envelope. Then they try to sort things out at the end of the year. We discourage this shoe box approach to record keeping.

First, the shoe box gives you no sense of where you stand financially during the year, and it provides no help in calculating your estimated taxes each quarter. You're forced to accomplish all your tax organizing at tax time, taking valuable hours and energy away from your daily business. In addition, it's too easy for some things to miss getting in the box. Keeping track of your expenses as they occur increases the likelihood that you'll claim all your deductions and thereby minimize your taxes.

Whatever record-keeping system you develop, the important thing is finding one that's comfortable and effective enough so you will use it routinely. If you don't want to do it all yourself, get the help you need during the year to keep on top of your financial records. See chapters 14 and 15 for specifics on developing a record-keeping system that will work well for you.

Forty-three percent of small-business owners say what they dread most about tax season is the time, hassle, and paperwork. Nearly half say they begin preparing their taxes three months in advance of April 15 each year! So the more consistently you've kept records throughout the year, the more time, hassle, and energy you'll save yourself at tax time.

GETTING THE HELP YOU NEED

"Look for an accountant or tax professional who speaks to your potential. Find someone who sees you as bigger than you are. Chances are good that that person will help you immeasurably in getting there."

MIKE RUSSO, CPA AND PRESIDENT, MICHAEL RUSSO & COMPANY

Tax law is not only complicated; it changes constantly. Unless you're a trained tax expert, we recommend getting professional help in preparing your taxes. When tax time arrives, you'll want to continue carrying out your work as productively and enjoyably as possible. You certainly don't need to get bogged down in tax complexities.

In fact, if your tax return is at all complex, having tax help is not only desirable but essential. In one case, the IRS actually leveled a negligence penalty against someone on the grounds that his tax return was too complicated to complete himself.

For tax help, you need someone who keeps up with the continually changing law, IRS code, tax rulings, and cases. The IRS alone issues a new ruling every two hours of each workday. You also need someone who has experience and empathy with home-based businesses in general and your type of business in particular.

Too often we've heard tales of home-based workers selecting professionals whose experience has been only with large traditional businesses. As a result, they have received advice that was either inaccurate for their situation or contrary to their best interests. Although you really don't want someone whose main experience is with larger companies, according to CPA Michael Russo, "You don't want to use someone who insists that you are a 'small' business. Your tax person should work toward helping you grow and reach your full potential."

Although there are other alternatives, including tax attorneys and tax consultants, we believe an accountant or an "enrolled agent" is generally your best choice for tax help. Accountants not only prepare your tax returns at filing time but also can be considered, along with your lawyer, as part of a team of professional advisers to whom you can turn throughout the year. They can set up your record-keeping system, perform certified audits, represent you to the IRS, prepare financial reports or statements, and help you with tax-planning decisions.

Accountants may be one of the more expensive sources of tax help, but in the long run their assistance can save you more than they cost. A Certified Public Accountant, or CPA, has had formal training in accounting, earned a college degree, and passed a tough state certification examination.

Charging about one-third less than a CPA, an enrolled agent can prepare your return and is eligible to represent you before the IRS and the tax court as your tax preparer. These agents have received their "enrolled" status either by passing a two-day examination given by the IRS or by working for the IRS full-time for at least five years.

Accountants who are not certified are called Public Accountants and may or may not be licensed by the state. They are qualified by experience and perhaps have had special training. They generally cannot represent you before the IRS as your tax preparer.

To find a tax professional, ask for recommendations from someone who's successful doing work similar to yours. We think it's a good idea to use someone whose practice is about the same size as your business. You might locate a CPA like that by contacting the American Institute of Certified Public Accountants society in your state for the names of accountants who serve on the Small Business Committee or its equivalent. Then communicate with firms on that list until you find an accountant who understands your tax situation and with whom you're comfortable.

You can locate enrolled agents in the Yellow Pages, or call the National Association of Enrolled Agents referral line at (800) 424-4339 to obtain a list of enrolled agents in your area.

For even less costly tax help, you can go to a tax preparation service.

The level of service you receive, however, is also limited. Tax preparation services are often so conservative and routine that they may advise against legitimate deductions.

The following checklist contains suggestions for questions to ask and things to look for when you interview to find your tax specialist. You may need to interview a number of firms until you find someone right for you. Although the usual guideline is to find a specialist you are comfortable with personally and philosophically, consider finding someone who balances your tendencies: If you are inclined to be creative with your deductions, find a tax preparer who focuses on documented facts and is a problem solver. If you are fearful about claiming tax deductions, find a more aggressive professional who will help expand your notions. But most of all, find someone who is knowledgeable. Tax law is constantly changing—there have been thirteen major changes in tax law since 1980—and you need someone who keeps up. In the process of meeting and interviewing these and others you choose to serve you, you will learn what other people do in presenting themselves effectively and not so effectively that you may be able to apply to how you present yourself to prospective clients.

 Checklist: Considerations When Interviewing a Tax Specialist

____ Is the tax preparer full-time or part-time? Tax law is so complicated, staying abreast takes a significant investment of time.

____ Is the tax professional available throughout the year or just during tax season?

____ How many tax returns does the preparer do each year? Eight hundred returns is about tops for an individual; too few returns is also a warning sign.

____ Does the specialist understand and believe in entrepreneurship?

____ Can the specialist communicate understandably with you about your business?

____ How often does the specialist quote the tax code to you rather than figuring out the best solution to your tax situation?

____ Does the specialist seem too good to be true?

____ Does the specialist belong to a professional association?

____ What is the specialist's training and experience in preparing tax returns?

____ How much will it cost and how is the fee calculated?

(Continued on page 308)

(Continued from page 307)

____ How does the specialist check returns for accuracy?

____ What type of continuing-education courses does the person take? Are they relevant to your tax or accounting needs?

____ Are you comfortable with how your questions are answered about the home-office deduction or some other subject about which you have some information? How does the information compare, and did you gain any insights?

____ Look at the books on the shelves. Is there a tax weekly or monthly newsletter? Loose-leafs like those from Research Institute of America and Commerce Clearing House? Tax information on CD-ROM?

____ Does the specialist have a Web site that you can check out before going to his office?

____ Are the specialist's self-employed clients never audited (the tax specialist may be too conservative) or audited too often (exceeding one chance in fifty-one if you file a Schedule C and make $25,000 to $100,000; or one in thirty-two if you earn over $100,000—this compares with 1 in 152 for all returns)?

____ Can the specialist represent you before the IRS if you're audited?

____ Has the specialist had experience appearing in IRS appeals?

____ Will the specialist pay any penalties and interest resulting from his or her errors, and has this ever happened? Has she ever paid a negligence penalty to the IRS for her own negligence?

USING YOUR COMPUTER
TO DO YOUR TAXES

Although we recommend using computer software for your business accounting, the records you create with your software are not sufficient to satisfy the IRS. Therefore, paper records are essential. Fortunately, tax-preparation software has gotten so user-friendly that some home-based businesspeople rely on it to calculate their own taxes. Among the best tax-preparation programs are Intuit's *Turbo Tax* and Kipplinger's *TaxCut*. These programs are updated and released each year to reflect changes in the tax laws, and each February or March, computer magazines review the various revised programs.

Because tax programs have built-in assumptions that may not apply to your unique business situation, we recommend that you still have your return reviewed by a tax professional.

Remember, accounting programs and tax-preparation programs are not the same. As New York accountant Irvin Feldman explains, "Tax rules and accounting rules are very different. Accounting rules have some logical basis as opposed to tax rules, which are designed simply to raise money and perform some social purpose." This means that there are no software packages that will do both. You must know the possible tax consequences of treating something a particular way before you do it.

WHAT IF YOU'RE AUDITED?

The self-employed are unfortunately more apt to be audited than salaried Americans. But need you fear an audit? No one wants one, but wise preparation and action can see you through an audit, and if you don't give the IRS an opportunity to exact more money from you, you'll be a less desirable target in future years.

The IRS conducts three types of audits:

• *Correspondence audits.* These are computer-generated adjustments. They come about because of discrepancies between what you report and other information the IRS has. For example, if you and your spouse are a partnership and one of your clients reports your fees using your Social Security number instead of the partnership's Federal ID number, you will get a deficiency notice from the IRS. You can respond to this by mail, supplying documentation of your position.

• *Office examinations.* You or your tax specialist is summoned to appear at an IRS office with your records. However, if the matter in dispute is

---

Difficult, or Impossible, Deductions

- You can't rent part of your home to your own corporation or to your employer in order to qualify it as income property eligible for deductions that you ordinarily would not qualify for as a home office.

- You can't claim your family dog as a watchdog because you have inventory stored at home.

- You can't take a home-office deduction for managing your stock portfolio.

- Deductions for landscaping and lawn care are no longer allowed, even if you have clients or customers coming to your home office.

- You can't deduct any tax penalties or interest.

unambiguous, your tax representative may be able to convince the IRS to resolve the matter by mail.

• *Field examination.* An IRS agent comes to your premises. If you have claimed a home-office deduction, an agent can come to your home, yardstick in hand, to measure the space you have claimed.

The most common are office audits, accounting for over half. Field audits and correspondence audits split the balance of IRS audits.

HEADING OFF AUDITS

You can head off an audit by providing lots of documentation with your return. Your tax preparer should be able to warn you if an item is likely to raise IRS scrutiny. Then you can include documentation such as notes of explanation and copies of canceled checks to circumvent the difficulty of locating records several years later and, more important, to avoid the time and trouble of an audit.

Besides being able to document all your deductions, here are some tips from experts:

1. *Respond to the IRS within the time specified,* although your response does not have to be immediate. Take the time to think things through and find the records you need. Make copies; don't send originals. Use certified mail, return receipt requested. That's an excellent idea for filing tax returns, too.

2. *Review key resources.* The IRS is required to provide you with information about your rights in notifying you of an audit. We suggest going beyond that and reading books like Frederick Daly's *Stand Up to the IRS* for invaluable advice on dealing with an audit.

3. *Don't go to an office audit yourself.* Have someone—a CPA or an enrolled agent—represent you. If you do appear yourself, don't volunteer any information. Someone on the Working from Home Forum once told about having his home-office deduction questioned. The part-time business qualified, but the taxpayer overjustified how he deserved the deduction by saying he not only used the office for his own business but also for after-hours work for his employer. The after-hours work did not meet the "convenience of the employer" test, and the whole deduction was disallowed.

4. *Never send or bring records that are not related* to the matter being questioned. To do so opens up the possibility that other aspects of your finances will be examined. It's not in your interest to arouse an agent's

curiosity about items not being questioned or about past years. For all practical purposes, the job of IRS personnel is to collect money, and consequently their position is an adversarial one. It is therefore to your advantage to get the best advice you can from the moment there might be difficulty.

Items That Invite IRS Audits

- High Schedule C losses from a part-time business.

- Deductions incongruous with your gross income. IRS computers are programmed to find discrepancies like a $15,000 entertainment deduction on a return from a home-based day-care center that grossed $22,000.

- Grossing less than $25,000 or more than $100,000.

- Making overt mistakes on your return such as errors in math or incorrect Social Security number.

- Not reporting all your 1099 income.

- Far-fetched business deductions, like claiming nylons because you must dress up for business meetings.

- Payments to family members as employees. Remember to keep records of when family members work and what they do.

- Items on the tax form preceded by solid black darts. These items are viewed with particular care by the IRS.

LETTING CONGRESS HEAR FROM US

We estimate that there are some seven million people in the "underground" economy today—people who are engaged in legal business activities but who are not filing or paying income taxes.

We believe that two principal reasons for evading taxes are the complexity of the tax system and the heavy burden of the higher Social Security and Medicare taxes that are imposed on the self-employed.

The laws and interpretations of the IRS relative to home-office deductions, however, may change as a home-office constituency begins to exert its influence on Congress and the executive branch. Squeaky wheels do produce reform. We have been told that each letter received by a representative or senator is perceived as equaling the sentiments of 27,000 constituents. Thus it is clearly in your interest to express your views on the tax system and to suggest ways it can be altered to improve the situation of home-based workers.

RESOURCES

BOOKS AND OTHER PRINTED INFORMATION

A Common Sense Guide to Retirement Plans for Self-Employed People. Fidelity Investments, free booklet; (800) 544-4774.

Cut Your Taxes (**annual**). Kevin McCormally. Washington, D.C.: Kiplinger Books. ISBN: 0812929438.

J.K. Lasser's Face to Face with the IRS: Successful Strategies for Dealing with Audits. Robert G. Nath. New York: MacMillan General Reference, 1997. ISBN: 0028616065.

J.K. Lasser's Tax Deductions for Small Business. Barbara Weltman. New York: MacMillan General Reference, 1995. ISBN: 0028603133.

J.K. Lasser's Taxes Made Easy for Your Home Business. Gary Carter. New York: MacMillan General Reference, 1997. ISBN: 0028620267.

Pension Plans for Small and Mid-Sized Businesses (**CPA's Practice Guide Series**). John B. Wollenberg. New York: Wiley, 1996. ISBN: 0471133914.

Stand Up to the IRS, **3d ed.** Frederick W. Daily. Berkeley, Calif.: Nolo Press, 1996. ISBN: 0873373375.

Tax Planning and Preparation Made Easy for the Self-Employed. Gregory L. Dent, Jeffrey Johnson, and Jeffery E. Johnson. New York: Wiley, 1995. ISBN: 0471114936.

Tax Savvy for Small Business: Year-Round Tax Advice for Small Business, **2d ed.** Frederick W. Daily. Berkeley, Calif.: Nolo Press, 1997. ISBN: 0873373723.

SOFTWARE

AgreeMentor. Jian Tools, 1975 W. El Camino Real, Suite 301, Mountain View, Calif. 94040. Software for independent-contractor agreements. (800) 346-5426; (650) 254-5600. Web: *www.jian.com*

The following tax programs include Schedule C and supporting forms, along with the ability to calculate depreciation. You may also import financial data from your accounting program (e.g., **Quicken, Peachtree Complete Accounting,** and **SOHOMaster,** as described in chapter 14) directly into your tax program. You can use one of these programs to organize piles of receipts and to get an idea of what forms you will need from among those included with the program. Then you can calculate how much tax you owe and take the results to a tax professional and see how close the program came to the professional's conclusions.

Kiplinger's TaxCut. Block Financial, P.O. Box 9211, Boston, Mass. 02205; (800) 457-9525; (800) 235-4060. Web: *www.taxcut.com*

TurboTax. Intuit, Inc. 2535 Garcia Avenue, Mountain View, CA 94043; phone: (800) 796-2600. Web: *www.intuit.com*

ON LINE

Price, Waterhouse, Coopers. This well-known accounting firm has answers to taxpayer questions at *www.taxnews.com/tnn-public*

Deloitte & Touche. Tax help and work sheets. *www.dtonline.com*

Intuit. The manufacturer of *Quicken* and *TurboTax* offers tax help at its on-line tax center. *www.qfn.com/taxcenter*

IRS Online. All IRS publications and forms are available online. *www.irs.ustreas.gov*

L.A. Times Online. The *Times'* burgeoning Web site offers much helpful tax and business information. *www.latimes.com/taxes*

State tax forms. *www.1040.com/state.htm*

OTHER FORMS OF HELP FROM THE IRS

The Internal Revenue Service provides assistance in a number of ways. These include:

Telephone assistance: (800) 829-1040.

Tax Forms and Publications:

For IRS Publications and tax forms call (800) TAX FORM. These will be mailed to you. Publications addressed to specific tax topics pertinent to a small business include: *Basis of Assets* (#551), *Business Expenses* (#535), *Business Use of a Car* (#917), Circular #E, *Employer's Tax Guide* (#15), *Depreciation* (#534), *Employment Taxes and Information Returns* (#937), *How to Begin Depreciating Property* (#946), *Selling Your Home* (#523), *Tax Guide for Small Business, Taxpayers Starting a Business* (#583), and *Travel, Entertainment, and Gift Expenses* (#463).

RECORDED TAPES

The IRS's Teletax provides prerecorded information on over one hundred topics on tape. You can also find out about the status of your refund by calling (800) 829-4477. For a directory of tapes, press 123.

CLASSES AND WORKSHOPS

Classes and workshops are offered by the Internal Revenue Service. Call your nearest IRS office for subjects, dates, and locations.

CHAPTER 11

Insurance: What You Need and How to Find It

Goals

1. Identify your home-office insurance risks.

2. Discover what's covered and what's not.

3. Decide what kind of and how much insurance you need.

4. Find the best insurance companies.

5. Save money on your insurance.

6. Find affordable, reliable health and disability insurance.

7. Plan adequately for your retirement.

8. Keep accurate records.

9. Find needed help.

It was shocking! We conducted a series of interviews with entrepreneurs to find out what types of insurance home-based businesses buy. We expected a routine litany of basic home-office insurance coverage that we've written about since the first edition of *Working from Home*. The answers we got revealed several startling and disturbing realities:

- Over two-thirds of the home-business owners we interviewed had no business insurance of any kind!

- Most of those without insurance didn't know they needed it!

- Many without insurance mistakenly thought they were automatically covered by insurance they already had!

- Others wanted insurance but couldn't get it!

A recent study conducted by the Independent Insurance Agents of America confirmed our findings:

- Over 60 percent of in-home businesses are not properly insured.

- Entrepreneurs between the ages of fifty-five and sixty-four are the most at risk in terms of having inadequate business insurance.

- Forty-four percent of those surveyed stated that they didn't have business insurance because they mistakenly believed that their private insurance provided adequate coverage.

Who are these uninsured home-business owners? Many of the people we spoke with run highly successful, professional businesses. Most are equipped with state-of-the-art computer and home-office technology. Some are doing over $100,000 a year in business.

Yet, surprisingly, only one in four of those we talked with had any protection against theft, damage, or other loss of their business equipment. Not only do those without coverage lack endorsements on their homeowner's or renter's (sometimes called "apartment dweller's" insurance) insurance to cover such losses; some don't even have homeowner's or renter's insurance in the first place. In fact, one man whose home office is filled with thousands of dollars' worth of expensive biofeedback equipment and elaborate proprietary computer systems didn't even know there was such a thing as renter's insurance.

This is not the only area of insurance protection that home-office workers neglect. We found that one in six home businesspeople were operating without health insurance. This compares with other recent findings that 46 percent of all self-employed people in California, for example, lack health insurance. Our research also showed that most didn't have insurance covering business use of their automobiles even when they regularly transported business products and equipment. And only one in ten had disability insurance.

The reasons people gave for not having coverage varied. Some open-collar workers went without business insurance because they judged their risks to be too small to justify the cost of added insurance. Others found the cost of insurance was simply beyond their budgets. This was particularly true with regard to those without health insurance. One of the most common reasons people weren't adequately insured was the mistaken belief that their business activities were covered under their homeowner, auto, etc., plans.

We were equally startled to discover that many people are desperately trying to get insurance but can't seem to obtain what they need. Some have spent months searching, with no results. Others have purchased insurance only to discover that it didn't cover certain key things they needed. One man, for example, purchased business property insurance only to find that it didn't include loss from theft or water damage. A computer programmer insured his computer with a special separate policy only to find that the insurance didn't cover loss of his stored data, only the cost of the media itself. Still others are being turned down for insurance because they work from home. This is particularly true regarding disability insurance.

At first glance, it seems that we're in the midst of an insurance crisis, partly of our own making and partly due to a lack of awareness by the insurance industry of the needs of home-based business activity. In this chapter we will attempt to clear up the major misconceptions, myths, and misunderstandings we've uncovered about insurance for the home office. This will help you to identify what you do need, how you can get it, and when you should have it.

INSURANCE MYTH #1: *It Won't Happen to Me*
FACT: Bare Bottoms Can and Do Get Burned

Insurance is simply one of many strategies available to manage the risks of doing business from your home. Preventing the risk in the first place is, of course, the best method. Staying healthy, keeping your property in good repair, securing your home and auto, doing a high-quality job, and maintaining your equipment are a few examples of how you can protect yourself from risks. Planning to absorb any risk that occurs is another alternative. If you virtually never have business visitors come to your home, for example, or if you never carry business equipment in your car and don't have inventory, you might feel that your needs for specialized insurance covering these risks are so low that you might opt to "take your chances." In some cases you can find ways to shift the risk to others. For example, suppliers can carry the risk of materials or equipment in transit to you; customers can carry the risk on items you ship to them.

> *In 1997 more than 1.5 million desktop and laptop PCs were stolen, damaged, or destroyed with losses of more than $2.5 million.*
>
> SOURCE: SAFEWARE

Let's consider a few all-too-real-life examples that illustrate why being insured can save you money, put your mind at rest, and in some cases save your business. A computer consultant who specializes in hardware was delivering $20,000 worth of equipment to a client when he was held up at gunpoint. Both his car and the equipment were stolen. Loss of the equipment was not covered under his insurance because he didn't have property insurance that protected his business equipment off the premises. The consultant wound up having to pay for the stolen merchandise in order to provide it to his client. The resulting cash-flow crunch nearly put him out of business.

Thirty-seven-year-old marriage and family counselor Nadine Barney was stricken with the Epstein-Barr virus after five years of managing a successful counseling practice. She was unable to work, and as a single woman and head of her household her loss of income led to the loss of her busi-

Work Sheet: The Ounce-of-Prevention List

It's much easier to prevent problems than to defend yourself against them once they've occurred. Here is a list of things you can do to avoid ever having to use your insurance. Check off those you're doing and star those you should institute.

____ Keep your home in good repair. Inspect wiring, plumbing, water heater, and air ducts and clean chimneys regularly.

____ Don't overload your electrical circuits. Upgrade or reroute circuit breakers if they start going out frequently.

____ Repair cracked sidewalks, banisters, stairs, doorways, eaves, and overhangs.

____ Eliminate potential hazards like icy steps, slippery rugs or floor surfaces in halls and entryways, file drawers that open into doorways, decorative or art objects that could easily fall over on someone, etc.

____ Install smoke detectors and replace the batteries regularly. You might even consider installing a sprinkler system.

____ If your dog bites, your cat scratches, or your pet boa squeezes a little too hard, make sure to take the proper containment measures.

____ Follow the steps outlined in chapter 7 to secure and protect your property from burglary and vandalism; e.g., install outdoor lighting and secure door and window locks.

____ Take measures to protect your computer data and office equipment described in the Resources list in chapter 8; e.g., make sure that you back up data, have a surge protector, provide an uninterruptible power supply (UPS), install a virus protector, etc.

____ Install an automobile security system to prevent break-ins. Systems range from low-cost devices that lock your steering wheel to sophisticated tracking systems like Lojack or others with alarms, etc. Even with insurance, you can only replace the equipment you've lost, not the work you had in your briefcase; so preventing a theft is doubly important.

____ Don't accept work that is beyond your capabilities or skills.

____ Live healthfully, exercise regularly, get enough sleep, eat sensibly, reduce stress, and create an ergonomically and ecologically sound environment for yourself (see chapter 8).

____ Do any of these sound familiar to you?

ness, her savings, and ultimately her apartment. She lived with her mother while she recovered and after three years was able to rebuild her business. She wishes she'd had disability insurance but admits she had never even thought about it until it was too late.

In recent years, fires have swept through northern and southern California. Many hundreds of homes were burned to the ground in seconds. We were touched by a story in the *Los Angeles Times* about one woman, an author, who was in her home office proofreading chapters from a book she was writing when the kitten in her lap tensed up and began to act strangely. She looked up and saw a huge cloud of smoke billowing across the canyon. Suddenly a neighbor was yelling for her to get out. She looked at the VCR, the computers, the antiques, and the clothes. She was still clutching the first few chapters of the book she had been working on and, in the end, that's all she took when she jumped into her car as a police officer ordered her to leave.

Having only recently completed our survey on home-office insurance, we wondered if she had insurance to cover the business aspects of her loss. If so, did it cover her computer? Did it cover the data? Did it cover the other losses she would experience from the interruption of her business? The answers to those questions would have made a major difference in her life. They certainly did for pioneering information broker Sue Rugge.

 True Confessions: Outstanding Invoices Up in Smoke

Sue Rugge lost everything in her home and home office in the 1991 Oakland, California, fires including tens of thousands of dollars' worth of accounts receivable for information research she had completed for her clients. She thought her home-owner's insurance policy would cover her home-office loss. It didn't. That's what publicist George Craighton discovered, too, when a fire swept through the home office he'd set up in the back of his garage. Fortunately none of his clients sued him for failing to complete his contracts on schedule. But what if they had? This possibility didn't occurr to him until after the fire.

Sue's and George's situations, and those of others we've talked with or read about whose home offices were destroyed in the Florida hurricane or the L.A. earthquake, prompted us to think about our own situation. What if these catastrophes had befallen us? Our home and business equipment is covered, but our data isn't. What if this manuscript and our research were destroyed? What if we were injured and couldn't keyboard for several months, as happened to our son? We don't have business-interruption insurance, and at the time we didn't have disability insurance.

How would we live? Where would we start? We had to ask ourselves which risk is cheaper in the long run: taking our chances that these disasters won't happen to us, or investing in insurance we hope we will never need to use? Of course, each of us must answer this question on our own. But here's our conclusion.

Rule of Thumb: *Only risk what you can afford to lose.*

INSURANCE MYTH #2: *I Don't Need That Coverage Because . . .*
FACT: You're Probably Not Covered

We were amazed at the reasons people gave us for not having insurance. Here are just a few of the most common ones: "I don't do anything dangerous." "I'm very conservative." "I don't take risks." "I'm only doing this part-time." "I'm just a freelance consultant." "I don't need that protection because my homeowner's insurance already provides it." "I don't need that coverage because I never have anyone come to my house." "I don't need that coverage because I don't use my car for business." "That's covered through my auto insurance." Do any of these sound familiar to you?

Like the emperor with no clothes, many home-business owners make these assertions with astonishing confidence, certain they're safe or already covered when clearly they are not. It's one thing to decide to take your chances on not being insured, but it's quite another to discover that you needed insurance for a risk you didn't realize you were taking, or worse, to think you're covered when in fact you're not.

The most common misunderstandings concerned business-property insurance, liability insurance, and auto insurance. So let's straighten out the facts about these.

Your homeowner's or renter's insurance probably doesn't cover your business property. People often think they don't need additional insurance because they believe their existing homeowner's or renter's insurance will cover any loss or damage to their business equipment, furniture, and supplies in the event of fire, theft, or other catastrophes.

In fact, basic homeowner's or renter's policies do protect you from damage or loss to your personal property, but they usually explicitly exclude coverage for any business uses of your premises. The standard form for homeowner's coverage lists as an exclusion: "business property pertaining to a business being conducted on the residence proper." Also, if your home office is in a separate, detached structure, the structure and its contents may not be covered.

Always check your policy for restrictions and limitations to make sure you have ample coverage for damage or loss to your business property. You might even find that running a business from your home voids the coverage of your policy altogether or that there are limits as low as $200 on what you can recover in case of loss from fire, burglary, or other damage to "property used or intended for use in a business." If you are unsure of any of your coverages, discuss your questions in detail with your agent.

When adding up the value of your computer, printer, software, answering machine, filing cabinets, desk, chair, fax, and copy machine, you'll find that you have thousands of dollars' worth of business property to protect. In such circumstances, the limits on your policy could mean negligible compensation.

If you are only able to get homeowner's insurance with these kinds of limitations, you can broaden your coverage by getting an endorsement, also called a rider or a floater, that raises the amount of coverage to include your business equipment. You can also purchase a separate policy to cover your business equipment. A separate policy may have the advantage of covering "mysterious disappearance" of property, whereas homeowner's policies don't usually allow for this contingency in the event of theft. Also, a separate policy can pay off at the stated value or the replacement cost of an item without figuring in the depreciation factor included in many homeowner's policies.

If you own a computer, you may want to get either an endorsement to your homeowner's policy or a special "floater" policy (also called a rider) to cover risks unique to computer owners. In the event that a power surge wipes out your $600 software or destroys six months' work on disk, this kind of policy can be well worth the expense. An alternative to a rider is to get special computer insurance from a company like Safeware, (800) 848-3469 (Web: *www.safeware–ins.com*), which costs from $50 to $159 a year and also includes protection against fire and theft of hardware, software, and other media; however, policies covering data loss will be more expensive. You can even get a policy that covers portable computers, personal organizers, and personal assistants. Safeware offers an international policy that replaces portables should disaster strike while you are on the road. Premiums for such insurance run from $60 to $400 with a $50 deductible.

Standard homeowner's or renter's insurance doesn't cover liability for accidents or injuries to customers and other business visitors, including delivery of packages related to your business. These policies only protect you from *personal* liability if a guest is injured while visiting your home. Even if you never have clients, customers, or colleagues who come to your home, you may still need to have additional coverage.

The good news, however, is that many homeowner's or renter's policies can be broadened to protect you by covering injuries to business visitors from such everyday mishaps as slips and falls, dog bites, and tripping on stairs. This liability coverage for home-business activity is available even if you live in an area not zoned for home-office use. If your business is such that you get the coverage you need by adding an endorsement to your homeowner's policy, you may pay only $20 to $40 a year for the additional coverage. Such endorsements are referred to as an "incidental business option," "incidental office occupancy," and a "business pursuits rider." Typical language for such an endorsement is "The residence premises shall not be considered a business property because an insured occupies a part thereof as an office, school, or studio."

However, if you have employees in your home, work outside your home, are incorporated, or use a name other than your own, incidental office coverage will not be enough. Some companies also take the position that full-time businesses cannot be covered by an extension of a homeowner's policy. In this case, a business owner's policy, or BOP, costing $250 to $500, will probably cover most of your insurance needs, including coverage while you're away from your home; however, many insurance companies may not be willing to insure some home businesses, such as catering, in which liability risks are perceived as significant. In these cases, coverage needs to be sought from companies that specialize in insuring the particular business. A home-based caterer, for example, should look for companies that specialize in insuring catering services and restaurants.

Companies like Cigna, Continental, and Traveller's offer policies that are tailored to the needs of home-based businesses. Continental Insurance's HomeWork option to their homeowner's policy combines a variety of business coverage, such as business property on and off premises, loss of income if your home is damaged and you cannot do business, and various liability coverage for less money than you would pay for individual policies.

Excluded from liability coverage, however, are claims for injuries or damage that result from the actual rendering of services or sale of products. Protection for these kinds of claims requires additional coverage such as malpractice, errors and omissions, or product liability insurance, depending on your particular business. One of the best sources for locating them if you are in a business that exposes you to such risks (i.e., psychotherapy, software design, programming, accounting, etc.) is through your trade or professional association. Note that such professional liability policies can be expensive.

Your existing insurance probably does not cover business losses in your car. Sometimes people are surprised to discover that if they have an automobile accident while on a business trip or if business property is stolen from their car, the damage or loss may not be covered under their existing property insurance policy. We've talked with people who had computers and other more specialized business equipment stolen from their cars, only to find that it was not covered. Musician Tony Atherton was rear-ended on the way to a rehearsal. Fortunately he was unharmed. Sadly, the same couldn't be said for three saxophones in the trunk of the car. The company paid to fix the car, but the $5,500 he had to pay to replace his horns left a year-long imprint on his cash flow.

Auto insurance poses some additional considerations. Let's say you're delivering the food and trimmings for a banquet you're catering and someone rear-ends your van. Will your auto insurance cover the injury? Risk management consultant Fred Carter from San Francisco tells us that the carrier will probably cover that particular accident. But, if you've led your carrier to believe you're using the car only for private use or travel to and from work, when a claim occurs that clearly reflects business use, the carrier may discontinue your policy or increase your premium.

Carter advises, "Be sure that your car is rated as a business auto if it's used to transport equipment to be sold or used in your work or if it is used to transport employees, clients, or customers."

And even if you don't use your car to carry equipment or clients, because you will undoubtedly be traveling for business purposes at some time or another, we advise that you review your insurance with your agent and determine if you need to make adjustments in either your auto or property insurance to cover your business travel. That's what we did and, indeed, our rate did go up somewhat when our car was listed for business, but the increase was minimal.

Without general liability insurance you may be safer at home than out of it. Insurance broker Toby Haynes of Pasadena, California, considers the risks of liability for home-based entrepreneurs to be greater when they're working away from their offices than when they're working at home. If you do any of your work in the homes of your customers, you might, for example, accidentally knock over and break an heirloom vase. Or suppose you're sponsoring a training program in a conference facility at a hotel and a participant slips and breaks a leg on the polished conference room floor. You would probably be named, along with the hotel, as a defendant in any resulting lawsuit.

Rarely would any of the personal insurance you now have protect you from risks such as these, but general liability insurance will. It costs only several hundred dollars a year. If you are self-employed and do any part of your work away from home, this coverage is a wise investment. And you're not just protecting yourself from your own clumsiness or oversights; in today's litigious environment, you're protecting yourself from situations over which you may have no control, like slick floors, fragile chairs, and clumsy clients.

General liability can also be obtained by adding an endorsement or rider to your homeowner's policy, a small-business insurance package, or one of the home-office packages. Companies also offer custom products, like special-events coverage, to fill in additional gaps.

Exercise caution when you shop for a general-liability policy. You need to be certain it will pay for attorneys' fees and other costs of defending yourself in case you are sued. Unfortunately, anybody can sue anybody else in today's world, but not everyone can afford an adequate defense. Traditionally, defense costs have been covered without limit, but now some carriers are setting limits.

Rule of Thumb: *When it comes to insurance, assume you need it unless you find proof you actually don't.*

INSURANCE MYTH #3: *I'm not Running a Business, I'm Just . . .*
FACT: **Business by Any Other Name Is Still Business**

Part-time, full-time, sideline, moonlighting, teleworking—it doesn't matter. For insurance purposes, any type of business-related activity probably means you are not covered for the necessary insurance protection on a personal policy.

This is particularly true with regard to partnership insurance. Under the law, you are liable for the actions of your business partners. This is the case in both formal and informal partnership arrangements. Yet business or personal insurance does not cover your partners. If you are operating a business in partnership with anyone else or undertaking a joint venture of some type, it is wise to consider having partnership insurance to protect you against suits arising from the actions of your partner(s).

Many everyday situations are considered "business" as well. For example, if a UPS delivery person brings a business package to your home, it's considered business even if you didn't intend for him to come. If a colleague or customer drops by unexpectedly to discuss business, it's still regarded as business even if she wasn't invited. And what if a repairman comes to fix your computer? That's business, too.

> **Rule of Thumb:** *Never assume you're covered for business purposes on any personal policy. If you are doing any business in your home, have your existing insurance reviewed by a knowledgeable insurance professional to see what risks involved in your business activities are not covered.*

INSURANCE MYTH #4: *It Costs Too Much*
FACT: **Many Types of Home-Office Insurance Are Surprisingly Affordable**

Attorney Arnold Goldstein states in his book *Starting a Business on a Shoestring* that the average cost of conventional business insurance can run from $8,000 to $10,000 per year. Only rarely would a home-based operation require such an investment. Some types of coverage will cost only a few additional dollars a year.

The same is often true of extending your auto or liability insurance. Covering your vehicle for business use may cost $100 or less a year. And general-liability insurance costs only several hundred dollars a year. Insuring yourself against such risks will become more expensive, however, when you have sufficient inventory, equipment, or business activities for which an extension on your homeowner's or auto insurance is not feasible. Even then, your cost is apt to be in the hundreds, not the thousands.

A small-business policy provides more extensive coverage than you can get from adding a business endorsement. It will compensate you for your property damage from disasters like fire, theft, vandalism, and lightning but will also cover loss of business data and lost income from occurrences that riders do not. It also protects you from lawsuits that claim personal injury or damages resulting from defective goods or breach of contract.

Discuss with your insurance agent which choice is best for your business, particularly if more than 20 percent of your residence is used for business purposes or when your business activity has a high risk of liability, such as catering or manufacturing handmade toys for children. Also, if you have over $3,000 in business inventory on hand, you should consider a small-business policy or separate business-inventory insurance.

> **Rule of Thumb:** *Phase in your insurance as you grow, adding additional coverage as your profits increase.*

Even though insurance is less costly when you operate a business from your home, getting all the insurance you ideally need can be a daunting expense at start-up time. This is particularly true if you add in the cost of health and disability insurance. Therefore, we asked financial consultant Dan Silverman of the Silverman Group in Los Angeles to recommend a plan for phasing in your insurance costs as you grow. He recommended the following:

• *Start-up.* If your budget is limited, get only the essential coverage at first: property, liability, auto, and medical.

• *Growth and expansion.* As your business grows, increase the limits on the essential coverage and add disability, term life insurance, and basic financial planning.

• *Established and profitable.* Maximize limits on all essential coverage and obtain equity life insurance, retirement planning, and a complete financial plan.

INSURANCE MYTH #5: *I Can't Get Insurance*
FACT: Of Course You Can!

Unfortunately we found that, far too often, people working from home run into problems getting insurance once they decide to buy it. We have a gigantic file from the *Working from Home* Forum on CompuServe filled with messages from people who tried to find various types of insurance, but to no avail.

This was particularly true with regard to securing health insurance, disability insurance, and errors-and-omissions insurance. It seems that some companies will not issue certain types of insurance to someone who is home based. Other companies may issue the insurance, but at a prohibitive cost. To make matters worse, we've also heard that occasionally months can pass before a company will notify someone that they won't provide coverage.

Warren Whitlock, who sells and services printers, told us that after going out on his own, his health-insurance policy rose to $500 a month. Due to claims on her prior policy, management consultant Sharon Connell hasn't been able to get health coverage at all after leaving her tenured university position. Private investigator and information broker Russell Koogler was unable to renew an errors-and-omissions policy. Most companies balked at issuing him a policy because he works from home. Mercury Auto Insurance denied us auto insurance on the basis that we worked from home! But 20th Century Insurance was happy to insure us.

Despite the frequency of such problems, the insurance agents we spoke with assured us that a good broker who is sufficiently interested in you and your business will take the time required to locate policies that meet your needs. We agree.

Sometimes problems in getting insured arise because working from home is still somewhat unconventional. It doesn't fit the long-established pattern. That means the agent must make a special effort to work with the insurance company to find out what additional steps need to be taken. In our case, for example, Bruce Norman, vice president of Mercury Insurance, told us that when someone's occupation can't be verified by an employer, they request that an additional application be submitted for review and approval. He therefore advises people working from home to allow at least thirty days for their applications to be processed.

If you're having trouble finding the insurance you need, locate a general agent who will take the time and make the effort to produce results for you. Don't settle for anything less. Silverman worked on behalf of Sarah for over nine months before he found her a good, affordable disability program—but he did it! So don't give up, and find an agent who won't either.

Your clout as a business consumer is growing. You are part of the fastest-growing segment of American business—small business. As we mentioned earlier, companies like Hartford, Fireman's Fund, and Travelers realize this and tailor policies to meet our needs. So if you encounter problems getting the coverage you need, keep looking. There are companies that will eagerly welcome your business.

Rule of Thumb: *The right agent can probably find what you need. Expect results or change agents until you get them.*

One note of caution, however. Using several policies, underwritten by several companies to create a patchwork of coverage, has its drawbacks. Often one company will withhold a payment on a claim and justify it by stating that claim falls under protection provided by another company. You will then need to coordinate between two (and sometimes more) companies and fight for your payment. This can be a long, frustrating process.

You'll find there are many different companies with a wide variety of policies to offer. Availability varies from state to state. Terminology also differs from company to company, policy to policy, and state to state. Nonetheless, these guidelines should serve as a starting point for talking with your agent to find out if you're covered where you need to be!

ASSESSING YOUR INSURANCE NEEDS

Now that you're familiar with the myths and the facts of insuring your home office, you can fill out the *Home Office Insurance Work Sheet* below to see if you, too, may unnecessarily be going bare without knowing it. Then discuss the work sheet with your insurance agent.

Note: The average premiums and coverage we describe on the work sheet are purely guidelines and may not be applicable to you. They were developed for us by chartered financial consultant Dan Silverman of the Silverman Group in Beverly Hills, California. He based these figures on a composite of the average home-office worker: a male, age thirty-eight, in good health, married with children, a sole proprietor working from home in a service-related business like computer consulting, public relations, word processing, or desktop publishing owning between $5,000 to $7,000 of business property, and living in a large metropolitan area. Silverman estimates someone living in a smaller community may pay 30 percent less.

 Work Sheet: Home-Office Insurance Work Sheet

Indicate in the status column below which types of insurance you think you Already Have (H), Don't Need (D), and Want But Can't Get (W). Then use this work sheet to review your insurance needs with your lawyer and/or insurance agent.

STATUS	TYPE OF INSURANCE	WHAT IT COVERS WHO NEEDS IT	ESTIMATED AVERAGE COST
_____	Liability	Costs of injuries occurring to business-related visitors while on your property—if you ever have delivery people, clients/customers who come to your home	$15–$100 per year when added as a rider to homeowner's policy

(Continued on page 327)

(Continued from page 326)

STATUS	TYPE OF INSURANCE	WHAT IT COVERS WHO NEEDS IT	ESTIMATED AVERAGE COST
_____	Business Property	Protects you from damage or loss to your business property—if you have equipment in your home office used for business	$100–$150 per year for $5,000–$7,000 of equipment
_____	Small Business	Provides coverage for losses when you have more extensive inventory or equipment than you can protect by adding a business endorsement or rider to your homeowner's insurance. Also covers general liability, business interruption and loss of earnings, errors and omissions, and product liability, although these policies can be purchased separately.	$250–$500 per year
_____	General	Damages from accidents occurring while you are on someone else's property. Useful if you do some portion of your work on someone else's premises.	Part of small-business insurance or several hundred dollars if purchased separately
_____	Business Interruption	Protects you against losses not being able to do business due to damage from fire or disaster causing you to close, relocate, or cut back your business while you recover, for example, funds for loan payments, payroll, relocation costs.	$100 per $10,000 in coverage or included as part of small-business insurance

(Continued on page 328)

(Continued from page 327)

STATUS	TYPE OF INSURANCE	WHAT IT COVERS WHO NEEDS IT	ESTIMATED AVERAGE COST
___	Special Computer	Risks related to your computer hardware, software, and data. Applicable if computer-related losses can't be adequately covered under your property or small-business insurance.	$89 yearly for $5,000–$8,000; $109 yearly for $8,000–$11,000; $129 yearly for $11,000–$14,000
___	Malpractice, Errors and Omissions, or Product Liability	Insures you against claims or damages that arise out of services or products you offer. You need to consider this if the work you do could inadvertently inflict an injury or loss on clients or customers.	Varies by the risks involved. Runs from hundreds to thousands annually.
___	Health	Cost of illness or injury. Everyone needs health coverage.	Premium is based on age, health status, and where you live.
___	Disability	Protects you from loss of income when you are unable to work due illness or injury. Necessary if you would need to have some form of income should illness or injury prevent you from working for an extended period of time.	Premium is based on age, income, and health status. Salary of $35,000 yearly; $2,000 monthly payment after 90 days = $682 per year; salary of $100,000 per year; $5,000 monthly payment = $1,562 yearly
___	Workers' Compensation	Compensates you for costs work-related injuries. Available primarily for employees. State regulations vary. May be called State Disability Insurance.	Provides bare-bones coverage for about $200 per year.

(Continued on page 329)

(Continued from page 328)

STATUS	TYPE OF INSURANCE	WHAT IT COVERS WHO NEEDS IT	ESTIMATED AVERAGE COST
_____	Auto Related	Loss of business property while in your car and costs of accidents arising while you or someone on your behalf is driving your car for business. Necessary if you drive for business other than to and from work, especially if transporting equipment or goods or if someone else drives for business.	Average auto policy costs $725 yearly up to $100 for business coverage.
_____	Partnership	Protects you against suits arising from the actions of any partners in your business.	$500 fidelity bond

Obviously, your rates and premiums will vary depending on your age, type of work, where you live, and so forth.

Because, as we have mentioned, certain types of insurance present particular problems or are more of a challenge for home-based business operators to obtain, the following information about specific types of insurance can assist you and your agent in meeting your needs.

HEALTH INSURANCE

If we were writing this book at the turn of the century, when most people worked from home or very near it, we would not have much to say about health insurance. Few people had it. Blue Cross didn't begin until 1929 when a group of Dallas schoolteachers started paying a hospital fifty cents a month to prepay for their maternity care if and when they had children. Now, as we write this, health care consumes one in every seven dollars of our national economy and is rising.

National debate on health-care reform is a near constant. We do not know if a national health-care plan will ever be adopted. We do know that health reform is happening in some individual states in an effort to address the problems that have developed over the last several decades. States like Hawaii, Oregon, Vermont, and Florida are in various stages of offering their citizens a "universal" plan.

Chances are, however, that until things change, you will have to find your own coverage and meet the challenge of obtaining a good policy. Nevertheless, a self-employed person or couple has many choices these days. Blue Cross and Blue Shield plans pride themselves on offering policies for individuals, including the self-employed. Pacificare has developed plans specifically for self-employed individuals. Other companies serve the self-employed as well. If you cannot find satisfactory and affordable coverage through such companies, there are options, each with its advantages and disadvantages.

FIVE FALLBACK HEALTH-INSURANCE OPTIONS FOR THE SELF-EMPLOYED

1. Joining a health-maintenance organization (HMO), like Kaiser Permanente, or a preferred provider organization (PPO). Although we list managed care as an alternative, the fact is that better than four out of five Americans have one form of managed care or another. So chances are this is what you will do.

2. Check out hospitalization policies available from professional and trade organizations, trade unions you're eligible to join, college alumni/ae associations, and chambers of commerce—your own or even one in another area.

3. Explore possibilities of getting coverage under the company of an employed spouse.

4. Investigate policies offered by nonprofit organizations that seek to provide affordable health insurance to the self-employed.

5. Consider establishing a Medical Savings Account (MSA)

Until health coverage becomes easily available to the self-employed, we must fend for ourselves. So whatever options we choose, we need to get the best deal we can and avoid the hazards too many of us now experience. The following lists discuss what to look for in health-care coverage, the principal hazards, and what to do to prevent or deal with them.

A Word About Medical Savings Accounts (MSAs)

Medical Savings Accounts (MSAs) were created to address the problem that to find affordable health insurance, many self-employed people must choose policies with high deductibles. MSAs allow you to put the amount of the deductible into a tax-exempt savings or investment account that you use to cover medical expenses not paid for by your health plan. Money you do not spend from this account can be rolled over from year to year and eventually used for retirement.

To be eligible for an MSA you must be self-employed, the spouse of a self-employed person, or an employee of a small group employer. Individuals must have a health plan with an annual deductible of at least $1,500 but no more than $2,250. For a family, the deductible cannot be lower than $3,000 nor larger than $4,500. However, the amount that is tax-exempt is limited to 65 percent of the individual deductible and 75 percent of the family deductible.

To set up an MSA you must do it through an approved financial institution separate from the health-insurance company. Mellon and Wells Fargo are large banks that offer MSA accounts. Congress only authorized a pilot program with a maximum of 750,000 subscribers, which restrained the number of institutions and major insurance companies (about fifteen) willing to develop MSA programs and policies. Lack of competition has limited what's available, particularly with respect to the high deductible insurance policies, so that after a year and a half, fewer than 100,000 people have set up MSAs. So whether Congress will authorize the creation of more MSAs after 2000 is in doubt. For more information, contact Mellon Bank (888) 256-3722, Wells Fargo Bank (800) 544-8880, or search the Web using the term "Medical Savings Account."

HOW TO AVOID THE SIX MOST COMMON COMPLAINTS ABOUT HEALTH INSURANCE

These are the most frequent complaints we hear from self-employed people and what you can do about them:

1. The policy excludes from coverage entire organ systems, such as reproductive, respiratory, or digestive. As one person on the Working from Home Forum on CompuServe said, "When I got my policy, it had riders attached that exempted any part of my body a doctor had ever looked at with more than a passing glance. Another rider exempted any problem of any kind having to do with a kidney or anything attached to it! I had naturally passed a kidney stone about five years ago, had no surgery or complications, but spent two days in the hospital."

Keep shopping. Don't buy a policy that doesn't protect you.

What-to-Look-for Checklist: Health Insurance Providers

Although selecting health insurance is apt to be a series of trade-offs between what you can afford or are willing to pay and what is desirable, here are some characteristics to seek.

___ Quality of care

___ Coverage if you become sick or injured without major exclusions, such as limiting coverage to in-hospital care only.

___ Rates and deductibles you can afford. Of course, the higher the deductible, the lower the monthly premium, and you may qualify for an MSA. You should request a rate sheet that tells you the rate based on your age and location and how long that rate will be in effect. If the company requires other information about you in order to give you the rate, that's a company to rule out.

___ Guaranteed renewability. Look for phrases such as "guaranteed renewable" or "not cancelable by the company for any reason except nonpayment of the premium."

___ An insurance carrier that is licensed in your state, offering an accredited health plan, that has superior ratings by one or more of the insurance-rating services.

___ Pay benefits based on customary costs, not by a fixed schedule. Rigid limits on what the insurer will pay is how people wind up with medical bills far beyond their deductible.

___ Choice of doctors

2. *The policy denies claims, delays payment, or only pays part of the charge.* This is an all-too-frequent experience: "Eventually they covered a part of the bill, but it has taken a year to collect. Meanwhile we paid the whole thing out-of-pocket" is an often-heard refrain.

Notorious for this practice are companies whose policies are sold in conjunction with membership in business associations, but this problem happens even with national insurance companies that have good ratings.

To prevent this from happening to you, before you buy a policy, check out the company with your state insurance commission. Many states provide information on a company's history of complaints. California, for instance, publishes comparative listings of justified complaints against insurers for property insurance as well as health and life. These ratings are expressed in terms of complaints per million dollars of premiums and allow comparison with the prior year. They also provide the dollar volume of premiums collected. As a general rule, it's wise to do business with larger companies. Other states calculate the number of consumer complaints received per thousands of policies in force.

Other items to find out about are the company's payment ratio/percentage and what percentage of physicians and health-care providers will accept the company's coverage as payment. Ask these and other questions of the insurance agent or salesperson. Don't let a loose or evasive answer pass; verify critical information by calling the insurance company after the sales representative leaves. This means you won't be a one-appointment sale. Resist any salesperson who pressures you into an instant decision.

If you are having problems getting an insurance company to pay your claim, you can either use the services of a medical claims assistance service, file a complaint with your insurance commission, or in extreme cases, use an attorney. Some insurance carriers make a practice of stalling and stonewalling in the knowledge that many claimants will simply give up. But as is exemplified in the movie *The Rainmaker*, juries have made significant awards of damages against insurance companies for operating in bad faith, so squeaky wheels can get attention.

3. *The policy costs $200 to $500 a month above what a group plan would cost.* To get around this, many self-employed people have purchased polices through group plans. Sometimes this results in a decent policy, but often today you can get as good a policy on an individual plan as a group plan.

As a general rule, insurance sold by or provided through associations' packages offers limited benefits. These plans are attractive to small businesses because they typically offer to insure employees at rates 10 to 50 percent or more below health insurance from major carriers. But there are a number of reasons to be wary even if you are willing to compromise by taking the limited benefits.

First, some national associations and chambers of commerce have been sponsoring health insurance plans for decades and doing a satisfactory job. However, some of these plans are not underwritten by an insurance company, but instead by a Multiple Employer Trust or Multiple Employer Welfare Arrangement (MEWA). MEWAs may have inadequate capital, be owned by a foreign corporation that does not meet U.S. standards, and may evade U.S. regulation or be subject to only limited supervision by the Department of Labor under the Employee Retirement Income Security Act (ERISA). After ERISA was passed, some associations were invented as a way of selling insurance. Some offer real membership benefits beyond insurance; others do not. Because of increased enforcement by federal and state officials, abuses are waning.

In addition, an association health plan will probably not be regulated by your state's insurance commission. Therefore, you cannot obtain financial information and complaint records on the plan from your state insurance commission. This also means that if the association's plan becomes insolvent, you will not be eligible for benefits from your state guaranty fund—a safety net that covers individuals when insurance companies become unable to pay claims.

Finally, if members of the association make many claims, rates are apt to be increased dramatically, then large numbers of people will drop out as they find better insurance, and the rates go up even higher. If you wish to drop out, too, but have made a claim, you may find replacement insurance even more prohibitively expensive because you will be deemed to have a preexisting condition by other companies.

An alternative to association coverage if you have employees or are a corporation is to lease your employees, including yourself, from an employee leasing company. The leasing company is apt to be eligible for large group rates, but check out the insurance company underwriting the leasing company plan. Employee leasing companies are listed in the Yellow Pages.

4. *The insurance company offers a reasonable rate when you sign up but then boosts the rate.* Some companies make a practice of providing a "low ball," that is offering an initial rate far below their cost and then doubling, tripling, or even quadrupling your premiums the next year.

To avoid this, assure that your rate is being pooled with a sizable population and that the experience of that entire population will be the basis for new rates. You might experience a 20 percent increase if that's what the trend is, but you'll be pooled with a large-enough population so that if you or one of your employees gets ill, it won't substantially affect your rate.

This is another reason to check a company's complaint history with the state insurance commission. You can also often find out about companies' track records by asking about them on line.

5. *The company boosts your premium after paying a claim.* "The claim was settled, but when the policy came up for renewal they almost doubled the premium" is another all-too-frequent complaint.

If you don't want this to happen to you, avoid a policy that uses an *experience rating*, because one bad claim and your rates will skyrocket. You want a policy that is based on *community rates*.

6. *You are told your health insurance is no good and find out that the bills are unpaid.* Having once served as a trustee in bankruptcy cases, Paul remembers cases where bad health insurance led people to financial ruin. With medical costs being so high, virtually everyone is medically indigent without good health insurance.

You need to invest the time to check out any health-insurance carrier—be it a Blue Cross plan, an insurance company like CIGNA, or an HMO. Chances are when you think of stable health insurance, you think of Blue

Cross. After all, Blue Cross companies cover nearly two out of every five Americans, but even some Blue Cross companies have had financial problems. West Virginia Blue Cross went under and Blue Cross of Illinois was under a credit watch. Another mistaken assumption is that "big is safe." This is not necessarily the case, either. Major insurance companies like Mutual Benefit Life, Executive Life, Monarch, First Capital, and Fidelity Banker's Life have failed.

HOW TO DETERMINE THE FINANCIAL STABILITY OF AN INSURANCE COMPANY

Most insurance companies have a rating that reflects their financial stability. But even before turning to a rating service, if you haven't heard of a company, you should first determine from your state insurance commission office if the company is licensed to do business in your state. If not, you are at risk. If so, go on to check its rating.

Five services rate life- and health-insurance companies. They are the A. M. Best Co., Duff & Phelps, Moody's Investor Services, Standard & Poors, and Weiss Research. The rating systems vary somewhat, but all are now based on letter grades. For your peace of mind, you want to get an insurance company with at least an "A+" from Best, an "AA+" rating from Duff & Phelps, an "Aa3" from Moody's, an "AA" or above from Standard & Poors, or a "B-" from Weiss. Fewer than one in four or five insurance companies will achieve these ratings. Not all the rating services rate all the companies; this is because, with the exception of Weiss Research, insurance companies pay for being rated. Blue Cross companies are rated by Weiss Research, and some are rated by Standard & Poors.

To find out how your insurance company or one you're considering is rated, first ask your agent. Also Best's Insurance Reports can be found at most libraries. Duff & Phelps ratings may be found in the National Underwriter Profiles described in the Resource list. A. M. Best ratings are offered via a 900 number at $2.50 a minute; the number is (900) 424-0400. To get the rating, you need to know the company's ID number. You can get it by calling Best at (908) 439-2200 or look up the company in a directory found at library reference desks entitled *Best's Agents Guide to Life Insurance Companies.*

Weiss Research charges $15 for a verbal report, consisting of a letter grade with brief explanation; $25 for a one-page report mailed to you; and $45 for a complete report on a company. Weiss now also rates property and casualty carriers.

You can also find consolidated ratings in *Insurance Forum,* a monthly newsletter that costs $75 per year. Its annual ratings issue shows the letter ratings by company from all the ratings services except Best. For the ratings issue, send $20 to P.O. Box 245, Ellettsville, IN 47429; (812) 876-6502. *Insurance Forum* also publishes what the publisher, Joseph Belth, calls a "watch list" of companies that fare poorly on four or more of the dozen key ratios that indicate the financial health of insurance companies. These ratios are developed by the National Association of Insurance Commissioners, which collects the information on which the ratios are based from insurance companies.

A number of companies now provide price comparison services. Some are also agencies; others link you to local agents. Here are some of them:

- *4freequotes.com*—automobile, homeowner's, renter's/condo/co-op, flood, motorcycle, watercraft, and life insurance. Links to brokers and agents in all fifty states.

- AccuQuote—life insurance. Comparisons include price, features, and financial strength of over 1,100 life insurance products. You can get quotes over the phone. 3180 MacArthur Boulevard, Northbrook, IL, 60062; phone: (800) 442-9899. Fax: (847) 480-7380. Web: *http://www.accuquote.com*

- BestQuote—life insurance companies, 23600 Mercantile Rd., Suite E, Beachwood, OH 44122. Quotations list the assets, industry rating, and years in business of companies quoted. Phone: (800) 896-8006. Fax: (800) 896-8007. Web: *http://www.bestquote.com*

- Quotesmith Corporation—life insurance companies and Blue Cross and Blue Shield plans for health insurance, term life, individual and group dental, single-premium-deferred annuities, long-term care, and the Medicare supplement. Comparisons include rates, coverages, and financial stability ratings and are mailed or faxed the same day. Each request is $15 and each product category and deductible amount is an individual request. Quotesmith is also a general agency that sells many of the policies it compares. Quotesmith, 8205 S. Cass Ave., Suite 102, Darien, IL 60561; phone: (800) 556-9393. Web: *www.quotesmith.com*

- Other services on the Web that offer comparisons are: Insurance resources online, *quickquote.com, insweb.com, insuremarket.com, itechusa.com, answercenter.com*

After shopping and checking out your options, you are apt to decide on a major company or Blue Cross and Blue Shield that may cost you more. But what good is insurance coverage if you can't collect on it or it's not accepted by the hospital when you need care?

> ## If You Now Have a Job That Provides Health Insurance, You May Be Able to Keep It with COBRA
>
> If you are currently employed by a company with twenty or more full-time employees, you may be able to maintain your present group health coverage by paying the premium plus 2 percent yourself for up to eighteen months following the end of your employment, whether you quit on your own or were involuntarily terminated. This is thanks to COBRA, which stands for Combined Omnibus Budget Reconciliation Act, which was passed in 1986. At the end of the eighteen-month period, you can convert your COBRA coverage into an individual policy. You must elect to take COBRA within sixty days from the date you leave your employer. At the end of the eighteen months, you may wish to find a lower-priced plan. But if you or a member of your family has had a recent medical problem, you will probably find it to your advantage to stay with the company after COBRA expires, even though an individual policy may cost more and offer fewer benefits. Your state, however, may have a COBRA-like law that extends benefits to you beyond those of the federal law.

DISABILITY INSURANCE

Statistically, an executive at age thirty has a 48 percent chance of being disabled for ninety days or more before reaching the age of sixty-five. Working at home should lessen the chances of a disabling accident or illness, but the possibility of being disabled without income is sufficient motivation to get self-employed people to pay for the protection disability insurance provides. Also known as loss-of-income insurance, it's particularly important to the self-employed, who have no sick leave to draw on in case they do face illness or accident.

Another type of disability insurance is credit disability insurance. It's usually designed to continue loan payments should you become disabled.

The cost of disability coverage can seem high, but that's because with other forms of insurance, claims are paid in one lump sum. Disability payments, should you need them, can stretch out over many years. For several ways you can reduce the cost of disability protection, see Insurance Money Savers on page 341.

What-to-Look-for Checklist: Disability Insurance

There are a number of factors to consider in selecting a disability plan. They include:

___ *How "disabled" you must be to receive benefits.* If a plan defines disabled to mean "totally disabled," you need to be unfit for any kind of work. If you are highly trained, you may consider yourself disabled if you cannot pursue your chosen career. You might not want to work at something you would be "able" to do, such as telephone solicitation. Therefore, a more advantageous definition of disability is "unable to engage in any gainful occupation for which the insured is suited by education, training, or experience."

___ *How long after a disability you must wait before payments begin.* The waiting period may range from seven days to six months. The longer the waiting period, the less you should have to pay for the policy.

___ *How long after disability the payments continue.* Payments may continue for any time from thirteen weeks to throughout one's lifetime. But statistics indicate the average disability lasts for five years.

___ *How much it will cost.* Cost of disability insurance depends on the factors stated above, the company you choose, and how much the policy will pay you. You can calculate how much coverage you need by adding up your cost of living and subtracting any income from investments, royalty payments, Social Security, or spouse's earnings.

___ *Is the policy both "noncancelable" and "guaranteed renewable"?* Both these terms refer to whether the policy can be terminated after you become sick or make a claim. A policy that is noncancelable and guaranteed renewable can only be canceled if you fail to pay the premiums. The premiums can't be increased so long as you are current in your payments, and the policy must be renewed by the company but not necessarily at the same rate.

EMPLOYEE-RELATED INSURANCE

If you have employees, there are various kinds of insurance you may be required to provide for them. For example, you may need to provide workers' compensation insurance, employee insurance benefit plans, or nonowned auto insurance.

Workers' compensation protects workers should they be injured on the job. Whether this coverage is required for a small business varies widely from state to state. For example, California requires an employer to have workers' compensation coverage if one person comes in to work only a few hours a week, while some states don't require this insurance until an employer has more than ten employees. If you hire people to help you in your business, check with your insurance agent, your attorney, or the appropriate state agency to find out what's required in your state.

At the same time, you can consult your attorney or agent regarding other benefits you may need to give your employees. There are federal regulations for providing employee benefits like pension plans, retirement plans, group-life and health-insurance plans, and employee welfare benefits. These regulations may apply to your business, too.

If your employees ever use their own cars while working for you, your family or personal automobile insurance policy will not cover accidents; however, you can get nonowned auto insurance to protect yourself in this situation. This kind of policy covers you against damages that result while employees are driving for any purpose related to your business and is particularly important for businesses with sales representatives or delivery personnel. This insurance is also necessary for a nanny or a child-care helper who drives your car for any purpose connected with her work for you. For other issues relating to employee requirements see chapters 10 and 21.

LIFE INSURANCE, RETIREMENT, AND FINANCIAL PLANNING

Even though you're working from home, you probably won't want to work full-time forever. Often in the prime of one's career, that time seems far away. Studies show, however, that by the time people reach fifty, more than half of them begin to worry that inflation will reduce their standard of living when they retire, and 40 percent worry about becoming financially dependent on others. So thinking about a financial and retirement plan is another form of insurance open-collar workers should consider, because any plans for your retirement will be entirely up to you.

We were startled to read that consumer health experts are now predicting that anyone who expects to be sixty-five years old by the year 2000 should plan to have from $50,000 to $200,000 in savings just to pay for long-term health care. This a lot of money to accumulate after you're fifty, and it's for medical care alone. So setting up and following a comprehensive financial and preretirement plan that begins well before the age of fifty is all the more important, but whatever your age, the time to start is now.

It's never too soon for people who are self-employed to begin funding their retirement. "Retirement" perhaps isn't the best word since many of us may never retire in the way the World War II generation has done. To keep your standard of living, however, without working you'll need about 80 percent of your current income. Historically Social Security has accounted for less than 40 percent of average retirement income. Many doubt Social Security will provide this much in the future. So we'll be working as well as living longer, but with our prime earning years behind us, lacking employer pensions, we must plan to take care of ourselves.

A rule of thumb is to save 10 percent of your personal income each year. But keep in mind that thumb sizes vary and so do individual financial needs. Fortunately, Congress has shown some recognition of the needs of the self-employed, and you can invest pretax money in a variety of tax-sheltered savings plans.

Retirement plan options are discussed further in chapter 10. Essentially, as financial writer Linda Stern describes in her book *Money-Smart Secrets of the Self-Employed,* there are nine kinds of tax deferral plans: Individual Retirement Accounts (IRA), Simplified Employee Pension or SEP-IRA, SAR-SEP, Profit-Sharing Keogh, Money Purchase Keogh, Paired Keogh, 401(k), SIMPLE, and Defined Benefit Plan. Which type of plan is right for you will depend on your age, your overall financial situation, what kind of retirement you want, and whether you have employees.

While these are all tax-deferral plans, the 1997 Tax Act introduced the Roth IRA which you fund with after-tax dollars, so with this plan there is no tax deferral. The trade-off is that if you keep your Roth IRA for at least five years, all withdrawals, including what you earn on your invested funds, are free of income tax. This is attractive since you are apt to be paying income tax on much of your Social Security income.

So, as you can see, there are many decisions to be made that cry out for help. There are many software programs like *Prosper, RetireReady, RetireASAP,* and the *Wall Street Journal's Personal Finance Library* that can help you with retirement planning (see Resource list at end of this chapter). You can also go directly to banks, which now offer brokerage services; insurance companies or companies like Charles Schwab (800) 435-4000 (*www.schwab.com*); Fidelity (800) 544-9697; Jack White (800) 233-3411 (*www.jackwhiteco.com*); and Vanguard (800) 922-8327 (*www.vanguard.com*) that operate both as brokerages and mutual funds "supermarkets." Or you can go to a full-service brokerage. They can all set up a retirement plan for you.

Many people feel best served, however, with the personal attention of someone they hire. To find a financial person, talk with your accountant and as with other professionals you hire, get recommendations from people whose judgment you trust. Several associations accredit financial counselors. These include: the Society of Financial Service Professionals (610) 526-2500 (*www.financialpro.org*); the International Association for Financial Planning (404) 845-0011 (*www.iafp.org*); and the Institute of Certified Financial Planners (800) 282-7526 (*www.icfp.org*). You can get the names of practitioners in your area and also consider these as credentials for whatever professionals you consider using.

If you are a single parent, the primary breadwinner in a two-career family, or a person supporting anyone other than yourself, life insurance is also a must. Dan Silverman recommends beginning with a basic term insurance policy, which provides benefits if you die during the term of the policy. Then as your revenues grow, he suggests adding equity or whole life insurance in which part of your premium goes toward that insurance and part is set aside as savings that you can cash in or borrow against. Robert Hunter, president of the National Insurance Consumer Organization in Washington, D.C., recommends that for most families with young children the rule of thumb is to purchase insurance equivalent to five times your annual income.

 Work Sheet: A Dozen Insurance Money Savers

There are steps you can take that will cut your risk and your insurance rates.

Property Insurance

Sometimes discounts on insurance rates are available if you protect your home as follows:

___ Fire-smoke alarms or smoke, heat, or ion detectors approved by Underwriters Laboratories.

___ Deadbolts on exterior doors.

___ Alarm system that notifies the police.

Disability Insurance

The longer the period after illness before the insurer begins payments, the lower the premium.

___ Costs can be halved if you cover the possibility of being disabled only up to age sixty-five rather than for your lifetime.

___ Some credit card suppliers like American Express's Corporate Card provide lump-sum benefits of $10,000 to $50,000 for small-business owners for an annual tax-deductible fee of $45.

___ Buying yourself a Workers' Compensation Policy if you're incorporated can be a low-cost form of disability insurance for work-related disabilities.

(Continued on page 342)

(Continued from page 341)

Health Insurance

___ To deduct 100 percent of health insurance costs as a sole proprietorship, employ your spouse, so that your insurance premiums become a business expense. You can then become a dependent on your spouse's policy. If you do this, expect scrutiny and document your spouse's work with time sheets. Because this is a loophole in a changing area of the law, check with your tax professional before proceeding.

___ Some companies write policies that charge lower premiums if you are a non-smoker and nondrinker and if you exercise regularly.

Auto Insurance

___ If you drive a minimum number of miles, as many do who work from home, you may be able to be placed in a lower-risk category and thereby pay lower premiums.

___ Purchase umbrella insurance to increase your coverage to a million dollars or more.

___ Good Sam, an organization for recreational vehicle enthusiasts, allows anyone to join for about $35 a year and offers special rates on auto insurance from National General Insurance.

SMALL-BUSINESS INSURANCE

Buying a small-business insurance policy can save you time and money if you would otherwise be buying a variety of individual policies like business property, general liability, business-interruption, errors-and-omissions, and special computer insurance. If, however, you only need one or two of these, you may save by buying just those you need (although remember the cautionary paragraph on pages 325–26).

Insurance companies have been somewhat slow to adopt small-business insurance packages for the home-based business, but several are doing so. The Hartford, for example, offers a home-business policy that covers the insured's property and provides third-party and business-interruption coverage, plus a package of business coverages including product liability. Firemans Fund, Travelers, and CNA, to name a few, also offer umbrella policies and endorsements designed specifically for the home business.

KEEPING ADEQUATE INSURANCE RECORDS

In the case of loss, it is always the burden of the insured to prove the value of what has been lost. Some insurance companies can be very rigid about this, requiring bills of sale and receipts. After a theft or fire, it's difficult to itemize everything that is missing and document what you paid. Here are several methods for keeping a current inventory:

• *Retain receipts of every durable item you purchase.* If you depreciate business property for tax purposes, you'll already have some of these records.

• *Keep a written inventory.* Organize the inventory room by room. List each item in a room, its date of purchase, its price, and its present value. Insurance companies give away booklets that will help you organize this information.

• *Keep an inventory of your business equipment (as well as articles in your home).* Videotaping or photographing items close-up will help establish that you owned them; however, a video or photos that make something look in worse condition than it actually is can lead to disputes about its value. You can use a database or specialty software to keep your inventory records.

A good agent can direct you to companies that are reasonable in processing claims, and in the event of a loss, the agent can run interference for you in collecting on your policy. A complete and accurate inventory of your property, however, is needed to make sure you can collect what you're entitled to.

FINDING THE PROFESSIONAL HELP YOU NEED

Insurance is a highly competitive industry. Companies differ in their rates, premium payment plans, and insurance packages, so it's important to find an agent who is willing to investigate all your options until the best ones have been located.

Insurance agents do not charge you for their services; they receive their compensation from the insurance companies for whom they write policies. Therefore we suggest talking to several insurance agents and comparing the different plans they propose. There are independent agents who deal with multiple companies and there are agents employed by a given company who write policies only for it. Often agents specialize in particular kinds of insurance (health, auto, liability, etc.) or they may have considerable experience in writing certain kinds of insurance. When selecting agents, find out if they have a specialty, and ask what type of insurance they write most frequently. Check out how many companies they represent and what kind of commissions they would get if you bought a particular package they're recommending. Normal commissions would be 15 percent or less. And, of course, be certain that they are licensed in your state.

Agents are listed under "Insurance" in the Yellow Pages, or you can ask your attorney, accountant, or colleagues for a referral. Be sure, however, to find out how familiar the agent is with your particular kind of business and with home business in general. An agent may have been quite well suited to the professional who referred you, but you want to work with someone who understands as much as possible about your field. You can even ask to talk with other clients he or she's served in your field. Find someone who is willing to invest the time to answer your questions, search for the best policies for you, and discuss the pros and cons of the various options. In fact, ask the agents you talk with for a spreadsheet with at least four possible packages. This way you can compare the many features of each policy.

Use the insurance checklist with your lawyer and insurance agent. Discuss your needs in each area. If you work from home for someone else, you can review the list with your employer as well. Put together an insurance package that meets your current needs within your budget limitations and develop a plan that can grow with your business.

Remember that insurance is inherently a gamble between you and an insurance company. The insurer is betting that bad things won't happen to you. So don't wipe out your protection by buying from a shaky company. Be sure to check out the financial stability of whatever insurance company you're considering.

How much insurance do you need? You should insure against what you can't afford to lose, but you don't need to pay for insuring what you can afford to risk.

Once you find the insurance package you need and it is in force, you can work at home knowing you're protected from many of the pitfalls that may occur along the way.

RESOURCES

BOOKS

The Complete Book of Insurance: The Consumer's Guide to Insuring Your Life, Health, Property and Income. Ben G. Baldwin. Probus Publishing, 1996. ISBN: 1557388806.

The Employer's Legal Handbook. Fred S. Steingold. Berkeley, Calif.: Nolo Press, 1998. ISBN: 0873373707. Web: *www.nolo.com*

4 Easy Steps to Successful Investing. Jonathan D. Pond. New York: Avon, 1998. ISBN: 0380791811.

How to Insure Your Income: A Step by Step Guide to Buying the Coverage You Need at Prices You Can Afford. The Merritt Editors, eds. Merritt Publishing, 1997. ISBN: 1563431483.

How to Retire Rich: Time-Tested Strategies to Beat the Market and Retire in Style. James O'Shaughnessey. New York: Broadway, 1999. ISBN: 0767900731.

Insuring the Bottom Line: How to Protect Your Company from Liabilities, Catastrophes and Other Business Risks. David Russell. Berkeley, Calif.: Nolo Press, 1996. ISBN: 1563431157.

The Millionaire Next Door, The Surprising Secrets of America's Wealthy. Thomas J. Stanley and William D. Danko. New York: Pocket, 1998. ISBN: 0671015206.

Money-Smart Secrets of the Self-Employed. Linda Stern. New York: Random House, 1997. ISBN: 0679777113.

The Nine Steps to Financial Freedom. Suze Orman. New York: Three Rivers Press, 1999. ISBN: 0609801864.

Standard & Poor's Insurance Company Ratings Guide (serial). New York: McGraw-Hill, annual.

10 Steps to Financial Success: A Beginner's Guide to Saving and Investing. W. Patrick Naylor. New York: Wiley, 1997. ISBN: 0471175331.

Top Dollar Property Claims: Secrets to Successful Insurance Claim Settlements. Les Watrous. TGWB Publishing, 1998. ISBN: 0965453715.

What Do You Mean It's Not Covered?: A Guide to Understanding What Your Insurance Does—And Doesn't—Cover. James Walsh. Berkeley, Calif.: Nolo Press, 1995. ISBN: 156343072X.

Other Printed Information

Health Insurance Association of America. 555 13th Street NW, Washington, D.C. 20004; phone: (202) 824-1600. Web: *www.hiaa.org*

Insurance Information Institute. 110 William Street, 24th Floor, New York, NY 10038; phone: (212) 669-9200. Web: *www.iii.org*

Insuring Your Home Business. Free pamphlets from the Insurance Information Institute available through National Consumers Insurance Helpline (800) 942-4242, or send a self-addressed stamped envelope to the Institute at 110 William Street, New York, NY 10038; *www.iii.org*

ORGANIZATIONS THAT ARE NOT INSURANCE COMPANIES AND ATTEMPT TO PROVIDE GOOD-QUALITY HEALTH INSURANCE AT AFFORDABLE RATES

Small Business Service Bureau offers 170 Blue Cross, Blue Shield, and HMO plans in fourteen Eastern states; phone: (800) 222-5678. Web: *www.sbsb.com*

Small Office Home Office Association (SOHOA) 1767 Business Center Drive, Ste. 450, Reston, VA 20190. Offers comprehensive business and personal insurance, including health plans. Phone: (888) SOHOA11. Web: *www.sohoa.com*

Support Services Alliance. P.O. Box 130, Scoharie, NY 12157; phone: (518) 295-7966, (800) 322-3920. The Alliance offers Blue Shield and SSA Life Insurance plans. Web: *www.ssainfo.com*

FINANCIAL PLANNING ORGANIZATIONS

Society of Financial Service Professionals, 270 Bryn Mawr Avenue, Bryn Mawr, PA 19010; phone: (610) 526-2500. Web: *www.financialpro.org*

Institute of Certified Financial Planners, Certified Financial Planner Board of Standards, 3801 East Florida Avenue, Denver, CO 80210; phone: (303) 759-4900, (800) 282-7526. Web: *www.icfp.org*

International Association of Financial Planning, 5775 Glenridge Drive N.E., Ste. B-300, Atlanta, GA 30328; phone: (404) 845-0011. Web: *www.iafp.org*

SOFTWARE

Prosper. Ernst & Young LLP, 787 7th Avenue, New York, NY 10019; phone: (301) 571-7070, (888) 321-3331. Web: *www.ey.com*

RetireReady. Individual Software, Inc. 4255 Hopyard #2, Pleaston, CA 94588; phone: (800) 822-3522, (925) 734-6767. Web: *www.individualsoftware.com*

RATING SERVICES

A. M. Best Company. Ambest Road, Oldwick, NJ 08858; phone: (908) 439-2200. Web: *www.ambest.com*

Duff & Phelps Credit Rating Company. 55 East Monroe Street, Chicago, IL 60603; phone: (312) 368-3157. Web: *www.dcrco.com*

Moody's Investor Services. 99 Church Street, New York, NY 10007; phone: (212) 553-1658. Web: *www.moodys.com*

Standard & Poor Corporation. 25 Broadway, New York, NY 10007; phone: (212) 208-1146. Web: *www.ratings.standardpoor.com*

Weiss Research. 4176 Burns Road, Palm Beach Gardens, FL 33410; phone: (800) 289-9222. Web: *www.weissratings.com*

ON LINE

The Blue Cross and Blue Shield Association. From this site you can tap into locally operated Blue Cross and Blue Shield plans across the country. *www.bluecares.com*

Handilinks to Insurance provides extensive links to insurance companies, ratings services, information providers, and software companies. *http:// ahandyguide.com/cat1/i/i23.htm*

The Health Insurance Association of America (HIAA) is a trade association with 250 member insurers and managed-care organizations. Its Web site has consumer information about health insurance and directories of member companies organized by type of policy (*www.hiaa.org/consumerinfo/ index.html*). One of these directories lists insurance companies offering Medical Savings Account (MSA) High Deductible policies. *www.hiaa. org/consumerinfo/medical.html*

Health Scope enables you to compare health plans with one another. It's operated by a nonprofit coalition and rates California HMOs, hospitals, and doctors. "Report cards" are also available on physician groups in the Pacific Northwest. Information on choosing a doctor and insurance is applicable to anyone. *www.healthscope.org/core.htm*

Kaiser, the nation's largest HMO, uses its Web site to provide information on its health plans, a directory of administrative offices, and advice for staying healthy. *http://www.kaiserpermanente.org*

The National Committee for Quality Assurance's site enables you to determine if your health plan is accredited. *www.ncqa.org.*

TELEPHONE HELP

National Consumers Insurance Helpline, (800) 942-4242, is co-sponsored by the American Council of Life Insurance, the Insurance Information Institute, and the Health Insurance Association of America. Besides answering general questions about auto, health, and life insurance on a toll-free hot line and sending free brochures, if a question cannot be answered or if the matter involves a dispute with an insurance company, callers are referred to consumer specialists. Web: *www.iii.org*

Managing Your
Home Office

CHAPTER 12

Getting Organized and Staying That Way

Goals

1. Become a self-organizer.

2. Evaluate what's working for you and what's not.

3. Organize your home office.

4. Set goals and priorities.

5. Create productive work routines.

Although the single most frequently mentioned advantage of working from home is the freedom and flexibility to do what you want when you want the way you want, when one actually lives with the joys of near-total freedom, it's not uncommon to hear comments like the following.

"My work is taking over the house. There are stacks of paper everywhere and I can't find what I need. I'm not getting as much done as I should and I'm always behind. There's so much to do, I don't know where to start!"

This common refrain has led a few who begin working from home to move back to an office before drowning in overdue projects, missing receipts, and backed-up paperwork. For some, just the fear of such havoc is enough to keep them from thinking they can successfully work from home in the first place.

Its important to keep in mind that most of us have had little or no experience in running our lives with complete freedom. No matter how much we think we're ready for 100 percent control of our lives, when we actually get the opportunity, it can be somewhat overwhelming.

Those who have faced the chaos of total freedom, however, and gained experience working from home find that success comes from creating a system for managing work and home life. With a system tailor-made to your needs, goals, values, and preferences, you can get both your work and your home organized and keep them that way. You'll be able to find the things you need when you need them. You'll have the time to accomplish your priorities. And you'll be able to enjoy the extra time you've saved by not commuting to work.

If using a system immediately makes you think of clean desks, rigid schedules, and hours of filing, sorting, and cleaning, STOP! Don't confuse having a system with being chained to an inflexible regimen. Rather, think of a system as a way of resolving competing demands on your time and space so that what's most important gets done easily and efficiently.

The routine that people are most familiar with, of course, is the eight-to-five office system. Chances are you've arranged your work and home around this framework for most of your professional life. If so, going to the office organized your day for you. Everything else in your life was managed after work and on weekends. This is only one of many possible systems for organizing a workday, however, and it's one many of us want to get away from. Part of the joy of working from home is the freedom to create systems that are more suited to our personal preferences and desires.

There is one stipulation: To work at home successfully without the familiar office routine, you have to become a self-organizer, someone who can create and operate your own systems. In talking with people who work at home, we met some who were natural self-organizers. Organizing their work seemed to come effortlessly. Others we've met have struggled with how to reorganize their lives around their new work schedules and have still come out winners.

In this chapter we want to share what these people either knew already or learned along the way. From their experiences, you can glean the essential features of creating your own successful systems.

BECOMING A SELF-ORGANIZER

As we talk with people about how they organized their work at home, the prototypical self-organizers, regardless of the type of work they did, typically describes their routines something like this:

"I don't have trouble working at home because I have a routine I follow every day. I get up at five every morning and run. Then I make long-distance calls from seven to eight. During the rest of the morning I do paperwork. In the afternoon I meet with clients. Every Monday morning, I pay the bills and update my records."

"At first I was quite disorganized. Then I realized that if I work just as if I'm at the office, I'm very productive. So now I'm at my desk by nine sharp and I usually quit working by five. If I have lunch I take no more than an hour, but I usually take a short break in the morning and the afternoon."

"I work best with deadlines. Whenever a project is due, I count backward from the due date and figure out how much I'll need to accomplish each day. When I've gotten that amount done for the day, I stop."

These prototypical self-organizers are choosing to follow formalized systems similar to those practiced in a traditional office setting. But those of you who want to break away from formal routines will be glad to know that there are less typical, yet equally effective, self-organizers who do not follow such traditional structures. At first these people sound rather disorganized, often describing their daily routines something like this:

"I don't like schedules and things like that. I like to roll with the punches and do whatever comes up."

"I don't have any particular schedule. Sometimes I take off the whole afternoon. But then there are times when I work all night, too."

"I do the things that need to be done. Some days are very light and I don't do much work. Others are quite busy. A lot depends on how I feel."

When we pushed further about how they decide what to do or when to take time off, we found that, indeed, these seemingly disorganized workers are actually quite organized. In fact, their systems are sometimes more complex than the formal ones we're more familiar with. It's not uncommon, for example, for such workers to create a different system for different days of the week or for different aspects of their work. One management consultant and trainer told us:

"People who work in an office may think I'm not organized because they see me with such a variety of schedules. But actually I know exactly what I'm doing. Today, just because it's five o'clock, I don't have to stop working. But tomorrow will be different. Tomorrow I will be training all evening. So to be at a peak, I'll probably take off in the afternoon."

SEVEN PRINCIPLES FOR DESIGNING A SYSTEM THAT WILL WORK FOR YOU

In organizing a home office, you're actually creating a system that will coordinate many different aspects of your professional and personal lives. Your system should include a plan for using your time, managing your money, keeping track of the information you need or the flow of paper through your office, and getting the help you need to keep everything running. Whether you're setting up a system to handle your mail, manage your schedule, or keep track of your files, the basic principles are the same and you will find them throughout all the chapters in this section.

Work Sheet: Are You a Self-Organizer?

Whether their systems are conventional or unconventional, the self-organizers we spoke with share four key characteristics. As we describe each of them, evaluate your own self-organizing skills. To what extent on a scale of 0 to 10 would you say you possess these traits, with 0 being not at all and 10 being absolutely true of you most of the time?

___ *1. People who are organized realize they can be in charge of how they do things.* After years of many rules and regulations while growing up, going to school, or working in an office, it's possible to feel you must do things in certain ways whether you want to or not. Too often, the result is that "being organized" takes on a negative connotation. It comes to mean doing things someone else prescribes and may even prompt resentment, rebellion, and a desire to sabotage all efforts at organization.

Self-organizers, however, have discovered that even if it doesn't seem so, they're free to choose how they do things. They also live with the consequences of their choices. Often self-organizers only gain this wisdom after they start working from home. As one man who started a rug-cleaning service told us, "The first three weeks after I quit my job, I goofed off most of the time. Then it dawned on me, I could goof off forever. No one was ever going to tell me I was fired or give me a failing grade. If I kept this up though, I wouldn't be able to pay the rent and I'd have to get another job."

Or as someone who is now telecommuting told us, "I hate to admit it, but I used to try to look busy so I wouldn't get assigned any more work. But after I started working at home, I realized no one was watching me. I was either going to exceed my quota or I wasn't. It was all up to me."

___ *2. Self-organizers keep their priorities in mind and orchestrate their work around these goals.* Knowing what's really important to them pervades everything self-organizers do, from which hours they spend working to their choice of tasks. A salesman who started his own sales company expressed his priorities this way: "I want to make this business go. That's the most important thing to me right now. I don't care how many calls I have to make or how many letters I have to send out, I'm going to do it."

A woman who runs a part-time business designing flower arrangements has a different set of priorities, to which she is equally committed. "Being here to nurse my daughter is what's really important to me. I've built my day around her schedule. But I still get my work done."

A graphic designer told us, "Everyone thinks my office is a mess just because you can't see any clear space on the desk. It may not look great, but that's not what's important. When I'm working on a project, I need everything at arm's reach."

And a mail-order merchandiser laughed when we asked how he decided what was most important to him: "Knowing how much each item is costing me is what's crucial. Any overage will eat away my profit. You better bet I keep a record of my expenses

(Continued on page 355)

(Continued from page 354)

on a day-by-day basis. I never get behind on that. Knowing what other companies are doing is important, too, but if I have to make a choice between keeping my records up and reading the trade journals, there's no doubt which one will have to wait."

___ *3. Self-organizers take responsibility for what happens in their work.* Because they realize that they can usually structure their work the way they want to, self-organizers have also learned that they're responsible for whatever results they get. If they aren't getting what they want, they realize it's because their approach isn't working. They take responsibility for problems as well as solutions, like the freelance editor who told us, "My son is still interrupting me. I haven't gotten this worked out yet. I'm going to have to do something different."

Or like the consultant who admitted he has a hard time finding things once he's filed them: "It happened again this morning. It took me fifteen minutes to find something I was looking for. So I'm setting up a better filing system."

___ *4. Although self-organizers often don't realize it, they have made a habit of following the basic principles of good systems organization.* Natural self-organizers have learned the principles of good systems organization by osmosis. They picked it up from their parents, a teacher, or on the job. The most common way people learn organizing habits is from the way they were taught to clean up their rooms as young children.

Think back to the time when you were nine or ten years old, and remember how whoever was rearing you got you to clean your room. Were you effectively taught how to organize your things? Or:

- Did your parents give up on getting you to clean your room and do it themselves?

- Did they condemn and nag you, saying, "What's the matter with you, anyway? Why haven't you cleaned up your room?"

- Did cleaning your room become a dreadful battle of wills between you and your parents?

- Did your room become an embarrassing shambles that was hidden behind closed doors?

Whatever your experience with cleaning up your room was, don't be surprised if you use that same approach with yourself when you begin working from home on your own and want to get organized.

If you weren't blessed during childhood with learning the basic skills for creating and using systems, don't despair. There's no need to struggle through the hazards of learning by trial and error. You can use the seven principles set forth in this chapter and other principles in subsequent chapters to design systems that will work for your home office. You'll find as you work on your own that when your systems meet your needs and suit your personality, you can develop the self-organizing habits you need to succeed.

1. Set Specific Goals

To create a workable system, first establish what you need it to do. Career counselor Ines Beilke discovered this principle when she began her long-awaited sabbatical. "At the college where I work, I have a very tight schedule. My sabbatical was going to be my chance to do so many things I'd been wanting to do. Two months later, working at home without the schedule I'd been used to, I almost panicked because I'd gotten nothing done."

Ines found that the only way she could get back on track was to remind herself of the goals she had set for the year: to complete a project she had undertaken and to spend time relaxing and going camping with her husband. She told us, "I kept reminding myself every day of what I wanted to accomplish with the time I had. Then I could make a plan to be sure I got it done."

In creating a system for managing both your household and your office, we recommend that, like Ines, you define your goals for both your work life and your personal life. Ask yourself questions like these:

- What does success mean to me?

- What are the five most important things in my life?

- What do I want to accomplish in my work?

- What is important to me about my home? My family? My friends?

Make a list of goals you have for your career, your personal development, your relationships, your children, your home. Be specific. Precisely how much money do you want to make? How large do you want your business to be? What skills do you want to develop? What do you want to provide for your children, or for yourself in terms of your own personal development? When do you want to have achieved these goals? What do you want to accomplish this year? Next year?

2. Turn Your Goals into Specific Tasks

The more specific you are about what you need to do to achieve your goals, the easier it will be to create a system that will help you meet them. For example, after Ines set her personal and professional goals, she realized that to reach them she would have to start establishing priorities. She set dates for the camping trips she and her husband wanted to take. She made appointments with each of the people she wanted to contact for the project she was doing, and so forth. She also had to turn away certain requests made of her in order to stay focused.

In designing a system for your office, identify the specific tasks you will

Five Proven Steps to Better Goal-Setting

Ken Blanchard, author of the popular *One Minute Manager,* says you set goals so you'll know when you're doing something right. After all, you can't know if you're on course if you don't know where you're headed.

1. Begin by visualizing or imagining in full detail the result you want as if it's already occurred.

2. Then, to state your goal, describe the situation you desire using an action verb in the present (not the future) tense. For example, "I earn $50,000 a year." "I deposit $10,000 a month into my bank account." "I speak to three associations each month and receive my full fee. They are pleased with my performance and invite me back." "I complete twenty pages of reports each day." Write these goal statements in your daily planner or personal organizer, and keep them visible at the top of each day's TO DO list.

3. Add a definite date by which you intend to accomplish this goal. For example, "By December 31 of this year, I will have closed six accounts." "By next Friday at 5 P.M. I will have made twenty calls." Best-selling author Harvey MacKay puts it this way: "A goal is a dream with a deadline."

4. Write out a list of the steps you will need to take to accomplish this goal and decide when you will perform each of them. Put them on your calendar.

5. Post your goals where you will see them regularly and review them daily. **Do at least one task related to achieving your goals every day.**

need to do in order to achieve each of your goals. Ask yourself questions like these:

- What will I need to do to get this accomplished?
- How much money will it take?
- How much time will I need?
- When do these things need to be done?

Watkins distributor Sharon Hayes keeps track of her goals by writing in a diary. She says, "I set goals in the diary and spend a few minutes each day going back to these goals and keeping track of what I've done to reach them. I also keep a daily log of how much time I spend on various tasks and decide ahead of time how much time I should be spending on each one. Then I reward myself when I make headway on my goals."

3. Set Priorities

The principle of setting priorities is expressed by the familiar adage "First things first." It involves putting the tasks you have to do in logical order.

If, for example, you have to run errands, make phone calls, do paperwork, and hold a meeting, decide which of these activities needs to be done first, second, third, and so on. If you have ten phone calls to make and only half an hour to make them before you must leave for a meeting, order the calls in terms of importance and make the most essential calls first.

Or when you're organizing your filing cabinet and have ten different types of records to keep track of, decide which ones are most important and which you will use most often. Then place them so they will be accessible in order of importance and frequency of use, saving the lower and more-difficult-to-reach drawers for the infrequently used and least-important files.

When you have a series of errands to run, save both time and gasoline by ordering the errands in terms of their location in relation to one another. We organize our business and personal errands into what we call our "standard errand routes." We do errands along an "eastern route," going to the gas station first because it's nearest, then to the printer, and last to the grocery store so perishable items won't spoil. At a different time, we do errands along the "western route," going first to the bank because it closes early, then to the dry cleaner, which is near the bank, and finally to the post office, which is on the way home.

4. Put Like Things Together

Putting like things together can be called the "combining principle." It's not a new idea. We've all heard it expressed as "killing two birds with one stone." It's a matter of figuring out which similar things could be done together.

Whether you're planning your day, organizing files, or setting up a way to handle your mail, put similar tasks together. For example, when you have to go out of the house for a business meeting or to make a bank deposit, carry out all other activities that need to be done outside the house on the same trip. You can go to the post office and the print shop while you're out, or you can arrange your outing to correspond to the time you have to pick up a child from school.

Other examples of using this principle at work would be storing all files and materials related to financial record keeping in one place, and setting aside time to do all your paperwork at one time during the day. When you pay bills, you could combine that task with checking your bank statement. Likewise, you can set up one time to make phone calls and keep all the files you use in conjunction with your calls close to your phone.

5. Create Routines

Quite contrary to the popular belief that following routines is dreary, routines actually bring your system to life. A routine is only dreary when it becomes an end in itself rather than a vehicle for taking you toward your goals.

By structuring your activities into regular routines, you save the time and energy spent making hundreds of little decisions every day and trying to remember today what you decided yesterday. Once you've discovered when, where, and how best to do something, turn it into a routine and you'll find you can operate more easily through your day according to your goals.

In setting up our routines, for example, we've found that it's easier to reach people by phone first thing in the morning, so now we have a regular routine of making phone calls from 8:00 to 9:30 A.M. On the other hand, if we do errands during prime business hours, we miss important calls, so we have a regular routine of doing errands after 4:00 P.M.

In setting up routines, however, be sure they match your style of working. If you like precise schedules, make yours very exact: "I'll do this every morning at 9:00 A.M." If you prefer more flexibility, make yours less specific: "First thing every morning I'll decide which things to do," or "I'll do my filing sometime during the first week of each month."

Once you've implemented a routine, set up ways to remind yourself of it. Use calendars, timers, tickler systems, "to-do" lists, posters, index cards, or computer programs to help you remember specifics of the routines you've set up. For example, if you have a routine for closing out the end of each week on Friday afternoon, you might keep a checklist posted on your file cabinet to remind you of each of the tasks you need to complete before the afternoon is over. Finally, make your routine a habit by doing it the same way repeatedly until it becomes second nature.

6. Remain Flexible

Although you will need to follow your routines consistently to make a system work, you will soon find yourself wavering from a system that is too rigid. Life is simply too unpredictable for any system to operate flawlessly without at least occasional changes. So allow yourself leeway for emergencies and unanticipated events. But then resume your routines the next time around.

7. Evaluate the Results

At least once a month take a look at the system you've designed and see if it's working. Are you achieving your goals? Can you see daily progress? Are you feeling satisfied with your business and your lifestyle?

Work Sheet: Is Your System Working

The following are fourteen signs that you need a better system. Check off any that apply to you:

___ Feeling as though you never have enough space (In her book *Getting Organized,* Stephanie Winston claims that 80 percent of overcrowding is the result of disorganization.)

___ Never having enough time for what most needs doing

___ Finding too much paper lying around and working its way into the rest of your home

___ Not having any time away from work

___ Not finding what you need when you need it

___ Being late for appointments or deadlines

___ Doubting your ability to manage your work

___ Feeling things are getting out of hand

___ Discovering overdue bills

___ Not knowing your bank balance

___ Failing to return phone calls because you feel embarrassed that it's been so long since the person called you

___ Feeling that you have to do everything yourself

___ Procrastinating

___ Not getting important things done because of endless interruptions

Evaluating how your system is working isn't a time for criticizing and condemning yourself; it's a time for acknowledging what's working and what needs attention. So take time at the end of each month to review your accomplishments and the insights you've gained.

In reviewing your efforts, pay attention to whether you're following your system. If not, then the *system* isn't working well enough to meet your needs and you must change it. A good system is easy to use and should make life simpler, not more complicated. Finally, decide whether or not it's helping you to get the results you want. If it isn't, adjust and revise your system until you can achieve your goals with ease by following it.

CUSTOMIZING YOUR SYSTEM

Below we've identified fourteen decisions you should make to set up a comprehensive home-office system that's tailored to your unique preferences and work demands. There's no one right answer, but most people run into trouble if they haven't addressed the issue each of the following questions raises. So decide:

1. How many hours will you work each day and each week? If the nature of your work is such that you cannot set a precise figure, define clearly how you will decide on the amount of time you'll spend working from week to week or day to day.

2. Which hours of the day will you work? As we'll discuss in the next chapter, unless your work demands it, there is no reason to limit yourself to typical hours. You can work at hours better suited to your circumstances.

3. How many breaks do you plan to take each day and when will you take them? Some people like to break for five minutes each hour. Others prefer taking longer breaks after working for several hours. Still others break when they come to a stopping point in their work.

4. When will you do household chores? Some people like to take a break for household chores and find that the change of pace allows them to come back to the office refreshed and ready to work. Others find that if they stop to do a household chore, the next thing they know the whole morning has slipped away.

5. When will you eat lunch and will you snack while working? Having the kitchen only steps away often becomes a problem for people who work at home. Consciously deciding how you will handle this should make it easier to keep your weight and concentration in bounds.

6. When and how will you dress? Some people find that to work effectively they need to get dressed as if they were going to the office. Others relish the freedom to stay in sweats all day.

7. Will you watch TV during daytime hours? If so, how much and when? Some people find it's easy to get hooked on game shows or soap operas and claim they work best while watching TV. Still others can't work well with the television on but get hooked nonetheless. Even if you wouldn't be caught dead watching a soap, the variety available on daytime TV today can lure you with movies, sports, and news.

8. Under what circumstances will you take off a day, afternoon, or a morning? Sick leave and days off take on a new perspective when you work at home. If you're self-employed, establish your own leave policies, consistent with the nature of your business. Just keep in mind that you deserve the same leave benefits you'd expect from any good employer, but you can't allow yourself excesses no good employer would accept either. If you're employed at home, you'll be on your own to coordinate your work with the established leave policies.

9. When do you decide to get someone to help you with your work? Many work-at-homers try to do everything themselves. Some can. Others end up saving money by spending it to hire help.

10. If you have children, when will you be available to them? Most people find they cannot allow children to have unlimited access to them during working periods. So you will need to make age-appropriate arrangements for their care and set boundaries regarding when you will and won't be available to them.

11. What information do you need to keep track of? Usually, in-house office procedures include policies for records you need to keep. Working at home, however, you will probably have to establish your own record-keeping procedures.

True Confessions: When Exceptions Become the Rule

"Once when my neighbor was in a jam," a home business owner wrote, "I offered to pick up her son from preschool. She has since asked me to repeat this favor several times. How can I explain to her, without damaging our friendly relationship, that just because I'm working at home doesn't mean I'm *not* working as hard as her corporate acquaintances?"

The truth is, you don't need to explain. The way to let family, friends, and neighbors know that you're working as hard as corporate acquaintances is to tell them that even though you'd like to help, you can't pick up her son because you're working. Be warm. Be sincere. But be clear and definite that your business is such that you can't take time off during working hours. They will probably be disappointed, especially if they have come to rely on you as their stand-in. But if you want them to take you off their emergency-help list, you will probably need to reinforce your message several times, repeating that you're sorry and wish you could help, but, because of your work, you simple can't.

Friends and relatives who have relied on you may call several times just to be sure you mean what you say. But, if you continue to be clear that you'd like to help, but cannot, they will find new resources.

12. *How will you manage your money?* If you're self-employed you will need to establish a system for managing the financial aspects of your business. Even if you're working at home on a salary, you'll have to arrange a procedure for managing your home-office tax records.

13. *What interruptions are you willing to allow?* There will be phone calls. There may be people coming to the door to repair things, sell things, or make deliveries. Neighbors may want to visit, have you accept deliveries for them, or get you to help them out by picking up their kids from school. It's easier to have your own policy in mind as a guideline for such interruptions than simply to respond to each interruption as it occurs.

14. *Do the decisions you make in answering these questions apply to every workday or are there exceptions?* This will depend on your work style and the nature of your tasks. A psychotherapist may not allow any interruptions during client hours but may be more flexible while doing paperwork. While working on a deadline, a writer or manufacturer may need to keep very strict hours, but the same person can be much more flexible in slower periods.

Unless you address these questions and incorporate them into your system, you will probably be faced with answering them afresh every day. That can be a tiresome and sometimes disastrous situation. For a closer look at the major issues we've raised, read the chapters that follow. They contain ideas and suggestions that will help you make the best decisions for creating a system that's right for you.

RESOURCES

BOOKS

Beyond Time Management: Business With Purpose. Robert J. Wright and Robert A. Wright. Portsmouth, N.H.: Butterworth-Heinemann, 1996. ISBN: 0750697997.

Creating. Robert Fritz. New York: Fawcett, 1993. ISBN: 0449908011.

Getting Organized. Robyn Freedman Spizman. New York: Ivy, 1998. ISBN: 0804116822.

The High-Tech Personal Efficiency Program: Organizing Your Electronic Resources to Maximize Your Time and Efficiency. Kerry Gleeson. New York: Wiley, 1997. ISBN: 0471172065.

Organized to Be the Best!: New Timesaving Ways to Simplify and Improve How You Work. Susan Silver. Los Angeles; Adams Hall Publications, 1995.

Secrets of Self-Employment: Surviving and Thriving on the Ups and Downs of Being Your Own Boss. Sarah and Paul Edwards. New York: Tarcher/Perigee, 1996.

Taming the Office Tiger: The Complete Guide to Getting Organized at Work. Barbara Hemphill. New York: Times Books, 1996. ISBN: 0812927125.

The 10 Natural Laws of Successful Time and Life Management: Proven Strategies for Increased Productivity and Inner Peace. Hyrum W. Smith. New York: Warner, 1995. ISBN: 0446670642.

365 Ways to Simplify Your Work Life: Ideas That Bring More Time, Freedom and Satisfaction to Daily Work. Odette Pollar. Chicago: Dearborn Trade, 1996 ISBN: 0793122813.

True Success: A New Philosophy of Excellence. Tom Morris. New York: Grosset/Putnam, 1994.

TAPES

The Goals Program. Zig Ziglar. Carrollton, Tex.: The Zig Ziglar Corporation; (800) 527-0306.

The Psychology of Achievement. Brian Tracy. Chicago: Nightingale-Conant; (800) 323-5552.

Secrets of Self-Employment, Paul and Sarah Edwards. Chicago: Nightingale-Conant; (800) 323-5552.

SEMINARS/SELF LEARNING

Robert Fritz, Inc. For information, self-study programs, seminars, software, and other goal-setting and organizing resources, contact Robert Fritz, Inc., P.O. Box 116, Williamsville, VT 05362; phone: (800) 848-9700 or (802) 348-7176. Web: *www.robertfritz.com*

CHAPTER 13

Managing Time:
Working on Purpose

Goals

1. Set up a successful work schedule.

2. Get started and stick to business.

3. Use home-office shortcuts and time-savers.

4. Avoid interruptions and procrastination.

5. Stop overworking and make room for your life.

6. Stay cool, calm, and collected.

7. Develop good work habits.

Overwhelmingly, people working from home find they have a greater sense of control over how they use their time. They have fewer interruptions and more flexibility to work in ways that are most productive for them. On the other hand, some also encounter difficulties managing their time, difficulties that they either didn't have at the office or had to a lesser degree. Primarily, we find that three-quarters of the people who have trouble with time report difficulty getting down to work, while the other quarter have trouble getting away from work. We hear problems like these:

"I have a hard time getting started. By the time I've eaten breakfast and read the paper, done my exercises, gotten dressed and put things away, half the morning is gone."

"I can't stick to business. It's too easy to think of something else I need to do when I get tangled up in a tough problem. The plants always need watering, the trash always needs emptying, there are always errands that need to be run instead."

"It's not infrequent that I start the morning with a clear day ahead, no appointments, no place I have to be, just a whole day to get my work done.

Then something will happen. The dog will get sick. The plumbing will break. And there goes the day."

"My problem is just the opposite. I'm always working—morning, noon, and night. The other day I overheard my son asking my wife, 'Why doesn't Daddy ever do anything but work?' That got me to thinking, but I don't seem to be able to get away from it. It's always there waiting to be done." For those who are already working from home, these problems may sound all too familiar. In this chapter we will address each of the most common problems people have with time when working from home and provide specific recommendations about what you can do to take charge of your time and avoid the problems you're most likely to encounter. You can begin by using the following checklist:

Diagnosing Your Time-Management Problems

Place a check by the problems you encounter most frequently:

___ Getting started and sticking to business

___ Organizing your workday

___ Procrastinating

___ Being interrupted

___ Getting away from work

___ Overworking

GETTING DOWN TO WORK
AND STICKING TO BUSINESS

It's so easy and enjoyable to sleep in on rainy mornings, spend extra time over the newspaper, take the day off, go out with your toddler to the park, sign up for a midday tennis class, or work in the yard during the cool morning hours.

The opportunity to pursue these kinds of activities when you want to may be precisely what attracted you to working from home. The question is, With no boss in the office next door and all these opportunities to do something else, can you get to work and stick to business on a regular basis?

Fortunately, it is possible to have the best of both worlds. You can combine the many activities in your personal life with effective and efficient work habits. But it takes a new way of working. It may require new skills, some fresh attitudes about work, and a few new tricks of the trade. You'll need to set up a work schedule, arrange ways to cue yourself to get started, and master the art of working efficiently.

FIVE WAYS TO SET UP A
SUCCESSFUL WORK SCHEDULE

We've found that only about 10 percent of people who work at home follow the same schedule they had at the office. Most people take advantage of the rich opportunity working from home provides by devising their own unique work schedules. The quality of your life can change with a creative schedule, so open your mind to all the possibilities. Don't limit yourself to the old ideas of what makes up a workday.

Here are a variety of ways you can approach designing your schedule.

1. Establish your schedule around the demands of your work. Let the work itself serve to get and keep you going. This may happen naturally, or you may have to make it happen by organizing what might seem like an atypical workday.

When psychotherapist Greg Rohan first opened his practice, he found his clients preferred appointments in the late afternoons and evenings, after traditional working hours.

"Since I was home anyway, I began setting up appointments throughout the entire day, a few in the morning, a few in the afternoon, and a few in the evening. I was very disorganized and I wasted most of the time in between. I finally decided to limit all my appointments to between two P.M. and nine P.M. This way everybody's happy. I'm free in the mornings and very efficient from one o'clock on."

Data-entry clerk Helen Gillis begins her day when her supervisor calls to transmit her workload for the day. "I never have any trouble getting going, because Marge calls at eight-thirty A.M. sharp. So whether I'm dressed yet or not, I'm at my terminal and ready to work through to my first break."

Janet and Carl Jeninski, who operate a bed-and-breakfast inn at their home, worked out a more unusual arrangement. When they're at home, they feel as though they work twenty-four hours a day. "We put in eighty-hour weeks. Our work is our life, and we love working side-by-side. But we need time away, too, so we work three weeks a month and take the fourth week off at a cabin we own with several other people. We hire someone to come live in our home and manage the inn while we're gone."

2. Establish your schedule around those times of the day when you work best. Everyone feels more alert and energized at certain times of the day. During these high-energy periods, it's easier to get to work and produce a higher-quality job. Our high-energy periods come at different times of the day. Paul is a morning person. He's up at dawn and ready to work. By mid-afternoon, he's running down. He does his prime work during the mornings and saves the afternoons for errands and other less-demanding activities.

On the other hand, Sarah doesn't usually get going until mid-morning. For years, when she worked for the federal government, she would sit at her desk at 8 A.M. nursing a cup of coffee to keep her eyes open until around 10 A.M. By 3 P.M. she was raring to go, but the workday was winding down. So now she usually reads and does less-demanding activities in the morning and saves her prime work activities for the afternoon and early evening.

Thor Thorensen, vice president of Advanced Computer Techniques Corporation, has a highly unusual pattern that makes having his office at home ideal for him. "I prefer working from late afternoon until two in the morning. When I was working at other companies, I had to work from eight to five like everybody else. Now I can pick my hours." And because he picks them, he finds it easy to stick to them.

3. *Establish your work schedule around the other priorities in your life.* Raising a family, exercising, painting, or another activity that's important to you can serve as an effective way to structure your workday and make those things you value a regular part of your lifestyle.

Twila Carnes, for example, who works from home on line, has established a schedule that allows her to devote sufficient time to other priorities. A single parent, she logs on to the computer at midnight, works until seven in the morning, gets her kids up and off to school after breakfast, and goes to sleep until around three in the afternoon, when they come home. "With this schedule, I get to be a full-time mother and still earn a living. That means a lot to me."

One common pattern among people who work from home is to work long hours four days a week so they are free to pursue their personal interests over a long weekend. Engineering job-shopper Kevin Maher loves to ski. He gladly works from nine to nine Monday through Thursday so he can go to the mountains over the weekends. "I'm motivated to get everything done before Thursday night. If I leave early Friday morning, I can beat the crowds to the slopes."

4. *Organize your schedule around particular work tasks.* Landscape designer Joseph Turner teaches Monday, Wednesday, and Friday at a university. His time on campus defines the schedule for those days, and he limits everything involved in his teaching to those three days. On Tuesdays and Thursdays he works with customers and completes their landscape designs. He finds that by separating these two aspects of his work into different days, he stays focused on the tasks he needs to do for each.

5. *Set up an arbitrary schedule.* Establishing any schedule is always better than having none. Whatever schedule you initially set up will help you define the one you'll ultimately want to adopt. Once you begin to adhere to an arbitrary schedule, you'll notice the times when you have difficulty working and can then begin tailor-making a more compatible one.

USING RITUALS TO GET STARTED

Even with an established and workable schedule, many people still find they need to prompt themselves to get started at the appointed time.

Working from home, you don't have the forced ritual of shave, shower, and dress that millions of office workers experience between 6 and 7 A.M. daily as they get themselves off to work. Some commuters have to resort to a pot of strong coffee or a shot of vodka to get going. Usually open-collar workers don't have to go to such extremes, but without the pressure of having to arrive at the office on time, they still have to find a way to be sure they get out of bed and into their work.

If you can arrange to have your business cue you, this is a surefire work starter. Because we live on the West Coast and our publisher and many other business contacts are on the East Coast, we begin getting calls by 8 A.M., for example. Our employee arrives at 9. These cues are a big assistance in our getting up and ready for the work day. Of course, such work cues are not always possible, so people create a variety of rituals they use to cue themselves that "it's time to work." Here are some:

- Hearing the closing music of *Good Morning America* or the *Today* show

- Getting into your work clothes

- Simply walking into your home office

- Scheduling regular networking breakfast appointments

- Pouring a thermos of coffee to take into the office

- Starting when your spouse leaves for work or when your kids leave for school

- Setting a clock radio to go off at the selected hour

- Scheduling an early-morning aerobics class, meditation, or workout session at the gym and beginning work immediately afterward

- Hiring a reminder service to call when it's time to start

- Walking or driving around the block and starting to work when you get back

- Starting each day by making long-distance calls before 8 A.M.

These rituals can help you get to the desk, the drawing board, or the computer screen. Once you get there, however, if you're still faced with the horror of the blank page, the overflowing in-box, or the "Start a new Document?" prompt, you may still need an action plan for really getting to work.

If you're still having trouble starting out in the morning, try this tip from business consultant Dan Shafer: "Leave something half done when you quit for the day. That runs counter to your upbringing, right? Like fingers scraping a chalkboard? But it works. As a writer, I've used this trick dozens of times. I just leave off in the middle of a sentence and I know exactly where to start in the morning."

Seven Quick Tips for Getting Started

1. **Take action:**
   Sit down at your desk.
   Clear the desk.
   Turn on the computer.
   Get out the pertinent files.
   Sharpen your pencil.
   Make up or review your schedule for the day and "to do" list.
   Dial the first phone number you need to call.

2. **Begin with the most interesting thing** you have to do.

3. **Start asking questions:**
   At the end of the day, what do I hope to have accomplished?
   What tasks am I most concerned about getting done?
   What needs to be done next?
   What will happen if I don't get this done?

4. **Set a deadline** for yourself or tell someone else you will have completed a project by a certain time.

5. **Bribe yourself.** "If I get such-and-such done today, I can . . ."

6. **Make a game out of your work.** "Let's see how many of these I can finish before noon," or "Can I make three calls in ten minutes?"

7. **Use positive aphorisms with yourself.** "This is the first day of the rest of my life." "The early bird gets the worm." "The sooner I start, the sooner I'll be done."

STICKING TO BUSINESS
AND WORKING EFFICIENTLY

Once you get started, your work can develop a momentum that keeps you going all day. But sometimes it can be as difficult to keep working as it is to get started in the first place. Household distractions and interruptions, poor work habits, lack of planning, or procrastination can thwart your efforts. Before we consider these problems, however, let's take a new look at what it means to "stick to business."

Traditionally, it meant sitting at your desk riveted to work tasks without interruption and looking busy even if you weren't. Actually, once people start working at home with no one looking over their shoulders, they're often surprised to find they work better when they don't "stick to business" in such a traditional way. This is how one writer describes the way she gets her work done: "When I'm writing intensively I don't sit at the typewriter without moving for six hours. I typically write for half an hour, and then I'll start thinking about something I'm developing and get up and wander around the house, make a cup of coffee, or water a plant. It's part of my thinking process, wandering and pacing around for ten minutes or so and then going back to the typewriter."

Publisher and magician Mike Caveney describes a similar process for using a time-out from his office while ideas gestate in his mind. "When I'm working on something, I might go mow the lawn, but I'm thinking about what I was working on."

When graphic designer Nancy Rabbitt started her home business, she was relieved by the change she was able to make in how she keeps herself working: "I discovered that when I'm stuck or my mind isn't sharp, I can go on to something else. We've been taught to sit there and struggle with a work problem. But you go nowhere when you do that. It takes longer if you try to force a solution. And to handle the responsibilities of my business, I have to go on and come back to the problem later when I'm ready."

From reactions like these, we've identified a more flexible work pattern among successful home-office workers that confirms our own experience. Since we began working at home in a more flexible way, we've become more creative, and the quality of our work is immeasurably better. We've given birth to some of our best ideas while jogging, reading, or driving somewhere.

Although the flexible pattern we're describing is not the way we're used to thinking about work, management consultant and psychologist Tom Drucker argues that "if they have the choice, most people will work this way. The truth is, most people do. At the office they just have to look like they aren't."

Still, flexible work patterns like those we've described strike fear in the hearts of many supervisors and some workers. Although they may allow that such flexibility might be fine for artists or professionals, they doubt it would be efficient for most office workers. Their fear is "Will the work get done?" Many home-office workers we've talked to argue that it does.

One telecommuter who does data entry at home told us she had tried working both ways, and "when I take a break at least every hour and go do something totally different, I actually get more done in the same amount of time than if I work straight through to a mid-morning or mid-afternoon break."

Freed from sticking to business in the strict sense, people generally find shortcuts that get the work done more efficiently. The secret to doing this, however, lies in being able to make the distinction between breaks and distractions, and between shortcuts and diversions. Supervisors can't make these distinctions, because to an onlooker they often appear the same. But you can tell the difference, and when working from home you will probably have to.

A classic research conclusion known as the "Hawthorne Effect" has shown that people are more productive when there are changes in their work environment. You can improve your efficiency by occasionally moving

Nine Steps for Maximizing Your Efficiency

Taking the following steps can dramatically improve your work habits while still providing for the flexibility that makes working from home so appealing. Read on for how to make them a regular part of your day.

1. Plan the workday.

2. Safeguard your work from unwanted distractions and interruptions.

3. Recognize and sidestep procrastination.

4. Set reasonable work goals.

5. Praise yourself frequently for your work.

6. Reward yourself for a job well done.

7. Take frequent, regular breaks.

8. Schedule work so it won't conflict with your favorite extracurricular activities.

9. Arrange for a change of scenery.

around while you work, changing the room arrangement or decor of your home office, or working in a different place for a while. If your work allows you to move around while you work, you can do certain tasks by a pool, in the living room, on the porch, in a restaurant, or at the park. A cellular phone, portable dictating unit, or portable computer are all tools that make it possible to effect a change of scenery.

PLANNING YOUR DAY

Planning your workday at home is not much different from planning a day at an outside office, with one important exception. Since your home and office are so closely interwoven, we recommend planning your entire day at one time—work, household responsibilities, social activities, and so on. Otherwise it's too easy for one to interfere with another.

Time-management experts claim that the best approach to planning your day is to use a time-planning system of some kind. There are many systems available at stationery stores or through the mail. They range in price from under $20 to over $100. Three popular systems are the Day Runner, the Day-Timer, and Franklin Planners. Alternatively, you can use an electronic personal organizer such as Sharp's Wizard line; Casio and Royal also offer different models costing between $40 and $200. With many of these organizers you can buy add-on program cards or EPROMS that will give you a dictionary, thesaurus, language translator, time/expense manager, and more.

A third option is to manage your day on your computer using calendar and appointment software like Microsoft *Outlook,* Lotus *Organizer, Maximizer* by Maximizer Technologies, or *Ascend* by Franklin Quest. Contact management software such *Act* (Symantec) or *Goldmine* (Goldmine Software) is also quite helpful in organizing your day.

Organizing and appointment software also enable you to set priorities, create "to do" lists, and outline and track goals. Many programs also have the ability to print out your schedule on one of the popular paper systems like Day Runner, or Day-Timer, so you can manage your calendar on your computer and then carry a printed version with you when you're out of the office.

Personal-information managers are a step up from calendar and appointment programs in that they let you create more extensive records and search for them by keywords. They also feature extensive Internet and E-mail interconnectivity. Contact-management software provides even more extensive functions that let you track not only appointments but also client records and sales calls. Personal-information managers and contact managers are described in chapter 15.

In selecting time-management tools, make sure that the one you choose is more than a simple monthly calendar and address book. Time management involves much more than just entering phone numbers and appointments. A time-management system should include a calendar for the year, month, and week, a daily planner, a place for setting goals, building and prioritizing "to do" lists, and planning projects. If you are using a paper system, it should allow you to add, subtract, and rearrange pages to suit your needs.

 Checklist: The Basic Requirements of a Home-Office Time-Management System

We consider the following to be the essential elements of a time-management system when working successfully at home:

____ *One All-in-One System.* Unless you have employees to help you manage your schedule, we strongly advise against trying to manage yourself using multiple systems; i.e., one calendar at your desk, one you carry with you, a one-year planner on the wall, a monthly planner in your computer, a daily pocket planner, etc. Such a system not only wastes time but also risks the inevitable missed appointment or double scheduling. So while it may take you awhile to find just the right system for your needs, we urge you to seek out ONE system that will work and use it and only it.

____ *Portability.* Whatever system you work out for yourself, make sure it enables you to take it with you if you work even periodically away from your home office. Because the average home business is only conducted "at" home sixteen hours a week, most people need a portable system. Certainly there are people who use only one master calendar and planner at their offices. These are invariably the people who have to get back to you to schedule something when they're away from the office. Again, this is time-consuming, but even more important, it often results in missing out or not following through on important opportunities. With the availability of computers, subnotebooks, personal digital assistants, Day Runners, personal organizers like the Wizard series, there's no need to have to get back to someone in order to schedule an appointment. Alternatively, you can use software like *PC Anywhere* to link up with your home-office desktop computer when you're on the road.

____ *Long- and Short-Range Planning.* Your time-management system should have yearly, monthly, weekly, and daily planning capability all in one. By using a computer, you can enter an appointment once and it will appear on all four such calendars.

(Continued on page 375)

(Continued from page 374)

___ *Multipurpose Daily Planning.* Working from home, you are most likely carrying out all the functions that many people would perform in a larger office. Your daily planner should have more than just one "to do" list and an hourly appointment schedule. It should also have a place to sort, itemize, schedule, and organize the following types of activities you may need to carry out each day and display them on one page:

- Appointments and meetings by time of day

- Correspondence, billing, invoicing, and filing tasks you must do

- Phone calls you need to place

- Contacts you need to follow up on

- Major projects you want to accomplish that day

- Errands you need to run and odd jobs you should do

- Plans you need to make and things you should read or write

Such a daily planner prevents you from feeling like one frustrated woman who told us, "I have so many 'to do' lists I need a list of my lists." A daily planner like our specially designed Time Manager (Figure 13-1) saves you the hassle of having multiple "to do" lists. You can even design or customize such a form for yourself using form-generating software like *PerFORM Pro Plus* (Delrina/Symantec).

___ 5. *A Think-of-Everything List.* Your time system should provide you with a place to record or jot down future tasks, ideas, and thoughts that are not time specific. We call this the "Think of Everything" list. The Day Runner has a "Memory" section to serve this purpose. *Ascend* calls it the Master Task List. This is the place where you put everything for which there is no other place. It's the place of last resort, where you put something instead of resorting to making notes on the backs of envelopes or paper napkins, or instead of having multiple sticky notes pasted all over your desk, computer, and walls. You can use the back of your daily planner or the notes section for this purpose if you're using a paper system. If you're using an electronic organizer, you can put such items in the "memo" section.

Figure 13-1

A SUREFIRE DAILY PLANNING PROCESS

Now here's a step-by-step process for putting the system to work on a daily basis. Each day:

1. Use your daily planner to build one "to-do" list. Find time either at the end of the day or first thing in the morning to fill out your daily planner, listing all the tasks you need to do in each category: appointments, correspondence, phone calls, major projects, errands, reading.

To be sure you're including everything, go through the day in your mind, review your appointment calendar, go over your list of things to do in the future on the "Think of Everything" list, check deadlines in your current project files, and review upcoming-event or tickler files you have.

2. Screen your items. Once you have identified the things you need to do, screen them to be sure they need to be done. Ask yourself these kinds of questions: Does this have to be done today? What will happen if it isn't? Can someone else do it? Is this task worth the time required to do it? If not, could I do a scaled-down version that will take less time?

3. Assign all tasks an "A" or "B" priority. "A" priorities are tasks that should be done today; "B" priorities are those that might well be done today, but are not crucial.

4. Identify your top-three "A" items and rank them first, second, and third. The top-three "A" items are those tasks you feel are most important to get done before the end of the day. They will take priority during the day.

5. Plan to do your top-three "A" items first. Block out your day around these three tasks and indicate on the planner the times during the day you will spend completing them. Leave larger blocks of time for creative work. When possible, schedule these creative tasks to coincide with your peak energy periods.

6. Plan to do the remaining "A" tasks next. You can save time by doing the "A" tasks in each category together: making all "A" phone calls at the same time, running all "A" errands together, and so on.

7. Plan to move to the "B" tasks after you've finished all the "A" items, again saving time by doing those in the same category together when possible.

8. Check off the items as you complete them.

9. Carry over to the next day tasks you didn't have time to do. List the tasks you didn't get done on the daily planner for the next day. If you carry over tasks more than a week, consider whether you should drop them.

MAGIC TIME-SAVERS

Once you begin working on the tasks for the day, whatever you're doing—whether it's writing a letter or attending a meeting—your goal should be to "work smarter, not harder." Here are some time-savers to build into your daily routine:

An Organized Information System

Keep track of names, addresses, phone numbers, and files. The number-one time-waster is not being able to find the information you need when you need it. A simple-to-use filing system that keeps this information at your fingertips will save you more than a two-week vacation. You'll find many ideas for creating such a system in chapter 15.

Use Technology to Save Time

That's what it's here for, after all. Of course, complex technology can be more trouble than it's worth, but so much of the equipment in today's home office really can save us a lot of time. A computer, fax, and high-speed printer are musts in almost any home office. But little things can make a big difference, too, like:

___ a Touch-Tone telephone with a redial button and the ability to program frequently called numbers

___ A photocopier

___ E-mail

___ An electronic postage scale and a postage meter if you do a lot of mailings

___ An electric stapler

___ A letter-opening machine

___ A letter folder if you do lots of direct mailings

For more ideas for streamlining your office, see the list Technology Time Savers on the work sheet that follows this list.

Learn to Say "No"

A simple "no" can save you hours of time. Evaluate the requests for your time from clients, family, and friends. You may find that many requests are in keeping with your goals, while others are clearly at odds with them. Although saying "no" may be difficult at first, with practice you will find it easier to draw the line tactfully and protect your time.

Make Use of Idle Time

Take advantage of idle moments, like the times when you're waiting for a call, an appointment, a Web site to load, a fax to go through or a printout. Read the journal articles you've highlighted, change the ribbon you've been meaning to replace, take a mini–mental break, or slip out to put on dinner during these downtimes.

Build a Time Cushion into Your Plans

In estimating how long it will take to do something, include the time it takes not only to do the actual work but also to get ready, set up, drive to and from where you're going, and put it all away. Then add in some leeway for the inevitable delays in getting the job done.

Make Quick Decisions on Small Matters

Decisions take energy. When the stakes aren't high you can afford to make snap decisions. So, when deciding things like which brand of paper clips to buy, save your energy and act impulsively.

Multi-Task

Do two or more things at once. This is the time-saver of the era. Women have been good at doing many things at once for years. Kids now are becoming true pros at doing lots of things at once. So, learn to multi-track. Plan a project or listen to an informational tape while shaving, driving, or cooking dinner. Scan periodicals at night while watching TV. But never lose your ability to focus intently on giving the most important things your 100 percent undivided attention.

Keep a List of Fill-In Jobs or Five-Minute Tasks

When you're between projects and waiting on hold, there are myriads of mini-tasks you can do: jot down the agenda for a meeting, write a note, clip an article, sort incoming mail, proofread a letter.

This is not to say you should be working every minute of every day; breaks and idle time throughout each day and week are important to refresh your mind and spirit. So never get so organized that you don't have time for spontaneity and relaxation.

 Worksheet: 19 Technology Time-Savers

Are you getting the most from today's home-office technology? It can streamline many of the most time-consuming, routine administrative tasks you have to do to run a home office. Here are a few examples from Making *Money with Your Personal Computer at Home.* Check those you're not using and consider whether they could make your life simpler.

___ *1. Use integrated software* (suites) when you need to make intermittent use of multiple software programs. With integrated software like Microsoft *Office Small Business* or Lotus *SmartSuite,* you get a word processor, a spreadsheet, presentation graphics, and a database program as well as many other modules. All these components have similar command structures and tool bars so you can

(Continued on page 380)

(Continued from page 379)

learn to use them more quickly. You also can move simply and easily from one to another and transport information or data among the various applications.

___ **2. Find it on line!** No matter what you are looking for: a resource book, a marketing fact, a government agency or law, up-to-the second news, the latest version of a software program, where to stay in almost any city in the world, a replacement cartridge for that twelve-year-old dot matrix printer, what *not* to feed to a depressed horse—just about any fact or product is available on line. Save time by using the Internet to actually buy items and make reservations, or just compare prices and features before you buy. We can't overstate how much time and effort you can save by doing research on the Internet. So, before you look anywhere else, log on and try to find it on line using one of the popular search engines like Alta Vista (*www.altavista.com*), Excite (*www.excite.com*), Hotbot (*www.hotbot.com*), LookSmart (*www.looksmart.com*), Lycos (*www.lycos.com*), or Yahoo (*www.yahoo.com*)

___ **3. Use macros.** On a word processor, macros save time by stringing togeth-er sequences of keystrokes that can be activated by entering one short command. Each sequence—be it several words, a sentence, or a paragraph—is associated with just one or two keys that you can press to get the entire sequence. For instance, you might program your word processor so that whenever you press the Alt and C key simultaneously, it writes out a standard closing for your letters; e.g., Paul and Sarah Edwards
Sincerely,
Paul and Sarah Edwards

___ **4. Automate as many functions as possible.** Programs such as AutoMate from Unisyn Corp. allow you to set up a schedule of tasks the program will auto-matically perform for you, such as backups, close routines, or other tasks you rou-tinely do.

___ **5. Use templates for standardized documents**. Programs like Microsoft *Word* and *WordPerfect* already have predefined templates or style sheets for things like business letters, faxes, memos, proposals, and more. Desktop publishing pack-ages like *Microsoft Publisher* and *PageMaker* also have predefined templates for creating such documents as newsletters, cards, and catalogs. When you use one of these templates for a letter, for example, the program automatically inserts the date, sets up the "Dear . . ." salutation, lets you select from a library of names and addresses you've already keyboarded, and signs "Sincerely" and your name, thereby saving you hundreds of keystrokes.

(Continued on page 381)

(Continued from page 380)

___ **6. *Use the outlining feature*** of a word-processing program that lets you move entire sections of a report around just by moving the title associated with that section.

___ **7. *Use a spell checker, grammar checker, dictionary, and electronic thesaurus*** that come with many word processors to save the time of looking up words in reference books.

___ **8. *Link documents if you are operating in a Windows environment.*** With linking, anytime you revise the numbers in one document like a spreadsheet, they will be automatically updated in your other documents like reports, overheads, or proposals that have incorporated those numbers.

___ **9. *Use the automatic addressing and envelope printing capability*** that comes with most word-processing programs or purchase an add-on software utility with additional powers like *Office Accelerator*. These save keystrokes because you don't have to type a name and address twice, or spend time setting up your printer for an envelope.

___ **10. *Use a separate label printer*** such as Avery's *Personal Label Printer* and *Label Pro* software to print rather than hand-type or write out individual mailing labels. These dedicated label printers also enable you to print out labels for file folders and make index tabs for proposals.

___ **11. *Use form design software for your standard business forms.*** A package like *PerFORM Pro Plus* (Delrina/Symantec) or *Formworx* (Power Up Software) includes predesigned form templates you can use either as is or customized to your needs. You can print out and use these forms or you can save paper by filling them out on your computer screen, for example, while interviewing or collecting information by phone. *PerFORM Pro Plus* enables you to do calculations while filling out a form, look up information in a database, or turn the data you've collected into a database file that can be used in programs like *Microsoft FoxPro* and *Paradox*. Using electronic forms is saving some companies over 70 percent of what they would be spending to print paper forms.

___ **12. *E-mail documents instead of mailing, if possible.*** If the document contains only text, you can attach it as a file to any E-mail transmission and send it to any E-mail address in the world. This saves a great deal of time and expense for approving terms and conditions on contracts, approving content for publications and any form of business or personal correspondence.

(Continued on page 382)

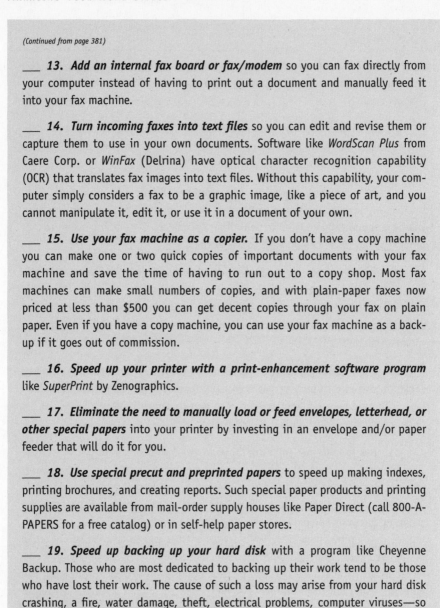

(Continued from page 381)

___ **13. Add an internal fax board or fax/modem** so you can fax directly from your computer instead of having to print out a document and manually feed it into your fax machine.

___ **14. Turn incoming faxes into text files** so you can edit and revise them or capture them to use in your own documents. Software like *WordScan Plus* from Caere Corp. or *WinFax* (Delrina) have optical character recognition capability (OCR) that translates fax images into text files. Without this capability, your computer simply considers a fax to be a graphic image, like a piece of art, and you cannot manipulate it, edit it, or use it in a document of your own.

___ **15. Use your fax machine as a copier.** If you don't have a copy machine you can make one or two quick copies of important documents with your fax machine and save the time of having to run out to a copy shop. Most fax machines can make small numbers of copies, and with plain-paper faxes now priced at less than $500 you can get decent copies through your fax on plain paper. Even if you have a copy machine, you can use your fax machine as a back-up if it goes out of commission.

___ **16. Speed up your printer with a print-enhancement software program** like *SuperPrint* by Zenographics.

___ **17. Eliminate the need to manually load or feed envelopes, letterhead, or other special papers** into your printer by investing in an envelope and/or paper feeder that will do it for you.

___ **18. Use special precut and preprinted papers** to speed up making indexes, printing brochures, and creating reports. Such special paper products and printing supplies are available from mail-order supply houses like Paper Direct (call 800-A-PAPERS for a free catalog) or in self-help paper stores.

___ **19. Speed up backing up your hard disk** with a program like Cheyenne Backup. Those who are most dedicated to backing up their work tend to be those who have lost their work. The cause of such a loss may arise from your hard disk crashing, a fire, water damage, theft, electrical problems, computer viruses—so many things can go wrong. But you can protect your files by backing up in one of multiple ways.

Now let's talk about specific time-savers for handling those tasks that are notorious for consuming—and too often wasting—much of our time.

Shortcuts: Reading.

There is more information in a highly specialized field than any one person can keep up with. To cut the time you spend reading without losing out on vital information, skim tables of contents, directories, and headlines and read only pertinent material. Learn to read more quickly by taking a speed-reading course. Use a clipping service that will clip pertinent articles for you, or subscribe to specialty newsletters or digests that summarize developments in your field.

 Shortcuts: Meetings.

Before scheduling a meeting, ask yourself if the matter could be handled by phone or by mail. Also, speakerphones, call-conferencing, and inexpensive Web-based video-conferencing technology are making phone meetings easier and more cost-effective.

To keep meetings efficient in person or by phone or computer, limit their length. Fax or E-mail the agenda in advance. If you don't complete your agenda within the allotted time, you can schedule another meeting or follow up by phone or mail. Time limits force people to say what they have to say and hear what they have to hear quickly, with fewer diversions into nonessential details.

If you must attend outside meetings, try to schedule them so you will not be traveling in rush-hour traffic. When you have business that relates to more than one person, arrange joint meetings, if feasible.

For formal meetings, plan to use an agenda, have a leader who keeps the meeting on track, and generally restrict meeting time to decision making rather than actually working on projects. Have a system of referring such work to individuals or subgroups to do outside the meeting. For more casual meetings, begin by agreeing on what you want to accomplish. When conversation strays from the goals, bring it back politely.

Learn to use body language to signal the end of a meeting or appointment. Shut your notebook, pick up your papers, rise and begin moving toward the door, using closing comments like "I'm glad we could meet," "We got a lot done," and "I'll look forward to hearing from you soon."

Shortcuts: Correspondence.

Set up an efficient routine for processing your postal and electronic mail. To cut time spent on correspondence, include checklists on outgoing mail on which people can quickly indicate their answers. Write your own responses to inquiries on the bottom of the original request and return it to the sender. Use standardized forms, and form letters, and keep all correspondence materials together in a convenient location. Programs like *Organizer* and *Outlook* have extensive features that allow you to sort and organize E-mail.

Use the phone instead of writing a letter when it will accomplish the same outcome in less time. Fax or E-mail instead of using regular mail whenever you can. Ask for information you need immediately to be faxed or E-mailed to you.

Use form-making software to create a variety of standardized letters, responses, inquiries, etc., that you can use again and again. Buy a book or two of sample letters to cut down on the time you spend thinking of what to say. *The 100 Most Difficult Business Letters You'll Ever Have to Write, Fax, or E-Mail,* by Bernard Heller, is a large handbook of sample letters for the busy executive, and *Letters That Sell,* by Edward D. Werz, provides ninety ready-to-use letters to help you sell your products, services, and ideas. Also, to make sending out form letters a snap, computerize your mailing list. In chapter 15, you'll find a variety of suggestions of how to use your computer to make handling correspondence more efficient.

You can even save time buying stamps by phone or mail. You can order them by phone from 1-800-STAMPS24 and charge them to MasterCard or Visa. To order stamps by mail, use the order forms you can pick up at post offices. Many banks offer stamps for sale through their ATMs as well.

 Shortcuts: Errands.

Keep time spent on errands to a minimum by taking care of as many things as possible in one trip. Do errands during your low-energy periods. Avoid rush-hour traffic and go when you are least likely to encounter lines and crowds. For example, avoid the post office while the twelve-to-two-o'clock lunch crowd is there. Take other work with you to do while you're waiting in lines you cannot avoid.

Call ahead to make sure the person or material you need is ready and available before you take the time to drive by. If you're spending too much time on errands, schedule biweekly or monthly trips for supplies, or consider finding an office-supply store that will deliver goods to you.

Shortcuts: Phone Calls

Keep names and phone numbers current and within arm's reach so you won't have to spend time looking for the numbers you want to call. Use the auto-dialer feature available on most phones. It holds frequently called numbers in its memory with one-number codes. All you need to do is punch one number to put a call through. Or use the address-book feature of your time-management or contact-management software to dial your phone number for you. You can call up the names, addresses, and phone numbers of business contacts in your computer immediately even while you're working in another file and keep a record of your conversations.

Or to better manage calls, you can screen your voice mail just like an answering machine by using Casio's two-line cordless PhoneMate. It will also tell you when you have voice mail waiting so you're not wasting time calling to check your voice mail. Also, Casio's IT-380 PhoneMate will let you screen your E-mail and log on without a PC connection or booting up.

Keep phone conversations in bounds by having a set time of day for making and returning calls. Use an answering machine or service to protect yourself from untimely interruptions. In fact, you can use an answering machine to screen your calls, only picking up those that are high priority and returning all others at a designated time.

Limit time on the phone by telling callers you only have a few minutes. Rather than discussing points in detail over the phone, ask for or send written materials to be reviewed later. Arrange to call back after you or your caller has had time to think over ideas brought up.

Learn to use closing comments like "Thank you for calling," "It's been good talking with you," and "I'll get back to you soon" to bring conversations to an end.

Shortcuts: Projects

To manage large projects efficiently, break them down into smaller tasks and list them in the order in which they need to be completed. Assign deadlines to each task and set up a Project File (paper and/or computer based) that will serve as the clearinghouse for the entire project. In the file or on the inside cover keep the following information:

　　Names, phone numbers, and addresses of all people involved
　　Tasks to be completed
　　Schedule and deadline for each task
　　Dates and locations for project meetings

(Continued on page 386)

(Continued from page 385)

All correspondence, proposals, and contracts

Summaries of phone calls and meeting notes

Keep all correspondence and material related to the project in this file. As work progresses, check off the tasks you complete and note any modifications in your project schedule. To track project tasks most efficiently, consider using project-management software. In the planning stage, this software enables you to set goals for the project and divide the work into smaller tasks. It helps you identify the resources you will use, determine the costs involved, track your progress, and evaluate your results. Popular project-management programs include Microsoft *Project*, *SureTrak Project Manager* from Primavera, and *Inspiration Professional Edition* by ACE Software.

STAYING CALM, COOL, AND COLLECTED

Planning your work ahead of time is clearly the best way to avoid the panic of getting behind schedule or becoming overwhelmed with too much to do. Knowing what you have on hand and what you have to do also helps you say no to projects and activities that you can't realistically handle.

It's not uncommon for new open-collar workers, eager for business or the opportunity to prove their worth on the job, to take on everything that comes along. In reality, taking on more than you can do, and do well, sets you up for failure.

 True Confessions: Taking On Too Much

The first time Joyce Green started a word-processing service, she actually put herself out of business by agreeing to do more than she could. She took on the typing of several doctoral theses simultaneously, thinking this would launch her business. Instead, her son became ill and she ended up being unable to deliver. Trying to juggle the typing and the care of her son put her further and further behind. Two months later her customers were furious and demanded their deposits back. They took their business elsewhere and spread the bad word about Joyce on campus. Their deposits, of course, had been spent, and she had to borrow the money to repay them. "I ended up going back to another job. But this time it's different. What I learned from that horrible experience is to take on only what I know I can do. Now I refer business out when I'm busy. I also try to stay ahead of schedule because I know there will always be some unexpected interruption."

(Continued on page 387)

(Continued from page 386)

Writer and editor Nancy Shaw works with her husband, Jim, from their ocean-front town house. She keeps her sanity with her demanding schedule by planning all her meals for the week on the weekend. She gets the groceries in on Saturday and cooks most of the main courses on Sunday. "This way, I can relax during the week and just concentrate on the work I need to do. When we're ready to eat, I just go to the freezer, and everything is ready."

In the midst of deadlines, delays, competing priorities, unforeseen emergencies, and demands from family, customers, and friends, even a well-organized day can get pretty hectic. It's on just such days that you realize that you don't actually manage time, you manage yourself.

With the pressures of the day, you can lose precious time stewing, floundering, and storming around the office. There are moments when chaos reigns despite the best-laid plans. So we've collected a list of things you can do to keep your wits about you and stay in the right frame of mind in the midst of it all.

 Nerve-Savers

1. ***Take a deep breath.*** In the pressure of a stressful situation, most people start holding their breath or breathing more shallowly. This leaves them with less oxygen to think clearly and signals the body that it's under stress. The adrenaline starts pumping, the heart beats faster, the palms begin to sweat. By taking a slow, deep breath, you bring oxygen into your system and fool your body into thinking it can relax. Immediately you begin to feel more relaxed and at ease.

2. ***Count to ten.*** This old chestnut still serves us well. When your mind starts racing and there are more problems than you can handle at once, slowly counting to ten will give you a few moments to recover your perspective.

3. ***Use aphorisms.*** Studies of highly successful executives show that they have slogans or mantras they repeat to themselves to get through rough situations. In other words, they give themselves pep talks with sayings like these: "Hang in there, Charlie." "You can do it." "Inch by inch everything's a cinch." "When the going gets tough, the tough get going."

   Psychologist Shad Helmstetter calls these aphorisms "self-talk," and his book *Self-Talk Solutions* is filled with many useful things you can say to yourself to get through the most challenging of times.

(Continued on page 388)

(Continued from page 387)

4. ***Project the best.*** Instead of worrying about what you fear might happen in the future, use the techniques of Olympic athletes and concentrate on what you want to have happen. Visualize things going precisely the way you want them to.

5. ***Look for the learning experience.*** Instead of worrying about mistakes you've made, think of what you can learn from them. The road to success is lined with mistakes. So rather than chewing yourself out for getting in such a mess, be your own fan club. Congratulate yourself for getting one step closer to success, and cheer yourself on.

6. ***Take a five-minute break.*** Take a walk, get a hug, play with your dog, or throw a private tantrum. Then ask yourself, "What's the best thing to do right now?"

7. ***Slow down and take one step at a time.*** Just because things are happening at a breakneck pace around you doesn't mean you have to be caught up in the same whirlwind. Concentrate on doing one thing at a time.

8. ***Remind yourself, ". . . and this too shall pass."*** Nothing lasts forever. You've been through tough times before and you're still here. Tomorrow is a new day.

TAKING CHARGE OF INTERRUPTIONS AND DISTRACTIONS

Even the most carefully laid plans are vulnerable to interruptions and distractions. Like financial consultant Michael Fey, most people find this is true even when they are working at home: "There are interruptions you can't even contemplate."

The most common interruptions and distractions you are likely to encounter fall into three categories: being distracted by household responsibilities, by other family members, and by your own lack of focus. Let's take a look at each of these and some steps you can take to tackle them.

 The Problem: Escaping from Household Responsibilities

When you're working from home, the various aspects of your life can become so interconnected that it can sometimes be hard to tell whether you're working or you're busy doing other activities.

(Continued on page 389)

(Continued from page 388)

Errands and household responsibilities become part of the workday. They can be insidious, monopolizing the best part of your day before you know it. Writer Marcia Seligson recounts what often happens: "You could spend half a day, every day, doing trivia—the laundry, the errands, taking the car in. You can spend days paying the bills, arguing with the phone company."

Certainly all the trivia Marcia refers to is work. And it needs to be done. Therefore, while you are doing it, you feel productive. Career consultant Marilyn Miller describes this feeling: "Originally I had problems focusing, because whether I was doing household duties or whether I was doing my work, I kept telling myself, 'It's okay, you're working.'"

Many of the business errands you run are the type that someone else would have done at the office—getting supplies, taking out the mail, delivering a package, and so forth. Now, when you have to do them yourself, they fit in naturally with stopping to get a birthday card and dropping off the dry cleaning.

When you were working at the office, your household responsibilities weren't there staring at you. You didn't know about the broken pipe until you got home. Somehow you squeezed in all the major responsibilities and just let the rest go. And that's what you will have to do when you work from home. It's just harder, because everything is there in front of you.

 ## The Solutions

Your daily planning process and priority system should help, but the best safeguard is your attitude and determination. You will need to cultivate the attitude that even though you are at home, you are at work. You must train yourself to operate as if you were at an outside office.

Calligrapher Jean Hilman handled her problem this way: "When I first started working at home, I'd tidy up the house before I got to work, but I would always find one more thing to do. Finally I decided that come nine A.M., wherever things were, that's the way they would stay until my work was done. After all, that's the way it was when I had a job."

Marilyn Miller found she had to get over the old rule "You always answer a ringing phone" and turn over her personal line to the answering service. Obviously you don't have to answer your personal phone while you're working. You wouldn't be answering it if you were away at an office.

Simply closing the office door is helpful to many people. Some take coffee and other things they'll need into their office first thing in the morning so they don't have to go out later amid the many household items that need attention. Others are comfortable doing housework during a break or during their natural downtime.

The Problem: Getting Solid Family Support

Since your family is probably accustomed to your being accessible when you're at home, discovering they can't talk to you during large blocks of time can be quite an adjustment. "I had to learn to pretend he wasn't here," one wife reported about her spouse. "That took awhile, but now I only interrupt him during those times I would have called him at the office anyway."

And what a surprise for a child of any age to discover that Mommy's home, but can't be seen. "I really didn't need to talk to her," one sixteen-year-old told us, "but I kept interrupting her just to see if I could. Now I'm used to it and I only bother her if I need to."

 The Solutions

Work out a clear plan with your family and get their support. Let them know when you will be working and what your expectations of them are during that time. The plan should define the following:

- ✓ *How everyone will know when you are working* and when you aren't. How you'll signal your family that this is work time.

- ✓ *When you can be interrupted or not and during which hours and activities.* What emergencies will you want to know about? What type of problems should you be interrupted for even if you're working? What household events will you be willing to handle?

- ✓ *Other expectations you have:*

  Areas of the house that must be kept neat.
  The sound level you expect in the house while you are working.
  Who is responsible for taking care of household events while you are working.
  Whether you expect anyone else, such as a spouse or an older child, to be responsible for making sure you aren't interrupted.
  Whether you want anyone else to answer your business phone.
  Whether you have any special expectations when you have business visitors.

- ✓ *How any young children will be cared for* while you are working.

In setting up your plan, remember, you want to work at home, not become a police officer. When someone is opposed to doing something you expect him or her to do, problems will usually develop. Most people find that in order to get the support they need, everyone involved needs to be consulted before a plan of operation is decided on.

Expect a lot of testing in the beginning. At one time or another, everyone will forget the plan. Everybody will push and explore the limits. Even you will probably forget sometimes. Be prepared to discuss exceptions. Like most people, you will find that if you simply keep your expectations to yourself, the plan will go out the window. "I wasn't able to work at home because of the kids," an entertainer told us. "If I had set and kept the limits in the beginning it might have been different."

Often family members find it helpful to have cues or signals that remind them when you are not to be interrupted. Marketing consultant Robbie Bogue finds that getting dressed in professional work attire in the morning is one way he can signal his family that he's at work. At the end of the workday, he changes into "comfy" clothes, signaling that now he's "at home." Here are some other signals people use:

✓ Posting a schedule on the office door

✓ Closing your office door

✓ Hanging up a DO NOT DISTURB sign

✓ Posting an OUT sign on the door, meaning "Don't interrupt," or an IN sign, meaning "It's okay to come in"

I'm-Available Signals

You will probably find you'll have fewer interruptions if you let people know exactly when you are available. When family members hear a vague "Later" or "When I'm done" too often, they just make further interruptions to see if "later" has arrived. So if it's "not now," let people know exactly "when."

✓ Post the time of your next break on the door.

✓ Ask family members to knock once when they need something, and let them know you will come out at the first opportunity.

✓ Put a plastic WILL RETURN AT sign on your door as shopkeepers do to signal when you'll be available. You can find these at office-supply stores.

✓ Draw a clock face. A speech therapist who works at home with small children draws a picture of a clock showing what the face of the clock will look like when she's free to see them. She tells them beforehand to look at the clock and "When the little hand is here and the big hand is here, just like this, that's when I'll be available."

✓ Put up a mock traffic signal. Buy a small three-canister track-lighting strip and mount it on the door frame. Put a green bulb in the top canister, a yellow bulb in the middle one, and a red bulb in the bottom one. The green light signals "Come on in"; the yellow light says, "Knock" or "Ask before entering"; the red says, "Don't bother me unless this is an emergency."

Of course, you need to make clear to your children what constitutes an emergency.

Avoiding Interruptions While on the Phone

Many parents of small children find that the child is fine entertaining herself around the home until the moment the parent gets on the phone. A parent on a business call seems to attract interruptions the way honey draws a bear. Here are several clever ways parents tell us they deal with telephone interruptions when there's no other adult around to handle the child's need for attention.

✓ **Create a "phone box"** for your children to play with while you're on the phone. Fill the box with interesting toys or intriguing objects the child has never seen. Get it out only when you're on the phone. So, when your child starts whining or begging for attention while you're on the phone you can pull out the "phone box" and present some irresistible distraction.

✓ **Use a cellular phone with a mute button.** This can be a helpful tool as well for getting the glass of water the youngster must suddenly have the minute she sees her mom on the phone, or going into the living room to see the new Lego creation that just has to be viewed now that Dad's on the phone.

✓ **Set up a "twin" office** for your young children: a small desk with mock (or actual, depending on the age) computer and telephone, paper, pencils, and pens. Your kids can "play" at work right alongside Mom or Dad.

To guard against kids' deciding to "play work" on Mom or Dad's real computer, you can get a disk lock that prevents the child from booting up the computer. Of course, this means you can't leave your computer on with open files unattended.

Rule of Thumb: Putting an End to Interruptions

The most important thing to bear in mind is that when the family and friends do follow your plan, let them know how much you appreciate not being interrupted. Be sure you don't make the mistake one advertising executive did: "Every time my ten-year-old would come to the door and interrupt me, I'd talk to him about what he wanted and how he shouldn't be interrupting me. We'd have an out-and-out argument. A friend pointed out to me that he got more attention by interrupting me than he got if he waited until I was free."

Giving a lot of attention to someone who interrupts, even if it's negative, will only encourage more interruptions. So when you're interrupted, keep your responses short and sweet and give family members more attention before and after business hours.

Most people find that by sticking with it, through what is usually a bumpy beginning, they can eventually evolve a creative and individualized plan that will work for them. For more ideas, see chapters 19 and 20.

How Do You Avoid Your Work?

Interruptions from other people aren't the only reasons people sometimes have difficulty getting to work and sticking to business at home. Each of us can invent our own reasons to avoid work. What diversions are you most apt to use?

- Socializing on the phone
- Visiting with friends and neighbors
- Daydreaming, planning a glorious future
- Worrying, but not acting
- Working on other, less-important projects
- Getting sick
- Watching TV
- Starting later, stopping earlier
- Cleaning out all the file cabinets
- Taking longer, more frequent breaks

The Problem: Keeping Focused on Your Work

Many people interrupt themselves. A phone call reminds them of someone else they should call. The dog barking in the backyard reminds them they need to put out the trash. Hearing the kids squabbling, a parent wants to get involved.

 The Solutions

Set up your environment to help you stay focused on the job at hand. Put temptation out of sight. Close the door. Soundproof your office in one of the ways suggested in chapter 7. Close off the TV room. Close the kitchen door. Put away books or magazines.

Psychology Today once described a surgeon who was concentrating so intently on his work that he was unaware that the ceiling had collapsed around him. When he finished he asked the nurse, "What's all this plaster doing on the operating room floor?" This story highlights how effective the power of concentration can be.

The ability to maintain deep concentration can safeguard you from almost any interruption. Working with psychologist Frederick Robinson's ideas about concentration, we've identified four simple principles for developing improved attention and concentration:

✓ *Cultivate a zest for the work you are doing.* Become involved in mastering it, taking it to its limits, finding a new or better way of doing it. Become fascinated with the possibilities. Make the work come alive. See it in relation to the big picture, the difference it makes in the world, in the lives of others. There's nobility in all work; discover the nobility in yours.

✓ *Keep thinking about your immediate goal.* Sift out everything that doesn't relate to it. At other times, seek to find a relationship between everything and your goal. This is how people can be watching TV or reading an article and suddenly discover a better way to do their job.

✓ *Take it easy.* Don't push. The most economical use of your mental and physical energy is also generally the most effective.

✓ *Let your subconscious work for you.* Grapple with whatever you're focusing on. Really get in there and wrestle with it. Then take a break. Often ideas and solutions will appear to come from nowhere. This is the key to how people are able to take productive breaks while mowing the grass or running an errand.

Last-Ditch Strategies: Sticking to Business

If disruptions continue to be the bane of your workday, despite all efforts to control them, there are several last-ditch approaches you can try.

✓ Consider relocating your office to a different area of the house.

✓ If your work allows you to move around, work somewhere else during certain periods. Public libraries are good places; college campuses, hotels, or restaurants are other possibilities.

✓ Consider changing your office hours, too, perhaps working after the children are asleep or early in the morning before other activities have started.

✓ Rearrange your schedule, moving tasks to different times of the day.

✓ Finally, learn how to tolerate the interruptions you can't avoid. Set up reminders or cues to get back to work easily after you've been interrupted. Leave yourself a short note about where you stopped. Mark the page or the file you're on. Leave your work as it was so you can step right back into it when you return.

Put an End to Junk Mail

Opening, perusing, and tossing out stacks of unwanted junk-mail solicitations can eat into your ability to work productively. How much junk mail do you have to sort through every day? If it's more than you want, you can cut it off at its source. The nation's largest credit bureaus sell names and addresses of consumers to direct-mail marketers, and they have all agreed jointly to delete names of consumers who do not want their names and addresses to be sold by direct-marketing agencies. You can request that your name be removed by contacting the following:

The Direct Marketing Association
Mail Preference Service
P.O. Box 9008
Farmingdale, NY 11735
Web: *www.the-dma.org*

Equifax Options
P.O. Box 740123
Atlanta, GA 30374-0123

(Continued on page 396)

(Continued from page 395)

TRW Target Marketing Division
Mail Preference Service
901 N International Parkway, Ste. 191
Richardson, TX 74081

Trans Union Corporation
Consumer Relations Department
TransMark Division
555 W. Adams
Chicago, IL 60606

A simple letter will do; e.g.: "Please have our names and addresses deleted from your members' direct-mail lists." For additional information about ending junk mail, you can call the Direct Marketing Association at (212) 768-7277.

To be removed from prescreened credit card solicitations call (888) 567-8688.

End Unwanted Telephone Solicitations

Responding to unwanted phone solicitations can eat into your ability to work productively. How many times a day are you interrupted by a call from someone wanting to sell you siding or carpet cleaning? Well, you don't have to take it anymore. The Telephone Consumer Protection Act provides us with some protections. First, companies are to call only between 8 A.M., and 9 P.M., and they must tell you it's a sales call before proceeding. Also you have the right to notify solicitors that you don't want to get their calls. If you tell a telemarketer that you don't want them calling, by law they must not make any future calls to you.

The FTC enforces this regulation, and fines for violations run up to $500 per call. If a telemartketer continues calling, contact the Direct Marketing Association Telephone Preference Service in writing requesting that your name be removed from their national solicitation lists. Write to: P.O. Box 9014, Farmingdale, NY 11735; *www.the-dma.org*

Additional resources:

Center for the Study of Commercialism has a step-by-step guide on using the Telephone Consumer Protection Act to stop unwanted calls. Send $3 to 1875 Connecticut Ave. NW, Ste. 300, Washington, DC 20009.

You can add yourself to the Private Citizens' list of consumers who don't want calls from telemarketers by calling (800) Cut-JUNK.

Prefone Filter Company offers filters for telemarketing messages. Call (800) NO-2-JUNK.

True Confessions

Like most of us, San Diego–based consultant Bob Beken hates junk mail. He considers it an invasion of privacy when companies collect information from purchases he's made and use it for future marketing or to sell to others. But, unlike most of us, Beken doesn't put up with it. When paying for merchandise, he writes a simple contract on the back of the check that reads: "By cashing this check, you agree that I will be damaged in the amount of $1,000 if you subsequently send me junk mail." When a company violates the contract and sends him junk mail, he sues. He claims to win about half the claims. So far he's netted $8,000 in damages.

PREVENTING PROCRASTINATION: GETTING DOWN TO THE CAUSE

With all the freedom you have working from home, it's far too easy to procrastinate. Procrastination arises from a number of causes, and recognizing the reasons can keep you from succumbing to it.

Perfectionism

In the face of impossibly high standards, we're all likely to put off what we fear can't be accomplished. Therefore, to avoid procrastinating, think performance, not absolute perfection. Set manageable, concrete goals to be achieved at specified times.

Fear

In their book *Procrastination: Why You Do It, What to Do about It,* Jane Burka and Lenora Yuen say the major cause of procrastination is fear of something, whether it's fear of success, fear of failure, or fear of change. Finding out what you fear, and then deciding whether it's realistic, or how you could handle things if your worst fears came true, can free you to go ahead with the task.

Large, Overwhelming Tasks

When what you're doing seems so large and complex you don't know where to start, procrastination is often the result. In a situation like this, break the work into small chunks that will take you no more than ten to thirty minutes each. Take one small step at a time.

Unpleasant Tasks

If you hate doing something, you're likely to procrastinate tackling it. When possible, delegate or hire someone to do the tasks that are most distasteful to you. If you must do them yourself, think about how good you'll feel when the task you've been avoiding is done. Bribe yourself with the promise of a reward when you finish, and keep your promise. You might offer yourself small rewards for doing each part of a larger task. Also use the tactic of doing unpleasant tasks first to get them out of the way and free the rest of your day.

Creating Pressure to Perform

Some people motivate themselves by creating the pressure of a crisis atmosphere. They procrastinate until the last minute and then dramatically complete the work. Since this strategy actually helps them get the work done, they're often confirmed procrastinators. The emotional expense, however, is great and detracts from the kind of consistent, concentrated effort a successful business needs. So instead, motivate yourself by working at a reasonable pace to finish one step at a time rather than getting yourself into a panic to do it all in one last-ditch effort.

Waiting for the Right Moment

People get entrenched in procrastinating by telling themselves they can't start something until something else has happened. Their thought is, "I'll do this as soon as . . ." (For example: "I'll clean out that storeroom as soon as my son moves out.") The way out of this trap is to do it now. Now is not only the right moment; it's the only moment. Tomorrow has a way of never coming, so start today.

 Warning!!

Sometimes procrastination is a warning signal, a way to tell yourself this is not the right thing to do or that it is a waste of time and doesn't need doing. A potter we talked with, for example, kept putting off delivering a particular pot she had sold. All she needed to do was to take a picture of it for her portfolio and deliver it. After much delay, she realized that if she sold this pot, she would not be able to duplicate its unique and unusual finish. Once she realized this, she knew she did not want to sell it and called immediately to work out a new agreement with her customer.

When, for whatever reason, you find that you continue to avoid important tasks, identify what you're doing instead, and cut off your escape routes.

Last-Ditch Strategies: Procrastination

If you chronically procrastinate and find you can't cut off the escape routes, ask yourself these three questions:

- *Under what circumstances would I be motivated to do what needs to be done?* Listen carefully to your answer. Don't censor it. Think about what's stopping you from going on with what you need to do. If you're honest with yourself, you may recognize you're not willing to work as long or hard as it takes to get the job done. You may not have scheduled enough free time for yourself. You may not be willing to perform some of the tasks your work entails. In any case, now you have to face the truth. You are the boss; but you can't fire yourself. You have to learn to live—and work—with yourself. So you may have to compromise or strike a bargain with yourself about such things as setting up a different schedule, getting additional help, or allowing more free time.

- *Do I enjoy my work?* If the honest answer is "no," it's no wonder you are having difficulty getting yourself to perform the tasks involved. When you work at home, it is particularly important that you enjoy what you do at least most of the time. If you don't, seriously consider finding different work. As magician and publisher Mike Caveney says, money alone is often not motivation enough to get you to work when you're on your own. "I can't think of anyone who works harder than we do. At midnight or eleven o'clock we'll knock off and watch the news. If we were to do it just for the money, it wouldn't work. You have to love it."

- *Am I depressed?* If you chronically can't get yourself going, your procrastination may be a sign that you are depressed. Working at home alone, day in and day out, you can be more vulnerable to depression and it can grow on you gradually. Depression can arise from not having enough personal contact, excitement and stimulation, or structure for doing things. You can also become depressed from too much contact and stimulation, and a schedule that is too rigid or overloaded.

Avoiding the Inertia of Depression

The isolation, unexpected interruptions, uncertain financial conditions, loss of regular routines—all changes that people face when they work at home—can lead to depression. In fact, depression could be an occupational hazard of working at home unless you take preventive action. To combat the situation, here are practical steps you can take to avoid feelings of mild depression:

- Keep moving. Even though you may not feel like it, stay active. Physical exercise for twenty or more minutes daily is a good way to keep your spirits up.
- Make daily contact with people.
- Set up and follow a schedule that is neither too tight nor too loose.

Whether feeling depressed is related to working at home or other events in your life, if it continues or worsens despite your efforts, contact someone for professional help. It is important that depressions not deepen or continue for weeks on end. You'll find ways to contact professionals in the Resources at the end of this chapter.

CLOSING THE DOOR ON WORK

If you have more work to do than you can possibly get done in a regular workday (and who doesn't?), how do you put it aside if it's always there with you? At an outside office, you can close the door and go home, but some people who work at home find that's not enough when the door is right down the hall next to the bedroom.

Short of moving the office out of your house, there are several things you can do to get away from the work around you.

Separate Your Office Space

When you have an office space or work area that's as remote as possible from the rest of the house, it's usually easier to "close the door"—literally— the way you would when working away from home. Psychotherapist Richard Nadeau has his counseling practice in a separate wing of his home. "When my last client leaves, I put away the coffee cups, empty the ashtrays, and close the door to that portion of the house. I don't go back in again until the next day when I begin to prepare for my first client."

Graphics designer Mary Stoddard has to walk across an outdoor courtyard to get to her studio in the garage.

Lauren Brubaker has his recording studio in the basement so that "downstairs I'm at work, upstairs I'm not."

Whatever you do, if you have a tendency to overwork, make sure you don't put your office in your bedroom! Any other room in the house will be easier to get away from!

Set Up an End-of-the-Workday Ritual

Michael Warner, who operates his company, InfoSource, from home, has created a unique ritual to close his workday: "At the end of the day I walk to the garage, open and close the car door, walk in the front door and shout, 'Hello, dear, I'm home.' It gives me the feeling that I don't have to go back into the office until I 'leave' for work the next morning."

Here are some other rituals people use:

✓ Taking a walk around the block

✓ Running errands

✓ Taking an exercise class at the end of the day

✓ Taking a shower and changing clothes

✓ Picking the kids up from the baby-sitter or from school

✓ Having a snack while watching the five o'clock news

Set a Firm Schedule

If possible, set a fixed "closing hour" and do not compromise except for emergencies. This is usually easier to do when you're salaried than when you're self-employed. In our work, for example, we give many evening speeches and seminars. We have early-morning meetings with our editors. We give all-day seminars, too. If we're not careful in planning our week, we could end up working morning, noon, and night.

Put Nonwork Events on Your Calendar in Advance

There is another simple step you can take to close the door on work when you need to. Use your calendar to prepare yourself to take time off. Most people reserve their appointment calendars for work-related activities or special social occasions. Personal or family activities are usually fit in around business. Writing these activities on your calendar helps you give them equal time.

Rule of Thumb: Setting Reasonable Work Hours

For situations like ours when you're working at different times of the day during the week, here are two general rules:

1. Set aside the morning, afternoon, or evening of each day as "free" time during which you do not work. As you fill in your appointment calendar, block off the morning, afternoon, or evening of a day by putting a big "X" over the one free period.

Some days, of course, will be more hectic than others, but to make this system work, we've found we have to be fairly rigid about this rule. When we have X'd out an evening of a fully scheduled day and someone wants us to meet that night, unless it's crucial we have to say, "No, that evening is already filled." And it is. It's filled with time off.

2. Allow at least one full "free" day per week. For most people this is Saturday and/or Sunday; but it can be any day of the week. A family we know operates a swap-meet booth every weekend, and takes Monday and Tuesday off. A professional dog handler works at shows on weekends and teaches evening classes during the week. His free day is Friday, and during the rest of the week he doesn't go to work until one in the afternoon.

Get Out of the House

When work is home and home is work, people sometimes find they have to get away from the house to really get away from work. They come to feel the way graphics designer Nancy Rabbitt does: "When you commute to work, coming home is like a retreat, a refuge. But when you work at home, it's no longer a refuge. To relax and refresh myself I have to go someplace else, get away for an evening or go off for a weekend."

Getting away isn't always easy, however. Have you ever thought of planning an evening at the theater or taking a short trip, but then waited to see if you'd be free or if you'd feel like it when the time came? What happened? Too often, when the time came, you were too busy or too tired to go.

Genevieve Marcus and Bob Smith, who run an educational foundation from their home, have found that to get away from work they have to make reservations in advance. When they see an event that looks interesting, they buy the tickets right away. If they want to spend a weekend at a vacation resort, they pay for the tickets and the hotel room in advance. "Then we have to go. We have to drop what we're doing," Genevieve explains. "Right before it's time to go, I always wish I hadn't bought the tickets. I never feel like going. But since I've paid for them, I go and I always end up having a wonderful time. When I get back, I'm glad I got away."

Protect Your Free Time

Home-business owners frequently complain that clients, knowing they're at home, call or even drop by at any time of the day or night. If this sounds like your situation, you must create ways to protect yourself from business intrusions into your free time.

Nancy Rabbitt found a double solution to this problem. Although she had fixed business hours, she kept getting calls in the early morning or the doorbell would ring while she was still in the bathtub. "I now have an answering service, which I keep on before and after business hours. When

---

Eight Signs of Overworking

Watch for these signs that your work is taking over your life. The more of them you notice, the more likely it is that you need to find a better balance between your work and other aspects of your life.

____ Do your spouse, children, or friends nag and complain that you need to spend more time with them? Do frustrated children, friends, and other loved ones feel last on the list for your time? Do they sulk, badger, or act up for your attention?

____ Do you have many business associates but few friends? Are you always too busy to get together with people? Do you hear yourself saying things like "I can't make it," or "Sorry I had to miss it"?

____ Do you work even in nonworking situations? Do you "work" your social gatherings and talk shop wherever you go?

____ Do you work at your play? Is all your recreation as much work as being on the job, because you play to win every point and improve your previous performance, and you refuse to take losing lightly?

____ Do you feel uncomfortable if you're in a situation where you can't be productive, growing nervous as you wait in a grocery line or for a red light to change?

____ Do you think of non-goal-directed fun as frivolous? Do you feel that "doing nothing" is being lazy, and do you consider those who don't work as hard as you do unmotivated?

____ Do you let the clock run your life? Do you look at the clock often, wanting to cram as much as possible into every minute, or are you frequently late because you had to get just one more thing done before you left?

____ Do you take everything so seriously that you miss or resent humorous comments in a work situation?

customers call, they're told the hours they can reach me and asked to leave a message. I also have a box on the front door so if clients come by before I'm open for business, they can leave off whatever work they're bringing. Or in the evening, they can pick up their work after I'm closed."

If security is an issue, consider installing a Smart Box (*www.smartbox. com*) that lets people place deliveries in a security-coded compartment in your door. If you're one of those people who can't stand to hear a phone ring without picking it up, a phone with a button for turning off the ring may help you turn a deaf ear.

 Last-Ditch Strategies: Stop Overworking

Perhaps you're a person who simply can't stop working: a "workaholic." If many of the signs of overworking apply to you, an office at home may aggravate the situation. You don't have to move your office out of the house, however, to escape from overwork. You can get to the root of the problem.

People who overwork often link their self-worth and sense of well-being to whether or not they are being productive. They feel bad if they aren't always doing something. They fear the worst will happen if they let up.

Behavioral scientists have found that the constant drive to work is usually traceable to very basic concepts and beliefs about ourselves and about life. These convictions are related to what we unconsciously believe we must do to survive, to be loved, to succeed, to be worthy as a person.

Often workaholics have gotten the idea that they must overwork from their parents, or even grandparents, who lived through more difficult economic times. One woman we know traced her belief that she had to be working all the time to her immigrant grandparents' struggle to survive and rise above poverty. She recalls her grandmother working from dawn to dusk seven days a week. She remembers every family member being sent to work, and how her mother continued this tradition years after they were all affluent.

Similarly, a carpenter recognized how his tendency to overwork arose from having grown up in the Depression. His father never lost his job, but those around him did. The father worked long hours during that time and ever after. For years to come, the father would recount how being caught with an idle moment could have cost him his job and the family's livelihood.

In addition to the experiences in our past, societal conditioning also invites us to overwork and rewards us for doing so. Many men have been conditioned to believe that their value lies in how much money they can make or how high up the corporate ladder they can climb—both of which often seem to depend on putting in overly long and difficult hours.

(Continued on page 405)

(Continued from page 404)

In recent years, many women have found themselves in this trap, too, feeling they can't get ahead unless they overwork themselves as much as so many men do. Women also get caught in the "Superwoman" syndrome, working full-time and trying to be the perfect mother, lover, and housewife all at once.

If you're self-employed, concern about your economic security can drive you to think that you must keep working all the time or you'll never make it. Sometimes family and friends unintentionally intensify such concerns because of their own fears. Not wanting you to fail or suffer needlessly, parents may subtly suggest that you take another job. Worried about mounting bills, spouses can thoughtlessly comment that you should have kept your old job.

Usually overworkers are not aware of such patterns, beliefs, and conditioning, but once recognized for what they are, they can be changed. The overworker can develop new values that support a healthier, more balanced, and even a more productive and secure life.

SOLUTIONS FOR WORKAHOLICS

If you overwork, here are several steps you can take:

Change your ideas about success.

There's a difference between hard work and overwork. Success today does not require working yourself into the grave. In fact, success can be easy. A consistent, steady effort proves more successful than a stress-filled obsession. Reassure yourself of your ability to achieve your goals or get reassurance from others who will support you. When sales trainer Harriet Brayton left her job, for example, she was so frightened about whether she could make it on her own that at first she couldn't even sleep. She kept thinking of work she could be doing. She turned to her father for reassurance. "For a while I was calling him every day. A successful businessman himself, he kept telling me, 'Harriet, relax, You're doing fine. Just keep going.' And that's what I would say to others. It works. I'm doing fine now and I still take time to play."

Have a talk with yourself about the therapeutic effects of relaxing.

Convince yourself that you're entitled to relax and that there's more to life than work. In fact, you owe it to yourself. Your life will not only be just as good when you stop working so much; it will actually be better. Studies like the one by Dr. Charles Garfield of the University of California, San Francisco, School of Medicine show that workaholics not only have more heart attacks and other illnesses but also don't accomplish as much! You may be surprised to discover that you get more done and have more energy after you begin to take more time off.

If this is hard for you to believe, read about others who used to feel as you do. Writers like Norman Cousins and Jerald Jampolsky are good examples. They have both written about how, after a near-fatal disease or life crisis, they learned to change from inveterate overworkers to people who could relax and enjoy life while they had a chance.

Find out what drives you to overwork and give yourself permission to stop.

Below we have listed what psychologist Taibi Kahler has identified as the four most common messages people use to drive themselves and the messages they need to hear to stop.

How to Escape What's Driving You

Psychologist Taibi Kahler has identified the four most common messages people use to drive themselves unproductively and the new beliefs we can develop to replace these drivers so we can relax and enjoy life. Which ones, if any, apply to you?

DRIVING MESSAGE	NEW BELIEFS
Be perfect.	You can learn from making mistakes. Mistakes take you closer to success. No one is perfect.
Try hard.	Do your best, and you'll do a good job. Doing well doesn't have to be hard. You don't have to struggle to succeed. Success can come effortlessly.
Hurry up.	You can go at your own pace. You'll get more done when you go at a reasonable and steady rate. Slow down. Take a breath. Take one step at a time and you'll reach your goals.
Please others.	You can't please everyone all the time. You have to take care of yourself before you can take care of others. It's okay to say "no."

Explore how you became so driven.

Try to discover how you got the idea that you have to work so much. If you overwork, look back into your roots to find out what experiences or social pressures influenced you to overwork. Use the following Five-Step Change Process to recognize what keeps you overworking, why it's important to you, and how you can develop new, healthier, and more rewarding ways to accomplish what you want to do.

A Five-Step Change Process

You can use this five-step process developed by Richard Bandler and John Grinder to change any stubborn pattern of behavior that is preventing you from achieving your goals in life.

Step 1. Ask yourself, "What positive intention do I have for working so much and driving myself so hard?" What am I hoping to get? What am I hoping to avoid? Here are a few sample answers:

- To make enough money to relax someday

- To be somebody

- To keep from going under

- To avoid hassles in the family

Step 2. Ask yourself if you would be willing to consider other ways of achieving your positive intention besides overworking.

Step 3. Then, using your creative abilities, think of three other ways you could achieve your positive intention.

Step 4. Ask yourself if you are willing to use these three new ways instead of overworking.

Step 5. Check to see that you have no doubts about using the new alternatives. If you do, go back to Step 3 and come up with some other ways that will overcome your doubts.

Set up minibreaks.

Set aside five to fifteen minutes a day to "do nothing." Spend that time doing anything that you enjoy but don't have to do. It's surprising what people call "doing nothing." For example:

- Working in the garden
- Watching TV
- Taking a walk
- Sitting in the sun
- Playing ball with the kids
- Brushing the dog
- Taking a nap
- Reading a magazine

At first you may feel uncomfortable during these five to fifteen minutes, but make yourself take them. Don't expect "doing nothing" to feel good at first; you're going against your conditioning and years of habit. It takes awhile to shed the discomfort and develop new habits. To help the process along when you are feeling uncomfortable, take notice of the old beliefs your feelings stem from and mentally replace them with the new beliefs that will free you from overworking.

Also, initially you will probably have to schedule your leisure time by formally putting these five- to fifteen-minute work breaks into your day. Set a goal of taking one break at ten o'clock in the morning and one at three o'clock in the afternoon, for example.

Set aside part of each day for leisure.

If you are now working most of the waking day, build up to enjoying a portion of every day off. For example, graduate from minibreaks to setting aside a whole hour once a week for leisure time in the evenings. Then add one or two hours a week as free time begins to feel more comfortable. Eventually, you will be able to limit your work to eight or ten hours a day.

Avoid invitations to work on something else.

When you start taking time off, some people may see that you're free, for a change, and try to put you back to work—finally you're available to do some of the things they've been waiting for you to do! Tell them these "free times" are health breaks that will keep you alive longer, and send them on their way.

Raise your prices.

If the cause of your overwork is too much business, consider raising your prices. This is a better alternative than hiring an employee or turning work down because you earn more from your own efforts. You want to give existing clients plenty of notice, perhaps even extend your current prices for a period of time. For more information on pricing, see chapter 22.

Refuse to let anything interfere with the time you've blocked off for leisure.

Avoid the trap of working at your play. Engage in leisure-time activities because you enjoy them, not because they will produce some work objective for you. Your time off is for doing things that are gratifying in and of themselves. Play golf, for example, because it feels good, not because you can talk over a business deal. If you play golf with a prospective client, that's probably not leisure. If you jog to improve your time, you are probably working at it and not playing. So you'll need to include another way of relaxing.

Spoil Yourself.

Finally, as time-management consultant Dr. Terry Paulson advises, it's okay to pamper yourself when you relax. See that baseball game you've been itching to go to. Listen to your favorite album or radio talk show. Buy yourself that science fiction thriller you've been meaning to read. And read it. Or, in the good doctor's words, "Pamper yourself . . . there are no replacements."

RESOURCES

BOOKS

The Balanced Life: Achieving Success in Work and Love. Alan Loy McGinnis. Minneapolis: Augsburg Fortress Publishing, 1997. ISBN: 0806635703.

Feeling Good: The New Mood Therapy. David D. Burns. New York: Avon, 1999. ISBN: 0380731762.

Get a Life Without Sacrificing Your Career: How to Make More Time for What's Really Important. Dianna Daniels Booher. New York: McGraw-Hill, 1997. ISBN: 0070066469.

Get Out of Your Own Way: Overcoming Self-Defeating Behavior. Mark Goulston and Philip Goldberg. New York: Perigee, 1996. ISBN: 0399519904.

The How-to-Be Book: A Table with Exercises to Take the Stress Out of Your Life. Thomas Thiss. Minneapolis: Deaconess Press, 1994. ISBN: 092519073X.

If You Haven't Got the Time to Do It Right, When Will You Find the Time to Do It Over? Jeffrey J. Mayer. New York: Simon & Schuster, 1991. ISBN: 0671733648.

Letters That Sell. Edward D. Werz. Chicago: Contemporary Books, 1987. ISBN: 0809246848.

Problem Solving for Entrepreneurs: A Creative New Approach to Overcoming Your Business Problems. Bryan Drysdale and Julie Blau. Aptos, Calif.: S M D Publishing, 1995. ISBN: 0963950614.

Sales Letters that Sell. Laura Brill. New York: AMACOM Books, 1997. ISBN: 0814479456.

Secrets of Self-Employment: Surviving and Thriving on the Ups and Downs of Being Your Own Boss. Sarah and Paul Edwards. New York: Tarcher/Putnam, 1996. ISBN: 0874776465.

TAPES

How to Master Your Time. Brian Tracy. Chicago: Nightingale Conant, phone: (800) 323-5552.

TIME-MANAGEMENT SYSTEMS

Day Runner. Harper House, 2750 West Moore Avenue, Fullerton, CA 92633; phone: (800) 232-9786. Web: *www.dayrunner.com*

Day Timer. Day-Timer Concepts, One Willow Lane, East Texas, PA 18046; phone: (800) 317-9152. Web: *www.daytimer.com*

The Franklin Planner. Franklin Covey, P.O. Box 31406, Salt Lake City, UT 84131; phone: (800) 544-1776. Web: *www.franklincovey.com*

TIME-MANAGEMENT SOFTWARE

Anytime. Individual Software. 4255 Hopyard Road, #2, Pleasanton, CA 94588; phone: (800) 331-3313. Web: *www.individualsoftware.com*

Ascend. Franklin Covey, P.O. Box 31406, Salt Lake City, UT 84132; phone: (800) 877-1814. Web: *www.franklincovey.com*

CalendarWise. Blue Cannon Software, P.O. Box 7641, Charlotte, NC 28241.

Calendar Creator Plus. The Learning Company, One Athenaeum St., Cambridge, MA 02142; phone: (617) 494-5700. Web: *www.learningco.com*

Farside Computer Calendar. Delrina, 15770 Dallas Pkwy., Dallas, TX 75248; phone: (972) 715-2003.

Lotus Organizer. Lotus Development Corporation, 55 Cambridge Parkway, Cambridge, MA 02142; phone: (800) 635-6887. Web: *www.lotus.com*

Outlook. Microsoft Corporation, 1 Microsoft Way, Redmond, WA 98052; phone: (800) 426-9400. Web: *www.microsoft.com/outlook*

CHAPTER 14

Managing Money: Financing and Cash-Flow Management

Goals

1. Decide what you need to keep track of.

2. Set up an easy way to manage your finances.

3. Select the best money-management software.

4. Avoid feast or famine.

5. Collect the money you're owed.

6. Get credit.

If you're like the majority of the people who work from home—salaried or self-employed—you have neither the time nor the inclination to spend hours doing complicated record keeping. Fortunately, there's usually no need to get complicated, but you do have to spend a little time setting up a system for managing the records you need to keep in order to track the money you're making. Otherwise, it's all too easy for your income to slip through the cracks.

Picture this: A check bounces and your credit is marred. It's tax season and you're buried beneath a mound of receipts trying to figure out just how much you spent on supplies and equipment. You're at a party and overhear how you lost out on a way to make your money work for you by earning higher interest rates. With an effective money-management system you can avoid these and other problems of money mismanagement, which is the number one reason for small-business failures.

Unfortunately, many financial record-keeping systems for small businesses are scaled-down versions of those used in large organizations. They require too much time, too much energy, or too much money for a one-person home office. At the same time, systems for managing household money matters aren't adequate for home-business needs, either.

Faced with choosing between two extremes, some home-office people adopt the bookkeeping systems designed for larger businesses. Others, seeking to avoid the hassles of complex systems, fly by the seat of their pants, hoping everything will work out in the end. For too many, both of these strategies produce disappointing results. People frequently tell us: "I've tried several times to use a formal record-keeping system, but it takes so much time that I get behind after a few weeks. Then for the rest of the year I just try to keep up with what's necessary. The receipts and everything, they're all in a box in the corner of my office. I guess until I can hire someone to do it for me, I'm doomed to trying to straighten it all out at tax time." To avoid this dilemma, you need a simple system for managing your money that doesn't take much time or effort but keeps you on top of you money from day to day and month to month, not just once a year at tax time.

 Checklist: What You Need to Keep Track Of

The specific financial information you need to keep track of depends on whether you're salaried or self-employed and on the type of business you're in. Here is a checklist of the typical kinds of information you may need to manage. Review it and check off the items that apply to you:

___ *Banking transactions:* making deposits as well as keeping track of and balancing your savings or checking accounts.

___ *Bills:* paying and keeping track of your personal and business-related expenses.

___ *Time and expenses:* keeping a record of time and costs you need to bill to your customers, clients, or employer.

___ *Billing or invoicing:* keeping records of money that people owe you and sending statements to get paid for services or products you've provided.

___ *Inventories:* keeping track of products you have on hand.

___ *Sales records:* keeping track of the products you've sold and any sales tax you've collected.

___ *Tax information:* tracking the deductions to which you're entitled, knowing how much you owe, how much you've paid, and when you've paid it.

THE FOUR MUSTS OF GOOD
HOME-OFFICE MONEY MANAGEMENT

A good home-office money-management system should meet four criteria:

1. It should be simple and easy enough for you to use in the time you have. In fact, it should be so simple that it's as easy or easier to use than not to use.

2. It needs to have a fail-safe mechanism so that if you fall behind, there is a way of picking up again without undue effort.

3. It needs to be easily expandable into other larger systems if and when your business grows.

4. It has to do the job for you; it must enable you to keep track of all pertinent aspects of what's going on with your business.

EASY-TO-USE RECORD-KEEPING SYSTEMS

As with time-management systems, there are a variety of ready-made money-management aids available at stationery, office-supply, and software stores to help you keep track of the information you need. When you're salaried or affiliated with a sales organization, the company may have a system of its own for you to follow. If so, you'll need to incorporate it into a comprehensive system that addresses all aspects of your personal and business finances.

The right system will enable you to:

- Know how you're doing financially: if you're making a profit; how far ahead or behind you are each month.

- Keep track of how you are spending your money so you can adjust what you spend in accordance with your goals.

- Determine which of your business activities are the most profitable.

- Be prepared, save time, and avoid stress when you do your taxes, when you seek loans and investors, when you want to sell your business, or any time you need to prepare financial statements, profit-and-loss statements, or balance sheets.

- Provide your tax preparer with everything needed to complete your federal and state returns in the minimum amount of time, therefore saving you money.

- Minimize your taxes by enabling you to take the legal deductions to which you are entitled.

- If you're self-employed, estimate your quarterly state and federal tax payments so you can put aside enough to pay what you owe.

- Provide adequate records should you be audited by the IRS or state agencies.

- Have everything in one place so you know where to find it when you need it.

In this chapter we provide you with a framework to choose and set up a system that will meet these criteria and provide some guidelines for getting additional help when you need it. Take a look at how your existing system is working; then we'll review the basic tools available for creating a system that works for you.

 Worksheet: Is Your Money-Management System Working?

How does your current system measure up? Check off ✔ the areas that are working and star * the ones that need improvement.

___ Do you know your bank balance?

___ Are your bills paid on time—without late charges?

___ Are your tax materials already in order when tax time comes?

___ Do you get invoices out within the week the work is completed or product is shipped?

___ Can you locate a receipt, order, or payment record you need in less than five minutes?

___ Do you know exactly what you're spending your money on?

___ Do you have the money you expect to have on hand when you need it?

BASIC MONEY-MANAGEMENT SOFTWARE

The easiest way to keep track of your financial situation is to use a personal computer. With the proper software, you can write checks, reconcile your bank accounts, do budgeting and basic bookkeeping, and produce financial reports. There are hundreds of financial software programs; we recommend, however, selecting one that meets the level of complexity your business demands, is easy to learn and use, and will enable you to transfer your financial records to more sophisticated software when your business growth demands it.

Using these criteria, we recommend the following for finding the right level of software for your home office:

Level 1: One- or two-person business with no employees

Our choice at this level is a check-writing program like *Quicken,* by Intuit, or *VersaCheck Pro,* by MIPS. These programs are extremely easy to use and make keeping track of cash transactions (checks, money orders, and currency) as simple as writing a check. Although professionals agree that a double-entry bookkeeping system is more accurate and reliable, most single-person home offices find that a check-writing program works well at least in the beginning. If you have someone else doing your record keeping, however, be certain not to rely on a check-writing program. A double-entry bookkeeping system in this case is a must.

Level 2: Fewer than five employees, or a need for billing or inventory capabilities

If your business has fewer than five employees or you need to do regular billing or keep track of inventory, we recommend a program like *Peachtree Complete Accounting, Quickbooks Pro* by Intuit, and *SOHOMaster* from New Perspective Software. In addition to basic financial management, these programs enable you to do payroll and invoicing, pay your bills, and control your inventory. Of course, this greater capability requires greater effort on your part to learn the program.

Level 3: More than five employees and a need for accounts-receivable and accounts-payable capabilities

If you employ more than five people and your business involves a significant volume of credit purchases or sales, you will benefit from using a software program such as DacEasy's *Accounting and Payroll.* It's a complete bookkeeping system that provides you with all the invoicing, banking, communications, and reporting tools you need to manage your entire business.

ELECTRONIC SPREADSHEETS

In addition to basic money-management software, many home businesses also like to use spreadsheet software to forecast and manipulate financial information. These programs offer vastly more flexibility than is possible with pencil and paper. When you change an entry on an electronic spreadsheet, the software alters all the other affected figures automatically to reflect that change so you can easily:

- Do financial modeling—play "what if" with numbers

- Do tax planning

- Plan alternative budgets

- Project monthly sales, cash flow, profit and loss

- Do financial problem-solving

- Track and plan your project schedules

- Track your productivity

- Evaluate a stock portfolio

RECORDING TIME AND EXPENSES

Software may also be the simplest, quickest, and most accurate way to make records of your time and expenses. *TimeSlips,* by TimeSlips Corporation, for example, enables you to track every minute you spend working on a project for up to thirty thousand clients or jobs. With such a program, you can either:

• *Record the time yourself* by keeping track and then logging in the exact hours each day when you start and stop working on a particular project. The program will then tally the number of hours and minutes spent on that project.

• *Let the program track the time for you.* If you're working on the computer or nearby on the telephone, you can simply push a few keys and the program will begin tracking your time.

Time-and-expense software calculates the total hours you spend on a project and can automatically prepare your invoice according to whatever hourly or per diem rate you have specified. *TimeSlips* has many other features as well. You can arrange to have multiple billing schedules so one kind of work can be charged at one fee while another can be billed at a different fee. You can also record expenses billable to a certain project and add them to your invoice. There are many time-and-billing software packages available that are expressly designed for specific types of businesses, such as graphic designers, attorneys, architects, and many other professions. Check with your professional group or organization, or computer user's group to find out what may available for your business or industry.

If you prefer paper-and-pencil recording, you can, of course, use your appointment calendar or daily planner to record time-and-expense information. Or you might prefer recording it in a personal organizer that travels everywhere with you like *Sharp Wizard*. If you do keep paper records, use a pen, not a pencil, for your entries, because pencil entries are not acceptable in an IRS audit. Erasures are not acceptable, either. So make corrections by crossing out the erroneous entry with a single line so it is still visible. You can use similar systems for recording and calculating business mileage and travel expenses you won't be billing to anyone but need to use in calculating your business deductions for tax purposes.

Several long-distance services offer a free or nominally charged service that allows you to code all your outgoing calls for easy categorization later on. AT&T's program, for example, is called *Call Organizer*; however, it's only for business lines, and the calls, of course, must be made using AT&T. Once the service has been initiated, you enter any number from 1 to 9999 after a call you want coded. For example, if you're a consultant, punch 22 before you call a client whom you are billing on a time basis. When the bill comes, all the 22 calls will be grouped together and totaled for you, giving you the basis for billing your client. (To order, call [800] 566-2464.)

If you're using a residential line for outgoing calls or want to record incoming calls, you can get a device called *CallCost* that stores information about outgoing and incoming calls, including the duration of each call and the number dialed. Periodically, you can upload this information into your computer using software that comes with *CallCost*. *CallCost* ([800] 245-9933) also lets you assign account codes anytime during an incoming or outgoing call as well as preassign an account code to a group of numbers.

Financial Management Software Overview

Check-Writing Software

Purpose: Many home-based businesspeople can use one of these easy-to-learn programs to carry out most of their financial management tasks. You can pay bills, write checks, keep your bank balance, record and track income, and create financial reports.

For: One- or two-person service businesses with no employees and little inventory.

Examples:
   VersaCheck Pro, MIPS
   Microsoft *Money*
   Quicken, Intuit

(Continued on page 418)

(Continued from page 417)

General Ledger Accounting Software

Purpose: Makes double-entry bookkeeping and accrual-based accounting somewhat easier because it automates various accounting functions for keeping a general ledger. Accountants will often advise business clients to use a general-ledger system like these because they meet what is known as "generally accepted accounting standards." They reduce posting errors, and if you use an accountant for year-end work, your information will not need to be reentered into such a system by the accounting office.

For: Home-businesspeople who have employee payroll, considerable inventory, or wish to use the accrual method of accounting.

Examples:

DacEasy Accounting, DacEasy
One-Write Plus, One WritePlus
Peachtree Complete Accounting, Peachtree
QuickBooks, Intuit

Spreadsheet Accounting Systems

Purpose: Provide access to more powerful financial analysis including forecasting, modeling, and projecting.

For: Either cash- or accrual-based accounting for all types of businesses that prefer working with spreadsheet software.

Examples:

Lotus 1-2-3, Lotus Development Corporation
Microsoft Works & Excel, Microsoft
Quattro Pro, Borland

Time-and-Expense Software

Purpose: Tracks the time you spend on each job or client.

For: Any business that bills by the hour and needs to track time allotted to each project or client.

Examples:

Bill Quick, BQE Software
Timeslips, Timeslips Corporation
Time Logger, Westing Software

(Continued on page 419)

(Continued from page 418)

Invoicing

Seventy percent of all business communication is invoices and estimates.

Purpose: To create professional invoices easily

For: All businesses that must submit bills to clients.

Examples:

Dedicated time-tracking and invoicing software like *Timeslips*.

Word-processing programs like Microsoft *Word* or Lotus *AmiPro* that provide you with templates or design capability to create your own invoices.

Professional form-design programs like *PerForm Pro Plus* (Symantec) that contain invoicing templates and ways to design your own forms.

Accounting and management programs that include invoicing like *SOHOMaster* and *Peachtree Complete Accounting*.

 Features-to-Look-for Checklist: Financial-Management Software

The more sophisticated a program, the more features and flexibility it has, but generally the more complex and costly it will be. Select a package that has the features that best match your current and projected needs.

Check register

Check writing

Memorizes recurring transactions

Schedules future transactions

Reconciles accounts

Link to credit-card statements

Bill-paying reminders

Prints checks to laser, ink-jet, and dot-matrix printers

Prints out check register

Preset budget categories

Adds categories

Splits transactions among categories

Numerous reports and charts

Views supporting data of reports and charts

Financial planning

Portfolio management

Debt-management planning

Estimates tax liability

Data readable by or transportable to tax software

Generates invoices

Calculates payroll deductions

Customized reports

Calculator/calendar

Contact manager

Tasks minder

Help with accounting principles

Ease of use

Tutorial

Clarity and simplicity of documentation

Unlimited free support

Toll-free support

TAX-PREPARATION SOFTWARE

Tax preparation software enables you to prepare your taxes electronically. Financial records can be entered manually or imported directly from your bookkeeping or financial-management software. You can dramatically cut the time you must spend completing your taxes using packages like Kiplinger's *Tax Cut* or *Turbo Tax* by Intuit

---

Features-to-Look-for Checklist: Tax Software

❏ Capability and memory required

❏ Edition for your state

❏ IRS forms included and excluded

❏ Ability to import data from your financial package

LEAVING THE ESSENTIAL PAPER TRAIL

The Internal Revenue Service still requires a paper backup of all financial transactions. Computer records alone, because they can be altered, will not do. So to make yourself an easy-to-keep paper trail, we recommend using partitioned accordion files to keep records of paid bills and receipts for cash and charge-card payments of expenses. Simply place labels on the partitions of the accordion file to correspond to the categories of tax deductions you take—for example, advertising, automobile, Internet charges, dues, publications, entertainment, and so forth.

We keep our accordion files in a room right by our entryway. Then, filing receipts, along with taking messages off the voice-mail answering system located nearby, is part of our ritual when coming home. Receipts don't get lost or accumulate for filing at some other time. Another place to keep your accordion file is near the computer with your bookkeeping software. That way, it will be handy when you enter cash and credit-card expenses into your computer records.

MANAGING CASH FLOW

If you are self-employed, having a system for managing your cash flow is a matter of survival. Cash flow is to your livelihood as breath is to life. If the cash doesn't keep flowing, your business doesn't keep going.

We recommend a system that enables you to minimize what others owe you, utilize your cash on hand for maximum benefit, and hold on to what you have. That involves collecting the money you're owed, following up on overdue payments immediately, and making it easy for customers to pay via credit card when possible. Let's consider what's involved in each of these elements for keeping your cash flowing.

COLLECTING THE MONEY YOU ARE OWED

For ideal cash management, you should collect on services or products at the time you deliver them. Do this whenever you can. You may be able to do so more often than you think. When Sarah was in private practice, for example, she expected her clients to pay at the end of each session. Only on rare occasions did they request other arrangements. Because she was used to operating in this way, she continued this policy when selling advertising time on a Los Angeles radio show we were pilot-testing. Not a single advertiser objected, yet to her surprise, a radio consultant told her a year later, "No one ever pays for radio time up front."

Of course, there may be times when you will need, and want, to extend credit. Remember, credit is always a privilege. You owe it to yourself to check out if your client is credit-worthy. If you're working with a well-established company, you may be able to check their credit quite easily. Diane Sobotik has worked with *Fortune* 500 companies for years. She finds the easiest route to doing a credit check is simply to call the accounting office and ask them for credit references. She notes that most companies are commonly asked for such references and have a sheet that lists their regular vendors. With this list, you can call and check the company's payment history.

When this is not possible, you can and should ask clients desiring thirty-day payment to complete a credit application—just as you are asked to do when you want to obtain credit from those whose products and services you buy. Standard credit application forms are available on software such as *PerForm Pro Plus*, by Symantec. Your credit form should ask for the following information:

- Type of business
- Years in business
- Dunn & Bradstreet rating
- Names, addresses, and phone numbers of partners and corporate officers
- Bank references
- Person to contact regarding purchase orders and invoice payments
- Confirmation of accuracy
- Release of authority to verify
- Policy statements
- Trade references

In addition, depending upon who your clients are, you may be able to obtain credit information through several on-line sources, including:

1. Dunn & Bradstreet Web: *http://dbisna.com* Accounts can be set up through their Web site or over the phone at 1-800-552-3867, ext. 1067.

2. Equifax Web: *www.equidfax.com* Equifax offers on-line information on "consumer and commercial credit information, payment services, software, modeling, analytics, consulting, and risk management."

Another resource for checking credit is the National Association of Credit Managers (NACM), which has local offices throughout the U.S. that offer seminars on credit collection principles and information on obtaining credit reports. In addition, some companies are joining credit exchange groups, where companies operating in the same industry or related industries get together on a monthly basis to discuss credit concerns. This can be especially helpful in industries where customers may be playing one supplier against another. If you experience chronic collection problems with major clients, you might consider joining or starting such a group.

Even once you've decided to extend credit, there are a variety of steps you can take to make sure the money you're owed comes in as quickly as possible:

✓ *Get deposits,* retainers, or partial or progress payments.

✓ *Get payment up-front* for expenses or arrange to charge expenses to your client's account. Here's how consultant Molly McClelland handles this. When asked to travel for her clients, she says, "If you'd like me to make the travel arrangements, I'll be happy to take care of it. Whom in your office should I have my travel agent contact for a credit-card number?" She says it works like a charm.

✓ *Take bank cards* instead of extending credit. (See below for how to do this.) With new clients, information researcher Janet Gotkin uses what she calls her credit-card/cleared-check policy. She bills clients she's never worked with before through American Express or, if they prefer, she offers the option of their sending a check and waiting for the check to clear before proceeding.

✓ *Bill immediately* upon delivery of a service or product, instead of waiting until the end of the month. A thirty-day period usually begins from the date a customer receives your invoice.

✓ *Use a check guarantee service.* Telecredit is one of the largest in the country. They charge a small percentage for each check and have a monthly minimum, but you do not have to process all your checks through the service.

✓ *Whenever extending credit, have clear terms* for when you must receive payment. Offer discounts of 2 to 5 percent for receipt of payment within 20 days from the date of the invoice. Some companies are known for taking 90 to 120 days to make payment, so negotiate payment terms of 30 days as part of your sale.

✓ *Include a delinquent interest or financing charge* on overdue accounts as part of your payment agreement. In most jurisdictions it is illegal to charge such fees without written consent, but charging such delinquent fees can be important in offsetting the expenses that may be incurred in collecting on such accounts. So include information about these fees in all your contracts or as part of the credit application.

✓ *Act promptly on overdue accounts.* Don't let them slip by. The longer the account is overdue, the less likely it is to be paid. The first day a client is past due, get on the phone, refer to your contract, and ask for your money. Link any ongoing or future service to payment. Do not continue working for someone whose account is overdue.

✓ *Use a factor.* Factors are specialized privately owned finance companies that purchase accounts receivable. The factor offers some combination of the following services: provides immediate cash on accounts receivable, maintains ledgers and bookkeeping duties on accounts receivable, collects accounts receivable, assumes the losses that may arise, furnishes loan funds to its clients on a seasonal or term basis, and offers advisory services. One consultant uses a factor because expenses on behalf of his clients can get steep and his large clients particularly stretch out their payments. He couldn't find a bank to handle his receivables, but by using a factor, he gets paid in a timely fashion. He pays 4 percent in exchange for getting his money forty-five to sixty days earlier and he builds a service charge into his contracts to cover the cost of the money.

 True Confessions

Business writer Andre Sharp has established a fee schedule that helps him avoid cash-flow problems. First, he asks for 50 percent of his fee in advance. The balance is due upon delivery of a project. He requires that individuals and clients he doesn't know or about whose dependability he is uncertain pay all major expenses in advance. With new clients he always makes and keeps a copy of the check payment as further proof that there is a contract. These policies help his immediate cash flow, cover his expenses, and convey a high level of professionalism.

Last-Ditch Strategies: When the Check's Not in the Mail

Up until the time you've collected what you're owed, you've given your product or service away . . . and that's exactly how it feels when you end up having a hassle collecting the money you've earned. To inspire timely payments and avoid hassles, private investigator Bob Taylor adds a light touch by using a stamp on his statements that reads, "If you pay us, then we can pay them, and they can pay you." His favorite stamp, though, is a little angel in a praying position with the caption "PLEASE."

For those times, however, when even all your best efforts fail to produce the check, Leonard Sklar recommends the following ten tips in his book *The Check Is Not in the Mail:*

1. Lay the groundwork for prompt payment by giving your clients and customers a very clear and comprehensive payment policy right from the start that spells out exactly how and when bills are to be paid.

   TIP: *Include your payment policy on your fee schedule.*

2. Call the person who owes you money instead of sending another letter or bill.

3. Ask for payment in full, no matter how large the bill.

4. Create a sense of urgency that your bill must be paid NOW.

5. Follow up on overdue accounts immediately! The longer the account goes uncollected, the greater the chance you won't receive payment at all.

6. Pin down the debtor. Ask for exactly what you want and when you want it. Don't be vague and don't let him or her be vague.

7. Offer payment option: e.g., "Would you rather take care of this by check or cash?"

8. Blame a third party for your insistence that you receive payment now: e.g., "My accountant is insisting that I get this completed."

9. To make sure that you have a way to counter possible stalls, excuses, and evasions, role-play with a colleague what you're going to say before you place a collections call.

10. Don't do business with individuals, companies, or organizations that have poor credit records.

If all else fails, do not hesitate to engage a collection agency or take your case to small-claims court. Small-claims courts routinely handle such cases. Sometimes just filing the case will spur payment; other times you will need to wait until you get a favorable judgment. Should you have trouble collecting on your judgment, you can get help from a company like Lutz Asset Research. For $125 this company will locate judgment debtor bank accounts. They claim to find 50 percent of their accounts if provided with a valid current address. For information call (800) 999-CASH.

 Tip: How to Get Paid Immediately and Reliably by Check

You can get checks processed like credit cards by using a service called Electronic Check Acceptance. It takes a special terminal and software but results in quick payment automatically deposited into your account, and you never get a bounced check. The customer gets a printed receipt and his or her check back. The service is offered by TeleCheck, the same company that provides check guarantee and verification services. Telecheck, 5251 Westheimer, Ste. 1000, Houston, TX 77056; phone (800) 733-3400, (713) 599-7600. Web: *www.telecheck.com*

FOUR WAYS TO BE ABLE TO GET PAID WITH CREDIT CARDS

Sales go up when customers can pay you with a credit card. According to credit-card industry experts, a business can expect to increase its sales between 10 and 50 percent. Whether the increase is closer to 10 or 50 percent depends on the type of business, with mail-order and Internet operations particularly likely to benefit. Not only will your sales go up, but installment sales are also possible by billing someone's credit card over a period of months or collecting all your money at once while the customer decides to pay his balance over time.

Yet there can be few tasks more difficult for a home-based business than obtaining a merchant account. This is because many banks still discriminate against home-based businesses by lumping us in with the types of businesses that have been chargeback problems. This is especially true for new home businesses. Nevertheless, home-based businesses do manage to be able to offer their customers the ability to use their charge cards. Here are four basic avenues for securing a merchant account.

1. Financial Institutions

Banks. Even though banks, as a general rule, are not granting home-businesses merchant accounts for taking Visa and MasterCard, do try your own bank, particularly because they know you as a customer. If your bank denies you a merchant account, try small independent banks, particularly those that have their merchant accounts processed by an out-of-state bank instead of doing it themselves or using a larger local bank. Banks in smaller communities are more apt to work with home-based businesses.

Find out in advance what the bank's criteria are for granting merchant accounts. This information should be available in writing. Typically this includes but is not limited to:

- Your type of business. Mail-order and telephone-order businesses have a difficult time.

- How long you have been in business

- Your credit history both as a business and personally

- Your record with previous merchant accounts

- Your current banking relationships.

The bank will want to know about your business's financing, track record, and sales projections. You may need to show a business plan and will probably be well served to offer it and your marketing materials even if it is not requested.

Structure a presentation to meet the criteria established by the bank. Make as much effort as you would if you were pitching your services to a new client or applying for a loan. The key to convincing a banker to grant you a merchant account, says former banker John Witmer, is "to convince the banker that you are 1) professional, 2) serious, 3) knowledgeable, 4) persevering, and 5) profitable. Anything you do or say that contributes to that image will help you and anything you say that suggests otherwise is probably fatal."

In talking with bankers, you're more apt to display the self-confidence that produces respect if you keep in mind that you are giving the bank business rather than pleading for relief. Also be prepared to offer to establish a reserve account, which may range in size from a few hundred to several thousand dollars. This account, or guarantee of assets, will back up any refunds or other defaults that make banks extremely cautious in granting merchant accounts. Whether applying to a bank or another source of merchant accounts, be careful not to omit items from the application or fail to disclose what you will be selling. Merchant account issuers will terminate accounts once disqualifying information becomes known.

Savings and Loans, Thrifts, and Credit Unions. Most people think of banks as THE only financial institutions granting merchant accounts to businesses. However, savings and loans, thrifts, and even credit unions are increasingly offering merchant accounts. You may find these institutions more willing to work with you.

Remember, as Larry Schwartz and Pearl Sax, founders of the National Association of Credit Card Merchants, remind us: These institutions "need reassurance that handling your business will be both safe and profitable." It almost goes without saying that a presentation of your business, your financial ability, and yourself must make your banker feel absolute confidence in you. Home-business owner Ed Verry inspired this confidence by using what he calls the Security Deposit Method. First he pointed out that his business is not prone to large individual sales or the type of customers and products that cause credit-card fraud. Then he offered to use the electronic card-verification machines on every credit card sale. (The bank sold him this machine at cost, $250.) But finally, and most important, he offered to place an appropriate amount of dollars in a one-year CD account as a security deposit for the bank. He signed a common agreement form that he wouldn't withdraw the money for a specified period of time. He says, "This offer worked wonders for me!"

2. Business Organizations

Some business organizations provide access to credit-card vendor status as a member benefit. Here are two types of organizations where you may be able to find such benefits:

Trade Associations. Trade associations sometimes provide access to Visa and MasterCard accounts as a member service. Examples of organizations that may be helpful are the Retail Merchants Association and Direct Marketing Association and others specifically related to your particular industry. To find trade associations in your field, use *Gale's Encyclopedia of Associations,* found at the reference desk in most libraries and increasingly made available on line by libraries for library patrons.

Local Business Organizations. Chambers of commerce and local merchant associations sometimes help their members secure merchant accounts through a bank affiliated with the chamber or the association. These can be the least-costly merchant accounts with discounts as low as 2 to 3 percent on relatively small volumes.

Small Business Organizations. Many home- and small-business organizations have arrangements with independent selling organizations that enable members to get merchant accounts. The associations may be able to negotiate more favorable terms for members than you can buy from the same company on your own, and in the event of a problem with the independent selling organization, you may get the association director to go to bat for you.

3. Independent Selling Organizations

Perhaps the most likely way to get a merchant account, especially if you are just beginning, is to work through a bank agent or independent selling organization (ISO), which is a company that acts as an intermediary between small businesses and banks.

You will undoubtedly pay more using an ISO because these companies derive their income from fees and surcharges added to what you would normally pay if you were able to deal directly with a bank. So carefully go over the contract. Here are some typical costs and charges you may be quoted when going through an ISO:

- Application fees ranging between nothing and $200. These may or may not be refundable. Usually they are not, but find out under what circumstances all or part of the fee may be refundable.

- Card swap machines also known as point-of-sale terminals are available by lease or purchase. If purchased, the terminals range in price from $150 to $700. Leasing typically runs between $18 and $80 a month and usually are noncancelable. Some ISOs are offering software that can be used in place of a sales terminal, priced as low as $150. However, *IC Verify,* the leading software for credit authorization/draft capture, check guarantee and ATM/debit cards, is more likely to cost close to $500. Because *IC Verify* is compatible with virtually all networks, you can change processors and still use the same software. Still another option if you're able to swipe cards for all transactions, you can add a mag stripe reader to your computer for less than what you would pay for a terminal.

   Discount rates (sometimes called service fees) run from under 2 to 4 percent. The amount of the discount rate, deducted from every transaction, depends on a number of factors: (1) the type of business you are in, (2) your total annual volume of sales, (3) your average ticket sale, (4) the method in which you submit your charges, and (5) how good a deal you can negotiate with a particular ISO. Often a low discount rate is accompanied by other charges that will make up for a very low rate and may even result in your paying more than you would with an ostensibly higher discount rate. Following are the items for which typical additional charges are made:

- Per transaction charge: none to 25 cents

- Monthly statement fee: none to $10

- Minimum monthly fee: none to $10

- Voice authorization fee: none to 95 cents

As you can see, fees vary considerably among ISOs, so it pays to be a comparison shopper. Read the contract carefully for hidden charges and requirements. You may also be required to use a check-verification service provided by the ISO for an additional fee. Also note that if you have a seasonal business or have months with no or few charges, other fees can exceed your sales so that you owe money to the merchant account provider.

 Warning!!!

Although obtaining a merchant account is apt to be easier through an ISO, there are unethical people who falsely represent themselves as ISOs and take money from eager merchants. To determine if the ISO company you are talking with is "legit," ask for the bank with which the ISO is affiliated and contact the bank to verify the status of the ISO. You can also check with your local Better Business Bureau and the state attorney general's office.

Also, some salespeople for ISOs may be so eager to sign you up that they may inaccurately fill out your application with regard to items that would not be approved if reported accurately. If such a falsehood is detected later by the bank, your merchant account may be terminated and your name placed on a terminated merchant list that bars you from getting another merchant account in the future.

Subjects that are sometimes filled in inaccurately include whether the salesperson has personally inspected your premises and the percentage of your sales that are by mail order and telephone. So be sure to check your completed application for accuracy.

Finding an ISO

A list of independent selling organizations or agents for ISOs that have told us or we've been told accept home businesses for merchant accounts appears in the Resources at the end of this chapter. This list is updated regularly on *www.workingfromhome.com*

4. Options Other Than Visa and MasterCard: American Express and Discover

Keep in mind that Visa with 45 percent of the market and MasterCard with 28 percent will be the cards most customers will want to use. However, an American Express merchant account is easier for a home business to get, and with 16 percent of market share, a lot of people have them. You can contact American Express at (800) 445-2639. With the exception of a voice authorization fee, which can be avoided by using an electronic terminal, American Express charges no fees other than its discount rate. Rates vary, according to the company; however, expect them to be higher than other cards.

Taking Discover cards is another option. About one in twenty-five people has a Discover card. For a Discover merchant account, contact Novus/Discover at (800) 347-6673. Calling this number will result in your being referred to a sales representative in your area. Novus is the parent company of the Discover card, but it also functions as an ISO making MasterCard, Visa, and American Express available through it.

One avenue to avoid is running your charges through another company's merchant account. This is called "factoring" and will get you and the holder of the merchant account in trouble.

COMBATING CREDIT DISCRIMINATION

We regularly hear a loan company's radio commercial in Los Angeles that proclaims the company will lend money even if "you're unemployed, self-employed, or have bad credit." To us being self-employed means we're self-sufficient, but putting "self-employed" on a credit application often puts us automatically into the netherworld of creditworthiness. Here are several steps we can take to counter this:

✓ *Incorporate or register and use a business name* other than your personal name. Thus, when you fill out an application that instructs you to list your employer, you can list your company. A business name that describes the nature of your business can be helpful in marketing, too.

✓ *Have two phone numbers:* one for business, one personal. When filling out an application that asks for business and residential phone numbers, be sure to list both numbers even if you use only one of your numbers for incoming calls. With distinctive ringing, you can have two numbers on only one phone line.

✓ *Answer your phone with your company name* so when you are called to verify employment, the caller reaches your company. This enables you to believably answer that you are employed by your company. Someone who operates as a corporation *is* an employee of his or her corporation.

✓ *Rent an office suite or a miniwarehouse* if you would have use for one. It may also serve as your business address. This is particularly helpful if your residence is in an area zoned only for residences.

✓ *Put a sign with your business name on your mailbox,* if your zoning allows. If a banker, supplier, or prospective customer makes an on-site inspection, their first impression may be "This is a business." When they enter your home office, make it look as professional as possible and certainly remove personal items, such as toys and laundry, from view.

MAXIMIZING YOUR CASH ON HAND

Let your money make money for you while you have it. Don't just let it sit in a non-interest-bearing account. Here's why. Let's say you let $1,000 sit in a non-interest-bearing account. Five years later the buying power of your $1,000 will have shrunk to only $837 if inflation remains at even a minimal 3.5 percent. But if you invest that same money at 5 percent instead, in five years, you will have the buying power of $1,077. So here are some steps you can take to make the most of your money while you've got it.

✓ *Deposit money immediately.* CPA Barry Schimel, author of *100 Ways to Prosper in Today's Economy,* suggests making deposits as often as once a day. If your balance is large enough, an interest-bearing checking account will make money for you.

✓ *Avoid bank fees.* Avoid banks with ATM charges. Keep a high-enough monthly minimum balance to avoid monthly fees. If you have both your personal and business accounts at the same bank, arrange to use what's called "relationship banking"—that is, linked accounts, which allows you to save on fees and some minimum-balance requirements if you have more than one account in the same bank. Compare account fees, minimum-balance requirements, and interest-bearing accounts among banks. Also pay attention to whether the bank charges apply based on an "average balance" or a "low balance."

✓ *Use cash management services* provided by a bank if your business volume is large enough, i.e., $100,000 a year. A lock box, for example, is a program in which you have your customers mail their payments to a box maintained by the bank. The box is located so that in most cases payment is received the next day, and it is immediately deposited by the bank into your account.

✓ *Deposit surplus cash on hand* in interest-bearing certificates and money-market funds.

✓ *Invest excess cash.* Arrange to have excess cash transferred to funds with a higher yield. Some banks will also automatically transfer money back if your account drops below a certain level. You might consider placing short-term savings in money market mutual funds or tax-free investment funds. Tax-free funds are especially worth considering if you fall into one of the new top tax brackets. For longer-term savings, you might consider bonds. Talk with a financial advisor about what is best for you.

✓ *Grow your business.* Depending on interest rates, you may be able to bring in more money by investing in your business than by investing your money elsewhere. If a new voice-mail system or a part-time assistant will generate more or better-paying clients, you could come out ahead by putting your money to work in your business.

HOLDING ON TO WHAT YOU HAVE

Cash-flow problems arise because you need to spend money to make money and, of course, to live, while you're providing your services or products. To minimize your problems, you'll want your business to pay for itself as it goes. To do this, we recommend that whenever possible:

- ✓ Arrange for thirty, sixty, or ninety days of interest-free credit from suppliers.

- ✓ Use low-rate, no-fee credit cards for your personal and business transactions.

- ✓ Rent or lease equipment rather than tying up your capital by owning it.

- ✓ Make timely but not immediate payment of bills.

- ✓ Keep costs down. Don't overstock on supplies.

MAKING THE MOST OF CREDIT CARDS

For small and home-based businesses, credit cards can be among the only sources of credit. And credit cards can provide you with 30 to 60 days' free use of your money, though increasingly credit-card companies are reducing the grace period. Therefore, we encourage home-based business owners to have and use at least one business credit card to help maximize their cash flow and to finance marketing and other costs of business expansion.

Unfortunately, however, it seems that thanks to credit cards, most Americans are living beyond their incomes. Americans have run up credit-card bills of almost half a billion dollars. At the end of 1997, credit-card balances stood at a record high, over $1,600 for every man, woman, and child in the USA! So whereas wise use of credit cards is to your advantage, we don't advocate that you bury your business in overloaded credit cards.

The best credit-card policy is to limit charge cards to financing activities and investments that will pay for themselves in increased productivity or additional business. Even then, paying off your balance each month is the most cost-effective use of your cards. But of course, we can't always get that fast a return on our business expenses, so here are several other ideas for keeping credit-card costs down.

✓ *Look for low-rate cards.* Oftentimes, banks and other card issuers try to entice you into taking their card by offering a low introductory rate. If the rate is low enough and the introductory period is long enough (look for 6 to 9 months), you might consider using the card. Some people make a practice of moving their balances from one card to another that offers a low introductory rate and when the introductory rate expires, transferring the balance to another card with a low introductory rate.

✓ *Check how finance charges are computed.* Low credit-card rates won't save you much money if the issuer uses the "two-cycle method." Most issuers compute their financial charges based on the average daily balance in the prior month. This is referred to as ADB. But some issuers are charging interest based on your average balance over the last two months, so if you pay only the minimum balance each month you could end up paying twice on the same charge. Card issuers must disclose their computation method on applications, cardholder agreements, and monthly statements. So check out your existing cards and any future ones you consider.

✓ *Don't accept minimum purchase requirements.* Credit card minimum purchase requirements are prohibited under the standard contract merchants must sign with the issuing bank and Visa or MasterCard. So if a retailer refuses to accept your card, send a letter of complaint to your issuing bank. If that doesn't resolve the issue, write to the credit-card company.

✓ *Avoid minimum balance payments.* Minimum balance payments can cost you the most. For example if you charge $500 on your card and pay only the minimum each month at 18 percent, the item will cost you almost $800 and take six years to pay off. If you pay $50 a month, you'll save almost $250 in interest and be debt-free in only eleven months!

Low-Rate, No-Fee Credit Cards

Of course, when you're able to spend less by paying cash, you need to balance your cash-flow needs with the need to keep your costs down. But you can keep the cost of using credit cards down by using low-rate, no-fee credit cards. For monthly surveys of low-rate, no-annual-fee cards, as well as comparisons of secured cards and reward cards, you can subscribe to *CardTrak,* a newsletter that tracks bank credit cards. Cost: $5 a month. Write CardTrak, Box 3966, Gettysburg, PA 17325; Phone: (800) 344-7714. Web: *www.cardtrak.com*

Keep in mind that cards with low interest rates may have high annual fees. If you pay off your balance every month, look for no-fee or reward cards.

EIGHT STEPS TO RESTORING GOOD CREDIT

Robin Leonard, author of *Money Troubles: Legal Strategies to Cope with Your Debts,* points out that most creditors are just as interested in positive as they are in negative credit information. Creditors are looking for evidence and positive indications that a person is capable of repaying his or her debts. Leonard claims, for example, that most major credit companies will ignore a negative credit history if you can demonstrate two or three years of consistently responsible credit behavior. So here are the steps she recommends taking to repair a damaged credit rating:

1. *Secure a stable source of income.* Creditors generally look for a steady employment history, so when you're on your own, you have to create a record of steady income from your own business. If your business is struggling due to lack of funds to adequately market yourself, you may have to take a full- or part-time job or temporary work to secure a steady income.

2. *Create a budget you can and will live within.* Think of living on this budget as a temporary condition, until your business is generating greater income.

3. *Open a passbook savings account* at a local bank and begin saving as much as you can as quickly as you can.

4. *Apply for a savings passbook loan,* once you have $500 to $1,000 saved, or apply for a loan that is secured by your savings. Your goal in applying for this loan is to demonstrate that you can pay it back.

5. *Pay back this loan over a six- to nine-month period* so there will be time for the loan to appear on your credit report. Make sure that your bank reports this type of loan to credit agencies. If it doesn't, go elsewhere.

6. *Obtain a secured credit card.* Some banks automatically offer their savings account holders such a card. These cards give you a credit limit somewhat lower than the amount in your savings account. *CardTrak* newsletter does a monthly survey of secured credit cards.

7. *Use this credit card sparingly* and only if you're sure you can and will pay off the entire bill when it comes, because interest on these cards can be around 22 percent.

8. *Apply selectively for other cards* as soon as your credit will justify it. Department stores and gas companies are often more liberal than the major credit-card companies, so start there. Get only one or two such cards and charge minimal purchases that you can easily repay. Leonard suggests you might even run a revolving balance for a few months to prove that you can handle the interest charges and meet a regular repayment schedule.

For other information on rebuilding your credit, you can contact the National Foundation of Consumer Credit. They will refer you to credit counselors in your area. (See Resources at the end of this chapter.)

 Tip

Business Owners Debtors Anonymous holds meetings throughout the country. To find out about meetings near you, write Debtors Anonymous, General Services Board, P.O. Box 888, Needham, MA 02492; (781) 453-2743.

PROTECT YOURSELF FROM INCOME FLUCTUATIONS

The most difficult time to manage your money is when there's too little to manage. There are several things you can do to protect yourself from the woes of feast or famine, peaks and valleys.

Keep a reserve of cash on hand.

Bruce Michels, president of Management Advisory Services Consulting Group, advises small businesses to have $2 of current assets on hand for every $1 of current expenses. Accountant Michael Russo says your cash cushion should depend on your own comfort zone. Whereas some need a $10,000 reserve to feel secure, others require more. Still others need considerably less. Find your level of security and operate within it.

Market constantly.

Set aside at least 20 percent of your time each week for marketing activities and do this all year long, even when you have plenty of business. Don't slack off your selling effort when cash flow is great. There is always a lag time between marketing efforts and marketing results, so keep selling every week. If you generate more business than you can handle, you can refer or subcontract it to trusted colleagues who will do the same for you when they have surplus business.

Track your income and expenses.

Project your expenses and anticipated income at the beginning of each month. Post all due dates. You'll find that establishing this habit will prove invaluable. You'll always know exactly where you stand and you'll be alerted when you need to take action either by deferring costs or accelerating your marketing effort. You'll also know the moment someone is late with payments.

Plan to make the most of slow times.

Most businesses go through periods of time that are slower than others. For example, holiday seasons are great for party planners and gift-related businesses but not so good for business consultants or training professionals. Anticipate these periods and use your time during them to initiate special marketing efforts to attract business.

Word processor Evalyn McGraw finds Augusts are routinely slow, so she builds up cash reserves in June and July and plans her vacation for August. Before she leaves, however, she sets her late-August marketing plan in motion so that when she comes back there will be business coming in. Seminar leader Jerry Cane offers Early Sign-up discounts for the New Year during the December lull to fill his January seminars.

Create various income sources.

Another way Evalyn manages her cash flow is to offer several adjunct services. In addition to straight word processing she provides editing and indexing services. She also teaches university extension program writing courses at a local university. So if one area of her business is slow, she can rely on these other areas to carry her through. She finds they are rarely all slow at once.

You'll notice, however, that Evalyn is not offering a variety of scattered services that dissipate her efforts or confuse the public about what business she's in. She isn't selling real estate and offering fitness training simultaneously. All her services are related and, in some cases, ancillaries to word processing.

Continually upgrade your skills and improve your business.

Grow with your business. Don't get caught in the rut of offering the same services and products year in and year out. To spark sales add new lines, offer more advanced techniques. If your service or product applies, offer it on the Web. And you shouldn't wait for sales to wane. Every change you make in your business provides an opportunity for promotions and gives you a good excuse to contact present and past clients about what you're doing now.

Network, network, network.

Make regular contact with colleagues, clients, and associates part of your ongoing weekly marketing. Participate in professional and trade associations, on-line newsgroups, user's groups, and civic organizations so you'll be abreast of new market trends and the latest breakthroughs; this will also help you generate referrals and find out who needs you right now. Don't overlook regular congenial contact with your competitors. They may be overloaded just when you're slumping. Offer to help them on a subcontract basis with business they can't handle. More and more independents are forming consortiums to take on large projects and refer work to members. Consider joining or forming a consortium or affiliation of people you are comfortable working with.

Remember, you're in charge.

Sometimes it may seem as though your cash flow has nothing whatsoever to do with your efforts. You may feel you are being tossed about at the whim of fluctuations in the economy, the seasons, or your market's fickle passions. In actuality, if you take charge, you'll be in charge. You aren't dependent on the wishes of a single boss who can fire you on a moment's notice. All your clients would have to fire you before you'd be out of business. You're ingenious, talented, and creative or you wouldn't be in business in the first place. There is always some way for you to serve others and thereby keep the cash flowing in. If you start feeling out of control, just focus on that reality.

PAYING BILLS TO MAXIMIZE YOUR CASH FLOW

Here's a simple but effective manual system developed by Ray Martin, president of Microcomputer Applications, Inc., of Austin, Texas:

1. Check the day's incoming bills and invoices for accuracy and discounts offered for quick payment.

2. Determine the best date to make payment of each bill so that you will neither be overdue nor early in making payment. Then write a check.

3. Place the check in its envelope; stamp and seal it.

4. Code the envelope in the lower right corner with the necessary mailing date. Allow three days for local delivery, seven days for cross-country mail.

5. File the envelopes in chronological order.

6. Each day, mail those bills earmarked for that date.

Tips for Good Money Management

1. Keep business and personal finances separate. Have two bank accounts—one for business, the other for personal expenses. Have separate bank cards. Keep records and receipts for business and personal expenses separate.

2. Have one place where you keep all of your financial materials, records, equipment, and supplies.

3. Establish a time each day, week, month, and quarter to take care of needed financial transactions:

    - banking transactions

    - bill paying

    - invoicing

    - tallying monthly and quarterly summaries

    - filing tax and other necessary reports

4. Establish the habit of filing expense and income receipts immediately after getting them.

5. Keep inventory records as you add to or take from your supply.

WHEN TO GET HELP

With the tools and ideas suggested in this chapter, you can probably manage your own record keeping while your business is small. Depending on your experience and the size and nature of your business, however, you may want to get the advice of an accountant in setting up your system. Also, you will periodically want to evaluate how well your system is working.

Less-expensive alternatives to CPAs are franchised "business counselors" from companies like General Business Services and Marcoin. They advise small businesspeople on a quarterly basis for much less money than the typical CPA charges. They help prepare and analyze financials and do tax planning and tax returns.

If your business expands or is already too large for a do-it-yourself system, you will need to set up a more sophisticated system and get additional assistance. You can hire a full- or part-time bookkeeper or use a bookkeeping service. Finally, since many record-keeping tasks involve filing and sorting, you may be able to hire a full- or part-time secretary or file clerk whose duties would include various record-keeping tasks.

Checklist: Two Signs You Need Help

Here are signs that it's time to go beyond a do-it-yourself system. Is it time yet for you?

___ When you would make more money by paying someone to keep your records than the money you save by doing it yourself.

___ When you are operating under government or other contracts that require you to use a double-entry bookkeeping system. When you need to spend more than thirty minutes a day doing financial-management tasks.

Even when you have help in keeping your records, you will need to be responsible for providing the receipts, reviewing and evaluating the records regularly, and making financial plans and projections for your business. So you will still need to establish daily, weekly, monthly, and quarterly routines for carrying out these tasks.

RESOURCES

BOOKS

The Check Is Not in the Mail. Leonard Sklar. San Mateo, Calif.: Baroque Publishing, 1991. ISBN: 0962483346.

Guerrilla Financing. Bruce Blechman and Jay Conrad Levinson. Boston: Houghton Mifflin, 1992, ISBN: 0395522633.

How to Get Out of Debt, Stay Out of Debt, and Live Prosperously. Jerrold Mundis. New York: Bantam, 1990. ISBN: 0553283960.

Keeping the Books. Linda Pinson and Jerry Jinnett. Chicago: Upstart Publishing Company, 1998.

Money-Smart Secrets for the Self-Employed. Linda Stern, New York: Random House, 1997.

Money Troubles: Legal Strategies to Cope with Your Debts. Robin Leonard. Berkeley, Calif.: Nolo Press, 1997. ISBN: 0873373898.

Personal Finance for Dummies. Eric Tyson. San Mateo, Calif.: IDG Books, 1996. ISBN: 0764550136.

Quick and Legal Credit Repair. Robin Leonard. Berkeley, Calif.: Nolo Press, 1996. ISBN: 0873373545.

Small-Time Operator. Bernard Kamoroff. Laytonville, Calif.: Bell Springs, 1997. ISBN: 0917510143.

The Smart Money Financial Planner. Ken and Daria Dolan. New York: Berkley, 1992. ISBN: 0425134776.

Smart Questions to Ask Your Financial Advisers. Lynn Brenner and Mark Matcho. Princeton, N.J.: Bloomberg Press, 1997. ISBN: 1576600157.

Straight Talk on Money: Ken and Daria Dolan's Guide to Family Money Management. Ken and Daria Dolan. New York: Fireside, 1995. ISBN: 0684800497.

The Ultimate Credit Handbook: How to Double Your Credit, Cut Your Debt, and Have a Lifetime of Great Credit. Gerri Detweiller. New York: Plume, 1997. ISBN: 0452277124.

Your Money or Your Life: Transforming your Relationship with Money and Achieving Financial Independence. Joe Dominguez and Vicki Robin. New York: Penguin USA, 1993. ISBN: 0140167153.

NEWSLETTERS

CardTrak. P.O. Box 3966, Gettysburg, PA 17325; (800) 344-7714. Information on credit cards, including secured cards, and where low rates can be obtained. Web site: *www.cardtrak.com*

Extraordinary Results. A tax, financial, and entrepreneurial publication. Michael Russo and Associates. 9229 Sunset Boulevard, Ste. 303, Los Angeles, CA 90069; (310) 777-8825.

DEBT MANAGEMENT

Consumer Credit Counseling Service, National Referral Line. P.O. Box 51149, Riverside, CA 92517; (800) 338-2227. Provides information and referrals to credit counselors in your area.

CREDIT INFORMATION

National Association of Credit Management (NACM), 8815 Centre Park, Ste. 200, Columbia, MD 21045; (410) 740-5560. Offers seminars on credit collection principles and information on obtaining credit reports. Web: *www.nacm.org*

INDEPENDENT SELLING ORGANIZATIONS (ISOs) OR BANK AGENTS

Access Group, (800) 480-6694. The company reports it will serve "riskier" businesses. It places many accounts with Teleflora.

Cardservice International, 26775 Malibu Hills Road, Agora Hills, CA 91301; phone: (800) 456-5989. E-mail: *clee@csi-corp.com* Fax: (818) 878-8459. By dealing directly with the corporate office, you get corporate pricing. Web site: *www.cardservice.com*

Merchant Services, Inc., 231 Quincy Street, Rapid City, SD 57701; (800) 888-4457 and (605) 341-6461. Visa, MasterCard, Discover, and American Express are available through it. The company states that it processes applications quickly.

North American Credit Card (NACCA), 215 Salem Street, Ste. 12, Woburn, MA 01801; (800) 762-3782. Fax: 781-933-2334. Has a special program for dissatisfied merchants to change processors without new equipment at no cost.

NPC, 1231 Durrett Lane, Louisville, KY 40285, claims to be the second largest card processor in the country. Call (800) 928-2583 to be referred to a sales representative in your area. A reserve account of two months of receipts may be required for a company engaging in sales by mail order.

For an updated list of ISOs, visit *www.workingfromhome.com* You may find others who will work with home businesses in the Yellow Pages under the category "Credit Card Terminal Systems."

ON-LINE LOAN INFORMATION AND FINANCIAL RESOURCES

Quicken Business CashFinder. A free service which allows you to download software that will locate possible credit options for your business so you can compare them and actually apply electronically through secure on-line forms. *www.cashfinder.com*

CashFinder is one of a variety of financial services (mortgages, insurance, retirement funds, and investment) offered by Intuit, makers of Quicken and Quickbooks, through its Web site: *www.quicken.com*

CHAPTER 15

Managing Information and Other Stuff: Getting Rid of Clutter

Some people have felt pressured by information overload since the 1970s, but now most realize information is proliferating so quickly that we all feel as if we're probably missing something that's important . . . maybe a lot that's important. Just compare the amount of mail we receive with what our parents did; the size of the newspapers, the number of magazines, newsletters, and the various media that bring information to us—broadcast television, the Internet with its millions of Web sites, cable TV, satellite TV, videotapes, and more.

As Gertrude Stein has pointed out, "Everyone gets so much information all day long that they lose their common sense." In today's home office, that's not all we lose. Chances are that if you're reading this book, you have at least one pile of unread or unfiled magazines, newspapers, mail, business cards, or telephone notes somewhere in your house. And more likely than not, you suffer routinely from one of the most common symptoms of this information avalanche: that nagging question "Now where did I put that?"

How often this frustrating question interrupts the flow of work! Not being able to find needed information is probably the single most common form of home-office inefficiency. And it's not a minor problem. Think of the missed opportunities when you can't find a business card you need, the lost hours spent searching for correspondence you should refer to, the embarrassing moments when you lose the address of a meeting you're already late for, or the failure to return an important call or E-mail because you can't remember where you wrote the phone number or stored the address.

Nearly twenty-four million Americans suffer from "message overload," says a Yankelovich Partners survey for Casio PhoneMate, and spend over an hour a day handling phone, fax, and E-mail messages.

So no matter how small your home-office operation, it's helpful to have a system for processing and organizing the array of information you need at your fingertips. You must have a way to easily process your mail, handle phone messages, and store phone numbers, addresses, business cards, and mailing lists. You need a system for recording upcoming events and keeping track of subject matter of interest to you as well as key information relating to your clients and projects. And sometimes you have to track this information in both paper and computer files. You also need a way to conveniently store reference materials from magazines, books, and tapes that you want to keep.

FIVE STEPS TO HAVING THE INFORMATION YOU NEED AT YOUR FINGERTIPS

Because you probably don't have anyone to whom to delegate these administrative tasks and you're undoubtedly operating in limited space, your system for managing these details needs to be simple, easy to use, and compact. Having an effective system requires that you do five things:

1. Know what information you need to have access to.

2. Have a proper place to keep the information you need.

3. Set up a regular and convenient time for putting information where it belongs.

4. Establish a familiar routine for processing, storing, and using information.

5. Use equipment and supplies that make storing and locating your information easy.

Much of the information you receive in your home office isn't of sufficient value to devote precious time and space to addressing and storing it.

Such "information noise" just clogs up your office and interferes with your ability to access the information you want and need quickly. Therefore, we suggest that you use the checklist below to identify the type of information you need to have on-hand to do your work successfully. With this plan, you will have a place for everything and will be able to find everything in its place when you need it.

This chapter will address how, with a minimum of time and energy, you can manage the wide range of information needed by most home offices. We also provide guidelines for what to keep, where to keep it, when to throw it away, and when to get help keeping everything in order. Begin by assessing just what information you actually need to have access to on a regular basis to function effectively.

 Worksheet: Identifying the Information You Absolutely Need

Check off each type of information you need to work effectively. As you read through this chapter, develop a plan for when and where you will address and store it.

TYPE OF INFORMATION	PAPER	COMPUTER	WHERE	WHEN
Upcoming events and activities	_____	_____	_____	_____
Customer or client records	_____	_____	_____	_____
Financial and tax information	_____	_____	_____	_____
Project or task material	_____	_____	_____	_____
Business cards	_____	_____	_____	_____
Information on key subjects	_____	_____	_____	_____
A tickler system	_____	_____	_____	_____
Computer disks	_____	_____	_____	_____
Newspapers	_____	_____	_____	_____
Magazines	_____	_____	_____	_____
Tapes	_____	_____	_____	_____
Books	_____	_____	_____	_____
Mail	_____	_____	_____	_____
Phone messages	_____	_____	_____	_____

WHY YOU SHOULD BEGIN BY COMPUTERIZING YOUR INFORMATION

Certainly we haven't reached and may never reach the paperless office, nor would most of us want to. But so much information flows through even the most low-tech home offices, and most of us have few if any employees to help us manage it, that we really need electronic help to keep track of the most vital information that we need to have at our fingertips. Be it correspondence we're sending out, forms we must generate, update and use regularly, or marketing materials we must design and forever customize, we need a way to create, change, store, and locate information as quickly and simply as possible.

 True Confessions: Computerphobe Turned High Tech

Diedra had operated a family day-care program in her home for five years. She loves kids and is a natural-born nurturing teacher. She was a high-touch person. "I don't have any interest in computers and I don't need one," she told her husband. But her business was growing increasingly information intensive. She had to prepare enrollment forms, handle payments, provide reports to the state, send frequent notes home for parents, and create work sheets for the children to color and work with. She was spending more time than she wanted to at her old Selectric typewriter and the copy shop.

Finally her husband talked her into attending a free Working Smarter with Technology Small Business seminar. "I had to admit after attending that seminar that I was doing things the hard way. I broke down and got a computer, printer, and some software. My husband helped me set it up and learn to use it. Once I got over that hurdle, (it took a few weeks), I've been amazed at how much more organized my records are and how much less time I spend trying to find and change things. The time and money I'm saving at the copy store alone will probably pay for the whole thing eventually."

For reasons like these, we suggest that the first step to taking charge of your office clutter is computerizing as much of your key information as possible. Close to two-thirds of all home offices are computerized. One of the key factors driving the surge in home-office technology is the need to organize and process the rush of information that flows through even the smallest home businesses.

With proper backup and file storage, much of your correspondence, record keeping, contact management, billing, marketing, and other business records can be stored on your computer. In addition to the money-management software we mentioned in chapter 14, here are several other types of software that can help you organize and store the information you need to access quickly and easily.

WORD-PROCESSING AND DESKTOP-PUBLISHING SOFTWARE

With any sophisticated word-processing program such as Microsoft *Word* or *WordPerfect,* you can create and store correspondence, reports, manuscripts, and other types of written material. The mail-merge capability of these programs enables you to quickly personalize and address your correspondence to your entire mailing list right down to individually printed labels or envelopes. It also allows you to create E-mail messages and send them without leaving the programs.

With desktop publishing software like *Microsoft Publisher,* Aldus *Pagemaker,* and *QuarkExpress,* you can also create and design very sophisticated documents like newsletters, postcards, ad layouts, manuals, marketing materials, and forms of all kinds, even Web pages.

Both word-processing and desktop-publishing software programs often contain "templates" that serve as models you can use again and again to create such things as invoices, newsletters, price lists, and other page layouts.

INFORMATION-MANAGEMENT SOFTWARE

Each day you're in business puts you in contact with many people and ideas that you want to keep track of and find at your convenience. This ever-growing base of names and facts is among your most valuable resources, your lifeline to success. Unfortunately, many people find themselves too busy and disorganized to take advantage of the contacts and information they have.

For example, you might meet twenty or thirty interested contacts at a trade show or exhibit, and although some of them will bring you business from that first contact, a much larger number could become clients at some later time—if you continue to maintain contact with them.

Or, say you regularly read several magazines and clip articles of interest to your business. Although you can remember the most recent articles, you usually don't recall important facts and statistics from earlier ones. But if you don't have a full-time secretary or sales and marketing staff, it's easy for business cards, brochures, notes, and articles to become strewn throughout your filing system, and scattered amongst Rolodex cards, appointment books, business card holders, and other repositories of names, addresses, and phone numbers.

There are three computer solutions to this problem: You can use mailing-list software, contact- and personal-information management software, or even a full-fledged database-management program. The choice depends on your needs, the complexity of information you want to keep, and your computer's ability to learn and use sophisticated software. Here's an overview of the three categories of software:

MAILING-LIST SOFTWARE

Mailing-list programs are actually simplified database programs that are preformatted to record basic mailing and contact information like name, address, city, state, phone number, and E-mail address. If you primarily want to reach your contacts by mail, a mail-list manager like *Day-Timer Organizer* (Kensington Software), *My Mail Manager* from MySoftware, or Avery's *LabelPro* can be the simplest way to manage your contact lists. Some programs like *My Mail Manager* also include a built-in word processor and mail-merge capability that enables you to write brief letters to send to all the names on your mailing list, then print out the letter along with mailing labels complete with Zip + 4 bar code. It will also sort first-class and third-class mail to save you money with bulk mailings.

CONTACT- AND INFORMATION-MANAGEMENT SOFTWARE

No type of software is better suited for cutting clutter than contact- or personal-information management software. With such programs, you can enter the information you need and organize the many details that contribute to clutter before they get lost or out of hand. Here are the highlights of various options open to you:

Contact-management software allows you to set up and maintain extensive records of your business contacts. It combines mailing list management and mail-merge capabilities with features such as calendar and appointment logs, notepads, automatic phone dialing and call management, automatic E-mail management, alarms that alert you to when to follow up with a contact, daily to-do lists with priority settings, and faxing capabilities. You'll find examples like *Act, Goldmine,* and *Maximizer* listed in the Resource list at the end of this chapter.

Whereas contact management focuses on tracking contacts, personal-information management software enables you to locate, analyze, and cross-reference dates, activities, events, and subjects of all kinds. You can track goals, ideas, leads for future business, facts and quotes you want to have available for proposals and speeches, as well as business information such as inventory, sales, billings, and personnel records—any kind of information. The strength of this software is that, unlike database-management software, many of these programs free you from the constraints of formatting information in specified ways using mandatory fields with fixed lengths. Instead, you can enter your information freely, in whatever format or length you choose.

You'll find some of the most notable programs like *Ascent, Outlook,* and *Lotus Organizer* in the Resource list at the end of this chapter.

DATABASE-MANAGEMENT SOFTWARE

Another way to manage information is to use a full-fledged database program. Actually, mailing lists and contact and information managers are all specialized database programs that provide a predefined structure for keeping track of specific kinds of information, making them simpler to learn and use. With a full-fledged database-management program, nothing is predefined. You can set up the database any way you want to track whatever information (data, text, dates, etc.) in whatever customized ways you want and change readily when you wish.

Today's powerful database programs have become much easier to learn and use; so if you find preset versions of mailing-list and contact-management software too limiting, you can tailor the software to your particular needs. Popular database programs include *FoxPro* (Microsoft), *Paradox* (Borland), *FileMaker Pro* (Claris), and *Approach* (Lotus).

Database-management programs also have more specialized sorting and searching functions so you can call up complex clusters and patterns of information. Some "relational" databases can even join files so that changes you make in one will automatically make the appropriate adjustments in others.

SOFTWARE SUITES

If you the have need for a variety of software programs, as most small offices do, you may benefit from using "integrated" software package or software suite. Popular suites include the Microsoft *Office* family, Lotus *SmartSuite,* and Corel *Professional Office.* In addition to providing word processing, presentation graphics, database, spreadsheet, and other software programs in a unified "bundle," suites also offer the advantage of interoperability. This allows you to move data and documents created in one program easily and quickly into another, thereby saving you several steps in needless repetition. It also helps you learn to use them more quickly.

 Rule of Thumb: Compatibility

Even if you don't use integrated suites, in order to manage your information most effectively, the software programs you select should be compatible so you can easily and flexibly transfer information from one program to another. For example, it is useful to be able to import the information in your financial package into your tax software, or charts developed in your spreadsheet into your financial package, your desktop-published newsletter, or an overhead presentation.

Compatibility and importing among programs are certainly being made easier with each version of Windows that is released, but it is still an issue to be aware of, especially in database and financial applications.

Features-to-Look-for Checklist: Personal-Information Managers, Mailing-List Managers

The more sophisticated a program, the more features and flexibility it has—but generally the more complex and costly it will be. Select a package that has the features that best match your current and projected needs.

❑ Degree of flexibility in which data can be kept other than name, address, and phone

❑ Easy importing and exporting of data

❑ Import and export files from other programs

❑ Link to E-mail and the World Wide Web

❑ Phone dialer

❑ Utilize caller recognition telephone service

❑ Link to word processing and mail merge to print labels and envelopes

❑ Contact history with date and time stamp

❑ Follow-up reminders

❑ Follow-up alarm

❑ Yearly, monthly, weekly, and daily view calendars

❑ Address-book and calendar print-outs

❑ To-do list, drop, and drop to future dates

❑ Expense tracking

❑ Scheduling

❑ Ability to search multiple fields

❑ Ability to define contact groups

❑ Memo, notepad, daily journals

❑ Ease of use

❑ Tutorial

❑ Clarity and simplicity of documentation

❑ Unlimited free support

❑ Toll-free support

CREATING PAPER AND ELECTRONIC FILING SYSTEMS

Even though you manage and store much of your key information on computer, you will invariably still have plenty of paper coming in and going out of your office. You need an effective filing system for keeping track of all the paper, and of course, you need a system for organizing your electronic files as well. It's just as easy to clutter up a disk as it is to clutter up a desk, and it's just as easy to "misplace" a computer file as it is to misplace a manila folder.

If you've been working at home for any length of time, you undoubtedly already have a filing system. The question is whether the system you have works for you. Remember, the primary purpose of a filing system is retrieval, not storage. If you won't need to use a piece of information again, there's no reason to file it. So if you can't find your desk for all the piles of paper you have carefully stacked in descending order of importance, you have a filing system. It's just not a system that helps you find what you need when you need it. If you hear yourself saying "I know I have that some-where, but I'll have to look for it," take that as a sign that your system is not working.

To work effectively, any filing system—whether in your computer, on your walls, or in a filing cabinet—should enable you to find the information you've stored within a minute or two. It should also be easy to keep current. To create a system that meets these criteria, we recommend that you group the many types of information you use into clear and simple categories that correspond to the various aspects of your work. In other words, organize your files by function and, to the extent possible, use the same major func-tional categories and titles for both your computer files and your paper files.

 Checklist: Basic Filing Categories

Here are several functional categories of files that most home offices will need. You can create specific directories and designate specific file drawers or even whole file cabinets for each of these areas. As you read on about each area, use the following as a checklist to identify which specific files you should have for your business:

____ Client and customer files

____ Project files

____ Business card files

____ Subject files

____ Upcoming file

____ Tickler system

Client or Customer Files

If you provide a service or sell products to key accounts, create a file for each of the clients or customers in your contact-, database-, or personal-information management software. Each file should contain the client's name, address, phone number, fax, E-mail address, other contact names, sales history, notes, and other pertinent information. Then, if needed, create a corresponding section of your filing cabinet and paper file for each client where you can store written materials they send you such as brochures, annual reports, drafts they want you to look at, etc. Keep these files in alphabetical order by last name or company name.

As your clientele grows, you can subdivide your client files if you wish into "past" and "current" clients, or "active" and "inactive" clients. Or you can subdivide them by industry or type of work; e.g., "banking clients" and "ad agencies," or "transcription clients" and "training clients."

Tips for Organizing Your Computer Files

✓ **Create folders (directories) and/or disks with the same names as your paper files.** For example, if you have a Projects section in your file cabinet, create a corresponding Projects folder or disk. Keep your computer and paper records related to each other.

✓ **Back up the contents of your hard disk on floppy disks** or some other storage medium, such as tape or a removable hard drive, to avoid costly errors.

✓ **Erase unnecessary backup files daily and purge inactive files monthly** to keep your disk uncluttered.

✓ **Use file compression and archiving utilities** to expand the amount of space available on your disks.

✓ **Optimize your hard disk by using software like CheckIt** (Touchstone) to keep your system operating at top speed.

✓ **Use a software utility that enables you to find your files,** no matter where they are on the disk by name or key words in case you have forgotten the name of a file or can't locate it. *Smart DiskFinder* (Seiko Instruments) is a good choice.

✓ **Create macro commands** to cut down on the keystrokes required to perform complex and repetitive operations.

✓ **Use disk organization programs** like *Partition Magic* (Power Quest) or Norton's *Uninstall* to simplify moving, deleting, copying, and renaming files.

✓ **Keep disks you use frequently within arm's reach of your computer.** The cardboard or plastic holders in which disks are packaged can be used for storage and kept in desk drawers or on shelves. Special disk storage units are also available in multiple sizes, shapes, and designs (see p. 459).

Project Files

Create a folder and file cabinet space for your project files. Then create a separate file for every major project you're working on. For example, if you were writing an article on child abuse, you might create a word-processing folder entitled "Child Abuse Article." In this, you would store your query letters, content outline, interview notes, and so forth, along with the actual article itself. Your corresponding paper file would also be entitled "Child Abuse Article," and into this file you would put correspondence received from magazine publishers, the contract you signed when you sold the article, brochures from clinics you interviewed, etc.

If certain projects become voluminous, you can subdivide your project files. For example, if you begin to write many articles on child abuse, you can create a subdirectory and a special section in your project file drawer for all these articles and name them by magazine, date, or emphasis.

We recommend that you file paper project files in alphabetical order. On the inside cover of each file, you can record pertinent information related to that project—the names, addresses, and telephone numbers of contact people, your deadlines, meeting dates, work schedule, and so on. Or, if you're using contact- or information-management software, you can keep much of this key information in a file.

Business Card Files

The most effective way to store business card information is in your computer using contact- or database-management software. But until recently, that meant taking the time to input the data from the many stacks of business cards that have been collecting over time. Now, however, there is a quick and easy way to get business cards into your computer. There are quite a few software programs available that work with scanners (or sometimes provide their own palm-sized scanners, such as *CardScan* from Corex) to capture the information on business cards, translate it to database or text file, and allow you to quickly import it as a record for contact management or other software programs.

If you still want to keep the paper version of business cards on hand, there are lots of filing systems for business cards, names, addresses, and phone numbers. We recommend using a system that enables you to file business cards and other names and addresses in one place. The system you select should be easy to update so you can add to, change, and remove names in alphabetical order. Here are several popular systems:

1. Rolodex filing system. This is a familiar system for filing business cards in which the cards are attached to the center of a circular column so that you can flip to the one you're seeking. The uncovered versions are easier to use. Color-coated cards are available to easily identify certain clients, suppliers, or other key people. Adhesive dots can be placed on the upper right-hand corners of cards to highlight most frequently used or high-priority numbers.

2. *Metal business-card holders.* These holders store business cards in a metal tray that is separated alphabetically. Keeping spare cards in the back of the file enables you to write out a name and address when you have no business card for a client or customer.

3. *Calling-card files.* In this system, business cards slip into soft plastic walletlike inserts bound in a ten-by-fourteen-inch plastic notebook.

4. *Stapling cards to file folder jackets.* Instead of placing a business card into a filing system, you can staple it to the inside cover of a project or client file. This can be an efficient way to keep numbers or addresses you will only be using in conjunction with information in the file.

Subject Files

Create paper and computer files to keep information on subjects of interest to you. Personal-information managers (PIMs) are great for this purpose. If you like to collect favorite quotes to include in articles or proposals, for example, record them in your PIM. Or perhaps you like to collect great jokes to use in presentations. Again you can collect and store them in your PIM. Anecdotal stories, statistics, great ideas—essentially anything you would jot down on a napkin or sticky pad and then either lose or have cluttering up your desk space—all can be included using personal-information management software.

Designate space for subject files in your filing cabinet as well for such things as magazine and newspaper clippings on subjects of interest, product brochures, warranties, etc. Keep these files in alphabetical order. For example, if you will be buying a copy machine in the future, create a subject file titled "Copiers" for articles you have clipped, brochures on different brands, or notes you've taken when talking with a salesperson. When you have purchased the copier, clean out the file of materials you no longer need, and relabel it with the trade name of your copier, for example, "Canon Copier." Now you have a place for your instruction manual, warranty information, and supply order forms.

Upcoming File

This is one type of subject file everyone should have. Use a file folder labeled "Upcoming" to keep announcements, confirmation letters, convention programs you plan to attend, and so forth. Before you file anything, mark the date of the event in the right-hand corner of the first page with a bright-colored marker. File the material in chronological order, with the nearest event at the front of the file.

By using an upcoming file you avoid having to create a new file for each event you will be attending. Keeping the file in a desk drawer or somewhere near your phone makes information about upcoming events readily accessible. When you need to look up details or locations for these events, you can simply reach for your file.

Clean this file out periodically, discarding material on events that have passed.

Tickler System

When you have more activities that need to be acted upon by a certain date than can be managed in an upcoming file, you need a tickler system. Appointment, calendar, and contact-management software is ideal for alerting you to when certain activities need to be done and for making sure you follow through on commitments and plans you've made. Some of these programs simply fill in prescheduled activities on your calendar or "to do" list. Others have a beeper alarm that will actually call your attention to an action on the appropriate day.

You can also set up a paper tickler file for paying bills or following up on various announcements and materials you've received in the mail. You can buy one at a stationery store; they're called Everyday Files or Desktop Files. Or you can create your own.

To set up such a paper system, label one manila file folder for each day of the month (1–31). Have one extra folder labeled "Next Month" or, for a more extensive system, one for each month of the year (January–December). Then, throughout the workday, you can put materials in the file for whatever day in the future you want to act upon them, whether they're checks to be mailed, letters to be answered, phone messages to be returned, or monthly reports to be filled out.

Whatever combinations you work out for your filing system, follow these simple rules for filing most efficiently:

---

 12 Rules of Thumb: Filing

1. *File each folder, card, or record in one, and only one, designated place.*

2. *"If a file is out, use it or lose it."* Every file or record should be in one of two places: in use on your desk or stored in its designated space. Put files away immediately after use. Don't leave them lying around to get to later.

3. *File material immediately.* Whenever you have new information for your files, add it at the time you get it. Don't create "file piles." When you receive mail, read articles, or take phone notes that you want to save, file the

(Continued on page 455)

(Continued from page 454)

pertinent material as soon as you finish reviewing it. If you come home from a meeting with business cards, notes, or flyers you want to keep, file them when you arrive—at the same time you store your receipts for any expenses you've incurred.

4. ***Put the most recent materials in the front of the file folders.***

5. ***Remove all paper clips before filing materials.*** They fall off and get stuck inside the files. If papers belong together, staple them together.

6. ***Don't overstuff files.*** Keep three or four inches of extra space in file drawers so they will be easy to use and the files won't get damaged. When files get overly crowded, clear them of outdated material.

7. ***Label all file folders.*** Use a file name that is broad enough to cover all the materials you will want to put in the folder.

8. ***To keep from misfiling your folders when you return them,*** either remove the papers you need and leave the folder itself tilted up, or tilt up the file behind the one you remove, leaving the drawer open as a reminder to return the file.

9. ***Separate "active" files from "storage" files.*** Active files are those you use on a regular basis. They should be kept in an area near your work space. Storage files are those you need to keep for legal or tax purposes, but which you no longer use. Keep these in cardboard file boxes in more remote storage areas (see Figure 15-2).

10. ***When filing accumulates, catch up during "down times,"*** while watching TV or talking casually on the phone, for example.

11. ***Don't let file folders grow beyond three-quarters of an inch.*** Finding a single paper in a thick file takes too long. Break large files into subfiles.

12. ***Reduce legal and large documents to letter size for easier filing.***

 True Confessions: Digging Out From under the Paper Piles

Okay, we admit it. We've had one of the most common home-office afflictions: paper piles. We've been fighting this affliction for years, and we've tried everything. We've brought in several professional organizers to help us. They all had great ideas for how we could better organize and arrange our paperwork. One suggested using decorative baskets. That resulted in a houseful of attractive baskets

(Continued on page 456)

(Continued from page 455)

overflowing with papers. Another suggested moving toward the paperless office and scanning documents into our computer instead of keeping them around. That sounded good, so we bought a scanner. Then we had stacks of paper waiting to be scanned instead of waiting to be filed.

All such creative suggestions for managing paper buildup in a home office are fine . . . if you carry them out and, well, we didn't. When guests come, we've always managed to find a place to hide embarrassing paper piles, but only temporarily. Truth is a snoopy guest would have found piles of papers behind our living room couch, under our desks, on the dining-room table, at the top and the bottom of the stairways, and so on.

In desperation we considered just throwing out old piles sight unseen. After all, if we haven't needed them for months at a time, could they really be that important? But just peeking at their contents assured us that something vital was probably in there somewhere.

Now, at last, we think we've solved this problem once and for all. We purchased a rolling cart at Hold Everything composed of three see-through sliding wire basketlike drawers. The top two baskets are seven and a half inches deep and the bottom basket is eleven inches. This is just big enough to hold a week's backlog of newspapers, magazines, and other mail if we're out of town; but not so large that it can pile up endlessly. Here's how these rolling temporary files have helped us climb out from under a household of paper piles.

1. The cart is kept out of sight in a closet off the living room, but every day before the mail arrives, we or our assistant rolls the basket out to the dining-room table where we sort the mail.

2. Incoming mail is sorted into one of the three drawers as follows:

   - Top drawer: Must-Do Action—bills, checks, pending business correspondence

   - Middle Drawer: Look at and Consider—possible business correspondence and other materials of interest

   - Bottom Drawer: Reading Materials—magazines, newsletters and newspapers, books and products to review.

   Of course anything that's not of interest goes directly into the trash.

3. During the day, whenever we take a break, we come down from the loft where our offices are and take care of as many materials as time allows. Sometimes we don't get to the cart all day, but that's okay.

(Continued on page 457)

(Continued from page 456)

4. By evening, we roll the cart into the living room where we address as much as possible of whatever remains in the drawers while we're watching television or doing other leisure activities. Then sometime during the evening, we take them to our desks or file them away.

5. Before retiring, or whenever we don't want the cart around, we roll it back into the closet.

6. If we've been out of town or especially busy and a drawer begins filling up, we roll it out on weekends to catch up.

Although the drawers are rarely ever empty, they're never overflowing and we feel victorious! So, why is this system working when nothing else has? The answer is simple: We actually do it. It fits our work schedule and our lifestyle. It allows us to be in charge and prevents us from getting behind, so piles never get out of hand. This serves as a built-in motivator for us to use it faithfully.

Perhaps this system, or one like it, will work for you. If our solution doesn't fit your circumstances, however, don't despair. If we can conquer this problem after all these years, you can too. The key is finding a system that fits you as well as this one fits us. Make a list of your own prerequisites for handling paper work that you could honestly and realistically commit to. Then experiment until you find a way to meet your needs. You can just imagine how great it feels to have recovered our home from under the piles!

Using the Walls as Information Organizers

You can turn your walls into calendars, project planners, and information organizers by using:

Blackboards or whiteboards. Columns and lines for permanent headings can be drawn with indelible markers, paint, or tape. Different colors of chalk or markers can be used to highlight different types of information.

Plexiglass panels, plate glass, or see-through plastic. Clear panels of these materials can be mounted on the wall and held in place by a wood molding. Use grease pencils, crayons, or felt-tip markers of various colors and wipe them off easily with a moist cloth.

(Continued on page 458)

(Continued from page 457)

Movie screens or clear white walls. Using an overhead projector, clear plastic transparencies, and felt-tip pens, you can easily project and work with information displayed on walls and screens.

Newsprint. Sheets of blank newsprint from pads or rolls can be used to outline material you're working on and can then be hung on the walls for easy reference.

Bulletin boards or cork squares. Information can be tacked or pinned on commercial bulletin boards.

Planning boards. Commercial planning boards are sold as wall units made of magnetic material that can be written on with felt-tip markers and wiped off.

STORING NEWSLETTERS, MAGAZINES, BOOKS, TAPES, AND DISKS

The best system for storing newsletters, magazines, books, tapes, and disks depends on how many you have. One or two tapes can be kept in a drawer. A few newsletters can be kept in a subject file. A few books can be placed on a worktable or credenza between bookends. But, like file folders, once you get more than a few of these items, they can begin to stack up. So here are some tips for keeping them in order:

Newsletters. Using a three-hole punch, file newsletters in standard-size ring binders, keeping the most recent ones in the front. Some newsletters come prepunched. Put the name of the publication on the outside spine.

Magazines. Instead of stashing magazines in corners or under the bed, keep them in chronological order on bookshelves or in cabinets. For ease of access, standing them on end is preferable to stacking them. You can buy open-style magazine files to keep them standing upright (see Figure 15-1).

Books. Books can be kept on shelves in closets or cabinets or, more commonly, on bookshelves. Although there is a wide variety of styles to purchase, we made our first bookcase from three pieces of lumber and some bricks. You can arrange books on shelves in alphabetical order either by subject or by author, but always place the most frequently used books on the shelves that are easiest to reach.

Tapes. Special plastic trays are available for storing your tapes, or they can be placed in shallow drawers, wood cabinets, or cardboard boxes. The biggest problem with storing tapes is that they are usually labeled on the front rather than on the spine, which makes locating the one you're look-

Figure 15-1. Storing Information

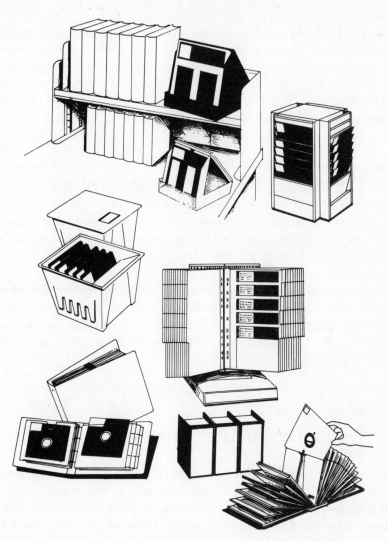

Disk storage units

ing for a time-consuming process. To avoid this problem, you can label them on the side yourself, with adhesive labels, and then organize them as you would books, in alphabetical order by subject or author.

Disks. There are a wide variety of holders for both 3½-inch floppy disks and CD-ROM disks (see Figure 15-1). We recommend keeping software disks and backup copies of software in separate holders from the disks you use to back up your hard drive. Label your data disks by topic or, when the data requires more than one disk, use the same names for the disks as for the directories they are backing up.

Eliminate Newspaper and Magazine Piles

If you're tired of having stacks of newspapers and magazines piled around your home office that you're going to get to some day, you can cut your reading time dramatically and shrink or eliminate those piles by using any number of customized news services available on the World Wide Web.

Every AOL user has the ability to create his or her own "new profile" that will provide up to fifty articles daily that contain any number of key words specified. Most major search engines, such as Yahoo, allow you to create personal news profiles, as do many of the major on-line news services such as Nandotimes (*www.nandotime.com*).

A DAILY ROUTINE FOR HANDLING MAIL

For most at-home workers, the mail brings the biggest influx of information into the home office each day. While some of it is vital business information, some may be personal or for other family members, and much is junk mail you would just as soon not receive. Whatever it is, you have to do something with the mail once it arrives at the door.

The first step is to designate one area where you process all mail, personal and business, incoming and outgoing. Often your desk is the best location. It's usually near both the phone and your files. Sometimes, another location is more suitable. If, for example, your mail usually includes orders that need to be shipped out, a storage area with a large table where you can pack and ship out incoming orders would be an excellent place for handling your mail.

If it isn't convenient to have these materials near your work space, you can keep them elsewhere in a drawer-organizer tray or rolling cart, and then bring it out when you're ready to deal with the mail.

✓ **Checklist:** Managing the Mail

Keep all the materials you need for handling both incoming and outgoing mail within arm's reach of the area you've selected. For example, we keep our mailing materials in the cabinets close to where we handle the mail. These are the materials we find useful to have nearby:

___ Manila folders	___ Postage scale
___ Stamps	___ Postage affixer
___ Mailing labels	___ Packing material
___ Envelopes	___ Postcards
___ Letter opener	___ Wastebasket
___ Filing labels	___ Marking pens
___ Stapler	___ Tape

Set aside a specific time each day to process the mail. Depending on the amount of mail you receive, fifteen to forty-five minutes a day should be sufficient. Many people like to handle the mail immediately after it arrives. If your mail arrives at an odd time for you, however, as ours does (2 P.M.), you may wish to handle it at a more suitable hour. Some people prefer to process the mail first thing in the morning, feeling it's a good way to get the day under way. Others like to do it during what they call the "after-lunch lull." Still others prefer to close the day with the mail.

You should set up a similar plan for handling E-mail. Some people check E-mail on the hour; others set aside a particular time each day. We check periodically throughout the day for urgent messages and answer all others late in the evening.

The telephone you select can actually help to facilitate E-mail processing. Casio's *Phonemate IT-380* with *Mail Call,* for example, alerts you when you have E-mail waiting. It also lets you check your E-mail as you would your voice-mail messages by displaying the header information of forty incoming messages so you can review them and listen to those deemed urgent or important without booting up your PC and logging on. You can then respond by using preprogrammed responses, notifying the messager of your phone number or by speaking a reply into the phone.

Which part of the day you set aside for handling mail is less important than doing it at some regular time and not letting it pile up from one day to the next. Avoid the temptation to let E-mail messages back up for days or scatter different pieces of mail hither, thither, and yon throughout the house. Keeping all your mail in one place and doing it at one time each day will make it much easier to manage. One exception to this is people whose work keeps them out of town or out of the office most of the week. They may prefer to set aside an "administrative day" once a week for processing all mail and other paperwork.

There are a variety of ways to pick up your E-mail when you're out of the office. The Casio *Phonemate IT-380* mentioned above, for example, also allows you to call in remotely and pick up your E-mail via the phone. Or you can dial in using a digital cellular phone and a notebook computer or a PDA (personal digital assistant).

 Time-Saver: The Sort/Act System for Handling the Mail

The "handle it one time" principle is truly a mail-processing lifesaver. Using the system we're about to describe, you can handle every piece of mail once, and trash it or stash it in its proper place within forty-five minutes.

Open the mail, sort it into the following four action piles, and handle it in one of these ways:

1. ***Throw it away.*** The wastebasket (or paper shredder) is our best friend in sorting the mail. Even better, keep a receptacle for paper recycling and throw "junk" mail into it. We usually throw away three-fourths of our mail, tossing out advertisements and announcements that aren't of interest. In fact, we don't even open mail we know will not be of interest to us.

2. ***Act on it.*** Whenever possible, take immediate action. Fill out forms, send any requested material, ship out orders, make out a needed check, call to make a reservation, read correspondence or short newsletters. If the necessary action will take more than a few minutes, however, put the mail into a pile to be filed in the proper place for handling at a later time.

3. ***Refer it to others.*** Sort out mail for other family members or employees who are to handle it. Designate some place where this mail will be put on a regular basis. We used to put our son's mail on the ledge by the stairway to his room, for example.

4. ***File it.*** Any piece of mail you have not thrown out or passed on to others should be placed in its proper location by the end of the time period you've set aside for processing the mail. It should be in one of three places:

    ✓ ***In the appropriate file.*** Put materials that require no further action in the subject, client, or project files discussed earlier in this chapter. Materials that need further action should be placed in the upcoming, project, or tickler files and flagged for when they need attention. If you wish, you can take this time to add these items to your daily planner or "Think of Everything" list (see chapter 13).

(Continued on page 463)

(Continued from page 462)

> ✓ *In an area set aside for reading material.* Find a place to put maga-
> zines, newsletters, and journals you want to read. Places people fre-
> quently use include a bookshelf, a nightstand, or a magazine rack in the
> TV room or bathroom.
>
> ✓ *In your financial record-keeping system* (see chapter 14).

Some people prefer to create a special place or file for personal mail
they want to handle after business hours. We often put our personal mail
on the nightstand, for example, since we prefer to read and write personal
letters at our leisure.

If you have more mail than you can finish filing in forty-five minutes,
you can set up a tray or box on top of your filing cabinet for materials to be
filed later. Generally speaking, we don't recommend this, because it's too
easy for this kind of "file pile" to get so backed up that it's out of control.

Unless you have someone else coming in to do it, leftover filing is too
often something that just never gets done. Then you're always having to
scramble through the "file pile" to find missing information and may even
overlook vital data that's become buried in the pile. When your mail takes
more than forty-five minutes to process, unless you're in the mail-order
business so that answering the mail is what you get paid for, it's a sign you
need to hire administrative help, even if it's part-time or once a week. Providing personalized office support services for very small businesses is a
growing field.

 True Confessions: Simplicity Works Best

"I don't like in-baskets and out-baskets or anything else that sits on my desk. I
have a hanging-file folder labeled "Accounts Payable." During the week, as mail
comes in, I pull out the bills, both business and personal, and put them in the
folder. Every week on Sunday morning while I'm watching *Face the Nation,* I pay
all the bills in the folder. If something is not due for a couple of weeks or more, I
leave it in the folder. I deal with junk mail immediately . . . it usually ends up in
the round file (the wastebasket). Magazines are read as soon as possible each
week. If there's an article I like or want to keep, I tear it out and throw away the
rest. My rule is keep junk off the desk, do a routine sorting every day, get tough
with junk mail and clutter. Just looking at it clogs my mind."

Check Sheet: Managing Phone Messages

Set up an area on or near your desk where you handle phone calls. If you're right-handed, place your phone on the left of your work space. This will leave your right hand free for writing while you're talking on the phone. Using a headset will enable you to enter information into your computer while you're talking. Keep the following within arm's reach in your phone area:

____ *A telephone message pad or computer and software for writing down messages.* The pink tear-off pads we're all so familiar with are designed for multi-employee offices in which a secretary takes messages for several people. There is no place or need for "pink slips" in the home office.

Instead, we recommend entering phone messages in your time-management software by day, recording each contact by name in your contact list or using a spiral-bound steno pad for recording all phone notes. Using either method, you won't have hundreds of little slips cluttering the desk and forever getting misplaced. You will always know exactly where all your messages are. Who called, when they called, who needs calling back, their phone numbers, directions to where you are meeting them—these will always be easy to find. In short, all the information you receive over the phone will be in one place.

If you use a notebook, put the date you begin using a particular pad on the front cover of the pad. When it is full, record the date of the last day's messages on the cover also. The pad can then be stored as a permanent record. Be sure to write the date beside the messages as you take them each day.

____ *Stick-on notes* for writing down information you want to take with you or put into a tickler file. Avoid the temptation, however, of replacing your time-planning system with little pieces of paper hanging all over your home and office. Besides creating a mess, they're too easy to overlook on the day you most need to see them. Keep as much detail as possible in your personal-organizer software or paper system.

____ *Pen and pencil with eraser.* Although this seems obvious, how many times do you end up saying, "Just a minute, let me find a pen"? We've found the only solution to this is to have a pen that does not leave the phone area. There are pens you can attach to your phone with a little cord, special desk pens with a stand, and, of course, pen and pencil holders you can use next to your phone.

____ *Business cards, addresses, and phone numbers.* Keep whatever filing system you have selected for storing this information near your phone for easy access.

Calls, of course, can come at any time of the day or night, but some people find it easier to manage an office at home if they set aside a time of day for placing and returning phone calls. Often they work alone and don't want the phone to infringe on their business at hand or, for that matter, on their personal lives.

Writer Kitty Freidman, for example, finds that phone calls disrupt her train of thought, so she places the calls she needs to make first thing in the morning before she starts writing. Then she turns on the answering machine and writes until the end of the day when she takes the messages off the machine and returns her calls.

You are more likely to reach people if you call before 9:00 A.M. meetings, at 11:45 A.M. before people leave for lunch, and in the late afternoon, between 4:00 and 5:00 P.M.

When working on the phone, record notes and messages on your telephone answering pad or directly into your contact-management or personal-information-management software. At the end of a phone call, you may want to set up a project file or client file relating to the call. If you need to follow up on a call, use the information in your notes to put the data into your upcoming or tickler system.

 Shortcuts: Organizing Tools

1. Use a letter opener.

2. Have a large wastebasket near the area where you process your mail.

3. Use memory-resident calculators on your computer so you can make quick calculations no matter what files you're working on.

4. Use a typewriter instead of your computer for filling out forms and simple response postcards.

5. If you send out lots of mail each day, use a ceramic wheel or automatic stamp applicator.

6. Use card extenders to turn business cards instantly into Rolodex cards.

7. Plastic silverware trays keep pens, pencils, Post-it pads, paper clips, rubber bands, scissors, stapler, and Magic Markers organized in your desk drawer.

8. Try plastic stacking trays to keep various types of stationery and documents you use too frequently to keep in a filing cabinet at your fingertips without cluttering your desk.

WHAT TO KEEP AND WHAT TO THROW AWAY

Deciding whether to keep a piece of paper, a file, a letter, or an announcement can consume undue time and energy. Some people have a tendency to keep everything, "to be on the safe side." Others, not wanting to bother with decisions, throw things away too hastily. We've found the following guidelines useful in making the right decision.

✓ *Keep materials you will use in relation to current projects or clients.* When a project is finished or a client or customer is no longer active, cull the file of extraneous material and retire it to storage.

✓ *Review files at least once a year.* If you haven't used a file in the last year, ask yourself whether you have a good reason to keep it.

✓ *Keep materials related to work you still do,* if reconstructing them would require a lot of effort. If you currently have no use for the materials but expect you could use portions of them in future work, retire the materials to storage files.

✓ *Keep irreplaceable materials.* If they are related to work you still do, materials that are not available elsewhere should be retained if reconstructing them would be difficult, expensive, or time-consuming.

✓ *Some documents should be kept permanently.* Keep legal documents, warranties for the life of a product, securities, licenses, capital assets, insurance policies, all tax returns, home improvement contracts, and so forth.

✓ *Keep tax records for six years after you've filed returns.* Records supporting a return filed on April 16, 1999, should be kept until April 16, 2005. After filing your return each year, you can retire the material to storage files, discarding materials over six years old. Real estate records and those relating to stocks must be stored indefinitely since records must be kept "as long as they are important for any tax law." Keep the tax returns themselves permanently.

✓ *When in doubt* about keeping something, ask yourself these questions:

- What will I use it for?

- When will I need it?

- Under what circumstances might I need it?

- What would happen if I didn't have it?

- Would I pay to rent extra space to store it?

Generally, we agree with what Stephanie Winston says in her book *Getting Organized:* If you haven't used something in the past year, and it has no sentimental or monetary value, but "it might come in handy someday"—toss it!

 Tip

If you do not have a copy of any of your tax returns, you can obtain a copy from the IRS by writing to request Form 4506 entitled "Request for Copy of Tax Form." This form is available on their Web site: *www.ustreasury.irs.gov*

Neat, Convenient, and Attractive Storage Systems

Despite all the paper, disks, books, files, magazines, and sundry other equipment and supplies an office brings into your home, you don't need to lose the "homey" look and feel you want your home to have. With manufacturers and retailers taking a growing interest in meeting our needs, even storage units and systems are being customized for the home office. Browsing through a Crate and Barrel or Hold Everything store or catalog, you'll find an array of attractive alternatives to gray steel and wire that could be perfect for keeping your home office organized. Here's a sampling:

- Various-sized handwoven natural rattan baskets for holding newspapers and magazines, or shelf baskets for collecting similar materials like print cartridge refills or booklets in one place on a shelf.

- Rolling hanging file trolleys in natural wood or forest green that glide from desk side or tuck neatly under a desk or table when not in use.

- A folding pine bookcase that can divide an office, sit against a wall, or be folded up and put in a closet if need be.

- A CD-ROM tower or flat disk case that fans out when the lid is opened.

- Plastic stacking media tubs with divided wells, for keeping disks dust-free and in order.

- Computer "screenies," corkboard, or wood frames for posting notes and reminders around your computer monitor.

- Wood wall-storage units for books, shelf baskets, disk tubs, paper supplies, and small equipment.

(Continued on page 468)

(Continued from page 467)

- Wicker and wood storage bins that can substitute perfectly for steel filing cabinets. In fact, in many cases they will work better for you because you can pull out a file drawer basket, and using the side handles, take it anywhere in your home office to file, update a file, or work on a project. They're available in double stacks of four or eight baskets.

- Hanging file boxes of paper-covered cardboard that can hang in your filing cabinet or be taken out, closed with Velcro and carried anywhere.

- Acrylic magazine butlers for organizing and displaying your magazines and journals.

And if you have lots of forms or paper to keep stacked and sorted, KwikFile F/S Open-Shelf Forms Cabinets can keep them neat and in order along any wall ([800] 368-1057).

 Checklist: Are You Ready for Audio or Video Teleconferencing?

The more of the following questions you answer "yes," the more likely it is that you should consider audio and video teleconferencing to make your workday more productive.

1. Am I using my speakerphone more often and finding it more irritating day by day?

2. Am I constantly traveling to nonpaying meetings away from my home office?

3. Do I often need to get together with people from other cities to work on joint projects?

4. Am I losing time and money faxing and overnight-mailing the same documents back and forth again and again?

5. Am I missing opportunities because I can't get together more often to work with colleagues, clients, or potential clients?

WHEN YOU NEED SOMEONE TO HELP

As your work expands, the first person you hire will probably be someone to help with your information management tasks. When is the right time to get this help?

One question we're frequently asked is "When should I hire office help?" Our answer: "As soon as you can afford it." Certainly, having someone else to take over many of the office housekeeping tasks makes life easier and frees you for more creative and profitable uses of your time.

A more direct answer to the question, however, is to think about getting help when you're spending more than forty-five minutes a day processing information. Finally, if you find that you're simply not able to keep your records up to date, investing in the expense of getting someone to help may be the best use of your resources.

Once you do get help, we recommend that you set up a system you can use yourself when you need to, and evaluate its effectiveness regularly. Someone else can handle the files, the mail, and the phone calls, but ultimately you need to be able to step in at any time and handle these things efficiently, because information is the lifeblood of any office.

RESOURCES

BOOKS

The Complete Book of Contemporary Business Letters. A book and disk from Round Lake Publishing, 31 Bailey Avenue, Ridgefield, CT 06877; (203) 431-9696.

File . . . Don't Pile! For People Who Write: Handling the Paper Flow in the Workplace or Home Office. Pat Dorff, Edith Fine, and Judith Josephson. New York: St. Martin's Press, 1994. ISBN: *0312102860.*

High Performace Through Organizing Information. Carolyn Simpson. New York: Rosen Publishing Group, 1996. ISBN: 0823922073.

The High-Tech Personal Efficiency Program: Organizing Your Electronic Resources to Maximize Your Time and Efficiency. Kerry Gleeson. New York: Wiley, 1997. ISBN: 0471172065.

If You Haven't Got the Time to Do It Right, When Will You Find the Time to Do It Over? Jeff Mayer. New York: Fireside, 1990. ISBN: 0671733648.

Information Anxiety. Richard Saul Wurman. New York: Bantam, 1990. ISBN: 0385243944.

Organized to Be Your Best. Susan Silver. Los Angeles, CA: Adams Hall Publishing, 1995. ISBN: 0944708366.

Winning the Fight Between You and Your Desk. Jeff Mayer. New York: HarperBusiness, 1995. ISBN: 0887307183.

CONTACT-MANAGEMENT SOFTWARE

Act! Symantec Corporation, 10201 Torre Avenue, Cupertino, CA 95014; phone: (800) 441-7234, (408) 253-9600. Web: *www.symantec.com*

Goldmine. GoldMine Software, 17383 Sunset Boulevard, Ste. 301, Pacific Palisades, CA 90272; phone: (800) 654-3526. Web: *www.goldminesw.com*

Maximizer. Multiactive Software, 1090 West Pender Street, Vancouver, BC, Canada V6E2N7; phone: (604) 601-8000. Web: *www.maximizer.com*

TeleMagic. Q & I, 115 Symons Street, Toronto ONT M8V 1V1; phone: 416-253-5555. Web: *www.qisys.com*

Sharkware. Multiactive Corporation, P.O. Box 500129, Atlanta, GA 30350; phone: (800) 947-5075. Web: *www.sharkware.com*

INFORMATION-MANAGEMENT SOFTWARE

Ascend. Franklin Covey, P.O. Box 31406, Salt Lake City, UT 84132; phone: 800-654-1776. Web: *www.franklincovey.com*

Ecco. NetManage, 10725 North De Anza Boulevard, Cupertino, CA 95014-2030; phone: (408) 973-7171. Web: *www.netmanage.com*

Microsoft's Outlook. Microsoft Corporation, One Microsoft Way, Redmond, WA 98052; phone: (800) 426-9400. Web: *www.microsoft.com/outlook*

Lotus Organizer. Lotus Development Corporation, 55 Cambridge Parkway, Cambridge MA 02142; phone: (800) 635-6887. Web: *www.lotus.com*

C H A P T E R   1 6

Cleaning Up:
Sixty-Second Housecleaning

"When the house is a mess . . . you certainly are not in touch with the very best in you."   PAM YOUNG AND PEGGY JONES

<table>
<tr><td>

Goals

1. *Fit keeping your home and office clean and tidy into your busy schedule.*

2. *Cut cleaning supplies to a minimum and make using them convenient.*

3. *Avoid eighteen messes you won't have to clean up.*

4. *Get family and roommates to pitch in.*

5. *Use cleaning services strategically.*

</td><td>

What a pleasant feeling to walk into a model house—no dust, no muss. But then model houses don't feel quite right, do they? They lack the sense of being lived in that makes a house feel like home. If there's one thing a home office is, it's lived in. And along with that lived-in feeling come the muss and the mess.

Now that you're working from home, unless you hire a cleaning service, keeping your home both livable and workable falls to you. But who has time to keep things up the way the woman of the house once did when she was a full-time homemaker? We certainly don't. You probably don't either. And if you take the time, you probably feel as though you're stealing it from yourself

</td></tr>
</table>

or your work. Let's face it, the demands of our schedules today simply leave very little time for cleaning.

AVOID THE HOUSEKEEPING CRISIS

A recent survey from *USA Today* confirms what most of us know—housework is the first thing to go when we run out of time. And when you're working on your own at home, is there ever a day when you don't run out of time?

The majority of American households now consist of two-career couples, singles, or single parents; and that means most of us are pressed for time. Certainly deciding to work from home frees you to spend your time more as you wish, but cleaning rarely comes out at the top of the list. We have found that successful home-based self-employed individuals work an average of sixty-one hours a week. That doesn't leave much "free" time. Even if, by working from home, you're able to save the twenty or more minutes a day you once spent commuting, who wants to do cleaning during that extra time?

So what does happen to that "free" time? Surveys show most Americans spend a full weekend day (about thirteen hours) trying to take care of housework, grocery shopping, doing errands, etc. But at what a price! When we cram cleaning chores into the little free time we save for weekends, we have even less leisure time. So we start off the workweek as stressed out and tired as we were when we closed the door on work at the end of the week. In a very real way, cleaning as the part-time job we've known it to be in the past no longer works for most households. But does that mean we have to choose between being dead tired or dirty?

We say NO! We say there's another way. It took us years to find it. And we had to try just about everything else before we did! First we tried the most obvious solution—hiring someone else to do it. In fact, a survey of the Mothers' Home Business Network showed that 39 percent of their membership listed having a maid as their most commonly cited need!

But like many others who work from home, we found that having someone come in to clean was disruptive whether they came during the day or at night. During the day, we couldn't take calls while they were vacuuming. And the clatter in the kitchen could be heard in the background. At night we were either out or wanted to have a quiet evening at home.

In addition, cleaning services can be expensive. The average professional cleaning service we interviewed ran $300 per month. Freelance individuals cost somewhat less. Of course, if you decide to hire someone to clean, you may be able to deduct part of your cleaning costs as a business expense. Still, in paying out that much money, we kept thinking of all the other great things we'd rather do with that $300 each month. Think of the equipment $3,600 a year would buy—a new notebook computer, a color laser printer, a copy machine—and there would still be money left over. Or how about the marketing $300 a month would pay for, or the fun we could have with it? We could take the whole family to Hawaii for $3,600! So like four out of five of the successful entrepreneurs we interviewed, we decided we'd rather spend that money on our business or ourselves than on cleaning up.

So, rather than bringing in a service to do occasional large-scale tasks such as cleaning windows, carpets, and venetian blinds and a seasonal housecleaning, we decided to stick with the do-it-yourself method. Besides, we've read it's good exercise!

First we tried setting aside a special time each week to clean our home and office. That lasted about a month. Then we tried a schedule for spreading the work out over the week; e.g., vacuuming on Monday night, dusting on Tuesday, etc. That lasted about a week. We also tried agreeing to do the cleaning randomly in our spare time. That lasted a long time. But no housework got done. We didn't have any *spare* time.

Ultimately we fell into what we call the *chronic crisis* method of housekeeping—that is, you put up with tolerably marginal levels of the mess until important "company" is coming. Then you drop everything and rush around like competitors in a supermarket contest who are trying to see how many groceries they can get in their carts in three minutes. Instead of throwing things in a cart, however, you're throwing things out of sight—paper, books, toys, mail, etc.—as fast as you can stash them somewhere before the doorbell rings. By the time your guests arrive, of course, you're exhausted. And either you vow never to have anyone come over again or you promise never again to let things get so out of hand—another promise that lasts about a month.

We even tried out some of the clever ideas in the "I-hate-housekeeping"–type books. You know, the ones with ideas like using a cleaning apron or a cleaning caddy to carry all your supplies and stuff around from room to room. None of those worked for us because they didn't deal with the real issue. The real issue is that we, like most self-employed individuals, have too many more important things we want to do than to clean. The truth is, we don't want to take the time to clean. So we certainly don't want to take time to create clever cleaning caddies.

Nonetheless we were getting fed up with the dirt and the periodic crises when we hit a turning point. We had just returned from a sixty-city media tour—the crowning glory of seven years of struggling to write and then promote the first edition of this book. You can just imagine how easily we came to rely, over that four-month tour, on returning at the end of each long day's work to an immaculately clean and luxuriously neat hotel room. The bathrooms were always sparkling. The beds were always freshly made—with *perfect* corners. And any dirty dishes were whisked away in moments. Dirty clothing and shoes disappeared at night to reappear laundered and shined. It was heaven! We felt like King and Queen for a Day!

But eventually we were home again, and guess what? We'd get up in the morning to dress for the day, and no one had cleaned up the bathroom! It didn't sparkle. We'd go into the kitchen for something to eat, and no one had cleaned off the countertops! They didn't shine. We'd come in late at night to drop into bed, and no one had made it up fresh and crisp!

The contrast was a shock! We realized for the first time on a gut level how wonderful it feels to enjoy a *really* clean home. Suddenly it was no longer something your parents tell you to do. It was no longer a social expectation, an outdated role demanded of women, a badge of "superwomanhood," a sign of the sensitive male, or a distasteful duty that proves you're an enlightened couple. No, instead, we realized at the gut level that a really clean, neat place to live and work is a treat, a compliment, a privilege, a reward. It says "You're important. You're special. You deserve to be honored and treated like royalty."

And we missed that feeling! We wanted it back. We wanted to feel like King and Queen for a Day every day. We deserve it. We work hard. We do good work. And so do you. But the question still remains, Where do you find the time? Our schedules hadn't changed. We still had very little time to devote to cleaning.

But we're firm believers that when you set a goal, when you're determined to have something in your life, the next thing you know a solution arises. And that's what happened. We developed a new perspective on housework and cleaning, and the result is a system that makes it possible for us to keep our home and office clean, neat, and tidy in only seconds a day. We call it Sixty-Second Housecleaning. It's easy. It works, and we think you'll like it too.

---

7 Steps to Sixty-Second Housecleaning

1. Adopt a new attitude toward cleaning.

2. Think in terms of preventing messes instead of cleaning them up.

3. Clean as you go through the day instead of waiting until you have a block of time.

4. Put your cleaning supplies "on a diet" and keep them near the multiple places throughout the house that need cleaning.

5. Let technology do the work for you.

6. Get everyone to pitch in.

7. Make strategic use of professional cleaning services.

We can keep our work and living space neat and clean enough in only seconds a day by doing seven things differently from the way housekeeping is usually done. And fortunately, because we work from home, we can make these changes. They probably wouldn't work for someone who is employed outside the home five-plus days a week. Here's a summary of the seven steps to Sixty-Second Housecleaning, followed by more details on how to put this method to work for you.

STEP ONE: ADOPT A NEW
ATTITUDE TOWARD CLEANING

First throw out all your old ideas about what you *have to do* and *should do*. Instead start thinking about what you *want done* and how you can do it most efficiently.

It's time we acknowledge that times have changed. Housekeeping was once a full-time career for most women. Today it's no longer necessarily a woman's responsibility alone, and whatever gets done must be squeezed in around full-time careers and perhaps a family too. A clean house is no longer an appropriate measure of how good a person you are—and that goes for both men and women. We believe housekeeping needs to be redefined to mean maintaining an environment to your liking, one you can live and work in comfortably and successfully. And the truth is that means different things to different people.

Nonetheless two-thirds of women answering a *Good Housekeeping* poll reported they're not happy with the way their homes are kept because they can no longer maintain the housekeeping standards they grew up with. Let's give ourselves a break and stop measuring ourselves by those old standards. It's time for us to set new standards. Let's think about how we want our homes and offices to be. Do we really need to pass the "white glove test"? Just what is "clean"?

For some people "clean" means there isn't a lot of "stuff" around. For others, it means an absence of dust or dirt. Take notice of what bothers you and what makes you feel good. If it bothers you, you deserve to take care of it for your own benefit. So do it. If it doesn't bother you—as long as it's not detracting in any way from the success of your business—let it go and get on with what matters to you.

We also need to alter our expectations about how much time we need to spend cleaning. An R. H. Bruskin survey shows that people spend about fourteen weekend hours on chores—six and a half more hours than they want to spend. Still one-third of people we surveyed think they spend too little time. In actuality, we only need to spend as much time as it takes to do what we want done. So start setting your own standards, and you'll find that it's much easier to motivate yourself to make the time to meet them.

STEP TWO: THINK IN TERMS OF PREVENTING MESSES INSTEAD OF CLEANING THEM UP

Half of housecleaning is unnecessary because a lot of the messes we have to clean up never need to happen in the first place. Just as in running your office, a little effort now can save lots of effort later. You can cut the time required to clean your home and office in half by avoiding some of the biggest messes in the first place. You won't need to clean the stove if you wipe up spills as they occur. You will rarely need to clean the refrigerator if you clean up spills and stains when they happen. You'll rarely need to scour pots and pans if you wash them the moment you empty them.

If you like using your time to clean—and some people do—then you can enjoy the luxury of being as messy as you like. But if you're like us, you hate doing most cleaning tasks so much you may prefer to take a moment to prevent a mess so you can avoid doing the time-consuming tasks of cleaning it up. Why should you spend time cleaning if you can easily keep things from needing cleaning? Use the following checklist to identify messes you could save time, energy, and money by avoiding in the first place:

 Checklist: 18 Messes You Can Prevent

The following list of common household messes can all be avoided. Check off those that you'd just as soon not like to have to clean up.

____ Dirt that doesn't get through the door doesn't need to be cleaned up. Good-quality mats at the door and covered or elevated entryways keep dirt, mud, and water out.

____ Well-insulated doors and weatherproofed windows let in less dust.

____ Using liquid soap dispensers instead of bars of soap prevents soap scum buildup on sinks.

____ Deep sinks prevent splattering.

____ Brushed brass plating on faucets doesn't show spots that must be polished.

____ A shower stall or tub wiped down immediately stays clean.

____ Mildew doesn't grow as much in well-lighted bathrooms with plenty of circulation.

____ Dishes cleaned off at the moment they're used don't get food caked onto them.

(Continued on page 477)

(Continued from page 476)

____ With today's fabrics, laundry folded when it comes out of the dryer usually doesn't need ironing.

____ Clothes hung up at the moment you take them off don't get piled up to be put away.

____ Magazines and papers read or skimmed, clipped, and filed when they arrive don't accumulate into a major catch-up project.

____ Receipts filed when you return from shopping don't pile up for sorting.

____ Semigloss latex enamel paint and vinyl wallpaper don't spot, and they clean easily.

____ Fabrics treated to resist stains are easier to clean and need cleaning less often.

____ Neutral colors for all surfaces are easier to clean than dark or white ones.

____ Tile with dark grout saves hours of bleaching and scrubbing.

____ Streamlined furniture and fixtures don't collect dust and dirt like ornate ones, and they can be cleaned more quickly.

____ Plenty of storage units, drawers, racks, cabinets, and closets prevent messes by making sure there's a place to put everything away in, on, or under.

We have what we call a *Backup Barometer*—that point at which things pile up or get looking sufficiently crummy that they start to bother us. That's the point to jump in and clean up before you find yourself with a major project that you'll have to struggle and sacrifice time to do. For more tips on messes that don't need to happen, see *Make Your House Do the Housework,* by Don Aslett and Laura Aslett Simons.

STEP THREE: CLEAN AS YOU GO THROUGH THE DAY SIXTY SECONDS AT A TIME

Don't wait until you can set aside a block of time to clean. Face it, chances are you don't have a day or a morning to set aside for cleaning every week. Realistically, who has big blocks of time to devote to housework? And anyway, if you miss a "block" one week, next week's block has to be even bigger. You probably don't have any "spare" time to squeeze it into, either. But cleaning as you go throughout the day literally takes only seconds, and nearly anyone can spare just a minute here and there.

Most repetitive cleaning tasks can be done by following the "sixty-second rule." It's true. We've actually timed them. For example, to clean your whole master bathroom and bath might take a half hour. But, let's say that while you're brushing your teeth, you notice that the mirror needs cleaning; it will take only sixty seconds to clean it. Or if you notice that the bookshelf is dusty; it will take only sixty seconds to dust it. If you notice that the bedroom floor is getting dirty; it takes only sixty seconds to vacuum it.

Actually this "do it when you see it" approach is the heart of our Sixty-Second Housecleaning Method. See it; do it; get on with your life. Because you work from home, this is much easier to do. Some tasks like washing the kitchen or bathroom floor will take a little longer. But there's a big difference between ten minutes and all Saturday morning. In other words, you don't have to clean all at once. Do what you can do when you notice it, and you'll be amazed at how much easier cleaning becomes. Your home and office may never be sparkling all at once using this method; but they will be generally clean all the time with less time and effort on your part.

 Warning!!! Housekeeping Perfectionists

If the sight of a dusty shelf, a few crumbs under the breakfast table, a crooked picture frame, or fingerprints on the mirror drive you up the wall, you can still do sixty-second housecleaning, but you will need to do two things:

1. *Firmly limit yourself to only sixty seconds* of cleaning at any one time and then get back immediately to whatever task was at hand when you noticed something needed cleaning.

2. *Limit yourself to no more than ten sixty-second cleaning chores a day* and let others go until tomorrow. Otherwise you could find yourself cleaning your way through every day and never getting down to business.

If you can't do these two things, don't use this method. You are someone who needs to hire a weekly cleaning service or to set aside a block of time each day or week to keep everything spick and span so you can be free to work without distracting housework staring you in your critical eye.

STEP FOUR: PUT YOUR CLEANING SUPPLIES ON A DIET AND KEEP THEM NEARBY IN MULTIPLE PLACES THROUGHOUT THE HOUSE

The sixty-second approach works best if all the supplies you need to clean are virtually within arm's reach. Having to traipse back and forth to a central cabinet where you keep your cleaning supplies and then having to rummage through an assortment of bottles, cans, sprays, polishes, waxes, and other cleansers is another hurdle that makes cleaning too time-consuming.

Instead we recommend limiting your supplies to the bare essentials and keeping a set of them in a convenient place in every major cleaning area of your home or office. Most people have four times as many types of cleaning supplies as they need. All this excess cleaning material just clutters up your cabinets, wastes your time, and squanders your money. If you cut down to the essentials, you can have them all in multiple places and still get more from less.

Bare-Bones Cleaning Supplies for Sixty-Second Cleaning

1. Turn a shelf, cabinet, or drawer into a Sixty-Second Mini-Cleaning Center in each of these key locations in the home:

   - Kitchen
   - Each bathroom
   - Laundry area
   - Office

2. Have these basic supplies handy in each Sixty-Second Mini-Cleaning Center:

   - A glass cleaner
   - An all-purpose cleaner
   - A dust remover/furniture polish
   - Paper towels and/or cloth

3. For bath areas only add:

   - A toilet-bowl cleaner and brush
   - A tub-and-tile cleaner (Some toilet-bowl cleaners do double duty as excellent tile and tub cleaners!)
   - A shower caddy stocked with tub/shower cleaning items such as:
     - Tub-and-tile cleaner
     - Sponge
     - Squeegee for wiping down shower doors
     - Mildew remover (in humid locales)

4. Additional supplies/equipment for each Sixty-Second Center could include:

   - A handheld or mini vacuum to clean floors and countertops
   - A box of disposable plastic gloves
   - A double-sided sponge: one smooth surface, one rough
   - Trash can liners
   - A full-powered vacuum sweeper on each floor or in each wing of your home/office.

STEP FIVE: LET TECHNOLOGY
CLEAN FOR YOU

As with running your office, the right appliances will do some of the worst cleaning tasks for you, and we believe they're worth the investment. It's surprising how some people can equip their offices with the latest office technology, but their cleaning appliances may still be no more advanced than the ones their parents used. Perhaps that's because office equipment is tax deductible. However, if you're using the Sixty-Second Housecleaning Method in your home/office, the cleaning appliances and supplies that you keep and use in your work space are also deductible as a business expense.

So when replacing appliances or doing remodeling, opt for time-savers whenever you can. Consider built-in wall vacuums, no-wax flooring, an au-

---

Sixty-Second Cleaning Secrets

Virtually every surface in your home and office from countertops to monitor screens, telephones to disk holders gets dusty and dirty, smudged and smeared. An easy way to avoid lugging out spray bottles, paper towels, and dust rags is to keep a supply of premoistened or reusable towels on hand everywhere you might use them. For example, Read/Right has premoistened pads called Klean & Dry for cleaning monitor screens. We keep a supply in our desk drawers. For other surfaces, we use moist towelettes, the ones that are actually for washing your hands and face while away from home. But they're great for quickly cleaning desktops (other than wood), telephone handsets, countertops, bathroom sinks. Pull one out, wipe, and toss! And because they're actually for use on hands and faces, they don't leave your hands covered with harsh, smelly chemicals. We like Wet Ones by L&F Products best. They're the moistest and come in a pop-out plastic bottle for under sink or counter or a travel pack that fits easily in a desk drawer. Nice'n Clean comes in individual packets.

Handi-Wipes also are useful for instant cleaning or dusting. They're actually reusable paper towels. You can use them for anything you'd use a paper towel for, but they're stronger than paper towels. You use them, wash them out, and use them again. We keep them around for instant dusting.

Unfortunately, dust doesn't settle on only the easy-to-reach surfaces. It has a way of getting into the nooks and crannies of electronic equipment where towels can't clean. But Dust-Off can. This air-spray canister enables you to clean out the hardest-to-reach areas, and it can even be transformed into a minivacuum. Dust-Off is made by Falcon and is often sold in the photography departments of retail stores for about $5.

tomatic vacuum sweeper, a frost-free refrigerator, a trash compactor, built-in appliances, and self-cleaning ovens. Even a built-in soap dispenser and drinking fountain on the kitchen sink counter can be a super cleaning saver when you have children. While some may consider such things to be luxuries—and they are usually somewhat more expensive than more time-consuming models—now that you're working from home, your time is money, but not when you're using it to clean things up.

STEP SIX: GET EVERYONE ELSE TO PITCH IN

Housemessing is always a joint venture. Why not housecleaning? Get everyone in your household (and your employees, too) onto the Sixty-Second Housecleaning Method. Here are some ideas for how to do that:

- Don't slip into letting cleaning become any one person's responsibility.

- Sit down together and talk about by whom and how the house-cleaning will be done.

- Discuss each person's idea of how the home and office should be.

- Determine which tasks are most important to each person.

- Discuss how you all can assist one another in making sure that those things that are most important to everyone get done.

- Present the idea of Sixty-Second Housecleaning. Find out if everyone would be willing to use it by comparing this method to alternative ones. You can use the following work sheet for comparing Housecleaning Methods.

- Set an example as someone who eagerly and cheerfully keeps things up the way you want them to be.

Children in particular need to understand why housekeeping is important. They need a reason; "Because I said so" is not enough. They also need to know, especially in this day and age, that it's not "mother's job." They need to be shown how much more enjoyable it is to live somewhere where you can find things when you want them. They need to see how inconvenient and unpleasant it is for more and more of your space to become uninhabitable and unusable because it's all taken up with clutter.

Having a sense of responsibility arises from feeling a sense of ownership and participation. It's hard to feel responsible for that which you're required to do. Slaves, for example, rarely feel responsible. They may feel

Work Sheet: Pros and Cons of Housecleaning Methods

No Particular Method

PROS

- You don't have to make any decisions.
- You don't become enslaved to any method.
- You have ultimate flexibility.

CONS

- Cleaning usually falls to one person who feels resentful.
- Housework often doesn't get done.
- House only sporadically clean.

Regular Schedule

PROS

- House clean all at one time.
- You don't have to think about cleaning at other times.
- Get housework done all at once.

CONS

- Hard to keep to schedule.
- Often fall behind.
- Can't find blocks of time to do everything at once.

Hire Someone

PROS

- Saves you time.
- Saves you energy.
- You don't have to do cleaning tasks you don't like doing.

CONS

- Disrupts the workday.
- Increases overhead.
- Takes away funds from other, more profitable things.

Sixty-Second Method

PROS

- You don't need to set aside blocks of time you don't have.
- House always reasonably clean.
- Much easier to motivate yourself.

CONS

- House never clean all at once.
- You are still doing the cleaning yourself.
- Have to create a new habit.

obligated, but only until they're free to do as they choose. Therefore, if you don't want to become the "cleaning cop," involving others in making decisions about which and how things will be cleaned up and asking them to decide what they will make a commitment to do is crucial. Once a commitment has been made, it's important to expect that it be kept or renegotiated.

True Confessions: The Ten-Minute Cleanup

Media presentation coach Kim Freilich developed a variation of the Sixty-Second Housecleaning Method. If she needs to get down to work, but the state of the house is driving her crazy, she sets a timer and gives herself ten minutes to clean up everything she possibly can. She says she's amazed at how much she can get done. It becomes like a game of beat the clock to see how much she can do before the buzzer rings.

We think this is a great idea, too, for getting the whole family involved in quick cleanups. Everyone could fan out to a different area and see who can get the most done before the buzzer goes off. Prizes or treats can be given out to all!

STEP SEVEN: MAKE STRATEGIC USE OF CLEANING SERVICES

Certain cleaning tasks are large scale by nature, and these are the ones that we recommend saving for a cleaning service. They take considerable time, energy, and even some specialized skill. We and about 20 percent of the owners of home businesses we interviewed hire a service to come in periodically for a thorough general cleaning and specialized tasks like cleaning windows, carpets, blinds, air ducts and drapes. We use such services quarterly, but we also spoke to people who have someone come in for some tasks monthly or even every other week. You can farm these tasks out to specialized services or you can use one service that provides them all.

RESOURCES

BOOKS

Clean and Green: The Complete Guide to Non-Toxic and Environmentally Safe Housekeeping. Annie Berthold-Bond. Woodstock, N.Y.: Ceres Press, 1994. ISBN: 1886101019.

500 Terrific Ideas for Cleaning Everything. Don Aslett. New York: Budget Book Service, 1997. ISBN: 0883659921.

Helpful Household Hints: The Ultimate 90s Guide to Housekeeping. June King. Santa Monica Press, 1996. ISBN: 0963994638.

Make Your House Do the Housework. Don Aslett and Laura Aslett Simons. Cincinatti: Betterway Publications, 1995. ISBN: 1558703845.

PART 5

Managing Yourself and Others

CHAPTER 17

Avoiding Loneliness

Goals

1. Identify if you're missing the kind of contact you'd get at the office and if so, what kind.

2. Keep in contact with colleagues and peers.

3. Make new connections.

I solated? Me? Impossible!" says Nick Sullivan, a senior editor working from home via modem for a computer magazine. "When I work, I work. When I socialize, I socialize. Whether I work at home or at the office, it doesn't make much difference. I couldn't isolate myself if I tried. I live in the world."

This expresses the amazement most successful open-collar workers experience when they are asked, as they frequently are, "Don't you feel isolated?"

Frankly, most people who work from home don't feel isolated once their business or job at home is under way and functioning. Their world is full of clients, customers, neighbors, family, friends, suppliers, business associates, and colleagues. But what if you start working from home and do feel that you're out of the loop? How do you get connected to a whole new world of contacts?

THREE STEPS TO GETTING CONNECTED

Although there's usually an adjustment period during which you may miss former office mates, working from home does not mean you will be isolated and lonely unless you are a hermit. It does mean you have to be active and take the initiative to be involved in the world around you. Should you begin to feel isolated and lonely, here are three steps to getting yourself back in the swing of things again.

Step 1: Admit you're missing some type of contact. Admitting you're feeling isolated seems to be the first step to getting past it. Since people usually start working from home for some important reason, sometimes they don't like to consider that it might not be satisfying to them. Bookkeeper Paulene Smith, for example, left her job because she wanted to be at home with her new baby. "I wanted everything to go well and certainly didn't want to think I'd made the wrong decision. But finally I had to admit

---

✓ Checklist: Things You May Be Missing

In a *Success* magazine article, Robert S. Wieder described how office gossip and the grapevine make a variety of subtle but important contributions to working happily and effectively. It isn't always easy to recognize these intangible but vital benefits of being part of an office culture. Here's a checklist of things you may miss. Check off those that could apply to you:

____ The inside information. The vital tips. The scuttlebutt about what's going on.

____ Esprit de corps. Exciting news or a lighthearted conversation that gives you the feeling of being part of a group.

____ Some helpful social pressure, a little incentive, to keep your mind on business and your hands off the potato chips.

____ Some help or moral support in the midst of an emergency.

____ Immediate feedback on your work.

____ A way to test out a new idea.

____ A pat on the shoulder, an understanding look, a word of encouragement.

____ Someone to complain to about how awful things are or brag to about a job well done.

____ A candid evaluation of how you're doing or a warning when you're about to make a mistake.

____ A chance to build self-confidence in your work by telling someone about what you're planning.

____ The sense of belonging that comes from being part of an organization.

____ The sense of importance that comes from having a formal title and a needed role in the organization.

to myself I really did miss the old gang at the office. I had to acknowledge that working on my own involved some special problems I hadn't expected."

Step 2. Recognize what you're missing. After admitting you're missing something, the next step in avoiding isolation is recognizing exactly what you miss. Isolation means different things to different people. For freelance programmer George Broady, not having people around wasn't the problem: "It isn't really people I miss. I work better by myself. What I miss is not knowing what's going on. I don't like feeling out of it."

Marriage and family counselor Sharry Cox agrees that "isolation" means more than being alone. "I'm with clients all day, so it took me awhile to figure out that it wasn't really contact with people I was missing. I get plenty of that. I miss seeing a friendly face that understands the challenges of the work I'm doing."

Step 3. Take action to get involved in activities that provide what you're missing. Once you know which benefits you're missing, you can set about finding the best way to replace them. A next-door neighbor can provide a friendly "hello" and possibly even a good ear for the joys and tribulations of your day. But only a respected colleague can give you feedback on what you're doing, share news in the field, or recognize and praise a brilliant effort.

You'll have to take action to replace the particular elements of office interaction you're missing. To stay in touch, you'll have to take the time and invest the energy to set up opportunities for the interchanges you miss. Sharry Cox expresses what so many people who work at home discover: "Unless I work at it, I get out of touch with what's going on in my field. I start missing opportunities, learning the hard way what I could easily learn from someone else. Unless I make the effort myself, unless I dial a phone number or drive to a meeting, I lose contact with the people I've known."

KEEPING IN CONTACT
WITH COLLEAGUES AND PEERS

In other words, whatever you're missing from contact at the office, chances are it won't find you. You'll have to find or create it yourself. Here are nine steps you can take to create the interaction you need.

Join and participate regularly in community organizations and professional, technical, or trade associations. Most fields have a national professional association, and many have local chapters. If there is not a local chapter in your area, consider forming one. Many chambers of commerce welcome home businesses and self-employed individuals. Some even have home-business counsels or special-interest groups that meet separately from the monthly chamber meeting. In addition, the number of home businesses has grown so dramatically over the past few years that independent Home Business Associations are forming spontaneously in communities all over the country.

When you join one or more such trade and professional organizations, of course, attend the meetings regularly, but in addition, participate actively in the organizations' leadership structure. Volunteer to serve on a committee (membership, hospitality, and fund-raising are good ones to become active with) or run for an office. Make presentations and attend local, state, and national conferences.

Read and listen. Specialty publications now number in the thousands and serve needs in almost every area of interest. Newsletters, professional and trade journals, and magazines keep you aware of what's happening and often inspire creative ideas. Audiocassette tapes are available from many sources on almost any subject. You can even subscribe to a tape library program. Two such programs are included in the Resources list at the end of this chapter. Workshops and conferences frequently come in tape format as well. If your work involves driving, listening to these kinds of tapes is a great way to make the best use of your time.

Attend workshops, seminars, and courses in your field, or explore new and related fields. Once you've attended a few of these programs, you will be on mailing lists for many others and receive announcements of the workshops in your area of interest. Begin by contacting the continuing-education department at your local college or university as well as your professional, technical, or trade association for workshops they may be sponsoring. Also, look through specialty or trade newsletters and magazines for workshops advertised in your area of interest.

Use the telephone. Stay in touch by phone with the people you've known. Call to say "hello," to get an opinion or reaction, or just to share some news. People are flattered when you think of them and enjoy being consulted. Use phone contact to discover what others are doing and when or where you might get together.

Call or write the interesting people you hear or read about. If you want contact with them, ask how you can get involved in what they're doing. We have met several of our most valued colleagues because they took the time to call us after reading about something we had done; we've met other important colleagues because we called when we read about them.

Take electronic coffee breaks. The proliferation of on-line services, E-mail, and the World Wide Web makes being tuned in and staying in touch easier and faster than ever before. It's as easy as using your computer to reach out and be in touch with other people who work from home, not only all over the United States and Canada but even in Europe, Asia, and

South America. On-line services, such as America Online, create a host of networking and socializing opportunities that you can plug in to any time of the day or night. On-line users' groups, chat rooms, and discussion groups organized around common business or personal interests are always lively, sometimes even informative places to go when taking a break.

Visitors to the Working from Home Forum we started in 1983 on CompuServe have used this resource to ask home-based people all over the country for all sorts of information—marketing advice, tax tips, how to work at home with small children, if a certain business is right for them. People on the Forum have made friends, made enemies, established strategic partnerships, or sometimes just quietly looked on; in short, developed a community. While we're no longer overseeing the Working from Home Forum on CompuServe, we host on-line discussions and resources on our Web site, *www.paulandsarah.com,* on the Alternative Career site in Jim Gonyea Career Center on AOL, and on Intuit's *www.quicken.com*

What you'll discover on line is a shrewd realism that's based on the experiences of people who are making it on their own each and every day, solving problems like getting health insurance or merchant accounts from MasterCard and Visa or coming up with ideas for projecting a professional image. Expertise in countless areas is only moments away. Just how specialized the help can be is illustrated by one request we feared might go unanswered. Someone had left a message asking about how he could get information for a client on Percheron horses. But within hours, an answer awaited him. Every day people reach out to share their moments of joy as well. Be it celebrating the birth of a child or closing a big contract, those in need receive support that would do any businessperson proud.

To find on-line resources and communities in which you can participate, start by pursuing your current business and personal interests. Most major trade, business, and lifestyle magazines have their own Web sites where they offer chat rooms and discussion groups. The working-from-home, entrepreneurial, and small-business worlds all offer a host of Web sites with on-line communications possibilities. We've listed a few of these in the Resources section at the end of this chapter. You'll find others among the Hot Links on our Web site. Most major search engines, such as Yahoo (*www.yahoo.com*), Excite (*www.excite.com*), and Lycos (*www.lycos.com*) offer their own forums, discussion groups, and chat rooms, as well as providing a good starting point for finding additional resources on the World Wide Web.

Schedule breakfast, lunch, or dinner meetings with peers. Even though this may mean breaking up your workday, set a goal to meet regularly with peers with whom you want to stay in touch. These business meetings may be partially tax deductible. To personalize the meal and save money, you may want to host your colleagues at home.

Invite others to visit your home office and arrange to visit their offices. You can invite colleagues over to see a new piece of equipment, to sit in on some work, or to talk over a new idea. Rather than fearing competition by sharing with people in your own field, consider the experience of a group of Pasadena, California, housewives who came together to support one another becoming writers when their children left home. Over a period of twenty years, their weekly Tuesday lunches, in which they critique one another's manuscripts and talk over story ideas and the ins and outs of publishing, have enabled them to produce hundreds of published books for children, juveniles, and young adults.

Join or set up a networking group to meet with on a regular basis. *Networking* is a widely used term referring to the informal or formal relationships that develop among people through which they make contacts and get information, referrals, leads, and various other forms of support. Certainly much "networking" gets done through professional, trade, and civic organizations, but as this concept has grown in popularity, groups are forming all across the country for the sole and exclusive purpose of networking.

Networking groups come together as study groups, "leads" clubs where you trade referrals and business contacts, or support groups where you can share horror and success stories and get moral support. In talking with people who are working successfully on their own from home, we have found that invariably they have joined or created some type of networking group for themselves.

Today there are a number of formal networking groups with chapters throughout the United States. These groups are primarily "leads" clubs, in that their primary goal is to do business with one another and provide mutual referrals. Normally these groups meet once a week, early in the morning so as not to interfere with the workday. They are composed of only one member from any one type of business (one desktop publisher, one chiropractor, one bookkeeper, etc.), so there is no internal competition. Another type of networking organization you can find in many communities is women's referral services, which are networks of women business owners who meet regularly to support and refer business to one another.

The Resources section at the end of this chapter lists several formal networking organizations. If none of these organizations has a chapter in your community, you may be able to set one up.

Alternatively many people form a more informal support group of their own. Author and publisher Peggy Glenn tells the interesting tale of how she created a network for herself when she began her first home business, a secretarial service:

True Confessions: Starting Your Own Support Group

"Although I wanted to work by myself, when I began my secretarial service at home," Peggy Glenn told us, "I did run up against feeling isolated. There was nobody to turn to when I was having a really bad day, nobody to say, 'Come on, let's go have some coffee.' I was two weeks into my business and one of my customers sent me roses! Who was I going to tell? My husband was at work. My kids were at school. None of my neighbors were home. There was nobody to talk to.

"So I got brave and called a few other people who also ran similar office-support businesses at home and invited them to lunch, dutch treat. Six or seven of them came, and right then and there was the birth of what has become a great network.

"We support one another. We help with overload. There is somebody to call on a bad day, somebody to call on a good day, somebody you can learn from if you've just received a job that is something you've never done, somebody to refer others to if you don't want to take the job."

When we moved to the Los Angeles area and first set up our home business, we felt isolated in such a large metropolis. But we felt certain there were lots of interesting people nearby, whom for some reason we weren't getting to know. So we decided to start a Friday night Community Network. Every second Friday Night of the month we hosted an open-house potluck dinner. We invited everyone we met whom we thought we'd like to know better—our neighbors, our suppliers, and so forth. We asked them to come, bring a dish and a drink—and their friends.

It worked! Each month about twenty people came to eat and talk. Midway through the evening, we had people introduce themselves, explain what they did, and the type of contacts they wanted to make.

Through this network, we made both business contacts and new friendships with people who work at home. We met a potter, a cartoonist, a word processor, a manufacturer of silk hats, a typesetter, and many more. The people who came also made valuable contacts and friendships. Realizing how much they miss the stimulation of working in a clinic, for example, several health practitioners who work alone at home met at one of our meetings and formed HealthNet, a network for health professionals in private practice.

In a similar vein, Sarah has long had what she calls a "peer mentor" group, a very small group of personal friends who are self-employed with whom she meets every other week for mutual moral support. They provide one another with the kind of interaction an employed person might get from having lunch with co-workers and the kind of advice and counsel an employee might get from a valued mentor. Mobile, Alabama, notary Mary Malloy has formed such a group for herself. She calls her group of peers a "spirit team." Home-business consultant Katrina Newby organized what she calls a "brainstorm" group.

Affiliate or form other joint business relationships. Drawing on the contacts you make, set up joint projects with people in your field. Think of ways you can collaborate with them. Do a program together. Write an article. Share the workload.

Two human resource development consultants we know, for example, have an interest in future trends in their field, so they've developed a program they offer several times a year at professional conferences. They've also written joint articles for professional journals on future trends.

We've known several artists who regularly share a booth at art fairs. Two other home-based entrepreneurs, Michelle Whitman of High Tech Humor and Debbie Grosshandler of Bit's and P.C.'s, were able to launch their businesses by jointly renting a booth at an important trade show. These joint ventures not only keep costs down but also provide some much needed moral support and involvement with others for those who are working alone.

Formal partnerships can provide similar benefits. Many husbands and wives, such as ourselves, find that working at home together prevents them from having problems with isolation. Sue Rugge, founder of Information on Demand, credits an early partnership with Georgia Finnigan for the initial success of her business. "Although I enjoyed being president and hundred-percent owner of my company, I doubt if I ever would have made it if I hadn't started as a partnership."

Programmer Lucy Ewell and psychologist Elizabeth Scott came together to do what they couldn't have done alone and started a software firm to develop computer games for girls. Barbara Elman began her word-processing service with a partner. She says of her initial partner, "He gave me the idea and the confidence that I could do it."

In many ways, a business partnership is like a marriage. You may spend more time with a partner than you do with your spouse. Unfortunately, the divorce rate among partners is even higher than among married couples. So pick a business partner with the same care you would take to pick a mate.

Short of a full-fledged partnership is the buddy system, or what Carol Hyatt calls a "planned partnership," in which you and your informal partner agree to meet at least once a week to help each other achieve your goals. In her book *The Woman's Selling Game,* Hyatt describes how the buddy system can work:

> The partner you select can be a friend or not, and preferably should come from the same area of expertise as yours so you can understand each other's problems and provide useful mutual assistance. He or she should be someone whose judgment you respect and who respects yours, so there will be productive interplay. The two of you should contract to meet formally and at regular intervals.

Your first meeting may be to define your goals and discuss their reality, with subsequent meetings devoted to reviewing your progress toward these goals. When you miss the fact that you've strayed from your purpose, been vague about strategy or laissez faire about precious time, it's your partner's job to spot what's happening and give you the feedback and constructive advice by which you can work through what you want. You, of course, will do the same in return.

Although planning and participating in such activities does cost valuable time and money, they are worthwhile investments in yourself and your work. Besides preventing the problems of burnout and isolation, they keep you fresh and competitive within today's ever-changing marketplace.

MAKING NEW CONTACTS

Establishing relationships, meeting people in a crowd, approaching business contacts you've never met before—these are all important skills for people working on their own.

Networking to make contact quickly and easily with people you don't know involves more than the customary "Hello-how-are-you?" handshake and exchange of business cards. Whether you're meeting people at a cocktail party or through a computer terminal, networking involves making contact with them in ways that enable you to assist one another in achieving your goals.

Here are several tips for becoming a master networker.

Step into the role of host. Adele Scheele, author of *Skills for Success,* suggests that successful networkers approach life as a "host" instead of as a "guest." Guests wait to be introduced. They feel ill at ease until someone makes them feel welcome. Hosts, on the other hand, assume responsibility for making sure everyone knows who everyone else is and for helping people feel welcome and at ease.

Tell everyone you meet who you are, what you're doing, and what you want to do. As consultant William Slavin has discovered, "I never know who my next client might be, so I treat everyone as a prospective client." Likewise, you never know who might be a future resource, friend, or colleague.

Make yourself and what you are seeking clear. Too frequently people introduce themselves like this: *"Hello, I'm Ralph Carnes. I'm the senior technical writer. My company is MicroProductions."*

After hearing this kind of introduction, do you know enough about what Ralph does to engage in a conversation? Do you have any idea how you might be able to work with him? It's easy to spend a whole evening introducing yourself this way and wondering why you aren't making any valuable contacts.

How about if Ralph introduced himself this way:

"Hello, I'm Ralph Carnes. You know how difficult it can be to get up and running with a new piece of software? Well, I write on-line instructions for software companies so people buying their software can feel like they have a computer consultant right there in the office with them to help them get up and running with their new software."

This type of introduction helps people know whether you share common interests and whether you can be of help to one another. Introducing yourself this way is a matter of putting together two things: a common problem most people can relate to and what you do to solve that problem. We call this kind of introduction a File Opening Soundbyte because it enables people to open a mental file folder for you and your business. You can find more about how to develop an effective soundbyte for yourself in our book *Getting Business to Come to You*.

Be interested in other people. The more interested you are in someone else, the more interesting you will seem. By finding out about other people, and their finding out about you, you will know how you could be valuable contacts for one another.

Offer to give people the very thing you want. If you're looking for someone to help with your office overload on occasion, offer to provide backup for them. If you're seeking someone to share a booth with you, offer to share one with those you meet.

Plan a follow-up meeting with people you want to know better. When you discover others who share a mutual interest, exchange business cards. Write notes on the backs of their cards about where you met them and what your joint interests are. Don't wait for them to contact you. Make a follow-up call or send an E-mail message proposing that you get together in person to find out more about what they do.

In summary, staying in touch with others is as important to people working from home as it is for the regular office worker. At the office, it takes relatively little time and energy. For those of us who work at home, however, it's something we have to plan for and work at throughout our careers. Yes, it does take concentrated effort to stay in contact, but there are ways to do it. You just have to use them.

RESOURCES

Books

Communicate with Confidence!: How to Say It Right the First Time and Every Time. Dianna Daniels Booher. New York: McGraw-Hill, 1994. ISBN: 0070064555.

Getting Business to Come to You: A Complete Guide to Attracting All the Business You Can Enjoy. Paul and Sarah Edwards. New York: Tarcher/Putnam, 1998. ISBN: 087477845X.

Power Schmoozing, The New Rules for Business and Social Success. Terri Mandell. New York: MacGraw-Hill, 1996. ISBN: 0070398879.

7-Second Marketing : How to Use Memory Hooks to Make You Instantly Stand Out in a Crowd. Ivan R. Misner. Austin, Tex.: Bard Press, 1996. ISBN: 1885167156.

Skills for Success: A Guide to the Top for Men and Women. Adele M. Scheele. New York: Ballantine, 1996. ISBN: 0345410440.

The World's Best Known Marketing Secret. Ivan R. Misner. Austin, Tex.: Bard Productions, 1994. ISBN: 1885167059.

Networking Groups

Business Network International. 199 South Monte Vista, Suite 6, San Dimas, CA 91773; phone: (909) 305-1818. Web: *www.bni.com*

LEADS. P.O. Box 279, Carlsbad, CA 92018; phone: (760) 434-3761, (800) 783-3761. Web: *www.leadsclub.com*

LeTip, International, 4901 Morena Boulevard, Suite 703, San Diego, CA 92117; phone: (800) 255-3847. Web: *www.letip.org*

National Association of Women Business Owners. 1100 Wayne Avenue, Ste. 830, Silver Spring, MD 20910; phone: (301) 608-2590. Web: *www. nawbo.org*

Directory

Encyclopedia of Associations. Detroit: Gale Research Company (see full citation in chapter 3).

Sources of Audiotape Programs

Nightingale Conant Audiocassette Library. The Human Resources Company, 7300 N. Lehigh Avenue, Chicago, IL 60648; phone (800) 323-5552. Call or write for a catalog.

Personal Progress Library. A membership club that enables members to rent and return a wide selection of business and personal-development tapes. 7657 Winnetta #331, Winnetta, CA 91306; phone: (818) 700-0817. Web: *www.successnetonline.com/clients/ppl/pplib.html*

Success Motivation® Institute, Inc. 5000 Lakewood Dr., Waco, TX 76710; phone: (254) 776-1230, (800) 678-6101. Web: *www.success-motivation.com/freetape.html*

ON-LINE RESOURCES

Access Business Online. A business information meta site that offers a number of different chat and discussion areas. *www.clickit.com/touch/home.html*

America Online. Now the biggest on-line service, America Online provides literally hundreds of ways to socialize and talk business on the Internet. You must be a paying member. *www.aol.com*

International Small Business Consortium. On-line information-sharing and discussion groups on a wide variety of business topics. *www.isbc.com*

Newsgroups. Newsgroups predate the World Wide Web on the Internet. With newsgroup reader software and a connection to the Internet, newsgroups provide thousands of specialty areas where people exchange ideas, information, and opinions. One tool for accessing the newsgroups quickly is the Dejanews Web site: *www.dejanews.com*

paulandsarah.com The place to be . . . on your own, but not alone. Daily information, inspiration, and support including chats, Q&A, and people you should know. *www.paulandsarah.com*

Quicken.com. A host of business and financial information and resources, including bulletin boards and round-table dicussions. *www.quicken.com*

Womenbiz. "Education, technology, marketing, events, profiles as well as information to all women to guide their strategies and business philosophies for success." *www.womenbiz.net*

Working from Home Forum on CompuServe Information Service, 5000 Arlington Centre Boulevard, P.O. Box 20212, Columbus, OH 43220. *www.compuserve.com*

CHAPTER 18

Staying Out of the Refrigerator and Away from Other Temptations

---

Goals

1. Pinpoint your bad work habits when working at home.

2. Avoid excesses and overindulging.

3. Break bad habits and create new ones.

4. Find positive ways to reward yourself.

At first, working at home can seem like Paradise Island. Life's greatest pleasures are at your fingertips. You can literally eat, drink, and be merry at will. Your refrigerator and kitchen cabinets are only steps away. Cocktails are there for your making. The bed is there for your taking. You have the freedom to sleep 'til noon, eat your favorite foods whenever you're hungry, have sex in the afternoon, share a beer with a neighbor at a moment's notice, or watch a favorite midday TV show.

Like tourists on a holiday, many people working from home start out living it up, indulging in whatever they want to do, but by the end of a few weeks, they realize that if they don't get down to work, they won't have any work. Then they begin to set up routines, time schedules, and effective boundaries to keep their pleasures in bounds.

Sometimes, however, without the structure of a separate office, even experienced open-collar workers indulge to excess. According to them, the enjoyable fantasy of sipping wine and munching culinary delights while working by the pool can become the ugly reality of unwanted pounds and foggy-headed afternoons. In fact, one question we're sometimes asked is

"How do you stay out of the refrigerator?" Some people do find this a problem, and when they do, we hear complaints like these:

"I've gained thirty pounds in the six months I've been working at home."

"When I have to work late into the night to get a big order out, I can eat two bags of potato chips without even knowing it."

"I'm having my 'afternoon' drink earlier and earlier in the day."

"A beer with lunch can become a six-pack by dinner."

"Our last baby wasn't planned. She came along about nine months after I began working at home."

In this chapter we will talk about what happens when excesses get out of control and what you can do to prevent such a situation. We will not talk, however, about chronic eating disorders or drug, sex, or alcohol addiction. Conceivably someone could engage in and conceal a serious addiction more easily at home, but any such problems are beyond the scope of this chapter and must be solved by seeking professional help.

> *Thirty-six percent of Americans who work from home or run a home-based business report that they eat more. Thirty-two percent say they gained weight, 51 percent indicate that their weight remained the same.*
> INCOME OPPORTUNITIES MAGAZINE

AVOIDING EXCESSES

Whether it's smoking, eating, sleeping, drinking, sex, or watching TV, overindulgence is generally related to the stress of having too much or too little happening in one's life. People overindulge most often when they are pressured, overworked, anxious, bored, don't like what they are doing, or are in dire need of contact with other people.

There's medical evidence, for example, that shows that eating causes the brain to release substances called endorphins, some of which actually relax the mind and body. Also, psychologists have found that repetitive, nonpurposeful activity like chain-smoking, finger tapping, drinking, and chewing fingernails, gum, food, or rubber bands helps discharge pent-up frustration and discomfort. So chances are that frequent trips to the refrigerator, munching away on snack food, or reaching for a drink begins as a way to make you feel better and help you get through the day.

Once someone begins to rely on a particular indulgence to deal with stress, what follows makes it difficult to stop. First, the eating, drinking, smoking, or whatever you're doing to excess becomes a habit. You end up doing it automatically, reaching for a cigarette or candy bar without even thinking about it, raiding the refrigerator without having made a conscious decision to stroll into the kitchen.

To further complicate the situation, many activities like smoking, drinking alcohol, taking drugs, and eating salty or sugary food produce a chemical reaction in your body that causes you to crave more. So as you indulge to excess, your body begins to demand greater amounts of what you're indulging in. Then instead of feeling better, you start to feel as if you "can't go on without it."

These factors combine to make breaking out of habitual excesses a challenging task. For this reason, the easiest way to avoid problems with excesses is to prevent them from happening in the first place, or to catch the problem as early as possible.

Checklist: The Top-Ten Bad Habits

These are the top-ten bad habits people who work from home can unexpectedly fall into. Have you developed any of them? Are there any you might take up if you don't watch out?

____ 1. Snacking

____ 2. Sleeping late

____ 3. Procrastinating

____ 4. Talking on the phone

____ 5. Watching TV

____ 6. Getting sloppy; staying in nightclothes all day

____ 7. Taking too long to read the newspaper

____ 8. Drinking alcohol while working

____ 9. Spending too much time visiting neighbors

____ 10. Working too much

Life Savers: Awareness Is the First Step

Take notice right away when you start to exceed a normal or familiar pattern. Most people do notice the difference. "I'm snacking more." "I'm having my after-work drink earlier in the day." "I've eaten a whole bag of potato chips! I don't usually do that."

Life Savers: Act Immediately

Before divergences from your regular pattern develop into a new habit, take steps to deal with the situation. Recognize what you have too much or too little of in your life that is causing stress, and find a different way to handle it. Here is how people working at home have managed to avoid the stressful situations that lead to excesses.

SIX STEPS TO AVOID OVERINDULGING
WHILE WORKING

Step One: Work at a relaxed and reasonable pace. The best protection against raiding the refrigerator or grabbing another drink is to take good care of yourself. Don't overwork. Take breaks. Learn to relax.

Barbara Bickford, for example, found that "the only way I could be sure I wouldn't turn to the junk-food snacks every night was to put an end to working all day and into the night. By taking on so much business that I had to work late, I was really abusing myself. Occasionally, yes, it's okay. But I was doing it as a matter of course. Eating was my way of buying myself off so I wouldn't complain about letting my work consume me."

Don't let your home office become as stressful a place to be as the worst of traditional offices. Take advantage of the fact that you have more flexibility about when and how you work. Use the time you would have spent commuting to relax in some way. Structure your day to keep the pressures from building up. It can be good for your health. Take the case of nationally known speaker and seminar leader Lee Shapiro, known as "The Hugging Judge," for example. When he went "from the courtroom to the living room," he found that his blood pressure went down.

Step Two: Develop "positive" addictions. Psychologist William Glasser coined this term to refer to activities like jogging, golfing, swimming, and knitting, which people enjoy and find helpful in handling everyday stress. Glasser found that people who regularly engage in such activities actually feel as though they are "addicted" to them. They miss the activity when something interferes with doing it. They crave it and feel depressed and out of sorts when they're deprived of it. Unlike an addiction such as smoking, drinking, overeating, or taking drugs, however, these activities actually improve your health.

Engineering consultant Jeff Knoghton found himself drinking more when he first started working at home. "I was used to having a drink to unwind when I got home from work. Once I was at home all day, whenever I felt pressure building up, I'd grab a can of beer. Then I started jogging for twenty minutes every morning. I heard it helped you become less tense." If it's a really bad day, he runs again in the early evening. "It just relaxes me, keeps me loose. It's better than beer, because it clears my mind rather than fuzzing it up."

Step Three: Be sure you have enough contact with people you enjoy. An office with other people provides stimulation, company, and people to share problems with. Working at home can be lonely at first. But the loneliness doesn't have to lead to overindulgence. Instead of heading for the kitchen, reaching for another drink, or turning on the tube, you can head for the telephone. Call someone or log on to the Net. Go visit a neighbor. Invite someone to come over. However busy you are, make time in your workday for some kind of interpersonal contact.

Step Four: *Treat yourself to something positive each day.* Plan something you can look forward to as a refresher after work, or once or twice during the day. Here's a list of treats we and others have developed. Build your own list.

Treats Instead of Sweets: Positive Ways to Reward Yourself

- Go outside. Walk through your neighborhood or visit your favorite outdoor spot. Notice the grass, trees, wind, sun, clouds, the sounds of birds, barking dogs, and children playing, the faces of strangers and friends.

- Buy yourself some flowers or pick a bouquet from your own garden.

- Take a stimulating shower or a relaxing bath, go to the spa or sauna, soak in a candlelight milk bath with music playing in the background.

- Do something handy around the house. Fix what's broken, build something new, work in the garden.

- Buy yourself a present, something you might not otherwise purchase for yourself but wish someone else would.

- Have a party.

- Enjoy your favorite sport. Take time out for a game of tennis, badminton, golf, or handball, or join a softball or bowling team.

- Curl up in your favorite spot and read an enthralling book or a magazine of your choice.

- Keep a journal in which you write down your thoughts, your feelings, and your goals; make a list of your accomplishments, describe what you've discovered about yourself and your work.

- Serve your favorite meal on your best dishes and invite someone special to join you.

- Take a class you've always wanted to take: photography, modern art, yoga, programming.

- Sit in the sun. Take a nap.

(Continued on page 504)

(Continued from page 503)

- Make a change in your day-to-day life. Rearrange the furniture, get a new hairstyle, go on a vacation.

- Do something childishly carefree. Romp with the dog, turn a cartwheel, buy a balloon, play a video game.

- Log into a chat room, and talk to the world through your fingertips.

- Go to a funny or suspenseful movie, take in a concert, a play, a ball game, a museum, the zoo.

Step Five: If you want to snack, set some guidelines. Deepak Chopra, physician and author of the book *Ageless Body, Timeless Mind,* suggests several such guidelines. He advises eating only if you're actually hungry. Sometimes the urge for a snack is actually a desire for something else, such as taking a break, getting a drink of water, or doing something different. If you are actually hungry, he proposes that you stop whatever else you are doing, sit down away from work with your food, take a moment of silence before you eat, and then eat with the intention of enjoyment.

Psychologist Dr. Nancy Bonus, founder of the Bonus Plan, has developed a nondiet weight-loss program that distinguishes between physical hunger and habit or emotional hunger and suggests eating only when your body actually needs fuel. She also advises eating exactly what you want to eat and enjoying it fully by taking very small bites, chewing them thoroughly, savoring the flavor, and pausing between bites. Then she recommends that as soon as you feel slightly full, stop eating immediately and return to work feeling completely satisfied.

Step Six: Keep whatever you want to avoid as far away from your office as possible. Data entry clerk Helen Willis told us, "I don't keep salty or sugary snacks in the house anymore because they just make me want to eat more. So I have lots of nuts and bananas and dried fruit around now. They're much more satisfying."

This is one of the pluses of working from home. Unlike office vending machines, your kitchen cabinets can be filled with whatever you choose. Here are a few more "out of sight, out of mind" tricks people who work at home use to keep themselves from overindulging:

"To avoid walking in and out of the kitchen all day for a cup of coffee, where I invariably grab a cookie to eat along with it, I've set up a coffeemaker in my office. I keep all the supplies—the cups, even the bottled water—on a small cabinet in the office closet."

"I close the kitchen door and think of it as a restaurant. It's only open between noon and one and after five o'clock."

"I don't allow smoking in my house. That way I have to take a break and go outside to smoke. This keeps my habit under control."

"We set up a little icebox and hot plate in the office, which is behind the garage. We 'bring' our lunch to work every day and usually don't go into the house while we're working."

"I work at the computer most of the day. I put the computer on a stand that doesn't have enough space to set down coffee cups, glasses, or food. To eat or drink anything, I have to get up and go somewhere else."

Guidelines for Snacking

1. Don't snack mindlessly. Snack consciously and only when hungry.

2. Take a break from whatever else you are doing. Go somewhere other than your office.

3. Select exactly the food you want to eat when you snack.

4. Sit down with your food and spend a moment silently relaxing before eating.

5. Eat with the intention of enjoyment.

6. Take small bites. Chew your food thoroughly. Savor the flavor. Pause between bites.

7. Stop eating when you feel slightly full and satisfied.

BREAKING OLD HABITS
AND CREATING NEW ONES

What do you do if you've already developed a bad habit? And what if it's a habit you've had for a long time? Again, awareness is the first step, and then comes corrective action. You must find another way to deal with the circumstances that led you to develop the habit in the first place, different ways of handling the stresses of your work. Then you have to replace your old habit with a new one. Here are five suggestions for breaking undesirable habits:

1. Anticipate when you are likely to indulge in your habit. Know the actions leading up to an occurrence. Do you snack or smoke at particular times of the day or in conjunction with particular activities?

2. *Create a new and competing habit to take the place of the old one*. For example, if you have a habit of going to the kitchen for a snack between projects or clients, establish a new habit by making phone calls or taking a walk instead.

3. *Interrupt the sequence of the habit or disrupt its pattern*. If you are used to smoking while you sit at your desk talking on the phone, for example, stand up while you talk on the phone. Clear away all the ashtrays. Keep your cigarettes away in another room, so you'll have to go through several involved steps to get to them.

4. *Set up cues or "anchors" that help you remember to change your habit*. Put a "No Eating Between Meals" sign on your refrigerator. Set the alarm for scheduled snack breaks.

5. *Think about how terrific you'll feel when you no longer have this habit*. Begin imagining yourself as a person without such a habit. Think of yourself as a nonsmoker, for example, or as someone who doesn't snack.

ENDING ADDICTIONS AND COMPULSIONS

If you have a particularly stubborn habit of overindulging, you may be suffering from an addiction or a compulsion—you feel enslaved. Recent findings from the emerging field of psychoneuralimmunology suggest that addictions (whether physical or mental, acquired or inherited) are the result of a fundamental distortion in the biological system. This research indicates that these distortions can be corrected by using your mind and your environment to return yourself to a natural state of health.

You'll find a variety of books and programs available to help you apply the methods from this new field cited in the Resources list that follows.

RESOURCES

BOOKS

Ageless Body, Timeless Mind. Deepak Chopra. New York: Crown, 1995. ISBN: 0517882124.

Beyond the Relaxation Response: How to Harness the Healing Power of Your Personal Beliefs. Dr. Herbert Benson and William Proctor. New York: Berkley, 1994. ISBN: 0425081834.

Boundaries Workbook: When to Say Yes, When to Say No to Take Control of Your Life. Henry Cloud and John Townsend. Grand Rapids, Mich.: Zondervan, 1995. ISBN: 0310494818.

Changes That Heal: How to Understand Your Past to Ensure a Healthier Future. Henry Cloud. Grand Rapids, Mich.: Zondervan, 1993. ISBN: 0310606314.

8 Steps to a Healthy Heart. Robert Kowalski. New York: Warner, 1994. ISBN: 0446394580.

Learned Optimism. Martin Seligman. New York: Pocket, 1998. ISBN: 0671019112.

SELF-STUDY PROGRAMS

Beyond Dieting: Non-Diet Weight Loss Home Study Course. A video, audio, and workbook program from Dr. Nancy Bonus. The Bonus Plan, Naturally Thin, P.O. Box 505, Chatham, NJ 07928; phone: (800) 760-5490.

Sante (for Your Health). An all-in-one weight-control, diet-planning, and exercise software program including recipes. Hopkins Technology, 421 Hazel Lane, Hopkins, MN 55343; phone: (612) 931-9376, (800) 397-9211. Web: *www.hoptechno.com*

SELF-HELP ORGANIZATIONS

Alcoholics Anonymous. P.O. Box 459, New York, NY 10163; phone: (212) 870-3400. Web: *www.aa.org*

Gamblers Anonymous. P.O. Box 17173, Los Angeles, CA 90017; phone: (213) 386-8789. Web: *www.gamblersanonymous.org*

Narcotics Anonymous. P.O. Box 9999, Van Nuys, CA 91409; phone: (818) 773-9999. Web: *www.na.org*

Overeaters Anonymous. P.O. Box 44020, Rio Rancho, NM 87174; phone: (505) 891-2664. Web: *www.overeatersanonymous.org*

SmokEnders. 666 11th St. NW, Suite 200, Washington, DC 20001; phone: (800) 828-HELP. Web: *www.smokenders.com*

TAPES

Alan Watts Teaches Meditation. Alan W. Watts. Audio Renaissance, 1992. ISBN: 1559272139.

The Art of Meditation: Creating Inner Peace. Jonathan Faust. Kripalu; (800) 967-7279.

Healing Meditation Cassette: Nourish Mind, Body and Spirit. Howell. Brain Sync Corp. ISBN: 1881451259.

Meditations for Overcoming Depression. Joan Borysenko. Hay House. ISBN: 1561701254. (800) 654-5126.

Morning and Evening Meditations. Louise Hay. Hay House. ISBN: 0937611042. (800) 654-5126.

CLASSES

Transcendental meditation. Classes available in many states. Call (888) 532-7686 for classes near you. Web: *www.tm.org*

Staying in Love and Saving Your Relationship

<table>
<tr><td>

Goals

1. *Avoid problems and prevent conflicts.*

2. *Prepare for changes in household routines.*

3. *Take a win/win approach that problems are solvable.*

4. *Build good communications skills.*

5. *Put love first.*

</td>
<td>

How do I know that if I start working at home I won't end up getting divorced?"

"I'd like to work at home, but how do you two stand being around each other so much?"

"What happened to your relationship when you started working at home? Was there an adjustment period? Did you fight all the time?"

Hundreds of people have asked us questions like these after speeches or at seminar breaks. We answer that when you're married, working from home is like

</td></tr>
</table>

opening a birthday present. It may be just what you wanted or it may not suit you.

Our files are filled with stories of couples who, like us, discovered that the best part of working from home is the extra time they have to be together. It's hard to build a relationship on weekends and in the few hours that remain when people get home from an exhausting day at the office. At the very least, working from home gives couples a better chance of building a good life together. Occasionally, however, it doesn't work; instead of things getting better, they go downhill.

For better or worse, you can count on undergoing some changes in your life and your relationship when you begin working from home. And, as with any change, there will usually be a period of adjustment. The question is how the adjustments will affect your relationship. We agree with Peggy Glenn, who had a new husband and three kids when she quit her job to start a home typing service: "If a person decides to work at home to salvage a dead marriage or revive a dying one, I think it will kill the marriage altogether. But if the relationship is strong and there is trust between the husband and wife, then they'll get through the change. Working from home will strengthen the relationship."

In this chapter we'll share the principles that we and other couples have found for staying in love when you work from home. Although there are many differences in how couples go about it, there do seem to be several key ingredients.

First, it's important to get off to the right start. It then helps to be prepared for the inevitable adjustments you must make, to realize they are normal, and to know some positive steps you can take to resolve the conflicts that arise. Finally, it's important to recognize the early warning signs of trouble and know what you can do when things aren't getting better.

GETTING OFF TO THE RIGHT START

Couples begin working from home for many different reasons. Sometimes it's by choice; sometimes it isn't. It may be opportunity, or it may be a necessity. Whatever the situation, you'll get off to a better start if you both agree that the best course of action is to work at home.

It's virtually impossible to work happily at home without the cooperation and support of your spouse, so a joint decision will most certainly work better than issuing an edict or even simply making an announcement that you've decided to work at home. Even if you already have an office at home, it's not too late to sit down and talk about whether it's working out.

Be honest about how you feel about using your home as an office and encourage your spouse to be honest too. Discuss your concerns openly. If you're worried that your spouse will never leave the office, say so. If you're concerned that the children will be neglected, say so. The potential problems you identify can help you develop a practical plan to guard against them.

Take each concern seriously and get the facts about it. Think of possible solutions and develop a plan for how to avoid potential problems. Test out your solutions. See if they work. Revise them when they don't work to your or your mate's satisfaction.

One woman told us she felt silly bringing up her real concern. She was afraid that if her husband worked at home, the house would always be a mess and she would become a servant cleaning up after him. Fortunately, she did talk it over with him and they decided to hire a cleaning service.

It's ignoring "silly" concerns like these that get us into the worst problems. Ignoring just such a problem precipitated one of the few marital casualties we know of. The wife who worked in an outside office couldn't stand coming home every day to a messy house. She'd tidy it up in the morning, and when she got home, exhausted from a day's work, she'd find another mess awaiting her. Failing to resolve this incompatibility ultimately contributed to their divorce.

So when your spouse brings up an objection, thank him or her on the spot for sharing it with you. That's just one more problem you can avoid. Once the objection has come up, you can start talking about the facts of the situation and work out various plans for ensuring it won't be a difficulty.

Avoid the temptation to discount the concern by saying "Oh, that won't be a problem. You don't have to worry about that." Even if it seems as though there would be no problem with a particular concern, explain your reasoning. Describe in detail why it won't be a difficulty; even create hypothetical situations to show that indeed there is no need for concern. You may discover something you overlooked.

 True Confessions

A radio announcer we talked with didn't think he'd mind having his mother use his office as a guest room when she came to stay on weekends. His wife wasn't sure. "Since she didn't think it would work, I decided to test it out. Although I wasn't yet working full-time at home, one weekend when my mother came up I had just put my equipment and a number of important files in my home office—that is, the guest room. My wife was right. We had to figure out some other solution before it would work for me to move everything home. Even though it required some construction, we decided to set up a basement studio for my office."

Specific Steps to a Smooth Transition

- Make the decision to work at home a joint one.

- Express your reasons for wanting to work at home.

- Discuss your concerns openly and encourage your spouse to do so as well.

- Thank your spouse for each concern he or she brings up.

- Respond honestly to each other's concerns.

ADJUSTING TO THREE INEVITABLE CHANGES

The inevitable changes that take place when you start working from home can strain your relationship. These changes don't have to become painful, however. The initial stress can be a sign of new and better things to come. But you must be alert and responsive to difficulties that arise while they are still manageable.

Here are some of the healthy reactions a couple can expect. They don't always feel good, but they are a normal part of the process of changing your lifestyle.

Change #1: New Identities

The decision to work at home is almost always part of a larger decision to change your life, which changes your identity. People who begin working at home are at turning points in their lives.

Assuming a new identity is a major adjustment in itself. Add working from home and the many accompanying changes in daily routine and you can begin to see why people going through so many adjustments may not be easy to live with. You can understand why they may be unsure of themselves, edgy, worried, or struggling to put up a good front.

Even when spouses want to be supportive, and actually think they are helping, they may not welcome all aspects of their mate's new identity. One woman, whose husband quit his job to become a professional performer, described the experience this way: "I didn't marry an entertainer. I married a lawyer. I don't know him anymore. He's a different person."

She wasn't so sure she liked this new person. She also wasn't totally sure who she was now, either. Among other roles in life, she had been a lawyer's wife. Now she was supposed to be an entertainer's wife. "He expects me to come to late-night shows and sit with a lot of other entertainers and their wives while he performs. I'm not sure this is something I want to do."

When she started her typing service, Peggy Glenn's identity changed from being someone's secretary in a nine-to-five job to being an entrepreneur and businesswoman. "It was very, very difficult for my husband. Not only was he unsure about the money I would make in this new business—and we needed the money from my work—he was also unsure about this new change in me. All of a sudden I was someone who was in demand by other people. My customers knew him as 'Peggy's husband.' That was kind of hard on his ego."

Change #2: Duties and Responsibilities

Working from home usually means changes in household routines. Arguments and conflicts can arise over day-to-day arrangements about:

Housecleaning. Living and working at home twenty-four hours a day means more mess and more wear and tear. Who does the extra work to keep the house in order? When does it have to be cleaned up or repaired? Do children now have to be neater because customers are coming to the house? If so, who gets the children to clean up? If the packaging department of your business is on the dining room table, how long can it stay like that, and who puts everything away—the person who made the mess or the person who wants it cleaned up?

Meals. Working at home usually means at least one extra meal there. So you need to discuss who plans it, who buys it, who fixes it, who cleans up after it. If you have been fixing the meals, for example, will you still have time to fix them all, or to fix the same kinds of meals now that you're working at home?

Space. Working at home can place certain limitations on what your family can do there or even on other things you want to do. If your family room is now your office, where does everyone go to relax? Can they have company while you are working? Can your spouse walk around the house in a bathing suit during business hours? You'll need to consider issues like whether your family can play the stereo or talk on the phone whenever they want, or if such activity infringes on your office space.

Children. Children need a lot of attention. They can be a distraction and an interruption that makes work next to impossible. A decision has to be made about who handles them. Does the one working at home take on more of these responsibilities than before? Who keeps the children quiet or out of your office?

Time. When your office is at home, you need to determine who gets to spend time with you and when. If you're away at the office all day, you clearly can't take the kids to the park after school. And of course you can't make love before lunch. But what about now? What will you say when someone you love asks, "Couldn't you just take a minute for . . . ?"

Money. Working from home is likely to mean a change in your income. If you've quit your job to start a business, the amount of money you're bringing in could go down at first. What gets cut—theater tickets, your tennis lessons, your spouse's night class? If you've taken a second job or started a new career at home, it could mean your income will go up. In that case, who decides what the additional money is to be used for?

Change #3: New Roles

When people decide to work from home, the nature of their role in the marriage often changes. Sometimes they like and welcome the new role; sometimes the new role is thrust upon them without their consent. Let's consider some of the adjustments individuals and couples can encounter.

A husband and father moving his work home. In our society, although a woman's place is no longer necessarily at home, a man's place is still at the office. As columnist Jim Sanderson wrote, the "Image of the Stay-at-Home Kind of Man" can create some humorous but uncomfortable situations. He found that his wife's friends, the neighbors, and repair personnel who came over either thought he was ill, implied he was lazy, or believed he'd married a "rich dame."

In addition to contending with the perceptions of others, a man moving his office home often finds himself confronted with household or child-rearing responsibilities he's not used to handling. Also, he may have difficulty adjusting to working without the support services he's been accustomed to getting at the office. He may feel angry or depressed about having to do everything himself, from buying paper clips to making copies. On the other hand, he might feel grateful for the independence and new responsibilities.

A woman starting or returning to work. When a woman who has been a homemaker decides to start working from home, she will have less time for household chores. Housework, meals, laundry, and possibly even children will not get her full attention. A husband who may be supportive of his wife's new work style may still not like the inconvenience of doing things for himself that she once did for him. He may have to start packing for his business trips, preparing his own lunches, or shopping for his own shirts. He may even have to forgo some of the conveniences he's become accustomed to, like freshly ironed and folded shirts.

The homemaker-turned-open-collar-worker may also have difficulty getting family, friends, or neighbors to take her new role seriously. After all, she's still at home. Everyone may expect her somehow to do everything she has always done. In fact, polls still show that homemakers who decide to launch a career do not get much additional help with household chores. They simply add to their existing responsibilities as wives and mothers.

If the woman who begins working at home tries to keep up with everything, she can get caught in the "Superwoman syndrome," trying to be all things to all people, which is a good way to become irritable, over-stressed, burned-out, or even sick.

The homemaker. The wife who is a homemaker may feel her husband's presence is an intrusion into her domain: "I married him for better or worse, but not for lunch!" She may feel pressure to become not only a

True Confessions

When Michael Fey decided to leave his hectic downtown job and work from his suburban home, his wife decided for the first time in their marriage to work outside the home.

"With my being at home and her starting to work away from home, we had a real shift in role responsibilities. Since I was there, I found myself handling certain domestic tasks." Now, before he sits down at his desk in the morning, he finds himself doing things he never had to do before: getting the house organized, getting the kids off to school, and monitoring their squabbles.

"It's been a real education. I would say it's been an advantage. The kids have gotten to know me better. My wife is glad that part of the responsibility for child-rearing has shifted to me. It's less of a burden on her and frees her to do what she wants. She's also glad because the kids do need to get to know me now. In a couple of years they'll be grown and gone."

Although Michael hadn't expected the changes that took place after he started working at home, he says, and his wife agrees, "We're happier as a couple."

wife and mother but also a receptionist and secretary. On the other hand, she may be eager to have her husband home, thinking he can take on more responsibilities around the house and that they can spend more time together. But will he have the time to take on these new roles? If he's like most at-home workers, he may actually work more, not fewer, hours—at least at first.

Two-career couples. Wherever they work, at home or away, two-career couples face an array of challenges and strains on their relationship. When one spouse works at home and the other works away, for example, it's easy to fall into "the grass is always greener" syndrome. The spouse who works away from home may be jealous of the one who's been home all day. Those at home may seem to have more free time and less pressure. After all, they haven't had to contend with traffic or wait for the train in the rain. Those working in an outside office may even feel disappointed to find the house a mess when they get home. They're likely to wonder why, with all that time at home, their partner wasn't able to get more done.

From the other point of view, the ones who work at home may feel burdened by household interruptions and responsibilities and jealous of their partner's freedom to get out in the business world and socialize with others during the day. Those who've been working at home all day long may be itching to get out in the evening, while their partner is looking forward to getting home to rest and relax.

When both partners work at home, they may have difficulties drawing lines between their roles as workers and their roles as spouses. It's hard to tell your spouse, "No, I can't talk now, I'm in the middle of a project." It's equally hard to resist the temptation to start sharing the events of your business day when you're excited, devastated, or just eager to talk.

 True Confessions

Even when he was an executive for Xerox, Tom Drucker was attracted to the idea of working from home. When he began working from home as a self-employed management consultant, one key motivation was to spend more time with his wife. Instead of trying to play catch-up each night about the events of the day, he enjoys "sharing the day with her while it's happening."

As a writer who had worked at home alone, his wife, Marcia Seligson, also likes having Tom home while she's working. "I enjoy his company, and it breaks the solitude of writing." At first, however, they were so thrilled to have each other there that they would eagerly interrupt work to talk about what was happening.

"On the job it was easy to create a boundary around myself," Tom recalls. "I had people screen my calls. If I was interrupted I could say, in a straightforward manner, 'Don't interrupt me now.' But when my wife comes in and says she'd like me to read this letter, I'm less likely to say those things. I'm just like everyone else, I'd rather go do something I enjoy than struggle with some difficult task I'm working on."

Aware of the problem, Tom and Marcia have learned how to respect each other's work space. They've begun telling each other when they don't want to be interrupted, and Marcia finds "we're getting better at it now. We save our news for lunch breaks together."

Couples working at home are also susceptible to each other's moods. Usually your spouse is the only one there to talk with about the feelings and events of the day. When one of you is down, it may pull the other down, too. When one of you is hassled, the other may pick up the frazzled feelings. When you are angry about something that's happening with work, you may take it out on your partner and disrupt his or her work as well. Or, in order to keep peace in the house, partners may try to hide negative feelings from each other and find there is no place to let off steam.

Partners who both work at home generally feel like getting away from each other once in a while, just as translator Bill Grimes and his partner, Isabel Leonard, do. "We tend to go our separate directions on weekends and evenings. If we didn't, we'd get pretty sick of each other." Bill and Isabel's reaction is a perfectly natural feeling for any two partners. Yet sometimes mates feel guilty or hurt if their partner is the one who wants to get away.

Rules of Thumb: Resolving Conflicts

While these adjustments are normal reactions to the changes that come with working from home, they can produce conflicts that need to be resolved so both your business and your relationship can be successful. Here are a few rules of thumb we and other couples have found useful in resolving conflicts before they become ongoing problems.

Remind yourself that the conflict is temporary. It helps to remember that this is a transition period. Your life won't be like this forever. Make an effort to be understanding and patient with both yourself and your spouse while you work out the initial conflicts. It's only for a while.

Approach problems as opportunities. Because adjustments and conflicts are an inevitable and normal part of striving to create a new life for yourselves, each of them is truly an opportunity to take another step toward that new life. Regard problems as obstacles to be removed on the way to reaching your goal.

Remember, you love each other. When your relationship is an important, indispensable element of your life, it's worth practicing restraint to protect it from the corrosive effects of thoughtless arguments. Although you may feel upset at the moment, remind yourself that this is the person you love. This is someone you respect. This person is probably the most important individual in your life.

The many small things married people get upset about are truly insignificant in the shadow of the love they can have between them. Don't overlook what's bothering you or simply put up with it in the name of love, but reach out to your spouse. Try to understand his or her position. Maybe if you can help your partner through the adjustment, he or she will be able to help you. As you discuss conflicts, keep the basic love you have between you in the forefront of your mind and concentrate on how important your relationship is.

Because it's often difficult to keep a positive perspective in the midst of a heated argument, here are a few things you can do to short-circuit flaring tempers. First, when you notice that communications are going from bad to worse, take a break. Go for a walk. Take a deep breath. Remind yourself that the opposite of love isn't hate; it's indifference. And anger is only part of the full range of feelings you have for your mate. Taking a moment to think of the loving feelings will make all the difference in the world in resolving the conflict.

Solve problems so that everybody wins. Sometimes in the midst of a conflict, the people involved think someone has to win and someone has to lose. Or they think someone has to be right and someone has to be wrong. In sports events and lawsuits this may be true, but, fortunately, solving problems with your spouse isn't a contest or a trial. It's possible for everybody to win.

(Continued on page 518)

(Continued from page 517)

Actually, if you approach a conflict as a win/lose contest when you're working at home, nobody will win. The "winner" has to eat, sleep, live, and work with the "loser" every day. Once you've done that, you realize you haven't won much. So whenever you feel that someone must win and someone must lose, know you are on the wrong track. Usually you haven't defined the problem correctly. For example, if there is only one spare room in the house and both spouses want to use it exclusively, it may look like a win/lose situation. Actually the problem is not who gets to use the room. The problem is that there are two people who both need space to do something that's important to them. When you've solved that problem, everyone has won.

When you define a problem in this way, there are almost always options for solving it so that everyone wins. It's amazing what two creative minds can come up with when seeking a solution that will benefit them both.

Make clear agreements. Making assumptions is the surest route to frustration, disappointment, and unnecessary conflict. When you work from home, the familiar assumptions people make about how things are done at an office no longer fully apply, nor do the assumptions people normally make about how things are done at home. Getting clear agreements about who is willing to do what is crucial, whether they concern how you want your partner to act when the business phone rings, or who will fix lunch.

It's easy to overlook telling your spouse what you expect and then proceed to get angry when he or she doesn't act accordingly. It's also easy to declare what you want and assume it will be done without further discussion. And when you're worried that your partner won't want to do something, it's awfully tempting to use coercion, manipulation, threats, shame, guilt, or pressure tactics to get your way.

Unfortunately, agreements made under such circumstances are either not kept or are kept halfheartedly or grudgingly. Sometimes they're actually sabotaged. Although it's easy to blame the other person for not being supportive, you will nonetheless have to take responsibility for instigating such behavior and will come to regret the day you extracted an agreement under duress.

Communicate, communicate, communicate. In addition to talking, listen open-mindedly to your spouse's feelings and concerns. As Peggy Glenn discovered in starting her typing service at home with a new husband and three children, "Communication is the key. If you communicate, you can overcome most of the problems."

You might use the time you once spent commuting to and from the office to listen to each other, not necessarily about problems, but about yourselves, your lives, and your dreams. Chances are that this kind of honest and open communication will strengthen your determination to succeed and keep your romance alive.

Tip: Getting Clear Agreements

Agreements that clearly define what each of you will and will not do can make working from home easier and more enjoyable. Here are a few tips for how to do that:

- Express precisely what you want and what you expect.

- Make it clear whether you will meet your spouse's expectations or whether you won't.

- Don't say "yes" when you mean "no."

- Accept "no" from each other as okay. A "no" is clearly better than a "yes" on which someone will not follow through.

Laugh a lot. Laughter is the sugar that can sweeten the bitterest moments in periods of adjustment. It can save the day. Be willing to step back to look at yourselves, to see some of the humor in your behavior and your situation. If laughing amid the pressures of life doesn't come easily to you, make a habit of going to funny movies together, going out with lighthearted people, and watching TV comedies.

Thirteen Ways to Keep Romance Alive When You Work at Home

Romance in a relationship is much like a garden. It can't be neglected; it must be tended if it is to grow and flourish. Here are several things you can do to protect, care for, and treasure your relationship:

1. Remember, love keeps you together. Don't dissolve it with acid remarks. Keep the bond strong with small kindnesses.

2. Enjoy each other's enjoyment.

3. Keep the positive regard you have for each other in the forefront of your interactions.

4. Compliment each other liberally every day for your individual accomplishments, contributions, and talents.

5. Solve problems when they are small. Don't let them build up.

(Continued on page 520)

(Continued from page 519)

6. Commit yourselves to solving problems so you both win, instead of defining problems so that one of you must win and the other must lose, or one of you must be right and the other wrong.

7. Work out clearly stated agreements. Don't assume. State what you need and ask for what you want from each other.

8. When you say "no," explain what you're willing to do instead, and when you're told "no," find out what the other person would be willing to do.

9. Close the door on work at the end of the day. Have nonbusiness time. In particular, separate the bedroom from business. Don't take business to bed and don't go to bed mad.

10. Don't hoard negative feelings. Express them when they develop so you don't have an overflow of bad feelings to unload on each other in an explosive argument.

11. Get out of the house together regularly to do things you enjoy. Take mini-vacations for an afternoon or weekend.

12. Follow the advice of Kahlil Gibran: "Let there be space in your 'togetherness.'" Have and pursue your own interests.

13. Take time out to celebrate and don't let a day go by without at least ten hugs.

A COMMUNICATION HANDBOOK

You may well be seeing a lot more of those you live with. Good communication is vital to assuring that you enjoy being around each other, so here is a short course in good communication skills that can go a long way to prevent tensions from building and to reduce them when they do.

General Principles

• *Be **nonjudgmental**.* A climate of trust is vital if people are to enjoy living and working together. Keep an open, accepting mind toward each other's ideas, opinions, and experiences. Never rain on each other's parade. While it may be appropriate and can be helpful to share information and your concerns, avoid put-downs and judgments.

• *Be empathic.* Try to see each other's point of view. Put yourself in each other's shoes. Do your best to understand the other person's motivation and reasoning as you listen and learn about each other.

• *Make feelings okay.* Often the most difficult aspects of being on your own are not the situations you encounter, but the feelings you have about these situations. Those you live with can be more supportive if it's permissible to express the whole range of feelings family members have. Everything from anger and frustration to elation and fear should be acceptable. In fact, family members can be most valuable by helping each other identify and clarify their feelings. Once clarified, feelings can become the basis for constructive action.

Listening

Often the most valuable role we can provide for each other is simply that of listener. Having someone spend the time to truly listen can help us to clarify values, express feelings, and explore the appropriate available options and solutions. In fact, it's been estimated that the average adult gains 90 percent of his or her information from listening.

"Listening," according to the Random House Dictionary, "is to give attention, to attend closely, for the purpose of hearing." For purposes of being supportive of each other, we would expand that definition somewhat. Listening in a way that is supportive means giving attention and attending closely to what someone is saying for the purpose of "understanding." Here are some guidelines for becoming a good listener:

• *Be attentive and interested.* Don't be distracted by your own ideas and thoughts or by the activities going on around you. Have a desire to listen and understand. If you cannot listen fully, say so and find a time when you can.

• *Put yourself in the other person's place* to identify what he or she is saying (the content), how he or she is feeling (the emotions involved), and what the situation means to him or her (the values involved).

• *As you listen, feed back what you are hearing* by restating what you understand to be the most important thoughts and feelings; e.g., "What I hear you saying is . . ."

• *Do not interrupt, offer advice or suggestions,* or bring up similar feelings and problems you have experienced yourself.

• *Don't argue,* either verbally or nonverbally, with the person talking or with yourself.

- *Listen "between the lines"* for not only what is said but also what is being implied. Listen for the underlying "music" as well as the words.

- *Don't antagonize* the speaker with hasty judgments or comments about what you're hearing.

- *Show your support* with appropriate nods, smiles, supportive comments, and encouragement.

Problem Solving and Decision Making

The goal of problem solving is for family members to assist one another in solving their own problems. Surprisingly enough, giving advice and suggestions is often not a helpful problem-solving tool, yet this is the way we are most likely to try to help our friends and colleagues. Here are seven steps to more effective problem solving:

- *Get an agreement.* Make sure whomever you're talking with actually wants you to help him solve the problem. Just because he starts to complain or discuss a problem does not mean that he actually wants you to start helping him solve it. He could simply want someone to listen or may need an "Ain't It Awful" session (see page 525). So if someone gets into a problem without specifically asking for help in problem-solving, ask him or her directly, "Can I help? Shall we have a problem-solving session or what would be useful?"

- *Don't own the problem.* Do not take responsibility for the other person's problem. Your goal is to assist the person in solving his or her own problem. Don't start giving "advice" or suggestions. If you have some initial ideas, write them down and bring them up near the end of your discussion.

Instead of taking on the problem yourself, help the person define the problem. Sometimes the initial problem is not the primary one, or the person isn't really clear about what the problem is. Begin by asking the person to describe the problem. Then, start asking "open-ended" questions (the most useful ones usually begin with "how" or "what") in order to:

  - *Clarify feelings.* Listen for how the person feels about the situation and help him or her sort out feelings.

  - *Gather information.* Find out as much as you can about the situation.

  - Then, based on the information presented, feed back as clearly as you can your understanding of just what the problem is until you get a statement that sums up the problem in a way that the person involved agrees with.

- *Determine the desired outcome.* Query the person to identify the ultimate outcome he or she wishes from the situation at hand. Help him or her go beyond shortsighted immediate desires like restitution, retaliation, or revenge and get to the ultimate goals.

- *Brainstorm alternatives.* By asking opened-ended questions, identify what actions the person has already taken or is considering taking. Then you can use a brainstorming process to generate new options.

- *Evaluate alternatives.* Focus the conversation on what can be done in the "here and now" and discuss the pros and cons of various solutions. Then help the person prioritize his or her best choices.

- *Predict consequences and reach a decision.* Discuss options so that the person with the problem can identify the best possible outcomes and select one to act upon.

- *Develop an action plan and follow up on the outcome.* Help the person list the things that must be done to carry out the decision he or she has reached. If it's not working, you can offer to go through these steps together again so the person can arrive at a new decision.

Asking for and Receiving Feedback

You may at times want to ask for feedback from those you live with about your ideas, thoughts, plans, or behavior. Remember, at such times, feedback is only useful if it's honest. So if you ask for feedback, you must be willing to accept whatever you hear graciously or you will probably not get honest feedback in the future. If you want to hear positive reactions and compliments only, admit it to yourself and ask accordingly. Otherwise, here's a process you can use:

- *Listen carefully.* Put your mouth on hold until you have gotten all reactions. Do not argue, disagree, or enlighten the other person as to "how it is."

- *Keep in mind as you listen that in giving you his or her feedback, the other person is trying to be helpful.* Do not take what you hear personally. It need not be the last word. You don't have to use or agree with feedback. But you may benefit if you accept, weigh, and appreciate the motivation for and energy spent in providing it.

- *Ask clarifying questions;* e.g., "Why do you say that?" "Would you say that if . . . ?" "What if I changed this . . . ?"

- *Thank those who offer their feedback.* Tell them you appreciate their opinion and will weigh it carefully.

- *If you don't find the feedback helpful, feel free to discard it,* but you need not point this out to the people who have been so kind as to give it to you. Before you discard feedback, however, consider that although you don't agree, your clients and customers or employer may. So you might want to solicit additional feedback from others.

- *If you did find the feedback helpful, report back* later on the value it has had for you. Such reports will make everyone feel good and reinforce the value of helping one another.

Giving Feedback

The general rule of thumb on giving feedback is "Don't give it unless it's wanted." Before giving feedback to anyone in your household, we advise asking if he or she would be interested in hearing your feedback. Then, if so, follow these guidelines:

- *Don't give "advice" and opinions.* Raise facts, observations, concerns, and reactions. Provide the reasons for your comments.

- *Try to balance positive with negative feedback.* Point out what you think works, as well as what you think doesn't. Discuss what you like and appreciate as well as what you dislike.

- *When possible, provide the alternatives* or changes that would correct or eliminate the negative aspects you identify.

- *Accept that your feedback may or may not be useful* and don't expect people to use it unless they find it helpful. Your concerns or reactions may be correct, but if the person is not disposed to hear and use them, just drop it.

Celebrating Wins

Success can be lonely in a harried, busy, and often frustrating world. One of the most rewarding roles household members can play for one another is to be a mutual-admiration society, serving as cheerleaders, dedicated fans, and an applauding audience. Home is a great place to share your "wins."

Make your home a place where everyone can brag and toot his or her own horn unabashedly. For this to be truly effective, everyone has to genuinely enjoy one another's success and be glad for one another's victories. This means that whenever any good news—big or little—is shared, everyone should:

- *Avoid negative comparisons.* As you hear the wonderful things your loved ones are reporting, resist the temptation to start thinking about how you're not doing as well as they are. Instead, say to yourself, "That's for me!"

• ***Momentarily set aside any problems or negative feelings*** you may be having so you can enjoy each other's success. Put your concerns on hold while you celebrate. If you find you simply cannot do that, tell those involved that you want to celebrate with them, but first you've got to get some support for the pressing concerns you're facing.

• ***Think of little gifts or tokens you can give*** to recognize one another's talents, importance, and contribution. It might be something like clipping a cartoon you know someone will value, picking up a book you know he would enjoy reading, or just sharing a thought you had during the week about her life.

Ain't-It-Awful Sessions: Telling War Stories

Sometimes we all need a chance to complain and ventilate our feelings about the things that bother us. We also need a place to share our "war stories," the disappointing, dreadful, discouraging things we have faced or are weathering. Of course, we can't, or at least we shouldn't, do this with our clients and customers. And often family and relatives would rather not hear about difficulties, especially when we express them with the vehemence and the detail that we feel. Nevertheless, home can be a place for us to let off steam, especially if we do it in a way that doesn't tax others' patience.

BUT . . . there is nothing worse than listening to someone complain on and on endlessly about all the details of his or her problems. Nothing will make home a more unpleasant place—more quickly. Habitual complaining makes us feel like screaming "Enough, already!" "Give me a break!" or "Get a life!" So we advise using the following "Ain't It Awful" process to meet each other's legitimate needs for complaining without killing the morale around the house.

• ***If you want to "bitch," ask first*** if those you're talking with will indulge you with a five-minute "Ain't It Awful" session. (If you really have a "biggy," you might ask for ten minutes.)

• ***If they agree, set a timer*** or have someone look at his or her watch. Then proceed to complain and complain until you feel empty. Tell about all the awful things that have happened to you. As a matter of fact, exaggerate the situation, give yourself permission to blow it all out of proportion if you wish.

• ***Those listening should be uniformly sympathetic,*** moaning and groaning at each added assault, adding on a chorus of "Oh, no. That's awful!" Since we've all been through hassles of some kind and we can summon the feelings about our own frustrations, it's possible to do this authentically.

- **When the time runs out, cease complaining** and thank those who were listening for their support. If everyone has really gotten into the spirit of this process, you may all be laughing your heads off before the "Ain't It Awful" session ends.

If someone begins complaining without asking for such a session and it starts to become tedious, whoever notices it first should comment that it sounds like the person needs an "Ain't It Awful" session. Suggest you devote five to ten minutes for out-and-out complaining. Sometimes a household may want to have a group "Ain't It Awful" session where everyone joins in with his or her complaints.

Crisis Management

At some time or another, most of us will be confronted with a crisis. Where better to turn at such times than to those we live with? If we respond appropriately at such times, we can help one another connect with our own inner resources and carry on with confidence and courage.

In other words, the crisis itself is not so much about the events that have occurred as it is about our reactions to them. In fact, one way to define a crisis is "a time in which our normal coping or adaptive mechanisms are no longer functioning." Here's how you can help each other at such times:

- **Begin with feelings; move to facts.** Usually we're quite emotional during a crisis even if we don't show it. It can be difficult to move right into talking rationally about what happened and what can be done. It's easier and wiser to start with the person's existing state of mind and listen to his or her feelings before asking questions about the facts. Usually the person will calm down when he or she begins talking and you can start asking questions about what happened. But if someone continues to be extremely upset, asking very simple questions will help him or her connect with the here and now—questions like "Did you drive home?" "How long have you been here?" "Can I get you a glass of water?"

- **Evaluate the current situation.** Once the person is calmer, find out as much as you can about the situation that precipitated the problem. Explore what it is about this situation that is different from the many other challenges he or she has handled in the past.

- **Help the person define the problem** (as described above for problem solving).

• *Explore alternative ways of coping* with the crisis and less cata-strophic ways of viewing what has happened.

• *Lend appropriate support* to the person in taking whatever action is needed. Sometimes those we live with can help by volunteering to ac-company the person in crisis somewhere, consulting with him or her on a particular action, or taking over some simple routine tasks like picking up a child at the sitter's or calling to cancel a dental appointment.

We hope these guidelines will assist you in enjoying the rewards and benefits of living and working together. We are indebted to Joan Sturkie and Valerie Gibson, whose ideas we adapted for a good number of these guidelines. They are the authors of *The Peer Counselor's Pocket Book*.

WHAT TO DO IF IT ISN'T GETTING BETTER

On occasion, the changes and adjustments of working from home seem to precipitate more serious problems than those we've been discussing. The tension and bad feelings build until the situation feels intolerable. What happens then? What has gone wrong? Has working from home destroyed the marriage?

Yes and no. Whether it's a new baby, a new job, or a new house, any new element introduced into a relationship can aggravate existing problems or bring them to the surface. Working from home is like this too.

It's easier to avoid problems when you don't see each other very much. When someone is at the office for most of every day, it's simpler to push the difficulties away. Working at home, couples usually see more of each other. This proximity, and the strain of adjusting to the changes involved, can stir up and bring out problems that were kept beneath the surface before.

In a relationship that's suffering from underlying problems, it's difficult to get in touch with the basic loving feelings that brought a couple together. Every little concern becomes a battleground. Even the smallest differences can become unsolvable, because the real problems are not being addressed. In situations like these, it's important to heal the relationship itself before a couple attempts to solve the more peripheral problems of working from home.

If you notice these warning signs either before or after you begin work-ing from home, we suggest you communicate with your spouse about them. Then, if the problems persist or go from bad to worse, get professional help to improve your relationship.

There's no need to settle for less than the relationship and lifestyle you want for yourself. You deserve it and so does your partner. Don't wait until things have deteriorated to a hopeless state. Act now. You can use the re-

---

Five Early-Warning Signals

If you're concerned about whether your conflicts are normal adjustments to the changes of working from home or whether these changes are bringing up more general problems, review the five early-warning signals that follow:

1. Your spouse begins blaming all the problems the two of you are having on your work.

2. Your spouse starts to feel jealous of your work.

3. You start using your work as a way to escape talking with your spouse.

4. You start using your work as a way to avoid sex.

5. You talk about everything but what's really on your mind.

If any of these behaviors start to become a pattern in your household, it could be a signal your relationship needs help.

---

sources listed at the end of this chapter or contact the following organizations for help.

There are many courses on building relationships. Marriage Encounter programs, for example, are offered across the country. You can usually locate them through local churches and synagogues. Otherwise, to find out about programs in your area call (800) 795-LOVE ([800] 795-5683). On the Web: *www.me.org* The American Association for Marriage and Family Therapy, 1133 15th Street NW, Ste. 300, Washington, DC 20005 (202) 452-0109, can put you in touch with trained professionals in your community who help couples solve problems. On the Web: *www.aamtc.org*

If your partner won't seek help with you, go yourself. Sometimes all it takes is for one person to have the courage to take the first step and lead the way.

RESOURCES

BOOKS

Couple's Business Guide. Amy Lyon. New York: Perigee, 1997. ISBN: 0399523006.

Couples at Work. E. W. "Dub" and Janet James. Denver: Boomer House Books, 1997. ISBN: 0965580490.

Honey, I Want to Start My Own Business. Azriela Jaffe. New York: Harper Business, 1996. ISBN: 0887307957.

The Relationship Toolbox. Robert Abel. Denver: Valentine Publishing, 1998. ISBN: 0965766623.

Working with the One You Love. Cameron and Donna Partow. Minneapolis: Bethany House, 1995. ISBN: 1556615329.

Tapes

How to Handle Conflict and Manage Anger. Denis Waitley. Nightingale Conant, 7300 North Lehigh Avenue, Chicago, IL 60648; (800) 323-5552.

CHAPTER 20

What to Do About Children

Goals

1. Learn how to introduce your working from home to your children.

2. Know what reactions you can expect from your children and what steps you can take.

3. Choose among a wealth of child-care options.

4. Use checklists to hire the help you need.

5. Balance parenthood and work.

6. Protect your children and avoid interruptions.

Many parents first begin to think about working from home as a way of pursuing both parenthood and a career. Studies show that 40 percent of men and 80 percent of women with children would stay home to raise their families if they could. And nearly half of all children with working parents say they wish their parents were at home.

Certainly bringing work home holds the potential of making juggling these demands easier for both mothers and fathers. Yet parents and others who want to work from home often worry whether they'll be productive enough, working with children in the house. In this chapter we want to affirm that working from home does indeed offer many rewards for parents. At the same time, we want to realistically address what you can expect as parents working from home, the difficulties you may face, and the practical steps you can take to avoid problems and take full advantage of the benefits.

IT CAN BE WORTH THE EFFORT

Our son, Jon, was eight years old when we moved our offices home. Having both worked long hours away from the house since shortly after he was born, we felt pleasure hearing him come in the door after school and call out, "Hi! I'm home!" We'd take a break to make him a snack and find out the highlights of his day.

Our being in the house so much was a real treat for him, too. Until we started working at home, he had only seen us at night and on weekends. From the time he was tiny, we had asked the baby-sitter to be sure he took a nap in the late afternoon so he could stay up late with us when we got home. So, at first, having us there in the afternoon was like a continual holiday for Jon.

> According to a survey conducted by USA Today, 71 percent of men with children under the age of eighteen said that being a father has become more difficult; 77 percent of the women surveyed agreed.

We liked knowing we were more available to him, too. Although at times he had trouble knowing when he could or couldn't interrupt us, we were all surprised to discover that he was often too busy with his own things to pay much attention to us. Jon is living in northern California now pursuing his own career as a computer game designer, and we often think that if we hadn't decided to work from home, we would be looking back on his childhood regretting how much we'd missed.

When financial consultant Michael Fey moved his office home, he found, just as we had, that being with his teenage children was surprisingly rewarding. "Being at home in the morning, helping the kids get off to school, being involved in their squabbles, it's been a real education! My kids know me better now. They may not like me any better, though, because I'm a real parent. I'm putting down certain prescriptions, not leaving it up to Mom. It's changed their image of what a father is. Daddy isn't just somebody who goes off to fight traffic and bring home a barrel of cash for everybody else to spend."

Both men and women who work at home describe this close involvement with their children as a real advantage. And indications are that it's also a benefit for the children. Often the adult world of work is so removed from the lives of children that it's literally a life apart. Alvin Toffler expressed this separation in his book The Third Wave. "Most children today have only the foggiest notion of what their parents do or how they live while at work." He tells this poignant story to illustrate his point:

An executive decides to bring his son to his office one day and take him out to lunch. The boy sees the plushly carpeted office, the indirect lighting, the elegant reception room. He sees the fancy expense-account restaurant with its obsequious waiters and exorbitant prices. Finally, picturing his home and unable to restrain himself, the boy blurts out: "Daddy, how come you're so rich and we're so poor?"

In contrast, when parents work at home a child not only gets to know them better but also experiences their world of work. Management trainers Linda and Bill Belisle have even involved their children in their home business. "Our kids know what it's like to be in business. They've grown up with it. We all work together, and when we have deadlines to meet, the kids pitch in and help. We think it's good preparation for them to succeed in life."

But although the rewards are potentially rich for most parents and children, it is also true that working with kids around is not always easy. Ken and Stephanie Wilson work from home and are the parents of two young sons. They agree that "it's just wonderful for the boys to have both parents here, but it's a real adjustment. It's a true test of living up to what we want as parents and professionals."

Noise, interruptions, and privacy are usually issues parents have to face, as well as knowing what's reasonable to expect of your children and yourself under the circumstances.

Children have an adjustment to make, too. We remember at least one occasion when Jon, feeling frustrated with our ever-present business conversation, asked angrily, "Is this a home or a business?" So let's talk about the different reactions you can anticipate from your children, what you can say to them, and how you can make practical, age-appropriate arrangements for their care.

WHAT YOU CAN EXPECT

Children's reactions to your being at home will vary greatly, depending upon their ages, personalities, your family, and the nature of your work. In most situations, children are glad to have a parent there more often, but they probably will not fully comprehend what it means to have a parent working from home. To them, you are Mom or Dad, and that's it. They probably don't know you as lawyer, doctor, bookkeeper, or whatever else you happen to be. If you want to make working at home with children both enjoyable and productive, you'll have to introduce them to your professional side and show them how to relate to you now that you're more than a mom or dad at home.

Whatever their ages, kids will be kids. Don't expect your children to act like grown-ups just because you're working at home. Don't expect them, for example, to be quiet. Remember, by nature children are not quiet, and to be so for more than short periods of time is unhealthy for their development. Constantly trying to hush them will be a losing battle for you in the short run and not good for them in the long run.

Rule of Thumb

Regardless of your children's ages, it's important to "child-proof" your home office instead of trying to "office-proof" your children. In other words, let your kids be kids. Let them engage in normal activities, but set up your office and your schedule so that having "normal" children around will not disrupt your work. Here are some examples of how people have "child-proofed" their work while letting their kids be kids:

Programmer William Keen solved his dilemma this way: "I put the business phone and a desk down in the basement because it just doesn't make any sense to try to keep two dogs and three kids quiet when I'm on the phone. By putting the desk and phone at the far end of the basement, under the master bedroom, I get very little noise. Even when the TV is going full blast, I don't hear it."

Artist Gary Eckart managed the problem another way: "I set my workshop up in an RV on the side of the house, because cutting stained glass just isn't compatible with having a toddler around. There's too much risk. If even once she crawled into my studio and got cut or put a piece of glass in her mouth . . . well, I couldn't take that chance."

If you have equipment or materials you don't want children to disrupt or damage, we suggest not allowing them to play in your office while you work. Otherwise they will then treat it as a play area they can use even when you are not there to supervise them. Judy Wunderlich, who runs a temporary agency for graphic artists in Schaumburg, Illinois, found a creative way of solving this dilemma. When her two young children were under five, she needed to have them in sight at all times. She didn't want them playing around her computer equipment, so she had the basement divided in half with a three-foot-high wall. Her office is in the back half; the kids' playroom is in the front. She could see and hear them and they her, but the office was off-limits.

The first step is setting up your work to accommodate the reality of children in the house. Then remember that you can fully expect your children to behave responsibly and appropriately for their age and level of development. They do not need you all the time and can grow and develop very well while you're working undisturbed at home.

Let's take a look at what you can expect at each age level and how you can get work done whatever ages your children are. Since the age groups we discuss are based on typical stages of childhood development, assess your own children's personalities and rates of development so you can adjust these expectations to your family.

Newborn to Six Years Old

With mothers of newborn babies going back to work earlier than ever before and 56 percent of all mothers going back before their children are six years old, working from home becomes increasingly appealing to parents eager to find ways of avoiding the risks of day care, not to mention the high costs of child-care services.

Research shows that day care poses both physical and mental-health risks for children under six, and surveys show that more than 75 percent of mothers are unsatisfied with child care for which they pay from $75 to $200 or more weekly. One of the most common misconceptions new mothers have, however, is that working from home will be a replacement for child care. Often it is not a replacement but it does open up many more flexible and rewarding options for combining motherhood and career. About 50 percent of parents working at home say they can do work while caring for infants and toddlers. Considering the fact that young children of this age need constant supervision, want and demand attention, and try to be part of everything going on around them, the other 50 percent who work at home find this unsatisfactory.

When working parents care for toddlers and preschoolers at home, little work may get done at times and/or the parents may end up expecting the young children to behave in ways beyond their abilities. This usually leads to a flood of yelling and unpleasantness. It can also result in emotional or behavioral problems on the part of the children.

Barbara Elman was operating a word-processing service bureau when she became pregnant with her first child. Her story is similar to that of many women who begin working at home with infants and toddlers. During the first six months, she found she could work fine while the baby was right there with her. "Then my daughter became mobile. She started crawling and moving around and needing more attention. I couldn't sit and nurse her anymore while I was proofing, because she wanted to play with the keys and everything else in sight. I couldn't work when she was around. It was difficult then and it's impossible now that she's two-and-a-half."

Experiences like Barbara's have led most people in this situation to the same conclusion: If they want to work without interruption for longer than fifteen minutes, they need either to work at night while the children are sleeping or to get some form of supplementary child care for children under six or seven.

If you do hire someone to help you with your children and they or others want to know why someone else is caring for them when you're at home, it's important to explain that you are working just as someone does who goes out to a job each day. When consultant Mary Smolinski started to work from home, her son was fifteen months old and she worked only part-time. "I hired a high-school student to watch him while I worked in my office. As he grew, he learned that when Mommy's office door was closed that meant he had to get permission from the sitter before knocking and getting my permission to enter because Mommy was busy. Now he's nine and I no longer need a sitter, but the closed door still means I'm busy. He knows I'm there when he really needs me (maybe to congratulate him on his latest super-fantastic Lego design). But he still has to knock and ask first."

As an added safeguard, now that there's no sitter, Mary also leaves her telephone intercom on in the background so she can hear what's happening in the house.

Keeping an Eye and Ear on Young Children While You Work

Often parents want to see and hear what's going on with their young children while they're working at home, but they don't want the kids playing underfoot or around their equipment. Here are six solutions:

1. Separate your office area from children's play area with shutters that you can open or close, depending upon how focused you need to be and the child-care arrangements you've made.

2. Replace your regular office door with a Dutch door, so when you want to supervise what's going on in the household you can leave the top open and still not have pets or kids running in. When needed, of course, you can close the door fully.

3. Use a baby monitor or telephone intercom to alert you to any problems you need to attend to. Keep the base unit in your office and add as many remote units as you wish to monitor or communicate with various other rooms of the house.

4. Divide a basement, attic, or family room into two rooms with a half wall so you can work in one room while the kids play within sight in the other.

5. Use a portable child-door divider which you can put up or take down as needed to make office or unsafe work space inaccessible to children without their being out of sight or sound. Such folding gates are plastic or wood, and they come in various heights and extend to various widths.

6. Use two-line cordless phones (with a mute button) so you can pick up business calls while you're in other parts of the house with your children, can follow the children around if need be, or get to them quickly while you're talking on the phone.

Seven to Twelve Years Old

Once children are over six, they are usually in school for a good part of the day, which leaves parents with considerably more flexibility in scheduling uninterrupted work time. Parents can arrange their schedules so they are not working while the children are home, or are doing tasks that require less concentration and can more easily withstand interruptions.

Children over six also require less direct supervision, so it becomes feasible to work in your office while they are playing in their rooms or in the backyard. Another advantage is that children this age often play in the homes of friends, although their friends are just as likely to come over to your house.

Ideally, you would have another adult available for children seven to twelve years of age when you need to work without any interruptions for considerable periods of over an hour or so. This is especially useful if there is more than one child in the family and bickering is likely. However, you can often handle the needs of children this age on short, intermittent breaks, and teach them to wait for those break times.

You can usually expect children from seven to twelve years old not to interrupt you when:

- There is some other person over twelve in the house whom they can ask for help.

- You let them know the home office has become your room and they need permission to be there.

- You tell them specifically when you will be available, and you are only unavailable for about an hour at a time.

- They understand that they can and should interrupt you for emergencies. (Beware, though, that what is an emergency to you and what is an emergency to an eight-year-old can be quite different, so you will need to spell out what you mean.)

Children of this age will probably do a considerable amount of testing in relation to these expectations. At first, they may push to find out if you mean what you say and exactly what the limits are. This will be particularly true when you have been with them full-time before you began working at home. But if you are both loving and firm, they can usually adjust to your expectations after a few weeks.

In the first few weeks after we began working at home, we told our son not to interrupt us if we were in a session with a client and had the door closed, but he did anyway. We explained that clients came on the hour, and asked him to wait to talk with us until the break between each hour. We would be free once the client had gone out the front door.

Whenever he disrupted a session unnecessarily, one of us would simply say, "I'm in a session now, Jon. I will be done at—," and then we would close the door. Later, on the break, we'd be sure to check out what he wanted. It didn't take long for him to understand he could get his needs met without interrupting us.

 True Confessions

Ken and Stephanie Wilson have two boys, ages seven and ten. Stephanie began working from home as a landscape designer. Ken left his job at a major utility company to begin consulting and writing from home.

The Wilsons have located their offices so they are less likely to be disturbed by their children's activities, but they believe that children should have free access to their parents. Therefore, they take a flexible approach to interruptions.

As Ken explains, "I don't want to make a rule, 'No, you can't come in and see me.' I don't want limits on their coming in and saying, 'Hey, Dad, what's this or what's that?' That's why I'm here. I'm glad they're coming in to see me. It means we're relating."

The Wilsons have avoided making rigid rules by letting their boys know in the beginning that an office at home is serious business, and by having frequent family meetings to talk about everyone's feelings. They agree that "it has worked out reasonably well, but it hasn't just happened. It does take effort."

Over Twelve Years Old

Children over twelve should be able to carry out agreements not to interrupt your work for specified periods as long as they know:

- When you do not want to be interrupted.

- What emergencies you do want to be interrupted for.

- When they will be able to have your attention to deal with their needs. (We've found this is important not so much because teenagers need your time but because they want to know that you are there.)

With children from age ten up, you may find that involving them in some aspects of your work is rewarding for you both. Teenagers, in particular, have many more talents and abilities than our society provides them with outlets for. They may well be our greatest untapped natural resource. We often had our son help with mailings, newsletters, or big projects of various kinds. We suggest, however, that such help be strictly on a voluntary basis,

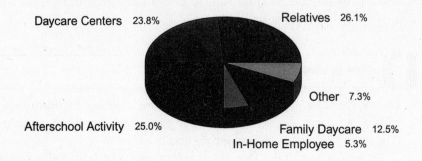

Who Cares for Our Children When We Can't Do It Ourselves?
55% of American Parents Get Help Caring For Their Children

Daycare Centers 23.8%

Relatives 26.1%

Other 7.3%

Afterschool Activity 25.0%

Family Daycare 12.5%
In-Home Employee 5.3%

1990 National Child Care Survey

Figure 20-1

if not for a set wage; you will get more willing and productive participation that way.

Sandee and Al Burger started an extermination business in their home when their two children were toddlers. Sandee says, "The family and the business grew together." When the children were old enough, they got fifty cents to sharpen pencils and do other office tasks. In high school, they worked for the business on weekends. The Burgers' daughter, now an adult, has taken a full-time job with the company, which long ago outgrew their home.

CHILD-CARE OPTIONS

The type of care you arrange for your children is a highly personal decision. What suits some people will not suit others. For working parents, having a wide variety of creative and flexible child-care options is one of the real advantages of working from home. You are no longer limited to only those arrangements that can provide care from 7 A.M. to 7 P.M. while you commute to work in a downtown office.

For example, Barbara Elman found that, in order to be productive, she needed to hire someone to take care of her daughter part of the day while she was working. Like so many women, Barbara originally wanted to work at home so she could take care of her daughter full-time herself and was hesitant at first about making other arrangements. But she discovered that trying to run a business and parent a toddler was too much to expect of herself, so she decided to explore the different kinds of support she could get. She urges women to give themselves permission to find child care that will best fit their needs.

Seven Child-Care Options

Working from home provides greater flexibility and more choices for making the best possible child-care arrangements for the family. Here are seven choices you can select from or mix and match.

____ 1. Call on other adults in the family: spouse, aunts, uncles, brothers, sisters, grandparents.

____ 2. Have siblings over twelve years of age watch younger children.

____ 3. Have a baby-sitter or nanny come into your home.

____ 4. Take the children to a private baby-sitter.

____ 5. Place the children in a child-care program:

____ a day-care center

____ a day-care home

____ a nursery school

____ 6. Join a child-care co-op.

____ 7. Trade baby-sitting with a friend.

Work Sheet: Making the Best Child-Care Choices

In deciding which options are best for you, review the following pros and cons of each and consider your situation, the nature of your work, the ages of your children, and the help available in your home.

____ ***Call on another adult in the family.*** The advantages of having a spouse or relative care for your children are that these adults know and are known by the children, and are aware of how you want the children to be treated. Often, too, there's no extra cost involved. The disadvantages are that spouses and relatives may not always be available when you need them. They also may resent your asking them to help on a regular basis; and even if they don't say so, relatives may expect to be paid.

(Continued on page 540)

(Continued from page 539)

If you do plan to use a spouse or relatives, be sure to let them know what you expect of them, and find out if they are actually willing to meet your expectations. You don't want help that's given out of duty, obligation, coercion, or guilt. Chances are these motivations will just lead to resentment and unreliable support for you, as well as possible negative experiences for your children.

___ *Use a sibling over twelve years of age.* The advantages of using older siblings are that they are usually close by; their help is free or they'll be earning spending money you might give them anyway; and by helping you, they have the opportunity to contribute to the family. The disadvantages are that they may not want to watch their younger siblings; they may not watch them very well; and they may sometimes even mistreat them. Another drawback is that older brothers and sisters are usually only available at certain times of the day. Also, sometimes younger siblings resent being "parented" by an older sibling, so they become disobedient and create more squabbles for you to police.

If you do use an older sibling, be certain to talk this over with all your children to get their agreement and support. If they really hate the arrangement, it's better—for your own benefit—to respect their wishes and use siblings only in special situations.

We strongly advise against using children under twelve years of age to supervise younger siblings, because they generally cannot get younger children to respect and obey them. One way you can measure whether a child is effective enough to watch younger children is to observe whether the child can get dogs or other trainable pets to obey him or her. Also, watch the child interacting with younger children from day to day. See if he or she demonstrates the skill and judgment that caring for a younger child requires.

___ *Hire a baby-sitter, nanny, or au pair to come into your home.* There are several options for having a caregiver come into your home and care for your child. You can hire a baby-sitter; usually this is someone who doesn't have any formal training, background, or licensing in child care but who by nature and experience is good at caring for children. Baby-sitters may be high-school or college students or elderly individuals in need of extra income. They may come into your home daily or live in. Most often you can find them through school placement offices, churches, or personal referrals.

Alternatively you can hire a professional nanny. A nanny has completed a professional training program and has studied child development, health education, safety, nutrition, and more. She or he will most likely have a repertoire of stories, songs, and games for children of various ages and will usually have had professional supervision in a variety of other child-care settings.

(Continued on page 541)

(Continued from page 540)

A baby-sitter may have baby-sitting experience, a love of children, and a caring nature, which can make for a terrific helper as long as he or she is willing to learn. In most cases, however, a baby-sitter is likely to need more supervision and training from you than a nanny. But as you might expect, a nanny will cost considerably more. If you can find a nanny through word of mouth from other families with nannies or through child-development programs at nearby colleges, your cost will be less than if you must go through a nanny agency (fees could run from $400 to $2,000). An agency can be worth the expense, however, if you don't have the time to locate and screen applicants. Nanny agencies can be expected to screen for training, health, driving and criminal records, family background, employment histories, and references. But do check references yourself anyway.

Another option is to hire an au pair. Au pairs are typically Western European women between the ages of eighteen and twenty-five who come to live in the United States with an American family for a year to care for the children. In return, the au pair must be provided with room and board, a minimum of $100 a week, airfare, medical insurance, and a $300 educational allowance. There are now eight agencies that place au pairs who have met federal guidelines and carefully screen and match au pairs with appropriate families.

Although the cost is lower than hiring a nanny or baby-sitter, the au pair can only stay legally for one year and is usually a young woman away from her family in a new country. So arrange to interview several applicants and make sure the agency will provide a replacement if your first choice doesn't work out. Here are several of the top au pair agencies recommended by *Parents* magazine:

- Au Pair in America. 102 Greenwich Avenue, Greenwich, CT 06830; phone: (800) 727-2437. Web: *www.aifs.org*

- EurAuPair. 250 N. Coast Hwy., Laguna Beach, CA 92651; phone: (800) 333-3804. Web: *www.euraupair.com*

- AuPairCare. 1 Post Street, Ste. 700, San Francisco, CA 94104; phone: (800) 4-Au-Pair.

- E. F. Au Pair. E. F. Center, 1 Education Street, Cambridge, MA 02141; phone: (800) 333-6056. Web: *www.ef.com*

Whichever of these options you choose, there are pros and cons of having a caregiver come into your home. The advantage is that you now have someone whose explicit job is to take care of your children while you work. You can also hire a person who clearly wants to work and who is available at the specific times you need child care. Having someone come to your home saves you the time of

(Continued on page 542)

(Continued from page 541)

taking the children elsewhere and also provides you with the opportunity to over-see what the sitter is doing.

The disadvantages are that you have an added expense, and since the children are still there at the house, noise and interruptions may continue to be a problem. Because you can probably still overhear some activities, you may have difficulty not going out to see what's happening when disturbances arise. To overcome this problem, some parents take their children out to the home of a private baby-sitter or family day-care home.

Technical writer Liz Danzinger chose working from home specifically so she could spend more time with her four children. She restructured her career so she could run her business only in the mornings and still earn the same income as when she was employed full-time. She has hired a live-in employee, not to care for her children, but to care for the house, so she can have the afternoons and evenings free for her family.

_____ ***Take your child to a child-care program.*** Although some parents are fearful of taking their children to child-care programs, many people highly recommend them. The advantages are that licensed child-care programs are generally reliable; they're open every day because they are businesses; and with the children not at home, you can work with total privacy. The disadvantages are that the child may not get the individual attention you'd like; the hours may not be as flexible as you want; and you'll have to make other arrangements when your child is sick.

There are many good child-care programs, including day-care centers, day-care homes, preschools, and after-school programs. Call your county offices for a list of licensed programs in your area. Then visit several of them while children are there. Talk with the operators and teachers and ask how they handle the various situations you're concerned about in child care.

Find out, for example, what the children will be doing during the time they are there. Will they be learning and playing, or only playing? How many children are in the program, what are their ages, and how many adults are present? How is discipline handled? Talk to other parents who have children in the programs you are considering. Find out how pleased these parents are and whether they have any complaints. And be sure to investigate the provider's credentials.

_____ ***Join a child-care co-op or trade baby-sitting services.*** In a child-care co-op, you join with other parents and take turns providing care for your children. Sometimes parents provide all the care by themselves and sometimes they only supplement the work of professionals who are hired to provide the care. The latter arrangement is called a "parent participation" nursery.

The advantages of co-op programs are that they usually cost less than other

(Continued on page 543)

(Continued from page 542)

options; you get to participate in the care of your child; and other parents often become close friends. The disadvantages are that participating in a co-op means contributing time that may take you away from work; you also have to invest time in organizing the co-op and energy in caring for other people's children.

When selecting a co-op program, shop for one that understands and appreciates the needs of working parents. This is particularly important if you are a working single parent and will have to contribute all the time yourself. If you cannot find a satisfactory child-care co-op arrangement in your area, do what many parents have done—initiate a co-op by getting together with other working parents in your neighborhood.

On a more informal basis, some parents also trade the task of baby-sitting with friends or neighbors. Finding someone to help out on the spot may not provide the kind of security you need to run your business reliably, however, so a more formal baby-sitting co-op might be more to your liking. A baby-sitting co-op doesn't have a separate facility like a co-op nursery where parents take turns working in the nursery. Instead parents usually care for one another's children in their own homes.

As Patricia McManus spells out in her book *The Babysitting Co-op Guidebook,* a baby-sitting co-op works on a point system. A family who needs a sitter calls another member of the co-op and asks for baby-sitting time. The family that receives the help is charged points for each hour of sitting service. The family that baby-sits is given points for future baby-sitting they need. Points are recorded by the co-op's bookkeeper, a position that rotates monthly throughout the membership. The bookkeeper gets paid with a few extra baby-sitting points, too.

 What to Look for Checklist: Selecting Someone to Care for Your Child in Your Home

Having someone come into your house while you are working from home can be an ideal child-care solution. Because often you will be on the premises, you'll be in a good position to make sure that the caregiver you hire is indeed giving the kind of care you want and expect. Here are several things you can do to make sure you find the right person the first time around:

____ **1. Decide what you're looking for in a caregiver.** Identify the personal traits, background, experience, and so forth that are most important to you. Also decide what you will want him or her to do; e.g., meal preparation for the children, driving, reading, teaching, etc. One major decision, of course, is whether

(Continued on page 544)

(Continued from page 543)

you'll be seeking a live-in caregiver or plan to have him or her come and go each day.

Prepare a list of questions you will ask all the candidates you interview that is designed to ascertain if they have the qualities and experience you're looking for. Be sure to ask the same questions of everyone, so you can impartially compare one to another.

____ *2. Get references.* Check out each and every reference thoroughly. Because people are often hesitant to give negative references, ask open-ended questions that will give you as much information as possible from which to form your own opinion. Ask, for example:

- What tasks did the caregiver do?

- Which ones was he or she best at?

- What did the parents like most about the caregiver?

- What did they wish he or she had done differently?

- Why is the caregiver no longer working there?

Before you end the conversation, make sure to ask directly if the former employer would hire the person again.

____ *3. Observe the interaction between the caregiver and your child.* We didn't know we should do this when interviewing the first woman we hired, who turned out to be very cold and distant with our son. It didn't take long for us to discover this and replace her, but the experience was disruptive and stressful. The second woman we hired was a wonderful caregiver who was with Jon for many years. However, he adopted aspects of her personality that we would just as soon have preferred he ignored. So also make sure that the person you hire is someone whose habits and personality you won't mind your child adopting.

____ *4. Make sure you put applicants at ease during the interview.* You want applicants to be forthcoming in talking about themselves. Ask open-ended questions like:

- Tell me about your child-care experience."

- "How did you choose to do child care?"

- "What do you like about it?"

- "How do you know when a child is doing well?"

(Continued on page 545)

(Continued from page 544)

After a candidate is talking openly and easily, you can ask the more detailed questions you have prepared. Be sure to ask candidates what they would do to discipline a child and when they think discipline is necessary. Also ask them to describe a child-care situation that gave them trouble and what they did about it. Watch facial expressions and body language as well as listening carefully to the content of their answers.

___ **5. Make all your needs and expectations explicitly clear in writing:** Specify such things as:

- Days of the week they will work

- The hours and activities you want them for

- The days off and sick leave they can expect

- What meals if any, they will be preparing

- What activities, if any, they will be driving to and from and when

Because you will probably be working at home at least part of the time, make sure you have a clear understanding with the caregiver about when you can be interrupted. And once your caregiver is on the job, avoid the temptation to run out and get involved whenever you hear your child crying or some other commotion in the house. In other words, let your caregiver do his or her job.

Also reach an agreement as to when you will be out of the office and what procedures are to be followed if for some reason you are unable to return at the agreed-upon time for the caregiver to leave.

___ **6. Make it legal.** Hiring a full- or even part-time caregiver makes him or her an employee, so you must comply with all state and federal hiring practices (see chapter 21). Even if you or your spouse never expects to be nominated for attorney general, be sure you're taking all the necessary legal steps.

SELECTING A DAY-CARE CENTER OR FAMILY DAY-CARE HOME

We have a bias toward licensed family day care, because it's a home environment more nearly like being in your home office. Whichever you choose, you should visit any child-care home or center you are considering and evaluate the quality of care carefully, including the facility, the personnel, and the activities.

What-to-Look-for Checklist: Day Care

Here are several things to look for provided from the *Parent's Guide to Choosing Quality Child Care,* by the National Association of Pediatric Nurse Associates and Practitioners.

____ Know the licensing requirements in your state and be sure the facility you're   considering meets them.

____ Find out if the caregivers are educated in child psychology and child development and/or early-childhood education.

____ Determine that the ratio of children to staff is appropriate for your child's age group. Here are their recommendations:

Infant to 18 months	4:1
18 months to 2 years	5:1
2–3 years	8:1
3–4 years	10:1
5–6 years	15:1
7 years and older	20:1

____ Be sure there is ample square footage of space per child indoors and for outside play areas. (For day-care centers thirty-five square feet is recommended indoors; seventy-five for outdoors.) Family day-care requirements vary by state.

____ Determine that the facility and equipment are kept clean and disinfected.

____ Make sure caregivers are careful about personal hygiene.

____ Ask whether there are appropriate facilities and procedures to take care of sick children.

____ Determine whether the activities program includes all the elements to foster child growth and development.

____ Be sure that your involvement in your child's activities and progress is welcomed.

____ Find out that corporal punishment, humiliation, or ridicule are never employed as disciplinary measures.

____ Review safety precautions and security procedures and determine that they are strictly observed. For us this would include assurance that there is ample protection of smaller children from abuse, extortion, or harm from older children.

(Continued on page 547)

(Continued from page 546)

A great deal about the climate and atmosphere of a facility can be ascertained by visiting for several hours. Look for these positive signs:

____ Are children generally happy, busy, and engaged?

____ Are they learning values and good behavior?

____ Is there time for rest, meals, and liquids?

____ Is the food healthy?

____ Is there room and flexibility for each child to express his or her own needs and personality without disrupting others?

The National Association for Family Day Care Providers (see Resources list) offers accreditation to day-care providers who meet their state's requirements and have been providing care in their own homes for eighteen months. It publishes an annual *National Directory of Family Day Care Providers*.

Whatever child-care option they choose, most people working at home with children under twelve find that the cost of the care is less than the cost of lost productivity and the stress of trying to parent and work at the same time. Then, too, the financial burden can be partially relieved by taking a tax credit for child- and dependent-care expenses if you have the proper receipts and the provider's Social Security or tax ID number.

CLAIMING YOUR CHILD-CARE TAX CREDIT

If you decide to hire help to take care of your children while you work, you are entitled to claim a tax credit for a portion of your child-care costs. A tax credit is more valuable than a tax deduction because you can take a tax credit right off your final tax liability instead of deducting it from your taxable income. For example, if you owe $10,000 in taxes, you can subtract the percentage of child-care credit you are entitled to receive directly from that $10,000.

How much you can take for a child-care allowance depends upon your adjusted gross income. It ranges from a 30 percent credit for an adjusted gross income up to $10,000 to a 20 percent credit for an adjusted gross income of $28,000 and more. There is a maximum of $2,400 you can deduct for one child or $4,800 for two or more children.

The following table shows the actual IRS percentage you can claim up to the maximum.

How Much of a Tax Credit You Can Get for Child-Care Costs	
ADJUSTED GROSS INCOME	**PERCENTAGE OF COST CREDITED**
Up to $10,000	30%
$10,001–$12,000	29%
$12,001–$14,000	28%
$14,001–$16,000	27%
$16,001–$18,000	26%
$18,001–$20,000	25%
$20,001–$22,000	24%
$22,001–$24,000	23%
$24,001–$26,000	22%
$26,001–$28,000	21%
$28,001 and up	20%

If one parent is employed, some companies have dependent-care assistance plans that allow the family to put away up to $5,000 for day-care expenses; this money is deducted from your paycheck before taxes are applied.

INTRODUCING THE IDEA OF WORKING AT HOME TO YOUR CHILDREN

Whatever ages your children happen to be, when you decide to work at home they will have some reactions to this new way of life. At the very least, they will be curious and have their own ideas about what your being at home will mean. Sometimes these ideas will be unrealistic. For example, children are likely to think you will be as available to them as you have been on weekends or during your other free times at home.

When you decide to set up a home office, remember to give your children as much information as you can about:

- When and where you will be working

- When you will and will not be available

- Who, if anyone, will be available to them while you are working

- Exactly what you will expect from them now that you are working at home

- Who might be coming to the house to see you

Develop a plan with your children like the one discussed in chapter 13 under "Taking Charge of Interruptions and Distractions" to provide all the above information. Be firm in carrying out the plan you agree upon, but give your children the opportunity to ask questions. Be sure to set aside times when you are not working and are fully available to be parents. Make sure your children know when those times are. If problems (crying, frequent interruptions, and so on) develop, talk with your children before you decide to punish them. Search for the underlying need a child may be expressing, and for underlying feelings of fear or anger about changes in your relationship. Offer support and information. Some questions children may be troubled about (often unconsciously) in connection with your working at home include:

- Am I still important?

- How much can I get away with?

- Is my parent(s) still available to me?

- Who is going to be in charge?

Some messages that help children adjust to parents working at home are:

- You and your needs are still important to me.

- My work is important to our family and to the world.

- You can think and solve problems yourself (for children over three).

- There is time for you to get what you need from me. (Specify when, and follow through.)

- It's okay for us to be mad, sad, glad, or scared and to express our feelings to each other.

- We can solve problems so we are both happy.

Listen to your children's needs and expect them to listen to your demand for time and space in which to work. With children over four years old, invite them to propose solutions that will satisfy both their concerns and yours. Propose such solutions yourself.

Books that can help you listen to children's feelings and understand them while still communicating your needs appear in the Resources list at the end of this chapter.

MAKING SURE YOU DON'T EXPOSE YOUR KIDS
TO TOO MANY ADULT CONCERNS

The seven biggest stressors for children, according to *Family Circle* magazine, are:

- Separation from parents
- Parents who are too busy to listen to their concerns
- School and homework pressures
- Anxiety and nightmares brought on by watching violent TV or movies
- Illness and pain
- Anxiety about parents possibly divorcing
- Death of a relative, family friend, or pet.

Perusing this list should comfort those of us who work from home that we should be better able to help our children through these concerns if we're home and available to them more often. But although working from home is a real plus for parents who want to be there more often for their children—and for kids, most of whom certainly need more from their parents these days—working from home also brings business problems and concerns into the household. It's important that we don't inadvertently expose our kids to too many additional stresses from the adult world of work. Here are several signs *Child* magazine identifies to alert us that our youngsters could be feeling overburdened by too many adult concerns:

- Repeated questions about how much everything costs.
- Frequent questions about whether parents are getting divorced.
- Anxious habits like hair twisting or thumb sucking while you're addressing work issues or arguing with your spouse.

Of course, we can't avoid having some work-related pressures and concerns, especially while we're building a business or career at home. But arranging for supplemental child care during especially stressful and tense deadlines or projects, and during peak work periods, can help keep tensions from spilling into your children's lives. So can making sure you get out regularly to meet with a support group of peers with whom you can let off steam, express concerns, and get complaints off your mind.

Although it's certainly okay to let kids know you are having a stressful workday, don't be tempted to talk over your work concerns with your children, even teenagers. If children express concerns about, or interest in, work problems that arise, feel free to explain them briefly. Also let them know that these kinds of things are part of being your own boss and that you'll be handling them. It's important to convey a sense of confidence even at times when you don't know exactly how you will handle problems and then to make sure you get whatever help you need.

HANDLING SPECIAL PROBLEMS

A variety of problems can arise when a family tries to combine work with having children in the house. Here are several of the most common problems and some of the things you can do about them.

Getting Off on the Wrong Foot

Sometimes a problem can develop and become entrenched in the family before people realize it. Then they not only have the initial problem to handle but also a bad habit to break.

If, for example, you start out allowing children to interrupt you whenever they want, you set a precedent. You will most likely have more difficulty convincing them not to interrupt than if the problem had been handled the first time it happened. Sometimes, breaking out of bad habits like this one takes a bold approach.

 True Confessions

When Peggy Glenn started her secretarial service, she discovered that her three teenage children expected more from her now that she was at home. They rebelled against the hurried meals and extra chores that they had put up with when she was working away from home. Not by arguing, however. Instead, they began leaving everything around the house for her to do. Because she was at home all day, they thought she should handle all the things a full-time mother would.

To put an end to this habit, she proposed two alternatives, either of which would have been acceptable to her: all five members of the family could do an equal share of the work, or they could get a housekeeper and everyone would pay a proportionate share of the cost, based on individual income.

"All of us had some income," Peggy remembers. "My oldest daughter had a job. The youngest was baby-sitting, and my son had his paper route. Not wanting to part with their money, they thought at first they would rather do a proportional share of the work. But when I didn't do anything more than my share, they soon decided it would be better to hire the housekeeper. Then an interesting thing suddenly happened. They no longer left the messes they had been making."

Resentments

At times, children or parents may feel resentful about a working-from-home situation. Children may resent having to pick up their things because of clients; not being able to make noise at certain times; having strangers in the house and being expected to be polite to them. Parents may resent interruptions; kids who seem uncooperative; and the pressure of having to do two jobs at home: working and parenting.

Most of these resentments are a normal part of life. Remember, if you weren't working from home, you and your family would be resenting other inconveniences, like driving on the freeway, getting up early, never having enough time together, and so on. The best way to handle resentments like these is to express them and get on with living and working from home.

Resentments that build up, however, are probably a sign that you need to make some changes. If you hear frequent complaining and whining about why you're always working or why your family can't be "normal" like everybody else's, it's a clue that work may be intruding too much on family life. If you're frequently doing the complaining, cursing, and yelling, it could be a sign that the family is intruding on your work.

Don't overlook these symptoms. Sit down and talk about the basic problem with your children and see if you can come up with some practical solutions, like locating the office somewhere else in the house or changing your work schedule.

Acting Out

Occasionally children will use the fact that you are working at home to act out their personal difficulties. For example, if you and a child have a bad relationship or the child is lonely, your working at home may be a chance for him or her to communicate the problem to you by doing things that will clearly get your attention, like being belligerent to business guests or damaging your business property.

Acting out is definitely a sign of a problem that needs to be solved. Talking it out can help sometimes. It may be especially helpful, now that you're home, to follow through on any solutions and keep a more watchful eye on the child. But if your efforts are not working, your pediatrician, family practitioner, or religious adviser should be able to refer you to someone who can help. Some counseling resources are listed in the Resources list at the end of this chapter.

Constant Interruptions

It's not uncommon for people to tell us that even after a few weeks of "testing," a child is still interrupting their work more than they would like. This can occur for a number of reasons. If it happens to you, consider the following possibilities:

First, you may not have arranged for the level of care your child needs. For example, you can't expect a four-year-old to entertain himself or herself alone for more than a short period. A television set or VCR will not substitute for a baby-sitter. Unless someone else is there with the child, you will continue to be interrupted. Sometimes, six- or seven-year-olds are "young" for their age and require more supervision than you initially thought. Making other child-care arrangements can solve this problem.

There are other possibilities. Maybe you're not letting your children know when you will be available. Or perhaps you're not giving them enough time once you stop working. Occasionally children will keep interrupting you because of personal problems they are having with your working at home. Talking with them about their feelings and arranging to spend non-working time with them should help when this kind of problem is at the root of the interruptions. Usually, however, continued interruptions occur because parents have not been clear and firm enough. They give double messages like "I told you not to interrupt me. Now what do you want?" And after responding to the child they say, "Now don't interrupt me again." With children, actions always speak louder than words. In this case, the words say "Don't interrupt," but the actions are saying "It's okay."

Thinking they are being firm, some parents get angry at the child and spend time and energy dealing with each interruption. Teachers and army sergeants have both learned this lesson the hard way: negative attention is better than no attention at all. Briefly notifying children that you are working, telling them when you will be available, and closing the door as if you expected the child to act accordingly is the best approach.

Consistency is important, too. Behavioral research shows that being firm 80 percent of the time, but lax the other 20 percent, only increases the chances of repeated interruptions. From the child's perspective, perhaps *this* time will be one of the exceptions. For a variety of specific suggestions for dealing with interruptions from children, see chapter 13, pages 391–92.

Inability to Say "No"

Some parents find it very difficult to say "no" to their kids. If this describes you, you will either have to get someone else to manage your children or learn to say "no" and mean it. Otherwise you will probably end up yelling and screaming and wondering why your children still don't do what you want them to. You can learn to say "no" without sounding harsh or cruel, by practicing with pets or salespeople. When you can use your voice firmly enough to get the pets to obey you or salespeople to accept "no" for an answer, you're well on your way to being able to make your children obey without screaming and physical punishment.

Guilt

"When I'm at work, I feel guilty that I'm not with my kids, and when I'm with my kids, I feel guilty that I'm not working." This is a dilemma many parents face. Certainly, working at home can help ease the discomfort of feeling that you should be in two places at once, but sometimes it intensifies a parent's guilt feelings instead.

As one woman told us, "When my daughter comes to the door and says, 'Mommy, please don't work anymore,' I could just cry." Of course, feeling this way splits her energy between her work and her daughter. The result is that she doesn't get to enjoy either one. With feelings like these, it's very hard to send a firm, clear, and consistent message to your children about the importance of not interrupting your work. So instead of getting their cooperation, you end up getting even more interruptions and feeling even more torn.

What can a parent do to combat guilt feelings like these? Recognize that pursuing your career effectively is actually important to your children's futures. Personally, we didn't feel guilty about working because we realized that the best thing we could have done for our son was to love him and care for him while pursuing fulfilling lives for ourselves. This way of acting shows him that it's wonderful to be alive and to grow up. It says that having children is a joy, and that you can love and care for them and live your own life to the fullest, too. For us, working at home made this possible.

When It Doesn't Work

If your needs, the needs of your family, and the needs of your business just don't match up, working at home can be more pain than pleasure, and finding another office location is the best solution. Single parent and publicist Kathy Hubbell encountered such a problem. When she opened her public-relations firm, she decided to work at home so she could be closer to her children, both of whom were in grade school.

"I never dealt very successfully with my guilt about my not being there when they got home from school," Kathy explains. "I've never particularly liked being a single parent. It usually means one provider, but no parent. So I thought working at home would offer a more cohesive way of life and I wouldn't feel so split."

She felt the kids did benefit from her being at home but found her own tensions only increased. "It was really difficult for the kids to understand that when I was in my home office, I was at work and couldn't be disturbed. They were so glad to have me home, they'd just launch in and talk away about their day."

The continual interruptions angered her, but she was torn because she felt they deserved her time after not having had it for so long. For her own sanity, she moved her office out of the house. She felt better, but the kids felt worse than ever. She finally found the solution when she placed an ad in a college newspaper for a male student to come serve as a big brother to the kids and adopted family member, in exchange for room and board.

When Doug joined their household, "the kids stopped fighting, chores were getting done, the whole atmosphere changed, and I began to relax about what I'd find when I came home from work."

Does she still like it better having her office away from home? "No, but since Doug is here, home has become a better place to be. I want to be here again."

Hubbell's story illustrates an important point about working at home with children around. It seemed impossible, yet she finally found a solution that made it feasible and even preferable.

When you work from home and live with children, there will almost certainly be adjustments to make and problems of one kind or another to resolve. Yet with firmness and love and time to share feelings, you're just as likely to find solutions that will make working from home rewarding for all of you.

RESOURCES

BOOKS

Normally, knowing how busy those of us who work from home are, we pick a very few titles we believe to be the best resources on a given topic. For this chapter, however, parents have such a wide range of needs that we have selected more resources than usual and provided some notes as to when a particular book would be helpful.

The age of your child is one factor in seeking the most helpful books, so we've tried to provide books that will be helpful with children at various ages. In addition, it seems that parents either have difficulties that arise from being too strict and rigid, which leads to one set of problems, or they have difficulty being too unstructured and laissez-faire, which leads to a different set of problems, so we've tried to suggest books to provide guidance for each extreme.

The Family Manager's Guide for Working Moms. Kathy Peel. New York: Ballantine, 1997. ISBN: 0345413113. Family-management expert Kathy Peel provides down-to-earth advice on how to involve the whole family in Mom's work schedule. Helpful skills and routines cover social life, food, finances, and much more.

How to Raise a Family and a Career under One Roof. Lisa M. Roberts. Moon Township, Pa.: Bookhaven Press, 1997. ISBN: 0943641179. Advice on how to launch a business while meeting the dynamic demands of a growing family. One interesting twist is a section on how to use your parenting skills to help you become a successful entrepreneur.

In Praise of Single Parents: Mothers and Fathers Embracing the Challenge. Shoshana Alexander. New York: Houghton Mifflin, 1994. ISBN: 039566991X. Practical, firsthand experiences of single parents and how they cope with the demands of raising their children on their own.

Kid-Friendly Parenting with Deaf and Hard of Hearing Children. Denise Chapman-Weston and Daria Medwid. Washington, D.C.: Gallaudet University Press, 1995. ISBN: 1563680319.

Mompreneurs: A Mother's Practical Step-by-Step Guide to Work-at-Home Success. Ellen Palapiano and Patricia Cobe. New York: Perigee, 1996. ISBN: 0399522336.

101 Things You Can Do for Our Children's Future. Richard Luv. New York: Anchor/Doubleday, 1994. ISBN: 0385468784. This is an amazing book outlining 101 things we can do to create the world we want so much to create for our children and be the parents we so much want to be. Helps parents keep their lives in perspective and discusses how we as parents can get support for our needs, too. Includes guidelines for selecting child care and setting up neighborhood co-op nurseries.

P.E.T. Parent Effectiveness Training. Thomas Gordon. New York: New American Library, 1990. ISBN: 0452264618. This is an excellent book for learning how to listen so that children will openly express what they really think and feel. It also teaches parents how to express their own needs so children will be more apt to listen than to tune out. Finally it provides guidelines for doing family problem-solving.

Playwise. Mark and Denise Weston. New York: Putnam, 1996. ISBN: 0874778085.

Siblings Without Rivalry: How to Help Your Children Live Together So You, Too, Can Live. Adele Faber and Elaine Mazlish, Avon, 1998. ISBN: 0380799006.

TeenSpeak! Linda Meyer. Princeton: Peterson's, 1994. ISBN: 1560793384. Examines teen life in America today and helps parents negotiate the difficult teen years.

The Work-at-Home Balancing Act. Sandy Anderson. New York: Avon, 1998. ISBN: 0380798018. A "classic" guide for working parents.

The Working Parents Help Book. Susan Crites Price and Tom Price. Princeton: Peterson's, 1996. ISBN: 1560795794.

Your One-Year-Old : The Fun-Loving, Fussy 12-To 24-Month-Old; Your Two-Year-Old: Terrible or Tender; Your Three-Year-Old: Friend or Enemy; Your Four-Year-Old: Wild and Wonderful; and Your Five-Year-Old: Sunny and Serene. A series by Louise Bates Ames, Frances L. Ilg, and Carol Chase Haber, Doubleday; 1995. ISBN: 0440506727.

CHILD-CARE REFERRAL ASSOCIATIONS AND INFORMATION AGENCIES

The American Council of Nanny Schools. Delta College, Room A-67, University Center, MI 48710; (517) 686-9417.

AuPairCare. 1 Post Street, Ste. 700, San Francisco, CA 94104; (800) 4-Au-Pair.

Au Pair in America. 102 Greenwich Avenue, Greenwich, CT 06830; phone: (800) 727-2437. Web: *www.aifs.org*

Child Care Action Campaign. 330 7th Avenue, 17th Floor, New York, NY 10001; (212) 239-0138. Publishes an information guide, *Finding and Hiring a Qualified In-Home Caregiver,* which you can obtain by sending a self-addressed stamped envelope. *www.kidscampaign.org*

Child Care Aware. 2116 Campus Drive S.E., Rochester, MN 55904; phone: (800) 424-2246. Child-care resources, information, and referrals.

E. F. Au Pair. E. F. Center. 1 Education Street, Cambridge, MA 02141; phone: (800) 333-6056. Web: *www.ef.com*

EurAuPair. 250 N. Coast Highway, Laguna Beach, CA 92651; phone: (800) 333-3804. Web: *www.euraupair.com*

NAPNAP Child Care Guide, by the National Association of Pediatric Nurse Associates and Practitioners. A free booklet provided by Lysol Products, P.O. Box 460, Westbury, NY 11592.

National Association for the Education of Young Children. 1509 16th Street, N.W., Washington, DC 20036; phone: (800) 424-2460. Web: *www.naeyc.org/naeyc*

The National Association for Family Child Care. 206 6th Ave., Suite 900, Des Moines, IA 50309; (515) 282-8192. This association offers accreditation to day-care providers who meet their states' requirements and have been providing care in their own homes for eighteen months. It publishes an annual National Directory of Family Day Care Providers. *www.nafcc.org*

The National Association of Childcare Resource and Referral Agencies, 126 Wood Lake Dr. SE, Rochester, Minn. 55904; phone: (507) 287-2020 or (800) 462-1660.

CHILD-CARE CO-OPS

The Babysitting Co-op Guidebook. Patricia McManus. 915 N. Fourth Street, Philadelphia, PA 19123.

A Parent's Guide to Child Care and Baby-sitting. Warm Lines, 492 Waltham Street, West Newton, MA 02165. A guide for establishing co-op, day-care, and baby-sitting clubs.

NEWSLETTERS & MAGAZINES

At-Home Dads. A quarterly newsletter providing tips and networking for working dads at home. $15/yr. 61 Brightwood Ave. North Andover, MA 01845. *www.athomedad.com*

Child. P.O. Box 3167, Harlan, IA 51593; Web: *www.parents.com* (800) 777-0222.

Parents. P.O. Box 3167, Harlan, IA 51593; (800) 777-0222; Web: *www.parents.com*

Working Mother and *Working Woman.* 230 Park Avenue, NY, NY 10169; (800) 234-9675; Web: *workingwomanmag.com*

HIRING CHILD CARE

Immigration and Naturalization Service offers the *Handbook for Employers* which guides readers in the requirements and documentation required for hiring child-care workers, among others. Call (800) 870-3676 and request the I-9 form and document number M274.

Internal Revenue Service answers questions about withholding taxes and provides the proper forms. Call (800) 829-3676 and request publication numbers 17, 503, and 907.

Nolo's Law Form Kit: Hiring Child Care and Household Help. 1994. Nolo Press Self-Help Law Books and Software, 950 Parker Street, Berkeley, CA. ISBN: 0873372298.

ORGANIZATIONS

Home-Based Working Moms. P.O. Box 50164, Austin, TX 78750; phone: (512) 918-0670. Web: *www.hbwm.com*

Mother's Home Business Network. P.O. Box 423, East Meadow, NY 11554; (516) 997-7394. *www.homeworkingmom.com*

ON LINE

www.partsplace.com
www.parentsoup.com
www.practicalparenting.com
www.divorceinfo.com
http://family.com

CHAPTER 21

Getting Help When You Need It

Goals

1. Identify the help you need.

2. Recognize when it's time to hire help.

3. Pick from six sources of help.

4. Know where to find good help.

5. Get the best from the help you hire.

Most home businesses are one-person or husband-and-wife teams. Yet, many of us have come from salaried employment where we've been used to having a host of supportive office staff. Some of us yearn to replace that support once we're on our own, while others of us are so self-sufficient and self-reliant we'd rather do everything ourselves. And though computers and other home-office equipment can do the work of one to two office personnel, in this age of information overload even the jack-of-all-trades can become burdened by having to do everything without additional help.

Certainly putting other people's efforts to work for you when you need help can extend your time, money, and peace of mind. Most people who work from home ultimately do call upon the skills and talents of a variety of other people to help them get their work done. They build a network of local vendors who provide business supplies and services. They build a team of professionals to handle legal, tax, insurance, and banking needs. They find support staff and personnel to help carry out the day-to-day operations of their work.

You may prefer to do most of the things that need to be done in your business yourself, particularly at first. Certainly the more you can do, the easier it will be to get under way. As a matter of fact, the desire to handle every facet of an enterprise is considered to be an attribute of successful entrepreneurs. But as your home business grows, the time may come when you simply can't, or no longer want to, do it all yourself. In this chapter we talk about how to know when that time has come, how to identify what help you need, where to find it, and how to make the most of it.

 Work Sheet: When Is It Time to Get Help?

How do you know it's time to bring in some help? Here's a checklist of signals that tell you the time has come. Check off any that apply to you

___ When you don't have the skills and expertise to do a job yourself.

___ When it will cost you more to do the job yourself than to hire someone else to do it.

___ When the job can't be done by one person.

___ When you hate doing a task, but it must be done and you can cost-effectively bring in someone else to handle it.

There maybe some necessary tasks you don't have the skills to carry out. Some of these skills, like keyboarding, selling, and marketing, you can and probably should learn.

If you don't type, you may be tempted to hire a secretary or a service to do all your typing for you. Resist this temptation. Typing or keyboarding is a basic entrepreneurial skill that saves time and aggravation and is essential to doing even rudimentary word processing, desktop publishing, E-mail and other basic computer functions. You can still use a secretary or service when you want to, but don't handicap your success by not being able to type when you need to. There are several great software programs for learning to type quickly and easily. You'll find two in the Resources listed at the end of this chapter.

Other skills, like graphic design or accounting, may not be feasible for you to acquire. These situations require hiring the expertise you need. Studies, like the one done by Thorne Riddell, show that successful business owners recognize when they need professional assistance and get it.

When you first begin working on your own, you will probably have free time to do the majority of tasks involved in running your business. Later, some tasks may no longer be cost-effective to do yourself. Writing and formatting a newsletter, for example, can be a good use of your time when you don't have much business. Once your workday is filled with business, how-ever, paying someone else to do these tasks could actually cost you less.

You may also start out being able to handle all the business you can generate, but a sudden burst of seasonal activity or one big order may be more than you can handle alone. At this point, your choice is to hire help or turn away business. You may find yourself forced to act like Van Von Middlesworth, who has a sideline business producing hand-painted toy sol-diers. For shows and special orders he has no problem producing what he needs, but when a large chain wanted a thousand soldiers during the Christmas season, he had to hire help to fill the order.

Finally, when there are tasks that you clearly dislike, neglect, or resist, it's very likely you can find others who are willing to do them. Finding some-one else to assist you under these circumstances will undoubtedly make your life and your work more pleasant and make you more enthusiastic.

The time to get help with unpleasant tasks is when you see that it will free you to generate the business you need to cover the added expenses involved.

Work Sheet: What Help Do You Need?

Here are a variety of tasks people working at home often dislike, can't do alone, or find more cost-effective to have done for them. Review the list for those that apply to you.

___ Accounting	___ Filing
___ Advertising	___ Marketing
___ Answering the phone	___ Office management
___ Assembly	___ Organizing
___ Bookkeeping	___ Pickup
___ Cleaning	___ Public relations
___ Computer maintenance/configuration	___ Research
___ Data entry	___ Shipping
___ Delivery	___ Tax preparation

SIX SOURCES FOR GETTING THE HELP YOU NEED

Working at home can present various roadblocks to getting the full range of help you need. Money certainly is one, because most people start working from home on a limited budget. Space is frequently another; the typical household can take only so much equipment and very few employees before it begins to feel overcrowded. Finally, finding the right people to do the work under home-office circumstances can also become a problem. But none of these obstacles is insurmountable. Here are six workable alternatives to doing everything yourself.

1) Using Other Business Services

Because the number and range of services available for small businesses continue to grow, you may be able to purchase what you need without hiring any employees.

Printing services are available in most neighborhoods. In addition to standard printing and duplicating, many of these shops offer design, Internet and Web consulting, and other services. You can also use computer consulting, secretarial, bookkeeping, answering, messenger, cleaning, and research services, to mention just a few. Many of these services are home businesses themselves.

In our neighborhood, we have been able to create a network of small home businesses with whom we trade. Our artist, cartoonist, audio technician, and researcher all operate home businesses in our area. It's like having our own organization, without the cost of an office building or the ongoing overhead of employing them.

By purchasing services, you pay only for what you need when you need it. And because businesses that don't provide a good service won't be able to stay in business, businesses are likely to want to please and stand behind their work.

Because these businesses have overhead to support, you will pay more per hour or per task than if you hired your own employee. You may also have to wait until a service can get to your work. Sometimes, when you need them most, they're too busy to help. The service will improve, however, if you become a regular customer. And the better a customer you become, the more willing they will be to extend themselves and help you out in emergencies.

You can locate services through your local business Yellow Pages, the Chamber of Commerce, networking groups, or on line. Once you find a service, try it out for a while. Then, if you're satisfied, keep using the same service so they'll pay special attention to you.

2) Hiring and Contracting for the Help You Need

When you need someone to come in and work with you shoulder to shoulder, hiring help is usually going to be the answer, and here are several different ways you can do it.

Full-time employees. If you hire the right full-time employee, you will have a loyal and hardworking person you can count on day in and day out to get the job done for you. Such employees are worth their weight in gold and may be the answer to ensuring that you'll have the help you need.

However, the primary reasons most people choose to work from home are to keep their overhead low and to simplify their working life. Hiring employees may deprive you of some of these benefits. There are payroll, tax, and insurance costs to consider, and unless you have enough work for a full-time person, you may find that the employee has nothing to do, and you need to manufacture something to keep him or her busy.

The decision as to when to add full-time personnel, therefore, is one of timing and personal goals. If you hire prematurely, you threaten your financial peace of mind because hired help always gets paid first! On the other hand, if you postpone hiring needed help, you may lose business. And sometimes that's a choice we must make. There are people who prefer to stay smaller rather than assume the responsibility and pressure of "meeting payroll."

One consultant told us, "At first I enjoyed having my own secretary. It made me feel like an executive, but paying her monthly salary really put me behind the eight ball. I had to support someone else before I could support myself! Finally I decided to let her go and hire an answering service and occasional office support services. It felt like someone had taken a weight off my shoulders."

In addition, you have to provide work space, equipment, and supplies for your employee. Unless you plan to rent separate space, this means you will have another person coming into your home every day. In some areas this can present a problem with zoning. Certain municipalities allow home businesses but prohibit having employees on the property. Finally, as C.P.A. Bernard Kamoroff points out in his book *The Small-Time Operator,* "Hiring employees will just about double the amount of your paperwork." When you become an employer, you must keep separate payroll records, withhold federal income and Social Security taxes, withhold state income and possibly state disability taxes, prepare quarterly and year-end payroll tax returns, pay the employee's portion of Social Security taxes and unemployment taxes, usually purchase workers' compensation insurance, and prepare year-end earnings statements for each employee.

You will also need to familiarize yourself with state and federal regulations regarding such things as minimum-wage laws, fair-employment practices, employee benefits including health insurance and unemployment insurance, and the federal disability act. See the checklist that follows for a summary of these many requirements. The costs of these requirements has been estimated to add 30 percent to the salary you pay an employee.

Work Sheet: Legal Aspects of Hiring an Employee

State and federal regulations for hiring employees vary according to the number of employees and/or the nature of your business. This checklist of issues to address is from *The Hiring and Firing Book: The Complete Legal Guide for Employers,* by Steven Mitchell, which provides detailed information about each of these issues. When hiring an employee, you can also use this list in checking with state agencies and your attorney or tax adviser to determine how and when these government laws and regulations apply to you.

Hiring and Firing Practices

These and other laws define what you can and cannot do in advertising, setting job requirements and job descriptions, screening and selecting job applicants, making a job offer, and terminating an employee:

___ Americans with Disabilities Act

___ The Civil Rights Act

___ Immigration Reform and Control Act

___ Fair Debt Credit and Reporting Act

___ Wage and Hour Regulations

Benefits, Financial Considerations, and On-the-Job Policies

The following laws and regulations affect your day-to-day operating practices, including such things as holidays, vacations, wages and salaries, overtime, privacy, draws and advances, personal liability, and privacy:

___ Social Security Tax and Federal

___ Income Tax Withholding

___ Federal Unemployment Taxes

___ State Withholding

___ State Disability Insurance

___ State Unemployment Insurance

___ Workers' Compensation

___ Insurance

___ Employee Benefit Plans (ERISA)

___ Federal and Health Insurance Requirements

___ Employee Safety and Health Requirements

___ Fair Labor Standards Act (FLSA)

___ Older Workers' Benefit Protection Act

___ The Sherman Anti-Trust Act

(Continued on page 566)

(Continued from page 565)

Employee Fringe Benefits and Personnel Policies

When you have employees, you need to determine the fringe benefits you will offer and establish policies for managing them. Common fringe benefits that employees may expect are listed below:

___ Health Insurance   ___ Vacations

___ Disability income insurance   ___ Sick leave

___ Life insurance   ___ Retirement plan

___ Paid holidays

Written personnel policies covering the following issues are also advisable:

___ Working hours   ___ Probationary period

___ Lunch hour   ___ Termination

___ Job description   ___ Payroll schedule

___ Breaks   ___ Confidentiality

___ Absences   ___ Tardiness

___ Harassment policy   ___ Grievance policy

Because of the complexities of having employees, you may prefer to use an employee leasing service (see page 569), or you can pay others to handle the excess paperwork. You can also contract a payroll service to manage many of the formalities involved in having employees, although you will still be legally responsible for them.

Our advice is to consider some of the other alternatives we'll be discussing before you decide to hire. If full-time employees are your best answer, consult your attorney and accountant for help in setting up the easiest and most workable arrangements for handling the responsibilities of being an employer.

Part-time employees. Although hiring part-time employees may pose some of the same problems as full-time workers does, many home-based businesses opt for part-timers, either to save costs or because several part-time employees can do a variety of specialized tasks that no one person could do alone.

Career consultant Marisa Magana, for example, has three part-time employees. A secretary works three days a week typing, filing, and returning phone calls. A training assistant accompanies Marisa to seminars and workshops to manage all the on-site logistical arrangements. And she has a research assistant who does library work for her.

Hiring part-time employees also helps meet short-term high-volume demands. For example, Paul and Gretchen Fava rented a warehouse and hired seventy part-time workers to achieve the high buildup of inventory needed to fill orders for their hand-painted Christmas decorations. After reaching the inventory level they wanted, operations returned to the reno-vated guest house behind their home where they maintain their inventory with the help of a handful of part-time college students.

Independent contractors. Many people prefer to hire independent contractors for specific tasks and pay on a fee-for-service basis. Indepen-dent contractors are self-employed individuals who usually work for more than one client. An independent researcher, for example, will work on proj-ects for various clients and charge individually for each task.

As Bob Baxter's business, Pet Organics, grew from twenty-four ac-counts to five hundred, he decided to expand by using independent con-tractors. Instead of mixing, bottling, and preparing to ship natural flea treatments in his garage, he contracts with someone to produce, bottle, and ship the products for him. Rather than call on only those retail stores he can visit himself, he has contracted independent salespeople to represent his line to retailers.

Designer Ben Lizardi contracts with an independent Web site devel-oper. "If a client asks me to build a site, I simply call in my contractor," ex-plains Ben. "That way I can concentrate on my forte, which is design, without having to take the time to keep up with the ever-changing techni-cal side of the Internet. And since Web sites are only a portion of my busi-ness, I don't have someone on staff who is only being utilized half of the time."

As these examples illustrate, using contractors can help you control costs while expanding your capabilities. Contractors generally provide their own facilities, supplies, and equipment. Another advantage is that using contractors provides you with the flexibility to find the best services possible for the specific task. Being small-business operators themselves, indepen-dent contractors may have a keen understanding of your needs as a small business. They face many of the same issues you do and may work at home.

Since an independent contractor is not an employee, you do not have to withhold taxes, pay employment taxes, or file payroll tax returns. When you pay an independent contractor over $600 a year, you do, however, have to file IRS Form 1099 with the Internal Revenue Service and send a copy to the individual.

Warning!!!

A word of caution. Do not think that you can simply employ someone and call him or her an "independent contractor." The IRS position is that if the person is an employee, the label you give that employee doesn't matter. In other words, to the Internal Revenue Service, an employee by any other name is still an employee. To help you understand exactly who is and who isn't an employee, the IRS puts out a free publication, Circular E—Employer's Tax Guide. We have summarized these points on pages 299–303 in chapter 10.

The disadvantage of using independent contractors is that your work may not be their first priority. They may not be available when you want them. There may be delays in getting your work done while they work for others. Also, independent contractors only become knowledgeable about your business needs if you use them frequently. They may fail to produce work done the way you want it, but unless you have a contract that covers this possibility, you may have little practical recourse other than to go elsewhere.

Technical writer David Treweek learned this the hard way. He hired two free-lance writers to assist him in completing a large contract. Coordination with their busy schedules was difficult, then one writer got bogged down in personal problems that nearly resulted in a business disaster. The writer submitted incomplete work directly to the client and charged Treweek for the work that hadn't been done. Only some fast talking saved the contract. He fired the writer and will be more careful in the future to screen those with whom he subcontracts. If you are planning to hire independent contractors, get and check out references and spell out procedures, deadlines, and work to be done in clear written agreements. Also consider using contractors for small, less-important jobs before trusting them with larger and more vital work.

Warning!!!

Some temporary help agencies will not send employees into a home office. Search out those that do and participate in local business organizations like the Chamber of Commerce to become personally acquainted with temp agency owners to establish the legitimacy of your home business.

Temporary-Help agencies. For certain short-term assistance, you can hire help through a temporary service. Temporary services are primarily limited to secretarial and office management personnel. On the other hand, these agencies have the advantage of being able to provide you with reliable help quickly, without your

(Continued on page 569)

(Continued from page 568)

spending the time and money to locate and select someone. The agency handles all financial arrangements with the employee and bills you for the service. The agency also stands behind the work. The cost is usually somewhat higher than using an independent contractor, and you cannot depend upon getting the same person again.

Employee leasing companies. One way to have employees while saving yourself the paperwork and legal responsibility of being an employer is to lease employees from a staffing company. Doctors and dentists have been using these services for years. You maintain substantial control over the employee, except that if the worker assigned to you must be fired, you send the employee back to the staffing company instead of releasing the person yourself. For managing all the legal and administrative responsibilities of your staff, you pay the leasing company a fee over and above the cost of the employees' earnings and benefits each month.

3) Bartering or Exchanging Arrangements

Barter is a cashless exchange of services that some home businesspeople find useful for getting the assistance or the products they need. It works by offering your services to someone who needs them in exchange for their providing services to you. In exchange for providing word-processing services, Barbara Elman, publisher of *Word Processing News,* set up a barter agreement with her answering service. They answer her phone; she does their mailing labels each month.

Barter obviously reduces your costs or enables you to have assistance you could otherwise not afford. To barter for services on your own, you can simply take the initiative and ask people who offer the work you need if they are willing to barter. You may be surprised at how many people will consider it. Marilyn Miller, for example, was surprised to discover that she could barter to have color slides made for her management-training presentations. When she realized she would need slides of higher quality than those she was presently using to accompany a planned fee increase, she decided to approach an audio/video service about training its staff in exchange for a set of top-quality four-color slides. They said "yes!" So go ahead and ask. You may be surprised at the response.

However, it may be difficult to find the appropriate person with whom to trade services or products. Barter clubs enable you to overcome this problem. They keep a credit balance for you, so if you offer a service to one member, you get credit to receive services from any other member.

There are over five hundred barter exchange networks in the United States offering virtually every possible personal and business service. Most barter networks charge a fee to join and a commission on each transaction, which is split between the two parties. Some networks also charge a monthly fee. The advantage of such an exchange is that you can collect barter credits so you don't need to locate someone who needs your service in order to take advantage of theirs.

As a designer, for example, you might provide design services for an ad agency in the network and then use your barter credit to have your printing done by a printer who belongs to the network. Keep in mind, however, that these clubs often require a considerable start-up fee, though, and may or may not have the business services you need in your area.

When bartering, make a clear agreement as to the value of the services you are exchanging and evaluate the trustworthiness and experience of those you barter with, just as you would when purchasing the service. As with all contracts, you're best protected against misunderstanding by putting the agreement in writing.

 Warning!!!

The IRS considers business services received through bartering as income, and business services you provide through bartering as deductible business expenses. So keep records of your exchanges, and make sure the values you claim represent actual market rates.

---

4) Teaming Up with Others

Affiliating with others whose skills support and supplement yours can be another way to find the help you need. In fact, this is fast becoming one of the most popular trends among self-employed and small business owners. According the National Foundation for Women Business Owners, over half of women-owned businesses are started with at least one other person.

Here are three common ways you can team up to help your business grow:

Calling on customers and clients. Explore the possibilities of using or buying the services of companies for whom you are working. These companies may be glad to see you purchase services like financial consulting or insurance to help offset their overhead costs. They may even be willing to let you use company services without charge, or as part of the fee they're paying you.

Sharing expenses or efforts. Pooling expenses with colleagues or competitors can provide you with help you might not otherwise be able to afford. Two women we interviewed share a secretary, each employing her part-time. Other home businesses are using what's called co-op advertising, in which several of them share the costs of advertising their related products and services. Lynne Frances found she could share certain expenses with an owner of another cleaning service, and they assist each other when short on cleaning crews.

Joint ventures. By entering into joint ventures with others who have skills or expertise you need, you can accomplish much that would be impossible to do yourself. In a joint venture, you affiliate with others to provide a service or produce a product, and then share together in any profits. No one individual has to make a large cash investment. Each invests primarily his or her own time and talents. But everyone involved benefits when the venture is successful.

A professional development consultant we know arranges joint ventures on all the training tapes he produces. He writes the material and joins with others who produce the film and still others who market it. They all share an agreed-upon percentage of the profits on the finished productions.

Since partners are often investing their time without payment or at a reduced fee, a joint venture usually becomes a side venture. Locating dedicated and honest partners is therefore crucial. You have to rely on their conduct and efforts for the success of your project.

 Warning!!!

Legally, joint ventures are partnerships. This means you will be liable for anything your partners do in relation to the project. Having a written contract or partnership agreement is a necessary safeguard.

The best way to locate people interested in sharing expenses or joint-venturing is through professional or trade associations in your field, networking, and relationships with competitors or other businesses that complement yours. For more information on a wide variety of ways to team up with colleagues and associates, see our book with Rick Benzel, *Teaming Up: The Small Business Guide to Collaborating with Others to Boost Your Earnings and Expand Your Horizons.* (It's listed in the Resources at the end of this chapter.)

5) Getting Assistance from Family Members

Using family members to do jobs that need to be done provides an opportunity for them to share in your work and is a way for you to limit your expenses. You can ask for volunteers or you can offer wages.

Hiring your children has a tax advantage too. When you hire your children to work for you, their salaries are a deductible business expense, while their earnings are taxed at a much lower rate than yours. In fact, there is no tax for earnings below a certain amount each year.

Family members may not always be reliable workers, however. Sometimes they don't want to help or may be too busy doing other things to follow through for you. Family squabbles may spill over into work activities, and vice versa. So when you hire a family member or ask your family for free assistance, we recommend that it be strictly a voluntary matter rather than something you expect, coerce, or finagle someone into doing.

6) Calling on Employers or Contractors

If you are salaried, working on a commission, or under a contract, explore the services your employer or contractor can provide for you. At-home employees are still not the norm, so companies are not always aware of their needs. So express your needs and ask for support.

If you are working with a franchise or are in direct sales, explore with the franchiser or the direct-selling organization what additional support services they can furnish you with. Different companies offer different levels of assistance. Many provide extensive training, promotional materials, and displays. If you are working under a contract, contractors are often more than happy to let you use their facilities and support services when doing so helps reduce the expense of the contract or improves the quality of the project.

 Checklist: Where to Find Help

To find employees, independent contractors, and employment services, you can use:

____ *Telephone Yellow Pages.* Various employment services are listed under "Employment." Independent contractors are listed by field—for example, Translation services. They usually have one-line listings under their own names.

____ *College placement offices.* Students seeking part-time work or contracting out their services are often listed with these offices.

____ *Referrals from associates.* Associates are good sources of information about independent contractors they have been satisfied with. Part-time employees of associates may also be looking for additional work.

(Continued on page 573)

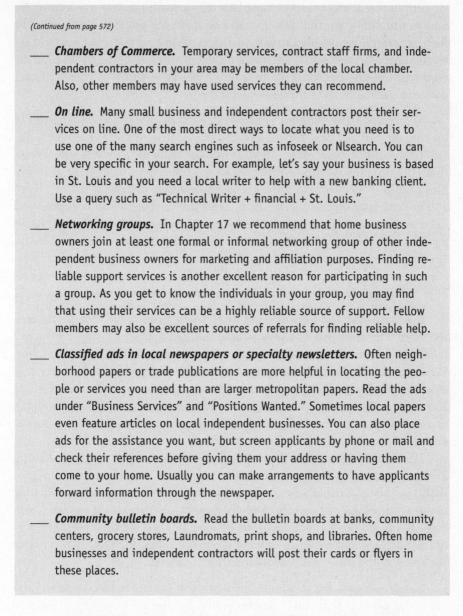

(Continued from page 572)

____ ***Chambers of Commerce.*** Temporary services, contract staff firms, and independent contractors in your area may be members of the local chamber. Also, other members may have used services they can recommend.

____ ***On line.*** Many small business and independent contractors post their services on line. One of the most direct ways to locate what you need is to use one of the many search engines such as infoseek or Nlsearch. You can be very specific in your search. For example, let's say your business is based in St. Louis and you need a local writer to help with a new banking client. Use a query such as "Technical Writer + financial + St. Louis."

____ ***Networking groups.*** In Chapter 17 we recommend that home business owners join at least one formal or informal networking group of other independent business owners for marketing and affiliation purposes. Finding reliable support services is another excellent reason for participating in such a group. As you get to know the individuals in your group, you may find that using their services can be a highly reliable source of support. Fellow members may also be excellent sources of referrals for finding reliable help.

____ ***Classified ads in local newspapers or specialty newsletters.*** Often neighborhood papers or trade publications are more helpful in locating the people or services you need than are larger metropolitan papers. Read the ads under "Business Services" and "Positions Wanted." Sometimes local papers even feature articles on local independent businesses. You can also place ads for the assistance you want, but screen applicants by phone or mail and check their references before giving them your address or having them come to your home. Usually you can make arrangements to have applicants forward information through the newspaper.

____ ***Community bulletin boards.*** Read the bulletin boards at banks, community centers, grocery stores, Laundromats, print shops, and libraries. Often home businesses and independent contractors will post their cards or flyers in these places.

MAKING THE MOST OF THE HELP YOU GET

Whatever type of help you use, there are several guidelines you can follow to ensure a top-quality job.

Clearly define what you want done. First, before you even decide on the type of help you want, define precisely what you need someone to do. We suggest writing or sketching it out. Sometimes you have to do some research to find out what you actually need.

Producing the covers for some tape albums we created was a good example. Originally we thought it would be a simple process. But before we
hired a printer, we decided to talk with several to find out what it would involve. There turned out to be many different ways of doing it, and having
reviewed the choices we were in a much better position to hire a printer
with experience in the process we preferred.

Select the right people. Finding the right people is usually a matter of
looking carefully at past experience and present capabilities. Getting referrals from satisfied customers in your field is probably the best way. When
that isn't possible, getting—and checking—references or looking at examples of past work can help provide the information you need.

In talking with prospective help, raise the problems and concerns you
have in relation to the work you're hiring them for. If you're under a tight
deadline, for example, express your concern that it be done in time. If you
need the worker to take certain precautions when dealing with customers,
explain what they are. Then listen and watch the person respond. Does he
have solutions? Is she confident about handling the situations you present?

Don't assume the help you get knows what you want. We discovered
the hard way that just because people are good at what they do doesn't
mean they know how to do what you want. Be specific. Draw sketches.
Write out a list. Bring in samples. Define the end product with care and
monitor the progress. Have checkpoints to look at, or talk with workers
about the progress they're making. Consider hiring someone for a small job
and reviewing the work before hiring that person for larger or more important projects.

Hiring a designer for a flyer is a good example of this process. Writing
out the correctly spelled text is only the beginning. Don't leave the designer
with the job of writing sales points, figuring out your market or learning
about your product or service. Specify exactly what you want to communicate. If you do not know enough to be specific, ask for the designer's recommendations and a sample of what the piece would look like. Then ask to
see the way the piece will look before it is finalized.

Set deadlines. Set deadlines for when the work is to be completed and
get an agreement that it will be completed by that time. To be on the safe
side, call or talk with the person along the way to see if things are on schedule. The more advance notice you have of problems, the easier it will be to
revise your plans.

*Get an understanding about what will be done if work isn't satis-
factory.* The best policy, of course, is to expect the person will stand behind the work and redo it if it isn't right. You do not have to accept less than
the quality you wanted, providing you were clear about what you were expecting in the first place.

Also identify who will pay for costs incurred from mistakes. After one costly error, marketing specialist Gene Call negotiates with all the designers he uses to ensure that if the mailings they design for him don't meet U.S. Postal Service requirements, the designers will be liable for the resulting cost. Added postage on 100,000 mailings, because the piece was oversize, is an expensive error. And more than once a designer has had to pay the extra bill.

Treat the people you hire like people. When you're considerate, thoughtful, and understanding of the people you hire, they go out of their way to do a better job. Greeting those who work for you, complimenting them when they're helpful, and listening to the concerns they raise are part of the honey that sweetens any business relationship. One sympathetic word that shows you understand the pressures or difficulties can win you work that goes above and beyond the call of duty.

Pay on time. The best way to have people begin dragging their feet or doing less than their best on your job is to delay or overlook payment you owe. Pay immediately in accordance with whatever arrangements you have established.

Reward good work. Reward good work with praise, repeat business, salary increases, bonuses or referrals. Under whatever arrangements people work for you, they generally appreciate recognition for a job well done. Giving it to them is a way of increasing their desire to please you again and again.

With the variety of possible arrangements you can make for getting help, you should be able to find whatever support you need while working from home. Whenever you want assistance, you can review the options we've discussed for getting the help you need, and then use the strategies given to make the most of the help you get.

RESOURCES

BOOKS

The Employer's Legal Handbook. Fred S. Steingold. Berkely, Calif.: Nolo Press, 1997. ISBN: 0873373707.

Hiring & Firing Book: A Complete Legal Guide for Employers. Steven Mitchell Sack. Mattituck, NY: Legal Strategies, Inc., 1996. ISBN: 0963630652.

Selling Through Independent Reps. Harold Novick. Saranac Lake, NY: Amacom, 1994. ISBN: 0814451462.

Small-Time Operator. See full citation under chapter 14.

Teaming Up: The Small Business Guide to Collaborating with Others to Boost Your Earnings and Expand Your Horizons. Paul and Sarah Edwards, with Rick Benzel. New York: Tarcher/Putnam, 1997. ISBN: 0874778425.

NEWSLETTERS AND PERIODICALS

Barter News. P.O. Box 3024, Mission Viejo, CA 92690; phone: (949) 831-0607. Web: *www.barternews.com*

Internal Revenue Service (see chapter 10 for full citation): Employer's Tax Guide, Circular E.

TRADE ASSOCIATIONS

The International Reciprocal Trade Association. 175 West Jackson Boulevard, Ste. 625, Chicago, IL 60604; (312) 461-0236. For information on how bartering can benefit your business and to identify barter exchanges in your area, send a self-addressed, stamped envelope. Web: *www.irta.net*

ON LINE

The International Reciprocal Trade Association (IRTA). *www.irta.net*

The National Association of Trade Exchanges (NATE). *www.nate.org*

PART 6

Getting Business
and Growing

CHAPTER 22

Pricing: Determining What to Charge

Goals

1. Avoid the common pricing mistakes.

2. Determine your costs.

3. Calculate your overhead.

4. Add your profit.

5. Know when and how to raise your prices.

6. Pick a winning pricing strategy.

On our way to teach a marketing seminar, we stopped at an out-of-the-way service station/general store/post office where a wizened old-timer in bib overalls asked us what we were doing all dressed up in three-piece suits. When we told him we'd stopped to get a soda on our way to give a marketing seminar he said, "Boys, I'm gonna tell you all you need to know about marketing in three sentences. You got to know what your stuff costs. You got to know what you can sell it for. And you got to learn to live on the difference.

Tim Rooney, Marketing Consultant

"What shall I charge?" This is one of the most common questions prospective home-based business owners ask at our seminars. If you've ever read anything about pricing or attended a seminar on pricing, you've undoubtedly discovered the question is not so much "What shall I charge?" as "How do I determine what to charge?"

Although you'll encounter a wide variety of complex "formulas" set forth by business experts, in reality there is no simple answer to what to charge. Even veteran businesspeople often find themselves wondering if they're missing sales by charging too much, or if they could get away with charging even more. That's why the range of advice novice entrepreneurs receive about pricing is often enough to make their heads spin. Here are a few examples of the type of advice we've been given:

> *"Set your price so low that they can't refuse."*
> *"Never discount your prices."*
> *"Charge the going rate."*
> *"Charge just below the going rate."*
> *"Charge just above the going rate."*
> *"Add up your direct costs, overhead, and profit and that's your price."*
> *"Find out what everyone else charges and position yourself in*
> *the middle."*

Does this sound familiar? Bob Wittenberg found out—there may not be a "going rate." When Bob set out to research what to charge for freelance copywriting, he found writers who were charging as little as $25 an hour and others who were charging over $100 an hour, and almost every amount in between. So how do you know what to charge? The answer is that you don't know what to charge, you discover what to charge.

Pricing, like marketing, is an experiment. It's like cooking without a recipe. You're balancing many sensitive factors and adjusting the combinations until you get one that suits the palates of your customers. Like diners choosing a restaurant, some customers want a no-frills cafeteria while others prefer only an elite tearoom or a trendy bistro.

In this chapter we want to provide you with a basic guide to consider in determining your own ideal pricing recipe. You'll learn from the experience of many successful home-based businesses how to avoid the most common mistakes open-collar workers make in pricing their services, and discover how taking the time and energy to find the right price can be a key to your success.

FOUR QUESTIONS THAT
DETERMINE YOUR PRICE

Occasionally, the price of a particular home-based product or service is driven, like the price of gasoline, by the marketplace. Clothing merchandising consultant Martina Polaski's specialty is such a business. "All the manufacturers pay the same thing for what I do. It's the rock-bottom price. They know what they can get it for and that's that." Under such circumstances, pricing is a matter of finding out how you can run your business successfully at the prevailing price.

Most home-based ventures, however, tend to be more personalized by nature. This means you probably won't be unduly constrained by what someone else is charging. More likely you'll have a great deal of flexibility, as we described above. Therefore, to find the right price, you need to begin by doing some investigation to determine the following:

1. *How much is your product or your service worth in concrete terms?* Value, like beauty, is in the mind of the beholder. It's highly subjective. The value people place on what you offer will vary according to their needs and their perceptions of what your product or service will do for them. The more concrete you can make the value of your work, the easier it will be to determine your price, and then get it.

Here are several questions you can ask to help set the value of what you offer. Can someone get this product or service elsewhere? How much are they paying now? What would they have to pay someone else? Does your product or service save or produce money for your customer? For example, if you're supplying dried flower gift baskets to local hospitals, the hospitals save the costs of having them shipped in from out of the area. Or, if hiring you to design a direct-mail campaign will generate $25,000 of income for your client, you could be a bargain at $5,000.

When the benefits of your business are more intangible in nature, think in terms of how much they are worth relative to other things people buy. For example, people might spend $50 for an entertaining evening at the theater. Paying $50 to attend your evening workshop on real-estate investing, however, could be profitable and might even be entertaining. Parents might pay $80 or more for a pair of shoes for their junior highschooler. Paying you the same amount for two tutoring sessions could help their child catch up in math.

2. *What will people actually pay?* No matter how much a product or service may be worth, if people won't pay a price they perceive as high, it won't sell. A good example of this problem is Carol Hartager's beautiful hand-painted greeting cards. Because they could each easily be framed as a work of art, she thought $10 was a fair retail price. Greeting-card store buyers didn't agree. They thought $10 was too much. When Carol placed them on consignment in a local store, she discovered that the customers thought so too. They didn't sell until she had reduced the price to $3.

Perception of value can be as important as the actual value. If the customer thinks your price is too high, you'll end up without work or with a garage full of inventory. At the other extreme, if buyers perceive something as too cheap, they either won't buy it or they'll worry about what the "catch" is. Many new entrepreneurs are surprised to discover they can actually sell more by charging more. A book, for example, that wasn't selling at $19.95 sold briskly when repackaged as a workbook at $99.95; a software package sold much better at $69.95 than it did at $30.00.

So don't rely on your own perceptions of what people will pay. Your perceptions are limited by your upbringing and experience, and may be outdated or at least different from those of your market. Find out what your clients and customers are accustomed to paying and match your price as closely to their expectations as possible.

Shirley Glickman learned this the hard way. As a teacher, she knew what public school systems paid for outside consultants. When she left her teaching job to conduct values-clarification workshops for corporate training departments, she set her fees based on her experience in the school system—and had a lot of trouble closing sales! Prospective clients seemed interested until she mentioned her fee. Then their interest cooled. She feared her price was too high. By asking around at professional associations for trainers, however, she was amazed to discover that companies were used to paying almost double her fee for outside consultants. With such cut-rate fees, they weren't taking her seriously. When she raised her prices to what was expected, she closed sales.

Underpricing is one of the most frequent mistakes home-based businesses make.

 True Confessions

As desktop publisher Matt McCaffrey advises, "Don't sell yourself short—I landed a design contract recently at a rate 35 percent above the prevailing wage in my area because I valued my time appropriately and was firm in my requirements."

Programmer Kristi Wachter agrees. She says, "I still feel weird telling people I'm charging $75 an hour when this little voice in my head keeps reminding me of all the jobs I've worked on at a salary of $10 an hour. But companies are used to paying this kind of money for the consulting help they need. And remember, they're paying for all the time you've put in to develop the expertise you have. You are not an employee any longer, you're supporting yourself. No one's paying for your coffee breaks, benefits, or anything else."

Marketing consultant John Elmer, writing for *Marketing News*, points out that each aspect of pricing serves a different purpose:

- Calculating your costs simply sets a baseline that enables you to determine if you can offer a product or service profitably.

- Ascertaining what your competition is charging orients you to what your marketplace has been paying and will consider to be a fair price.

(Continued on page 583)

(Continued from page 582)

- Determining what your customers or clients would "expect" to pay for what you're offering helps you avoid turning off your buyer with a price that's too high to be "worth it" or too low to be "worth anything." It can tell you when you can raise your prices or explain why sales have not been as brisk as you expected.

Elmer uses a research technique called PSM (Pricing Sensitivity Measurement) to gather the data he needs to let the marketplace set his prices. Using the PSM method, prospective buyers read a product description accompanied with pictures, samples, or diagrams. He then presents them with a pricing scale starting with $0 up to fifteen to thirty possible prices. Prospective buyers use the scale to indicate at which point they would consider the product or service to be too "expensive" for them to buy on the one end and too "cheap" to be considered of high-enough quality on the other end.

The result is a price range in which people will perceive value without "sticker shock."

3. *Are you charging enough to make it worth your while?* You can make a million dollars but if it costs you more than a million to make a million, you've lost money. As graphics designer Todd Minor found out, making money can be deceptive. He had two major contracts his first year in business that produced over a quarter of a million dollars. Things seemed to be rolling along. But by year's end, he was in debt. In his eagerness to be the low bidder on these contracts, he had unknowingly run his company into a hole.

When setting your prices, make sure you'll have more coming in than you have going out. That means charging a price that covers your direct and indirect costs with some to spare, in fact, here's a commonly used pricing formula for covering all your costs.

Popular Pricing Formula
direct costs + overhead + profit = price

Direct costs refers to costs you incur as a direct result of producing your product or providing your service. For example, if you are making and selling gift baskets, the supplies used in each basket are a direct cost. If you provide a mobile computer-repair service, the cost of driving to your customer's office is a direct cost. So is the cost of any parts you replace for them. If you are doing public relations, costs of telephone calls you make to book a client on out-of-town talk shows is a direct cost as is the cost of printing and mailing media kits on their behalf. And so is the time you spend on these projects!

Yes, your time is a direct cost. For purposes of doing business, you have to factor in the cost of your time as if you were an employee of your business. For the single-person service business, your time is all you have to sell. You can't make any more money than you can bill out. For example, as a psychotherapist, you have only so many hours a week in which to see clients; as a trainer, you have only so many days a month on which you can train people. Even if your business is manufacturing a product, your time is a labor cost.

To determine what to charge for your time, consider what you would have to pay if you had to hire someone with your background and experience to do what you do. Or if you are doing the same thing as you did on your last job, calculate your salary including the fringe benefits into your current rates.

Many new home-based business owners underprice themselves by leaving out the value of their time or by forgetting to include the cost of their fringe benefits when calculating their fees.

Also remember you can't possibly bill out every hour of the business week. Some portion of your time must be spent marketing and administering your business. You have to set the cost of your billable time high enough to compensate you for your time that isn't billable.

Overhead refers to all the costs of being in and doing business that are not directly attributable to a specific product or service, whether or not you have any business. For example, the cost of your computer equipment, your software, utilities, office supplies, an 800 number, advertising and marketing costs, tax preparer's and attorney's fees, even bank charges and other administrative costs, are all overhead costs. Everything you must spend to stay in business counts as overhead.

At first, of course, you may not know what your overhead is, but you can estimate those costs you are aware of. You can also go to the library to consult books such as *Annual Statement Studies* by Robert Morris Associates, Dunn & Bradstreet's *Industry Norms and Key Business Ratios,* Prentice-Hall's *Almanac of Business and Industry Financial Ratios,* and *Business Profitability Data* from Weybridge Publishing Company for a review of industry norms.

In doing interviews for our book *Best Home Businesses for the New Century,* we discovered that owners of most home businesses do not know precisely what their overhead is, and that average overhead ranged roughly from 20 to 30 percent of income. Standard overhead for larger businesses is from two and a half to three and a half times the wage rate, but someone who is home-based can usually beat that. Some tell us they multiply their hourly wage by 2.6.

Sometimes people have difficulty distinguishing between overhead and direct costs. The simplest explanation we've found is that overhead relates to costs you have when you're in business, whether you have any customers or clients or not. Direct costs are costs you incur only once you're actually providing a product or service for clients or customers.

EXAMPLES OF DIRECT COSTS:	EXAMPLES OF OVERHEAD:
Your salary while providing your service or product	Office supplies and equipment
Fees to consultants helping on a project for a client or customer	Marketing costs or consultant fees to advise you on advertising or sales
Travel and transportation	Basic business telephone
Copies made for a client project	Web site server fees, computer consultant fees to configure you new computer
Materials used for the project	
Postage used for the client project	Utilities
Equipment or facility rental to provide your service to a client or assemble a client order	Vacation, holidays, sick time
	Health insurance

Profit is any money that's left over after you pay all direct and indirect expenses. Many business experts advise adding 15 to 20 percent or more to your price over and above all your costs. This is considered your reward for the risk you take to be in business or as an allowance for development.

Many home-based businesspeople, however, do not include profit in calculating their prices.

Often this is because they aren't aware they could be adding in profit or because they fear that to survive they must cut their prices to a bare minimum. Others, however, feel that being self-employed is more a benefit than a risk. They reason that if they have charged adequately for their time, they're being compensated sufficiently. Viewed this way, profit is more like a tip. It's what you get because you haven't paid yourself enough.

You can use costing or spreadsheet software to experiment with various scenarios until you find your best possible price. Of course, you won't know how much you can really charge until you actually take your product or service out into the marketplace. The feedback you get there will guide you as to the changes you need to make. You may be able to charge more than you imagined, or you may find that you have to adjust your costs so you can lower your price.

Ultimately, the important thing in setting your price is that one way or another you are earning enough to provide yourself with a comfortable-enough lifestyle to make running your business well worth the effort. If you can't command such a price, then you should rethink your business choice.

 Rule of Thumb

If to cover your costs and produce the requisite quality of product or service you must charge more than people are accustomed to paying, build so much value into what you offer that people are so relieved to hear your price that they're willing to pay more than they otherwise would.

 True Confession

Here's a case in point for the above rule of thumb. While browsing through art shops, we found a particularly stunning piece and asked the price, hoping it would be reasonable. Instead of giving us the price, the clerk began telling us about the artist in a tone that conveyed great admiration. He had learned his craft from the three generations of artists in his family before him. He had now developed his own unique metal overlay on wood technique which the clerk described in mesmerizing detail.

As we listened, we could sense how special the piece was and understood why we were so attracted to it, but we grew increasingly apprehensive that it would be far more expensive than what we would be willing to pay. When the clerk finally came to the point of telling us the price, we were so relieved. It was considerably more than we would have planned to spend but so much less than we feared it would be that we eagerly paid the price, knowing its value was well worth the investment.

4. *Can I make more money doing a little for a lot or a lot for a little?* How much business do you want and need? Often pricing requires that you face directly just how you want to structure your business, how much you want to work, and what type of role you want to play in your business. If you want to make $65,000 a year as a psychotherapist, for example, you could see twenty people a week for $65 each. Or you could see thirteen people a week for $100 each. Or you could have five groups of about twelve people each, who pay $25 apiece each week.

Which would be easier and more cost-effective: getting sixty people who would pay $25 each to be in one of the groups you do five nights a week for three hours, or finding thirteen people who will pay $100 a week for one hour each? Your income would be the same, but the time and effort involved in achieving that income would be quite different.

If you are a public speaker and want to make $100,000 a year, you could give just one speech a week if you charged about $2,000 a speech;

Work Sheet: Fee Setting

Use this work sheet to gather the information you need in order to set your fees. You might want to put it into a spreadsheet to calculate various scenarios.

YOUR YEARLY SALARY:　　　　**ENTER YOUR AMOUNT**

Yearly salary you want to earn　　_____
Days per week you wish to work　　_____
Billable hours worked per day　　_____
Days worked per year　　_____

EXPENSES:　　　　**ENTER YOUR AMOUNT**
OPERATING OVERHEAD　　**MONTHLY**　　**YEARLY**

Marketing　　_____　　_____
Legal costs　　_____　　_____
Insurance　　_____　　_____
Postage　　_____　　_____
Repairs　　_____　　_____
Supplies　　_____　　_____
Taxes and licenses　　_____　　_____
Travel costs　　_____　　_____
Telephone　　_____　　_____
Utilities　　_____　　_____
Other　　_____　　_____

Total expenses　　_____　　_____

Desired profit %　　_____　　_____

CALCULATIONS:

Salary + Expenses + Profit ÷ days or hours worked =
Daily rate　　_____
Hourly rate　　_____

whereas if you could only get $1,000 a speech, you would have to give two speeches a week in order to make your goal. How much effort will it take you to book that many speeches? How much will it cost?

If you have a pool-cleaning service and charge $50 a month, you can serve sixty clients yourself and make $3,000 a month. Or you can hire, train, and supervise three employees and pay them $25 a client. Then, by keeping your fee the same, you could serve 180 clients and make $4,500 a month. Which work style and lifestyle would suit you better—the challenge of supervising three employees for a possible additional $1,500 per month, or the quiet satisfaction of working for yourself?

PRICING PRODUCTS VERSUS PRICING SERVICES

Although many of the principles are the same whether you're pricing a product or a service, some factors involved in pricing a product differ from those of services. Many service businesses, for example, have very few costs of doing business. Selling products invariably involves paying for your products up-front and keeping an inventory on hand. On the other hand, products hold the potential for passive income—that is, income that comes to you whether you're working or not. In providing a service, your income is directly wed to how many hours you can work. If you're ill or take a vacation, there's no income. And unless you add employees and the costs they bring, you can only reasonably work a fixed number of hours a week. Products, of course, can be selling while you sleep. All these factors have implications for setting your prices.

A Handy Formula for Pricing a Product

In pricing a product, you'll need to attend to manufacturing costs, setting wholesale versus retail prices, and providing for markups and discounts. The following is a formula many home-based businesspeople use to set an initial price for their products:

total material costs + overhead + minimum profit + retail margin = retail price

The reactions you get from this initial price can allow you to make the adjustments you need to find the optimum price you can command. For additional information on pricing a product, we recommend reading *Homemade Money*, by Barbara Brabec (see Resources at the end of this chapter).

FORMULAS AND STRATEGIES
FOR PRICING YOUR SERVICE

In setting fees for your service, you'll need to consider whether to charge by the hour, the day, the project, the piece, or the head. Whichever alternative you use, here are four formulas home-based consultants and people in service businesses have used to calculate their fees. Experiment with those that would be most appropriate for your industry.

1. Find out what others in your field are charging or what your potential clients are now paying or expecting to pay, and price your services accordingly. For example, if you are a copywriter and other copywriters in the area are charging between $60 and $75 an hour, you might test pricing your services at $65 an hour.

2. Figure what you were or would be making per hour as an employee and multiply this figure by two or three to cover your fringe benefits, overhead, expenses, and profit. A data-entry person earning $10 an hour on the job (about $21,000 a year), for example, should multiply the hourly wage by 2.5 and test charging $25 per hour.

3. Identify what you would like to earn annually, divide by about 2,000 hours per year, and then multiply this figure by two or three because you won't be able to bill for all 2,000 hours. For example, if you are a seminar leader and want to make $100,000 a year, divide $100,000 by 2,000 ($50), multiply by three. The result is $150 per hour or a rate of about $900 a day. If you averaged a little over two days a week of work, you'd hit your goal.

4. Quote prices on the lower end of the range others are charging and keep raising your prices until you get resistance. This is what Sandra Kurtzig calls the "flinch method" of pricing. In her book *CEO: Building a $400 Million Company from the Ground Up* she says, "We'd sit across from a customer and tell him the software cost was $35,000. If he didn't flinch, we'd add, 'And the financial package is $20,000.' Still no flinch, 'Per module.' And if he still hadn't flinched, we'd say, 'And the updates are $10,000.' Still no flinch: 'Per year.' The second we detected a flinch, we backed down one level."

Publisher Hal Schuster puts it this way: "Your fair price is the price point at which you can maintain sufficient business. Raise your prices slowly at intervals until you find a manageable point in your workload. Then stop raising them. Then if you are consistently attracting more business than you can handle, you can raise them again."

The following are a variety of commonly used pricing strategies: flat fee, value added top of the line, percentage of results, bargain-basement specials, a start-up price, and working on retainer.

Calculating Your Billable Days

In a service business not every workday will be billable, and many people who start home businesses are surprised to learn just how few billable days there are in a year. Yet the number of days you can actually bill will influence how much you'll need to charge. The number of days you can bill depends on many things: how actively you market, how much time is required to run your business, and what type of work you do. But here's a way to estimate the number of billable days you might want to project in pricing your services:

From 365 days—

1. Subtract weekends: 365 – 104 = 261

2. Subtract 2 days a month for running your business: 261-24=237

3. Subtract 4 days a month for marketing: 237 – 48 = 189

4. Subtract 13 days for holidays, vacation and sick days: 189 – 13 = 176

Programmer Mark Kleinschmidt, in setting his price, uses this formula: He determines how much he wants his annual income to be, multiplies by 2.6, and divides by the estimated number of billable hours.

Flat Fee Versus Hourly Wage

Many service businesses charge by the hour. On the face of it, that seems fair. Sometimes, however, customers and clients become nervous as they imagine the sound of your clock ticking. They have very little idea of what's actually involved in your work and envision their bill mounting out of control. You certainly never want clients to be shocked when they receive their bills. Some people find, however, that a flat fee is an invitation for the client to ask for increasingly more to be done under that one charge. So here are several ways to avoid the time-clock jitters:

Avoiding Clients' Time-Clock Jitters

- Make a bid that reflects your estimate of the number of hours you think the work will take and call the clients before proceeding beyond that estimate. If you come in under the estimate, they'll be pleasantly surprised; if you run over, you're giving them a chance to remain in charge of their cost before proceeding.

(Continued on page 591)

(Continued from page 590)

- Establish a flat price to provide price stability in your client's mind, but in your contract make it "subject to any change in orders." This will protect you from unexpected demands they make as the work proceeds that would put you in the hole because they would take more of your time or add to your costs.

- Set a fixed price, but designate a specific allowable percentage of overage. That is, 100 hours at x number of dollars with a possible variance not to exceed 15 percent. Or offer a fixed cost plus expenses not to exceed a specified amount.

- Establish an assessment stage for a project during which you are paid either a flat fee or an hourly rate to define the scope of the work to be done. Essentially under such an arrangement you are being paid to prepare a proposal that will outline the scope of the work, the detailed costs involved, and the work to be accomplished. Be sure to get a clear up-front agreement in writing that specifies what you will deliver by when.

These strategies are designed to protect both you and the client and to avoid fee disputes. Fee agreements spelled out in writing are essential. Writer Chris Adamec finds that no matter how much she wants to do a particular project, she needs to make her offer in writing and never begins doing any work on the project until she has received an acceptance in writing.

Problems can arise, however, if you have underestimated what you can do for the price you've quoted. Technical writer Raj Khera never bills by the word or the page because in his field, the shorter the better. To convey this point to clients, he sometimes paraphrases a quote from Abraham Lincoln, saying, "It takes me two weeks to prepare a twenty-minute speech, but if you want a two-hour speech, I'm ready now." He's done eighty-page projects for $7,000, 270-page projects for $25,000, and 8-page brochures for $2,000. Each was for a fixed fee and he made good money, but how much depended on how on target he was in estimating his costs. The more experience he's gained, the more accurately he's been able to estimate the time and costs involved, and the more money he makes.

One dilemma faced by those whose work depends upon the speed at which they can produce their services is that the quicker and more efficient they become, the lower they know their estimates can be, but to bid lower and lower doesn't compensate them for their increasingly improved skills. Yet bidding at higher rates can present difficulties when competing with others who are willing to charge less but will take longer. To solve this problem, the office support professionals' trade association has developed Industry Production Standards, an industry-wide formula members can use to define and communicate their rates so customers can readily see the value of their prices.

Programmer Ron Thompson uses a popular approach to making estimates that he calls the "fudge factor." When a client asks him how long it will take to complete a project, he figures the high side of how long he actually thinks it will take, doubles that estimate, and then tacks on a 100 percent safety factor. As often as not that "fudged" number is pretty close to what it actually takes.

Promotions specialist Rick Wallace has an interesting method of making appealing estimates without selling himself short. He gives a tentative quote of an hourly fee with an estimated time of completion immediately but makes it clear the estimate is tentative until he can see the actual work. After seeing the work to be done, he sends a one-way fax using a standard form he's created, confirming his initial quote. If he needs to charge more than the estimate, he gives the client a chance to change his mind before proceeding. He explains the difference and offers the client a choice: He'll do the more limited work for the original price or quote a new price for the more extensive work. This method helps educate the client as to the cost of various aspects of his work.

Often clients may have little knowledge of the value of your services or the various aspects of how you work, so any way you can demonstrate why prices vary or need to be what they are can be helpful. Here's an example of just how helpful such information can be. Judith Wunderlich, who runs a specialized temporary-help agency, lets the freelancers she places set their own prices, so when a client calls for help she quotes a range of prices from let's say $20 to $30 an hour. Human nature being what it is, most people jump at the $20 price at first. But Wunderlich doesn't stop there. She faxes copies of blind resumes and samples to clients with the hourly rate of each person clearly marked. When clients can "see" what they'll get, she finds they usually pick the middle range over the lower ones.

One final thought about making pricing estimates. Gerald Weinberg, author of *The Secrets of Consulting*, sums up our philosophy: Price your work so that you'll be glad if you get the business or if you don't. The last thing you want to do is get the business and then think, "Oh, my gosh, now I've got to do all that work for that little money!"

For details on pricing a service, we recommend *How to Set Your Fees and Get Them*, by Kate Kelly, and *Selling Your Services*, by Robert Bly. Both these books are listed in the Resources at the end of the chapter.

 True Confessions: Pricing Strategies

What to charge is a popular topic on the *Working Smarter* site on Quicken's Small Business Channel (*www.quicken.com*). Here are a variety of strategies people have shared for setting fees.

Value Added

Steve Singer owns a small business-forms company in the Chicago area. He advises considering three factors in setting your prices: (1) How available your product or service is: the more common the service or product, the less you can charge; (2) the value you add to what is normally provided: the more you've added, the more you can charge; and (3) the prevailing price range in the industry. He points out that you need to walk the tightrope of being neither too high nor too low: being too low hurts your credibility, but being too high invites competition. Singer has found that the more value you add, the more you will sell, and the less price will be a factor in the final sale.

Private investigator Alan Kaplan adds value by listening to the major complaints of his clients against his industry and then gives them something nobody else is giving to remove those complaints. He has noted, for example, that clients don't like the risk and uncertainty of an open-ended contract, or even a capped contract, with no guarantee of results. For one type of client, he sets a fixed fee with a guarantee that if he isn't successful, the client will get his money back. He admits it's a risky strategy, but he's betting he's as good as he wants his clients to believe he is. And he does have a fallback strategy. If he finds the case is much more complex than anticipated, he can cut his losses and bail out by giving the client his money back.

Top of the Line

George Hoeing discovered quite by accident that the more he raised his prices, the more he could sell of his Tribal line of designer workout clothing for body builders. Whenever he put his outfits on sale, his sales dropped. Puzzled, he began experimenting with raising prices. And, sure enough, the more he charged, the more people bought. With top-of-the-line pricing, people considered his sportswear more valuable. Programmer Tim Berry finds that the best time to charge top-of-the-line prices is when you are consciously trying to create a buyer perception of high quality, as in the case of BMWs and fancy resort hotels.

If you go top of the line, however, you have to maintain a top-of-the-line image and have entrée into circles with top-of-the-line budgets. And of course you have to have something special. You may have heard the Depression-era story about the man who was standing on a corner with a tray of apples marked $500 each. When asked if he had sold any, he said, "Not yet. But when I do, I'm going to make a killing!"

Percentage of Results

Sometimes when you're introducing a new service, you'll meet with skepticism and resistance. One way to overcome this resistance is to set your fee based on a fixed percentage of the results you will achieve for your client. This has been referred to as "impact pricing." People whose business is telephone audits, for example, could charge a percentage of the savings the audit produces. A sales trainer could charge a percentage of the increase in gross sales revenues for a specified number of months after his training program. Or a safety engineer might contract for a percentage of the money saved after his safety program is initiated. A variation of this would be to bill for your direct costs up to a specified amount in addition to some percentage of the results you produce. Be sure when using a percentage-of-results strategy, however, that you have a clear written agreement as to specifically how and when the results will be documented, measured, and validated.

The Bargain-Basement Special

You've heard the old joke "I may be losing money on every sale, but I'll make it up in volume." Well, losing 10 cents on every sale means losing $100 on every 1,000 sales and $1,000,000 on 10 million. Discounting your service can be just such a trap, especially for a home-based business, because even though you may have lower overhead as a result of working from home, your volume is usually limited. Home businesses usually can't handle sufficient volume to make only pennies on every sale.

In his eagerness to get in initial customers, for example, a desperate new graphic designer decided to price himself as a bargain-basement special. He told us, "After all, work does beget more work and therefore it's important to get work whatever the price. Which would I prefer: sitting on the porch reading a novel or being underpaid for working?"

 Warning!!

> Although charging bargain-basement prices may work to get some business coming in, if you're tempted to try it, keep this in mind: Once you set your price, your clientele will beget clientele from the same economic stratum. It is difficult to change upward once you have set your prices. When you raise your prices, your business will show slow or no growth because you've priced yourself beyond the budgets of your old customers and will need to start from scratch building a new clientele who can pay your new price.

That's exactly what happened to the graphic designer: he soon had a whole clientele of cheapskates. Stanton Kramer had a similar experience. He had to change his customer base three times before he got to the price range he wanted to be in. Interior designer Lillian Hamilton also discovered this phenomenon, but to help bridge the price gap as she raises her prices, she continues to serve previous customers at the original price for a full year. She calls this her "preferred client" price and lets them know it's a courtesy she offers to her steady customers.

If you decide to start out pricing yourself on the "low" side, remember that you'll never know how much more you could actually have charged. It's the reverse of buying something, knowing for sure you'll find it at a lower price sometime in the future. Setting prices is like fording a river; you never step in the same water twice. The important thing is that you feel sufficiently compensated each step along the way. If you're feeling resentful and taken advantage of, you need to figure out how you can raise your prices.

A Start-up Price

Rather than entering the market as a bargain-basement special, you might consider this approach to establishing a novice-business rate: Determine what established businesses in your field are charging. Calculate what you would be paid if you were doing this same work on a salary. Then pick the difference between the two and make that your start-up price. Let your clients and customers know that this is an "introductory" offer.

That's what facialist Laura Mars has done. She finds her clients like the introductory offer because they can sample the results and when they like what they see they're willing to come back at the full price.

Staying in Budget Without Cutting Your Rate

Many business experts will advise you: Never cut your rate. In radio, the saying is "Never go off the rate card." Obviously, you won't present a very substantial professional image if you quote a price and then agree to do the work for less when you meet price resistance. The solution is to offer a range of services or products and to break down the price of your service by type of activity. Then you can essentially cut and paste a customized price that fits your client's budget.

For example, career coach Marilyn Martinson offers private consultations, one-day seminars, a six-week workshop, a two-tape audio program ($29.95), and a six-cassette album at $69.95. With this menu of products and services she can meet her range of clients at a price point each can live with. You can do the same with your services. Consider having such price distinctions as a full-day rate and a half-day rate; a rate that includes a final report and one that does not; an in-town price and an out-of-town price. Offer a price for rush service (twenty-four hours or overnight); a price that includes workbooks and one that does not. A price for working from typed copy and another for working from handwritten copy; a price for short-term work and another for long-term projects; a paid-in-full up-front price and a thirty-day-credit price.

In other words, give your clients a range of options that in essence says: You can have it fast, you can have it cheap, or you can have it great, but you can't have all three. This "price-options" approach gives you lots of room to negotiate your price, and any reductions you make can be directly related to the effort demanded of you and the value your client receives. You will always be compensated fully for what you provide.

Working on Retainer

Ken Sobel, owner of For Your Information, Inc., a marketing-research company servicing *Fortune* 500 packaged-goods manufacturers, typically works on a retainer. His clients might pay for $20,000 of work over a twelve-month period, and to make his retainer more attractive Sobel provides $25,000 worth of services (that is, a 20 percent discount). To qualify for this discount, however, Sobel's clients must agree to two things: (1) they must commit to pay the full $20,000 regardless of the amount of work they actually use and (2) they must commit to pay in advance of the work.

Sobel requires that the first $10,000 be paid at the time his services begin and the second $10,000 after six months or when he's logged $12,500 of services, whichever comes first. He reports that so far none of his four retainer clients has ever had unused time at the end of the year. If they have used up the retainer value before the year runs out, however, they can pay on a project-by-project basis with no discount or open a new retainer at the special rate.

Working on a retainer can be quite desirable for a home-business owner because it comes close to duplicating the regularity and security of a paycheck. With the retainer, you agree to be on call for a specified number of hours for an agreed-upon monthly fee. Normally the retainer is paid in full or on a periodic payment schedule (i.e., monthly, quarterly, or annually) with each payment made in advance of the work to be done. In other words, the retainer operates like a "draw." The clients prepay to have your time available to them as needed up to a certain amount. If they don't use all the time, they lose it. Usually the retainer involves a quantity discount that is offset by the security of knowing you will have a steady income.

When working on a retainer, however, it's vital to have a contract or letter agreement that clearly spells out your fee structure and what work is to be done over what period of time. Otherwise, you may find yourself being called upon to work far more hours than your monthly fee can cover, or a client may stretch out the contracted number of hours over a longer period so that your quantity discount is no longer profitable. With a clear agreement, should the workload drop below a specified level, you can simply bill at a higher rate. If your client complains, you can point to your agreement.

Also, working on retainer you can become very comfortable, but keep in mind that clients often think of such consulting services as a temporary expenditure, not an ongoing commitment. So don't get too dependent. You may be wise to anticipate a natural attrition rate for retainer clients. As you do a good job for them, their need for your services may be progressively reduced and they may start looking forward to freeing up the funds they're now investing in your services.

Steps to Take As Work Is Coming to an End

Usually you can sense the time approaching when ongoing clients are beginning to feel they'll no longer be needing your help. Here are several action steps you can take when you sense that time is approaching:

- Look and listen carefully for additional types of work you could offer that clients may be unaware of needing and get them excited about the benefits of new services.

- Offer a smaller retainer with less of a discount or offer an annual subscription or maintenance fee as a way to continue providing some more minimal level of services.

- Introduce additional services or products based on new needs you've heard or observed your clients are experiencing.

- Begin preparing to accept and line up new business. Remember, satisfied customers make excellent referral sources and may even return for repeat business at any time in the future if you leave on good terms and keep up regular communication. So always accept inevitable cutbacks or terminations with grace and goodwill. And be sure to continue your marketing activities no matter how busy you get so that you'll have a stream of new clients waiting in the wings when you need them.

ADJUSTING YOUR PRICING STRATEGY TO YOUR CHANGING BUSINESS SITUATION

As you can see from the variety of the above pricing strategies, there are three factors that affect what you can charge: your image of yourself, your reputation, and the market for what you have services to offer. Each of these factors is subject to change over the lifetime of your business. Therefore, anticipate the need for adjusting your pricing strategy to different stages of your business.

Novice businesspeople, for example, may enter a field at a moderate price and raise it gradually as their reputation and self-assurance grow. But let's consider a less obvious evolution. If you're introducing a new product or service and discover that the response to it is strong, you may be able to charge a premium price right from the beginning because you have no competition. When others notice your dramatic success, however, they may well jump into the field and undercut your price. Then you may face having to adjust your price down in order to remain competitive.

As the developer of one of the first customer-service training programs in the country, Coleen Sager encountered such a dilemma. She found companies were eager for her information and the dramatic increases it could mean in their bottom lines. Her seminars and video programs sold briskly at a premium price. Over the years, however, many other trainers, seeing her success, added a customer-service training program to their offerings at much lower rates. Ultimately, her products and programs cost much more than everyone else's.

Of course, she still had her reputation as one of the leading authorities, but eventually cost sensitivity won out in the marketplace and her sales began to decline. Coleen was presented with a monumental challenge. Obviously she couldn't just cut the price of her existing programs without damage to her reputation and stature. The situation called for an innovative new pricing program. And that's exactly what she initiated.

Instead of promoting her three-day seminars, Coleen began marketing herself as a corporate speaker. Because of her reputation, she could command top speaking fees and still save her clients money. By bringing her in to speak, they could get the best for less. They got her most important information in a condensed form for less than the cost of the lower-priced multiple-day seminars on the market. When the speech went well, she could then work out customized follow-up seminars.

Another stage of business involves retraining long-term clients. We've already mentioned making provisions for guaranteeing some period of price stability for preferred clients. Another way to price for retention is to add on value to existing services when you raise prices, or retain your existing price but add on charges for additional services.

 Rule of Thumb: Raising Your Fees

Even though we all would enjoy bringing in additional income without increasing our workload, most of us hate to raise prices. We fear our clients will decide to cut back on what they buy from us or, even worse, will take their business elsewhere. Nonetheless, we know that periodically we owe it to ourselves to raise our rates. When that time comes, it need not be traumatic. Planning ahead can help. Here are eight rules of thumb for making raising your rates easier and even routine.

(Continued on page 599)

(Continued from page 598)

1. *Let your existing clients or wholesalers know well in advance* when you will be raising your fees.

2. *Provide information about why you need to raise your prices.* Relate rate increases to increases in service or to economic conditions your clients may or may not be aware of.

3. *Provide a grace period for existing clients and customers,* if you wish. For example, Sarah typically carried existing clients at the previous year's fees. No one ever complained because when their fees did go up the next year, they were still paying less than newer clients.

4. *Alternatively, you might offer a temporary incentive for your long-term customers;* e.g., "I'm raising my prices, but for the next month we'll include the shipping for free."

5. *Build anticipated fee increases into the contract,* so no one will be surprised when contract renewal comes and your fees are higher. Or include information about fee increases along with all fee information. That's what Chip Morgan, president of Chip Morgan Broadcast Engineering, does. Morgan believes that we should all plan to raise our prices annually, because, after all, we are one year more experienced and our cost of doing business usually goes up each year. Here's how he does it. He tells his clients up-front that he raises his fees each year when quoting them this year's fees. In this way, no one is surprised when the fee goes up in the new year. "They expect it anyway," he says. This makes the anticipated increase clear from the start.

6. *Announce price increases matter-of-factly and with confidence.* Do not be defensive or uncomfortable about your decision. Such negativity sparks precisely the type of reaction you most want to avoid.

7. *Be open to considering exceptions for long-standing clients* but always attach them to a specific deadline at which time your new prices will go into effect.

8. *Do not be overly concerned if a few clients do decide to go elsewhere.* Sometimes a fee increase simply catalyzes a decision that was already imminent. But, of course, don't let clients leave without making an effort to find out if they are dissatisfied and how you could continue serving them.

WHAT TO DO IF THEY SAY
YOUR PRICE IS TOO HIGH

When you're told that your price is too high, marketing consultant Laura Douglas advises simply asking "In what way is it too high?" Then ask, "What price did you have in mind?" You do this not to lower your price but to get a better idea of what the people with whom you're talking really want done. Remember, you can always offer reduced services.

Keep in mind, too, that people usually have no idea how much time is actually involved, much less the expertise required to do what you will be doing. Douglas suggests preparing a small graph that illustrates how much more it would cost the company to do the job in-house. Include factors such as how much more time it would take an inexperienced person, and other costs they may not think of. Such comparisons offer your prospective clients a more realistic idea of what they need, and their response provides you with a better means of knowing if and how you could help them.

 True Confessions: Developing the Confidence to Get Your Price

Many of the problems people have in pricing their products arise from limiting attitudes and beliefs they have about money. Often, we are not even aware that we have these attitudes and beliefs. Many arose during childhood from the assumptions our families held about money, and they can interfere with charging what we are actually worth.

Speech and diction coach Saundra Keen, for example, was barely surviving on the fees she charged for her private consultations. Even though as an actress Saundra had studied with the top speech coaches for many years and had crafted a beautiful voice for herself, she believed that no one would want to pay very much for her coaching because she didn't have a college degree in speech communication. With our help, her self-esteem grew, and she began to notice that her clients were improving dramatically. She finally realized that actual results were the bottom line of her value, not academic degrees.

She remembered that throughout her childhood her father had always told her that if she ever wanted to make any money, she would have to go to college. Little did she know that, once she'd decided to pursue her acting career directly from high school, her father's old admonition about making money would prevent her from earning a decent living twenty years later.

(Continued on page 601)

(Continued from page 600)

Saundra decided to raise her prices but was still fearful that no one would book an appointment once they heard what she was asking. You can imagine her surprise when she finally worked up the courage to state her new price and the response was "That's very reasonable."

Saundra's story illustrates both sides of the psychology involved in pricing: the seller's and the buyer's.

 Tip: Your Customer's Money Attitudes

Gregory R. Passewitz, of the Ohio State University Extension, has developed an entire course based on psychology from the buyer's perspective. The points he raises are well worth considering in determining what you will charge:

- A customer will never volunteer to pay more than what you ask for.

- The value of a product or service rests with the consumer.

- Value is determined according to the benefits received versus cost.

- Other factors that determine value include:
  weight, size
  packaging
  advertising, promotion, and referrals
  brand name

 Work Sheet: Your Money Attitudes

Close examination of your attitudes about money may show that they are often self-fulfilling prophecies and are reflected in the prices you set. Those who believe in themselves and their product and expect people to pay for it gladly are infinitely more successful than those who expect to have difficulty earning a living. Examples of common negative beliefs that prevent people from setting prices that enable their businesses to flourish include:

- People hate to part with their money.

- Making money is hard.

(Continued on page 602)

(Continued from page 601)

- You have to work your fingers to the bone to make even a meager living.

- Rich people are dishonest. They rip other people off.

- Anyone can do what I do, so how can I charge very much for it?

- The work I do is so much fun, I really shouldn't charge anything.

Have you ever noticed, that when someone really wants something, he or she will pay almost any price for it? They can't get the money out of their pockets fast enough. Or have you noticed that truly successful people almost always love what they do and talk about it as something they would do even for free? Also think about how many of the most successful people achieve the success they do because they enable others to enjoy life more. And can anyone else ever really do exactly what you do?

To identify other limiting attitudes and beliefs about money that may stand in the way of setting a price that will enable your business to thrive, we suggest making the following statement out loud. Say it several times and notice your internal reactions.

People will gladly pay me well for the work I love doing.

If you have a negative reaction to believing any portion of this statement, think about what you believe instead. How did you come to hold these beliefs? What would convince you to believe this statement? In being able to agree fully with each aspect of this statement, you'll find setting and getting prices you want to be much easier. List here any negative beliefs you have about money. Notice when they arise and consciously replace them with the above statement.

- _____

- _____

- _____

- _____

- _____

A SIMPLE STEP-BY-STEP PRICING GUIDE

Although, as you can see, there is no one pricing formula that will work for everyone, we offer the following process for determining which approach might work best for you at a given time.

STEP 1: Work out several possible pricing strategies from those mentioned in this chapter.

STEP 2: Test each alternative with several prospective clients.

STEP 3: Select the alternative that gets the best response.

STEP 4: Remember, pricing is an experimental process, so continue fine-tuning until you're satisfied with the results.

STEP 5: Keep track of your income and expenses and evaluate your pricing every quarter.

STEP 6: Make changes when the numbers or any of the following indicate the need to adjust:

- Many complaints about your price
- Many other complaints that may be dissatisfaction with your price in disguise
- A downturn in sales or the fact that people lose interest after hearing the price
- People often say, "Boy, that's a bargain."
- Your prices have been the same for a long period of time.
- You're turning away business because you don't have time for it all.
- Sales are fine, but profits are low.
- You feel resentful about working so hard for so little in return.

Pricing is like the pulse of your business. When it's working, you're working. And that means that life's working!

RESOURCES

BOOKS

The Contract and Fee-Setting Guide for Consultants and Professionals. Howard Shenson. (See chapter 9 for full citation.)

Homemade Money. (See chapter 2 for full citation.) Information on pricing products.

Power Pricing: How Managing Price Transforms the Bottom Line. Robert J. Dolan and Hermann Simon. New York: Free Press, 1997. ISBN: 068483443X.

ON LINE

www.brint.com—The Business Researcher's Interests is an extremely comprehensive meta site that includes articles, published papers, and publications all devoted to theoretical and actual pricing strategies.

www.cbsc.org/ontario/bis /7071.html—An on-line guide that helps small and home business determine pricing.

www.sbanet.uca.edu/docs/Publications/pub00133.tx—An on-line manual for price setting for consultants.

www.quicken.com—Intuit's Small Business site has a wealth of information on the financial aspects of running a business.

www.sba.gov—This is the official site of the Small Business Administration. Advice on pricing is one the many types of helpful information found here.

CHAPTER 23

Successfully Marketing Your Home Business

Goals

1. Develop a marketing mindset.

2. Avoid needless waste of your time and money.

3. Focus your efforts on a special niche.

4. Don't rely on passive means of marketing; take the initiative.

5. Target your marketing to those who will buy.

6. Choose among the best methods for home businesses.

7. Find marketing methods you enjoy and will do.

8. Get business coming to you.

If you're working from home in your own business now, you already know that unless you bring in some business you won't be working from home for long. Without customers or clients, you'll soon be back out looking for a job. For many people, the fear that they won't have enough business prevents them from ever pursuing their desire to go out on their own. For those who do proceed, getting business remains their number-one concern. Year after year, surveys report that issues related to getting business make up the bulk of the top-ten concerns of home-based businesses. And no wonder because, ultimately, the only true difference between those who succeed and those who don't is that those who make it have enough business to keep going.

Because marketing is such a concern to people who are working independently from home, we have completely updated and expanded our book *Getting Business to Come to You*, which we wrote with marketing expert Laura Clampitt Douglas. We titled the book *Getting Business to Come to You* because that's what we all need if we're going to survive and thrive on our own. We can't spend most of our time out marketing. To succeed we have to set up our marketing so that it develops a momentum of its own and business starts coming to us, leaving us free to concentrate on the business we get!

The biggest hurdle most people face in getting enough business is that they know little or nothing about how to put the word out about what they can do. This is not surprising because most of us don't learn anything about marketing in school or even on the job unless we've worked in that field. But since few people who have home businesses can afford to hire a professional to do their marketing, most of us must fend for ourselves.

The problem is compounded by the fact that much of what's taught and written about marketing is designed for larger businesses, and unfortunately many home businesses flounder trying to use the marketing methods best suited for bigger operations. So most of us have had to experiment and improvise. Sometimes what we try works; sometimes it doesn't.

Fortunately, however, with the right information, marketing a home-based business need not be complex or expensive. In fact, there are highly successful marketing methods for every home business and every personality type. We have interviewed owners of several thousand successful home businesses, and most tell us they get most of their business one way: by "word of mouth." In other words, they have become so well established that almost all their business comes from referrals. Prospective clients and customers call them, and that's exactly what we all want. But few successful home businesses start out with the phone ringing, so we set out to learn what they did to create the word-of-mouth momentum that brings in a steady flow of business.

In *Getting Business to Come to You* we outline over fifty-five marketing methods successful home businesspeople tell us they've used to get their businesses going. Some of the methods, like direct mail and advertising, are used by larger businesses, but if you use these methods, you will need to tailor them to fit the budget and scope of what works for a home business. Other methods, like gatekeeping and sampling, are used in ways that are especially suited to home businesses. Our goal in writing the new edition of *Getting Business to Come to You* was to give you the tools, skills, and how-to's to use these methods effectively. A summary of these low- or no-cost ways to get business follows. You'll notice they are all one form or another of four things we've all been doing since kindergarten: walking, talking, showing, and telling. Identify which of these four categories suits you best and pick out the methods you would enjoy most.

Best Low/No Cost Marketing Methods for Home-Based Businesses*

Making Personal Contacts

Direct solicitation

Free consultations

Networking

Speeches and seminars

Volunteering

Walking around the neighborhood

Getting Others Talking about You

Gatekeepers and mentors

Letters of reference, endorsements,
  and testimonials

Referrals

Sponsorships, donations, and events

Publicity:
  newspapers, magazines, newsletters,
  business and trade publications

Radio and TV

Cyberspace

Telling All about It

Classified and display print ads:
  newspapers and magazines
  newsletters and trade publications

Directory listings and ads:
  Yellow Pages
  Trade and specialty directories

Direct Response Advertising:
  reply cards
  inserts
  card decks
  coupons and coupon packs
  bounce backs

On-line advertising

Articles and columns

Catalogs

Articles and columns

Brochures and flyers

Bulletin boards, tear pads, take ones,
  and door-hangers

Fax back, broadcast fax, and E-mail

Newsletters

Phone and hold button messages

Postcards

Product packing

Point-of-sale displays

Sales letters and proposals

Web site

Your own book

Showing What You Can Do

Audiotapes

Business cards as samples

Compact discs

Demonstrations

Displays and door-hangers

House parties, open houses and
  occasion events

Media appearances

Multimedia Web sites

Photos and portfolios

Radio and television advertising

Samples and giveaways

Speeches and seminars

Trade shows and exhibits

Video brochures

Your own radio show

Your own TV show

*From Getting Business to Come to You, Paul and Sarah Edwards and Laura Clampitt Douglas (New York: Tarcher/Putnam, 1998).

Some people, like Elio Samame, have told us our book has been central to making their businesses successful. Elio came to the United States from Peru with less than $500 and a dream. He came to America to be a fitness trainer and to start his own gym. He began working from home. Every day he tried one marketing idea from our book. His operation grew from a home-based business to a gym, and then he had to move into a larger gym. That's the power of effective marketing. Others have had similar results, and you can too.

There are several mistakes, however, that we continue to notice home businesspeople making again and again that thwart even their best marketing efforts. Despite investing considerable time and money in marketing, too many people are disappointed with the results they get. Inadvertently they are sabotaging the time, money, and effort they put into their marketing. In this chapter we will identify these common marketing traps and the simple steps we can all take to avoid them.

DON'T LEAVE YOUR SUCCESS TO CHANCE: DEVELOP A MARKETING MINDSET

The greatest mistake someone can make in marketing is thinking that because you have a good product or service, people will buy it. For example, most people think that Christopher Columbus or Leif Ericson discovered America. But two thousand years before Ericson, Basques, Phoenicians, Druid priests, Libyans, and Egyptians may have visited our shores. Instead of becoming famous for discovering America, Columbus achieved his fame by *marketing* his discovery of America!

Like Columbus, you will need to get your name associated with whatever field you've chosen. Your job is to let those who need your product or service know about it, and to do so in a way that convinces them to buy it from you whenever they need it.

That means developing a marketing mindset. A marketing mindset means habitually thinking about how to get get the word out about your business and making a commitment that your business deserves the time, energy, and even the investment of some money to make sure people have the opportunity to use your products and services. Without such an investment of time, energy, and money, the world will lose out on the benefits of your talents and abilities.

The first step in making sure you have ample business is to view yourself and what you're doing as important enough to invest in. This investment includes promoting your business and the realization that, in fact, marketing is something that you can learn to do successfully—even if you don't think so at the moment. Many, if not most, people who go out on their own are initially reluctant marketers. Those who are successful discover they can not only do it, but can actually enjoy it. That's what this chapter is designed to help you do.

DON'T WASTE YOUR TIME: TEST THE WATERS

"I've been marketing my service for six months, and I'm just not getting any business. What can I do?" writes a woman in desperation. She has been trying to launch a service in which she would run the offices of professionals who are on the road most of each week. This sounds like an excellent idea and, in fact, we have talked with several people who have tried it. So far, however, we have yet to meet anyone who has made a go of this business. Evidently the people who need such a service either don't think they need it or are not willing to pay for it. As yet, no one has positioned this business in a way that people will buy it. (Let us know if you or someone you know has. We're eager to find out if it can be done!)

This illustrates the first thing you can do to make sure you'll have plenty of business. Be certain that there are enough people who need and will pay for what you are setting out to offer. All the effective marketing in the world will not sell something to people who are convinced they don't need it or are simply unwilling to pay for it. Before you even start marketing yourself, do some homework to find out what you can offer that people need and how you can provide and price it in a way they will pay for. Actually, this kind of work should be done before you even begin a new business venture!

 Work Sheet: Finding Out If People Need and Will Pay For What You Want to Offer

The following work sheet lists seven different ways you can discover whether or not people need what you offer and will pay for it. You can use it in gathering the key information you need.

____ *1. Talk to the competition.*

Find out if there are others doing something similar and how successful they are. Talking with such people can provide a wealth of information. Don't be shy about approaching them. They may soon be your colleagues, and if you approach them as such instead of thinking of them as the enemy, they will probably be willing to talk with you.

(Continued on page 610)

(Continued from page 609)

Find out as much as you can about what they offer and what they don't. How long have they been in business? What do they like best about their business? What do they like least? Ask their opinion about whether this is a good business to be in, what they specialize in, and if they ever need backup or someone to handle their overload. Find out if they would recommend this business to someone else.

You may find a few people who are forthcoming, but if most people are open and forthcoming, the business is probably a pretty good one. If most people are tight-mouthed and unfriendly, that's not a good sign.

If there is no one doing what you want to do, explore further. It could mean that there's an unmet need, or it could mean there is no need at all. You'll need to check it out.

> **____ 2. *Talk directly to people who would need or are using something like what you can offer.***

Often conversations with potential clients or customers will tell you exactly what you need to do to succeed. Here are the kinds of questions you can ask:

____ *Have you ever used this type of product or service?*

____ *If not, why not?* They may not have known about it. They may have heard it wasn't useful or that it cost too much. Continue exploring their answers with questions like:

____ *Would you be interested in finding out more about it?*

____ *What would make it useful for you? What would you want to pay for it?*

____ *If you have used something similar, were you happy with it?* Listen to what they liked and didn't like. Each comment can tell you possible things you will need to say to market yourself to others.

____ *Would you do it again?* Investigate further. Find out why or why not. Think about how what you offer could be different, better, more useful.

____ *Are you using one now?* Find out if they are satisfied and why they are or aren't.

____ *What would make it more appealing to you?* Find out if there are any circumstances under which they would be interested. This information will help you better define what you can do profitably.

(Continued on page 611)

(Continued from page 610)

____ *What do you expect to pay?* Finding out what people would expect to pay can help you set your price, but in addition, it can help you identify what you will have to do to get the price you need to charge.

____ *3. Get feedback on a prototype or sample of the product or service you have in mind.*

Show people what they will get and find out how they respond. This can provide you with a wealth of information. If you have a product, make up a sample and show it around using some of the methods that follow. If you have a service, you can also provide a sample in the form of a seminar, an article, a free consultation or demonstration, etc.

Listen carefully to all their reactions. Again, people will tell you exactly what you will have to do to meet their needs. Often they will tell you these things by complaining about what they don't like or telling you why this wouldn't work. Follow up on such comments. Always ask them what would make it appealing to them.

____ *4. Participate in a trade show, expo, or swap meet and take orders.*

Having a booth at a show where your potential clients and customers will be walking by can provide you with a wealth of information about what they will or will not be interested in.

____ *5. Advertise a preproduction offer.*

If you are starting a newsletter, developing a software program, preparing to offer a training seminar, or creating a product of some kind, for example, you can place a strategic ad or do a select direct mailing to find out what kind of response you get. If the response is not adequate to proceed, you can return the limited orders you did receive with a message that you are no longer offering the product.

____ *6. Use questionnaires and surveys.*

You can ask potential clients and customers to complete a survey or questionnaire providing you with their reactions to your business concept. You can mail such a questionnaire, but your response will be better if you have people fill it out in person, at a trade show perhaps or at a speech or seminar you conduct. In such sit-

(Continued on page 612)

(Continued from page 611)

uations you can give a prize or gift of some kind to those who will complete the survey. Or you can use the completed forms in a drawing for a valued prize.

___ 7. Hold a focus group.

Identify and then invite seven to ten people whom you would define as needing your service to join you for a discussion that can provide you with the information you need. To provide an incentive for their coming, you might offer a free one-hour workshop or demonstration followed by an hour-long discussion. This is what we recommended to the woman who wanted to run an out-of-town service. We felt she could get to the bottom of the resistance she'd been encountering by holding such a group and asking questions like these:

___ Have you ever heard of an out-of-town service?

___ Have you ever used one?

___ If not, why not?

___ If so, what was your experience?

___ Would you use one again?

___ What needs do you have while you're out of town?

___ How are you meeting those needs now?

___ How satisfied are you with what you're doing now?

___ What additional help could you use?

___ What complaints do you have about trying to run your business from the road?

___ How much would you expect to pay for such help?

___ Had you heard of my business before I contacted you?

___ How would you most likely hear about a service like mine?

___ Where would you turn if you were trying to find help while out of town?

In addition, we suggested toward the close of the evening telling the group that she hadn't been getting the positive reactions she'd expected from people who she thought would need her service and asking them why they think this might be and what they would suggest.

For more ideas on do-it-yourself market research see the Resources list.

DON'T TRY TO MARKET MORE THAN
ONE BUSINESS AT ONCE: FOCUS

An Indiana couple was described as follows by the Los Angeles Times: "They teach jobless people the printing business on nineteenth-century, hand-fed platen presses. They market and sell coffee from small-scale farmers in Nicaragua, baskets from Africa, and corn dolls from Appalachia. They recycle tons of garbage from the local neighborhood, take in boarders, run a direct-mail operation that posts newsletters for about thirty nonprofit organizations, and they sell bumper stickers."

Wow! At first glance you might think, "Oh, what an enterprising couple!" But consider this: they made $6,100 last year. How sad. So much energy, so much effort, so many good intentions, so little return. This is an extreme example of an all-too-common mistake—trying to market more than one business at a time. Depending on whether you count the various craft sales as separate businesses, this couple operates between six and eight different businesses. That means they are making less than $1,000 a year from each business! And what kind of life can you lead on $6,100 a year?

The saddest part of this story is that if this couple were to focus all their time, money, and energy on any one of these businesses, they probably could earn triple the income, if not more. It's very tempting to think "Well, now that I'm on my own I can do all the things I've wanted to do. Some of this and some of that." And it's easy to want to try doing several different things "just in case any one thing doesn't work out, there will be other things to fall back on." But actually failing to focus on one business at a time has just the opposite effect.

Instead of providing us with greater security, trying to run more than one business at once makes marketing yourself successfully much more difficult. First, marketing a business takes considerable time and effort as well as some financial investment. Spreading your limited time, money, and energy over two or three businesses (let alone six to eight) means that no one business is likely to get the full investment it needs to get going and start thriving.

In many ways, starting a home business is like having a baby. Just think about it: Have you ever known any woman who was doing more than one thing in the delivery room? Well, so it is with a home business. Bringing a new business into the world demands that we focus 100 percent of whatever energy and attention we have on that end.

Second, how would you respond if you were to meet someone who introduced himself as a real estate broker and then in the next breath told you that he also is a career counselor and sells a line of sports equipment? Most people's reaction would be to feel confused and skeptical. They would wonder, "Is this person serious about all these businesses?" "Could he be doing very well at any one of them?" Think about it, would you want to hire him as your coach? Would you want to refer one of your own clients to him for coaching? Or would you want to do business with someone who seems to be more focused?

Although it's very tempting to try to "cover all the bases" by having several things going at once, we strongly urge you to make a commitment to just one business at a time. Once you get that one business under way and going strong, then you can consider if you have the time and energy to launch a second one. Even then, however, you will need to be careful in marketing yourself not to confuse your potential clients about what business you're in.

A wedding makeup artist who attended one of our seminars learned this the hard way and is eager to tell others that our advice to focus is wise. She had established a wedding makeup service, and things were going so well she decided to add a line of cosmetics. To launch this new aspect of her business, she took a booth at a wedding show. To her dismay several of her clients came up asking in alarm, "Aren't you doing makeup anymore?" Others commented in a puzzled tone, "I thought you did makeup." She spent the whole show assuring people that she was still primarily a wedding makeup artist, but she was just . . .

Having learned her lesson well, she didn't drop her idea of adding a cosmetic line. Instead, she continues to market herself as a wedding makeup artist; then she sells cosmetics to her clients as a way to keep them coming back as clients after their weddings.

DON'T TRY TO BE ALL THINGS TO ALL PEOPLE: NICHE

Consider these two introductions. Which one helps you understand what this person does for a living? Which one would you be more likely to remember, to use or to refer to?

"I'm a facialist. Everyone has skin and everyone could look better if he or she took good care of it. So, anyone, man or woman, of any age, can benefit from having a facial."

"You know how as you age, you start to notice changes in your skin. With the proper care much of this can be prevented. I'm a facialist and I specialize in working with people who are starting to notice changes in their skin and want to preserve a more youthful appearance."

If you're like most people, you're more likely to take note of the second introduction. Most of us want to work with a specialist, someone we believe really knows how to solve a particular problem or meet a need we have. Yet when we go out on our own, too often we're so panicked about making sure we have enough business that we try to be all things to all people. Saying "I can work with anyone" not only makes us sound desperate; it also does nothing to help distinguish us from all the other people who do something similar to what we do. There are many facialists, many photographers, many Web site designers, many desktop publishers, many business consultants, and so on. It's much more difficult to market yourself to anyone and everyone, and equally difficult to market yourself as part of an undifferentiated pool of others who do generally the same thing you do.

It is much easier to market yourself as a specialist serving a special niche; e.g., as a facialist who works with aging skin, a photographer who specializes in weddings, a Web site designer who specializes in on-line catalogues, or a business consultant who works with family businesses that are passing their business from one generation to the next. In other words, if you want to stand out from the competition, if you want to charge a decent fee, then you must be more than a general "worker" someone would hire as an employee or get from a "temp" agency. As a specialist, you become more memorable. People are more apt to think of you when they need what you offer or meet someone else who does. And they are more likely to pay you what you're worth.

In addition, as a specialist, you are less of a threat to your competition. As a specialist you can refer business to them and they to you. So identify what you are best suited to provide to whom, on the basis of your experience, interests, contacts, and expertise, and specialize.

HOW TO CARVE OUT YOUR NICHE

Actually there are many ways to define your niche. You can specialize in WHO you serve, WHAT you offer, WHERE you do it, WHEN you do it or HOW you do it. For example:

WHO you serve—A computer consultant could work only with women. A PR firm could specialize in environmentally conscious companies. A caterer could provide parties and weddings for the Polish community. A desktop publisher could work only with ad agencies.

WHAT you offer—A computer consultant could work only with Macs. A PR firm could specialize in only doing publicity book tours for authors. A caterer could specialize in health food that tastes sinful. A desktop publisher could specialize in newsletters or resumes only.

WHERE you work—A computer consultant could be Eastside Computing. A PR firm could specialize in getting PR in foreign countries. A caterer could specialize in outdoor events. A desktop publisher could be a Mobile DTP and work on the client's site.

WHEN you work—A computer consultant could specialize in after-hours calls when everyone else is closed. A PR firm could specialize in helping companies promote their Web sites to increase traffic. A caterer could feature rescuing clients facing a last-minute dinner party; e.g., Spur-of-the-Moment Parties. A desktop publisher could specialize in fast turnaround; e.g., Same Day DTP.

HOW you work—A computer consultant could concentrate on building and maintaining networks for mutual fund companies; a PR firm could feature special Web site promotions and contests. A caterer could prepare meals on his or her clients' premises. A DTP could specialize in producing flyers and ads for real estate agents.

Clever Home Business Niches

Here are a few examples of cleverly niched home businesses:

- An insurance agent who specializes in writing policies for race horses, jockeys, and other stable personnel.

- An actress who specializes in conducting drama-based sexual harassment training programs.

- A Tupperware salesman who does all his parties in full drag.

- An ex-chef who designs and remodels kitchens.

- A graduate student in history who buys and sells medieval coins.

- A nurse who provides medical background material for litigation support to lawyers.

- A chiropractor who started a specialized temporary-help agency supplying backup personnel for chiropractic offices.

- A handyman who specializes in working for single women who don't have a man around the house to fix things.

- A social worker in private practice who specializes in managing the health care of elderly parents whose adult children are not able to do it.

DON'T RELY ON PASSIVE METHODS
THAT WORK FOR BIG BUSINESS: INITIATE

"I just spent all the money I have on a display ad in this great magazine. I even put in an extra phone line to be sure I could take all the calls I thought I'd get and I hired someone to come in during the day to answer the phone. But I'm not getting any calls. The only call I got today was from someone who wanted to sell me radio advertising!"

This comment was from the owner of a referral service. We'll call him Tim. But we hear similar complaints all too often. Because many of us know so little about marketing and we often really don't like doing it anyway, it's easy to gravitate toward what we call passive marketing methods like advertising and direct mail. After all, aren't these the advertising media of corporate America and if it works for them, why not for us? These are relatively nonthreatening ways to market. You take out an ad or you send out a mailing and wait for the phone to ring.

Although there are circumstances in which these more passive methods do work, more often than not, passive advertising methods do not work well for home businesses unless they are coupled with personal initiatives. Usually we don't have the budget to pursue these methods long enough and on a large-enough scale to get sufficient results. And more often than not, the kind of products and services home businesses offer are not the type that people will buy from an ad or a mailing. People are much more likely to buy services from home businesses like recording studios, wedding photographers, medical transcriptionists, pet-sitters, and business consultants, for example, based on referrals or a personal contact than from a flyer they get in the mail.

Usually the best ways to get business involve personal initiative. Methods that work particularly well focus on creating visibility and building relationships. Then direct mail and advertising can be used to follow up on the contacts you've made. In other words, use personal initiative to build relationships and to let those who need you get to know you and your business. Use mailings and even advertising to keep yourself and your business in mind so that when the moment comes when someone needs you, he or she will think of you immediately.

SEVEN TOP-OF-THE-MIND MARKETING METHODS

We call this "top of the mind" marketing. And it works. For example, the referral service we mentioned above would be better served by networking or speaking at various business and professional meetings and then following up each month by sending those potential clients who expressed an interest a snappy newsletter featuring the services available.

Here are seven of the best methods for building relationships and creating visibility:

1. Networking: Leveraging Your Contacts, New and Old

Networking is the most popular way to start and build a home-based personal or professional service business. Networking refers to using face-to-face or on-line contact to establish relationships that can lead to business. We've called networking "word-of-mouth marketing" because it's based on talking with people about what you do and listening to find out how you might serve them.

Once a business is established, "word of mouth" comes to mean getting referrals from satisfied customers who talk about you, but until a business is self-sustaining, "word of mouth" means moving your mouth, telling people about your business, speaking with everyone you already know (family, friends, vendors, and colleagues), and making a determined effort to meet and talk with lots of new people, too.

Family and friends are the oldest networks of all. They have launched many businesses as have members of civic and professional organizations. On-line networks are available, too. Membership in professional and trade associations is another way to find out what others are doing, what's working, what isn't, and where there are holes in the market that you might be able to fill. You can also join associations and groups where your potential buyers might gather.

Today there are networking organizations, business guilds, and "leads clubs" whose sole purpose is to generate business leads for their members. These groups usually meet at mealtimes, and membership is usually limited to one person in a given type of business. For example, as the only member of her women's network and her breakfast leads club to offer executive secretarial services, Dorothy Baranski was able to build her business from these two sources. Chellie Campbell, of Los Angeles, who offers Financial Stress Reduction seminars, gets 69 percent of her business from participating in just one such formal networking group, the Women's Referral Network.

Telecommuting consultant Gil Gordon summarizes how networking has worked for him: "Everything in business, whether it's getting an article published or finding a distributor, is a result of networking. I keep in contact with old friends, past co-workers, sales reps who used to call on me. I've joined a couple of carefully chosen small associations or discussion groups composed of the people I need to meet for my business and I'm fortunate enough to know a couple of people who pride themselves on being "matchmakers." They love to get people with common interests together. I can't stress this enough. Just as in job-hunting, your friends and contacts are your best assets."

Networking gives you a chance to show personally that you are interested in meeting your prospective clients' needs. It gives you the opportunity to find out what they need and show how you can serve them better. In the process, prospects also have a chance to discover that they like you, and almost everyone prefers to do business with someone they like—particularly when dealing with a service business.

To make the most of your networking activity, however, be sure you get out regularly, go to activities where your potential clients or referral sources gather, make a point of meeting new people everywhere you go, and follow up later on the contacts you make. Marketing consultant Robbie Bogue finds that getting dressed in professional attire at the beginning of the workday makes it easier for him actually to get out to luncheon and evening networking events because he's already dressed and ready to go when the time comes. Also, once you get to an event, don't stand around with appetizers and drinks in your hands or you won't get much networking done.

2. Direct Solicitation

Talking personally to people who need what you offer is the quickest and most reliable form of getting business. Of course, the dreaded words *cold calling* can send a shiver down the spine of even experienced salespeople. But we've been surprised to find that many home-based businesses have successfully marketed themselves by placing informal, personal exploratory calls to acquaint themselves with the needs of the people in their market niche.

When David Goodfellow decided to provide and sell mailing-list services to small businesses, he got started by going through the Yellow Pages and calling small companies in his community to determine whether they needed his services. He started with "A" and never got past "K." He generated a steady flow of business from the first half of the alphabet!

Bob Garsson did direct solicitation for years and found that the first call of the day was the toughest one. He says, "I could find hundreds of excuses not to make that first call, but once I got that one out of the way, I could go strong the rest of the day."

Because a sale usually isn't made until after the fifth call, the key to selling by phone (or to any other form of selling) is to keep at it. You can figure that every "no" you hear brings you that much closer to a "yes."

To help overcome your dread of direct solicitation, think of your calls as relationship building, because after all, that's what they are. You are introducing yourself to people who could use what you have to offer, getting acquainted with them, and finding out about their needs. What's the worst thing that can happen? They don't need you now. Okay, but they may in the future. Or they may run into someone who does. And you'll be foremost in their mind!

3. Sampling

Sampling means letting people experience a sample of your work as a means of getting them to buy. Debbie Fields and Famous Amos both launched their cookie businesses by letting people sample their cookies. Famous Amos told us that when he opened his first store, he carried fresh hot cookies everywhere he went. Debbie Fields started her business at home and told us that the first day she opened a shop, no one came in. There she was with trays piled high with cookies and no customers. In a moment of desperation, she carried a tray of piping-hot, freshly baked chocolate chip cookies down the sidewalk, giving away samples. The story goes that people followed her back to the store the way children followed the Pied Piper.

The effectiveness of sampling is not limited, however, just to gourmet delicacies you can give away. You can offer a free introductory seminar to give people a sample of what they would get if they signed up for a series of seminars. You can give a free consultation to help someone assess the need for your service. You can offer a demonstration. That's what facialist Lori Tabak does. She offers to do one side of a client's face for free so she can see the dramatic effects of her facial rejuvenation techniques. If a client likes the difference, she completes the facial for her fee. The results are so dramatic, everyone has to have the other side done at once!

The way Ted Laux began his book-indexing service with a TRS Model I computer is another excellent example of how to use sampling to get business. Laux looked through bookstores for books that didn't have adequate indexes. To demonstrate how much more effective these books would be had the publishers used his services, he indexed the books and sent copies to the publishers. Several liked the results, and he was in business. His indexing software gave him a unique advantage, and the sample became his platform for showing off just what he could do.

Participating in trade shows is also an excellent way to get customers to sample your product or service. It's not unusual for such shows to attract from twenty to one hundred thousand people. And, at many of them, you can not only generate leads but actually sell products and services. A moonlighting artist launched a new line of greeting cards by exhibiting at just one trade show. She booked over ten thousand dollars worth of orders from gift shops.

In addition to exhibiting at a trade show, you can speak or conduct a seminar there. If you speak, show promoters will sometimes give you free booth space in lieu of a presenter's fee. If your reputation warrants, you can sometimes be paid a presenter's fee and also get free booth space. You can also sell your books or products from the back of the room after your presentation.

Speaking at a trade show workshop, speech pathologist Dr. Roger Burgraff sold over $2,000 worth of books on communications to a group of health professionals. Another example is a sales trainer who offers to do free sessions for exhibitors on how to work a trade show. These exhibitors often become his new customers.

> Besides attracting customers, trade shows are good avenues for reaching retailers, wholesalers, reps, and buyers. And exhibiting is also a good way to test a new product, build your mailing list, and do informal market surveys.

If you haven't exhibited at a show before, attend some in your field first. Talk to exhibitors about how worthwhile exhibiting has been. At the same time, ask if any exhibitors are interested in carrying your product or sharing future booth space.

Consult the Resources at the end of this chapter to locate trade show information. Think about the various platforms you could use to show off your products or services.

4. Pricing Incentives

The way you price your service can be a route to quick business. When Arlene Daily started her business promoting restaurants on the radio she used a discount pricing strategy. She offered restaurant owners the opportunity to come on her show and promote their restaurants at a price they couldn't refuse. She gave lots of service for the price. She prepared their commercials. She featured them in live personal interviews and invited listeners to meet her at the restaurants for various publicity activities. This approach enabled her to break even immediately, and because she now had satisfied advertisers, selling to new ones at a higher price was much easier. For more information about pricing strategies, see chapter 22.

A photographer offered an apparently absurd service to advertising agencies: a huge 30-by-40-inch color print in an hour for $150. Obviously, if two customers took him up on it, one customer would get his color print on time and the other would get his print two hours later. But the photographer knew that the chances were that no one would order a rush color print of that size. However, the psychological impact was powerful. The idea was not to sell huge color prints fast but to instill in the minds of art directors that here was a photographer who could deliver photographic services unmatched by any other photographer.

Having your fee be contingent upon results is another way to make getting business easier if your business is suitable to this approach. Donald and Paige Marrs often operate their business Marketing Partners on a contingent fee basis. They do marketing for small environmentally conscious companies and take a percentage of the increase in sales that result from their efforts.

5. Publicity

Author and business expert Jack Lander claims that, square inch for square inch, free publicity is more effective than paid advertising. We agree. Here are a few examples of just how powerful publicity can be.

When Shell and Judy Norris began Class Reunions, Inc., they thought that managing college and high-school reunions would be a part-time venture. Because their business was novel at the time, the *Wall Street Journal* published an article about them. It began a landslide of publicity that has kept them busy full-time ever since.

Sally Van Swearingen also built her business using publicity. Sally is a wedding makeup artist. To get visibility for her business, she sent news releases to the local media talking about the kind of makeup brides must have now that most weddings are videotaped. The release resulted in many articles in local newspapers and magazines and ultimately a recurring spot on a local morning TV show. Her business grew so fast, she now has her own salons in multiple locations in Los Angeles.

You've heard the saying "Success attracts success." Publicity operates on that principle, too. It assumes that if you create enough momentum around yourself and your business and then provide a good-quality service or product, your business will grow. Another way of thinking about it is that people are attracted to a bright, shiny, fast-moving object, something that stands out in a crowd.

To take advantage of free publicity, however, you have to qualify for it by making yourself and your business newsworthy. Then you have to invest some time and energy in contacting local newspapers, magazines, and radio and TV stations, or hire a publicist or public-relations firm to do this for you.

Public-relations consultant Michael Baybeck suggests regularly setting aside a specific amount of time, preferably five hours a week, for "PR" efforts. He also advises treating PR like an investment account in which you send out one news release a month, make five PR-oriented phone calls a week, and have at least one PR lunch a month.

Becoming Newsworthy

Of course, to get publicity in any media, you have to present something that is sufficiently different or interesting to be newsworthy. If what you offer is itself unique like Pat Waters's company, Mementos, which sells customized baby shoes, the novelty of what you offer may be newsworthy itself. The fact that Susan Smith is starting a mailing-list service on 10th Street isn't particularly newsworthy, for example. But if Susan's new business opens by dedicating her first week's profits to one of the community's most heartwarming charities and her news release includes stories and photos of the animals or children the charity is helping, she may get some publicity for her new business.

Sometimes you can seize newsworthiness from a moment's opportunity. Joseph Cossman, the author of the book *How I Made a Million Dollars in Mail Order* and an expert on self-promotion, seized one such moment. One morning he awoke to find a mallard duck in his backyard swimming pool. He called the local newspaper and TV station who came out to cover this unusual event. The newspaper syndicated the report nationally and each time it appeared, Cossman was identified as the author of the book *How I Made a Million Dollars in Mail Order.* Not bad for just one phone call.

With a newsworthy message in mind, here are a half dozen great ways for a home business to garner some great publicity:

News releases. Effective publicity is not just a matter of getting your message out. The message has to reach your market. Sending a news release to selected publications can result in a product review or announcement about your business in the particular trade and professional publications, newsletters, magazines, or newspapers that you know your customers will be reading.

A news release is usually a one- to two-page statement of some newsworthy event or information. It announces a new product, releases the results of a survey, or reports on an upcoming promotional event such as an all-day art exhibit at a local shopping center or a free evening seminar on how to save the most money under a new tax law. Editors and producers expect news releases to appear in a standard format; for the specifics of preparing a news release, visit our Web site at *www.paulandsarah.com* where you'll find a free Special Report: *Writing Effective News Releases & Query Letters.* You'll find it listed on the Site Overview.

Interviews. News releases or calls to local radio, TV, print media, even the Web, can lead to appearances on radio or TV talk shows or to feature or news articles about you and your business.

A good example is Charlotte Hartman, who designs beautiful custom-made bridal dresses. To attract more business for the upcoming spring season, she scheduled a February fashion show at a nearby shopping mall. After reading an article about how more marrying couples are opting for elaborate weddings, she began calling local radio and TV stations to suggest a story on new trends in wedding gowns.

Her strategy paid off. She appeared as a guest on several radio and TV programs and, of course, talked about her upcoming fashion show. Before her PR event, she sent press releases to local papers and got news coverage of the show, complete with photographs.

Cable TV opportunities. An easy way to get TV exposure is to volunteer your product or service for a TV benefit auction. Another route is producing your own TV shows by taking advantage of "local origination" or "public access" programming. Local cable access shows provide high local visibility and give you valuable on-camera experience.

Martial arts instructor Steve Grody generates business with his cable show, *Self-Defense with Steve Grody.* Hairstylist Ed Salazar builds his reputation and clientele with his beauty and style show, *30 Minutes with Salazar.* Financial consultant James Irwin has developed a following in the business community with his *Business in the News.* To find out about public access cable TV possibilities in your area, contact your local cable station.

Writing articles. With over six thousand business and trade publications available today, not to mention the thousands offered on line, you can probably find a way to have an article you've written published in a magazine, newsletter, or Web site that your customers read. This builds your credibility and establishes you as an expert in your field.

To get an article published, send it to publications that your customers respect and read, or send a query letter proposing an article you could write. Remember to include a picture of yourself and a brief biographical sketch along with your name, address, and telephone number to be included at the close of the article.

Sometimes you can get paid for your articles, or you may be able to trade articles for advertising space. But no matter what arrangement you make with the publishers, always make sure they will include a brief description of you, and your name, company, address, and telephone number.

For additional information on the principles of being both informative and promotional, visit *www.paulandsarah.com* for a free Special Report: *Writing and Designing Materials That Sell.* You'll find it listed on the Site Overview.

Teaching Courses and Seminars. Adult education is growing at a rate of 35 percent per year and presents another great opportunity for publicity.

Teaching adult-education classes is another way to enhance your reputation, meet prospective clients, and make business contacts. You can find opportunities to teach courses in college continuing-education programs, adult-education organizations, churches, YW-YMCAs, and even department stores and hotels.

When management consultant Marilyn Miller wanted to expand her business into the gift-buying industry, she offered to do a seminar for the industry's annual convention. Her topic, leadership skills, turned out to be popular. Several hundred managers attended. Many asked for her card at the conclusion of her presentation, and by following up on their interest, Miller landed several consulting contracts. You may be surprised at some of the paying business opportunities that arise from offering seminars.

Books, Workbooks, and Anthologies. Writing a book or booklet, developing a workbook, or contributing a chapter to an anthology will not only increase your credibility but can also become an ongoing source of income. You can sell your books at seminars, use them as promotional items, give them away as incentives for people to buy your product or service, or use them to help you get appearances on radio and TV programs.

Writing a book saved Patricia Massie and Pauline Link's fledgling catering service, Adam and Eve. When business tapered off, they decided to write a book on how to cater a party and use it to get appearances on local talk shows. This worked. It gave them the exposure they needed for the phone to start ringing again.

Getting a book or workbook published doesn't have to be an arduous affair. You can publish a small, simply bound version yourself using desktop publishing software and following the ideas presented in *The Self-Publishing Manual,* by Don Poynter. Or you can send an outline and two chapters of your book ideas to established publishers. Another alternative is using book packagers who, for a fee, will sell your book to established publishers.

If you don't have time to write a book, but could squeeze in time for a chapter (that's only about three thousand words, or twelve double-spaced typewritten pages), you can reap the benefits of a book by contributing a chapter to an anthology.

For example, Dottie Walters, who heads Royal Publishing from her home in Glendora, California, publishes several anthologies every year, each on a different theme, from sales power and effective communication to stress management. A different person contributes each chapter, which includes a full-page biography and picture, along with the address and telephone number of the author. Authors buy copies of the anthology wholesale and sell it retail. The best part of this arrangement is that while you're promoting yourself with the anthology, every other author with a chapter in it is promoting you, too.

Since insurance specialist Wayne Cotton contributed to one of Walters's anthologies, he has used it to increase enrollment at his high-priced business seminars. He gives the book away free to each registrant. The "gift with purchase" concept can be used to build any business. Estée Lauder, the famous cosmetics mogul, built her entire business on this promotional concept.

Tips Booklets. Another great publicity tool, creating a tips booklet, doesn't take as much time or effort as a full-fledged book. So, if you would love to have many of the benefits of having written a book, but simply don't have the time or patience to write one, consider creating a tips booklet as professional organizer Elaine Ensign has done. When Ensign decided to move to another city, she was faced with the prospect of having to build a new clientele from scratch. To help ease the transition, she decided to synthesize eight years of experience into a booklet entitled *110 Ideas for Organizing Your Business Life.* Little did she know that this decision would change the course of her life.

Not only was she able to use the booklet to effectively market herself, but she has sold over 400,000 copies of her booklet which has been translated into three other languages. The ideas have been incorporated into a laminated product, as well as a calendar and seminar. Whereas writing a book and getting it published might have taken Ensign a year or more, she was able to produce her booklet in only one month. And it has been such a stunning success that she has begun teaching others how to write and develop such booklets.

One of her clients, a matrimonial attorney in Chicago, has created a booklet on divorce which has enabled him to increase business and entry price point by 50 percent. Another client, Joyce Cooper, is a professional speaker who has created a booklet on her speech topic, *The Enthusiasm Factor in Our Jobs and Our Lives.* She uses the booklet in marketing her services and sells copies of it as part of her training program and at the back of the room after speaking. After hearing her speak, companies also buy the booklets for employees who were not able to attend the program.

Michael Wyland assists his clients in grant writing and fund-raising. He now has two booklets: *20 Steps to Effective Grant Writing* for grant writers and *12 Steps to Yes* for fund-raisers. Writing the first booklets was much easier than he imagined. He simply used the outline from the lecture notes he refers to when he speaks on these topics.

Ed Voil runs a consulting company, Vertical System Analysis, for property owners and managers on improving and evaluating the elevator service. Of course, he wanted to target the high-rise commercial and residential building market. He turned to marketing consultant Carol Milano of New York City for ideas. She suggested creating a fourteen-page free booklet entitled *Owner's Guide to Better Elevator Service.* They sent a news release

Ideas for Free or Low-Cost Publicity

Producing brochures and flyers	Sending out news releases
Posting on-line notices	Placing yourself in directory listings
Giving speeches	Carrying your product with you
Writing articles	Wearing a symbol
Networking at social events	Bartering
Sending personal letters and E-mail	Donating and volunteering
Getting articles written about you	Writing a newsletter
Mailing announcement cards	Teaching classes
Placing periodic telephone calls	Giving away samples
Making slide presentations	Offering discount coupons
Submitting unsolicited proposals	Contacting past customers
Joining professional and trade organizations	Putting up signs and posters
Running promotions on your Web site	Participating in civic groups and churches
Exhibiting at trade shows, fairs, and conferences	Hosting your own cable TV show
Guesting on radio and TV talk shows	Placing classified ads

announcing the booklet to real estate trade publications. Most printed the announcement, and the result was an impressive list of new clients.

Speaking. You can also publicize your services or product by speaking before civic, trade, or professional groups. There are more than nine thousand daily speaking opportunities in the United States. Speaking on subjects related to your business is a particularly useful sales tool for such personal-service businesses as real estate, child care, consulting, or counseling, where people like to feel they have a trusted relationship with a professional.

Consultant Bill Slavin finds that speaking and leading seminars provide him with the high profile he needs to attract business. "You never know for sure who will be a client in the future," he says. "So I've found that you have to treat everyone you meet as a potential client. You can convert the acquaintances you have made at speeches or seminars into clients with a follow-up call and an appointment. But be sure you focus the follow-through conversations on your business or they will think of you as a speaker or seminar leader instead of as a business."

Making impressive visual aids and handouts to accompany speeches, seminars, and proposals is easy with desktop presentation software. Use this software to create 35mm slides and overhead transparencies for speeches. Or preferably now you can simply project your presentation, including animation and sound if you wish, from a laptop computer onto the screen with an LCD panel and overhead projector, including charts for proposals. Leading programs are *Harvard Graphics*, *Freelance Graphics*, and *PowerPoint*.

6. Using Gatekeepers

Another method used by successful home-based businesses is to build relationships with one or more key influencers in your field who provide you with all or most of your business. These people are your "gatekeepers." Woodworker Robert Livingston used this approach when he started a cabinet-making business as a way to support his work in the theater. He obtains his business from just a few key architects who refer their clients to him. Graphics designer Tom Dower gets all the business he needs from his publicist wife, Kim Freilich. Janell Besell's husband is an anesthesiologist, so when she opened her billing service his office became her first client. Through referrals to his colleagues, her business has grown rapidly.

At first glance you may think these individuals are unusually lucky to be so well connected. Actually, if you begin thinking about those you know who hold your work in high regard and value your talents, you'll undoubtedly find that you, too, have key connections. If you don't already have such contacts, you can probably make them by volunteering your skills for charity or civic activities that will attract such supporters to you.

To identify gatekeepers for your business, think of all the businesses, professionals, and others who come in regular contact with your potential clients and customers at the precise time they need your products or services. These are your gatekeepers. Make a list of them. Then, set about identifying as many such individuals as possible. If you are a mobile disc jockey, for example, and you specialize in providing music for nonprofit fund-raising events, your gatekeepers include event planners, florists, caterers, hotels, and tuxedo rental stores, among others. So you would make yourself known to as many such sources as possible.

In establishing relationships with gatekeepers, provide them with samples of what you do and be sure to approach them as colleagues with whom you can work mutually to help each other's business to grow. Talk about how you can help them; don't just ask them to help you.

7. Super Service

Nothing sells like service. If your results are "extraordinary," if your service is outstanding, people will quickly take notice and want to tell everyone they know. Suddenly you have the equivalent of a volunteer sales force. When Nathan Pritikin started his first Pritikin treatment program, he didn't even intend to go into business. He wanted to demonstrate the dramatic restorative effects of diet and exercise on seriously ill individuals. His results were so dramatic, however, that he found he had opened a floodgate of new clients.

Charlotte Mitchell's business is literally based on going the extra mile. As Notary on Wheels and Fingerprinting on Wheels she goes where her clients need her. Medical transcriptionist Vickie Fite believes her success is the result of the following business philosophy: "I go the extra mile for people. I work harder than I would for an employer." And home-based marketing consultant Linda Jagoda puts it this way: "Treat your clients, no matter what size, to royal service. Your smallest customer can bring you one of your biggest clients later on."

Norm Dominguez's success also demonstrates that service beyond what's expected is a low-cost but effective means of marketing. Dominguez operates Unicom Paging, Inc., a mobile communications service in Phoenix, Arizona, and says of his marketing approach, "The name of the game is service. Phoenix is highly competitive. So I focus on the smaller companies who need only fifteen to sixteen pagers, and we provide an incentive to our customers too, so they'll want to refer us to other people. Besides our seven-day-a-week, twenty-four hour service, our incentive offer is eight months of free service credited to their account. We also have a philosophy of trust. I don't do extensive credit checks and I don't get burned any more than the norm."

DON'T MARKET IN BARREN FIELDS: TARGET

Georgina creates elegant, trendy, custom-designed women's clothing, but she was disillusioned. "I've been networking like crazy for months. I went to five meetings this week alone. But I'm not getting any business." When Georgina expressed these frustrations to us, we wanted to know where she had been networking and why she'd chosen these groups. She told us she was attending meetings of small-business owners because she'd noticed how plain and dowdy their wardrobes usually were. "They really need me!" she exclaimed.

In fact, the response Georgina was getting said otherwise: the women she was meeting may need her, but from what she told us, they didn't know it. Evidently the women Georgina has been networking with were not particularly image conscious. At their luncheon tables, they talked excitedly about new equipment, hiring practices, and investment opportunities. Beautiful, sophisticated clothing was apparently low on their list of priorities, if it appeared at all. Georgina had been networking in barren fields.

For your marketing efforts to pay off, you have to market in fertile ground. You have to target your marketing to places and media that reach people who are actually experiencing a need for what you offer. In Georgina's case, we suggested that she network with groups of professional speakers, ad agency executives, or public-relations specialists—people in professions in which image and appearance are vital to success. Or she could network with beauty salon operators, wedding consultants, or fitness trainers—professionals who come into daily contact with people to whom image is obviously a high priority.

DON'T BET IT ALL ON ONE HORSE: EXPERIMENT

Unfortunately, there's no cut-and-dried formula for making sure you find the most fertile ground the first time around. Marketing starts as an experiment. You try some of this and some of that, sampling several targeted activities simultaneously on a small scale, experimenting until you find the several most fertile fields.

In addition, if you make a habit of using several methods simultaneously, those who need what you offer will keep running into your name, your face, and your message repeatedly in multiple contexts. That results in more "top of the mind" marketing that helps to make sure your name comes to mind at the moment when someone needs your product or service. You will be more likely to be the one who comes to mind if your clients and customers regularly read, hear, or see something about you.

We've found that if you select about five different methods and use each of them regularly, you'll multiply the impact of everything you do. Marketing is contagious. It spreads like dandelions. Each activity you undertake in fertile ground will seed others. The person you meet networking at a professional association, for example, might say, "Oh, I know who you are. I saw your article in the journal." Or when someone receives your newsletter, he or she might say, "Yeah, that's the person I met at the trade show demonstration!"

By specializing and then marketing yourself in a variety of ways, you can become known as a preeminent specialist in your field. In order to know which combination of marketing methods will work, you will need to track your results and then let results be your guide. The best way to track your results is to make a policy of asking each person who calls or contacts you how he or she heard about you. Then record the answers in your contact-management or money-management software, so you can print out a report regularly of where your business is coming from and then compare these results with how much money you're spending on each marketing activity.

 True Confessions

Helen Berman is a good example of how multiple marketing activities generate success. She wanted to become a consultant and sales trainer in the publishing industry, but the competition was tough. There were already a number of well-known consultants serving that industry.

She was sure that the cost of what she calls "push marketing"—that is, trying to get through to the thousands of her potential customers by telephone—would be too high. If she called a list of people who didn't know her, she was going to have to phone a lot of people before she'd be able to make even one sale. So instead, she chose to use what she calls "pull marketing"—building a high profile for herself with interested and qualified individuals. Then when she called, these individuals already knew who she was. The same calls led to a higher ratio of sales.

To implement her strategy, she contacted the meeting planners of upcoming conferences in her field and proposed that she give a seminar on her particular sales expertise. She got several bookings. Simultaneously, she began calling the trade magazines in the field to talk about writing a sales column for them. Soon she was writing a column for *Folio*, the leading trade magazine in the field. With this credibility and name recognition she now gets business from both her calls and her mailings. She's also writing a book and creating her own seminars, which not only are profitable in their own right but also provide a source of funds for a direct-mail campaign.

Linda Jagoda of Scottsdale, Arizona, has used multiple methods to market her own marketing firm and is now grossing half a million dollars a year from her 2,500-square-foot home. She, too, is an avid networker and started her business by giving seminars to attract clients. In addition, she uses a half-page ad in the Yellow Pages from which she got General Telephone as a client, advertises in four print publications, and makes frequent use of direct mail. She says, "Consistent marketing saves you when times are the toughest. It causes people to call you out of the blue. You never know what new business the next week is going to bring."

DON'T WAIT: FOLLOW THROUGH

Marjorie came up during a break to tell us how uncomfortable she felt about marketing and to share a disappointing story. She was trying to sell advertising specialties. Several months before, she'd met someone at a conference who seemed quite interested in her service, but only that week she'd learned he had placed a large order with her competition. "He told me he'd call as soon as their budget was approved," she lamented. "He asked for my card. It was only a couple of months ago. I don't understand what went wrong."

Obviously this woman had done everything right, up to a point. After all, she had sold her contact on placing an order, and he did. Unfortunately he placed it with someone else. She did the work; the competitor got the order. She had come face-to-face with the old saying "Out of sight, out of mind." To make sure a contact actually does call you when the moment comes that they need you, you have to follow through and keep in touch.

Follow-through is part two of "top of the mind marketing." Do give out your card, but more important, get cards from the contacts you make and call them back to arrange for a follow-up conversation within the week. Then send something appropriate every week or so. Nothing is colder than a long-forgotten contact, no matter how eager the person seems at the time you first talk. You have to follow through.

Of course, we get busy. We forget. We don't want to be bothersome. So we tend to just wait for them to call. "After all, they said they would call when they're ready." But don't leave business to chance. Think of how many other people may be contacting them while you're waiting. Think of Marjorie. Take action to keep your name ever-present in the minds of prospective clients.

Create a contact database using mailing lists, contact-management, or personal-information-management software like *Act!*, *Goldmine*, or Lotus *Organizer*. Then, set aside a specific time period each week to make follow-up contacts. Look through your database (or card file, if you prefer) for names of contacts you haven't spoken with recently. Call them or send them something—a clipping, a thank-you note, a newsletter, a novelty. Then once a month, or at least once a quarter, send a mailing to everyone on your contact list: past, present, and potential clients and referral sources. Consider holding a party or open house occasionally. Here are several ways to follow up and keep in touch:

Direct mail. Experience proves that following up mailings with a personal phone call does improve response. A similar result can be obtained with a triple mailing. The first mailing might entertain. Send an amusing clipping from *The Wall Street Journal,* for example, and include your logo but no name or address. The second, mailed a week later, might further pique the recipient's curiosity with an elegant solution to a problem that he or she may be having. No name and no address on this mailer, either, but do include your logo. Finally, send a third mailer that has your name, address, and logo on it and includes a brochure that lists your services. This campaign can be tricky because you have to know what kind of solution to offer. But if you know the problems people on your mailing list are having and target those, you can get results, especially because they already know who you are.

Newsletters. Newsletters filled with informational tidbits of interest to your clients and customers can be great as ongoing follow-up with networking contacts. Whereas brochures are often tossed out, newsletters, if they contain valuable information your customers need and can use, are more often read and even filed away, particularly in businesses for which there is a dearth of published information.

Personal letters and thank-you notes. Sales trainer Steve Maier advocates writing personal letters to prospective clients. He told us, "I could never isolate a job I got because the client was attracted by a brochure I sent out. I've discovered that a brochure is something you use to ensure that your name is in someone's file after you've talked to them."

Instead of mailing out brochures to attract business, Maier focuses on personal mailings. "I write letters to the people I want to talk to, trying to provide value in the letter, addressing to the extent possible the particular problems they have and offering ways they might solve their special problems."

Maier's strategy works. He has found that the simple thank-you notes he writes to follow up contacts he makes generate enough business to pay his $5,000 annual printing bill.

E-mail works almost as well in these situations.

While you cannot depend on networking to produce immediate prosperity, compared with other business-getting methods, the investment is smaller and the return surer. If you want to get more business, get your mouth moving and have a good time while you're at it!

DON'T TRY TO BE WHAT YOU'RE NOT: TAILOR

"I just don't have a sales personality. And, I really don't like marketing. But you're saying I have to do more of it. I'm good at what I do; I just want a chance to do it!"

This is a frequent lament from a growing number of gifted and talented professionals, artists, and specialists who are going out on their own in today's service and information economy. They aren't particularly interested in running a business. They aren't entrepreneurs in the classic sense of loving business enterprise per se. They want to create a job for themselves doing what they love and do best, and the more they hear about the importance of marketing, the more frustrated they feel.

We have good news for everyone who doesn't like to market. You don't need to have a sales and marketing personality to get plenty of business.

You do not need to be a natural-born entrepreneur. There are marketing methods suited to every person, and the most successful home businesses are those that find methods that are tailored to their personalities so that marketing becomes an integral part of who they are and they market their business naturally and comfortably.

We have met and interviewed plenty of successful home-business owners who are shy and introverted people; yet they are successfully marketing themselves using methods that are suited to their personalities. We have met and interviewed others who are highly technical problem-solvers and yet they have been able to market themselves successfully by calling upon those very strengths. They tailor their marketing to their personality and to their business.

Whatever your personality, no matter how you feel about marketing now, know that you can find methods that will make marketing second nature to you. If speaking before groups leaves you shuddering and stuttering, you don't need to feel inadequate. If you'd rather have a root canal than call a stranger on the phone, don't try to get yourself to do it. You'll just put it off, dread it, and find a million other things to do before you pick up the phone. Start with methods that actually appeal to you. Get in contact with the excitement and pride you feel about your work and identify your most natural way to share with the people you'd like to work with. Once you find that, do it and do it and do it some more.

If you would like help identifying which marketing methods you are suited to do well, you'll find information in the Resources list about *The Business Generator,* a tool we developed with psychologist Dr. Jessica Schairer to help you identify your personal marketing style and match it with marketing methods that can work for your business. *The Business Generator* also helps you know how much marketing you need to do each day, week, or month, and to be sure you actually do it! It includes our book *Getting Business to Come to You* with Laura Clampitt Douglas.

Keeping up your marketing efforts month after month, year after year, will make the difference. Once you identify the strategies that produce the most results, continue them even after your business is thriving. If you sometimes generate more business than you can handle, you can subcontract the work to others and still make a profit. Or you can refer it to reliable colleagues with or without a referral fee.

Ultimately, your happy, satisfied customers become your greatest source of new business. As marketing consultant Cork Platts reminds us, "Referrals are golden. Do something special for each customer or client and they'll remember you to everyone else who needs you." In business, as in all of life, what goes around comes around.

If you don't waste your time, if you focus, niche, target, experiment, follow through, and tailor your marketing efforts, and if you do these things regularly and service your clients and customers well, you will find that when you go into your home office every Monday morning, there will be ample business waiting there for you. And as you sit down to get started doing it, you will know that all the effort you've invested in your goals and dreams has been worth it. You'll be living them! You owe that to yourself!

MATERIALS AND SUPPLIES TO HELP YOU MARKET IN STYLE

The more easily you can let everyone you meet see, touch, or learn more about what you do, the more quickly you will become known for what you do and the more people will think of you when they need what you offer or meet someone else who does. Therefore, the more professionally, cost-effectively and time-efficiently you can show off your business, the better. Fortunately, today, there is a wide range of materials and supplies to help you market yourself more easily and effectively. Here are a few examples:

1. Predesigned four-color papers that enable you to create one attractive, coordinated professional visual image for your home business. With your computer, desktop-publishing or word-processing software, templates, and printer, you just add the text and you can have one professionally coordinated look for your:

- Letterhead
- Business cards
- Stationery
- Postcards
- Brochures
- News releases
- Overhead transparencies
- Presentation folders
- Laser signs
- Portfolios

2. Tabletop presentation binders that hold your presentations in clear plastic pouches and open up into a tabletop stand so you can flip the pages of your presentation one by one for everyone to see as you talk. It snaps closed into a carrying case.

3. A notebook or portable computer for showing your Web site or visual presentations. You can even digitize your video brochure (if it's under five minutes in length) and show it on your notebook, saving you the trouble of lugging a monitor and VCR to prospects who don't have playback equipment.

4. Acrylic display stands, easels, and literature holders in which to place your business cards, brochures, or flyers at expos or other locations where your customers will see them. Similar stands are available for collecting business cards from others for promotional drawings at expos or conferences.

5. *Flip pads you can hang anywhere* without a stand, easel, or tape. Called Static Images, these sheets by Avery Dennison adhere to any surface and can be erased by using special marking pens.

6. *White dry erase wallboards* for formal presentations or taking notes at impromptu meetings.

7. *A three-fold paper folder* for quickly folding brochures and flyers. It folds 500 sheets in twenty minutes.

8. *An envelope sealer* quickly opens the flap, moistens, and seals your mailings at a pace of up to thirty-five envelopes a minute!

9. *Presentation protectors* for covering overheads, samples, or other materials you want to show to lots of people to examine without damaging them. Simply slip your materials into these see-through protector covers and place them in a three-ring binder if you wish.

10. *Business card accessories.* Laminators that will instantly turn your card into magnets or luggage tags for premiums and giveaways. A special stapler called Card-It will instantly create "die cuts" so you can attach your card to any piece of paper, brochure, or folder without having to use paper clips or staples.

These practical materials for marketing yourself more effectively are available from companies like the ones listed in the Resources at the end of this chapter. Call or write to them for their catalogs or names of dealers near you.

RESOURCES

BOOKS

The Desktop Publisher's Idea Book. Chuck Green. New York: Random House, 1997. ISBN: 0679780068.

Getting Business to Come to You, 2d ed. Paul and Sarah Edwards and Laura Clampitt Douglas. New York: Tarcher/Putnam, 1998. ISBN: 087477845X.

Getting the Most from Your Yellow Pages Advertising. Barry Maher. New York: Aegis Pub, 1997. ISBN: 1890154059. Over 700 pages. Each chapter of this book contains a wealth of additional resources for learning more about the best methods for marketing a home-based business.

Getting Publicity. Tana Fletcher and Julia Rockler. North Vancouver, British Columbia: Self-Counsel Press, 1995. ISBN: 1551800306.

High Probability Selling. Jacques Werth and Nicholas E. Ruben. Dresher, PA: Abba Publishing, 1997. ISBN: 0963155032.

Look Before You Leap: Market Research Made Easy. Don Doman, Dell Dennison, and Margaret Doman. Bellingham, Wash.: Self-Counsel Press, 1993. ISBN: 0889082928.

101 Mix and Match Ideas for Maximizing Your Marketing Efforts. Paul and Sarah Edwards. Here's How, P.O. Box 5091, Santa Monica, CA 90409. $10.95. 1998.

101 Ways to Promote Yourself, Tricks of the Trade for Taking Charge of Your Own Success. Raleigh Pinskey. New York: Avon, 1997. ISBN: 0380785080.

Selling Through Independent Reps (Chapter 21 for full citation).

Seven Second Marketing: How to Use Memory Hooks to Make You Instantly Stand Out in a Crowd. Ivan Misner. Austin, TX: Bard Press, 1996. ISBN: 1885167210.

Speak and Grow Rich. Dottie and Lilly Walters. Paramus, NJ: Prentice-Hall, 1997. ISBN: 0134904001.

Taming the Marketing Jungle, 104 Marketing Ideas When Your Motivation is High and Your Budget is Low. Silvana Clark. Hara Publishing, Box 19732, Seattle, WA 98109. 1994. An excellent example of a promotional booklet for Clark's own business as a public speaker.

Telephone Tips That Sell! 501 How-to Ideas and Affirmations to Help Get More Business by Phone. by Art Sobczak. Business by Phone, Inc., 13254 Stevens Street, Omaha, NE 68137; phone: (800) 236-7721. Web: *arts@businessbyphone.com*

301 Do-It-Yourself Marketing Ideas from America's Most Innovative Small Companies. Dam Decker, ed. Boston: Goldhirsh Group, Inc., 1997. ISBN: 1880394308.

The World's Best-Known Marketing Secret: Building Your Business with Word-of-Mouth Marketing. Ivan Misner. Austin, Tex.: Bard Press, 1994. ISBN: 885167059.

Tapes

Getting Business to Come to You. Paul and Sarah Edwards, Nightingale Conant.

Paul & Sarah Edwards' Business Generator. Includes the Edwardses' book *Getting Business to Come to You,* a seventy-five minute video, *Top of the Mind Marketing,* and *The Marketing Partner,* a sixty-four-page workbook and guide for developing and following through on a marketing plan tailored to your personality and your business. Here's How, P.O. Box 5091, Santa Monica, CA 90409.

Directories

Broadcasting Yearbook. Reed Elsevier, 121 Chanlon Rd., New Providence, NJ 07974; (800) 521-8110; Web: *www.reedreference.com*

Directories in Print. Julie E. Towell, ed. Gale Research, Inc., 27500 Drake Rd., Farmington Hills, MI 48331; Web: *www.gale.com*

Encyclopedia of Associations. (Available in libraries and on Dialog Information Service.)

National Directory of Addresses and Telephone Numbers. Omnigraphics, Inc. 2500 Penobscot Bldg., 25th Floor, Detroit, MI 48226. Annual. (800) 234-1340; Web: *omnigraphics.com*

Standard Rate and Data Service, Inc. 3002 Glenview Road, Wilmette, IL 60091 (produces eleven directories). (800) 323-4588.

Trade Shows and Professional Exhibits Directory. Gale Research Inc., 27500 Drake Rd., Farmington Hills, MI 48331; (800) 877-4253; Web: *www.gale.com*

Marketing Supplies and Materials

Avery Dennison Consumer Service Center. 20955 Pathfinder Road, Diamond Bar, CA 91765; (800) 232-8379.

Ideal Art. P.O. Box 291500, Nashville, TN 37229; (800) 433-2278.

Paper Direct. 205 Chubb Ave., Lyndhurst, NJ 07071; (800) A-PAPERS.

Queblo Images. 131 Heartland Blvd., Brentwood, NY 11717; (800) 523-9080.

National Networking Organizations

Call or write to find out about the chapter nearest you of any of these organizations or for information on starting a new chapter.

Business Network International. 199 South Monte Vista Ave., Suite 6, San Dimas, CA 91733; (909) 305-1818; Web: *www.bni.com*

LEADS, P.O. Box 279, Carlsbad, CA 92018; phone: (760) 434-3761, (800) 783-3761. Web: *www.leadsclub.com*

LeTip, International, 4901 Morena Boulevard, Suite 703, San Diego, CA 92117; (800) 255-3847. Web: *www.letip.org*

WEB SITE

www.paulandsarah.com features daily tips on getting business and the lengthy free special reports *Writing and Designing Materials That Sell* and *Writing Effective News Releases and Query Letters.*

CHAPTER 24

Moving On: What to Do When Your Business Outgrows Your Home

Goals

1. Know when it's time to move out.

2. Decide if you want to keep working from home.

3. Continue expanding your business or career without losing the benefits of working from home.

Sooner or later, the day comes when you'll begin thinking about whether it's time to move the office away from home. Perhaps your business has grown so much it's bursting at the seams, and working from home feels more like living at the office. Or maybe you've had an intriguing job offer or promotion possibility that promises to take you back to a corporate skyscraper. Whatever the reason, many people who work at home eventually face the question of whether they should move on.

For some, the decision is easy because working from home is only a stepping-stone on the road to another goal. Computer consultant Bill Slavin explains that his dream had always been to build a big organization, so "as soon as it was financially feasible, I moved my business to a downtown office."

In contrast to Slavin, there are those for whom working from home is a cherished way of life they refuse to give up. They share the sentiments expressed by designer and consultant Ben Lizardi when he declared, "I wouldn't want to work any other way." Ben and others who feel this strongly about their home offices will do whatever must be done to keep working from home, even if it means moving to a larger house or restricting the growth of their businesses.

Then there are those who realize that they will be able to make significantly more money with less effort if they keep their business at home. Loan broker Robert Roboti found, for example, that by moving his office back home he was able to reduce his overhead to the point that he can keep an additional $10,000 of income each month. Telemarketing expert George Walther discovered that moving his business out of his home required that he generate two to three times as much work just to sustain the same income. As you might imagine, although Robert and George were initially eager to move out, once they did, both decided to return home and stay there.

For most people, however, deciding whether to stay or move out is less clear-cut. When faced with the choice, the great majority of people who work from home feel torn between opportunities to grow and expand on the one hand, and the convenience, comfort, financial benefits, and flexibility they get from working at home on the other. Medical transcriptionist Georgia Hahn, for example, sought our advice about her situation because she had the opportunity of taking on a large account that would require hiring several staff members. She feared this would mean moving her business out of her house.

"I've become very spoiled having the business here at home. I make enough money to live comfortably, and I've been with my kids since they were little. They're in school now, and I'm a successful businesswoman. I've had the best of both worlds, but now I have to make a painful decision. What's it going to be, my easygoing life or a bigger business?"

Fortunately, moving on doesn't have to be the either/or decision Georgia fears. For us, working from home started as an island of relief from high-stress careers that has turned into a satisfying lifestyle. And there's no need to move out just because the business is growing. You have a spectrum of options to choose from if you want to expand without leaving home.

In this chapter, we'll talk about how to know when it's time to move on, and the full range of options you have. We'll also share some of the creative solutions others have found for preserving the benefits of working from home while taking advantage of promising career and business opportunities.

WHEN TO MOVE OUT

When Gerald and Sandy McDevitt consulted with the Small Business Administration about their home business, they asked, "How will we know when it's time to move out?" The representative simply told them, "You'll know." We would agree. When it's time for a change, the signs will be impossible to ignore.

As the McDevitts discovered, the issue is usually a matter of space. Some years ago accountant Sandy McDevitt was having difficulty using the software she had purchased for her computer. There were too many commands to recall. In her frustration she had an idea: create a template she could lay over a computer keyboard that would display all the commands she needed to remember.

With part-time assistance from her husband, Gerald, a computer analyst for the U.S. Navy, Sandy turned this idea into a home business called Creative Computer Products. The object was to produce "keyboard templates" for the major lines of personal computers.

Sandy and Gerald ran the whole operation from their family room and kitchen, taking orders by mail or phone and then packing and shipping them. For shipping, they rented a mailbox and had daily UPS pickup. By the time they began getting twenty-five to thirty orders a day, though, several things happened that made it clear they had outgrown their home.

First, the mailbox service told them they had too much volume to handle. At about the same time, the McDevitts ran out of storage space at home, and the family room and kitchen started overflowing with materials. There wasn't enough space for eating, let alone working.

Then Sandy and Gerald rented a space they thought would be large enough to meet their needs and moved most everything out of the house. A year later, however, they had to rent a second space the same size as the first one, and now they still don't have enough room. The printing press they use to produce all their literature remained in the garage, and they had a fifteen-foot camera on order but no place to put it. The next step came later that year when the McDevitts bought a building of their own and consolidated the whole business in one place.

Aside from outgrowing the confines of a home, the quest for a different business image is the next most common reason for a change. In the early days of our consulting business, our firm, Public Affairs Assistance, won a major federal contract. Although we could do most of the work at home, the officials would not allow overhead expenses for a home office. We also needed a place for the contract officers to preview the materials we were developing. The basement office we had in our first home was next to the laundry room and just wouldn't have conveyed the right image.

Because we wanted to keep as much of our work at home as possible, we considered several options short of moving the office out. The answer that time was to rent a professional suite temporarily, but there are other possibilities we could have chosen. In fact, we've subsequently used several of the options that follow to preserve our work-from-home lifestyle.

12 WAYS TO GROW WITHOUT LOSING THE BENEFITS OF WORKING FROM HOME

If you can't face the prospect of giving up the convenience and comforts of working from home, but you don't want to miss out on your chance to grow to the next level, here are twelve solutions we and other people have found for these dilemmas. Some may be totally inappropriate for your situation, but others can be catalysts to help you resolve the issue of how to grow while working from home.

1. Rent a professional suite. If you find you need a place where you can create a serious business image, hold conferences, or get more extensive office services, consider renting a professional suite. Such suites are part of a complex that includes small offices, central conference facilities, and a full range of secretarial services available to anyone subleasing space from the complex.

When we rented a suite while working on the federal contract, we had a small office, a separate phone, and a receptionist at the complex to take our messages. The conference room there was useful for making presentations and holding meetings with the contract administrators. The cost of such suites varies by community but is generally less than renting a separate outside office and hiring the equivalent office services.

2. Rent private office space. Renting an office doesn't necessarily mean you have to say good-bye to working from home. Some people have rented a second office for certain activities (receiving mail or phone calls, working on large equipment, holding meetings) while still maintaining a home office where they can do creative or detail work. And you need not rent such space full-time. You can rent space part-time or by the day. In renting part-time space, you arrange for the hours you need the space each week and pay a flat monthly fee which can include some additional services like mailing, addressing, answering service, name on building directory, etc. Such rental arrangements are usually advertised in the Yellow Pages as "Business Identity Programs" under Office Rentals.

Hypnotherapist Nancy Bonus holds her weight-loss group meetings in office space she sublets from a private clinic, paying only for the hours her group uses the space each week. She sees individual clients and does all the management of her business at home. Bob Weil runs his part-time picture-framing business from his apartment but rents workshop time on Saturdays from a large picture-framing company. Marjorie Dahl does image consulting from her home, helping men and women "dress for success." However, when she holds workshops or brings together several clients to look over a number of garments, she rents a hotel suite.

Many homes simply can't accommodate the additional equipment and furniture involved in hiring staff. When necessary, home-business owners can rent space for their employees and continue to work at home themselves, either full- or part-time, or they can arrange for employees to work from their homes.

Writer Collin Gribbons, for example, who publishes eight newsletters and magazines for Canadian labor unions, needed a secretary and wasn't comfortable with having one come to his home. His business requires a seemingly endless parade of air-express trucks. He began to worry that his business would bother his neighbors. His solution was to rent outside office space where his secretary now works full-time.

Having an office doesn't preclude his working from home; it just provides another option. Collin says he still works at home, using his computer and modem to link up to his outside office. "I can always send material to the office by E-mail when I don't want to go in, but a lot of the more office-oriented tasks, like courier pickups and handling telephone calls, are now handled away from home." Todd Cuebas Cranston also works from home while administrative staff for SC Consulting, his Web design company, work linked seamlessly by their phone system.

3. *Contract work with other businesses.* Instead of moving his business to a warehouse, Bob Baxter hired a company to bottle and package his pet health-care products, jobs he once handled in his garage. When developing a large marketing program for a customer, consultant James Mc-Claren subcontracted with several small businesses rather than renting office space and hiring employees for the duration of the contract. Using a free-lance writer, a packager, and an office-services company, he got the program done without leaving home.

4. *Move to a bigger home.* Whether you buy, lease, or build, a new and larger home may provide the added or specialized space you need to continue living and working under one roof. We've moved more than once to better meet our home and office needs. Not only does your business change; your family also changes. What may have started out as the perfect home office may not meet your needs at another stage in your life. Faced with such a change, husband-and-wife team Theresa Arnerich and Tom Morrell decided to build a new house.

 True Confessions

Arnrich and Morrell were operating a seminar firm from their condominium, but space was tight. Their shipping department was in the garage, and the office they shared also doubled as a bedroom for Tom's daughter when she visited on weekends. Theresa threatened to find an outside office, but they decided that instead of paying for office space, they'd use that money to custom-design a new house to accommodate both their business and family lives.

Theresa says, "I'm actually glad we worked from the condo for a while, because

(Continued on page 645)

(Continued from page 644)

we found out what we needed before building. We learned, for example, that we need the offices on a separate level, away from the kitchen and other household activities. We want to be able to close the space off from social events and from household maintenance personnel who come in. We also need the offices near the bedroom so we can work late and make early-morning calls without having to go across the whole house." For Theresa, the best part about the new house will be the luxury of having an office she can call her very own.

5. *Hire employees who will work from their homes.* Some home-based companies, like MicroGraphic Images, a software firm, and Escrow Overload, a temporary help agency for escrow personnel, have expanded by adding staff who work from their own homes.

Commercial artist Diane Wessling Blake of MicroGraphic Images says, "By having our employees work at home, we can expand as rapidly as we need to and keep our costs to a minimum. In a fast-growing industry like ours, this is very important." The founders and chief executive officers of these companies all still work from home, too.

6. *Rent storage or warehouse space.* When potter June Wright had the chance to fill an order for over two thousand goblets for a special benefit, she knew she'd have to hire helpers. She also knew they wouldn't all fit in her studio behind the house, so she found a warehouse to rent and hired ten students, part-time, for one month.

This arrangement worked so well that if she can get more orders on such a grand scale, she wants to keep it up. She will continue running the business and creating pots from her own home but will have a supervisor overseeing operations at the warehouse.

7. *Add on to your home.* There are many options for adding on or converting unused areas of an existing house into extra business space. Many of these options are described in chapter 6.

We added on to two different houses in order to continue working from home. We bought our first house so we could move out of a two-bedroom apartment where there wasn't any room for a home office, but our new house didn't have a suitable place for Sarah to see psychotherapy clients. So we enclosed a side porch, providing a separate entrance and complete privacy for her clients.

Then when we first moved from our home in Kansas City to California, we tried sharing one office in part of our living room. It didn't work. Each of us needed to have our own private office space, so once again we added on. This time we built a second story.

8. *Rent an adjacent apartment or buy a second condo.* When lawyer Mark Cane passed his bar exam, he worked from his apartment but rented an office from a group of lawyers in a professional building where he could meet with clients. The cost of prime commercial space was high, however, and his overhead was consuming most of his income. When the studio apartment next to his became vacant, he talked to the landlord about renting it for his law office. He explained that his work was very quiet and would not disturb other tenants. The landlord agreed to the idea, and Mark's net income rose in his first month at the new location.

9. *Buy a duplex or apartment building.* Although this may seem like a rather extreme solution, it can be a successful one.

 True Confessions

Lynne Frances started Rainbow Cleaning Service from her apartment. She ran the business from a bedroom that also served as sitting room and office.

"I enjoyed it until the business just got too big," she admits. "I had to hire a secretary, and then the number of my cleaning crew employees kept increasing until finally I had worked my way up to twenty. Of course, they were all coming to the apartment for work assignments. Even then it wasn't such a nuisance until it got up to twenty-eight. Then if I'd have one of my kids or my folks come to visit, it was just people around at all hours of the day and night."

After five years of this, she decided enough was enough and rented an outside office. She was running the service from this office when we met her, but she wasn't happy. "People just don't realize what a great way of life it is to work from your home. To move out is a terrible shock!" She had forgotten what a chore it was to have to get dressed up in the morning and rush off in a car to be at the office before the first crew arrived. "And," she told us, "it seems I never get anything done at home now that I have an outside office. When I get home at night the dishes are waiting in the sink, the bed's unmade, and the trash is overflowing."

The next time we saw Lynne, she had reached what was for her the ideal compromise: she had bought an apartment building. She lived in one unit and ran the cleaning service from another. "Now," she says with satisfaction, "I've got it all."

10. *Negotiate to keep a job at home.* A tempting job offer or promotion can lure you back to the office, but if you're ambivalent, consider negotiating to take the position while working at least part-time at home. Develop a plan that demonstrates how this would benefit the company and increase your productivity without jeopardizing vital communication with the office. Suggest, perhaps, two days in the office and three at home, or propose a schedule for regular meetings in the office.

11. Limit your business growth. Sometimes staying at home means making a hard decision. What is more important to you—a larger business or the particular work style that only a home office can provide? A surprising number of people are opting to limit their businesses to those that can be contained within the walls of their houses. Some people we've met have scaled their businesses back in order to return to a home office after moving out of their houses.

Perhaps this is not so surprising after all when you consider a Robert Half International poll which showed that two out of three men and women said they would be willing to reduce their salaries an average of 15 percent in order to gain more family and personal time.

When collections negotiator Patricia Lineman's business grew to ten employees, she finally realized she had to move to an outside office. She found, however, that she didn't like the added pressure, inconvenience, and responsibility of supervising others. She discovered she wasn't a manager at heart, so she consciously decided to cut back her business, close her office, and return to the more comfortable lifestyle of being a one-person home-based business working one-on-one with her clients. She's making less money but enjoying it and her life a lot more.

Moving home and limiting growth doesn't have to result in less income.

Technical writer David Treweek found he actually could make money by limiting his growth. He discovered that in order to provide salaries, desks, and equipment for two writers in rented outside office space he had to double his gross income to retain 20 to 23 percent profit. Instead, he chose to make more by doing less business.

12. Raise your prices; refer or franchise additional business. When you have more business coming in than you can do yourself, raising your prices can enable you to continue your income growth without adding clients, personnel, or space. Or instead, consider referring business you can no longer accommodate to a competitor for a referral fee. When you consider that marketing costs can run 40 percent in many businesses, a re-

---

If You Move, Make Sure People Can Still Find You

If you do set up a new office outside your home and decide to change your phone number, lawyer Gerry Elman advises that you pay to keep the old number and have it automatically forwarded to your new one. Also, he suggests, if your expansion plans involve a change in the name of your business, pay for a second telephone listing with your old name so that when people look under your old business name, they'll find you there.

ferral fee is not unreasonable. Licensing or offering a franchise to others to carry out your business in other geographical locations is another way of expanding financially without necessarily expanding your space.

A FUTURE OF NEW OPTIONS

Establishing the right work arrangement at home is often like raising a family—you have to keep making adjustments for new developments, some of which can be foreseen and some of which can't. If, like many we've met with, your intention is to continue pursuing your career to the fullest and to do so from the luxury of your own home, combining a little determination with a little ingenuity should enable you to find a way to do both.

With the desire to work from home growing at such an accelerating pace and the cost and size of sophisticated office equipment shrinking every year, we're beginning to see new housing and community developments that open new options for those who want to pursue thriving careers from home.

So often when people talk about the "electronic cottage" of the future, science-fiction movies come to mind, with images of chrome and steel modules, hermetically sealed and controlled by a master computer. Consider the possibility that the electronic cottage will not look like that at all. In our opinion, the electronic cottages of the future will look more like Rohn and Jeri Engh's wood cabin on their farm in isolated Osceola, Wisconsin, where they produce a newsletter for photographers; or like Doug Hansen's second-floor apartment in West Hollywood where he writes screenplays for a living; or like Vicki McLane's ranch-style house in a Kansas City, Missouri, suburb where she works for Hallmark Cards.

Gradual updating of zoning ordinances and continuing telecommunications advances will make it increasingly possible for you to live and work in almost any location of your choice.

New living arrangements like Hoffices, part of a real estate development in Oak Creek, Wisconsin; Workman's Mill in Frederick, Maryland; and Shopkeeper Homes in La Jolla, California (see Fig. 24-1) allow families to conduct business from first-floor offices and shops while living in pleasant condos above. In the future we may see the emergence of rural housing developments linked electronically to urban metropolises similar to Tom McAnally's little home office on the Montana prairie. Perhaps ultimately our home offices will be staffed by robotic employees who will tend to both our home and office needs.

Before laughing too hard about such possibilities, keep in mind that the Smart House is already a reality and there's a long history of "famous last words" like these compiled by the editors of *Science* magazine:

Figure 24-1. Shopkeeper homes like these in La Jolla, California, are an example of a new living arrangement the future may bring as more people work from home.

"What can be more palpably absurd than the prospect held out of locomotives traveling twice as fast as stagecoaches?"

(QUARTERLY REVIEW, 1825)

"The ordinary 'horseless carriage' is at present a luxury for the wealthy; and although its price will probably fall in the near future, it will never, of course, come into as common use as the bicycle."

(LITERARY DIGEST, 1889)

". . . as a means of rapid transit, aerial navigation could not begin to compete with the railroad."

WILLIAM BAXTER, JR. (POPULAR SCIENCE, 1901)

"While theoretically and technically television may be feasible, commercially and financially, I consider it an impossibility, a development of which we need not waste time dreaming."

SCIENTIST AND INVENTOR LEE DE FOREST, 1926

So who knows what lies ahead? Much of it will be in or beyond the realm of our imagination today. Perhaps orbiting space stations will be among the home offices of tomorrow. As an open-collar worker, you could find yourself ideally prepared for the new frontier of living and traveling in space.

Whatever the future holds, in the meantime you can enjoy a comfortable, rewarding, and productive life by working from home. And in moments of frustration, when the cat has eaten the corner of your latest report, you haven't seen another human being in four days, or your two-year-old has just hung up the phone in the middle of a business call, take heart.

Remember why you decided to work from home. Consider the overhead you're saving. Reflect on what you can do in the time that used to be wasted commuting. Think of the tax benefits of working from home. Remind yourself of how it feels to be there watching your children grow. Recognize how much more control you have, not only of your business but of your life in general. Remember, most of all, that working from home is a ticket to realizing a new American dream for personal and professional success, a way to have your cake and eat it too! Someone's going to do it; it might as well be you!

RESOURCES

BOOKS

Bond's Franchise Guide—1998 Edition. Robert Bond. New York: Source Books, 1998. ISBN: 1887137076.

Franchising 101: The Complete Guide to Evaluating, Buying and Growing Your Franchised Business. Association of Small Business Development, Ann Dugan, ed., Upstart Press, 1998. ISBN: 1574100971.

Home Businesses You Can Buy. Paul and Sarah Edwards, with Walter Zooi. New York: Tarcher/Putnam, 1997. ISBN: 0874778581.

ASSOCIATIONS

American Franchisee Association (AFA). 53 West Jackson Boulevard, Ste. 205, Chicago, IL 60604; (800) 334-4232, (312) 431-0545, has only franchisees as members. Thus it follows that one of the things the organization says about itself is that it "protects and enhances franchisees' economic investment." Web site: *www.franchisee.org* AFA's Web page is part of "The Franchise Annual Online" site (*http://www.vaxxine.com/franchise*), which has a good deal of information about franchising.

International Franchise Association. 1350 New York Avenue, N.W., 900, Washington DC 20005; (202) 628-8000, is a membership organization of franchisors, franchisees, and suppliers. It publishes *Franchising World* magazine. Web site: *www.franchise.org*

NATIONAL NETWORKING ORGANIZATIONS

Call or write to find out about the chapter nearest you of any of these organizations or for information on starting a new chapter.

Business Network International. 199 South Monte Vista Ave., Suite 6, San Dimas, CA 91733.

LEADS. P.O. Box 279, Carlsbad, CA 92018; phone: (760) 434-3761, (800) 783-3761. Web: *www.leadsclub.com*

LeTip, International. 4901 Morena Boulevard, Suite 703, San Diego, CA 92117; phone: (800) 255-3847. Web: *www.letip.org*

ON LINE

www.virtualrelocation.com—Lots of information about moving including tools for comparing one city against another and a means of getting estimates from movers.

Index

Above-the-line tax deductions, 288
Accountant, 306
Acting out (children), 552
Adding on (office), 151–59, 645
After-hours work, 5–6
Ageless Body, Timeless Mind (Chopra), 504
Age of Unreason, The (Handy), 13
AGI deductions, 288
Air
  cleansers, 185–87
  quality, 185–88
American Express, 429–30
American Planning Association, 250
Answering
  machine, 214
  services, 207–9
Appointment software, 373
Architect, 159
Aromatherapy, 187–88
Artificial light, 176–77
Aslett, Don, 477
Association health plan, 333–34
Attic conversion, 148–49
Audit
  correspondence, 309
  field examination, 310
  heading off, 310–11
  office examination, 309–10
  risk of, 281
Au pair, 541
Automation, 380
Automobile insurance, 321–322

Baby sitter, 540–41
Babysitting Co-op Guidebook, The
  (McManus), 543
Babysitting co-ops, 542–43
Back-up program, 382
Bad habits, 499
  avoiding excesses, 500–501
  breaking old habits, creating new ones,
    505–6
  ending addictions and compulsions, 506
  positive rewards, 503–4
  resources for, 506–8
  six steps to avoid overindulging while work-
    ing, 502–5
  snacking guidelines, 505
  top ten bad habits, 501
Bank fees, 431
Bargain-basement special, 594–95
Bartering, 569–70
Basement
  building of, 152
  conversion of, 149–151
  daylight in, 153
Bedroom office, 143–44
Best Home Businesses for the 90s, The (Edwards and Edwards), 15, 73
*Best's Agents Guide to Life Insurance Compa-
  nies,* 335
Billable days, calculating, 590
Bill paying, 437
Blanchard, Ken, 357
Blue Cross plans, 334–35

Bonus, Dr. Nancy, 504
Bookkeeper, 438
Book storage, 458
Brabec, Barbara, 588
Breaks, 361, 490–91
Bredin, Alice, 108
Building designer, 160
Bureau of Labor Statistics surveys, 4, 21
Burglar alarm, 182
Burka, Jane, 397
Bush, George, 178
Business card
  accessories, 636
  files, 452–453
Business counselor, 438
Business Generator, The, 634
Business opportunity, 63
  evaluating, 64–65
  preventing getting suckered by, 66–67
  resources for, 68–69
  schemes, scams, and rip-offs, 65
Business organizations, 427
Business owner's policy, 321
Business phone calls, 121–23
Business plan, 88–89
Business Plan Pro, 50
Business Plan Toolkit, 50
Business property, depreciating vs. deducting,
  290–91
Business services, 563
Business Use of Your Home (IRS Pub. 587), 282
Business visitors, 126–28
Business Week, 101
Butler, Jo Ann, 249–50
Buying equipment, 291–93

Cable TV, 624
Calendar, 373
California, 258, 296, 315, 332, 338–39
  telecommuting study, 105–6
CallCost, 417
Calling-card files, 453
Call Organizer, 417
Capital improvements, 281
Card swap machine, 428
Cash-flow management, 80–81, 420–21
  cash-on-hand maximization, 431–32
  collecting money you're owed, 421–25
  credit cards
    four ways to get paid by, 425–30
    making most of, 432–33
  credit discrimination, combating, 430–31
  credit restoration, 434–35
  holding on to what you have, 432
  income fluctuation protection, 435–37
  paying bills to maximize, 437
  when to get help, 438–39

Cash on hand, maximizing, 431–32
Catalyst, 21
Celebrating wins, 524–25
Cellular phone, 211–13
*CEO: Building a $400 Million Company from
  the Ground Up* (Kurtzig), 589
Certified Public Accountant, 306, 438
Chair (desk), 167–69
Check guarantee service, 422–23
The Check Is Not in the Mail (Sklar), 424
Check-writing software, 417
Child, 550
Child-care options, 538–45
Children and home office, 530
  child-care options, 538–45
  child-proofing home office, 533
  claiming child-care tax credit, 547–48
  day-care center vs. family day-care, 545–
    47
  don't expose to too many adult concerns,
    550–51
  hiring to help, 571–72
  introducing idea of working at home to,
    548–49
  resources for, 555–59
  rewards of working at home, 531–32
  special problems
    acting out, 552
    constant interruptions, 552–53
    getting off on wrong foot, 551
    guilt, 554
    inability to say no, 553
    resentments, 552
    when it doesn't work, 554–55
  what to expect, 532–33
    newborn to six years old, 534–35
    seven to twelve years old, 536–37
    twelve years and older, 537–38
Chiropractic consultation, 172
Chopra, Deepak, 504
Chromalux bulbs, 177
Cleaning
  service, 472, 483
  supplies, 478–79
Clear agreements, 518–19
Client/customer files, 450–51
Climate control, 185–88
Closet office, 143
COBRA, 337
Coffee breaks, electronic, 490–91
Colleagues, 489–95
Collecting money you're owed, 421–25
Color and office decor, 184
Combining principle, 358
Commissioner of Internal Revenue v. Soliman,
  274, 278
Commissions, 106–7

Communication, 518
  celebrating wins, 524–25
  crisis management, 526–27
  feedback
    asking for and receiving, 523–24
    giving, 524
  general principles of, 520–21
  listening, 521–22
  problem solving and decision making,
    522–23
  telling war stories, 525–26
Community rating, 334
Commuting time, 23–24
Compensation, negotiating, 105–7
Computer, 218. *See also* Printer; Scanner;
    Software
  choices among, 219
  desktop features, 220–21
  getting when you can't afford, 224
  for information management, 444–45
  monitor features, 222
  rider to insurance policy for, 320
  for doing taxes, 308–09
  tips for organizing files, 451
  where to buy, 222–23
Computer consultant, 226
Conflict resolution, 517–18
Consumer Reports, 292
Contact-management software, 447
Contingent workers, 13
Contract, 268–69
Contracting for help, 563–64, 566–69, 644
Contractors, 160, 572
Conversions, 143–51
Coolidge, Calvin, 274
Copyholder, 171
Copy machine, 234–36
Copyright Handbook, The, 267
Cordless telephone, 210–11
Corporation, 260, 264–66
Correspondence shortcuts, 384
Credit
  disability insurance, 337
  discrimination, 430–31
  restoration, 434–35
Credit cards, 77
  four ways to get paid by, 425–30
  low-rate, no-fee, 433
  making most of, 432–33
Credit check, 421–22
Crisis management, 526–27

Daily planning, 376–77
Daly, Frederick, 310
Dark colors, 178
Database management software, 447–48
Day-care center, 545–47

Decision making, 522–23
Decorator, 161
Delaware, 296
Deliveries, 124–26
Demographic changes, 11
Depression, 399–400
Desk, 165–67
Desktop-publishing software, 445–46
Digital camera, 236–39
Dimmer switch, 177
Dining-room office, 142–43
Direct
  costs, 583–85
  mail, 632–33
  solicitation, 619–20
Direct-selling organization, 59–60
  complaints about, 62
  finding right opportunity, 61
  pyramid schemes, 60
  resources for, 62–63
Disability insurance, 337–38
Disabled, 104–5
Discover card, 429–30
Disk storage, 460
Display stands, 635
Distractions, 363, 388–97
Dogs, 129–32
Dormer office, 152, 156
Douglas, Laura Clampitt, 606
Dress, 361
Dressing-room office, 143

Easels, 635
Economic restructuring, 8–10
Electronic
  Check Acceptance, 425
  spreadsheets, 415–16
Eliot, George, 247
E-mail, 381
Employee leasing companies, 569
Employee-related insurance, 338–39
Employee Retirement Income Security Act
    (ERISA), 333
Employees, 128
Employer services, 572
Employment taxes, 296
Energy Star, 180
Enrolled agent, 306
Entertainment expenses, 290
Entry plan, 79–81
Envelope sealer, 636
Environmental consciousness, 178–80
Equipment, 188–94, 199–201
  answering services, 207–9
  computer, 218–24
  copy machine, 234–36
  digital camera, 236–39

Equipment (*cont.*)
  fax machine, 215–17
  multifunction unit, 217–18
  online access, 231–33
  printers, 227–30
  resources for, 239–44
  scanners, 230–31
  software, 224–27
  telephone, 202–4
    answering machine, 214
    cellular, 211–13
    cordless, 210–11
    headsets, 213
    two-line, 210
    voice mail, 203, 205–6
    well-equipped home office, 200
Ergonomic disorders, 164
Errand shortcuts, 384
Estimated tax payments, 295
Everyday expenses, 287–88
Excesses, avoiding, 500–501
Exchange arrangements, 569–70
Exclusive use test, 275–76
Experience rating, 334
Extraordinary service, 629
Eyeglasses, 172
Eyestrain, 177–78

Factoring, 430
Factors, 423
Fair Labor Standards Act, 258
Family
  conflicts, 109–10
  getting support from, 390–91
  hiring to help, 571–72
  as visitors, 128
Family Circle, 550
Family day-care, 545–47
Family-room office, 141
Famous Amos, 620
Fatigue, 177–78
Fax machine, 215–17, 382
Fear, 397
Federal laws, 258
Feedback, 523–24
Fees. *See* Pricing
Feng-shui, 184–85
Fey, Michael, 531
Fields, Debbie, 620
File Opening Soundbyte, 496
Filing cabinets, 170
Filing systems, 449–50
  basic filing categories, 450
  business card files, 452–53
  client or customer files, 450–51
  project files, 451–52

subject files, 453
  tickler system, 454
  tips for organizing computer files, 451
  twelve filing rules of thumb, 454–55
  upcoming file, 453–54
Financial
  counselor, 340
  planning, 339–41
Financing sources, 77–79
Fire protection, 180–82
Flat fees, 590–92
Flexibility, 359
Flip pads, 636
Fluorescent light, 176–77
Focus group, 612
Follow through, 631–33
Form design software, 381
Form SS-8 (IRS), 303
Fortune, 6
Fortune 500, 9, 205, 421
Four-color papers, 635
Franchise, 53–54
  determining if for you, 55–56
  evaluating, 58
  home-based, list of, 56
  resources for, 58–59
  selecting, 57
Franchising, 648
Free time, 403
Friends, 128
Fringe benefits, 274
Full-time employees, 564
  legal aspects of hiring, 565–66
Furniture, 165–70

Garage conversion, 148
Garfield, Dr. Charles, 405–6
Gatekeepers, 628
General
  ledger accounting software, 418
  liability insurance, 322
Gen-Xers, 11
Getting Business to Come to You (Douglas and
  Edwards), 605–6
Getting Organized (Winston), 467
Getzels, Judith, 250
Gibson, Valerie, 527
Giving up, 85
Glare, 178
Glare screen, 170–71
Glasser, William, 502
Glossbrenner, Alfred, 227
Goal-setting, 356
Goldstein, Arnold, 323
Good Housekeeping, 475
Gordon, Gil, 95–96, 98, 618

Graham, Lee, 63
Green Lights, 180
GroupWare, 99, 102
Guilt, 554

Hand, Learned, 275
Handy, Charles, 13
Hawthorne effect, 372
Headset, 171, 213
Health insurance, 329–30
  and COBRA, 337
  five fallback options for self-employed, 330
  Medical Savings Accounts, 331
  selecting providers, 332
  six most common complaints about, 331–35
Health-maintenance organization (HMO), 330
Helmstetter, Shad, 387
Help you need, 560–62
  ensuring top-quality job, 573–75
  hiring, 563–64, 566–69, 645
  resources for, 575–76
  six sources for, 562–73
HEPA filters, 185
Hobby rule, 304
Home assembly, 101
Home business, 42. *See also* Home office
  finding opportunities right under your nose, 45–50
  home-originated companies, list of, 43
  key questions to ask yourself, 43–44
  resources for, 51–52
  start-up steps for, 51
Home Business Associations, 490
Home equity loans, 78
Homemade Money (Brabec), 588
Homemaker, 514–15
Home Occupation Ordinances (Butler and Getzels), 249–50
Home office, 163. *See also* Equipment; Office space
  creating image and decor, 183–85
  environmentally conscious, 178–80
  ergonomic, 170–72
  eyestrain and fatigue, avoiding, 177–78
  function criteria, 164–65
  furniture choices, 165–70
  lighting, 175–77
  noise control, 173–75
  resources for, 196–98
  security and fire protection, 180–82
  supplies and equipment, 188–94
  temperature, humidity, and air quality, 185–88
  twenty ways to find bargains, 194–95
Home Office Computing, 19, 22, 24, 27, 30

Home-office deduction
  audit risk, 281
  deducting expenses, 277, 281–84
  IRS criteria for, 275–79
  for salaried and commissioned employees, 285–86
  traps and pitfalls, 284–85
  why you should take, 279–81
Homeowners' association regulations, 257
Homeowner's insurance, 319–321
Hospitalization policies, 330
Hourly wage, 590–92
Housecleaning, 471
  adopting new attitude toward, 475
  avoiding crisis in, 472–75
  cleaning supplies should be nearby in multiple places, 478–79
  clean throughout the day, sixty seconds at a time, 477–78
  getting everyone else to pitch in, 481–82
  preventing messes instead of cleaning them up, 476–77
  pros and cons of various methods, 482
  resources for, 483
  in sixty seconds, 474
  strategic use of cleaning services, 483
  technology cleans for you, 480–81
Household responsibilities, 361, 388–89, 513
Houseplants, air-cleaning, 187
How to Form Your Own Corporation, 265
How to Get Free Software (Glossbrenner), 227
HR-10 plan, 294
Hughes, Jr. v. Commissioner, 275
Humidity, 185–88
Hyatt, Carol, 494–95

Ideas but no action, 69–70
Identity, new, 512
Idle time, 378
Image
  home office, 119–21, 183–85
  marginal business, 83–84
I'm-available signals, 391–92
Impact pricing, 594
Incandescent light, 176–77
Income fluctuations, 435–37
Income Opportunities, 19, 135
Incorporation, 260, 264–66
Independent
  contractors, 297–304, 567–68
  Insurance Agents of America, 315
  selling organization (ISO), 428–29
Indirect costs, 72
Industrial Homework laws, 257–58
Industry Production Standards, 591
Inexperience, 82

Infants, 534
Information management, 442–43
    audio/video teleconferencing, 468
    computerizing information, 444–45
    contact- and personal-information manage-
        ment software, 447, 449
    database-management software, 447–48
    digging out from under paper piles, 455–57
    five steps to having needed information at
        your fingertips, 443–44
    information-management software, 446
    mail handling, 460–63
    mailing-list software, 446–47
    organizing tool shortcuts, 465
    paper and electronic filing systems, 449–55
    phone messages, 464–65
    resources for, 469–70
    software suites, 448
    storage systems, 467–68
        newsletters, magazines, books, tapes, and
            disks, 458–60
    walls as information organizers, 457–58
    what to keep/what to throw away, 466–67
    when to get office help, 469
    word-processing and desktop-publishing
        software, 445–46
Information technology, 11–12
Ink-jet printer, 228
Insurance, 314
    agent, 343–44
    assessing needs for, 326–29
    disability insurance, 337–38
    employee-related, 338–39
    health insurance, 329–35, 337
    life insurance, retirement, and financial
        planning, 339–41
    a dozen money savers, 341–42
    myths about, 316, 318–26
    ounce-of-prevention list, 317
    professional help, 343–44
    rating companies for financial stability,
        335–36
    record-keeping, 343
    resources for, 344–47
    small-business, 342
    uninsured, 315
Insurance Forum, 335–36
Integrated software, 379–80
Interior Design, 165
Interior designer, 161
Internal fax, 382
Internal Revenue Service, 275–79, 297–304,
    420
Internet, 98
    Service Provider (ISP), 231–33
Interruptions, 363, 388–97, 552–53
Interviews, 623–24

Intranet, 98–99
Inventory, 343
Invoicing software, 419
ISDN line, 218
Isolation, 30–31, 108. See also Loneliness

Joining organizations/associations, 489–90
Joint ventures, 571
Junk mail, 395–96

Kahler, Taibi, 406
Kamoroff, Bernard, 564
Keogh plan, 294
Keyboard, ergonomic, 171
Keyboarding skills, 561
Kitchen office, 141–42
Kneading ball, 171
Kurtzig, Sandra, 589

Label printer, 381
Laser printer, 228
Lawyer selection, 269–70
Leasing equipment, 291–93
"Leave" policies, 362
Leisure time, 408–9
Leonard, Robin, 434
Licenses, 259
Life insurance, 341
Light colors, 178
Lighting, 175–77
Limited liability company (LLC), 262–64
Limiting growth, 647
Line of credit, 78
Link Resources, 41
Listening, 521–22
Literature holders, 635
Living-room office, 141
Loans, 75, 77–79
Loft office, 152
Loneliness, avoiding, 487
    keeping in contact with colleagues and
        peers, 489–95
    making new contacts, 495–96
    resources for, 497–98
    three steps to getting connected, 487–89
Los Angeles Times, 24, 318
Lunch, 361

Macros, 380
Magazine storage, 458
Mail, daily handling of, 460–63
Mailing-list software, 446–47
Mail-order catalogs, 190–93
Make Your House Do the Housework (Aslett
    and Simons), 477
Making Money with Your Computer at Home
    (Edwards and Edwards), 24, 48

Marketing, 435, 605–8
  finding a niche, 614–16
  focus on one product/service, 613–14
  following through, 631–33
  low/no-cost methods, 607
  materials and supplies that help with, 635–36
  mindset for, 608–9
  misconceptions, 82–83
  multiple activities, 630–31
  passive vs. active methods, 617
  resources for, 636–39
  seven top-of-the-mind methods, 617–29
  tailor methods to your personality, 633–35
  targeting, 629–30
  testing the waters, 609–12
Marriage Encounter, 528
McManus, Patricia, 543
Medical Savings Accounts (MSAs), 331
Meeting shortcuts, 383
Merchant account
  from American Express and Discover, 429–30
  from business organizations, 427
  from financial institutions, 425–27
  from independent selling organizations, 428–29
Metal business-card holders, 453
Microloans, 78–79
Minibreaks, 407–8
Minicopier, 234
Mini-notebook, 219
Mobile home, 153
Modified Accelerated Cost Recovery System (MACRS), 291
Money
  attitudes about, 601–2
  problems, 70–81
  purchase plan, 294
Money management, 363, 411–12
  cash flow, 420
    collecting money you're owed, 421–25
    credit card payments, 425–30
    credit discrimination, 430–31
    holding on to what you have, 432
    making most of credit cards, 432–33
    maximizing cash on hand, 431–32
    paying bills to maximize, 437
    protection from income fluctuations, 435–37
    restoring good credit, 434–35
  electronic spreadsheets, 415–16
  four musts of, 413
  getting help, 438–39
  leaving essential paper trail, 420
  recording time and expenses, 416–17
  record-keeping systems, 413–14
  resources for, 439–41
  software, 414–15
    features to look for, 419
    for tax preparation, 420
    overview of, 417–19
  things to keep track of, 412
Money-Smart Secrets of the Self-Employed (Stern), 340
Money Troubles: Legal Strategies to Cope with Your Debts (Leonard), 434
Monitor, 171, 222
Mothers' Home Business Network, 472
Mouse, ergonomic, 172
Moving on, 640–41
  new options, 648–50
  resources for, 650–51
  twelve ways to grow without losing benefits of home business, 642–48
  when to move out, 641–42
Multifunction unit, 217–18
Multilevel marketing (MLM), 59
Multiple Employer Welfare Arrangement (MEWA), 333
Multi-tasking, 379

Nanny, 540–41
National Association for Family Day Care Providers, 547
National Association of Credit Managers, 422
National Directory of Family Day Care Providers, 547
National Foundation for Women Business Owners, 570
Natural light, 176
Neighbors, 128, 252–53
Networking, 100, 436–37, 492, 618–19
Newborns, 534
New contacts, 495–96
New England Journal of Medicine, 172
New Hampshire, 296
New Jersey, 258
Newsletters
  storing, 458
  writing, 633
News releases, 623
New York, 258
New York Times, The, 5, 10, 24
Niche marketing, 614–16
Noise control, 173–75
Notebook computer, 219, 635

Office. *See* Home office; Office space
Office space, 134. *See also* Home office
  adding on, 151–59
  converting or remodeling, 143–51

Office space (*cont.*)
  matching your work style, 137–39
  minimum requirements for, 135–37
  professional opinion, 159–61
  resources for, 162
  separating from rest of house, 400–401
  using available space, 139–43
Office support, 109
100 Ways to Prosper in Today's Economy (Schimel), 431
One Minute Manager (Blanchard), 357
On-line
  access, 231–33
  buying, 193–94
  service providers, 232
Open-collar workers, 4
Open-plan modular systems, 144, 146–47
Ordinary business expenses, 275
  business property—deduction or depreciation?, 290–91
  checklist of, 289
  entertainment, 290
  everyday expenses, 287–88
  travel, 288
Oregon, 255, 296
Organization, 351–52
  customizing your system, 361–63
  evaluating your system, 359–60
  flexibility, 359
  put like things together, 358
  resources for, 363–64
  routines, 359
  self-organization, 352–55
  set priorities, 358
  set specific goals, 356
  turn goals into specific tasks, 356–57
Organized Executive, The (Winston), 170
Outgrowing your home business. *See* Moving on
Overdue accounts, 423
Overhead, 72–73, 584–85
Overindulgences, avoiding, 502–5
Overworking, eight signs of, 403–5

Palmtop, 219
Paper trail, 420
Partnership, 261–62
  insurance, 323
Part-time employees, 566–67
Passive marketing, 617
Patent Copyright & Trademark, 267
Paulson, Dr. Terry, 409
Peer Counselor's Pocket Book, The (Sturkie and Gibson), 527
Peers, 491
Percentage of results, 593–94
Perfectionism, 397

Perkins, Wendy, 13
Permits, 259
Personal
  Digital Assistant (PDA), 219
  information manager, 373
  letters, 633
  loans, 77–78
Pets, 129–32
Phone calls, 121–23
  avoiding interruptions during, 392
  shortcuts for, 385
Phone messages, 464–65
Pittsburgh, 257
Point-of-sale terminal, 428
Porch/patio conversion, 151, 154–55
Portable computer, 635
Positive addictions, 502
Poynter, Don, 625
Presentation protectors, 636
Prevention, 24
Pricing, 579–80
  adjusting strategy to changing business situation, 597–99
  formulas and strategies for your service, 589–97
  four questions that determine, 580–88
  if they say your price is too high, 600–602
  incentives, 621–22
  products vs. services, 588
  raising, 647
  resources for, 603–4
  step-by-step guide for, 602–3
Principal-place-of-business test, 277
Print-enhancement software, 382
Printer, 227–30
Priority setting, 358
Pritikin, Nathan, 629
Privacy, 117, 119
Private mailing address, 253
Problem solving, 522–23
Procrastination, causes of, 397–400
Procrastination: Why You Do It, What to Do About It (Burka and Yuen), 397
Product pricing, 588. *See also* Service pricing
Profit, 585–86
Project
  files, 451–52
  shortcuts, 385–86
Psychology Today, 394
Public Accountant, 306
Publicity, 622
  books, workbooks, anthologies, 625–26
  cable TV, 624
  interviews, 623–24
  news releases, 623
  speaking, 627–28
  teaching courses and seminars, 624–25

tips booklets, 626–27
writing articles, 624
Pyramid schemes, 60

Raising your fees, 598–99
Reading shortcuts, 383
Receipts, 304, 343
Record-keeping
insurance, 343
money management, 413–14
taxes, 304–5
Referring business, 647
Registrations, 259
Regular-use test, 276
Relationship banking, 431
Relationships, 509–10
communication handbook, 520–27
conflict resolution, 517–18
getting off to the right start, 510–11
resources for, 528–29
steps to a smooth transition, 511
thirteen ways to keep romance alive,
519–20
three inevitable changes, 512
duties and responsibilities, 513
new identities, 512
new roles, 514–16, 518–19
what to do if it isn't getting better, 527–28
Relaxation, 405–6
Remodeling, 143–51
Renter's insurance, 319–21
Renting
adjacent apartment, 646
equipment, 291–93
private office space, 643–44
professional suite, 643
storage/warehouse space, 645
Repairs, 281
Resentments, 552
Resources
bad habits, breaking, 506–8
business opportunity, 68–69
children and home office, 555–59
demographic and technological changes,
15–16
direct-selling organization, 62–63
equipment and accessories, 239–44
franchises, 58–59
general home business, 89–92
help you need, 575–76
home office, 196–98
housecleaning, 483
information management, 469–70
insurance, 344–47
legal matters, 270–72
loneliness, avoiding, 497–98
marketing, 636–39

money management, 439–41
office space, 162
organization, 363–64
pricing, 603–4
relationships, 528–29
setting boundaries, 133
taxes, 312–13
time management, 409–10
work-at-home jobs, 110–12
Retirement, 339–41
plans, 294
Rewards, positive, 503–4
R. H. Bruskin, 475
Rituals, work, 369–70
Robinson, Frederick, 394
Roles, new, 514
Rolodex, 452
Romance, keeping alive when working at
home, 519–20
Roof-raising for office, 152, 156
Roth IRA, 340
Routines, 359
Rugge, Sue, 83, 88, 318, 494

Safes, 181–82
Salary, 105–6
calculating, 71–72
Sales taxes, 296–97
Sampling, 620–21
Sanderson, Jim, 514
Saying no, 378, 553
Scams, 65, 102–3
Scanner, 230–31, 237
Schairer, Dr. Jessica, 634
Scheele, Adele, 495
Schimel, Barry, 431
School-age children, 536–37
Schuster, Hal, 589
Science, 648–49
Screens, privacy, 143–44
Second phone line, 121, 203, 210
Second story, 152
Secrets of Consulting, The (Weinberg),
592
Security, 119, 180–182
Self-employment
advantages of, 39–40
buying a business opportunity, 63–69
buying a franchise, 53–59
creating your own business, 42–52
joining a direct-selling organization, 59–63
resources for, 89–92
roadblocks to avoid, 69–85
tax, 295–96
tips from successful entrepreneurs, 85–88
what it takes to go out on your own, 40–42
writing a business plan, 88–89

Self-management, 30
Self-organization, 352–55
Self-Publishing Manual, The (Poynter), 625
Self-Talk Solutions (Helmstetter), 387
Seller Assisted Marketing Plan (SAMP) laws, 64
Seminars, 490
Separate building, 153, 158–59
Service mark, 266
Service pricing, 589. See also Product pricing
   bargain-basement special, 594–95
   billable days, calculating, 590
   flat fee vs. hourly wage, 590–92
   percentage of results, 593–94
   start-up price, 595
   staying in budget without cutting your rate, 595–96
   top-of-the-line, 593
   value added, 593
   working on retainer, 596–97
Setting boundaries
   business visitors at your home, 118–21
   deliveries when you're away, 124–26
   between home and office, 115–18
   letting people know you work at home, 118
   for other people, 126–29
   pet-owner considerations, 129–32
   handling phone calls, 121–23
   resources for, 133
   tips for keeping home and office space separate, 132–33
   using home address for business purposes, 123–24
Sharp Wizard, 417
Simons, Laura Aslett, 477
Simplified Employee Pension (SEP-IRA), 294
Sixty-second cleaning, 477–78, 480
Skills for Success (Scheele), 495
Skills upgrade, 436
Sklar, Leonard, 424
Slow times, 436
Small Business Administration, 78, 80
Small-business insurance, 342
Small-claims court, 425
Small-Time Operator, The (Kamoroff), 564
Smart Box, 125–26
Smart House, 648
Snacking guidelines, 505
Social Security, 340
Software, 224–25
   contact- and personal-information management, 447
   database management, 447–48
   desktop publishing, 445–46
   features to look for, 227
   finding and buying, 226
   free, 227

information management, 446
mailing list, 446–47
money management, 414–15
   features to look for, 419
   overview of, 417–19
   tax preparation, 420
   time and expenses, 416–17
suites, 448
Sole proprietorship, 260–61
Sound control, 173–75
Spare bedroom office, 140–41
Speaking before groups, 627–28
Specialist, 615
Spreadsheet accounting systems, 418
Square footage of home, calculating, 282
Stand Up to the IRS (Daly), 310
Starting a Business on a Shoestring (Goldstein), 323
Start-up
   costs, 73, 75–81, 293–94
   price, 595
State and local taxes, 296
State laws, 257–58
Stein, Gertrude, 442
Stern, Linda, 340
Storage space office, 143
Storage systems, 458–60, 467–68
Stress, 24–25
Sturkie, Joan, 527
Subchapter S corporation, 263
Subject files, 453
Success, ideas about, 405
Suitability survey, 35–37
Sullivan, Nick, 94
Superstores, 189–90
Supervision, 109
Supplies, 188–94
Support group, starting, 493
Supreme Court, 277

Tabletop presentation binders, 635
Tape storage, 458, 460
Target marketing, 629–30
Tasks
   large, overwhelming, 397
   setting specific from goals, 356–57
   unpleasant, 398
Taxes, 273–75
   audits, 309–11
   changing laws, 311
   child-care credit, 547–48
   computer for doing, 308–9
   demonstrating self-employment status to IRS, 297–304
   getting help with, 305–8
   home-office deduction
      audit risk, 281

deducting expenses, 281–84
   IRS criteria for, 275–79
   for salaried and commissioned employees,
      285–86
   traps and pitfalls, 284–85
   why you should take, 279–81
ordinary business-expense deductions,
   287–91
record keeping, 304–5
renting, leasing, or buying?, 291–93
resources for, 312–13
responsibilities of self-employed, 295–97
retirement contributions, 294
software for preparing, 420
start-up costs, 293–94
Tax-free funds, 431
Taxpayer Relief Act (1997), 274, 278, 285–
   86
Teaching courses/seminars, 624–25
Teaming up with others, 570–71
Technology, as time saver, 378–82
Teenagers, 537–38
Telecommuting, 6–7, 19
Teleconferencing, 468
Telephone, 202. *See also* Answering services;
   Voice mail
   answering machine, 214
   calls
      avoiding interruptions during, 392
      handling, 121–23
      shortcuts for, 385
   cellular, 211–13
   cordless, 210–11
   hardware, 209
   headset, 213
   messages, 464–65
   for staying in touch, 490
   telephone tag, 207
   ten ways to save time and money on your
      bill, 208–9
   top four home-office needs, 204
   two-line, 121, 203, 210
   unwanted solicitations, 396
Television watching, 361
Temperature, 185–88
Templates, 380
Temporarily Yours (Perkins), 13
Temporary-help agencies, 568–69
Temptations. *See* Bad habits
Thank-you notes, 633
Third Wave, The (Toffler), 5, 531
Three-fold paper folder, 636
Tickler system, 454
Time-and-expense software, 418
Time management, 365–66
   basic requirements of home-office system,
      374–75

closing the door on work, 400–405
daily planning process, 376–77
getting down to work, 366–67
interruptions and distractions, handling,
   388–97
planning your day, 373–74
procrastination, preventing, 397–400
resources for, 409–10
rituals to get started, 369–70
shortcuts, 383–86
staying calm, cool, and collected,
   386–88
sticking to business and working efficiently,
   371–73
successful schedule set-up, 367–69
time savers, 377–79
   technological, 379–82
workaholics, solutions for, 405–9
Time-planning system, 373
Time-savers, 377–79
TimeSlips, 416
Tips booklets, 626–27
Toddlers, 534
Toffler, Alvin, 5, 531
Tools for organization, 465
Top-of-the-line pricing, 593
Track ball, 172
Trademarks, 266–67
Trade shows, 620–21
Travel expenses, 288
Two-career couples, 515–19
Typing skills, 561

Underpricing, 582–83
Universal Product Code symbol, obtaining,
   267
Upcoming file, 453–54
USA Today, 9, 13–14, 472, 531
Use permit, 253

Value added, 593
Variance, 253–54
Vermont, 255
Virtual corporation, 101–2
Virtual Office Survival Handbook (Bredin),
   108
Voice mail, 203, 205
   answering machines, 205
   on your computer, 206
   through phone company, 206
   private service, 206

W-4 adjustments, 77
War stories, 525–26
Watson, Thomas J., 85
Weinberg, Gerald, 592
White dry erase wallboards, 636

White House Conference on Small Business, 278

Winston, Stephanie, 170, 467

Woman's Selling Game, The (Hyatt), 494–95

Word processing, 445–46

Work
 schedule, 367–69, 402
 style, 137–39

Workaholics, solutions for, 405–9

Work-at-home jobs, 93–94
 bringing current job home, 94–96
 companies with at-home employees, 103–4
 compensation negotiations, 105–7
 convincing employer to let you work at home, 96–98
 determining whether your job can be done at home, 99
 and disabled, 104–5
 and isolation, 108
 office-support arrangements, 109
 opportunities on the nets, 98–99
 possible family conflict, 109–10
 resources for, 110–12
 salaried jobs to do at home, list of, 95
 schemes and scams, 102–3
 and supervision, 109
 ways to find a job to do at home, 99–102

work-at-home agreement negotiations, 107–8

Workers' compensation, 338–39

Working for yourself. *See* Self-employment

Working from home
 advantages of, 18–27
 deciding if it's for you, 31, 33
 disadvantages of, 27–31
 motivation for, 34–38
 roles neeeded for, 33–34

Working From Home Forum, 491

Working hours, 361

Working on retainer, 596–97

Workshops, 490

Wrist
 rest, 172
 splint, 172

Writing articles, 624

Young children, 534–35

Yuen, Lenora, 397

Yurt office, 157–58

Zoning, 248
 ordinances vary by location, 248–51
 preventing problems with, 251–57
 violation of, 251

Complete Your Library of the Working from Home Series
by Paul and Sarah Edwards

These books are available at your local bookstore or wherever books are sold. Ordering is also easy and convenient. To order, call 1-800-788-6262, prompt #1, or send your order to:

Jeremy P. Tarcher
Mail Order Department
P.O. Box 12289
Newark, NJ 07101-5289

For Canadian orders:
P.O. Box 25000
Postal Station 'A'
Toronto, Ontario MSW 2X8

		Price
____ The Best Home Businesses		
for the 21st Century, Revised Edition	0-87477-973-1	$17.95
____ Finding Your Perfect Work	0-87477-795-X	$16.95
____ Getting Business to Come to You,		
2nd Revised Edition	0-87477-845-X	$18.95
____ Home Businesses You Can Buy	0-87477-858-1	$13.95
____ Making Money in Cyberspace	0-87477-884-0	$15.95
____ Making Money with Your		
Computer at Home,		
Expanded 2nd Edition	0-87477-898-0	$15.95
____ Secrets of Self-Employment	0-87477-837-9	$13.95
____ Teaming Up	0-87477-842-5	$13.95

Subtotal _____
Shipping and handling* _____
Sales tax (CA, NJ, NY, PA) _____
Total amount due _____

Payable in U.S. funds (no cash orders accepted). $15.00 minimum for credit card orders.

*Shipping and handling: $3.50 for one book, $1.00 for each additional book. Not to exceed $8.50.

Payment method:
Visa   MasterCard   American Express
Check or money order
International money order or bank draft check

Card # _____ Expiration date _____

Signature as on charge card _____

Daytime phone number _____

Name _____

Address _____

City _____ State _____ Zip _____

Please allow six weeks for delivery. Prices subject to change without notice. Source key WORK

Do You Have Questions
or Feedback?

Paul and Sarah want to answer your questions. They can usually respond to you if you leave a message for them at their Web site, *http://www.paulandsarah.com*

If you wish to write, you can write to Paul and Sarah in care of "House Calls," Entrepreneur's Home-Office, 2392 Morse Avenue, Irvine, CA 92614. Your question may be selected to be answered in their column; however, they cannot respond to every letter.

Other Books by Paul and Sarah Edwards

Use the table below to locate other books that contain the information you need for your business interests.

Subject	Best Home Businesses for the 21st Century	Finding Your Perfect Work	Getting Business to Come to You	Home Businesses You Can Buy	Making Money in Cyberspace	Secrets of Self-Employment	Teaming Up
Advertising			Yes		Yes		
Business opportunities				Yes			
Children and child care							
Closing sales			Yes			Yes	
Credit							
Employees							
Ergonomics							
Failure						Yes	
Family and marriage issues						Yes	
Financing your business						Yes	
Franchise							
Getting referrals			Yes	Yes			
Handling emotional/ psychological issues						Yes	
Housecleaning							
Insurance							
Legal issues							Yes
Loneliness, isolation							
Managing information							
Marketing	Specific techniques by business		Yes Focus of book		Yes	Yes Attitude	Yes
Marketing materials			Yes				
Money						Yes	Yes
Naming your business			Yes				
Negotiating							Yes
Networking			Yes				Yes
Office space, furniture, equipment							
Outgrowing your home							
Overcoming setbacks						Yes	Yes
Partnerships							Yes
Pricing	Yes Specific				Yes		
Profiles of specific businesses	Yes				Case studies	Yes	
Public relations and publicity			Yes				
Resource directory	Yes			Yes		Yes	
Selecting a business/ career/business opportunity	Yes*	Yes Focus of book		Yes			
Software					Yes		
Speaking			Yes				
Start-up costs	Yes						
Subcontracting							Yes
Success issues						Yes	Yes
Taxes							Yes
Time management						Yes	Yes
Zoning							

* *Finding Your Perfect Work* is a career guide with extensive appendices listing more than 1500 self-employment careers and a method for matching your personality with a career, and includes worksheets and inspiring stories.

About the Authors

Paul and Sarah Edwards, authors of eight books that have sold over a million copies, are often described as the nation's self-employment experts. They have worked from home for over twenty years. Their weekly column is syndicated by the Los Angeles Times News Syndicate and they write monthly columns for *Enterpreneur's HomeOffice* and Price Costco's *Connection.* Since 1988, they have produced and broadcasted their hour-long show *Working from Home* on the Business News Network.

Since 1990, their mission—which they express through print, via electronic media, and as speakers—has been to help people make the transition from the job economy of lifetime employment to the faster changing but potentially more satisfying world of self-employment. They live in California.